THE
NORMAN
ACHIEVEMENT

For Annie and Kevin
because I love you

THE NORMAN ACHIEVEMENT

Richard F Cassady

Foreword by John Julius Norwich

GUILD PUBLISHING LONDON

This edition published 1987 by
Book Club Associates
by arrangement with
Sidgwick & Jackson

The Norman Achievement was edited and designed by
Thames Head Limited, Avening, Tetbury, Gloucestershire, Great Britain

Editorial and Marketing director
Martin Marix Evans

Design and Production director
David Playne

Art editor
Heather Church

Editors
Stephanie Mullins   Gill Davies

Designers
Tony De Saulles   Nick Allen   David Ganderton

Illustrations by Terry Thomas

Typeset in Bembo by
Avonset, Midsomer Norton, Bath

Printed by
New Interlitho, Milan, Italy

All photographs taken by Richard Cassady except the
following which were taken by David Brueggemann

page 117 Hercules and the Nemean Lion, Canterbury Cathedral
page 118 Chapel of St John, Tower of London
page 119 Lincoln Cathedral, England
page 154 Durham Cathedral from River Wear, England
page 155 Interior, Durham Cathedral
page 239 St Bartholomew the Great, London
page 276 Chapter House, Bristol Cathedral
page 293 Buildwas Abbey Church, England
page 295 Kilpeck Church, England
page 332 Goodrich Castle, England
page 396 North Transept, Winchester Cathedral, England
page 414 Temple Church, London

Acknowledgements

When Pasenda City College (California) granted me a two-year leave in 1968 to pursue private studies in Italy, neither the administration nor my family and I anticipated the take-over of my whole being by a consuming interest in things Norman. The Pasadena City College administration I thank profoundly for that leave and for the later sabbatical which allowed me to visit and photograph all the places herein mentioned.

A loving thanks is extended to so many English friends who gave of their time, interest and open-hearted hospitality during the 'agony of creation'. First on the list, I extend a grateful hug to John and Doreen Cutler for their sympathy, endless enthusiasm, an unshakeable belief in my project, and for a hospitality beyond measure. Thank you to Christopher and Sue Gordon (and family) for their interest and willingness to arrange themselves in the name of bed and board, to Bonham and Phyllis Bazeley for steering me in the right direction, and to Ant and Kate White for their perpetual willingness—while still struggling Cambridge students—to open the door to their kitchen and a snug, dry bed. My new friend Eileen Crosby has been understanding and kind in her reading of certain difficult passages mainly having to do with strange inconsistencies in English and American English. I direct a special bow of gratitude and respect to busy John Julius Norwich for his willingness to read a manuscript by a totally unknown author, and for his enthusiastic encouragement ever after. And to Pamela Willis, curator of St John's Gate, London, I say 'thank you' for her interest, time and cordiality.

My cousin, Nini Dickinson, deserves my deep-felt love and gratitude for her critical reading and re-reading of the manuscript. Robert Scott's criticisms and erudite observations were more than helpful—they were indispensable. Carmen Mion proved more than a loving friend; her amused (and kind) understanding of my awesome ignorance of the nuances of the Italian language and her critical twice-over readings of the manuscript deserve my everlasting gratitude. Jan Littler, who worked with me from the start, is praised for her patience, love of research, knowledge of things English and shrewd insights. And every author should have an editor like Stephanie Mullins—who must be the kindest in the business—and an illustrator like Terry Thomas—who must be the most amicable.

A host of Italian friends—Dino and Mariella Campana, Franco and Guiliana Pedrina, Enso and Carla Paoletti, Raffaele and Ketty Spada, Nora and Maria Orioli among others, are remembered for endless kindnesses, as are *i Siciliani*, Alfio and Ida Maugeri. The various workers and librarians at the British Library, the Los Angeles Public Library, The South Pasadena Library, and the Pasadena City College Library and the University of California Library are all here remenbered. I am especially grateful to the considerate and patient designers and workers at Thames Head Limited who were so long-suffering when I was being difficult. My further thanks is extended to all who read this book, especially those who do so without complaints that I have ignored their own favourite Norman spot—an omission due to a compulsion to write mainly of my own.

R.F.C. Los Angeles, 1986

Contents

Foreword

When Philip the Bastard, at the close of Shakespeare's *King John*, gives it as his opinion that 'This England never did, nor never shall, Lie at the proud foot of a conqueror' he is guilty, whether he knows it or not, of an outrageous piece of wishful thinking. Since his day, admittedly, no such fate has befallen us—though we probably had a narrow enough escape during the Napoleonic Wars and an even narrower one in 1940; but before it, England (or large parts of England, at any rate) saw herself in this humiliating position not once but many times. Julius Caesar arrived in 55 BC, on a reconnaissance for the eventual Roman occupation of this island that was to last some five hundred years. Even while the Romans were still in power, there were troublesome incursions from the Picts and Scots, who were to become even more obstreperous after their departure. Later we found ourselves obliged to submit to Jutes and Saxons, Angles and Danes. Only after all these disparate peoples had been assimilated and digested came the grandest and most momentous invasion of the lot: the invasion which constitutes the supreme watershed of our political and cultural development—with which indeed, for many people, English history begins. On 28 September 1066 William the Bastard, duke of Normandy, landed at Pevensey; and less than three months later, on Christmas Day, he was crowned at Westminster as king of England.

So much, of course, every schoolboy knows; a fact, on the other hand, which nobody ever seems to be taught is that this date precisely coincides with another conquest, of far greater importance to contemporary Europe than William's ever was—a conquest which, within little more than half a century, was to give rise to the most dazzling kingdom of the middle ages. Five years and four months before William's arrival—in May 1061—Robert de Hauteville, called Guiscard, the son of an obscure Norman knight from the Cotentin, crossed the Straits of Messina with his young brother Roger and some two thousand men; precisely the same period after it, in January 1072, the two made their triumphant entry into the city of Palermo.

'No chapter of history', wrote John Addington Symonds, 'more resembles a romance than that which records the sudden rise and brief splendour of the house of Hauteville'; and he was right. In the space of a single generation, a family of penniless freebooters became, in all but name, sultans of an oriental capital, masters of a rich and prosperous kingdom in which, for the first and last time in history, the three great civilizations of the Mediterranean—the Latin, the Greek and the Arab—were fused together in harmony and concord, collaborating in works of art and architecture that still have the power to catch the breath. Nor did this achievement go unnoticed by their cousins in England; all through the twelfth century, the links between the two Norman kingdoms grew steadily closer. England sent Sicily two of her greatest ministers: Thomas Brown, who served as chancellor to King Roger before returning home to assume a similar position under Henry II, and Walter of the Mill—his name was later delightfully italianized to *Offamiglio*—chief minister of King William the Good and the only man in history regularly to sign himself 'Emir and Archbishop'. England even provided Good King William with his Queen—Henry II's daughter Joanna, thanks to whom we possess, among the mosaics of her husband's cathedral at Monreale, the earliest known portrait of Saint Thomas of Canterbury.

How, one wonders, can it possibly be that one of the most fascinating epics of European history between the ages of Julius Caesar and Napoleon should be so little known to the world at large, and to the English-speaking world in particular? In the first half of the twentieth century there were, so far as I could discover, only two non-specialist works in English which told the Norman-Sicilian story in any detail; both were American, both were out of print, and neither covered the whole period. When, nearly twenty years ago now, I set out to try to remedy the deficiency, it was with the comfortable feeling that I had the whole field practically to myself.

In my two volumes, however, I stuck firmly to the shores of the Mediterranean; my old friend Richard Cassady has set his sights a good deal higher. In the pages that follow he tells both sides of the Norman story, interweaving the English and Sicilian strands to make a single narrative; and he brilliantly sets that narrative against its natural and architectural background, describing the two countries, their landscapes and their monuments, with humour and perception. No wonder that the jacket of this book should feature a superb photograph of the Chapel of St John in the Tower of London; it was in their architecture that the Normans left the most visually dramatic proof of their own particular genius, and there is no other building, anywhere, in which that genius finds fuller or more perfect expression.

Ironically enough, by some strange paradox of historiography, the most energetic, vital and gifted people ever to burst upon the European continent have seldom infected their historians with anything of their own exuberance. The vast majority of books about the Normans, whether of the north or the south, are quite paralysingly dull. No one, however, will ever say that about the book you now hold in your hands. Richard Cassady is, thank heaven, an unashamed enthusiast; his academic training and background have done nothing to take the edge off his excitement—indeed, his sense of wonder—at the people and the events he describes. It is that excitement, that sense of wonder, that has carried him to the end of the tremendous task he has set himself; and he has succeeded with a triumph worthy of his subject. One cannot say more.

John Julius Norwich.

Introduction

Handsome they were, these Vikings from the north, exuberant in their emotions, valiant, fearless adventurers and insatiable marauders. Perhaps it was their blonde hair and blue eyes that gave them such appeal so far as the swarthier people of France were concerned; or maybe it was their height and the enormous breadth of their shoulders that made eager wives of so many of the native women. Whatever the reason, and regardless of their propensity for deviousness in personal, even familial relationships, in spite of conscienceless cruelties and selfish determinations for private aggrandizement, they were still appealing enough to the Frankish people to have become, in a single century, almost entirely assimilated. 'Whichever way we turn we have to admit that the Viking society of Rollo [tenth century] and his companions was something quite different from the Norman society of the eleventh century. The one developed from the other, but the development was not effective until the two races had merged and the Northmen had, for all practical purposes, become Frenchmen'.[1]

In the physical sense there is nothing about Normandy to encourage the establishment there of a people even today different from the rest of the French, a distinction to which the average Frenchman will not admit. But the cider-drinking Norman will own it readily enough, augmenting his argument with fist-thumping emphasis and hostile glances toward Paris some 150 miles away. No mountain barriers, no limitlessly sweeping seas, no swift rivers mark the boundaries, either in the exclusive sense of keeping out 'foreign' influences, or in the inclusive sense of allowing the development of a native society with a strongly individualistic flavour in religion, social organization and politics. There is nothing about this rich, smiling countryside to account for the good-natured stubbornness, the tight-fisted devotion to thrift (so often exaggerated by the tourist into avarice). Nor can it explain the friendly oneupmanship or the political astuteness that enabled its people not only to conquer England but also to weld together four of the most quarrelsomely misallied peoples of the Mediterranean as citizens of the most opulent, cultured and enlightened kingdom of the Middle Ages (the Norman kingdom of Sicily). And all this was achieved in a period of less than two hundred years!

The landscape of Normandy tends to be benign and rather cheerful, but it can at times be fearsomely violent and given to terrible moods. The lovely Pays de Caux, that coastline of the English Channel just north of the River Seine, is often at the mercy of the sea; and it was by way of this same boiling sea that the men from the north, the Vikings, had entered the middle European theatre, eventually to set up their land of the Northmen—Normandy. One likes to imagine these robust scavengers—for that is about all that can be said for them at the time they started their southern meanderings in the late eighth century—as arriving all frost-encrusted, wrapped in furs and shivering from the cold of their native Scandinavia. And that picture is probably fairly accurate. But they were also a restless and energetic people, forced to their ships by overpopulation and food shortages, as well as by dreams of wealth

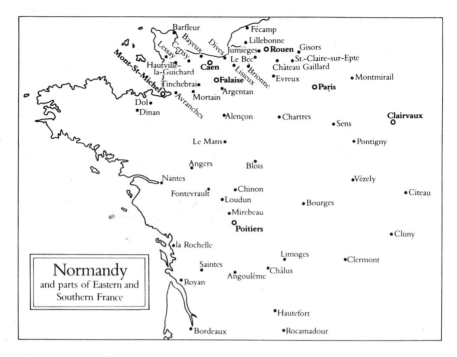

Normandy
and parts of Eastern and
Southern France

and glory. The Vikings flooded outward from Scandinavia in every direction, taking what they coveted, envying no one, practising pagan rites and offering human sacrifices. They founded the cities of Novgorod and Kiev, laid the foundation of modern Russia, and then moved on to Constantinople, Baghdad, India and China. They went westward as far as Newfoundland. The Danes hit the coasts of Spain and France, navigating the Seine as far as Paris. They lashed out at England over and over, attacking York and London, and even claiming certain settlements as their own.

They have a leading place in our story, these rough, imaginative adventurers. The first thirteen Viking ships to arrive off the coast of France in AD 820 were driven away without too much effort on the part of the defenders and with only a minor loss of life. Still, the pattern was started then, becoming more successful—that is, profitable—in the ensuing years. As spring followed spring the raiders became more persistent. The frost in the fields along the Seine had barely started melting, about 845, when a certain Reginherus or Ragnar, whom it would be pleasing but implausible to equate with the saga hero Ragnar Lodbrok, appeared, anticipating the habitual springtime raids so as to utilize the element of surprise. Charles II, the Bald, sent out divided forces to protect both sides of the Seine. Attacking the smaller of the two forces, Ragnar took 111 prisoners whom he hanged in full view of the defending divisions. With that the opposition collapsed, and Ragnar moved upstream to plunder Paris on Easter Sunday. 'He was now more than 200 miles from his element the sea, and it would not seem past man's devising to have hindered his return. Instead Charles paid him 7,000 pounds of silver to depart in peace and take his plunder with him'.[2] With such perquisites as that, word got around. Thus was the trickle of springtime migrations and departures increased to flood proportions.

With every new spring larger fleets of *snekjja* (longships) were launched in the north, headed in all directions, especially to France, with the upshot that eventually the target lands were almost destitute of portable booty. Is it any surprise that the church-going locals of northern Europe would write into their services, 'From the fury of the Vikings free us, O Lord!'? And with the scant booty available, along with the discomforts of the monotonously repetitious voyages which would have been boring had they not been so risky, was it any wonder that these men of the cold took to wintering along the comparatively warm Seine, whence they could foray into the Cotentin and the Bessin, even setting up permanent bases in these places? It is true that our picture of the Vikings between the eighth and the eleventh centuries has been gained largely through the naturally unsympathetic work of non-Scandinavian writers, producing 'for the contemporary world and posterity alike a picture at once incomplete, lurid and distorted'.[3] But the fact remains that in Viking literature itself—those lusty sagas which they told and sang to one another around the warming winter fires or while sailing their wave-tossed longships, brightly painted, shield-bordered and dragon-prowed, through drenching spring storms—we read of their barbarous pride in their ability to ravage the land, to burn and pillage cities, to rape, kill and enslave the unfortunate inhabitants.

A milestone of history was reached in 911 at Saint-Clair-sur-Epte when an agreement was concluded between King Charles III, the Simple, of France and the Viking chief Rolf, or Rollo. It is not that there had been no previous treaties and truces to pave the way; but this one was especially important because by it the men of the north were deeded actual land, the region on either side of the lower River Seine. The only concessions made by Rollo were his agreement to protect the land against all comers, even against other Vikings, and his swearing an oath of loyalty to the king. To these was appended his willingness to embrace Christianity, which he did with transparent alacrity. The Vikings were accustomed to baptism as requisite in any treaty with Christians; earlier, one Northman had claimed to have undergone 'twenty such washings'.

Legend relates that 'Rollo refused to kneel and kiss the king's foot, crying out in his own speech, "No, by God!" and that the companion to whom he delegated the unwelcome obligation performed it so clumsily that he overturned the king, to the great merriment of the assembled Northmen'.[4] In the face of the laughter Charles the Simple, probably frightened and certainly humiliated, pretended to see it all as a bit of friendly horseplay. It is debatable whether Charles was as simple as his sobriquet would have us believe, or as weak as historians sometimes make him. The agreement with Rollo was made so that he would be free to take advantage of political developments east of his kingdom, in Lorraine. In any case, his action in legitimizing the Norman presence probably brought to the French nation some of its more vigorous elements. The Normans adopted Frankish ways and institutions, to which they added their own gutsy elements; and within slightly more than a century after the treaty had set up a dukedom notably more advanced than the kingdom of their feudal overlord.

So Rollo the Viking became what is generally considered to be the first duke of Normandy, though he and his two immediate successors used the lesser designation 'count'. We know little about Rollo other than what later chroniclers say about him—that he was immensely large, with strength to match, and that he manifested a capacity to rule, demonstrated by wisdom and justice in all things. He was probably one with Hrolf the Ganger, known thus exotically 'because he was so huge that no horse could carry him and he must needs gang afoot'.[5] Scandinavian for sure, he was probably Norwegian, though the Danes try to make him Danish and the Swedes Swedish. At home he had been a pirate. Now in France he became a noble—a not unworthy achievement, all things considered.

Hyperbole aside, Rollo headed a society where order was maintained by strong men capable of striking down any form of insubordination without qualm and by the cruellest means. In the end friendship and family ties meant little. Book-length statements were made concerning sacredness of blood bonds, of friendship and the brotherhood of man—mostly lip-service rituals meant to perpetuate the myth that all men were not out to get one another in the end. Yet there was an established social organization, rigid and with occupations clearly delineated, as was normal in every society of the period.

At Saint-Clair-sur-Epte Rollo and his followers had accepted Christianity for reasons of their own which can be seen as unworthy, although pardonably so. In itself the willingness of the Northmen to go along with Christian Charles serves as a pertinent indication of their noteworthy ability to adopt the ways of the 'natives', to utilize existing institutions and to make both work in their favour. A willingness to hypocrisy lies not deep beneath the surface of the agreeable smile, the placing of hands between those of the liege lord and the swearing of sacred oaths. Agreements reached may be broken when it is advantageous to do so. Rollo ostentatiously made extensive grants of land to the various churches and monasteries within the confines of his new realm. Yet he clearly remained unconverted at heart, and at his funeral sacrifices were made to Norse gods. Throughout the Normans' story we cannot help but notice their propensity to deny treaties, to turn on friends, to sever familial ties—brother would fight against brother, son against father or mother, wife against husband. It is a tale of such unrelenting frequency as to be almost wearying, except that it is so terribly human.

But they were not ungifted, these Northmen. An eleventh-century writer, Geoffrey of Malaterra—a Norman, a Benedictine monk, on speaking terms with the royal Normans of Sicily, and a fairly reliable recorder of history, though he writes mostly from oral tradition—gives us a picture of the Normans that is both optimistic and unfavourable.

They are to be sure a cunning race, vengeful of injuries, despising their own patrimony in the hope of gaining more elsewhere, eager after gain and domination, given to imitation of every kind, holding a certain mean between ostentatious luxury and avarice—their leaders are very lavish in their desire to make a good impression. A race skilful in flattery, much attracted by the studies of eloquence, so much so that their very boys are something of orators; a race entirely unbridled unless restrained by the yoke of justice. They are enduring of toil, hunger and cold, when need be; devoted to hunting and falconry, delighting in extravagance of dress, horses and warlike accoutrements.[6]

Geoffrey's assessment was echoed by the English Henry of Huntingdon, who wrote in the first half of the twelfth century: 'For their character is such that when they have so crushed their enemies that they can reduce them no lower, they bring themselves and their own lands to poverty and waste . . . which is apparent, with continually increasing directness, in Normandy as well as in England, in Apulia, Sicily, and Antioch . . .'[7] History tells us that we must accept these judgemental assertions, for smells of fire and blood run through the Norsemen's own poetry; their sagas are full of the furious love of battle for its own sake, of adventure and of an almost prideful suffering.

Château Fort Pirou, France

13

Not long after the Saint-Clair-sur-Epte agreement of 911, further concessions from the Frankish kings were forthcoming. By the year 1000 much of historical Normandy was in Norman hands, in no way due to any further large-scale migrations from the north. Mainly the Normans were clever and adaptive. They seemed perfectly willing, indeed eager, to marry freely with non-Scandinavians. Rollo himself married one Popa, the daughter of a Frankish count of Bayeux. Their son William, called Longsword, married to the daughter of yet another Frankish count, felt compelled to send his son to Bayeux to learn Norse, for it was no longer being spoken at their principal city of Rouen.

Yet they never entirely lost their roots. They created their own art and architecture. Barely off the sand dunes of the western coast of the Cotentin stands what may very well be the oldest castle in Normandy, called Château Fort Pirou. The Vikings were the builders of this stronghold, at least the earliest parts of it, which retain today a feeling of almost savage honesty. The *stoneness* of the stone is so obvious, the compactness and solidity of the not huge but still massive structure express exactly those characteristics of stone in the abstract. The walls are almost cyclopean in their irregularity; they are walls from a time out of human memory. The moat at Pirou serves now only as a refuge for ducks and geese which, according to ancient legend, return every year to their rightful manor. The tranquillity of the site, a fine picnic spot, is so complete as to make the purpose of the fortress seem ridiculous.

A new line of French kings came into existence in 987 when Hugh Capet, duke of the Franks, persuaded the nobles and churchmen to recognize him as lawful king. The bloodless coup took place in Senlis, that city on whose cathedral façade clumps of wallflowers grow out of the cracks in the stone in mid-spring, giving it the appearance of a particularly handsome, carved stone Christmas tree. Hugh Capet's move came on the death of the last Carolingian ruler of France. At this point there was practically nothing to suggest the remarkable history that was in store for the Capetians.

Thought of as little more than upstarts, the Capetians were destined to survive well past the time of the Norman kings, through the sheer luck of producing a continuous string of heirs, by manipulating the feudal system of oaths, reciprocal rights and duties—and by a bull-headed adherence to purpose. The Capetians created a dynasty that, aided by circumstances a few centuries later, was to bring down the house of the Normans and confine their kings, courts and parliaments to the great islands just off the French coast. There they would remain, isolated by the Channel which the English would always think of as theirs and by a climate the French would always think of as English, too.

The year 1010 was the possible birth year of Robert I, duke of Normandy, the great-great-grandson of Rollo. At that period Normandy was prosperous, well-governed and violent, alternatively friendly and at odds with both the Church of Rome and the new line of Capetian overlords. A mere fifty-six years later Robert's son William was to earn his sobriquet the Conqueror on the southern shores of England. And in 1016, nineteen years before Robert's death, a group of forty shabbily clad Norman pilgrims at a shrine on Italy's Gargano Peninsula tentatively enlisted themselves to aid a certain exiled

Southern Italy and Sicily

Lombard noble from the southern Italian city of Bari, thus unwittingly setting the stage for the Norman kingdom in the south.

'Saturn's Land' it is called—*Saturnia tellus*—a land at once inviting and forbidding, salubrious, warm, welcoming (but guarded against the European hordes both ancient and modern by high-ranging mountains with snowy crests lost in turbulent clouds). It is edged by beaches under skies of incomparable blueness, and kept inviolate by expansive seas, rocky projections, legendary monsters and whirlpools lurking in narrow straits, formidable and disheartening discouragements to even the most adventurous hero.

Mortals and immortals have sought the blandishments of this sacred, benevolent land, some to return broken spirited to their homelands, others to find their earthly paradise, their love, their calm. No land has been so coveted and rejected, so loved and hated, so fortunate and so abused. People through the ages have been pulled to this divine promontory that projects like a great boot from the underside of Europe. They have left families behind, risked fortunes and deserted lovers to find their places in the Italian sun. Merchants and bankers, heroes and hippies, artists—droves of artists!—thinkers, writers, emperors, kings, saints and sinners, refugees, soldiers, wastrels and just plain

15

tourists, arrived and continue to arrive, singing troubadour-like their praises of Italian people and places; all hymning the land that everyone thinks of as his home, and dramatizing past history while creating that of the present. It is all 'very old, so old it could be considered part of the very nature of things. Its beginnings go back to the dawn of time, to the days when Saturn, the father of all the gods, after being deposed and humiliated by his son Jupiter, fled from Olympus. He is said to have found refuge in Latium, the territory embracing the yet unfounded city of Rome, where he became king and ruled in the golden age. He, too, was a disillusioned refugee trying to forget mis-understanding, ingratitude and defeat'.[8]

In the early eleventh century four main groups or authorities contended for or shared power in Italy. External suzerains were the German Holy Roman emperors, the political descendants of Charlemagne, and their Eastern counterparts, the Byzantines. Although the kingdom of the Lombards, established when they had invaded the peninsula in the mid-sixth century, had been annexed by Charlemagne, Lombard nobles still held power, most notably in the southern principalities of Benevento, Salerno and Capua, and spora-dically in the north. German imperial authority, exercised chiefly through the bishops in Northern Italy, waxed or waned accordingly as political conditions at home allowed the emperors to visit Italy. Greek power, at one time extensive, had by now been effectively reduced to the provinces of Calabria and Apulia, and the area around Otranto. The fourth element in the power mix was provided by the papacy, now largely controlled by the Roman nobility, but technically exercising authority in the Roman duchy and, by virtue of a gift from Charlemagne, suzerain of Benevento.

While recognizing papal authority, Benevento maintained the old Lombard traditions and manners. The dream of a revived Lombard kingdom loomed ever large in the minds of these southern 'foreigners'—for that is what they always remained in their three centres of power at Benevento, Capua and Salerno. For the time being they would admit vassalage alternately to the Holy Roman emperor in Germany and to the Byzantine emperor enthroned at Constantinople. But the Lombard rulers were perceptive enough to recognize that their strongest competitors for Southern Italy were the Greeks of the Byzantine empire. Conspiracy was the name of the game, along with attendant assassinations, mutilations, pillagings, familial under-cuttings, feuds, sales of daughters as political pawns and (always masked by religious devotion) alms and grants to monasteries, churches and the papal treasuries.

For the moment the Greeks had to content themselves with their power bases in Calabria and Otranto, along with a smattering of cities on the Italian west coast. Amalfi was the most persistently aggressive of these holdings, but all of them maintained their Greek customs and loyalties even though they had, by the eleventh century, evolved into hereditary dukedoms. By the year 1000 Apulia, Calabria and the area around Otranto had been transformed into a wealthy and politically powerful Byzantine province called the Capitanata, forming for the Greeks the single most potent political and mercantile force in the entire peninsula. Yet all was hardly a bed of roses. As an added affront, Saracens from the north coast of Africa had been performing piratical raids along the coasts of Southern Italy for generations, sometimes even making hit-

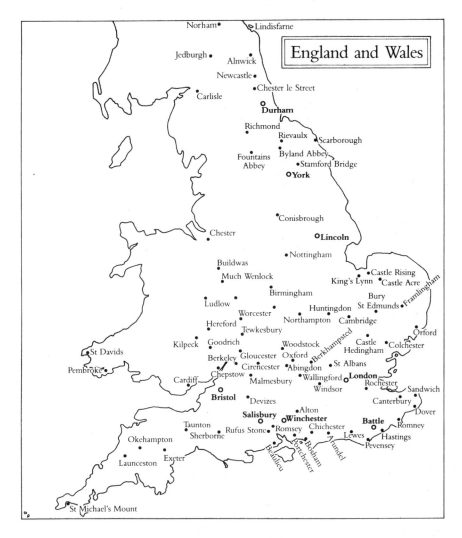

England and Wales

Norham
Lindisfarne
Jedburgh
Alnwick
Newcastle
Chester le Street
Carlisle
Durham
Richmond
Rievaulx
Scarborough
Fountains Abbey
Byland Abbey
Stamford Bridge
York
Conisbrough
Chester
Lincoln
Nottingham
Buildwas
Much Wenlock
Castle Rising
King's Lynn
Castle Acre
Framlingham
Birmingham
Bury St Edmunds
Ludlow
Worcester
Huntingdon
Northampton
Cambridge
Hereford
Tewkesbury
Kilpeck
Goodrich
Woodstock
Castle Hedingham
Orford
Colchester
St Davids
Berkeley
Gloucester
Oxford
Berkhampsted
Pembroke
Cirencester
Abingdon
St Albans
Cardiff
Chepstow
Malmesbury
Wallingford
London
Windsor
Rochester
Sandwich
Bristol
Devizes
Canterbury
Dover
Alton
Salisbury
Winchester
Chichester
Battle
Romney
Taunton
Rufus Stone
Romsey
Lewes
Hastings
Sherborne
Beaulieu
Bosham
Dorchester
Arundel
Pevensey
Okehampton
Exeter
Launceston
St Michael's Mount

and-run sallies many miles inland. The island of Sicily was already under their control, a fact not unrelated to their earlier expansion into Spain and Portugal. From Sicily they were perpetrating their atrocities against the cities of Southern Italy with alarming, sometimes predictable frequency.

Poor Southern Italy! Torn apart by powerful contending forces— Lombard, Greek, Saracen and German—pussyfooting its way through the violence of the centuries, always unable to establish a lasting continuity under a securely functioning benevolent rule. Security and benevolence were simply not the ways of the time, since even the Church, the body in theory best equipped to lend a strong, kindly touch, was interested in things more temporal than spiritual, and consequently was indulging itself in a perpetual stirring of the political witches' brew that bubbled steadily on the fiery coals of native Italian emotion. Indeed, it would seem to be an ideal situation for the advent of yet another outside force, immensely ambitious politically, greedy for power, and uncommonly adaptive to other peoples' ways.

Moisture seeping everywhere. A verdant greenness to challenge the tropics; to Shakespeare's John of Gaunt a 'demi-paradise', an 'other Eden'. To those of us from other lands it seems to nestle in the sea, heavy under wet, grey, usually chilly and always glowering skies. Even some of her own hold that any alleged faults in the English psyche are due to the darkly hostile climate, which results either in a prostrating depression of energy and attitude, or a tribal clamour to move to brighter lands, hence the British Empire. Perhaps. The fact remains that England has been hotly contested, valiantly defended, cultivated every inch, babied and passionately loved from the days of remotest antiquity.

The tourist from Europe realizes quickly enough that England is not all that different from the western continental coast, which seems to stand in a kind of face-down with the shores across the Channel. There are the same full rivers, the same trees, flowers and orchards, the same vertical chalky cliffs and grey stone, the same chill air. If Normandy seems more colourful it is because it enjoys more sunshine, though it can be from time to time prohibitively bleak. The two lands are not twins but only siblings. Both sides of the Channel are rude, rugged. The luxuriant springtime crescendo of daffodils, narcissi and tulips is Nature's way of accenting the starkness; it will, almost perversely, manufacture sunshine from the ground, frustrating the light-blocking canopy of clouds.

Unlike Italy, England, although many times invaded and conquered, formed a political unity at the time of the Norman Conquest. In turn Celts, Romans, Anglo-Saxons, Danes and Norwegians had poured into the country. The Danish invasions, best known from the exploits of the 'Great Army' against which Alfred, king from 871 to 899, so doggedly fought, perhaps provided the catalyst through which unification of the realm was eventually achieved in the mid-tenth century. Although ruled by Scandinavians from 1016 to 1042 (by Cnut, also king of Denmark and Norway, and his sons Harold II and Harthacnut), the unity of the state was maintained; it was, however, in their period that the great earldoms were established which, by the rivalries of their incumbents, weakened royal authority during the reign (1042-66) of Edward the Confessor. Structurally a kingdom of established royal administrative and judicial procedures, and of strong local government, England had also seen great flowerings of art and literature. But, in Edward's time always under threat from Scandinavian invasion and the turbulence of overmighty subjects, it was clearly ripe for Norman plucking.

PART ONE

The Three Mounts
of
Saint Michael

Factum est silentium in caelo, dum draco committeret bellum:
et Michael pugnavit cum eo et fecit victoriam, alleluia.

Princeps gloriosissime, Michael Archangele, esto memor nostri:
hic et ubique semper precare pro nobis Filium Dei, alleluia.

There was silence in heaven, while the dragon was waging war:
and Michael fought with him and was victorious, alleluia.

Most glorious prince, Michael the Archangel, be mindful of us:
here and everywhere always pray to the Son of God for us, alleluia.

Antiphons for the Feast of Saint Michael.
Translated by Carmen Mion.

Chapter One

*. . . it appears to me that so many things
concur to favour a new prince that I never
knew a time more fit than the present.*

Machiavelli, *The Prince.*
Translated by W.K. Marriott

1016

On sight the Gargano Peninsula, forbidding, rocky, dry and sterile-looking, fairly invites discouragement. Carved by nature out of a wasteland, it seems a place predestined for battle and pilgrimage. The only things alluring about the Gargano Peninsula are the sea and the heights. The spur of the boot of Italy, which is the Gargano, intrudes itself eastward as though to divide the Adriatic in two, north from south; it then drops abruptly from the dry but green heights into the sea which surrounds it on three sides. And what a sea it is!—shimmering hotly in a midsummer glare, or heaving dangerously in a winter storm, its countless white caps frothily protesting the absence of a tranquillity that has never come to this part of the world. A sea-swept peninsula, yes; but for landlubbers the panoramic view from the heights over the vast green and fertile plains of Apulia is more beguiling. This natural richness did not go unappreciated by forty Norman pilgrims recently landed on their way home from the Holy Land. Close as they were to Gargano's sacred shrine honouring the Archangel Michael, it seemed proper to pay their respects to their favourite warrior saint. Monte Sant'Angelo was a pilgrimage shrine of the archangel, second in importance only to the Normans' own Mont-Saint-Michel, and not to visit it would be tantamount to courting fearsome troubles on this last dangerous leg of the journey home.

The Gargano had enjoyed a reputation for the miraculous, an aura of the supernatural, from times as remote as those of classical antiquity, when Monte Sant'Angelo was already a pilgrimage spot. A Greek oracle had been set up in a cave there in the name of Calchas, Homer's soothsayer of wide repute. The story of how this holy place was converted from pagan to Christian fame is as improbable as is its location.

In the late fifth century AD, on a day famous for nothing but a miracle, a local cattle owner shot an arrow in the direction of a vagrant bull in an attempt to frighten it out of the ancient cave. The arrow, to his surprise, turned in mid-flight and embedded itself in his own thigh. Understandably uncomprehending, the local limped off to consult Bishop Laurentius of Siponto (ancient Roman Sipontum), a rough journey for a man with a gimpy leg since it is almost entirely vertical, downwards several thousand feet. Intrigued, Laurentius, after three days of fasting as though in preparation for a foreseen miracle—and who in those ages did not anticipate the miraculous?—went to the cave just in time to catch a visit by the Holy Michael, who appeared in full armour to announce that the shrine was henceforth to be dedicated to himself and his brother angels. As a token of his appearance he left one of his iron spurs. Returning a few days later, Laurentius discovered that the cave had been miraculously transformed by angels into a chapel (though how he was assured of the identity of the decorators remains undisclosed). Another version of the story has it that Michael appeared to some shepherds in the grotto in the year 491, leaving with them his red cloak. A piece of this garment was supposedly carried away by an eight-century bishop, Saint Aubert, who housed it in the Norman shrine he erected—Mont-Saint-Michel.

Such was the start of this pilgrimage centre, the popularity of which is attested by the crutches, artificial limbs and primitive paintings of accidents left behind as tokens of the miraculous cures worked in the name of the archangel. Not to be outdone by their inferiors, emperors, kings and princes have visited the shrine in droves; Pope Gregory the Great was there in the sixth century, and Saint Francis of Assisi, apparently as destructive as the worst of tourists, allegedly carved his initials on the altar.

So here, in the Gargano Peninsula in 1016, the Norman pilgrims, ill-clad and tired, made their wearying ascent up the steep slopes of the southern face of the mountains overlooking the sites of the future Manfredonia and the ancient Roman Sipontum. The air was dry, probably, but not without a bit of a tang from the sea which looked to be almost at their feet. Except for their flat-sounding speech—which they seemed to speak off their lips, in the very front of their mouths—and their clothes, they would have deserved barely a second glance from the few other pilgrims climbing the heights. They all wore homespun linen; and, since none of them was of the Norman upper class, their tunics were dark and unobtrusive, a hangover from Charlemagne's decree that the peasants would thus distinguish themselves from the aristocracy. Short tunics were the order for the men, coming to about mid-thigh, with some wearing tights; others, the younger ones especially, going bare-legged—it was, after all, warm in Southern Italy. They cinched in their tunics with leather belts, emphasizing their hips and deep chests while narrowing their waists attractively. The few women in the group—there were probably only three or four, if that many—wore linen outer garments, long, with sleeves to the elbow, allowing the longer sleeves of the under-garments to show on down to the wrists. If there was a married woman present she wore a scarf over her hair and tied, not without elegance, under her chin. The younger, unmarried girls went bareheaded, their hair braided, or maybe falling loosely over the shoulders. Knowledge of the Normans who would come later to Italy and Sicily—and to England as well—tells us that there were thoughts other than religious ones passing through the minds of more than a few of those pilgrims, the first of waves of Normans that were to prove unstoppable even by the combined powers of a Holy Roman emperor, a pope and an emperor of Constantinople.

Having attained the summit, the eleventh-century pilgrims then had to descend a rough path, treacherously steep, through an ever-narrowing ravine until they reached the cave entrance. Today a flight of eighty-six steps leads downward from the street-level gate to the enormous bronze doors which are the portal of this cave, now a dedicated cathedral. They were hung there sixty years after the Normans of 1016 paid their respects (in a visit which was to prove significant to every succeeding generation) by a wealthy merchant of Amalfi, who lived in Constantinople. He donated these towering doors to the shrine, in lieu of a pilgrimage, as his way of ensuring eventual salvation. His name, Pantaleone, appears in an inscription asking for prayers for the repose of his soul, as well as making a demand that the local priests keep the doors clean and polish them at least once a year, an admonishment which, to judge from the lovely soft patina, has gone unheeded.

The Norman pilgrims would have been impressed by these doors had they been able to see them. There is something miraculous about the sumptuousness of this medieval work, still largely intact. Rich decorative effects and illustrations from the Old and New Testaments supply ample material for hours of contemplative study. There is even a representation of Saint Michael appearing to Laurentius of Sipontum. Lions in three dimensions, and holding rings in their mouths, act as knockers, which the natives use vigorously before entering. In all, there are twenty-four panels, twelve on each door, and all of them marvels of the ancient art of metal inlay known as niello.

The earliest specimens of niello work date from ancient Rome; but it was in the medieval period, especially in Italy, that the art reached its most sublime. Niello work is the inlaying of a powdered amalgam of silver, lead and copper into scratches or wider gougings engraved in a metal plate. The amalgam is mixed with sulphur and the whole plate with its dry inlay material is heated, using borax as a flux. By adjusting the proportions of the three basic metals, various colours can be achieved in the inlay. When the plate has been cooled it is then scraped and polished to remove the excess niello, leaving a smooth, often elegantly decorated surface. On the doors of Monte Sant'Angelo, the flesh areas of the figures—the faces, hands and feet—are represented by silver inlay.

Perhaps because of the limitations of the technique of niello, the representations of different biblical stories sometime follow a similar format, though all of them are interesting and display variations. One of the more complicated panels shows the three men in the fiery furnace, watched over by the protecting angel of God. The artist was more concerned that we notice the angel, a fittingly larger presence, than the men with the red flames licking at the hems of their robes. Each of the three raises silver hands to the angel while looking at us, unemotionally, calmly asking us if we expected anything else. There is something naively sweet about those three silver faces; the angel seems a trifle disbelieving, gazing at us out of a strangely Picasso-esque face that simultaneously presents both frontal and three-quarter aspects.

The cave-church of Monte Sant'Angelo has not changed much since the visit of the Norman pilgrims; it has the same slippery wet floor, so treacherous to the unsuspecting tourist and so unimportant to the piously kneeling worshipper. There are works of art from many ages, some good, some atrocious, the most handsome of the lot being the marble bishop's throne resting on two carved lions. The Archangel Michael is on one side slaying a dragon; except for his wings he looks not unlike Saint George. The geometric patterns, so typically Arabic, on the back of the throne suggest that it is a product of Norman Sicily.

Cave church, Monte Sant'Angelo, Italy

If the church has not changed much, the city of Monte Sant'Angelo has. The year-round tourists, along with the summer visitors to the nearby resorts, have at last brought changes to this promontory. Prosperity is evidenced everywhere in the streets, and there is a smile on the face of the people. The brilliant light of the heights—the Italians have such a wonderful word for this particular kind of transparency: *limpido*—reflected from the sea below with a clarity to rival a diamond, bathes every nook and corner. The toothless little old grandmother minding the *frutteria* for her son and daughter-in-law during a lunch break could afford to laugh. In a light that seems to transfigure everything it touches, melancholy is inappropriate, an affront. And her eyes! How they lit up with pleasure when our two American *furbi* (con artists) spoke to her as *nonna* (grandmother)! They knew what they were doing—Italian chocolate is delicious! Monte Sant'Angelo and its Gargano Peninsula may be known as 'the spur of the Italian boot'; better it should be called 'the throne of the sun'.

At Monte Sant'Angelo the Normans struck their first Italian deal, one that would lead to so many others. A Lombard nobleman, Melus by name, was at the shrine also, driven into exile from his home city of Bari after having been accused of leading a revolt of a good part of Southern Italy against the Byzantine masters. A descendant of the former rulers of the northern districts, he had been reduced to straits which he found unworthy. Melus longed for the old days, for the permanent removal of the Byzantine presence, which would surely open the way for his return to glory, power and riches. He was a man of education and culture, though as unprincipled and treacherous as the very men with whom he bargained.

The forty Norman visitors were peasants, at best small landholders, but their reputation for prowess on the battlefield, not to speak of conscientious ruthlessness and unabashed treachery, had preceded them. It is easy to conjecture the meeting: Melus enticing with gifts—rare silks, strange foods, probably some gold and silver thrown in—coaxing, persuading them with his cultivated speech and delicate manners, that they could gain unimagined wealth if they would but remain in Italy and fight for him and the re-establishment of Lombard power; the Normans, rough, suspicious but interested, unshaven, wrinkled and soiled from travel, disliking Melus for his expensive clothes but respecting his wealth. And his manners they saw as prissy. They were anxious to get back to Normandy, to see their families again, they told him. They would, however, mention Melus' enterprise to their friends at home. Some of those present, along with others, would be sure to return the following year, they promised. History bears out that they kept their word. Melus had chosen his allies well—too well as it turned out!

1017

True to their word the Normans were back in Italy, at Capua, the following year. Having broadcast news of Lombard beneficence, they brought their brothers and friends. It was a gleeful Melus who greeted this first motley crew to descend on Southern Italy, a small group of toughs looking for ready cash, adventure and a fight. This handful of would-be brigands, mercenaries without a cause, and just plain alley fighters, was a mere harbinger of the flocks which were to follow shortly. They brought encouraging word that more were on the way, that it should not be too long before their ranks would be swelled. Melus, seeing his dreams materialize before his eyes, wined them royally and gave them gifts of the perfumes for which Capua had been famous since ancient days, a gesture lost on the hardened northerners who regarded such amenities as feminine.

There is no doubt that the Normans must have awed their hosts who, shorter and slimmer, could only look up to them and from their more mundane level admire the wide shoulders, the square jaws, and the tight thighs so lean from extensive horseback riding. The Lombards must also have thought the foreign armour unwieldly: those long broadswords, those short lances and enormous kite-shaped shields. Strangest of all must have been the Normans' conical helmets with the curious iron projections down the front—nose protectors, prominent enough to cause the uninitiated to wonder how these men of the north avoided developing crossed eyes. Along with the usual chain-mail to protect their necks and shoulders, the Normans also fancied a heavy chain-mail byrnie, an overall garment from neck to calf, though some preferred them waist length. All of this seemed terribly cumber-some to the Lombards and Italians who geared their attire to the intense southern heat. But the Normans endured hardship with the willingness of their Viking ancestors. The cold they were accustomed to; the heat they would grow accustomed to also. Certainly it would take more than a climatic condition to make them change their traditional battle garb.

Capua, where Melus met his new friends, was a Lombard city refounded by a Bishop Landulf in 856, after the ancient Capua, which dated back to Roman days, had been destroyed by Saracen raiders, probably from Sicily. Capua had been the ancient 'sin city' of the Campania, so notorious that even the heroic Cathaginian, Hannibal, could not withstand its sensual blandishments and is supposed to have grown so lethargic with Capuan luxury that he lost all will to fight and hence missed his chance to conquer Rome. This is not entirely true, though it does seem that once he decided to return to the field against the Roman legions his forces were decimated by desertions, attributed to the wanton women of Capua who were recognized as the most handsome of the Campania. We may be sure that Melus laid on for his new-found friends the famous Capuan pulchritude!

With their eyes on the fleshpots, the Normans probably had no interest in the ancient Mithraeum, small as always, and underground, still visible today (in the town known as Santa Maria Capua Vetere), and still showing vivid remnants of the old frescoes. Nor were they carried away intellectually or emotionally by the great amphitheatre of Roman Capua, second in size only to the Colosseum in Rome. Startlingly like twisting sun-bleached remains of some ponderous prehistoric beast, the arena skeleton looms skyward, extending its piers upwards as though struggling to be free of the soil. Etched dramatically against the distant mountains, these rough remains of a society sick with a sadism unmatched in history show a quality that is defiant, bold, rebellious and daring; they perhaps symbolize their greatest local hero and performer, the slave gladiator Spartacus.

The Normans were not to achieve instant victory in Italy, but neither were they in the long run destined for defeat. And what they were doing in Capua this year, little as they realized it, was certainly indicative of a changing motion in history.

1018

If they saw it at all, the Normans paid little heed to the crude, natural-looking prehistoric menhir which bore lonely witness to the first large-scale meeting of Greek and Norman forces on the already historic battlefield of Cannae, near Barletta, on the east coast of Italy. Even today, understanding of the function of menhirs is at best meagre, though they are one of the persistent evidences of prehistoric cultures in many places of the world. These vertical stones, sometimes arranged in long, precisely positioned rows, and often ponderously large, could be related to an ancient sun-worship or to a system of astronomical observation. Very early in its history the Church saw them as idols of a foregone time, idols not easily replaced by Christianity, 'for church records beginning with the Council of Tours in AD 567 and continuing into the tenth century contain several references to the problem of menhir worship. The church's solutions seem to have been two: the carving on the menhirs of Latin crosses, many still in evidence today, and the uprooting of other menhirs for subsequent re-erection atop the roofs of Christian churches'.[9]

Unlike the temporarily victorious Hannibal, whose elephant-reinforced army administered a resounding defeat to the larger Roman host on this same battlefield of Cannae in 216 BC, the Norman-Lombard forces were cata-strophically vanquished, ironically by fellow Vikings. The leader of the triumphant Byzantines, the great catapan (governor) Basil Boioannes, had augmented his forces with the formidable Varangian Guard, a regiment made up of Russians and Scandinavians, mostly the latter, which had been sent to him as a gift from Prince Vladimir of Kiev. What a sensible irony to pit Viking against Viking, 'barbarian' against 'barbarian', thus saving the more deserving and civilized Eastern Greeks.

The dispirited remnant of Norman adventurers, led by one Rainulf, took to the hills to regroup—and wait. Vengeance would be theirs. By now Melus was gone, finished, wandering around Northern Italy, attempting in his whining way to arouse others to his cause. He died two years later at the court of the Holy Roman emperor, Henry II, and was buried in an elaborate tomb in Henry's new cathedral at Bamberg. Even assuming that Melus' motives had been patriotic, he had performed the most disastrous disservice of all to his people. He had brought in the Normans. Now nothing was going to get them out. And being what they were, they would have their day!

1020

Rainulf was one of the cleverer among these Normans, and certainly the most able when it came to seeing relationships between the present and the future. Unlike so many of his compatriots, he was willing to lie quietly in obscurity, working patiently, confident that sooner or later advantages would come his way. His fellow Normans were flitting from employer to employer, unashamedly shifting their services—it is impossible to say loyalties—to the highest bidder. He knew how to wait, Rainulf did, and he was content to remain virtually unnoticed in the employ of Prince Gaimar IV of Salerno. Except for a few loyal followers, the pathetic little band he had led off the field of Cannae had dispersed to other power centres. There they distinguished themselves as able soldiers, and as often as not found themselves facing one another from opposite sides of the battlefields. What matter? They were being paid, were they not? And the prospects of plunder were always good. Only Rainulf waited. 'At heart he was the same as the others but he placed a higher price upon his treachery'.[10]

Basil Boioannes, alarmed at the steadily growing numbers of Normans arriving in the land he had been called upon to defend, and with the almost infinite Byzantine wealth behind him, mounted a massive programme of fortification building, starting with the stronghold of Troia. Named after the ancient city of Troy, this Italian fortress city, which was designed to defend the northern reaches of Apulia, had been built just a few years previously by the Greek prefect Basilius Bugianus, on the site of the ancient Aecae. Boioannes, of course, had no way of knowing that he was setting the stage for one of the great Norman Apulian cathedrals (*see* 1129).

In addition to his new fortress of Troia, which was the most important of several, Boioannes resorted to a typical bit of Byzantine bargaining. He enticed the newly arrived Normans into *his* service, an interesting reversal of the original plan which had brought them to Italy in the first place, and which paradoxically gave them the ultimate advantage. Their very disunity paved the way to success. 'By splitting up, constantly changing their alliances and contriving, in all the petty struggles in which they were involved, to emerge almost invariably on the winning side, they were able to prevent any single interest from becoming too powerful; by championing all causes they succeeded in championing none; and by selling their swords not just to the highest but to every bidder, they maintained their freedom of action'.[11]

Pilgrims entering the church of Mont-Saint-Michel in Normandy cannot help but sense the momentousness of the experience. Pocked by age it is, but not badly; soaring to the heavens from its towering rock (*see page* 33), it has been more out of the reach of man than many other structures. But the gorgeous, echoing vastness is an eleventh-century vastness, and heady with memories of other tongues, other times, and the struggles of the agonizing formation of what we call modern Europe. And of all the Norman sacred places none has had lavished on it riches in greater excess, a more opulent love, a more persistent adoration. When Abbot Hildebert laid out the floor plan for his mighty church this year he was simply acknowledging the personality and temperament—maybe even the eccentricities—of the angelic warrior of heaven, as well as the character of his worshippers.

Above all, Michael had flair. He had a way of getting about. One of his most spectacular flights was to this conical-shaped island just off the coast of Normandy, where he left a pool of miraculous water as his mark. Instant pilgrimage!—and the establishment of the most famous of all his shrines, one of the most breathtaking monumental sites in all of Europe.

There is something terribly Norman about Saint Michael, always aspiring upward as he does. It is an interesting fact that his three main flights, to Italy, Normandy and England, invariably terminated on great heights. Being warriors themselves, the Normans would be bound to see in him an ideal of their own breed. He was a warrior, too—he did, after all, lead the heavenly host against the fallen Lucifer.

The founder of the original oratory on the island was Saint Aubert, an eighth-century bishop of Avranches, from where, on a clear day, the mount can be seen in the distance. It was to this place that Saint Aubert supposedly brought a piece of Michael's cloak which he had obtained at Monte Sant'Angelo; so now the shrine could boast two relics: the pool of sacred water and a piece of Michael's clothing. In 966 William the Conqueror's great-grandfather, Duke Richard I, founded an abbey on the island, which raised its status even more as a centre of pilgrimage. Kings, saints and scholars, warriors, gentlefolk and children, all flocked to the sacred mount.

Only a rich, heavily endowed abbey could have built a cloister such as that at Mont-Saint-Michel. The cloister was an important centre of activity in any medieval monastery; this one is especially reassuring of the quiet contemplation of the brothers. A quadrangle of slender columns—not tall, but elegant—casts strong shadows on the bright sunlit paving. There is a pleasant garden in the centre and, on one side, an open arcade allowing a dizzying view of the surrounding flats, alternatingly dry and awash with the sea. 'The architect meant it to reassert, with all the art and grace he could command, the mastery of love, of thought and poetry, in religion. . .'[12]

Rebuilt, added to, altered by the centuries since Saint Aubert founded his oratory and Duke Richard his abbey, Mont-Saint-Michel was always the leading shrine of Normandy. Atop his tower at his dizzying height, Michael was never very far from the doings of his people. If the cloister is the place of contemplation in his name, if the needle-like tower is his perch, then Hildebert's church is Michael's turf (*see page* 33). He knows where he belongs, and he belongs right here, in the vast spaces of such exquisite proportions as only the Normans can manage, in the dusky light under arches of such proud simplicity as to make one almost wish for a world without decoration. There is such a masculine vigour about the four great piers that support Michael's central tower—which in its turn supports him at its pinnacle—as to make one feel that they are mere extensions of the muscular energy of this defender of righteousness, the very purest of the chivalric ideal. Even their placement (their bases are 240 feet above sea level) suggests the aerodynamics which seemed to propel this holy warrior to such rarified levels.

The whole bastion stands against a sea that twice a day does its best to drown it with frightening advances of the tides. He who is familiar with the Mount of Michael in Peril of the Sea experiences the struggle. For under the *baldacchino* of clouds that swirl around the head of the angel with Baroque intensity the onrushing breakers of the sea beat against the sacred mount, enraged as though possessed by the fallen angels themselves in their eternal quest for vengeance. Symbol of Michael it may be, but it is also a manifestation of the soul of the Normans; that restless, delightful and at once altruistic, mean, cruel and vengeful spirit which was to drive them on to such contradictory achievements.

1027

In this year the slow decline of Byzantine power in Italy began with the recall of Catapan Basil Boioannes to Constantinople, an enormous tactical blunder on the emperor's part. And this year saw the beginning of Rainulf's rise. All these years he had patiently bided his time in the service of the principality of Salerno, ruled for the last few months by the sixteen-year old Gaimar V with his mother acting as regent. With Boioannes gone Italy seethed again with the forces of insurrection so endemic in this unhappy land. Prince Pandulf III of Capua—the viciously motivated Wolf of the Abruzzi who had only recently been freed from the chains of a German prison—lashed out at Duke Sergius of Naples. Salerno also fell like a ripe fruit into Pandulf's hands; after all, the regent mother there was his sister. An uneasy shudder passed through Southern Italy, which was calmed only when Sergius put the brakes on Pandulf's aggressions by persuading Rainulf and his small band to join him in resisting them. In return for his services Sergius gave Rainulf the hand of his sister; and granted him the hamlet of Aversa.

In the circumstances Rainulf's shift of allegiance away from Salerno was an act of almost rudimentary simplicity. It was what he had been waiting for. The older, more time-entrenched nobility of the land saw him as an upstart and newcomer, but now he could claim with justification that he belonged. From freebooter and rough-and-tumble adventurer he had been promoted to a man of means, the tenant of a fief, a noble, whether or not the others admitted it.

But in the confused, free-wheeling world in which he operated, even Rainulf, far-seeing as he was, could not have guessed at the diadem of royalty in the future of his countrymen, for whom he had now achieved the first important step towards a throne.

The stream in the Norman valley of the River Ante was a pleasant place for the girls and women of Falaise to gather for 'girl talk', to gossip and exchange impressions of their rustic lovers, to help one another arrange assignations under the disapproving eyes of their mothers and grandmothers, and only incidentally to wash clothes. So the gathering place was frequented by Herleve (or Arlette), the comely daughter of the town tanner, a God-fearing man accustomed to hard work and frugal living and consequently given to neither the easy living of the rich nor their loose morals. He would probably have been the last one in the world to suspect that his lovely Herleve was enjoying a liaison of extreme intimacy, contrary to everything he and his wife stood for. As a further excursion into improbability, well—what if the partner was the younger brother of the duke of Normandy?

Castle at Falaise, France

Over the years the ducal ancestors of hot-blooded Robert of Normandy had fortified the sixteen-towered castle at Falaise, and indicated by their frequent presence there that it was the preferred residence. Not an especially attractive structure, it still maintains a kind of beauty in its heroic proportions, and a vaunting, almost defiant, architectural arrogance that can best be described as Herculean. And the true romantic finds it pleasing to accept the window, with its chipped stone mouldings and high window seats, as the very one from which Robert caught his first glimpse of the young Herleve. Not especially imaginative (perhaps not even completely sane) Robert had no way of knowing that his youthful idyll would change the course of history. Looking down into the fragrant green and sun-drenched valley of the Ante from his towering vantage-point, Robert had only one thought in mind; and it was more than a single hit-and-run proposition. From that young infatuation was born William the Bastard, later to be nicknamed the Conqueror.

To many a medieval chronicler William was predestined to be a king. The chronicler William of Malmesbury records the legend that on the instant of his being born the future conqueror of England filled his hands with the reeds that covered the floors both for fragrance and for avoiding contact between bare feet and the cold stone. He held so determinedly to his reeds that the midwives had all they could do to wrest them away. This was taken as an omen that he would some day be king, though the logic of this particular connection is not really explained.

There was to be yet another child born of the passionate interludes of Robert and Herleve, a daughter named Adelaide. Eventually Robert put Herleve aside, but not before helping to find a man of means for her, one Herluin de Conteville. By Herluin, Herleve produced two more offspring, one of whom was the warrior bishop *par excellence*, Odo of Bayeux. William and Odo were to enjoy a long, intimate, sometimes stormy, relationship before William, for reasons not entirely understood, felt compelled to clap his power-hungry half-brother in prison.

Wood was the most frequently used building material at this time, so it is doubtful that much of the castle of Falaise was made of stone when William first saw the light of day. But it was converted to stone soon afterwards. It is also debatable whether the centrally located donjon was built by William, or by his son Henry Beauclerc (Henry I of England). The Falaise château, especially when deserted and the air sweet with the odour of blossoming apple trees, or oppressive with the moist heaviness of a recent rain, is conducive to imagined echoes of history. Though the cold seat of the stone latrine in the tower may jarringly erase the romantic historical emotions of the moment, still the superb towers, the twelve-foot thick walls, the outer ramparts pierced by a single massive gate (itself flanked by guarding towers of ponderous girth) all bear eloquent witness to another, more heroic age. Falaise has seen its share of horror, the Allied advance in 1944 being the latest. But there is a noble calm about it today, a small-town quiet, a kind of gentle brooding—perhaps a pondering on the most famous of its children, that son who came into the world snatching up the products of the Norman soil and who would go out of it holding between his palms all of Normandy as well as the island kingdom to the north.

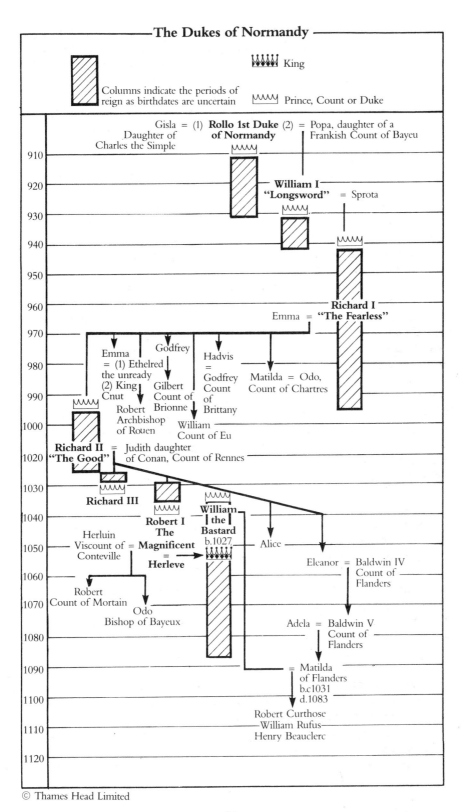

The Dukes of Normandy

King

Columns indicate the periods of reign as birthdates are uncertain

Prince, Count or Duke

Gisla = (1) **Rollo 1st Duke** (2) = Popa, daughter of a
Daughter of **of Normandy** Frankish Count of Bayeu
Charles the Simple

William I
"Longsword" = Sprota

Richard I
Emma = **"The Fearless"**

Emma Godfrey Hadvis
= (1) Ethelred = Matilda = Odo,
the unready Godfrey Count of Chartres
(2) King Gilbert Count
Cnut Count of of
Robert Brionne Brittany
Archbishop William
of Rouen Count of Eu

Richard II = Judith daughter
"The Good" of Conan, Count of Rennes

Richard III

Herluin **Robert I** **William**
Viscount of = **The** **the**
Conteville **Magnificent** **Bastard**
= b.1027 Alice
Herleve
Eleanor = Baldwin IV
Robert Count of
Count of Mortain Flanders
Odo
Bishop of Bayeux
Adela = Baldwin V
Count of
Flanders

= Matilda
of Flanders
b.c1031
d.1083
Robert Curthose
William Rufus
Henry Beauclerc

910
920
930
940
950
960
970
980
990
1000
1020
1030
1040
1050
1060
1070
1080
1090
1100
1110
1120

© Thames Head Limited

Some distance beyond the heavy gate, past the exaggerated, heroic bronze statue of a fierce-looking William, and then to the right (not a forbidding walk and well within the city), presiding over its own quiet little *place* is the handsome church of Notre-Dame-de-Guibray. Walking through as fine a Norman doorway as one is likely to find anywhere is perhaps experience enough for most of us; but it is one unfortunately somewhat mitigated by the incongruity of finding an interior which, formerly solid Romanesque, has, alas, been given a Renaissance veneer, as well as a horrific, overdone Baroque altar. There are some nice Romanesque capitals though, decorated with foliage, human and animal heads, and, looking down on us earthlings from their loftiness, two fine, virile bulls. With a little effort one can still feel a tug to another, darker age.

No less of a fortification than the castle at Falaise is another built by Duke Robert near Orival, just south of Rouen. Today the fortress is more redolent of pleasure than of war, complete with pinball machines, ice-cream and sweets, juke-boxes, miniature golf, an excellent reconstruction of a Viking ship, and the usual spectacular view of the surrounding Norman countryside. Le Château Robert le Diable—he was known as both Robert the Magnificent and Robert the Devil, apparently depending upon which side you were on—is fun to visit, but not for purposes of feeding one's historical imagination. A sunny afternoon there will give the foreigner a pleasant picture of French life outside the congested cities, and of the intimate family life that is as warm, shining and attractive as the sun-blushed apples of the Norman landscape.

The French folk who live south and west of Rouen in this agricultural area dotted by old castles and monasteries, battlefields long given over to vegetables, and orchards that suggest they were planted in the time of Robert (such is their gnarled and twisted age), are about as charmingly Norman as Normans can be; heaven help us all if they should succeed at being more so! They are a breed apart from the merely French, quick-witted, friendly, independent in the extreme and always on guard. Here eating becomes an almost spiritual realization of such exquisite proportions that thoughts of entering a cloistered community, on grounds of having experienced all, do not seem inappropriate. The good Norman wine, or cider if you prefer it, plays the proper supporting role to the food, roles which are too often reversed these days, even in French eateries.

Gastronomy was already considered a regional art of an advanced order by the time William the Bastard was born. True, he had come into a world of appalling violence and inequities, but one also of sheer animal pleasures. As a boy he could not but enjoy this fertile land of his, where every kind of edible growing thing abounded, was there simply for the picking and eating— raspberries, strawberries, and blueberries of such blueness and succulent sweetness that one would think them possible only in the imagination. Orchards of pears, peaches and cherries, whose warm colours are reflections of the sun itself, were grown in such profusion as to allow the drying of the surplus against harder times. There were probably apples, too, but not the varieties we see today which, we are told, did not appear in Normandy until the fourteenth century, imported by the kings of Navarre who owned vast estates in the area. Who has not tasted the Norman *cidre* has not tasted; and it

Mont-Saint-Michel, France

Church interior, Mont-Saint-Michel

Abbey at Jumièges, France

Matera, Italy

Southern Italy

is a pity so many people never do. The delicate combination of tiny cider-apples, one-third sweet and two-thirds sour and acid, is what makes their cider what it is, the Norman will tell you with just a hint of the braggart, a slight shrug as though to rid himself of thoughts of lesser brands, and a vaguely raised eyebrow as though to question your belief in his dogma. A distillation of the juice of the Norman apple produces Calvados, a spirit whose burn is so delicate, whose fire is so soft as to make one question the meaning of fire. It takes fifteen to twenty years to achieve the aged perfection of Calvados and, when taken in tiny quantities between the courses of Norman meals, one wonders how such magnificence can be achieved in so short a time. Pity that William's contemporaries had neither the cider nor the Calvados, enjoying instead their own heady mead, a product made of a fermented mixture of honey and water.

The local markets of William's Normandy were noisy, colourful and alive with good-natured, two-fisted bargaining—as they are today. There were festoons of strips of salted fish of every kind, taken from the Channel or, closer by from the freshwater rivers and lakes. The people of the north were always enthusiastic eaters of seafood, but they enjoyed meat too, a taste which could be assuaged by bear meat, a variety of fowl, pork, and even hedgehog and squirrel. Along with these lip-smacking delicacies, the eleventh-century housewife could haggle over cheeses of myriad diversity, rich butter and creamy milk from the famous Norman herds. True, not everyone enjoyed such varied fare as was served at Falaise Castle, William's family being nobles. But the succulent goodies were there for anyone who could afford them.

1028

Duke Richard III had presided over his domain only a year when he suddenly died, perhaps poisoned on the orders of his younger brother Robert —now we see why he was called the Devil! Richard's young son was sent to a monastery and Robert immediately became Duke Robert I, a man actively committed to violence and to a ruthless subjugation of the duchy to his will. Anything went in his book, even the giving away of Church properties to his vassals who, as greedy as he, would eagerly snatch them up in exchange for cross-fingered oaths of loyalty. He was excommunicated for his sins at least once, and through a decree issued by his own uncle Robert, the archbishop of Rouen, at that!

Legend has endowed Duke Robert, mostly unjustly (his life was disreputable enough without fictional exaggerations), with a reputation for every crime, outrage and eccentricity, every wicked impulse, even with a birth that resulted from prayers addressed to the devil. He has been made out to have been a fool (which he was not), a madman (which he probably was—he was certainly unstable), a hermit who ate food from the mouths of dogs, and finally the hero of an opera by Giaccomo Meyerbeer, all of which are gross elaborations on the life of a man who seems in any case to have been pretty well detested. Yet, knowing all this to be largely fiction, we are still left with the annoying question: 'What could Herleve have seen in him?'

1030

Duke Sergius of Naples formally presented Rainulf with his new fief, the town and territory of Aversa, which was no doubt more important to the ambitious Norman than the accompanying token of esteem, Sergius' sister. Thanks mainly to Rainulf, Sergius was now securely back in his ducal chair. But no one was fooled, least of all the ruffian defender of ducal rights. Sergius had enfeoffed Rainulf because he calculated that the Norman's presence at Aversa, just eleven miles north of Naples, would serve as an efficient barrier against further encroachments by Pandulf of Capua, the Wolf. What Sergius failed to see was that Aversa would make an efficient jumping-off place for an attack on Naples, should its owner be so inclined. Every sign available to him should have indicated that a breakdown in his relations with Rainulf, family ties or no, was at least a possibility. It is highly improbable that Duke Sergius missed the obvious signals that Rainulf was building his own little power-block. It was mostly on Rainulf's invitation, for example, that the numbers of Normans in Southern Italy were increasing as they were, far beyond anything poor Melus, now lying in his new tomb in Bamberg, could have imagined even in his wildest misbegotten dreams of power. True, the new arrivals were still of the cut-throat variety, hardly more than a rabble of booty-seeking highwaymen; but they could be managed. And Rainulf was the man to manage them.

It is difficult to resist using Robert's nickname the Magnificent when we think of him as the builder of the abbey church of Cérisy-la-Forêt. His other nickname, the Devil, should be reserved for the conceiver of the plan to raise money for the restoration of the central tower which had been damaged by lightning early in the nineteenth century. The west façade of the church, along with four bays of the nave, was demolished by the restorer, the stone being sold to pay for the work and materials in what must surely be one of the most questionable fund-raising schemes of all time.

The apsidal end of Cérisy-la-Forêt is lighted by three tiers of windows, a common feature of Norman churches, causing a flood of light to wash with sunrise fire what would otherwise be a sombre interior. The proportions of the apse in relation to the whole create a perfection that is breathtaking, the

Cérisy-la-Forêt, France

kind one learns to expect in this part of France. But proportional perfection is obvious outside too, especially in the trunk of the solid central tower where the typically blind arcading is used to such a refined and simple decorative advantage. A late afternoon winter sun, concentrating its dazzle on the already warm-coloured Norman stone, does wonderful golden things to the fabric of this badly treated church. William himself may have completed the original building, and it is pleasant to report that most of the inane destruction of the nineteenth century has been repaired.

1034

Robert of Normandy's mode of living was as quixotic as his two nicknames—one moment wealthily ostentatious, the next debilitatingly, penuriously repentant. Mentally unbalanced as he may have been, he was not so much so that he did not periodically despair over the hideousness of his crimes. He built monasteries—Cérisy-la-Forêt was one—to atone for his sins; but finally even that sort of thing was not sufficient to relieve his despondency. His many transgressions, perhaps including the fratricide of which he may have been guilty, finally forced on him the opinion that nothing would do but an exonerating pilgrimage to the Holy Sepulchre, barefoot and 'in fear of God'. His was one of the more flamboyantly eccentric journeys of the age, even for a people who 'were notoriously the most energetic pilgrims of the eleventh century and became the leaders of the early crusades.'[13] Robert, desperate as he was for absolution, went so far as to pay the expenses of his entire retinue—the bishops, nobles and abbots, all of whom could well have afforded to pick up their own tabs. 'The official historian of the dukes of Normandy recorded that such was the magnificence of Duke Robert when passing through Constantinople—and such the largesse which he dispensed to the inhabitants, that they concluded that he was the king of France'.[14]

In a rare and mysterious burst of accurately prophetic foresight, Robert had performed a surprising and fateful act before leaving his homeland: he had persuaded his Norman magnates to recognize the young William as the rightful heir to the duchy should he not return from the Holy Land. Only six years old at the time, William can hardly have been expected to understand what all the fuss was about, or the seriousness of the infighting and politicking which no doubt took place before such a promise would have been made to this unstable man.

Meanwhile William was maturing rapidly. He was growing up in a world more civilized by far than any his Scandinavian ancestors had known, a world of more genteel society, grander castles and burgeoning cities. He would often have accompanied his father on hunting trips to the Brotonne Forest. And he would have gone with the troops to Caen, which he was later to regard as his favourite city. He would have been to Rouen and Bayeux; and to Brionne, about twenty-three miles southwest of Rouen and lorded over by his great-uncle Gilbert. A typical warlord of his day, Count Gilbert had in his employ a young knight of uncommon ability in arms, and the possessor of a modesty as becoming as it was rare among the strutting members of his class. He has come down to us as Herluin. He gave up his profession, and casting his world-weary eyes in the direction of the religious life, around this year he established a small community which in 1039 moved to Le Bec-Hellouin near Brionne.

Though only the bare outline of the foundation and the base stones of the columns remain, there is still something starkly monumental in the remains of the enormous church that Herluin put up at Bec. There is a stillness about the ruins of this important abbey, a quiet perhaps symbolic of the peace so diligently sought by this knight-turned-monk. Reactivated only in 1948—it had been closed and abandoned during the French Revolution—Bec was in its day a leading centre of learning, supplying England with three of its most important churchmen after the invasion of 1066; Lanfranc and Anselm, the first two Norman archbishops of Canterbury, and Gundulf, bishop of Rochester and designer of the Tower of London. Herluin had unknowingly founded a monastery of enormous future clout.

While Duke Robert was preparing his pilgrimage, the luxuriousness of which seemed hardly appropriate in the circumstances—but such were the ways of the century—Sergius of Naples was undergoing the rude awakening of his lifetime. Albeit aware of the Norman propensity for shifting loyalties, he must nevertheless have been astounded at the alacrity with which Rainulf, on the death of his bride (Sergius' sister), leaped to accept the hand of Pandulf of Capua's niece, whose father just happened to occupy the throne of Amalfi; surely it was an eagerness unbecoming to a grieving widower! Once again Sergius got the unmistakable message: he was being surrounded by the wily Capuan and this Norman climber of little or no loyalty, now Pandulf's adherent by virtue of family ties. Betrayal was not a new experience to Sergius, but this was simply one too many. Disillusioned and bitter, he retired to a monastery where, in the quiet of the cloister, he could meditate on the perfidy of man and the meaninglessness of political power, at least in Southern Italy. He died soon after entering his place of retreat.

1035

Hauteville-la-Guichard! This characterless village on the Cotentin Peninsula of Normandy has so little to recommend it to the modern tourist that never to have heard of it is not only forgivable but understandable. Hauteville-la-Guichard? Even its eleventh-century inhabitants could not have suspected that from their backward community of farmers and cattle-raisers would march one of those indomitable families whose eyes are ever on the peaks, whose only philosophy is pragmatism, whose loyalties are loose, and whose future is unquestionably in the sun. There is nothing there now but the name to suggest any connection with that family of brawling brothers, all of whom were known throughout Europe as far as Constantinople, and at least a few of whom had such power as to rock the thrones of Christendom, causing the occupants, be they kings, popes, or emperors, to battle occasional bouts of queasiness on feeling the insecurity of their positions.

Tancred de Hauteville, a man of petty nobility, had to have been a crusty

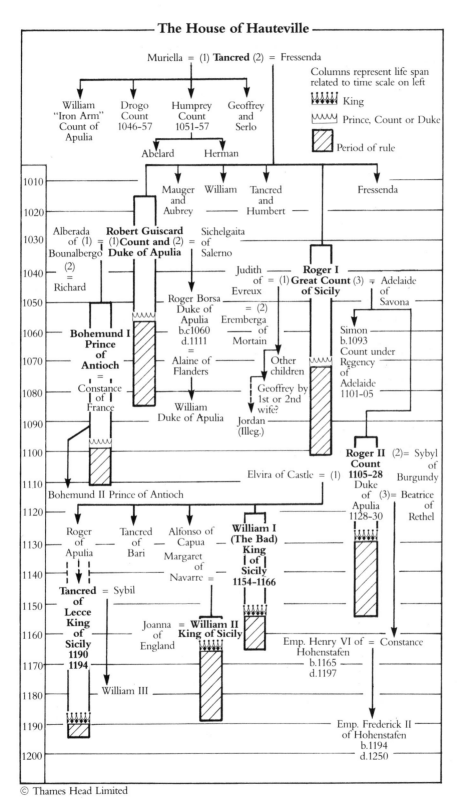

The House of Hauteville

Columns represent life span related to time scale on left

- 👑 King
- 👑 Prince, Count or Duke
- ▨ Period of rule

© Thames Head Limited

old goat. If he had any fears of impotence they were demonstratively proven to be misguided. Tancred was the progenitor of a raft of swaggering, bullying, troublesome, but sometimes likeable young marauders who this year began a veritable migration into Southern Italy on the invitation of Rainulf, count of Aversa; and for this reason alone is Tancred de Hauteville remembered, though there are probably worse reasons for immortality. One by one he produced his swarm of gifted, active sons with remarkable regularity. His first wife, Muriella, bore him five stalwart heirs. His second wife (it is hardly surprising that he had become a widower!), a lass by the name of Fressenda, went two better than the first.

Having satisfied himself as to his own fertility, Tancred informed his sons that the modest family resources were simply not adequate, taking the reasonable stand that dispersal was the only alternative. Thus it was that the three eldest, seeing the world as their oyster, left the Cotentin and found their way to the gates of Norman Aversa. The world was not their prize, of course; but they would do everything in their power to make it so.

Word was received this year that Duke Robert had died of unknown causes in faraway Anatolia, so unmourned that even his burial place is a mystery. William the Bastard thus became duke of Normandy. With his great-uncle Robert, archbishop of Rouen, offering a strong protection that had the weight of the Church behind it, serenity reigned in the duchy, no small achievement in a day when every baron was a potential duke, oaths, allegiances and bloodlines notwithstanding. Things were so comfortable, in fact, that William was almost certainly sent to the Parisian court of Henry I, his overlord, to perform the expected homage and to establish the proper vassal-lord relationship. Certainly the king accepted William as the new duke. Once mature and able to set up his own rule in his realm, William was to benefit from having established the appropriate feudal ties—but only for a time, kings being no less fickle than barons.

1037

Two years later a power vacuum too enticing to be resisted was created by the death of Archbishop Robert. Instant chaos! But through the ten years of anarchy that followed, William's realm somehow remained miraculously intact, due primarily to the protection which King Henry I of France afforded his young vassal. In this Henry was aided by his brother-in-law, Count Baldwin of Flanders, soon to be father-in-law to William himself.

1038

Rainulf of Aversa could do no wrong, at least so far as getting ahead was concerned; this is not to speak of moral right and wrong, but rather of pragmatic trial and error in the amoral world of politics. His rise to power was inexorable. Anyone as hated as Pandulf, Wolf of the Abruzzi, could not last long. His own treachery finally brought him down, without a friend to come to his aid. Gaimar V of Salerno, young, active, an insatiable woman-chaser with a virility usually spoken of as lust, united with Rainulf and the German emperor, Conrad II, to run the Wolf out of power once and for all. Following a series of political manoeuvres too complicated to interest any but the most devoted student of intrigue, Pandulf fled to the Eastern court of Constantinople where, to his chagrin and incomprehension, he was stashed away in goal. Certainly no tears were shed for his departure. As usual Rainulf was again on the winning side, despite the fact that his wife was Pandulf's niece and had been presented to him precisely for the reason of establishing family ties to prevent his sort of shilly-shallying. But all this shifting back and forth was acceptable behaviour to Rainulf, a simple getting what he wanted. He had, by turning on Pandulf, earned the favour of Emperor Conrad II, who saw him as a stabilizing influence in the south until such a time as it could be brought under tighter imperial control. With Conrad's goodwill, Rainulf also gained imperial confirmation of his possession of Aversa, along with bestowal of the noble title of count.

This year also saw the Hautevilles come to the public attention in a place which even they could not have anticipated: Sicily. The three eldest brothers, William, Drogo and Humphrey, had joined Rainulf's forces and watched his consequent rise to nobility. Now they were pressed into service by Gaimar V of Salerno who, kowtowing to the Eastern emperor, was willing to supply some men for an attempted Greek recovery of Sicily from the Saracens, who had been occupying the island since the ninth century. So the Normans make their first venture into this largest island of the Mediterranean, ostensibly under the flag of the Eastern emperor, but under the direct command of the great Byzantine general, George Maniakes.

During this campaign the Normans met a man of story-book dimensions, a prince of Norway (his father was King Sigurd of Eastern Norway and his half-brother King Olaf, the saint), Harald Hardrada (best translated as 'ruthless'). Everything about Harald is of heroic proportions, his build, his adventures, and even the role he eventually played in facilitating William the Conqueror's victory at Hastings. In 1030 Harald Hardrada had fled from Norway after sustaining wounds in the Battle of Stiklestad. But he was made of saga stuff. He took refuge at Novgorod and finally ended up at Constantinople 'during the period known as the "reigns of the husbands of Zoë", the empress who alternately exalted and murdered her lovers. According to the Norse sagas, Hardrada, with his long blond hair and gigantic frame, made a sensation in Byzantium, where he was appointed commander of the Varangian Guard, recruited from volunteers from Scandinavia'.[15]

In ancient times Sicily had been occupied in turn by Phoenicians, Greeks, Carthaginians and Romans. Following the breakdown of Roman power in the West, it had come into the Eastern orbit and was ruled from Constantinople until the Saracen conquest. As in Spain, the Saracens had proved basically tolerant of other religions, even allowing the Christian monasteries to flourish. Commerce and agriculture were encouraged, thus raising Sicily to new heights of prosperity. More stunning than any of these accomplishments, though, was the Saracen success in bringing together the four normally antagonistic principal cultures of the Mediterranean world—Greek, Muslim,

Jew and Christian—to live more or less gregariously and with mutual respect. Yet political stability was never achieved under the Saracens, its absence their most notable failure; an anarchic situation very similar to that in Southern Italy was endemic under their hegemony. And anarchy was an ideal void for the Normans to fill.

1040

Two years after landing on Sicily, the Greek forces, with their three hundred Norman reinforcements, were still struggling for possession. The best of their trophies, and a worthy one, was Syracuse, a city of such importance in the ancient world that an observer during the fourth century BC could be forgiven for mistakenly concluding that it, rather than sublime Athens, was the centre of Greek culture. It was here at the very gates of Syracuse that William emerged as the first Hauteville hero, earning the name Iron Arm (*Bras-de-fer*) for the battlefield slaying of the emir of the city. According to the monastic chronicler Amatus of Monte Cassino, who may have known him, William was a large man, fearless and handsome. We get the feeling that most of old Tancred de Hauteville's brood were a pretty good-looking bunch and of formidable build, following the physical tendencies of their Viking ancestors. That the Normans fought hard is not an unrealistic assumption. The Greeks of Syracuse, no doubt anticipating with eagerness Maniakes' eventual victory, but being forced to act the defenders by their Saracen overlords, lived up to the ancient Syracusan tradition of fierce resistance.

After fighting so hard to take the city, it is difficult to imagine the Hauteville heroes slighting the local sights (especially since the large Greek population regarded them as liberators), or not enjoying the local wine, rich and nut-coloured, a legacy of the ancient Greeks, rather resembling Madeira. Doubtless they created no small stir, not only as the victorious conquerors, but because of their size. William, Drogo and Humphrey *en route* to view the ancient arena and the Greek theatre must have cut a curious spectacle: one can visualize the children of the city following after them, awed as if by some giant gods suddenly in their midst.

Sightseeing in Syracuse is an interesting experience, intriguing in its historical and legendary associations. Who has not heard of the brilliant Archimedes running naked through the streets shouting 'Eureka' after discovering the principle that a body immersed in water loses weight equivalent to that of the water displaced? And remember the admittedly hard-to-swallow story that he set fire to the attacking Roman fleet by focusing the sun's rays on it through a system of lenses? It did not prevent the Romans from taking his city, though, and they ran the great mathematician through with their swords as he worked at his calculations, unaware of their presence.

There is a splendid Greek theatre in Syracuse, built between 238 and 215 BC. Though serving as a convenient stone quarry for later centuries, it remains today an impressive sight, cut as it is out of solid rock. If Sicily has a lot of anything, stone surely tops the list. And here we have a whole theatre—seats, aisles, steps—carved from living stone. It is one of the largest of the ancient world, 440 feet across. The cypress and pine trees which are so much a natural part of the Sicilian landscape add a classic touch of the romantic, seen by many nineteenth-century artists in countless excursions into emotional fantasy! The Quarry of Paradise, so named by the Italian painter Caravaggio, is nearby, as is the rock-cut Road of the Tombs.

The ancient city of Syracuse was actually on an island called Ortygia. It was here, in Greek legend, that the nymph Arethusa was loved by the Greek river god, Alpheus, whose waters were believed to flow beneath the sea from their place of origin in Arcadia to merge with the spring waters of Arethusa. The spring is still there in modern Syracuse, eternally monumentalizing the spot where the lovers emerged from the earthy passage into open sunlight. Ovid tells the story in his *Metamorphoses*, while the composer Karol Szymanowsky commemorates it in *La Fontaine d'Arethuse*.

Some medieval evidence is still visible on Ortygia—sombre, heavy with age, venerable vestiges of more exuberant youth—but Baroque palaces and intricate ironwork are more the order of the day. Remnants of the seventh-century cathedral can be found, too, but one must search for them on the north exterior wall of the present cathedral. Nine columns from the ancient temple of Minerva, on whose foundation it was built, are easily seen, constant reminders of the frailty of even the finest of man's work. Inside, nineteen columns of the nave are from this same ancient temple. The old cathedral seen by Maniakes and his Hauteville fellow-conquerors was later replaced by a Norman structure which, in its turn, was laid low by an earthquake in 1693. The present Baroque structure was built on the old, much-used foundations.

Near the town of Maletto, and on the site of one of George Maniakes' most stunning victories (which in Sicily were few enough) was erected the church of Santa Maria di Maniace. It is said that the grateful local Greek population of the area built it as a salute to their Byzantine deliverer. Long after Maniakes' time, in 1174, it was richly endowed as a Benedictine abbey by Queen Margaret of Sicily, wife of William I. There is a persistent legend that George Maniakes himself built a castle on the site and in its chapel installed its greatest treasure, a portrait of the Virgin Mary painted by Saint Luke the Evangelist. What is left of this historic abbey, regardless of its origin, is at least in part much as Queen Margaret knew it. The Virgin's portrait is there, along with a portion of the old wooden roof and a splendidly carved doorway.

The curious student of such medieval lore will be hard put to find the place, even harder put to enter it. The way leading to the old abbey is tortuous, muddy and threatening to the underside of even a trusty little Fiat 124 built to brave such hazards. Considering the time spent in simply locating Maniakes' church, any amount of consternation is justifiable in the face of the curt, ugly, 'No! Chiuso!' in response to a well-meaning and serious request to see the inside. Rudeness does not come easily to the Sicilians. There is a smile on this land, and a good-natured acceptance of the visitor, especially when he makes a mildly successful attempt to speak the language. That the guardians of Santa Maria di Maniace should take such a hostile stance, even keeping in mind the annoyances of tourists' intrusions at any hour of the day, is lamentable; the more so when one remembers that in a sense it is the English owners who are intruders from a foreign land.

Santa Maria di Maniace today forms a part of the English Brontë estate, a situation which came about in a curious manner. The land on which the old church stands was given to Horatio (Lord) Nelson—he of the Battle of Trafalgar—in 1799 by Ferdinand IV of Naples (or III of Sicily, and from 1816 I of the Kingdom of the Two Sicilies; he is all the same man) who was grateful to Nelson, as well he might have been, for the admiral's assistance in restoring him to his throne. 'The Dukedom of Brontë was a poverty-stricken piece of rough country with a few peasant holdings, and some dilapidated dwellings. It was not even, as represented, Crown property but really belonged to the Church from whom it had been stolen by the Bourbons a century before'.[16] The ownership of the estate has been retained through Nelson's niece

Charlotte, 'who married in 1810 Samuel Hood, 2nd Baron Bridport. The Sicilian dukedom has thereafter stayed with the Hood-Bridport family to this day.'[17]

Of the little that we know of the Sicilian campaign we are certain that it finally collapsed in confusion and frustration because of the almost ungovernable temper of Maniakes himself. In a fit of rage which must have been awesome to behold in a man the size of Maniakes, the general physically abused the Greek admiral, Stephen, a little man who has been likened to one trying to play the part of Hercules but is defeated by the weight of the club. So much for George Maniakes. He was called home to prison, the Normans would find other vacuums to fill on the mainland—and Sicily, by default, was returned to Saracen rule.

While William Iron Arm and his brothers struggled to gain mastery of an island to which they had no right, another and totally different war was being waged at home in Normandy. In that war the victory to be won was a spiritual triumph over the self, achieved by a complete withdrawal from the very world the three Hautevilles were so valiantly fighting to conquer. A remarkable flowering, the monastic development of the Middle Ages, which would reach a peak in this century and the next, is splendidly represented at the abbey of Jumièges, standing so quietly eloquent in the shade of a lush grove, majestic on its dais of verdant green.

Almost the entire area of the little town of Jumièges is at one time or another shaded by the towers of the ruined abbey which even in their decline rear themselves proudly—almost defiantly—in the face of the abuse of centuries; and it is man, not nature, who has twice destroyed this stately preserve of learning and sanity, originally set up by Saint Philibert in 654 as an antidote to a world given over to base self-interest, hypocrisy and lip service. It is hard to imagine Philibert caring. He was a kindly man, less interested in mundane matters than in working his spiritual way through the

Abbey at Jumièges, France

earthly trial. Jumièges later became established as one of the leading alms-houses of the day. The person in need, no matter who, when entering beneath the low but sweeping arch into the abbey precinct, had reached a refuge where shelter, food or medical help was available. In a day when charity was not big business, when survival was often a matter of sheer courage and luck, it must have been a last-ditch salvation to many a lonely soul wandering in from the highways to find at last a warm dry place to rest, and some hot, albeit plain food to fill the emptiness.

The abbey founded by Philibert was destroyed in 841 by Osker the Northman, so by the time Rollo arrived in Normandy in 911 it had already been abandoned and was being slowly depleted, serving conveniently as a stone quarry for anyone who needed building materials. Under the impetus of the growing Benedictine presence, a new abbey church was begun this year to replace Philibert's razed original. True to Philibert's ideal, the new church re-established its reputation for almsgiving. The abbey was also a centre of sanctity and scholarship, and remained so until the monks were dispersed by the anti-religious demonstrations of the French Revolution. The final humiliation came in 1793 when it was bought at auction and the new owner dynamited a large part of the church in order to obtain stone to put on the market; thus for the second time Philibert's foundation was supplying building materials for the architects of another age.

Jumièges is now the centre of a refreshing tranquillity (*see page* 33), a place of quiet beauty and calming dignity. Magnificently pocked by time, cruelly desecrated by man, it still stands as obstinate evidence of man's belief in intellect, introspection and reason, even in the face of contradictory history.

Castle at Melfi, Italy

But Jumièges was only the beginning of a Norman magnificence that, by the time of William the Conqueror's reign, was to flower in a veritable architectural garden on both sides of the Channel. Those bold round arches and simple capitals of Jumièges, the solid columns (some now seeming tragically negated by their lack of load to carry), the mouldings of intricate geometric design, and, above all, that unmatched feeling for space so much a part of every Norman construction—all these things give us our first major hint of Norman ecclesiastical architecture in its full maturity. And Jumièges was to extend itself, reaching across the Channel to plant its seed on English soil. Well before the Conquest, Edward the Confessor, a fan of all things Norman, had followed the plan of Jumièges for his new abbey church at Westminster.

1041

In the southern arena the Lombards, with a hope that loomed eternal, persisted in their efforts to dislodge the Greeks from lower Italy. Seeking to keep the Normans on their side, they turned over to them the small city of Melfi which, located high on a hilltop even today difficult of access, became more a lair than a headquarters. Still highwaymen at heart, the Normans could now spread over the countryside in all directions, looting and plundering, and then swarm back to their remote eyrie, secure from retaliation.

Not much of the Norman castle remains at Melfi, what is there mostly having been remodelled by that greatest of all rebuilders of Southern Italy, the Hohenstaufen emperor, Frederick II. So frequently washed by the damp fogs that are characteristic of these high mountains of Apulia, especially in winter, the block form of the building hangs to its perch, glowering sombrely over the town, not evil, but threatening, forbidding, dour. The stone is green with moss, much in keeping with the town that seems so devoid of colour, where even the inhabitants dress largely in black. It was a good place for the Normans to settle: there was no way they could have gone soft with luxury at this remote height. It is the kind of land to make one tough.

Three times this year the Normans (in company with their Lombard employers) met the Greeks in battle. And three times the Greeks were defeated: at a field near Venosa; on the old 1018 battlefield of Cannae; and lastly at Montepeloso, where the Greeks were intercepted while attempting a march on the heights of Melfi itself. While the hero of the Norman forces was invariably William Iron Arm, there was yet a secondary hero, and a more entertaining one, whose action just prior to the first encounter smacks strongly of a Mel Brooks comedy. He was Hugh Tuboef, who was seen to incapacitate the horse of a Greek messenger who obviously rubbed Hugh the wrong way. Annoyed at the messenger's manner, Hugh struck his horse mightily between the eyes with his fist, leaving the poor beast senseless on the ground and the panic-stricken messenger, supplied with a new horse, scurrying back to his own lines. Obviously Hugh's victory was of no strategic importance. But the three large battles were. If the Byzantine ruler had ideas of holding on to that particle of his empire, then prompt and appropriate steps needed to be taken, and taken as quickly as possible.

1042

Imperial favour was an elusive prize in the Byzantine world, a mark of esteem or gratitude which was turned on and off with dizzying frequency, depending on palace revolutions and the urgency of constantly fluctuating situations. This year George Maniakes was restored to the fair-haired set once again, and was immediately embarked to Italy to redress the Greek defeats in Apulia. His vengeance was terrible.

One of the first cities to declare for the Norman-Lombard forces in their most recent rebellion against the hated Greeks, Matera served as the first object lesson on Maniakes' list. Old and young alike, the citizens of both sexes were struck down, buried alive, hanged or tortured to death in any of many exquisitely Byzantine fashions. Already a desolate-looking cityscape, Matera, when Maniakes finished with it, must have resembled even more closely one of Dante's hellish circles. By Maniakes' vengeance Matera was turned into a huge graveyard, its habitations empty caves, its few remaining citizens abject scavengers creeping in and out of their troglodytic dwellings, as pathetic, as tormented, and as without hope as any Dantean sinner.

But Byzantine justice was not divine justice. Matera (*see page* 34), against all odds, recovered, was slowly reinhabited and became again a centre and source of life. Until a few years ago when it was abandoned, the people being moved out to more modern and healthful apartments, it remained an enormous settlement of troglodytes, with houses, stores, even churches, carved into the faces of vast, eroded gorges which had been cut by nature into the dung-coloured soil. Here in these comfortless ravines there are none of the lush chestnut forests so typical of the area known as the Basilicata; no pastures for grazing sheep and goats; no luxurious vistas of joyous oleanders, always so much a part of the southern landscape. There are vistas, yes, but mean and inhospitable vistas that by their very nature seem to weep. Arid and depressing it may be, but there is something terribly determined about Old Matera—old as opposed to the modern city situated on a giant outcropping that overlooks the gorge-shadowed ghost city. It was a more interesting place when it was still a centre of life, when the streets winding downward as though to Dante's eighth circle were still alive with noisy animation and the stores opened for daily business. In the terrible pride of poverty the Materans constructed sometimes elaborately plastered and painted street façades to their caves. A bouquet of flowers on a table or window-sill, a boxed fern or palm by an entrance way or a trailing geranium's colours, any number of little refinements served to erase the gloomy airlessness and congested tightness of this city literally dug out of a hole in the ground.

Even the old church of Santa Maria in Idris is deserted now, its Byzantine-styled frescoes peeling from the rock-cut walls, its earth floor now settled with dust and littered with papers, discarded plastic objects so much a part of every Italian locality, and—the final mark of total abandonment—heaps of reeking, fly-covered human excrement. No wonder the twelve- or thirteen-year old boys who press their guide services on you whistle away the evil spirits while they are in the depressing cave—a veritable chapel of the damned. But outside the sun still shines as it must, resplendently, burning the now quiet streets which in climbing the steep walls of the gully act as roofs for the houses on the lower level. They are scorched with an ancient heat, those old streets and alleys that meander back and forth, rising from the depths, the one escape from Dante's lower circle.

There is nothing unreasonable about the assumption that George Maniakes would have successfully established the Byzantine hegemony over Apulia had he been allowed a continuing free hand. But once again he fell victim to Byzantine court intrigues. Aggravated beyond endurance when he was called home a second time, he decided to take matters into his own hands by declaring himself emperor. With his loyal troops behind him he crossed the Adriatic and headed for Constantinople to seize the throne. Unfortunately for him, he fell in battle in Thessaloniki, suffering the final indignity of having his head carried on to Constantinople, there to be presented to the emperor, and then publicly exhibited.

George Maniakes' excursion into Southern Italy was not without benefit to the Greeks, in that it effectively destroyed any dream of Lombard nationalism. But that the Normans were destined to triumph should have been clear to anyone able to read the signs. Among them William de Hauteville, he of the iron arm, emerged from this year of strife with so great a reputation for successful leadership that he was given the title count of Apulia. A momentary awkwardness was overcome handily; within the feudal pecking order a count must have a suzerain. So Prince Gaimar V of Salerno was declared duke of Apulia and Calabria, and William became his vassal. Along with his title William was given Gaimar's niece as his bride, and his chiefs were awarded all the land which might in future fall into their hands. Only the blind could have missed seeing that the Normans were planning a long stay in Southern Italy. They had demonstrated their ability to take what they wanted; they were now given official permission to keep it.

In this year Edward the Confessor, last of the royal line of Anglo-Saxon kings, succeeded to the English throne. An exile in Normandy throughout the period of Scandinavian rule in England, he had in 1041 been summoned home to join his childless half-brother King Harthacnut (both were sons of Emma of Normandy, wife first to the English Ethelred the Unready and then to King Cnut), who designated him as his successor. Harthacnut died suddenly in June 1041, after collapsing in his cups at a wedding banquet; Edward's accession was at once accepted by popular acclaim. Despite the general judgement of history, Edward proved to be a stronger king than anyone has reason to expect. On occasion he was a skilled statesman and a man of courage, who at least managed to keep his realm intact over twenty-four turbulent years.

In the same year that Edward crossed the Channel to receive the crown of England, a young Italian, who would, perhaps, prove more important to the intellectual life of the times than any ruler, had arrived at the abbey of Bec. The great teacher and scholar Lanfranc was just starting his meteoric rise to a position of power in the political, religious and scholastic worlds, eventually claiming as his students some of the most intelligent men of his day, among them Anselm (the future archbishop of Canterbury) and the future Pope Alexander II. Born into a noble Pavian family, and with, at first, every intention of remaining in the lay world, Lanfranc had applied himself from childhood to the study of the liberal arts and civil law, proving an astoundingly successful orator. He later turned his back on worldly interests and submitted himself to the disciplines of monastic rule at Bec, where he soon became prior.

This was the year, perhaps, that saw William the Bastard, aged about sixteen, enter the world of men when he was dubbed knight by King Henry I of France. According to chronicler William of Poitiers, all France had dreaded the day when the young duke of Normandy, only a few generations removed from the terrorizing and marauding Vikings, was to be given the blows and take the oath of knighthood. It was a justifiable dread as it turned out. For with the ritual of knighthood commenced a train of events that would eventually pit against each other the kings of France and their overmighty vassals, the dukes of Normandy.

William of Normandy must have made a splendid sight astride his charger, wearing the typical conical helmet, girded about with his sword and carrying a spear and tapering shield. And the long chain-mail tunic added just the desired overt masculine imagery, covering him from the top of his helmet to at least his knees with tightly woven links. Even at this age he was tall and of great physical strength. He was graceful in his movements, giving not a hint of that burliness and corpulence which were to become his chief physical characteristics in later years. Already he had achieved a reputation throughout his domain for stamina and bravery, to which later generations would add the adjective cruelty. He looked every inch a man of his times, a man who adapted well to an environment steeped in savage violence and intrigue.

William and his contemporaries saw fighting as a gentleman's trade. From the time of earliest childhood the boy of means was educated into it, leaving study and more peaceful arts to his lessers. War was life. Peace was boring, and life in a cold castle dull. Hunting was the only diversion of the noble's existence, for most of them were devoid of cultural interests. The fight was everything—and often the end of everything.

William was a knight. He was the duke of Normandy. For a time, despite constant unrest, he was safe, protected by his lord, the king of France. His battles were yet to come. His countrymen in the south, not so well placed by birth as he, had been fighting their own battles for these twenty-seven years. With Maniakes gone and Lombard power crumbling, was there a southern Norman who doubted that he and his brothers-in-arms could take twice their number in Saracens and rout them in half the time it took to recite an Ave Maria? The fragile tranquillity could not last—nor did the Normans in either theatre of operations want it to, Normans being Normans. Southern Italy especially would have done well to brace itself. It was about to make the acquaintance of the second-to-last Hauteville to come that way. And he was the most ambitious of them all.

Chapter Two

. . . land that nature and art have equally blest,
destined to be the mistress of all the world! . . .

Petrarch, 'Ad Italiam.'
Translated by Bishop in *Petrarch and His World*

1046

It was a fateful day for Italy, that windy autumn day in 1046, when Robert, the sixth son of Tancred de Hauteville, rode down the Via Latina toward Capua. Riding through the dust-blown Campania he hoped only for a welcome from his older brothers, a chance to prove himself in the forces of William, now count of Apulia. He was exactly thirty years old, inexperienced if measured by his brothers, and certainly unfamiliar with the strange ways of Southern Italy. Neither he nor his brothers had any ideas that he was 'destined to shake the very foundations of Christendom, to hold one of the strongest Popes in history within the hollow of his hand, and to cause the imperial thrones of East and West alike to tremble at his name'.[18]

By his conical helmet and his kite-shaped shield Robert would have been easily marked as a Norman—the people of the Campania had seen enough of them these days to know one when they saw him. But he was more striking to look at than most Normans, or than most other men for that matter. Years afterwards Anna Comnena, the daughter of the Eastern emperor Alexius I who was later called upon to defend his throne against Robert, wrote of him with undisguised admiration and more than negligible desire:

This Robert was Norman by descent, of insignificant origin, in temper tyrannical, in mind most cunning, brave in action, very clever in attacking the wealth and substance of magnates, most obstinate in achievement, for he did not allow any obstacle to prevent his executing his desire. His stature was so lofty that he surpassed even the tallest, his complexion was ruddy, his hair flaxen, his shoulders were broad, his eyes all but emitted sparks of fire, and in frame he was well-built . . . and was neatly and gracefully formed where less width was necessary.[19]

But when Robert presented himself at the Melfi stronghold he did not receive the effusive welcome he had hoped for, Count William dying almost simultaneously with his arrival. And although Robert's half-brother Drogo succeeded as count of Apulia, he was willing to accept Robert as no more than just another Norman knight, newly arrived and without experience in Southern Italy. Norman to the hilt, Robert would have none of Drogo's unbrotherly hedging. He turned to free-lance soldiering, willingly renting himself out to any petty baron able to pay his price. He had no trouble finding work for the next several years.

51

With Robert there arrived in Italy another Norman, the nephew of Rainulf of Aversa, who had died just the previous year. Richard was destined to do his uncle one better: he would eventually become prince of Capua. According to Amatus of Monte Casino he was 'well-formed and of fine lordly stature, young, fresh-faced and of radiant beauty, so that all who saw him loved him . . . It was his habit to ride a horse so small that his feet nearly touched the ground'.[20] Richard's welcome at Aversa was no warmer than Robert's at Melfi. Rainulf II, also a nephew of old Rainulf, wisely saw him as a threat to his own position, and to that of his son Herman. Richard responded as had Robert, taking himself off to the hills where he worked for anyone willing to meet his price.

1047

While the future strong man of Southern Italy was struggling mightily to assure mere survival, Duke William of Normandy's position seemed equally insecure. With King Henry I of France still acting as his protector, along with Baldwin V, count of Flanders, the first years following his knighthood were survivable, albeit anarchic. But Norman barons were never content to endure long periods of quiet and extended absence from the battlefield. An organized rebellion broke out this year, spearheaded by William's cousin, Guy of Burgundy, who was laying claim to the ducal throne through his mother's line—Guy's mother, Adeliza, was sister to William's father, Robert. William was not yet twenty. This uprising against his authority was a serious threat to him. Were it not for Henry I's unhesitating response in his role as William's protector, the young duke might very well have been deposed. As it turned out, the rebel forces were decimated at Val-ès-Dunes, near Caen, with William for the first time making a spectacular display of his skill at arms, a prerequisite for manhood. The plain of Val-ès-Dunes is featureless, and the battle fought there was unspectacular. Leadership on both sides was a good deal less than noteworthy.

In October young William presided over an ecclesiastical council held outside Caen, at which the Truce of God, a Church-inspired device to minimize warfare, already in force in some other parts of France, was imposed on Normandy. Comic enough by later standards, the Truce was nevertheless a serious attempt to bring some order into an unruly society. By it private wars were not permitted between Wednesday evenings and Monday mornings, as well as during the seasons of Lent, Easter, Pentecost and Advent—with the king of France and the duke of Normany exempted in the interest of maintaining order. Since excommunication was taken seriously by the baronage only to a point, the threat of such punishment for breach of the Truce was effective only in so far as the various nobles weighed secular power and material gain against ecclesiastical anathema. Nevertheless William's nobles swore their oaths to respect the Truce on the relics of Saint Ouen, the seventh-century bishop of Rouen, from where they had been specially brought. William was later to transform the armistice and expand it throughout his entire, much enlarged realm.

1048

Unable to persuade his half-brother Drogo to give him anything better than a malaria-ridden, mosquito-infested mountain guardpost near Cosenza, Robert de Hauteville determined to set out on his own. With a carefully chosen group of followers he established himself at San Marco Argentano, whence he moved out in ever-widening circles, terrorizing the farms and villages, filching from monasteries and desolating the land. San Marco Argenti (its modern name) is important solely as the first headquarters Robert was able to establish for himself and which he proudly maintained as his 'capital'. An old tower is still there, but surrounded by modern buildings which are dull in the extreme, it will scarcely engross the traveller with historical interests.

There is a bleakness about this land, an uninviting rockiness (*see page* 34). Though the valleys below the early Norman mountain retreats are now largely cleared of brush and turned over to agriculture and rolling green vistas, the upper regions are still steep, jagged, arid and dusty in summer, coldly grey and of a penetrating dampness in winter. Here leafy, dancing summer to naked, chilblained winter is never a comfortable distance in time; there is not much warning, the one from the other. There are patches of green, streams in season, trees like welded strips of iron they are so black and skeletal against the blue, grey or blue-grey skies. Did fire come late to this brigand land? And what of the wheel? It is astonishing that it got here at all. To eke out an even perilous existence in the very headquarters of malevolent Nature seems impossible. Better to turn to banditry.

In this inhospitable landscape Robert earned the nickname he was to bear for the rest of his life and which would be used in combination with or in place of his surname: Guiscard, the sly, the cunning. Roberto Guiscàrdo! The very name from the mouth of a short-tempered parent was enough to cause a youngster to lie awake and trembling half the night; a signal for the desertion of village streets and piazzas; the slamming and barring of monastery doors, those of God's own territory. News of Robert's daring became regional gossip. Gossip, magnified by simple retelling, became tall tales; tall tales, legends. Perhaps it was the legendary rather than the real Robert Guiscard who figured in this story of his take-over of a local monastery.

It is related that a band of monks were interrupted from their work and prayers one day by an approaching funeral procession, a not uncommon sight in this region where the very landscape seems to mourn. Under the direction of their abbot they scurried about, readying the chapel for the funeral, putting together a few meagre bouquets of wild flowers, lighting the candles. The wide gate of the monastery was thrown open to admit the bereaved party. Would the fathers give the blessing and say a requiem over the mourners' fallen comrade? It was Robert and his Normans pulling long faces and pointing to the coffin. The lid was removed to expose the corpse, a sure guarantee against trickery. No sooner had the mass started when the 'corpse' came alive and leaped from the coffin, exposing a cache of weapons with which the villains promptly belaboured the stampeding and scandalized monks. The monastery became a Norman garrison, though according to the traditional telling the monks were allowed to remain in residence unmolested.

Successful brigandage in Southern Italy required all the knavery that Robert was capable of mustering, a problem that did not seem to present him with undue difficulty. He even managed to take his first bride, a young lady by the name of Alberada, of a well-to-do family from nearby Buonalbergo. Although later cast off in the interest of political expediency, she first gave birth to Robert's finest son, Bohemund, who was destined to extend the Norman field as far east as Antioch.

By this time Richard, who had set his sights on Aversa, achieved his goal when Rainulf II died, leaving as heir his baby son Herman. Nominally Richard took over the government as regent for Herman, but within a year or two no more was heard of the child.

On 12 February Bruno, bishop of Toul in Upper Lorraine, then part of the kingdom of Germany, was elevated to the throne of Saint Peter. As Pope Leo IX the new pontiff showed himself not so much interested in politics as in reform, emerging as one of the most outspoken upholders of the new 'reforming conscience' which sought to abolish any secular interference in purely spiritual matters. Following time-honoured procedures, the German emperor Henry III had been pivotal in the selection of the new pope; himself a reformer whose episcopal appointments were, as a rule, above reproach, he was setting the stage for a drama of political-ecclesiastical entanglements that were to shake the foundations of the Church and the empire before being resolved. Leo may be said to have started the ball rolling. He issued decrees enjoining clerical celibacy and denouncing simony, brought into the papal curia a group of ardent zealots, and also stimulated a vital revival of canon law.

While the Normans to the south at first saw the budding struggle as just another contest between Church and empire, they too were soon to learn that Leo was a militant pope. Within a short while—Leo reigned only five years —they found themselves resisting papal efforts to dislodge them from their hard-earned holdings. The pope received endless complaints of their depradations on pilgrims and residents of Southern Italy alike. Moreover, their territorial expansion was becoming dangerous; in particular, they posed a threat to Benevento, long ago granted to the popes by Charlemagne. For obvious reasons the Normans must go!

1051

Edward the Confessor was on a Norman binge this year. He had appointed Robert of Jumièges archbishop of Canterbury, a connection that led Edward to plan his great Westminster Abbey after the pattern set by Jumièges. For his opposition to the influx of Norman officials and churchmen, Edward exiled his own father-in-law, Godwin, earl of Wessex, for alleged insubordination. With Godwin went his sons, including Harold the future short-lived king. Furthermore, Edward sent his wife Edith, Godwin's daughter, into a nunnery. He was leaning heavily in the direction of increased Norman authority in his island kingdom. It was probably about this time that Edward deeded the island fortress of St Michael's Mount to a group of Norman Benedictine monks.

Saint Michael, true to his penchant for travelling, and around the same time as his appearance to Bishop Laurentius on the Gargano Peninsula, had touched down on a small island in the bay of Penzance in Cornwall (*see page 67*). This pyramid-shaped island rises four hundred yards from the shore, and is united with the town of Marazion by a causeway passable only at low tide. After being given into the care of the Benedictines of Mont-Saint-Michel by Edward the Confessor, it remained in their hands until the fifteenth century; and like its parent abbey in Normandy it was a focal point of pilgrimage during the eleventh century.

As part of his Norman enthusiasm, Edward the Confessor proclaimed William the Bastard as his heir. Austere in his private life and not happily married, Edward was childless and it was common gossip that he was notoriously inactive in the bedroom. In these circumstances it was not unnatural that Edward should designate a successor. Edward's full brother Alfred had been murdered in 1036 (almost certainly with Godwin's complicity), and the only other surviving member of the old English royal line was Edward the Atheling, a grandson of Ethelred the Unready by his English first wife Aelfgifu. He was, in any case, in exile far away in Hungary. Edward the Confessor, with his strong Norman associations, would have been influenced by the fact that his own mother, Emma of Normandy, Ethelred's second wife, had also been William's great-aunt. So if Edward did promise the throne to William, as William later so loudly claimed, it was probably at this time, one source even implying that William made a visit to England.

Three years after assuming the papacy, Leo IX was already on a collision course with the Normans in Southern Italy, posturing bravely, if misguidedly, at the head of a vast conspiracy to remove their hated presence from the entire peninsula. He was encouraged in his crusade by the assassination of Drogo de Hauteville, who was immediately succeeded as count of Apulia by his brother Humphrey. Leo knew that local hatred for the Normans was genuine and deserved. Abbot John of Fécamp had written to him at about this time: 'Italian hatred of the Normans has now become so great that it is near impossible for a Norman, even if he be a pilgrim, to travel through the cities of Italy without being set upon, abducted, stripped of all he has, beaten and tied with chains —all this if he does not give up the ghost in a foetid prison'.[21] Had the dissatisfied members of the population pooled their resources they would have had little trouble driving out these most recent interlopers. By now the haters had become organized, at least to an extent, into three groups: a pro-Byzantine party; a contingent that would have been pleased to see Southern Italy under the control of the pope; and an Italo-Lombard segment.

Drogo's assassination was undoubtedly part of a large conspiracy to do the Normans in, for many of his chiefs died on the same day and in similar circumstances. As for Drogo himself he was struck down while alone at early morning prayer in the chapel of his own castle of Mont'Ilari, near Bovino in Apulia. But even with the Norman leader dead the three power-hungry groups, although all desiring the same thing, simply could not function as a unit. Perhaps Leo IX and his temporary allies—Emperor Henry III of Germany and a large Byzantine army—could fight their battle for them.

1053

Pope Leo IX set out to launch his offensive against the Normans. However, Henry III backed out at the last moment—his army was actually on the move, heading for Italy, when he recalled it. But Leo still had an alliance with the Byzantines. Agreement was reached between Leo and their leader, Argyrus, to meet at Siponto, on the Adriatic coast, 2,755 feet below the mountain shrine of Monte Sant'Angelo.

Siponto, of Grecian origin and identical with Roman Sipontum, had fallen to the Normans in 1039. It all but ceased to exist in the late thirteenth century when the handsome and ill-fated Manfred, illegitimate son of Frederick II, razed the town to force the inhabitants to vacate the malaria-infested area. He established the new city of Manfredonia (political figures of any period are not usually noted for modesty) a mile or so away, for the dispossessed citizens. Only one building in Siponto survived Manfred's destruction, the lovely church of Santa Maria, which had been consecrated as the cathedral in 1117. It is more than merely reminiscent of Byzantine prototypes in its square plan and central dome, its echo of oriental feeling. The richly carved porch in the centre of a comparatively plain façade is Romanesque; its blind arcades and abstract diamond patterning Norman, and the sleepy-looking guardian lion at the door Lombard. Sleepy he may be, even benign, but he was looked upon by his creators as a symbol of watchfulness, and is therefore often found at the doors of medieval churches or at the entrances to cloisters. It was the medieval belief that a lion slept with its eyes open—the perfect sentry—though this one gives the lie to that noble idealization. It is easier to see this unferocious beast lying contentedly on the hearth, fetching the morning newspaper or being tugged on by small children, than maintaining an uneasy sentinel duty and holding up a good portion of the church porch besides.

Santa Maria di Siponto, Italy

Portal lion, Santa Maria di Siponto, Italy

Standing alone, a few miles west of Santa Maria, is an even finer church, San Leonardo di Siponto. Its delicate carving may suggest the East again, but the doorway is unmistakably Apulian-Romanesque, with its hierarchical sculpture over and to either side of the main door. Saint Michael is there, on the left jamb of the door, killing a dragon in rather elegant fashion, though his manner in no way negates his warrior masculinity. On the right jamb the Adoration of the Magi (*see page* 67) shows Mary and the Infant accepting the proffered gifts of the kings while Joseph sits asleep in the background, unabashedly tired after the strain of assisting at the birth. In some of the most exquisite line contour imaginable the artist fairly sings a hymn of love, praise and belief, so graceful and fluid are the figures. This Adoration of the Magi reaches rarified heights of sweetness and gentleness, providing a ballet in stone, an ethereal poem in the hardest of mundane substances. The fact that time has despoiled several of the faces, including that of the Baby Jesus, does not really detract from the sinuous movement of the figures, the gentle interrelationships; these kings *believe* that this Child is a special child, a Saviour, a Prince of Light and Peace. But they are not put off by it; they welcome Him with gifts and tender gestures, the age-old responses to the birth of a baby any place in the world. And the anonymous sculptors, they believed too; the stone appears to have been caressed into its present form. Life is not here; but the *spirit* of life is, lovingly breathed into these several figures and announced to the world with a quiet joyousness. Such works are the best we have to offer, incontestable evidence of man the believer, the creator, the lover—man, the everlasting searcher.

On the same jamb with Saint Michael is Balaam, disloyal, anger-ridden, cruel—the disobeyer of God's command. God had forbidden Balaam to go with the princes of Moab, yet here he is riding out, contrary to God's word. Suddenly the way is blocked by 'the angel of the Lord standing in the way, and his sword drawn in his hand'.[22] The ass on which Balaam is riding sees the divine apparition and refuses to go further; with what a lovely gesture she lowers her head! A stubborn, grumpy Balaam, adamantly astride his extrasensory beast, hails the angel with an outsized hand—suddenly recognizing that there may be more here than at first had met his eye. And the angel, sword in hand as described, leaves no room for manoeuvre, no retreat, no advance. Whether or not Balaam has yet received the message of the Lord, the angel is getting the signals loud and clear.

The church of San Leonardo is dedicated to the sixth-century (?) founder of the monastery of Noblac, built on the site of what is now Saint-Léonard-des-Bois, about twenty miles southwest of Alençon, Normandy. Supposedly he was the godson of Clovis I and had gained notoriety by ensuring through his prayers that Clovis' queen would be safely delivered of her child. The grateful king promised that any prisoner Leonard visited would be set free. For these stories he was regarded as the patron saint of women in labour and of prisoners. He is shown over the main doorway of his church here at Siponto holding a chain of enormous links.

It was a rag-tag army that Pope Leo IX had gathered as he moved southward through Italy, spoiling for a show-down with the Normans. As it turned out he never made it to Siponto. His route from Benevento was blocked by carefully observing Normans, and he was headed off, finally coming face to face with the enemy in a valley below the papal palace of Civitate, within sight of the River Fortore and about ten miles northwest of San Severo.

Robert Guiscard was there with his half-brother Humphrey. Richard of Aversa had brought along his troops. As they surveyed the massive papal forces—the Byzantines had not arrived, and would not arrive—they realized

Balaam, San Leonardo di Siponto, Italy

that the odds were against them. They sent a delegation to the pope pledging loyalty to him and begging forgiveness for their past territorial transgressions. But Leo was intransigent. He was unmoved by the Norman overture and informed them that death or exile was their only choice. 'Flight they disdained, and, as many of them had been three days without tasting food, they embraced the assurance of a more easy and honourable death. They . . . descended into the plain, and charged in three divisions the army of the pope'.[23]

Wielding their heavy swords from horseback, and protected by their kite-shaped shields—almost wrap-around in their concave form, back towards the body—the Normans hacked at their enemies from above. Others of them, on foot, fought in short uncomfortable chain-mail shirts, carrying round shields which had been strengthened by iron edging, though the main part was leather-covered wood. Add to their armour the usual conical, nose-pieced helmet, and they were a formidable sight to their opponents, so much so that at the first sound of the Norman battle-cry, *Dex ais* ('God aid us'), much of the papal army fled, except for the Swabian mercenaries that Leo had recruited from Germany. As far as Richard of Aversa was concerned, the terrified fleeing troops, leaving the battlefield in such haste and confusion that they trampled their companions-in-arms, were not to be let off so easily. He pursued them, and cut them down almost to a man.

Pope Leo IX's forces were utterly decimated that eighteenth day of June. The Swabians, who before the battle had been insultingly contemptuous of the Normans, were vindictively slaughtered. High in the papal palace in Civitate Leo watched his army as it was divided, hacked to pieces and finally routed.

Humphrey was credited by the chroniclers for a valiant fight, as was Richard of Aversa. But Robert Guiscard was the hero of the day, and was proclaimed so by the poet chronicler William of Apulia, who wrote near the close of the century:

Just as the ravening lion, that falls on inferior creatures,
Grows more wildly enraged if he finds his authority challenged,
Rising huge and superb in his wrath and, admitting no quarter,
Tears and devours every beast in his path, as he scatters the others,
So the great Robert dealt death to the Swabian hordes who
    opposed him.[24]

Seeing that the battle was clearly lost, the inhabitants of the now threatened city of Civitate handed the pope over to the Normans. Astonishment would be an understatement to describe their reaction when they beheld these unpredictable and distrusted Normans, who had just butchered the papal forces with such animal ferocity, now falling respectfully to their knees and tearfully begging papal forgiveness. These bloodstained heroes threw themselves at the feet of the vanquished pontiff, kissed his sandals and implored his blessing. Then the pope, like the dove of peace, gently admonished his odious enemies, and they swore to remain faithfully in his service. They then 'escorted' the dejected vicar of Christ to his palace at Benevento, where, prisoner and yet not a prisoner, Leo was to remain stubbornly holed up until he was willing to acknowledge the reality of the Norman conquests to date.

Civitate is a sorry ruin today, windswept, sun-bleached and deserted, so neglected by time that even the highway passes it by at so great a distance that the tourist is unaware of the melancholy dilapidation. A relic of Leo IX's church is still there: a mere shell of an apsidal wall, crowning a rise of ground now given over to pasture. Lonely it is, silently eloquent, a kind of architectural sphinx. On this hilltop even the most romantic of us can hear no echoes, no voices from dim history; there is nothing to recall the all but forgotten chants of unforgotten rituals, the strident claims of a vain and ambitious pope. It is not like Pompeii, say, or the Forum of Rome, where one feels the brush of history with little effort, sometimes no effort at all. Leo's cathedral, the largest remains of his city—indeed, the only remains—has been abandoned even by the spirits of its inhabitants, who have had done with it so utterly that many of the local people do not know of its existence. The soft moaning of the wind passing through the broken arch and empty window does nothing to suggest the historic magic. The desolation is so complete that human activity seems never to have been a part of it. It is hard to believe that it was built by man. Of course it was. Intelligence tells us that, just as intellect tells us that it was destroyed by man, though not at the time of the Normans. It was destroyed in the fifteenth century, and as completely as were Leo's dreams of taming the detested Normans. There are a few column fragments lying about—a capital or two, here and there a base, a shattered remnant of a carved acanthus leaf—evidence of a mosaic floor and the shallow groove of a drain trough. It has been said that mute stones speak; perhaps—but not at Civitate.

One can ruminate on the personality of a pontiff who so unwisely under-estimated his adversaries. But his willingness to take on the fight against simony and other abuses indicates a strength that had recently been too often lacking in elected vicars of Christ. He had called his campaign against the Normans a 'holy war', attracting knights to his cause by assurances of eternal rewards. In this way he anticipated the crusades later in the century.

While the Hautevilles were doing their bit to keep Southern Italy in turmoil, even while patiently playing their waiting game with their captive pope, in northern Europe Duke William of Normandy was nothing loath to keep his realm in a state of perpetual spasm, not the least of the provocations being his marriage to Matilda of Flanders. It is hard to tell just why William was so persistent in his courtship. So far as the older heads of Europe were concerned he was barely more than a post-adolescent upstart, brash and bullying, the possessor of a young person's terrible energy which would see him through situations that sager minds would regard as impossible. The German emperor, Henry III, was against the union with Matilda, fearing a too strong Normandy on his western flank as the marriage would create an alliance with Count Baldwin V of Flanders. Pope Leo took up the emperor's cause, and in 1049 forbade the marriage, probably on the grounds of some relationship between the two which was within the Church's prohibited decrees. Nevertheless it took place, probably in 1051 or 1052. King Henry I of France was so angered by the mere thought of his vassal's presumptuous aspiration (Matilda was his niece) that he led his army into the realm of his former protégé. Even Matilda is said at first to have spurned her hot-blooded wooer. She was a tiny woman, barely four feet tall, and only seventeen years old. Eventually, however, she accepted him, but according to tradition only after a sound thrashing which taught her respect for his mastery.

By this time William and Lanfranc had met and, immediately attracted to one another, had developed an intimate friendship to the eventual advantage of both. Yet Lanfranc stood against the projected marriage too, mainly out of deference to the papal view. But William was to be cowed by neither pope nor scholar. In a display of petulance he ordered his friend to leave the realm, and even went so far as to harass the abbey of Bec as gratuitous punishment. It is told that William chanced to meet Lanfranc as he was leaving Normandy, and urged him to greater speed. Lanfranc's disrespectful rejoinder, asking the duke to supply him with a swifter steed, caused William to laugh, and soon the two were in one of their friendly discussions. Lanfranc became convinced that the match was a reasonable one, and vowed to do what he could to get the papal prohibition reconsidered. It took time, but he was ultimately successful, though not until 1059, well after Leo's death.

The marriage of William and Matilda proved to be a good one, as good an alliance as he would ever make. It is difficult to think of it as a love match; such a condition was almost unheard of among the nobility of the eleventh century. He was the only one of his line who maintained a single wife and proved faithful to her to the end. Certainly the marriage was politically astute, his father-in-law being his former co-protector, Count Baldwin V; and because it was advantageous for William it was bound to be regarded with suspicion not only by the German emperor but also by the king of France. They must have made a remarkable picture, the towering William and the diminutive Matilda. But size had nothing to do with her potential. In due course she presented her husband with four sons, and at least five (probably six) daughters, and proved herself an attentive, loyal and loving wife to boot.

Across the Channel in England, Earl Godwin of Wessex, whom King Edward the Confessor had recalled from exile the year before, died. With the death of their father, Harold and his brothers now exerted new powers in the kingdom, with Harold acting as principal royal counsellor and right-hand man. Harold's role in history is often lessened, even denigrated by historians, but the man cannot be ignored. His sister Edith was married to Edward the Confessor. Had she been the prime object of a more affectionate king, the relationship might have stood Harold in better stead; in view of the exile of the entire family of Godwin just two years before, it is incredible that he managed to worm his way back into Edward's good graces at all, much less ultimately to become king. Yet for all the treachery of the Godwin family, a contemporary account of his election stated that Harold was in fact appointed by Edward in a deathbed abrogation of his promise to William the Bastard. Equally astonishing is the virtuous picture that Harold cuts according to some chroniclers: '. . . A second Judas Maccabeus: a true friend of his race and country, he wielded his father's powers even more actively, and walked in his ways, that is in patience and mercy and with kindness to men of good will. But disturbers of the peace, thieves, and robbers, this champion of the law threatened with the terrible face of a lion'.[25]

1054

Nine months after the annihilation of the papal forces at Civitate and the consequent ruination of Pope Leo IX's plans for Southern Italy, the leader of Western Christendom was still 'in residence' at Benevento, frustratingly confined to his city by Norman forces beyond the gates. He was free within his city: but only there. Wandering the corridors of his palace in futile irritation, calling impotent assemblies of politically doddering churchmates to formulate useless plans, he gradually had to face the actuality of his situation. Simply put—but a realization so hard to take!—there was no one willing to come to his aid. In all of Christendom there was not a leader willing to take on these sons of the north, at once so gregariously charming and so un-hesitatingly brutal. After the decimation at Civitate they seemed invincible. No one who thought twice would try to drive them from this their adopted land.

Unable to stand the frustration further, a sick and exhausted Leo IX finally surrendered to the patient but firm Norman pressure. He agreed to recognize a *modus vivendi* between the Church and what amounted to a new Norman nation; in effect he legitimized their holdings. In March he was allowed to return to Rome, lonely, disillusioned and shatteringly defeated by life and his high office. Yet when he died the following month even his most ardent detractors would admit that he had been a courageous pope. He was not without certain successes, particularly in some hotly contested Church reforms. But because his labours did not reach fruition until later, Leo was unaware of even these accomplishments. 'Least of all could he have suspected that within only thirty years of his death those same Normans, against whom he had staked all and lost, would emerge as the sole friends and preservers of the resurrected Papacy'.[26]

Years of widening differences between the Churches of Constantinople and Rome finally weakened the structure of the 'Universal' Church so severely that rupture became inevitable. Hostility was now so overt, especially on the part of Leo IX after the Byzantine no-show at Civitate, as to be an unquench-able firestorm of anger and recrimination. Both theological and political differences divided the two—arguments on the nature of the Trinity, accusa-tions of papal arrogance, and charges of Eastern perfidy and betrayal. The moment of separation, July 16, plays like a comedy of errors. It was per-petrated by ill-chosen and bigoted papal emissaries who had been sent to Constantinople ostensibly to patch up the rift. In the course of the arguments, and in a moment of Christian heat, the Roman legates (who in fact had no authority since Leo was already known to be dead) excommunicated the Eastern Church dignitaries. The action took place in Justinian the Great's majestic, floating-domed sixth-century cathedral of Hagia Sophia, an action unworthy of that emperor's proud boast during the dedication ceremony: 'Glory to Thee, O God, who enabled me to such an achievement! Ho, Solomon! I have surpassed thee!'

The Byzantines retaliated by solemnly burning the bull of excommunica-tion and in turn anathematizing the offending Roman legates. Although both excommunications (the former in any case invalid) were of persons only—not of whole churches—and could have been retracted, the breach was never healed. From then on the Christian world was divided between those in Western Europe, who owed allegiance to the pope in Rome, and those belonging to the Eastern patriarchates—all the Eastern Empire and eventually Russia as well—who conceded to the papacy only a primacy of honour and denied its right to interfere in their affairs.

Henry I of France was worried. Slowly he realized that his vassal William was looming suddenly too big for his ducal station. There was only one answer: crush the upstart before he became unmanageably dangerous!—and perhaps in the process, he, Henry, could slice off a neat chunk of Normandy to add to his royal domain.

In an attempt to cut his vassal down to vassal size, King Henry sent two armies into Normandy; he dispatched one to the north under the leadership of his brother Odo, while he himself led the southern contingent. With typical Norman canniness William watched, patiently allowing both armies free rein until he learned that Odo and his troops were in the small town of Mortemer, in the northeast of the duchy, feasting, drinking and wenching. At the most unexpected hour—dawn—he set fire to the town and immediately declared himself victorious; on receiving the news Henry withdrew from Normandy.

With this daring flexing of his muscles William came to enjoy a new position of renown. Not only had he firmed up his own power in Normandy by forcing his fellow Normans into line, but he had ignored papal anathema by marrying Matilda of Flanders, had antagonized both the German emperor and the French king by the same marriage, and had attracted the envy of the world by thoroughly trouncing his own overlord who had attempted to bring him to heel. On top of it all, William made no bones about anticipating the English throne which had been promised to him. There was nothing star-crossed about this darling of the gods!

1056

One of the jewels of Norman Romanesque architecture, the small (only seven bays long) abbey church of Lessay, was founded in this year. Romanesque architecture takes on an even more intense virility in Norman hands, yet maintains an elegance and grace—standing out like a dancer among football players. Built by the barons of La-Haye-du-Puits (a small town about five miles north), the church successfully withstood the battering of the centuries until the last war in Europe, when it was severely damaged. An excellent job of restoration from the existing materials has returned the lovely church to its original form. The simplicity of this Norman Romanesque can best be appreciated from the adjacent memorial square, a vantage-point which allows one to experience the magnificent understatement of the style. The moss-covered, central square belfry rises in stubby majesty, proof of the greatest truth of Norman Romanesque—that simplicity is less wearisome than ornate complications, even when they are Gothic.

The interior, almost Spartan in its uncomplicated directness, is like some flute sonata in stone, an easy-to-follow melody of wide arches and un-

Abbey church,
Lessay, France

decorated capitals, subtle variances of light and dark timbre without the embarrassment of confusing sculptural configurations and needless gingerbread ornamentation. But then perhaps the flute is too light, too soprano an instrument to be used as a simile for such strength, for lines which dominate without being overbearing. Bassoon says it better—perhaps Mozart's Concerto in B-Flat Major, especially the Andante, gracefully slow, without needless flourish, baritone, adroit. Every part of the church contributes to the total orchestration—the simple arches, the encircling gallery, the groined vaults of the aisle in concert with the gently pointed arches of the nave. Few buildings in France are more thoroughly satisfying than this little-frequented church, located remotely on the moors of the Cotentin. And the modern stained-glass windows, displaying motifs from Celtic manuscripts, do nothing to detract from its austere grandeur.

1057

If Humphrey de Hauteville had felt threatened by brother Robert's acquisition of power, his anxiety was short-lived; he died in the spring of the year. Savage, mean and vengeful he had been most of his life—according to at

*Interior
of abbey church,
Lessay, France*

least one chronicler he had even cast the Guiscard into prison during a high point of jealousy. Yet Humphrey had known that Robert was the only one of his kinsmen strong enough to maintain his son's holdings against his ever-threatening countrymen. He therefore appointed him guardian of his young son Abelard, and adminstrator of all Abelard's territorial holdings. Inevitably, however, Robert had taken possession of Abelard's birthright before even a few months had passed.

Humphrey was buried beside his brothers William and Drogo in the church of Santìssima Trinità, in the city of Venosa, by now the Hauteville family shrine, and already a place of pilgrimage for the Normans in Southern Italy. Venosa, 'a place more illustrious for the birth of Horace than for the burial of Norman heroes',[27] is barely mentioned, if at all, in most guidebooks. Even so erudite a traveller as H. V. Morton waves it off with a sentence or two, while others simply credit the town with being the ancient Roman Venusium, a convenient overnight stopping-place on the Via Appia. Despite being short-changed by traveller and historian alike, the town is interesting for the church of Santìssima Trinità, a worthy ruin, capable of conjuring a bit of the grandeur of the basically shabby, yet strangely noble, Hauteville clan. The walls are sculptural masses flung against the sky, dramatic chunks of whiteness in an unfriendly landscape redolent of pagan antiquity, human sacrifice and the struggles of the people.

By this year Robert Guiscard, already the most powerful of these rough foreigners in Italy, and the biggest landowner south of the Papal States, was headed for even greater things. He must have sensed, as he stood at the new grave of his brother Humphrey, that things were finally coming his way. And perhaps he even saw Santìssima Trinità as the visual symbol of his glory and the apotheosis of his family. There is the unmistakable feeling of scale, of the heroic deed, the fortuitous creation of an oasis in a hostile land, and a turning of that oasis into a tribal pilgrimage shrine—reflections of the Hauteville family itself. Underneath a rough, self-seeking exterior, the family had class. And Robert had his share of it—but not, as it turned out, so large a share as that of his younger brother Roger.

To add to the endemic fears and miseries of the native population, there now rode into Southern Italy, cutting a figure of unbounded energy and with looks to cause female palpitations, a man of heroic dimensions, Roger the last of hoary Tancred de Hauteville's twelve sons, and the eighth to come to Italy, destined to rise to the highest position of all of them. But for the moment he learned the same lesson that Robert had on his own arrival in 1046. As his older half-brothers Drogo and Humphrey had responded to their own aggressive sibling, so Robert in turn reacted to his junior. And when he once realized that Robert did not really want him there, Roger followed his example and turned to freebooting brigandage.

As Norman as the best of the Hautevilles, Roger garnered the usual booty from the lawless rapine that his family had raised virtually to an art. Before long he was able to build his first donjon on a ridge in Southern Italy, high enough to enjoy the cooling airflows from the Gulf of Joy (Golfo di Gioia) which saves the area from a breathless humidity. Later he was to add solid square towers connected by massive stone curtain walls. A handsome castle, it became Roger's strategic headquarters, and always his favourite residence. It was more comfortable and modern—more civilized—than Melfi; and he called it simply Mileto.

There is nothing left of Roger in Mileto today, nothing to remind us of his marriage there and his death. Destroyed by earthquakes in 1783, 1905 and 1908, the modern town is uninteresting in the extreme, not much more than a long, dull street, near a few ruins of an abbey where Richard Lionheart once spent a night while on his way to the crusades.

The country surrounding Mileto is glorious though, undulating, green, lush, alternating fields and groves of olive and orange trees. The farmers and grove workers look up from their chores to watch the occasional car drive by, not so frequent an occurrence as one would think now that the Autostrada del Sole effectively links this formerly remote area with its richer neighbours to

*Saint Michael's
Mount, England*

*Adoration of the
Magi, San
Leonardo di
Siponto, Italy*

SS. Annunziata dei Catalani, Messina, Sicily

Bosham, England

Interior, Church of the Holy Trinity, Abbaye aux Dames, Caen, France

the north. They wave and smile, good-natured people, not yet used to the steadily growing influx of tourists, and still exercising their natural instincts of friendly hospitality.

Unconcerned with Roger's activities, the Guiscard had ample time to devote to his own ambitions. Thus it was during this year that his marriage to the faithful Alberada was proclaimed illegal on the trumped-up ground of kinship. He was not truly married, he claimed, thereby in a single stroke dismissing his wife and turning his son, Bohemund, into a bastard. By such reasoning he opened the way for his marriage to Sichelgaita, sister of Prince Gisulf of Salerno, the last remaining Lombard with so much as a shred of prestige left. Both men benefited: Robert widened his sphere of influence to include Salerno, while Gisulf achieved a new sense of security knowing he was protected against other, less stable Norman barons. Alberada lost a husband. But Bohemund was the real loser, cheated out of his rightful inheritance. Why he did not emerge more cynical, more angry and more vengefully determined to retrieve his stolen realm than he did is one of the miracles of the man's personality. As it is, we see him in later years as a likeable giant of a man, magnificent in his maleness, loyal to his father's causes, and the only one of Robert's sons worthy of being identified with him.

And Sichelgaita was not unworthy of her compulsively active husband. She was with him constantly: in battle, on the sea or atop freezing mountains —it made no difference. Battle, indeed, seems to have been one of her preferred occupations. A veritable goddess of war, she would don the armour of a man, and wielding the arms of a knight, ride with the best of them. Byzantine princess Anna Comnena calls her 'a second Pallas, if not an Athene'.[28]

Eleventh-century kinship laws may have been on the side of Robert when he put Alberada aside, but they are not understood by twentieth-century historians. To add to the enigma, soon after the annulment Alberada married Robert's nephew, Richard, son of Drogo. Furthermore, when she died, after a long life of indeterminate age, she was buried in the Hauteville shrine of Santìssima Trinità, in a columned tomb which seems strangely classical and out of tune with the surrounding Norman ambience. Perhaps Alberada was out of tune with her first husband, though she was, according to most sources, a good wife and seemed to bear him no ill will, even as a cast-off wife. Certainly she gave Robert the most prized of all male possessions, a worthy son, if not his most worthy child—and he had many, ten by Sichelgaita alone! But Alberada's tomb, looking so lonely and sadly out of place, is also mysteriously self-effacing, displaying an epitaph which states that should the visitor be seeking Bohemund he can be found at Canosa di Puglia where he is indeed buried.

Norman power in Southern Italy was further strengthened when Richard of Aversa, as grasping as the best of them, snatched the throne of Capua on which he had long cast his eyes. When in this year the young Prince Pandulf, son of the Wolf of Abruzzi, died, Richard attacked immediately. The citizens of Capua were unprepared for a prolonged blockade and submitted. Lombard rule, which had lasted for over two hundred years, was terminated on the day that Richard took the title of prince of Capua. Radiantly good-looking (according to the chroniclers was there ever such a thing as an unattractive

Norman?), he was now able to add strategic power to personal charm; from Capua he was better placed to expand his territory, using the most transparent excuses for making war on his neighbours. Richard never equalled Robert in terms of the area he controlled, but as long as he lived he now posed an increasing threat to Hauteville power.

On the death of the emperor Henry III, his not quite six-year-old son, Henry IV, inherited the kingdoms of Germany, Italy (Southern Italy only in theory, of course, though the emperors, with imperial optimism, always claimed it) and Burgundy. Henry IV would come of age in 1065, his mother and two archbishops having meanwhile acted as regents in his name. In his youth Henry was rather a free-wheeler, something of a paragon of licentiousness. Once settling into his reign, however, he was to prove himself diplomatically able, a good military leader and more generous than many of his equals. That is not to say that he was above some sudden and surprising reversals of decision, and immune from defeat. By nature opposed to papal pretensions, he started out on a collision course with the Roman pontiffs. And he was to prove much more successful in handling his northern lords than he was the wayward Normans in Italy.

1058

It is impossible to forget that Robert Guiscard was a Norman—and a Hauteville Norman, at that. True to the breed's capacity for adaptation, he was able, at need, to shrug off his natural jealousy of his youngest brother Roger and enlist his services when the going got really rough. A general revolt against the Norman occupiers, triggered by a widespread famine (which in its turn had been caused by the years of Norman depredation and Norman-Greek-Lombard warfare) now brought a hard-bargaining Roger back into the service of the Guiscard. The famine was disastrous.

> Even those who had money found nothing to buy, others were forced to sell their own children into slavery . . . Those who had no wine were reduced to drinking water, which led to widespread dysentery and often an affection of the spleen . . . They sought to make bread with weed from the rivers, with bark from certain trees, with chestnuts or acorns which were normally kept for pigs; these were first dried, then ground up and mixed with a little millet. Some fell on raw roots, eaten with a sprinkling of salt, but these obstructed the vitals, producing pallor of the face and swelling of the stomach . . .[29]

In this emergency Roger consented to help Robert, but only on condition that his brother cede to him half his troublesome territory plus *all* that had not yet been conquered between Squillace and Reggio. As further inducement, as well as evidence of really tight-fisted brotherly bargaining, Roger was offered equality of rank in all the cities of the area, a step which must have been not merely difficult but galling for the proud Guiscard.

1059

The consecration this year of Pope Nicholas II inaugurated a short, troubled and extremely important reign. His elevation was a major victory for the reformist party within the Church as opposed to the conservatives, who had already elevated their own 'pope', Benedict X, to the papal throne. While the papal chair is no doubt ample, it tends to be overfilled when two men claim rights of occupancy. It was Cardinal Hildebrand (the future Gregory VII), perhaps the only Church leader with the power and the guts to do it, who called in the Normans to settle the dispute. The Normans, always willing to give aid when it could be used to their own advantage, were in this case not only willing but eager.

Enter the fray they did, under the leadership of Richard of Capua and Aversa, to besiege poor Benedict X who had holed up in the small town of Galeria just north of Rome. Following the usual Norman scorched-earth devastation of the entire area, Benedict X was captured, unfrocked and imprisoned in Rome. Benedict was a good man basically, who had merely made the mistake of accepting the papal throne when it was offered to him.

At this point in troubled medieval history there started an era of remarkable friendship between the Normans and the papacy, an era soon to reach a violently destructive climax of loyalty during the coming reign of Gregory VII. It was the kind of 'odd couple' relationship that Leo IX, had he been alive, would have been unable to comprehend. Pacing those lonely corridors of his palace at Norman-surrounded Benevento during the long months of his detainment, presiding over fruitless meetings, pining for friends who were not forthcoming, Leo can be forgiven for having been incapable of envisioning a day of such an unlikely union of interests. But times had changed radically during the passage of only five years. Now both parties stood to gain by compatibility; so compatible they would be. And it was Cardinal Hildebrand who officiated over the union.

Destined to be one of the most controversial pontiffs in the history of the Church—and for that reason one of the most interesting—Hildebrand had been born about 1020. His family was not aristocratic, but he later had connections with the Pierleoni family of Rome, Jews who had embraced the Catholic faith. There is reason to believe that he may have been related to them, and so partly of Jewish origin himself. He had a rigid religious background gained in part, at least, while he served as monk, probably at Cluny, where he adopted the new reform ideals currently becoming the vogue within the Church. He had returned to Rome with Pope Leo IX, and from that time worked in the service of the papacy, eventually becoming the real power behind the throne. During the reign of Pope Nicholas II, Hildebrand continued as one of the principal manipulators of the power structure. Remembering that there was a mere child on the German throne, Hildebrand did his part to persuade Nicholas II to play the trump card and to win once and for all the dangerous game of reform that Leo IX had opened with such daring bidding. The deck was stacked for a grand slam.

Since the ninth century papal elections had been conducted in a complicated and uncertain manner, mainly involving the Roman nobility and clergy, but also usually involving the right of the German emperor to confirm the selection. This made both the pope and the emperor the key figures; the pope often needed the imperial nod, and the emperor in turn needed the pope to lay the imperial crown on his head. Now the reformists wanted to rid all Church appointments, starting at the top, from what they considered lay interference. To them the papal office—and therefore the Church—should stand supreme. The electoral decree that Nicholas pushed through this year was clearly an attempt to rid the Church of secular control, and was certainly the highlight of his short pontificate. It specified that the first choice of candidates would be made by the seven original cardinal-bishops of Rome, after which the final selection would be made by the entire group of cardinals. The rest—approval by the clergy and the nobles—would be a simple formality, as would the approval by the German king-emperor, who no longer held the right of veto. The consternation among the Roman nobles must have been awesome; and in the German court the anger must have been, well—imperial.

Henry IV of Germany was growing up in a world of titanic power struggles. Sooner or later a head-on collision between temporal and spiritual power was inevitable. And the Normans would have their part to play, a leading part as it turned out, one that would leave the two principals in straits which, this year, they would not have imagined in their wildest dreams. Henry IV would be shown to the world as something of a paper tiger, cowering from Norman might behind his Alpine wall; and Hildebrand (by that time Pope Gregory VII), ostensibly the victor, would be utterly broken and shocked to the point of death.

In June Pope Nicholas arrived in Apulia with an enormous train, making a progress through the southern country, dispensing honours and repaying debts which he had contracted by accepting Norman help in dislodging Benedict X. Here he was in the very stronghold of Norman power, and it was at Melfi that Robert Guiscard was invested by the pope as duke not only of Apulia and Calabria—but also of Sicily! Robert had never set his foot on the island. And it seemed to bother no one that Sicily was simply not the pope's to give away. But Robert, not batting an eyelid, swore fealty to the pope in exchange for this most questionable investiture.

Following Robert's investiture, Richard was confirmed as prince of Capua. Whether or not it was clear to the Greeks, their chances of regaining power in Italy were now doomed, while the Lombard political presence was dwindling, preparing the way for the creation of a Norman kingdom. In truth, with the exception of the city of Bari, whose turn was still to come, the Normans had completely destroyed the Greek presence in Italy. Bari could wait. The pope, now triumphantly back in Rome, had invested Robert with Sicily; perhaps the time was ripe to assert Norman claims in that island.

Chapter Three

The spears punctuated what the swords wrote,
the dust of battle was the sand that dried
the writing; and the blood perfumed it.

Ben Said Al-Magribi, 'The Battle'. Translated by Kemp.
In *An Anthology of Medieval Lyrics*

1060

Acting in brotherly unison, Robert Guiscard and Roger took the city of Reggio di Calabria. A few skimpy remains in Reggio today attest its existence in ancient days; and the Norman stronghold has been replaced by the Aragonese castle. But it was and still is a perfect jumping-off place to Sicily. From the promenade at Reggio there is a view of Sicily which seems to encompass the whole of the eastern coast—the city of Messina, and soaring Mount Etna, always snow-covered and smoking, glowing at night like a ventilator of hell.

Brooding magnificently, Etna has dominated the eastern half of the island perhaps from the days of the 'big bang' creation. It has been the subject of endless legends and an object of fear and superstition ever since there have been men to behold it. It can be viewed from an infinite number of vantage points, the two finest being from the sea or from the town of Taormina. The view from the sea gives a clear, uninterrupted sweep of the flat cone; but that from Taormina allows comparisons both in the colours of the landscape and in scale—the mountainous shape looming over and behind the by-comparison insignificant man-made town. When the wind is right during an active season, when we can not only see the flames and lava pouring from the gaping wound of a mouth, but can also hear the drum-like booming that seems to announce a Day of Wrath, we can accept it as

That windswept mount where Typhon
The monster hundred-headed
Is held in thrall . . .[30]

Typhon was the personification of hot windstorms and the largest mythical monster ever born. He almost conquered Zeus and his pantheon of gods, but was finally himself vanquished when Zeus buried him beneath Etna. So Pindar (who died *c.* 440 BC) could write with obvious relish:

. . . that tall pillar rising
To the height of heaven, contains him
    close—Aetna
The white-clad summit
    Nursing through all the year her frozen snows.

73

From the dark depths below she flings aloft
Fountains of purest fire, that no
Foot can approach. In the broad light of day
Rivers of glowing smoke
Pour forth a lurid stream,
And in the dark a red and rolling flood
Tumbles down boulders to the deep sea's plain
In riotous clatter.[31]

Standing side by side on the shore of Reggio di Calabria, the Guiscard and Roger were tempted beyond the point of self-denial as they looked across the Straits of Messina at the island basking in the southern sun, awaiting, indeed inviting conquest. Already in their time it was known as an island that devours its inhabitants; more recently it has been called a place 'where all the songs are sad'.[32] One hopes, though, that before the brothers became too involved in invasion plans they had the pleasure of a relaxing evening over a platter of Reggio swordfish. There is nothing more delicious!—and a mug of white wine on the side tops it off. If Robert and Roger missed this exquisite pleasure, then all their suffering, hardship and struggle was somewhat in vain.

It is said that, one day while staring across the narrow straits at the island with that old Norman acquisitive glint in his eyes, Roger saw a vision of the *Fata Morgana*—Morgan le Fay—the rather troublesome sister of King Arthur. She emerged from the waters and laid at Roger's feet the illusion of a city, bidding him to cross over and claim it as his own. Roger refused, saying that he would win Sicily all right, but on his own, by the power of his strong right arm, not by means of magic. The illusion may have been genuine enough, for there is a mirage almost unique to Reggio when, under ideal atmospheric conditions, small houses on the opposite shore appear in reflection to be magnificent castles rising from the sea and soaring into the air. (Such an illusion is said to appear also over Toyama Bay in Japan, and is sometimes seen over the North American Great Lakes.) *Fata Morgana* is the name the people of Reggio use for the illusion, *fata* being the Italian word for fairy. Magic, illusion, or strong right arm, it was to Sicily that the Normans were going.

And here they were, Robert Guiscard and his younger, athletic brother, poised on the shore of Reggio. There, less than two miles away, was the plum, the island which to Göethe, when suffering from seasickness, seemed a place not bathed 'in a very rosy light', and bitter evidence of 'the hopeless struggle of men with the violence of Nature, the malice and treachery of their times, and the rancours of their own factions'.[33] But the brothers did better by taking a view similar to Göethe's earlier statement: 'To have seen Italy without having seen Sicily is not to have seen Italy at all, for Sicily is the clue to everything'.[34] Beguiling as their view of the island may have been, the actual Hauteville conquest was to take them thirty-one years!

Henry I of France died on 4 August. Aside from his dealings with the Normans we know little of him. Shortly after his death the archives were destroyed, which has left his era largely in the dark. Since Henry had been at war with William the Bastard intermittently from 1047, his death was no pain to William. In fact, from his point of view, things could not have been better because the new French king Philip I—he was only eight—was placed under the protective regency of William's father-in-law, Count Baldwin V of Flanders. The regency was to continue until 1066.

1061

It was on Sicily's gloriously rugged northeast coastline, near Cape Farò, that Roger de Hauteville landed his first small force of conquest. He had decided to set out on this expedition without Robert's help. Initially all went well, with the Normans fighting their way to the very gates of Messina. Then disaster! Logically, Roger had felt that the city's inhabitants would welcome these rugged 'liberators' who were pledged to free them from the 'godless' Saracens. But the population of the city, old and young, men and women of every religious persuasion, had risen valiantly to defend their walls and gates, finally driving the badly outnumbered Normans back to their boats at Cape Farò. The Saracens were fine fighters; the Normans learned that fact here if they had not done so already.

After defending themselves while waiting on the beach three days and nights for the sea to calm sufficiently its springtime storm, having braved the surf and reached their boats, the Normans put out to a stormy sea, only to have to fight their way across the straits to Reggio harbour. They disembarked minus one ship, a battered, exhausted, demoralized contingent of would-be conquerers—victims of a grave miscalculation. One error of judgement was understandable, or could at least be taken in stride; a repetition would be totally unacceptable. Coiled on their side of the straits for another strike, the Normans licked their wounds, and planned for the future. The story, they promised one another, would be different the next time. In the meantime, the Saracens could make a romance out of victory. Their poets had ways of making even their spears objects of tender death.

It was dark till the dust of battle covered
　its head with white hair:
old age has always followed after youth.

When I thrust it toward the enemy, it seemed
　the rope with which I drew
blood from the deep well of a hero's heart.[35]

A little later in the year, in May, and this time with the more experienced Guiscard taking a hand in the planning, a second Norman invasion was launched. They set about, first of all, to collect a workable fleet. Though not far removed from their Viking ancestors, the Normans had already lost the knack of boat building, and were thus reduced to employing ships that they had found in the various ports they had conquered, probably galleys similar to their own ancestral longships.

Sailing from Santa Maria del Farò under cover of darkness, Roger landed a few hours later with his first contingent about five miles south of the city of Messina. The crossing had taken longer than anyone, including the watchful Saracens, had expected, possibly because the sea was so tranquil, actually hindering rapid transit. The defenders were looking for the enemy to land north of the city as they had before. By ferrying back and forth across the straits, Roger managed to collect five hundred men on his beachhead, with yet another fifteen hundred to come later with Robert; and all of this without arousing the suspicion of the intently guarding Saracens! Before Robert had disembarked to take possession of his new domain, Messina was in Norman hands.

For this second assault on Sicily the Normans had strengthened their hand by ferrying horses across the straits in greater numbers than before, a trick they are thought to have learned from the Byzantines, possibly as far back as the days of Rainulf and George Maniakes. The Normans were used to fighting from horseback; they would, naturally, benefit by having their steeds with them. The question immediately comes to mind: how did they manage to load and unload war-horses—and certainly ones that would be nervous after the sea crossing? There is no definitive information on this, though Geoffrey Malaterra offers, insufficiently, that they sometimes constructed ramps on the shore to board the animals. How they unloaded them is not mentioned. That they transported their horses across open water is certain; how they did it is not known, even for William the Conqueror's invasion of England.

Encountering little opposition, Roger and his men made short work of the first step of conquest. The Normans achieved their foot-hold at Messina, beginning a total take-over, within sight of Scylla and Charybdis, those monsters located one on either side of the narrowest point of the straits, those monsters which were so terrifying to Odysseus and his companions as they ravelled out their long Odyssey homeward in the wake of the Trojan War:

> Of these two rocks the one reaches heaven and its peak is lost in a dark cloud . . . In the middle of it there is a large cavern . . . Inside it Scylla sits and yelps with a voice that you might take to be that of a young hound, but in truth she is a dreadful monster and no one—not even a god—could face her without being terror-struck. She has twelve misshapen feet, and six necks of the most prodigious length; and at the end of each neck she has a frightful head with three rows of teeth in each, all set very close together, so that they would crunch anyone to death in a moment. She sits deep within her shady cell thrusting out her heads and peering all round the rock . . . No ship ever yet got past her without losing some men, for she shoots out all her heads at once, and carries off a man in each mouth.
> . . . The other rock[s] lie lower, but they are so close together that there is no more than a bow-shot between them. A large fig tree in full leaf grows upon it, and under it lies the sucking whirlpool of Charybdis. Three times in the day does she vomit forth her waters, and three times she sucks them down again; see that you be not there when she is sucking, for if you are, Poseidon himself could not save you . . .[36]

It is a different, more tranquil scene today at the harbour of Messina. The *Madonnina del Porto* watches from her sickle-shaped spur that forms the entrance to the harbour, blessing, counteracting the call of the ancient barking Scylla and the water-vomiting Charybdis. Her benediction is for her citizens and for all seagoers, who pass by her in enormous numbers as they enter and leave one of the most animated harbours in the Mediterranean: 'We bless you and the city'. Ferryboats, freighters, liners, hovercraft, sailboats and dinghies of assorted sizes and means stream past the kind Madonna, better for having received her blessing, more able to face the terrors, that lie out of her sight perhaps, but not beyond her sphere of influence.

Messina has been badly used by the centuries, certainly the worst of its disasters being natural. There were the decimations of its population by plague in 1743, and of the town itself by earthquake in 1783. There was an outbreak of cholera in 1854. And then in 1908 another earthquake demolished the city again. Over eighty thousand people were killed in Messina alone, the survivors not necessarily being fortunate, in that they had to face a renewed onslaught of cholera. With all their ruthlessness, surely the Normans were among the least of Messina's troubles!

No one familiar with its history can affect surprise that Messina boasts few remains prior to the twentieth century. There are some, however, the finest—a jewel of Norman architecture—being the church of Santìssima Annunziata dei Catalani (see page 67), built in the second half of the twelfth century, during the last great flowering of Norman religious architecture. There are Pisan decorative elements here, and Arabic devices in the blind arcading, elegantly slender columns and pierced screen windows. But it is characteristically Norman in its strength and directness, its modest size and its superb proportions. No architectural proportions satisfy so completely as do the Norman—solid against void, simple against ornate—executed with a mastery that in other styles becomes merely fussy. Size has nothing to do with it. The vast cathedral nearby, restored in modern times in the manner of the original Norman structure built by Roger II and consecrated in 1197, is no more, no less inspiring or satisfying. Or perhaps it is a bit less satisfying; it is so vast, so spacious as to be difficult to digest. Santìssima Annunziata dei Catalani has none of these problems. A tiny gem, it is as easy to understand as a simple-cut diamond. The cathedral with its beamed roof is majestic, and was meant to be so—as much a political as a religious statement, a bragging Messina flaunting her power at her rival, Palermo. And that is the cathedral's problem. Propaganda does not become architecture, as basilicas and cathedrals and temples around the world so clearly prove. And Santìssima Annunziata dei Catalani, by going the other way, toward spirit and belief, proves the point.

With Messina as securely in the Norman fold as was possible in that day of loyalties so tenuous as to appear little more than vehicles of self-indulgence, the Hauteville brothers set out for Enna, the stronghold of their most fomidable Saracen opponent, Ibn al-Hawas. The mountain town of Frazzanò lay in their path. Here Roger, later in the century, was to erect his abbey of San Filippo di Fragalà, silent in lofty majesty, dejectedly surveying the stupendous panorama at its feet—a large portion of the north coast of Sicily, and the sea beyond Cape Orlando toward the Lipari Islands. At one time it was one of the most heavily endowed Basilian monasteries of Sicily, its riches coming from the Hautevilles, by then a royal family. Almost deserted now, but not utterly neglected since it serves as a convenient outbuilding for a nearby farm, San Filippo di Fragalà rejoices with quiet dignity in its encrustations of age, a kind of leprous patina of time. One wonders how any aspiring monk could have found his way on foot, or at best on donkey-back, to this remote location.

Today the visitor picks up the key *and* the caretaker at Frazzanò, even that initial step pivoting on a degree of luck: a chance enquiry to a black-garbed peasant lady as to the location of the abbey, eventually leading to the house of her friend the caretaker, whom she 'just happened to be going to see'. Following the enjoyment of a cup of tea in a typical massively furnished Sicilian dining-room, and a drive of several tortuous miles beyond the confines of the town, only then is one properly prepared to be ushered into the presence of one of the sweetest of Norman remains, perched royally on its hill-throne, small yet stunning in its natural trappings, still quietly authoritative on its green-carpeted and stepped terraces. Only after entering and exploring the richly mouldering ruins festooned with decay and delicate fungus, does it become clear that the cloister and the adjacent communal rooms now act as rabbit-hutch, chicken-coop and stable. But the church, small and exquisitely proportioned as we have learned to expect—no, demand—of a Norman church, has been restored with taste, reminding us that men, even during this hectic destructive century, do, after all, have souls. To enter San Filippo di Fragalà is to feel a stirring of the soul, a surge of spirit, a feeling that at least in some place in the eleventh century things were as they should have been.

Paternò was an easy mark for the Normans, falling without so much as a struggle. The fortress built there by Roger in the following decade is among the most Siculo-Norman looking of defensive structures, so bleak and solid as it postures on its mound, scowling over the lower city. It has been much restored since Roger's day and there is nothing youthful about its musculature, its arrogant, even hostile, mien. Even a trio of twentieth-century adolescents sitting blissfully on the balustrade enjoying the warm March sun cannot dispel its anger; but neither will it cast a pall over their animated conversation. Its badgering usefulness has long since been spent.

When it became clear to the Normans that they were simply not going to shake the Saracens from their stronghold at Enna, Robert turned his attention elsewhere. For one thing, Sichelgaita was waiting for him in Messina; for another, endemic troubles on the mainland urged a return to Italy. He might not be able to best Ibn al-Hawas, but he could leave a garrison on the island to maintain the Norman presence. Thus arose the first Norman fortress to be

San Filippo di Fragalà, Frazzano, Sicily

Castle, Paternò, Sicily

built in Sicily, San Marco d'Alunzio, named by the Guiscard to recall the first of his centres of power in Calabria, San Marco Argentano, established thirteen years earlier.

The new San Marco was a mountain fortress, presiding over the most used pass in northeastern Sicily. In a position to observe and control Saracen activity, it afforded security both to the local natives not already under Saracen domination and to the Norman forces whom Robert planned to leave behind. The castle was remodelled later by Frederick II, and maintains to this day a character both lived-in and repelling. Drying laundry and the comfortable banter of housewives does nothing to conjure up images of more heroic times, and of the ancient wars between Christians and Saracens. But the rough-hewn stones, the very lay of the blocks and the expanse of arches speak of war-ravaged centuries, while the physical appearance of the women reminds us of Sicily's chequered past, for many Sicilians still possess that very striking nut-stained colour of the Saracen, the subtle almond eye and the elegant grace of movement. And their dialect sounds strangely un-Italian.

The town that grew up around the fortress, clustered compactly on the steep hill of its foundation, is the stuff of story-books. The narrow, irregular streets—some of them too narrow for even the tinier Fiats and VWs—often stepped, and always twisting through a warren of white-washed houses replete with window plants, clothes-lines and brightly coloured doors, persuade one to thoughts more innocent than those nurtured by our own age. The friendly inhabitants of San Marco d'Alunzio have created for themselves a thriving little community, prosperous and animated, riding its blunt-topped mountain in a limpid atmosphere. That alone makes the Hauteville brothers' struggles for possession of the island seem reasonable.

By the end of the year Robert was back in Apulia, spending Christmas in the comforting—and one suspects brawny—arms of Sichelgaita. Roger had

*Castle ruins, San Marco
d'Alunzio, Sicily*

intended to spend Christmas in Mileto, but the pull of Sicily was more than he could withstand. He returned with two hundred and fifty loyal followers, and by the holiday he was ensconced in the town of Troina which, though more formidable than Enna, had opened her gates to him, thanks to the mainly Greek inhabitants who bore no love for their Saracen overlords. It was while he was in Troina that he learned that Judith of Evreux, an old flame from Normandy, had arrived in Calabria. She was waiting for him. She hoped to become his wife.

Sicily was reasonably secure. It could wait. But neither Roger nor Judith could. Roger returned to Calabria to claim his bride. Then he took her to Mileto. Life was good. The Hautevilles had already surpassed anything Rainulf of Aversa, or even their own brothers and half-brothers had imagined. Setbacks had been experienced; but these had been offset. With the spring their campaign would get going again. Why not sit back awhile and enjoy the pleasures of power?

1062

While Roger was lolling in the arms of his new bride, while Robert Guiscard, duke of Apulia, Calabria and Sicily, was firming up his position in Italy—and attracting little notice from most of Europe save from the pope and the German emperor—William the Bastard was consolidating his power preparatory to his lunge for the English throne. The Hautevilles, regardless of how successful they were proving in their aggressions, were little more than upstarts. William had the blood-line right to reward or dispossess his vassals in Normandy, to manipulate this body of men who had not made much of a political impression until the early part of the century. He had already (in, or about, 1055) displaced the count of Mortain, and put his own half-brother Robert, son of Herleve and Herluin, in that seat.

Now, in the year 1062, on the death of Herbert II of Maine, an ancient county adjacent to his own duchy, and following years of political manoeuvring and agreements of betrothals, as often as not involving infants too innocent to be so sworn and too young to care, William claimed that county on behalf of his son Robert. His claim was not uncontested; troops were drawn up on both sides, and William himself led the invasion of Maine. By the beginning of 1064 he had established his power in the county. His programme of absorption and expansion was under way.

Roger de Hauteville's marriage to Judith did nothing to assuage his lust for possession of Sicily. So Norman was he that he felt no guilt in leaving his wife shortly after settling down to what should have been the first glow of a new marriage. As one of the leaders, albeit the youngest, of the most powerful family in Southern Italy, Roger had no doubt that he should provide his new wife with properties and creature comforts befitting her position. The Guiscard, who in 1058 had agreed to share his Calabrian holdings in exchange for Roger's co-operation, had since found more and more reason to regret ever having made such a pact. Roger seemed now always in the ascendancy. In any case his was the more attractive personality. He was vigorous and fearless, and terribly athletic in his every action. Roger himself had realized that his elder brother had not been honouring the stipulated division of power. For a while he had been content to wait things out. But his marriage to Judith of Evreux changed all that.

Judith of Evreux was not just another little Calabrian trollop, or even pretty female pawn whose father was attempting to build power by a 'good' marriage. She was related to William the Bastard, duke of Normandy, no less—a daughter of one of his first cousins. In her case, however, blood proved no thicker than water; she had been forced to leave Normandy under duress with her half-brother and guardian, Robert de Grantmesnil, after he had quarrelled with William. Robert had brought her to Southern Italy, along with eleven of his monks who were faithful to him during his tribulations—he had been abbot of the monastery of Saint Evroul-sur-Ouche.

The Guiscard set Robert de Grantmesnil at the head of the newly endowed monastery of Sant'Euphemia, thus introducing into Calabria the Norman traditional liturgy and music, both rightly famous in their day. He could not have been expected to anticipate that his welcoming of the abbot and his half-sister would lead to her almost immediately becoming his own sister-in-law, or that this in itself would cause him to be beset by a host of problems. His surprise and anger were colossal when, without warning, Roger bade him hand over twenty-five per cent of their agreed holdings or expect to have them taken from him by force!

It was a furious Robert Guiscard who turned on his demanding younger brother, first besieging him at Mileto, and then pursuing him to the southern hill town of Gerace. Robert's rage could only be fuelled when, expressing both their displeasure at his presence in their neighbourhood and their loyalty to Roger (they simply liked him better), the inhabitants of Gerace slammed and barred their gates in the ducal face. After the usual killings and violence of siege were over, the brothers, on finally confronting one another vis-à-vis, publicly patched things up by embracing tearfully and promising fraternal loyalty against all comers in the future. This was hardly what the common man—the farmers, the local shopkeepers and their sons—had been fighting for; and it could only expand an already entrenched cynicism. The central piazza in Gerace, where the famous hug is supposed to have taken place, is in commemoration called to this day Piazza del Tocco ('Piazza of the Touch').

Having re-established familial peace, the brothers Robert and Roger marched off, arm in arm, to the castle of the city. In all of romantic Italy there is no more magical site for a castle then that of Gerace, called by H.V. Morton a *'posizione panoramica stupenda'*.[37] Looming protectively on the highest rock above the city, which itself is located fifteen hundred feet above the Ionian Sea, it has clung to its perch throughout the centuries, so shaken to its Byzantine foundations by earthquakes as to make one marvel at the divine force that holds it to the precipitous cliff. But hold it has, though huge chunks of it have crashed into the dry moat and the main entrance, and, on occasion, rolled on down the sides of the mountain. Stunning to behold from across the over-grown moat, now, alas, little more than a ditch, it is unapproachable, protected by a jungle of thorny entanglements probably more effective than ever was the water-filled moat. Besides, there are signs a-plenty—*ingresso vietato! pericoloso!*—to discourage the foolhardy. By the time Robert and Roger indulged in their famous 'touch' they had been in possession of Gerace for about three years. It turned out to be one of their prizes, favoured by both of them, though Roger was later to make additions to the high-perched fortifica-tion, including a grand room which he called *sala di Mileto* after his own favourite creation.

The cathedral of Gerace is no longer the seat of authority it once was, the last bishop having departed the town on orders from Pope Pius XII in 1954. It is obdurately medieval, and vigorously Norman in feeling, the largest church in Calabria. Since the city had been established by Greeks from the coastal town of ancient Locri—about five miles away and several hundred feet below—who had been fleeing a ninth-century Saracen invasion, it is not surprising that the church was a centre of the Greek ritual. This was not displaced by the Latin ritual until 1480, further evidence of Norman, and later Angevin and Aragonese religious toleration.

The cathedral may be of Byzantine origin, and its twenty granite columns may have come from the ancient temple of Persephone at Locri, as they say, but the air of the solid structure smacks of the Normans, and especially the simply formed geometric capitals which cushion the nave's rows of arches, springing vertically before they curve gracefully over to the next column. The columns are varicoloured, soft in hue, with a silvery patina overlay. The pastor of the church, delightfully enthusiastic and as proud of his tiny realm as the most land-hungry Norman lord, will admonish the visitor to notice the subtle ancient colours and the softening effects of the silvery Calabrian light. Nothing changes much in these out-of-the-way southern towns, not even colour. It is assuring to think that some ancient Greek, a fervent worshipper of Persephone perhaps, gazing on these columns and seeing the same low-key colours burnished by the same gloss of light, was as moved spiritually as the glowingly lovely modern 'madonna' sitting quietly with her sleeping *bambino* in the shadow of the noble arches.

1063

The winter of 1062-3 was the most trying period thus far experienced by the Normans in Sicily. Roger had gone back to campaigning there; with Judith by his side and suffering the rigours of war along with the most hardened soldier, he led his troops into a potentially hazardous situation. Starvation and

*Former cathedral,
Gerace, Italy*

cold took their toll and they were hungry and tired; but morale remained high. With the adoring, hero-worshipping Judith to encourage him, Roger finally emerged victorious; but he took the citadel of Troina only because the Saracens themselves suffered from the severe winter and, in blatant and traitorous disobedience of the Koran, had over-imbibed on the good Sicilian wine. That victory, and another one at Cerami a short time later, allowed Roger to claim possession of Sicily from Messina to a point roughly a third of the way across the island (in short the entire northeastern corner—no small claim considering the odds against him). It was decided then to bypass Enna on the grounds that it was simply too formidable; when it was ripe it would fall—which it did, but not until 1087!

The projected conquest of all Sicily and the overthrow of the Muslim presence there took on the aspects of a crusade when Pope Alexander II (Nicholas II had died in 1061) presented Roger with a papal banner to be carried at the head of his troops when they moved into battle. Furthermore, he granted absolution to any common soldier who would fight for the Hauteville brothers in their efforts to free Sicily from the grip of the hated infidel. These gestures may have been made in response to the gift of four camels which Roger had captured from the Muslims and sent to the pope. If diplomacy came easily to Roger, it was also hardly foreign to Alexander. He was in trouble, as was almost every pope of that time, his rule disputed by the antipope Honorius II, who had imperial support. It was clearly to Alexander's advantage that he could claim the assistance of the Hautevilles, for no one now saw them as other than a power to be reckoned with.

1064

There is a good deal of disagreement among scholars as to whether Edward the Confessor had, in fact, promised his throne to William of Normandy back in 1051. Evidence both pro and con is inconclusive, and it is not the nature of this treatise to prove one or the other. We can be assured, however, that the idea was at least turning over in William's mind, major invasions—and that of 1066 is surely one of the most monumental—not being a matter of casual overnight planning. His dreams may suddenly have become more feasible when an unforeseen chance put Harold Godwinson firmly in his control. On the death of his father in 1053, Harold had inherited the position of earl of Wessex. By ingratiating himself with King Edward (they were brothers-in-law, remember), he achieved a quasi-royal status, and became the trusted confidant of the king. Then, probably in 1064, he made a journey to Normandy.

The chronicler William of Poitiers was a devoted admirer of Duke William, and in fact his chaplain during the invasion. He asserts that on the very eve of the Battle of Hastings the Conqueror was still insisting that Harold had acted as ambassador for King Edward to confirm his offer of the throne by oath.

> ... Edward, king of the English, who loved William ... established him as his heir with a stronger pledge than ever before. The king ... felt the hour of his death approaching, and wished to anticipate its inevitable consequences. He therefore dispatched Harold to William in order that he might confirm his promise by an oath. This Harold was of all the king's subjects the richest and the most exalted in honour and power ... The king, indeed, here acted with great prudence in choosing Harold for this task, in the hope that the riches and authority of this magnate might check disturbance throughout England if the people with their accustomed perfidy should be disposed to overturn what had been determined.[38]

Detractors of this theory insist that Harold was too important for the mission, and also so much in a position for skulduggery that the king would not have trusted him. Furthermore, would Harold even have consented to be the royal errand boy? He considered himself as Edward's successor since Edward, ascetic that he was, had no offspring. Harold had only to wait. In addition, he hated the Normans, seeing them as usurpers of Edward's affections, and had, on his return from exile in 1052, persuaded the king to send all the recently appointed Norman officials packing. (One version of the story even claims that Harold was merely on a fishing trip, which would negate any ideas of his 'intentionally' winding up in William's hands.)

A unique visual chronicle of the story is provided by the Bayeux Tapestry. It is most valuable, however, as a depiction of the life of the times—sailing and shipbuilding, feasting, preparing for war, actual battle. Factual though it is supposed to be, according to one writer it is 'little more than a mendacious propaganda "strip-cartoon" designed to justify William's unjustifiable invasion of England in what an earlier historian has described as a "piratical venture"'.[39] Yet it remains an exciting account of a day that shook the medieval world, and of the events preceding it, told in yarns of eight colours embroidered on a natural linen backing.

Most of us have little trouble in accepting the legend of William's duchess, Matilda, and her ladies-in-waiting embroidering the clumsily shaped strip (231 feet long and 20 inches wide) while William was off establishing his control in his new realm. More probably, though, the tapestry was made in England by English craftsmen, an assumption that is based on the English spelling of names in the Latin inscriptions and by a comparison with contemporary English manuscript illumination. Furthermore, it is almost a certainty that William's half-brother, Bishop Odo of Bayeux, gave the order for the work, intending it as a hanging for his cathedral currently being

Shipbuilding, Bayeux Tapestry

built. But it is hard to imagine how the unwieldy strip narrative would have been hung in the cathedral, and it may have been intended as a purely secular decoration. At best it would have proved an awkward church decoration, and unsuitable for a house of God, with two scenes of outright nudity and lewdness. But it had the political advantage of showing Bishop Odo, as good a mace-swinging man-of-arms as ever there was, at his best, doing just that.

To follow the tapestry scene by scene is to make a progress through history. There is Edward, regal and sad (some say sick), on his throne, appointing Harold Godwinson as his messenger. We see Harold and his entourage feasting at Bosham (*see page* 68), a fishing village in West Sussex, but not before he stops off at a church to pray for a safe journey; and well he might have done, as it turned out. The church, depicted in such basic abstract terms in the tapestry, is the Saxon church of the Holy Trinity, which still stands, with its sturdy chancel arch and pre-Conquest tower. While the greater part of it has remained Saxon, there are some noticeable later additions: the spire, some stained-glass windows, and a thirteenth-century tomb showing a recumbent figure of a young girl. Harold's party then boards some handsomely painted Viking-like ships, and later wades ashore on a French beach, to be captured on the spot by Guy of Ponthieu, one of Duke William's more tumultuous·vassals. Chronicler William of Poitiers tells the story:

> Whilst travelling upon this errand Harold only escaped the perils of the sea by making a forced landing on the coast of Ponthieu, where he fell into the hands of Count Guy, who threw him and his companions into prison . . . When Duke William heard what had happened he sent messengers at speed, and by prayers and threats he brought about Harold's honourable release. As a result Guy in person conducted his prisoner to the Castle of Eu . . . William in gratitude bestowed upon him rich gifts of land and money, and then took Harold with proper honour to Rouen. This was the chief city of the Norman duchy, and there William sumptuously refreshed Harold with splendid hospitality after all the hardships of his journey. For the duke rejoiced to have so illustrious a guest in a man who had been sent to him by the nearest and dearest of his friends; one, moreover, who was in England second only to the king, and who might prove a faithful mediator between him and the English.[40]

Harold (right) at Mont-San-Michel, Bayeux Tapestry

William then invites Harold to accompany him on a martial expedition to Brittany for purposes of putting down a hard-to-manage vassal, Count Conan. In the course of the Brittany adventure Harold rescues two of William's men in a sudden high tide that has surrounded Mont-Saint-Michel. He is shown endearing himself to William by bodily carrying one man out of the soft sands, while at the same time dragging another toward shore. The scene is vigorously animated, with a horse and rider going down in the surf, and soldiers struggling to cross the estuary, carrying their shields over their heads as they push against the current. Of particular interest is the almost comic-book representation of Mont-Saint-Michel in the background, propped up on its conical rock like a table astride a mole-hill.

There follows the telling of the campaign against Count Conan; and then the clincher, the part of the story on which William relied so insistently in asserting his claims to the English throne:

> When they had come together in conference at Bonneville, Harold in that place swore fealty to the duke, employing the sacred ritual recognised among Christian men. And as is testified by the most truthful and most honourable men who were there present, he took an oath of his own free will in the following terms: firstly that he would be the representative of duke William at the court of his lord, king Edward, as long as the king lived; secondly that he would employ all his influence and wealth to ensure that after the death of king Edward the kingdom of England should be confirmed in the possession of the duke; thirdly that he would place a garrison of the duke's knights in the Castle of Dover and maintain these at his own care and cost; fourthly that in other parts of England at the pleasure of the duke he would maintain garrisons in other castles and make complete provision for their sustenance. The duke on his part, who before the oath was taken had received ceremonial homage from him, confirmed to him at his request all his lands and dignities. For Edward in his illness could not be expected to live much longer . . .[41]

No matter that the tapestry cites Bayeux as the place of the oath; the important consideration is that Harold must have known that he was, by swearing these oaths to William, creating a grave impediment to his own chances at the throne. The English always maintained that the whole story was Norman propaganda, or that Harold was tricked or acted under duress.

While William was striving to ensure that he would in due course attain 'his' kingdom, Robert and Roger de Hauteville were itching for 'their' land. Probably neither Hauteville aspired so high as royalty. Exalted nobility, even of the new-rich variety, would suffice. In view of the crusading nature of the Sicilian venture it was only natural that Roger should think in terms of next attacking Palermo. So energetic was he that the city of Pisa, itself a long-time victim of Saracen encroachments and piracy, saw in him a possible liberator from the yoke of terror, and offered to join the fight for that centre of Muslim rule, wealth and culture. The time seemed ripe. So this year Roger and his brother met at Cosenza for purposes of planning their campaign and con- solidating their operations.

One of the three provincial capitals of Calabria (the others being Reggio and Catanzaro), Cosenza was once the headquarters of the Bruttii, a mountain people never totally assimilated into Roman Italy. A boomingly progessive city today, it enjoys a site in full view of the Sila Massif—'Italy's Little Switzerland'—while nestling at the confluence of the Bussento and Crati rivers. Cosenza is mainly famous as the burial place of the Visigoth chieftain Alaric. Gibbon tells the story that, after having looted Rome in AD 410, Alaric moved south, loaded with rich booty, his ranks swelled by newly acquired fighters.

He defeated the Bruttii and proposed to move on to Africa via Sicily; but his purpose was frustrated because a sudden tempest damaged or sank a large number of his ships. The Visigoths'

> courage was daunted by the terrors of a new element; and the whole design was defeated by the premature death of Alaric, which fixed, after a short illness, the fatal term of his conquests. The ferocious character of the barbarians was displayed in the funeral of a hero, whose valour and fortune they celebrated with mournful applause. By the labour of a captive multitude they forcibly diverted the course of the Busentinus, a small river that washes the walls of Cosentia. The royal sepulchre, adorned with the splendid spoils and trophies of Rome, was constructed in the vacant bed; the waters were then restored to their natural channel, and the secret spot where the remains of Alaric had been deposited was for ever concealed by the inhuman massacre of the prisoners who had been employed to execute the work.[42]

Nothing of Alaric is evident in Cosenza today. The *Città Vecchia*, with its narrow streets and cathedral piazza, seems more theatrical than real. Even with the late afternoon sun full on the front façade, the area around the cathedral, made mysterious by dark doorways and sombre shadows, smacks of assassinations and assignations, deeds of a sordid and secret nature. Colourful laundry, even a child's red shirt and tiny panties, strung overhead between buildings in the age-old Italian fashion, cannot quite alleviate the operatic mood. Had he not lived in Rome, Scarpia would have been at home here, lurking in the shadows near the church, waiting to catch a glimpse of Tosca coming to visit her Cavaradossi. 'Tosca, for thee I forget God!' Scarpia cries at the end of Act I; in such surroundings, who could doubt it?

About five hundred knights and a thousand foot soldiers accompanied Robert and Roger to Cosenza. The Norman castle which sprawls over the hill above the city was the meeting place. It has fallen on hard times now. But the Italians, so respectful of their ruins (and they have so many!), try not to meddle too much with them, preferring to preserve their *character*, to arrest decay rather than reconstruct. Ruins are marvellous conjurers of romantic rumination. One needs only to slow down and to be unafraid in the face of the decay.

Here at Cosenza were laid the plans for the capture of Palermo, the brothers having decided to go directly for the highest stakes. It was, however, an undertaking which would prove to be, at best, a failure—at worst, a comic failure. Used to larger modern military operations, we sometimes lose sight of the smallness of some of these nevertheless devastating battles. They were terrifying to the people, undeniable proof of Satan's presence, disruptive to any kind of sane living pattern, as well as destructive to the land. The brothers assumed that Palermo would be an easy trophy, and that on its capitulation the whole island would fall into their ready hands. On this occasion they had badly misjudged—nor had they foreseen the intervention of Nature at its most bizarre. In any case, the Sicilian population, Christian as well as Muslim, was on the whole not enthusiastic about a change of rulers.

Cathedral Piazza,
Cosenza, Italy

Within weeks after Cosenza, the Guiscard was encamped on the hills ringing Palermo, belatedly realizing that siege was impossible, as the city was magnificently fortified and he had not the forces to blockade its harbour. But most horrifying of all for the Normans, and guaranteed to cause shudders of revulsion in the most dauntless warrior, was a plague of tarantula spiders, a malevolent infestation inducing tragi-comic symptoms in the person bitten. The *taranta* possessed a poisoned sting which, among other distresses, caused the recipient to be filled with a foul gas. The discomfort was magnified until the wind forced itself from their bodies 'noisily and indelicately', hardly the type of ailment befitting a conquering army. And it must be one of the few, if not the only, instances of military defeat suffered because of flatulence!

In the north William the Bastard was poised for one of the greatest conquests in history. Here in the south were the Hauteville boys, compelled to lead their broken, disillusioned—if noisy—army back to mainland safety; safety, but not security, since Calabria and Apulia were always within an ace of shrugging off their control. Temporarily the Norman military machine ground to a halt, bogged down in petty little revolts, jealous uprisings, mean and vengeful antagonisms. They were all part of the Norman game of life. For the next four years it would be all Duke Robert and his brother could do to hold on to what they already had, much less add to it.

Chapter Four

Normans, but bastard Normans, Norman bastards!

Shakespeare, *Henry V*, III, 5

1065

The crowning work of Edward the Confessor's life, Westminster Abbey, was consecrated during the Christmas season, on December 28, a mere eight days before the king's death. Despite the fact that Harold Godwinson had persuaded Edward to rid his court of Norman officials, the king's sympathies were unmistakable when it came to church building; though larger than most Norman churches of the time, Edward's abbey was Norman in style and owed much to the abbey of Jumièges for its design.

Legends abound concerning Westminster Abbey. One says that a British king of the second century, named Lucius, built a Christian church on Thorney Island, which has long since been absorbed into the north bank of the River Thames. Another mentions Sebert, a (genuine) East Saxon king of the seventh century, as the builder of a church there, and that Saint Peter himself consecrated it. To commemorate that prestigious occasion local fishermen, until the fourteenth century, presented the monks of the abbey with an annual tribute of salmon, an appropriate offering considering Peter's background. It is certain that a Saxon monastic church was built near the present abbey, facing from a distance London's St Paul's. Saint Dunstan enlarged the Saxon church; then, a century later, Edward the Confessor made his notable contribution, which was actually a re-foundation. Ancient Roman Watling Street ran by the site. It was an important location, destined to become the nucleus of the entire Church-State governmental precinct that we know today.

Edward's church sufficed for a while. But it was not big enough for the grander-thinking Henry III who in 1245 tore the old building down and constructed his own around the remains. Edward's richly endowed monastery buildings were generally left intact and can still be seen in part today. The present church at Westminster has none of the brawnier vitality that Edward's abbey no doubt displayed. Henry III was an admirer of the French Gothic style, and consequently his Westminster—more soaring and graceful than the Romanesque—owes a stylistic acknowledgement to the delicate contemporary cathedrals across the Channel. Henry III did not live to see his church completed, but he had the pleasure of seeing Edward the Confessor's remains ensconced in a shrine of glass and gold, and placed behind the high altar, where they still rest. Except for the towers, designed and begun by Sir Christopher Wren in 1722 and completed by Nicholas Hawksmoor in 1745, the abbey is still much as Henry planned it.

It is a solemn place, Westminster Abbey, with its Tomb of the Unknown Warrior; its Poet's Corner; the Coronation Chair bearing, under the royal seat, the Stone of Scone; the myriad monuments and memorials to greatness. But

Westminster is not all pomp and circumstance. It has, from the start, been the scene of more than a few moments of levity. Gervase, a monk of Canterbury, records the following anecdote concerning a council held at Westminster Abbey in 1176 in what would still have been Edward's building. The arch-bishops of Canterbury and York had long been striving with one another for precedence. A most unseemly scuffle occurred during the visit of a papal legate to London. The prelates assembled in one of the abbey's chapels.

> When . . . the Papal Legate had taken his seat on a raised throne in the midst, and Richard Archbishop of Canterbury, by right of his primacy, had sat down on his right, then Roger Archbishop of York, puffed up with his own innate arrogance to reject the left-hand throne that was destined for him, strove irreverently to sit down between the Legate and his Grace of Canterbury, thrusting with the more uncomely quarters of his body so that he sat down upon the lap of his own Primate. Yet scarce had he struck my lord of Canterbury with that elbow of his wherewith he had been accustomed to fight, when he was ignominiously seized by certain bishops, clerics, and laymen, and torn from the Archbishop's lap, and cast upon the floor. But, when staves and fists were now wielded on both sides, the Archbishop of Canterbury sprang up and returned good for evil, snatching away from this disastrous conflict his own rival and the inveterate enemy of his see. At length the contumacious Archbishop of York, rising from the pavement with his cape torn ignominiously by the struggle, fell down at the king's feet and belched forth lying calumnies against the Archbishop of Canterbury.[43]

1066

With the passing of Edward the Confessor the succession question became urgent. The opponents squaring away for this 'battle royal' were Harold Godwinson, William the Bastard and Harald Hardrada, with Tostig Godwinson as an additional factor. He had ruled his earldom of Northumbria so cruelly that his subjects had risen up against him and he had been banished by Edward the Confessor. He could be expected to seek vengeance, to try to regain his earldom and, of course, to retain an opportunist eye on the throne itself, should the more obvious contenders be eliminated.

Harald Hardrada, too, was a threat to the island's stability, because he believed that he was the rightful successor by virtue of an agreement reached more than twenty years before between King Magnus of Norway and Harthacnut, king of Denmark and short-time king of England. These two Scandinavian rulers had contrived between them that whichever of them survived the other should inherit his kingdoms. When Harthacnut died in 1042 Magnus took Denmark, but was too preoccupied with a war in its defence to press his claim to England; so Edward the Confessor, who had been favoured by Harthacnut, was elected king of England. Magnus himself died in 1047 and had been succeeded by his uncle, Harald Hardrada. Now, at fifty-one years of age, Harald was the most notorious warrior of his time, a giant among men, and a king to whom any denial of his wishes was totally unacceptable.

War was clearly in the offing. Action had to be taken at once. Edward the Confessor was buried in his new church on January 6. And then with unseemly haste—on the very same day—Harold Godwinson had himself crowned king. Obviously he had planned his coup, though it is possible that Edward, on his deathbed, nominated Harold as his successor, thus abrogating his alleged promise to William. The *Anglo-Saxon Chronicle* indicates that the nomination was freely made, approving the Confessor's choice of a successor:

> . . . the wise ruler entrusted the realm
> To a man of high rank, to Harold himself,
> A noble earl who all the time
> Had loyally followed his lord's commands
> With words and deeds, and neglected nothing
> That met the need of the people's king.

And Earl Harold was now consecrated king and he met little quiet in it as long as he ruled the realm.[44]

Castle, Lillebonne, France

Even the Norman chronicler William of Poitiers did not fault Harold for his taking of a still 'warm throne'. Nevertheless Harold had sworn a solemn oath to William. The alacrity with which he accepted the crown must have caught William off guard. There were, after all, censures of withering force, both secular and religious, to be flung at oath-breakers. The whole feudal structure was based on the sanctity of the oath. For once William's barons were loyal to him. In several hurriedly summoned councils they agreed to join their duke in his efforts to secure the throne of England. Councils were held at Lillebonne, Bonneville-sur-Touques and Caen.

Lillebonne possesses the ruins of a great theatre, meagre enough remains of the Roman town Juliobona. Its castle is but a fragment of the formidable, brutishly-placed fortress that once stood in this strategically important corner of northwestern Normandy. Even the pleasant park which now surrounds it does little to ameliorate its basic haughtiness, its strident self-importance. The meeting of barons called to this castle was reportedly one of the most difficult for William, and needed all his powers of persuasion, cajolery and threats, which were extraordinary, according to his contemporaries. Even

the Almighty, reaching down from his heavenly sphere, made an ambiguous gesture. The tailed comet [shown with such a delightful ill-

King Harold, with Halley's Comet, Bayeux Tapestry

grace in the Bayeux Tapestry] or 'hairy star' which appeared at the time of Harold's coronation [but actually on April 24] is now identified by astronomers as Halley's Comet, which had previously heralded the Nativity of Our Lord; and it is evident that this example of divine economy in the movements for mundane purposes of celestial bodies might have been turned by deft interpretation to Harold's advantage. But the conquerors have told the tale, and in their eyes this portent conveyed to men the approaching downfall of a sacrilegious upstart.[45]

William prepared for war. Under his leadership Normandy was not to be stopped. From where he stood he could afford to be arrogant. Thus William of Poitiers tells a story of a captured spy being brought before the duke. He disdained to punish him, instead sending him back to Harold of England with these words: 'Tell him that if he does not see me within one year in the place which he now strives to make safe against my coming, he may rest quiet for the rest of his days and need fear no harm from me'.[46]

Arrogant William may have been, but he was also intelligent enough to know that, to achieve the ultimate success, he needed approbation. His barons he could manage; he had already tamed them. The feudal society's dim view of the broken oath made his job of enlisting the sympathies of his fellow rulers a not impossible or even difficult one. Having received assurances of at least moral support, if not outright aid of material and personnel, from most of the leaders of Europe (even Harold's cousin, King Swein of Denmark, agreed not to interfere), William turned to the most important one of them all. Pope Alexander II, with Hildebrand at his elbow, received William's emissaries. They no doubt explained to the pontiff William's side of the broken-oath story. No records of the interview or deliberations survive, but it is likely that William's already proven good work for the Church militated in his favour. Alexander II gave the nod of approval to William, recognizing him as the lawful king of England and blessed his coming enterprise with a consecrated banner and a holy relic—one of St Peter's hairs.

Papal approval notwithstanding, the Church normally exacted penances for killing others in battle, even when a knight or soldier had participated merely because he owed service to his overlord. When Bishop Ermenfrid of Sion visited England four years after the Battle of Hastings he issued a list of penances for those Normans who had taken part in William's invasion. Among them:

> Anyone who knows that he killed a man in the great battle must do penance for one year for each man that he killed.

> Anyone who wounded a man, and does not know whether he killed him or not, must do penance for forty days for each man . . .

> Anyone who does not know the number of those he wounded or killed must, at the discretion of his bishop, do penance for one day in each week for the remainder of his life . . .

> The archers who killed some and wounded others, but are necessarily ignorant as to how many, must do penance as for three Lents.[47]

Trees were felled throughout the realm, to be shaped into planks by carpenters, hauled to the coastal region where shipwrights would form them into long, narrow, strikingly-painted ships which, as shown in the Bayeux Tapestry, still displayed the old Viking dragon-prow. Supplies of infinite variety were stockpiled on the shore at Dives, today a resort-fishing village whose tranquillity makes the stories of William's eleventh-century bedlam impossible to imagine. The sturdy Norman chapel where he and his barons attended mass at Dives is still there. He accumulated wagon-loads of sails, arms, bulging wineskins, and fresh water supplies, and there was food enough to last at least through a beachhead landing.

And of course there were horses. William had heard of the Hauteville success of transporting horses to Sicily, probably from Normans who had been on that campaign. (Things were a bit slow in Southern Italy at the moment; therefore, always spoiling for a fight and rather than sitting around waiting for something to happen, many southern Normans had moved to this new theatre of activity.) Not the least of William's problems was how to manage the approximately three thousand knights and mounted esquires, along with their horses, and the seven thousand foot soldiers who were gathering around the seven hundred or so ships on the beach at Dives. Training them to fight was not the problem; they all knew that from experience. But this swarm of rough-necks had to be paid and fed. William must have been an organizer without eleventh-century parallel, taking it upon himself to see that these amenities were forthcoming. 'He made generous provision both for his own knights and those from other parts, but he did not allow any of them to take their sustenance by force. The flocks and herds of the peasantry pastured unharmed throughout the province. The crops waited undisturbed for the sickle without being trampled by the pride of the knights or ravaged by the greed of the plunderer. A weak and unarmed man, watching the swarm of soldiers without fear, might follow his horse singing wherever he would'.[48]

While William of Poitiers' picture is idyllic to the point of disbelief, it probably does record basic truths. In any event, the army was gathered and cared for, the fleet was built and assembled, and by 12 August William was ready to go. His army now faced across the Channel the defending militia and ships that Harold had gathered on the south coast of England. But on 8 September Harold dismissed the local levies, unable to retain them longer, and sent his ships back to London. Four days later William moved his troops to Saint-Valéry on the Somme estuary, so that his cross-channel trip would be shorter. Having fired the imagination of his subjects, having obtained papal sanction and encouragement, not to mention the approval of most of the leaders of Europe, only Nature now stood in his way; for over a fortnight longer William remained a prisoner on his own shores, kept there by gales, mountainous surf and lashing rains.

Feverish activities at Dives had not prevented William and his duchess from taking time off for some unfinished business at Caen. William had, in 1059, through the good auspices of his friend and minister Lanfranc, reached a reconciliation with the then pope, Nicholas II, concerning his marriage to Matilda. Though the union had been forbidden, Nicholas was enough of a realist to know it was a *fait accompli*. He agreed to acknowledge it provided William and Matilda each built and endowed a religious house at Caen.

It was in June that William and Matilda led a solemn gathering of clergy and magnates to the consecration of her church of the Holy Trinity at Caen, that of the Abbaye Aux Dames. To enhance the solemnity of the occasion further they gave their daughter Cecilia to the convent of nuns who would administer the new foundation. William's promised abbey, begun three years before, proved not to be ready for consecration until 1077. In the meantime the gathering at Caen gave William a chance to hold a strategy planning meeting with his barons.

Matilda's church is no longer in the pure state it once enjoyed—the spires, destroyed in the Hundred Years' War, were replaced in the eighteenth century by the clumsiest of balustrades. But Holy Trinity remains a remarkably fine example of Norman Romanesque architecture of the eleventh century. Its nine-bay nave (*see page* 68) is a triumph of the style, and a fitting last resting place for Matilda who is buried there before the high altar. There is a monumental solidity about the vast interior, a ponderousness, a Norman sturdiness that seems lost on the sweet nuns who people the church.

The putting together of the parts—the articulation—is handled with subtlety and grace, a nobility in keeping with Norman architecture generally. To enter the church of the Holy Trinity is to be impressed by the direct simplicity, the harmony of the various parts of what is a most complicated structure, and a positive defining of space. When the builders threw up these walls they did so with comfortable confidence in their ability to create a space that is never too high for its width, nor so squat that one would feel crushed. As Michelangelo in his sculpture four hundred years later, the Normans brought to their architecture a system of masses and voids, the masses giving form to the voids, the voids accentuating the solids, each unable to exist without the other. Consummate masters of the void, and of the solids housed in it, they were little interested in elaborate or flamboyant ornamentation. They spent their energies on enormous emptinesses hovering in absolute balance, with just enough decoration—usually relegated to columns, capitals and borders—to tease the imagination and arrest the attention. This is the greatness of Norman architecture.

Below the altar of Holy Trinity, the eleventh-century crypt of Saint Nicholas (was the saint chosen because of the pope who lifted the marital ban?) is in an excellent state of preservation, though one wonders how, but for a miracle, considering the almost total destruction of Caen during World War II. The rough figurative decorations which adorn many of the supporting sixteen columns prove, if nothing else, that Norman sculpture is invigorating, full of verve and bluntly direct. The church stands on a hill on one side of Caen, looking down on William's Abbaye aux Hommes on the other side.

Fortune intervened in favour of William when in mid-September Harold Godwinson's attention was distracted by the arrival of an invading army of Norwegians and Scots under the joint leadership of Harold's brother Tostig and King Harald Hardrada. It was no small force, the combined fleet numbering about three hundred vessels. Having ravaged the coast of Yorkshire and butchered the citizens—the people of Scarborough were killed to the last one—they finally cast anchor on the left bank of the River Ouse, nine miles from York. King Harold was summoned from London. The dilemma was awesome. But Harold was a man of quick decision and instant action. The threat from William was, so far as he knew, still theoretical; but the northerners were already in his realm. He mobilized his forces and set off with immense speed. While he was *en route* York fell to the invaders. In lieu of sacking the city, Hardrada agreed to accept 150 children of prominent families as hostages, to be delivered to him at Stamford Bridge, seven miles to the east.

Early the next morning Hardrada and Tostig waited at the bridge with only part of their army, and that spread out in a holiday mood on both sides of the narrow River Derwent, enjoying the taste of victory. In the madness of over-confidence about a third of the army had been left behind with the boats; and those troops who were at the bridge now were only partially equipped, having left their leather battle jackets, iron-studded and tough, stored uselessly on the ships. Before long they noticed a spiralling cloud of dust rising through the early morning damp. Even after the large body of soldiers making the dust took shape, Hardrada and Tostig hesitated, thinking that perhaps they might be friendly. Instead, it was Harold, newly arrived with his army from London. He gave the order for immediate attack.

> The noble king [Hardrada], that never feared danger in his life, made an inroad with a little band; but from the south of England there came a mighty host to battle with the good king. They met forthwith. The king's rashness in battle prevented him from awaiting old age, that king who never spared himself in fight . . . His was a steadfast breast in battle; the

bold king's heart never trembled when the bloody brand bit the lord of barons . . . His . . . mailcoat *Emma* did not save the king from the spears. Sooner than take quarter of the people [the English], his men rather chose all of them to fall with the king.[49]

A renewed attack by the defenders had already laid Tostig low by the time Norse reinforcements arrived; but by then the battle of Stamford Bridge was already lost. It was while Harold Godwinson was enjoying the customary victory celebration in York, probably on 1 October, that he learned by special messenger that William the Bastard had landed at Pevensey on the south coast on 28 September.

On touching shore William first disembarked his foot soldiers to reconnoitre the area. Having been prepared by lurid stories of these Norman ogres, the peasants fled in terror, taking with them what they could of their livestock: what was left behind was quickly rounded up and just as quickly ended up on Norman spits. When no resistance was forthcoming, William allowed his knights to go ashore, with their horses for which special ramps were built to allow for shifting tides. The whole operation was carried off swiftly and without incident, except one involving the Conqueror himself. As he was stepping ashore from his command ship, the *Mora*, he slipped and fell to his hands and knees. This was immediately regarded as an evil omen by his superstitious followers. 'By the Glory of God!' he swore to calm them, 'I have taken possession of my kingdom. The soil of England is in my hands!'

With his unerring eye for tactical advantage William had chosen a good place to land in his new domain. It was a site on which the Romans, those other masters of military logistics, had built one of their great fortresses to guard Britain's vulnerable southeast coastline. Immediately occupying the ruined but imposing fort, he set his men to work reinforcing the crumbling walls. They spent only their first night enjoying this ancient security, but William never abandoned the site, seeing it as a key to his coastal defence.

Pevensey's enormous bastions overlook an oval yard—rare in that most Roman fortifications were rectangular. In the days following the Conquest, William's half-brother Robert of Mortain was to build additional defences, a small inner bailey as well as a new keep. The fortress could have endured as an important defence mechanism for a longer time had not Nature intervened in the fifteenth century; the sea began a gradual movement away, the harbour silted up, and the structure was rendered pointless as it became farther and farther removed from the coast it was created to dominate. Pevensey Castle enjoyed a moment of renewed life during World War II, when it served as a Home Guard command post. Now it simply broods over its moat, shading with its great towers and square-cut stone foundations the silently contemplative men and boys who fish in its brackish waters, and the young farmer who has driven his tractor into the ancient compound and now sleeps off a too heavy lunch in the dappled shade of a few scraggly oaks.

The Norman landing in England was one of the best planned, most complicated manoeuvres of its kind in history. A bivouac was set up, fires lighted and the spits started turning. William intended his visit to be a lengthy one. Every act was premeditated, every contingency anticipated—except for

Pevensey Castle, England

William's fall, of course. It is even reported that he had transported a pre-fabricated wooden fort to England to set up on his beachhead. With guards on duty, and look-outs a little farther afield, the invaders could rest, for the moment unopposed, on the shores on which their sights had been set these past months.

So far fate had been on the Bastard's side; but he must have thought it was the calm before the storm. By the next day he had moved his troops to Hastings where they literally dug in, constructing an earth and timber fortification—a motte-and-bailey—typical of the Normans and the kind of structure that would later evolve into the castle. Many of the motte-and-bailey fortifications were subsequently converted to stone. According to Ordericus Vitalis, William's success in this incredible adventure was due in part to the fact that there were so few castles in England that could be used as defensive strongholds; and the ones that were there had been founded by those Normans brought to the island by Edward the Confessor.

By simply digging in and waiting at Hastings, William lured Harold to his south coast beachhead. There were some in Harold's party who tried to talk him out of an immediate confrontation,

> . . . his brother, Earl Gurth, thus addressing him: 'It is best, dearest brother and Lord, that your courage should be tempered by discretion. You are worn by the conflict with the Norwegians from which you are only just come, and you are in eager haste to give battle to the Normans. Allow yourself, I pray you, some time for rest. Reflect also, in your wisdom, on the oath you have taken to the duke of Normandy. Beware of incurring the guilt of perjury, lest by so great a crime you draw ruin on yourself and the forces of this nation, and stain for ever the honour of our own race . . .'

Harold was very indignant ... Holding in contempt the wholesome advice of his friends, he loaded his brother with reproaches for his faithful counsel, and even forgot himself so far as to kick his mother when she hung about him in her too great anxiety to detain him with her ... .[50]

Ordericus, born in England but educated in Normany, and writing some seventy years later, had every reason to paint Harold in an ugly light; but *kicking his mother?*

Eventually Harold walked into William's trap. The duke waited patiently while Harold called together such English as could rapidly be assembled, and force-marched them to Hastings. It was Harold's 'design to take them unawares, and crush them at once ... and, that they might not escape by sea, he caused a fleet of seventy ships, full of soldiers, to guard the coast'.[51] William was expecting them. He heard Mass; 'he also reverently suspended from his neck the holy relics on which Harold had sworn'.[52] William then swore an oath of his own: should God see fit to give him the victory, he claimed, he would found and endow an abbey on the spot of the battle.

Following their custom the English decided to fight on foot, and accordingly formed on a hill called Senlac (Sand Lake), about six miles from Hastings. To ride a horse into battle implied notions of a quick getaway, desertion of the cause, defeat. But William's use of mounted troops was not the sole deciding factor in his ultimate victory. Equally important to the outcome of the battle was the equipment of his knights with stirrups. These, taken for granted by the modern equestrian, were in eleventh-century Europe not yet thoroughly understood or tested. The stirrup may have been invented in Asia during the second century BC. It arrived in Europe, in the kingdom of the Franks, in the eighth century. William's horsemen were able to use their main weapon, the spear, so effectively only because they were securely anchored to their horses by means of the lowly stirrup, which enabled the rider to keep his seat at the moment of impact. His cavalry thus became a formidable shock troop, able to charge and ride down the Saxons.

William's was the flashier of the two armies—but then his men were not fatigued from battle and long marches—and with spears embellished by colourful pennons it made a stunning sight, a discouraging fact not lost on the defenders. Besides, the Normans were extremely well-equipped, offensively as well as defensively. On the Bayeux Tapestry we find seven different kinds of body armour, using a variety of materials, from the usual metals of the day to cuir-bouilli and horn. (Cuir-bouilli was leather that had been boiled in oil, in which condition it was moulded into body form. Extremely hard, it was used in England until the end of the fourteenth century.) Even William's common foot-soldiers cut dashing figures in their quilted gambesons, in which wool, tow or other fabrics were reduced by shredding and then sewn between two pieces of cloth. The gambeson was sometimes worn under chain-mail as extra protection, but, among the foot-soldiers, was more often used alone. It was not much good against a lance thrust but was useful protection against the sword slash or an arrow shot from a distance. Hurled stones and swung maces could, despite the gambeson, still wreak damage in broken bones.

According to tradition—and one that fairly screams of Norman inspiration—William's minstrel-knight, Ivo Taillefer, claimed first crack at the defenders. He is said to have sung the Song of Roland to his companions-at-arms before the battle; then, after performing some martial tricks with his weapons before the astonished eyes of the English, was the first to plunge into their ranks—to be promptly slain.

It was nine o'clock in the morning, Saturday, October 14, the day of the Feast of Saint Calixtus. In the ebb and flow of battle word got out that William had been slain. Sections of his army began to fall back. 'The duke . . . rode up to the fugitives and checked their retreat, loudly threatening them, and striking with his lance. Taking off his helmet, and exposing his naked head, he shouted: "See, I am here; I am still living, and, by God's help, shall yet have the victory"'.[53] Larger than life he was, astride his horse, his red hair redder in the sun and cascading around his shoulders—a man to make legends; indeed, a legend unto himself.

By feigning retreat, the Normans twice tricked the English forces into pursuing them, then cut them off from their companions and slew them. The Bayeux Tapestry weaves an exciting, if gory picture of attack and retreat, of cavalry against infantry, of decapitated bodies and showers of arrows and flying lances. We see Harold's brothers, Leofwine and Gurth, toppled by the Norman onslaught. The English and the Normans fall together intermingled in death, a condition they could not achieve in life. We see William lifting his helmet to prove that he is alive, and Eustace of Bologne, carrying what may have been the papal banner, pointing to his duke as though to encourage the men. Then there is Bishop Odo, William's half-brother, swinging a mace with wicked intensity. (By the marvellously abstruse reasoning of the medieval mind, a churchman was not guilty of breaking the commandment 'Thou shalt not kill' so long as he stuck to such a weapon, thereby not literally shedding blood, but only striking down with a blow.)

If a key is needed to explain William's decisive victory, then his archers serve as good a one as any. Most of his foot-soldiers carried bows; and we know he utilized a vast number of them. At some point he ordered the archers to shoot into the air; the arrows fell on the heads of the Saxons instead of uselessly hitting their shield wall. According to one tradition Harold was killed by an arrow that pierced his eye, though the Bayeux Tapestry shows what could be him being hacked down by a mighty blow from a Norman broadsword. The English knew

> . . . that their king with two of his brothers and many of their greatest men had fallen. Those who remained were almost exhausted, and they realized that they could expect no more help . . . Dismayed at the implacable bearing of the duke who spared none who came against him and whose prowess could not rest until victory was won, they began to fly as swiftly as they could, some on horseback, some on foot, some along the roads, but most over the trackless country . . . Many left their corpses in the depths of the forest, and others were found by their pursuers lying by the roadside . . . Many fallen to the ground were trampled to death under the hooves of runaway horses.[54]

Death of King Harold, Bayeux Tapestry

As though horror enough had not been perpetrated, there was one further disaster, this one suffered by the Normans. Pursuing their fleeing enemies, a contingent of Norman knights plunged headlong into a deep ravine, so overgrown that it was indiscernible. In their wild pursuit they dashed full tilt into the declivity, meeting their end in a hideous confusion of men, arms and horses. To this day the ravine is called Malfosse after the disaster.

Following the battle, itself one of the decisive events of Western history, William, for all his experiences in war,

> ... could not gaze without pity on the carnage ... The bloodstained battle-ground was covered with the flower of the youth and nobility of England ... And Harold himself stripped of all badges of honour could not be identified by his face, but only by certain marks on his body. His corpse was brought into the duke's camp, and William gave it for burial to William, surnamed Malet, and not to Harold's mother [whose four remaining sons had all been killed within the last three weeks], who offered for the body of her beloved son its weight in gold. For the duke thought it unseemly to receive money for such merchandise, and equally he considered it wrong that Harold should be buried as his mother wished, since so many men lay unburied because of his avarice.[55]

William had his victory—and, in due course, his crown; and England had a new abbey. William erected his promised abbey on the battlefield, placing the high altar precisely on the spot where Harold was cut down. Standing at the abbey ruins to survey the battlefield (*see page* 117), the visitor must work hard to imagine the carnage, clatter and agony of that fateful October 14, so tranquil, almost Elysian, seems the site of combat after a heavy rain on a spring day.

The town that grew up around William's monastery is called Battle; and Battle Abbey, a spacious religious house which was immediately entrusted to the care of Norman Benedictines, was the first foundation of the occupation, but only one of many yet to come. None of William's buildings at Battle remains standing today; even those in ruins are of a later date. But the spot is impressive, the ruins emotionally touching. England already had Norman-style churches—Westminster Abbey for example. But here, for the first time, a founder, Norman to the marrow of his bones, was calling on Norman designers to devise a church to be built by Norman workers and Norman money, and be maintained by Norman monks; and all this was to commemorate a Norman victory and symbolize the Norman presence on alien soil.

William tarried for five days at Hastings and then, realizing that the English had no intention of immediately offering him the throne, set out on the mopping-up process. Another leader might have headed straight for London, where organized resistance was still active. Instead, William decided to isolate that concentration of antagonism. He headed east, stopping off briefly at Romney to administer a lesson in butchery, a reprisal for the citizens having fought off a company of Normans who had mistakenly put ashore in the vicinity. The lesson was so explicit that Dover Castle, sitting haughtily atop its chalk-cliff pedestal, gave in to him almost without a struggle.

The castle William found at Dover was heavily fortified, and had been since the remote Iron Age. Dover has always been a key defensive postion of England, especially perhaps during the fourteenth-century Hundred Years' War, and even as recently as World War II when it was used as a look-out station in the defensive network surrounding London. The conspicuous site of the Dover heights made it an ideal place for a Roman lighthouse, the Pharos, which still stands imposingly on the castle grounds. By the Middle Ages it was being used as a belfry for the Anglo-Saxon church of St Mary in Castro,

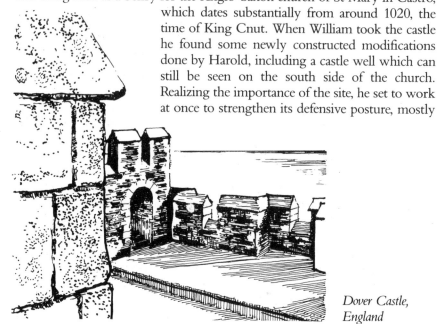

which dates substantially from around 1020, the time of King Cnut. When William took the castle he found some newly constructed modifications done by Harold, including a castle well which can still be seen on the south side of the church. Realizing the importance of the site, he set to work at once to strengthen its defensive posture, mostly

Dover Castle, England

by earth and timber construction. Nothing remains of William's additions, except perhaps the earth mounds near the church. He also constructed the moat, now oddly enough inside the *castrum* (encampment), a curious feature which is accounted for by the fact that later on Henry II encircled the moat with an enormous curtain wall, suspended from fourteen open-backed towers, two sets of which were coupled to form imposing gatehouses.

Most of what we see at Dover today was built by Henry II and his successors, who completely transformed the castle complex. Mainly it was the keep and the inner curtain wall which occupied Henry's builders; the man in charge was one Maurice, thought to be the same overseer who was responsible for the contemporary remodelling of Newcastle upon Tyne (*see* 1178) and who was paid 8d a day, later raised to 1/-.

The cube-shaped (98 × 96 × 95 feet) central keep which Henry II erected as the ultimate stronghold is composed of four floors of spacious halls connected by spiral staircases. With walls seventeen feet thick at base it is a maze of large halls, latrines, storage areas, a 240-feet deep well incorporating a sophisticated plumbing system, and two chapels—the whole structure more than ample to house a sizeable body of men. The large castles of England were often used as royal residences, but there is no evidence that Dover was even visited by royalty until Henry II himself arrived preparatory to invading Brittany, followed, perhaps, by Richard I when he was getting ready to set sail on crusade. With the fourteenth century, however, it was used more frequently by royalty, both native and foreign.

Ironically enough, considering its location and the money lavished on its modifications (Henry II's alone costing more than £3000), Dover Castle's history has been surprisingly calm. Its most dramatic moment occurred during the reign of King John, when Prince Louis of France (later King Louis VIII) invaded England in 1216 on the instigation of a clique of John's disloyal barons. Dover, one of the few castles to hold out against the invaders, put up a gallant defence under Hubert de Burgh, chief justiciar and warden of the Cinque Ports. But the attackers eventually took the barbican (the outer defences of the main gate) and burrowed under the gatehouse itself, the tunnel still visible at the northern end of the castle. On attempting to enter the castle precinct through their passageway, the French were driven back by such withering fire that they hesitated for reflection on the wisdom of their strategy, thereby giving the defenders time to pull themselves together and repair the breach with rocks, wood and tree-trunks. The castle was probably saved by the death of King John, which led to Louis' eventual return to France.

Garrison life is rough and tumble in any culture, with discipline a first prerequisite. The precinct of Dover Castle affords a good impression of the setting of medieval military life—the protecting bastions, the large halls and dark narrow corridors, spiral staircases, the high battlements and the obvious prominence of comforting places of worship. From a fragmentary copy of the statutes of the castle, the original in Norman French, we can pick up details of the military routine that prevailed. A few of the articles:

At sunset the bridge shall be drawn and the gates shut: afterwards the guard shall be mounted by twenty warders on the Castle walls.

Any warder found outside the walls or otherwise off his guard shall be put in the Donjon prison, and punished besides in body and goods at the Constable's discretion . . .

It is established by ancient rule, that if a chief guard discover a warder asleep, he shall take something from him as he lies, or carry away his staff, or cut a piece out of his clothes to witness against him in case the warder should deny having been asleep, and he shall lose his day's pay.

Either sergeant or warder using vile language shall be brought before the Constable, who shall have the matter considered, and the offence fairly enquired into. He who was wrong shall lose his day's pay—if the Constable so wills.

If a sergeant or warder strike another with the flat hand, he shall be liable to a fine as high as five shillings, and shall for the rest be held at the mercy of the Court. If he strikes with his fist he shall be liable to a fine as high as ten shillings and be at the mercy of the Court. If a sergeant or warder wound another the fine shall be as high as fifteen shillings and the offender shall forfeit his station in the Castle, if the Constable so adjudge.[56]

Having secured the coast from Hastings to Dover, William turned inland. It was towards the throne that he moved, and he so convinced the city of Canterbury of the seriousness of his purpose that it submitted without a struggle. Historians are unanimous in their agreement that a prime cause for the success of the Normans both here and in Italy was their uncommon ability to understand local traditions, to preserve them and make them work within the framework of the new order. William was moving over historic ground, and there is reason to think that this fact was not lost on him.

Canterbury had been important under both Romans and Saxons. Its cathedral had first been established by Saint Augustine, leader of Pope Gregory the Great's mission to the Anglo-Saxons in 597. During the period between Augustine and William I there were various attempts at remodelling and rebuilding the cathedral, futile activities in the end since it was accidentally burned down the year after the Conquest. A building momentum was achieved again under that man of optimism and energy, Lanfranc, when he was appointed by his friend William to be archbishop of Canterbury. Already perhaps approaching seventy years of age when he arrived from Bec, he plunged into the energy-consuming task of rebuilding the fire-ruined church and re-establishing the ecclesiastical authority of Canterbury. Lanfranc's church was finished in the incredible time of only seven years, astonishing in itself, but more so in that the building season lasted a mere seven to eight months—from March to October.

Lanfranc ordered his stone from Caen, the builders finding it easier to float it, already cut and dressed, across the Channel to Fordwich (two miles northeast of Canterbury) than to haul it overland from English quarries. Hordes of workmen, skilled and unskilled, and mostly recruited from Canterbury and its environs, clambered over the fabric of Lanfranc's new cathedral. A large number of the unskilled were farmers, pressed into service, but also probably attracted by the pay. The skilled masons would often work on through the winter, for they could carry on shaping blocks and carving statues and mouldings in the shelter of temporary workshops. These were used also as rest areas during the active building season; they became known as 'lodges', a term kept in use for our Freemasons' Lodges.

When Lanfranc died in 1089 another Italian, Anselm of Aosta, also from Bec, became the new archbishop of Canterbury. He has been called the greatest thinker ever to occupy the throne of Canterbury; but he was also zealous for the Church and its position and he immediately set his mind to the task of enlarging Lanfranc's cathedral, much of which was already falling into disrepair. Following a second disastrous fire in 1174, Canterbury cathedral moved into its 'golden age' with an enormous building programme initiated to accommodate the hordes of pilgrims who, foreshadowing Chaucer's raucous bunch, were descending on the town to pay homage to their favourite saint, Thomas Becket, martyred in his cathedral in 1170. It was with William of Sens, the great architect of the new choir at Canterbury, that English Gothic first appeared, obviously derived from the French but maintaining its 'Englishness' through generally lower proportions and typically Norman restrictions on the use of ornament and sculpture.

Clearly not much of the Canterbury Cathedral of the twentieth century is

Grotesque capital, Canterbury Cathedral crypt, England

Norman—though there is a solid tower dating from 1096 to 1115—but the crypt is thoroughly so. And what a crypt it is! The largest in England, built by Prior Ernulf, a contemporary of Archbishop Anselm, it has a nobility that is paradoxically both refined and barbarous, the kind of thing we find in Matilda's church of the Holy Trinity in Caen, and which is a primary ingredient in Norman art. The vigorous carving of the columns is the crypt's most noteworthy feature, and the variations possible within the simple forms of their capitals are both intriguing and beguiling. How utterly staggering was the imagination of these people who otherwise seem so lusty, so vindictive and so cruelly aggressive. Lurking under the arches which they cushion are monsters, two-headed and grotesque, sometimes riding on equally fantastic combinations of birds and animals. Here an acrobat poses insecurely on another's shoulders, while holding a chalice in one hand, a fish in another. There a friendly lion smiles openly, perhaps enjoying the performance of a nearby absurdly extravagant animal orchestra. Unexpectedly a cruel dragon kills a pathetically howling dog, looming over it, cursing—or is he taunting? —while he kills. Even Hercules is there, locking a fatal stranglehold on the poor Nemean lion (*see page* 117). There are some capitals representing simple or complicated patterns, decorative and always lively, some almost Doric in their simplicity, others baroquely excessive. These are not expressions of the soul—that part of us which medieval man was doing his best to push into heaven—but they are certainly things of the spirit, the unconscious, the imagination and the emotions. One would think it almost impossible to express that hidden part of ourselves—so soft, so light and mysterious, so ephemeral—in brittle, chunky stone. It seems an incompatible marriage—at the very least one incapable of enduring. Yet here it is, not only a happy fusion, but one lasting through, and perhaps beyond time.

Once Canterbury was in his clutches, William was ready to isolate London, the city which from the days of Tacitus has been rhapsodized and according to Doctor Samuel Johnson, has 'all that life can afford'. London was too large for William to contemplate its capture by direct assault. The encirclement was completed with his taking of Berkhamsted in Hertfordshire. The hopelessness of the English cause was at once apparent to the chief men of the land, a dilemma which they solved by offering the victor the crown. William finally acquiesced, and moved into London for a Christmas coronation in Westminster Abbey, a ceremony not without its evil omens. There,

> . . . in the presence of the bishops, abbots, and nobles, of the whole realm of Albion, Aldred the archbishop consecrated William, duke of Normandy, king of England, and placed the royal crown on his head in the church of St. Peter the apostle, called Westminster Abbey, where the venerable king Edward lies interred . . .

> Meanwhile, at the instigation of the devil, the enemy of all good, an unforeseen occurrence, pregnant with mischief to both nations, and an omen of future calamities, suddenly happened. For when Aldred the archbishop was demanding of the English, and Geoffrey, bishop of Coutances, of the Normans, whether they consented to have William for

their king, and the whole assembly loudly gave their willing assent, with one voice though not in one language, the men-at-arms, who formed the guard outside the abbey, upon hearing the shouts of joyful acclamation raised by the people in the church in a language they did not understand, suspected some treachery and imprudently set fire to the neighbouring houses. The flames quickly spreading, the people in the church were seized with panic in the midst of their rejoicings, and crowds of men and women, of all ranks and conditions, eagerly struggled to make their escape from the church, as if they were threatened with immediate danger. The bishops only, with some few of the clergy and monks, maintained their post before the altar, and trembling with fear completed the coronation office with some difficulty, the king himself being much alarmed . . .[57]

It was the Normans who established Westminster as the site for coronation ceremonies, there being no place especially allotted under the Saxon kings. With the exception of the boy king, Edward V, who was murdered just after his throne was usurped by his uncle Richard III, and the recent Edward VIII, who abdicated before his coronation took place, every English monarch has been crowned in that hallowed spot.

1067

Marching triumphantly into London the previous December, William had been impressed by its size, its crowds, its history and its location. What he saw through the dust and smoke was an urban sprawl of wooden houses, most of them one storey, facing on to narrow streets that were alternately powdery dry and impassably muddy. Life was more refined across the Channel, but then the climate itself was more friendly. Normandy had its grey days and fogs to be sure, but nothing to touch the unmoving opaqueness that oppressed the cities of the English—damp, unbreathable and depressing—with a frequency that made most of William's successors pine for the continental blandishments. But the London of William's day was exciting, too, in touch with the medieval world through its inland port. Its population numbered around twenty thousand, with most of them living within the three hundred and twenty-six acres enclosed by the original Roman walls—or about sixty-one people to an acre. Beyond the gates were small monasteries, a few ramshackle inns, one or two bishop's palaces and an occasional rich man's house. There was a slum-like huddle of brothels and taverns along the waterfront called Southwark. London was a seething hive of craftsmen, shopkeepers, soldiers, monks and prelates, ne'er-do-wells and just plain tourists.

Staring with his icy blue eyes at the English aristocracy who had met him at Berkhamsted, William was too cynically alert to have been taken in by their mollifying behaviour, their obsequiousness, their offer of the crown. An eleventh-century king survived because he was stronger and cleverer than his subordinates, and because he never concealed the iron fist in the velvet glove. Accordingly, the new king determined that there would be evidence aplenty of not just naked power, but power malevolent enough to badger recalcitrant nobles into submission. William of Poitiers claimed that the White Tower was needed to scare London's citizenry into docile acceptance of Norman rule. And certainly one of William's first undertakings was to order a timber castle to be built near the Thames in the southeast corner of London, the predecessor of the White Tower, and later the Tower of London.

Roman Londinium had been enclosed by a three-mile stone wall. At the southeastern angle of this wall three bastions had been erected overlooking a bridge across the Thames. It was the site of one of these towers—the one said to have been picked by Julius Caesar himself (who in fact was never there) —that William chose for his short-lived castle. Within three months of William's coronation the wooden tower and rampart was finished, and in March William felt free to return to Normandy.

When William was back in London later in the year he gave the order for the demolition of his new fortress in order to create a castle both outwardly formidable and appropriately grand. For his architect he chose Gundulf, later the militant bishop of Rochester, an enterprising and aggressive engineer, a designer of both fortresses and churches.

A Norman, Gundulf had been born near Rouen around 1024. He became a monk at Bec, where he met Lanfranc and was immediately captivated by the older man's modesty and intellect. The feeling was apparently mutual, for Lanfranc, as archbishop of Canterbury, brought Gundulf to England, where he achieved his renown, ultimately being consecrated bishop of Rochester in 1077.

Gundulf supervised the building of the White Tower, a structure so menacing that Londoners believed it was mortared with blood, a rumour sparked by the colour of the mortar in which the Normans used ground-up Roman bricks. It was a mutually satisfying bit of gossip to have

The White Tower, London

spread around, at once reinforcing the people's distaste of their conquerors while achieving the Normans' goal of cowing the population. For his materials Gundulf used imported Caen limestone along with ragstone from Kent, arranging them into an almost square-shaped structure, 118 x 107 feet at the ground. The southeast corner is curved to allow for the apse of the chapel of St John, a softening line which somewhat tempers the overt severity of the rest of the structure. The windows too, larger than the original slits characteristic of purely military architecture, soften the brutally massive walls which soar to intimidating heights—or at least seemed to do so in the eyes of William's subjects. Buttresses extending from foundation to battlements add to the architectural beef so that the whole thing stands as an overbearing, surly bully, ugly by intent and massive of form. A coat of whitewash added to the exterior shortly after completion did nothing to erase the image of malevolence, but instead made it appear more forbidding than ever. The white has been washed off now, but aside from that and the larger windows, the building remains essentially what Gundulf designed.

In the thirteenth century the White Tower was encircled by a double line of walls, giving the complex basically the form it enjoys today. It has been used as both fortress and palace. It has served as the Royal Mint, as a house for public records, and the home of the Royal Observatory. More infamously, it has gone down in history as a prison, having housed many an illustrious guest, as well as those who were not quite so illustrious. Among the better known of these royal residents are Henry VIII's second and fifth wives, Queens Anne Boleyn and Catherine Howard; the Lady Jane Grey; Queen Elizabeth I (then princess); Robert Devereux, earl of Essex; Sir Thomas More; and certainly its best known—or at least most pitiable—inmates, the child king, Edward V, and his brother Richard, the young duke of York, who were murdered in the Bloody Tower, their bodies probably buried beneath a staircase in the White Tower. Shakespeare calls this 'The most arch act of piteous massacre that ever yet this land was guilty of'.[58]

The finest of all the rooms of William's White Tower is the chapel of St John (see page 118). How quietly restrained, how dignified and solemn Norman architecture can be is stated here in terms so eloquent as to be clear to the most cynical sceptic. It is not large (though it is large as *castle* chapels go) being only 55½ × 31 feet. Standing in noble austerity, magnificently spanned by a superb barrel vault, it is Norman from the base of its columns to its arches, which spring vertically from the columns before assuming their curves. The chapel is a hymn to the so-called age of chivalry. A moment of hesitation there is worth more than hours in some other more ostentatious houses of worship. A young knight performing his vigil here, his eyes turned by nobility, his mind preoccupied by deeds of glory, and his emotions captivated by a courtly lady, would still have yearned for a union with the Divine; more than some other grander edifices, this is truly a house of God. And even today, in that softly lit interior, among those solid columns so precisely joined, and under those high-springing arches supporting the superb barrel vault, we know it too. Because that is the kind of place the chapel of St John is.

Following his coronation, William set himself to the task of ruling. He confirmed many of the laws of Edward the Confessor, and maintained Anglo-

Saxon institutions and legal machinery. Trial by ordeal continued, although to it was added the Norman trial by battle. Even William's law prohibiting a man from selling another outside the country under penalty of a fine payable directly to the king was the echo of a much older Anglo-Saxon law. Ordericus Vitalis' estimation of William's administration of justice clearly smacks of eulogizing. William, he says, ordered 'many affairs with prudence, justice and clemency . . . He enacted some laws founded on admirable principles. No suitor ever demanded justice of this king without obtaining it: he condemned none but those whom it would have been unjust to acquit'.[59] Nevertheless William did acquire a reputation for so effectively enforcing the laws that a man could walk the highways in comparative safety. But although the retention of Anglo-Saxon law and administrative practice helped to mollify his new subjects, William's harsh game laws and stringent protection of the royal forests did not endear him to them. Certainly it was a throwback to his more barbarous forebears that prompted him to pass a law of mutilation: 'I also forbid that anyone shall be slain or hanged for any fault, but let his eyes be put out and let him be castrated. And this command shall not be violated under pain of a fine in full to me'.[60]

He was indeed a Norman, and a conqueror, and proved it by the grants he made to his loyal Norman followers and retainers. English estates were freely granted to them, as were positions of power within the machinery of government, which he took over almost intact from his forerunners. Yet it took some time to pacify the country. Although his barons, once well settled in their new properties and perquisites, became interested in seeing things run smoothly, they at first followed the example of countless invading armies throughout history and rode roughshod over the native English. It was not long after the Conquest, therefore, that a series of revolts broke out, especially in the West Country, touched off in the main by one Edric the Wild, around whom fantastic legends developed. It is said that while strolling through the woods one night, perhaps walking off the effects of a hefty meal, he encountered a group of fairies dancing in the wild. He fell in love with one of them and married her. When William heard of this he ordered her to be brought to court. 'A conversation between William the Conqueror and the Queen of the Fairies would have been worth hearing'.[61]

William, confident of his control of his island, had returned to his duchy and his queen, leaving control of the realm in the hands of William fitzOsbern ('son of Osbern') and Bishop Odo, a man dangerous in the extreme and, as would be proven in time, ambitious. Odo was still well regarded by his half-brother and had recently been awarded the title of earl of Kent. Taking advantage of the king's absence, Edric the Wild, with the help of two Welsh princes, set out to take the newly fortified castle at Hereford. They were unsuccessful; but the tocsin had been sounded. William was back in London for Christmas, 'treating the English bishops and nobles with great courtesy. He received each with open arms, gave them the kiss of welcome, and was affable to all . . . By these arts the numbers of treasonably disposed were reduced . . . but, on the frontiers of the kingdom, in the northern and western districts, the same wild independence prevailed which formerly made the people insubordinate except when they pleased . . .'[62]

1068

If an eleventh-century king expected to survive he needed to put down every revolt as quickly as possible and preferably in person. With the hardening of resistance to William's rule during his absence in Normandy, the citizens of Exeter had formed a league against him. So William sallied forth from his castle comforts and headed west in the very teeth of winter, itself an indication of his determination to subdue his new subjects. He laid seige to Exeter, 'a rich and ancient city, built in a plain, and fortified with much care'.[63] After a futile display of bravado and eighteen days of assault William took the city. The citizens prostrated themselves abjectly at his feet, and he, 'with great moderation, extended his clemency ... and pardoned their offences'.[64] Clement or not (it apparently never occurred to Odericus that royalty could offend, too) and remembering that a fundamental reason for his victory over the English in the first place was their lack of defensive fortresses, William ordered a castle to be constructed within the city walls, which he called Rougemont from the colour of its rock foundation. Unlike most of the early post-Conquest castles, which were mainly earth and wood structures, the one at Exeter was built at least partly of stone. When he left Exeter for further disciplinary action against the local populace, William detailed a garrison to finish and man this fortress as a reminder of the consequences of further demonstrations of misguided independence.

William's gatehouse, which, apart from a section or two of curtain wall, is all that now remains of his Rougemont, is a handsome structure. It is not easy to find, tucked away from the main traffic of the modern city, but its location is almost precisely across the street from the Rougemont Museum, and just to the left of the entrance to the Exeter Courts of Law, which now occupy the site of the Norman castle. The colour from which it received its title is unmistakable, a clear, deep red that gives it a special identity and continued importance despite the anachronism of its existence as a gatehouse, yet now walled up and set to the side of the working entrance to the ancient keep. Nevertheless, it had its day, and its day was heroic.

The cathedral of Exeter is the city's finest monument, established in 1050 when the see comprising Devon and Cornwall was moved there from Crediton. Except for the two Norman towers and parts of the outside nave walls, it is Decorated Gothic in style and dates from 1280 to 1369. These are mighty Norman towers, and are shown to best advantage by being located at the ends of the north and south transepts, thus being separated from one another by a greater distance than the usual front façade location would allow. The transept towers are emphasized further in that there is no central tower as is customary in English Gothic cathedrals. Originally they stood apart from the building, but with later addition and remodelling they were incorporated into the transepts, becoming the only such towers in England except for those of the collegiate church at Ottery St Mary in Devon, for which they served as a model. To this day one of the towers nightly peals forth the reminder, *couvre feu*, the Norman injunction to cover the fire and go to bed.

Neroche, near Taunton in Somerset, was one of the first castles William reinforced to subdue the West Country, a typical motte-and-bailey of wood

North Tower,
Exeter Cathedral,
England

and earth. Presumably it was never converted to stone, so not much is now left of it but the central mound, overgrown with beech and European larch, shaded by Lawson cypress, red oak and mountain ash, and almost totally returned to its verdant beginnings. Archaeological evidence suggests that the fortress originated in the late Anglo-Saxon period around 1050-2. But this year, 1068, William's horse-mounted knights took the earth ramparts, then set to work on a series of inner concentric ramparts, each containing a bailey (courtyard). On the rim of the bluff overlooking the Taunton vale—on the

112

north side of the Blackdown Hills that the locals call 'back-sunded' because of the slanting angle of the sun's rays—they raised their motte (mound), and on top placed a wooden tower surrounded by a protective wooden wall. At the bottom of the motte the new owners dug a ditch, a kind of empty moat. The Domesday Book (*see* 1086) indicates that Neroche was held after the Conquest by Count Robert of Mortain, William's half-brother. He apparently used it as a residential castle until 1087, when he abandoned it. For a time, then, Neroche was a centre of the Norman presence in the southwest. Further evidence of this is the completely lovely little church at nearby Staple Fitzpaine (a fine Norman name) which, although fifteenth-century, boasts as superb a Norman doorway as one has the right to expect.

To keep his expanding realm in line William set out on a massive road-building programme—distance itself never being much of an intimidation to a Norman. He built his roads—not the engineering feats of the Romans, but useful and durable—to aid him in his conquest of the remote southwest and Wales. One such roadway was unearthed in Taunton in April 1978 on the site of a new building for the Inland Revenue. A flurry of interest was created but, alas, the road disappeared forever under the foundations of the new structure.[65] In the violent eleventh century Taunton was an important cross-road in a system meant to weave together a network of fortified strongpoints.

One such fortified strongpoint was Launceston in Cornwall, still today dominated regally by an abruptly rising mound, which in turn is crowned with an imposing circular stone keep. Dunheved, as the castle was called in William's Domesday Book, became the stronghold of the earls of Cornwall and, at the time of its building, was held by Robert of Mortain. With the general disintegration of obedience to recognized authority in the West Country the Normans were feverish in their building of defensive structures. The beauty of the motte-and-bailey was that, being made of wood and earth, it could be quickly erected. It played a key role in the evolution of the elaborately and concentrically walled castles of the thirteenth century, of which so many still survive, especially in Wales. In William's eleventh-century shelter, a keep (later a castle) was constructed atop an earthen motte which was then surrounded by a trench. The trench (later a moat) also encircled the bailey, the timber enclosure which protected the stables, the barracks, a well and other necessary outposts of the keep, which was the ultimate defence position.

Launceston
Castle, England

The importance of William's new castles can be judged by running through a list of the magnates to whom he assigned the job of managing them, usually the most trusted and responsible of his followers. It was during this time that the castle, as conceived by the Normans, first became a real instrument of war in England. Aside from those already mentioned there were castles thrown up at Warwick, Cambridge, Nottingham, York, Lincoln and Huntingdon. Soon they would multiply even further, so that by 'the end of the eleventh century there had been erected in England at least eighty-four castles, and a few of these were even then being reconstructed in stone'.[66]

William knew he could not afford to ignore the western march, that lawless frontier territory separating his new domain from Wales, which had never been integrated into Anglo-Saxon England, although occasional Welsh rulers had become vassals of English kings. A somewhat isolated appendage to his kingdom, clumsily stretching westward as though making an inept pass at Ireland, Wales appeared to him as a breeding ground of organized incursion into his realm, a landing-place for foreign invaders as well as a jumping-off point for his own possible future expansive pretensions. But for the time he simply wanted to isolate the Welsh to their fog-enshrouded, slaty hills. The men he chose to barricade the frontier were experienced in his methods and totally trustworthy, William fitzOsbern being the most noteworthy of these trustees, one of several whose assumption of duties eventually would lead to the creation of a group of powerful barons known as marcher lords.

William fitzOsbern's family had for several generations been intimate with the ducal family of Normandy. Osbern had been steward to William's father, Duke Robert I, and a guardian of William himself during his minority. FitzOsbern had therefore matured in the ducal household, becoming one of the leading young warriors dedicated to its defence, and eventually steward in his turn. He was always close to Duke William and tradition says that he was one of the advisers who supported the project of invading England. FitzOsbern was made responsible for establishing a ring of castles along the southern Welsh border, wooden most of them, to be replaced later by stone. Chepstow Castle is the exception, for here stone defences were thrown up in the initial Norman guarding of their territory.

Earl William showed masterful understanding of the problem, placing his castle on a ridge on the Welsh side of the River Wye (*see page* 118), overlooking both a principal land crossing into Wales and a natural harbour by which the castle could be supplied from Bristol all the year round. The architectural layout is singular in its long, curving occupancy of a ridge following a bend in the Wye. The site slopes downward to the east, thus allowing for an upper bailey and barbican at the western end and two baileys at the opposite, lower end. The eastern baileys became central to life in the castle, and there in due course were located halls and living-quarters, a cellar, buttery and pantry, guard-rooms, a dungeon and the handsome Marten's Tower (this last not built until the latter part of the thirteenth century).

The most spectacular of Chepstow's offerings, however, is the Great Tower, one hundred feet long by forty feet wide, the lower part entirely built by William fitzOsbern. Originally it stood two storeys high, with a sloping cellar beneath. Later a third storey was added, and a study of the materials and their treatment in the three floors allows for an understanding of the increasing preoccupation of the late Middle Ages with creature comforts and additional light. The lower floor was lighted, if that be the word, by a few small, round-headed windows. There is little decoration of any kind. The second storey was slightly better lighted in that there were more windows, but even these were later enlarged and made more elegant. The top floor, though added at two different building periods, is in every way less austere, more amiable to civilized living. Handsome mouldings give evidence of greater ostentation, and bits of coloured plaster still cling precariously, telling, inadequately

Chepstow Castle, England

perhaps, of a more colourful castle existence. The ruins suggest that the large tower rooms were divided down the centre by wooden partitions, which in turn supported the floors above. Defence may have been the original reason why Chepstow was built, but in later centuries defensive efficiency did not automatically preclude ideas of comfort. Chepstow Castle was furthermore an ideal base for frontier advancement; indeed, by the time Earl William died in 1071 he had taken over much of the present county of Gwent, doubtlessly with Chepstow Castle playing a significant role in his campaigns.

In this same year of 1068 'King William sent persons of high rank to Normandy to bring over his queen Matilda, who quickly obeyed her husband's commands with a willing mind, and crossed the sea with a great attendance of knights and noble women . . . Matilda, before a year was ended, gave birth to a son named Henry [later Henry I] . . . This young prince had his attention turned to a learned education as soon as he was of age to receive instruction, and after the death of both his parents, had a bold career in arms'.[67] Son Henry, surnamed Beauclerc, was the third born to William and Matilda, not including one Richard who died young. The eldest son was Robert Curthose—a jesting nickname since it poked fun at his short legs— who became duke of Normandy; the next surviving son was William Rufus. Neither one of these elder boys would amount to anything remotely comparable to Henry. Maybe Matilda had a femininely intuitive feeling about Henry: he was always her favourite.

By the end of the year William could allow himself a certain feeling of pride and satisfaction. His new kingdom was, if not exactly peaceful, at least taking on a semblance of order which was more than merely cosmetic. He had his queen at his side, a fine counterpart to his lusty energies—she had already also borne him two daughters and was to bear three or four more. He had his castles built or in the process of completion across the realm, and his armies arrayed protectively around him. But trouble was still in store.

Chapter Five

O shameless pride, O luckless arrogance that cast an angel from heaven and man from paradise!

Otto of Freising, *The Deeds of Frederick Barbarossa*
Translated by Mierrow and Emery

1068

The year 1068 saw a revival of Norman fortunes in the Mediterranean, a success story to match William's in England. 'Stalemate' is perhaps too static-sounding a word to describe the situation in Southern Italy and Sicily during the years since 1064; however, the Norman ship in the south did seem, if not to have foundered, at least to have been becalmed. But this impression is in a way misleading; things were happening all right, but mostly internally, the usual Norman string of mutinies that occurred when there was nothing better on. That most Norman of Normans, Robert Guiscard, expected and knew how to handle insurrection; but it took time and energy. For four years it was all he could do to get around Apulia and Calabria, the Amazonian Sichelgaita ever at his side, putting the damper on a fire first here then there, at Conversano, Molfetta and Montescaglioso. These were serious challenges to his authority, and cohesive only in that the Norman barons were encouraged and supplied by the Byzantines, who still had their Varangian Guards in Bari, Brindisi and Taranto. Then, in 1068, the year that William was scouring the West Country and otherwise bringing England into line, the balance of power in Southern Italy tilted in the direction of the Hautevilles. And the weight brought to bear on the Guiscard's side of the scale came from an unexpected source: the Turks.

For years the Seljuk Turks had been making advances on Byzantine turf. They seemed, this year, about to threaten Constantinople itself, where a new emperor sat on the Byzantine throne: Romanus IV Diogenes. With his attention diverted to more immediate emergencies the Greek initiative in Italy collapsed, and with it the revolts of Guiscard's barons.

In Sicily Roger de Hauteville was doing his part by administering a resounding defeat to a large contingent of Saracen troops which he met at Misilmeri, about seven miles southeast of Palermo. The summer battle was so devastating to the defenders, for once acting under a unified command, that any organized resistance was henceforth impossible. The Saracen leader, Ayub ibn Temim, fled the island with his followers, of which there were few after the terrible slaughter of battle. With what horror the inhabitants of Palermo must have received the flock of carrier pigeons, captured by Roger from the decimated Saracen army, bearing bits of material which had been dipped in the blood of their dead husbands and sons! Malaterra wrote that the very air was heavy with Saracen lamentations, alleviated only by the rejoicing of the Normans. Poised, ready to administer the *coup de grâce* to Palermo, Roger

Site of the Battle of Hastings, England

*Hercules and the
Nemean Lion,
Canterbury
Cathedral*

117

Chapel of St John, Tower of London

Chepstow Castle, England

Cain and Abel, cathedral floor,
Otranto, Italy

Adam and Eve, cathedral floor,
Otranto, Italy

Lincoln Cathedral,
England

Trani Cathedral, Italy

St Etienne, Abbaye aux Hommes, Caen, France

decided to wait for his elder brother. Surely two heads were better than one. And he could do with the extra support of the Guiscard's troops as well as his advice. But in fact Roger would have to wait for three years. The Guiscard had decided to eliminate once and for all the Greek threat to his authority. Before turning his attention to any other adventure he decided to take from them their last major stronghold—Bari.

As an industrial-fishing city of Southern Italy, Bari is second only to Naples. Going back to Illyrian times, and then to ancient Greek and Roman occupations, it had been taken by the Byzantines in the ninth century. Since it was the major focal point of the Greek presence in Italy, it stood to reason that their power in Apulia would be broken once the city was in Norman hands. Those old Greek bulwarks which rose so menacingly out of the sea on one side and out of the flats of Apulia on the other, interrupted by stout towers from which fluttered the Greek pennants, at once mocking and challenging, must have loomed forbiddingly over the Guiscard and his ruffians as they surrounded the city with both ships and troops on 5 August. Robert knew that it would take a supreme and co-ordinated effort on his part to bring Bari to its knees. He was willing to persevere—so willing that he continued the siege for almost three years.

Even for a medieval city, where adequate defence was the first require-ment, Bari was exceptional in the strength of its fortifications. It would take a man with a plodding singleness of purpose to challenge a fortification which was thought of by all as impregnable. The original of the sea-facing castle that we know today is Norman, but the Greek defences surely centred on the same spot, overlooking as it does the great harbour and a sweep of the Adriatic Sea. Surrounded now, at least on the land side, by a dry moat-park, the castle stands as one of those moodily operatic monuments of architecture that one learns to expect in Southern Italy. The exactly hewn, moss-covered stone walls—so four-square as to smack of eternity—the shadowed archways and sweeping

Castle, Bari, Italy

staircases, all seem more suitable to legend than to history. Yet we know that the Norman castle was later modified, by Frederick II of Hohenstaufen, to pretty much its present indomitable form.

In his maraudings around Italy, and especially in his struggle to take Sicily, Robert had learned a lot. He had built up a large navy—large for its time, though nothing compared to what he would muster a few years later—and confronted the Bariots with a manoeuvre so imaginative that we can understand their not anticipating it. He encircled the promontory of the old city with a barricade of boats, all chained one to the other. With his army surrounding the city on land, he had achieved a complete blockade, making it even more surprising that the citizens held out for the incredible length of time they did. It was to be April 1071 before they finally capitulated.

1069

'Uneasy lies the head that wears a crown'[68] might well have been said by William I as well as by Henry IV. During a year of exceptional peril he was faced with trials from all corners of his realm: York, Durham, Dorset, Chester and North Wales all attempted uprisings which were at least successful enough to distract the king and, most of the time, cry for his presence. Pressures from beyond the realm presented themselves in the person of the Danish King Swein, who actually managed to take York and penetrate Lincolnshire before being harried out of the kingdom.

The Scandinavian forces at large in England had been joined by Malcolm of Scotland and certain of William's Saxon magnates. When York fell to them it must have been a period of terrible anxiety for William, a time turgid with the latent possibilities that a new Scandinavian kingdom might be established on the island. After lashing out in several directions, quelling first this revolt then that, William moved on York. Along the way he stripped the land of its life-sustaining properties, savaging the towns and leaving hardly a man alive. On reaching York, a burnt-out island in a sea of desolation, he celebrated the Christmas season. It is claimed that marks of his rampage were visible for yet another twenty years.

York was not unfamiliar with great men. The Roman city of Eboracum had been visited by the emperors Hadrian, Septimus Severus and Constantius (the latter two died there) and Constantine the Great (who was proclaimed emperor at York in 306). It had been noted as a centre of learning and boasted a famous school headed by Alcuin before he was called into service by Charlemagne. Located as it is at the junction of the rivers Ouse and Foss, it was destined to play a large part in the affairs of history. Yet the city that William visited for his Christmas celebration could then boast hardly a vestige of its centuries of culture and commerce. William had, in 1068, built a timber castle there, to which, earlier this year, he had added a second. Now even these were gone. But they were replaced at once with the usual Norman efficiency.

One of these castles was in 1190 burned down in a terrible holocaust directed against the Jews of the city, who had sought refuge there from a violent mob. When the castle was rebuilt it was placed, for reasons of security,

*Clifford's Tower,
York, England*

on a higher mound. But this structure, too, was demolished, by a great gale that occurred in 1228. Finally, in 1244, Henry III commissioned a new castle, this one in stone, placed on William's original mound and known today as Clifford's Tower, after the family whose coat of arms hung with the royal arms of Charles II over the main entrance. 'It was gutted by fire in 1684 when a salute of seven guns had a greater effect than intended. That did not deter the military; another salute a few years later blew the gunner into the moat'.[69]

The construction of 1244 is quatrefoil, of French origin, with a fore-building housing the entrance, and approached by a long flight of steps. When completed, with its bailey walled in by stone and fortified by five stone towers and two gateways, it was formidable indeed; exactly what was needed, from the royal point of view, in this population centre where revolt was endemic.

York—the name stems from the Danish Yorvik—is a prosperous railway centre, and boasts a wide enough variety of sightseeing interests to satisfy the most inveterate tourist. There is Roman stone-work from the beginning of the fourth century; medieval houses abound, along with some Georgian. The church of All Saints dates from about 1350; the Debtors' Prison of 1750 is now part of the Castle Museum (one of the finest folk museums in England). The churches of St Denis and St Margaret both have Norman doorways, and the first has Norman tower arches. For the train buff there is the fine Railway Museum. The two-and-a-half mile circuit of city walls is partly Norman, but mostly fourteenth-century; and four old city gates lend a medieval touch, including Micklegate Bar from which were hung the heads of enemies from both sides of the Wars of the Roses, including that of the duke of York, Edward IV's father, which prompted one of Shakespeare's most grizzily humorous lines from the mouth of Queen Margaret:

'Off with his head, and set it on York gates;
So York may overlook the town of York.'[70]

From the very beginning of its history York Minster was a cathedral, that is, it housed the *cathedra*, the bishop's throne. Little of the Norman building remains because, as one might easily suspect from the history of the city, there have been several minsters, the present one usually counted as the fourth. The oldest part of the building is the crypt, from where one can catch glimpses of some of the original Norman columns, enormous and decorated much like those at Durham, which formed the nave of the Norman minster. They are, sadly, truncated within a few feet of the ground to allow room for the flooring of the present-day church above.

Frustrated and weary, Robert Guiscard waited outside the walls of Bari. Had he known how long he was going to have to cool his heels before those great ramparts, he might have lost patience and given up. Nor was the situation without its humiliations. In the first months of this year a Greek convoy had broken his sea blockade, entering the harbour with supplies, military reinforcements, a new catapan and a fresh military commander. Norman morale was low, and sank even lower when the Greeks managed to break the blockade a second time, allowing the new commander to sail for Constantinople to request additional aid. And then, as though to rub salt into a festering wound, the Bariots made a bravura display of contempt by daily parading the city's treasures atop their walls in full view of an almost slavering Guiscard. The Norman wooden military machines were being burned almost as a matter of course every time they were wheeled within striking distance of the walls. Robert himself barely escaped an assassination attempt. But if morale was low outside the walls, Robert asked, what must it be like inside? And if the Greeks had it in mind to demand reinforcements, then Robert could do likewise. He sent for Roger, who he knew would be eager to help, since he was also waiting for the Guiscard to join him at Palermo. And it was a good thing that Robert called for his brother, since it was not too long before a relief force was heading towards Bari from the Eastern emperor.

1070

King William may have been living in a man's world, but even in those macho surroundings he was suddenly made aware of the power that lurks behind thrones, that launches ships, shapes empires—and disbands armies. With all of his kingly troubles he was soon faced with a new one: the Norman women waiting for their men across the Channel, who 'were so inflamed by passion that they sent frequent messages to their husbands, requiring their speedy return, adding that, if it were not immediate, they should choose others'.[71] William was caught between belligerent and vengeful English on the one side and noisily angry Norman wives on the other. 'The king naturally wished to retain his soldiers while the country was in so disturbed a state, and made them great offers of lands with ample revenues and great powers, promising still more when the whole kingdom should be freed from their opponents . . . On the other hand, what were these honourable soldiers to do, when their licentious wives threatened to stain the marriage bed with adultery, and stamp the mark of infamy on their offspring?'[72]

The pull of the marriage bed was stronger than the promise of wealth, and some of Williams's best and most trusted soldiers 'returned obsequiously to their lascivious wives in Normandy'.[73] As though this were not trouble enough—William's 'red-haired temper' must have been spectacularly pyrotechnical!—the year was recorded as one of disastrous famine across the land. English weather at this time was at least as bad as today. Crop failure was frequent, especially if the summer was wet, a condition that can be regarded as normal. Animal hunting had been greatly curtailed by the Normans, who set aside enormous tracts for themselves, and these private warrens were protected by cruel and stringent laws.

> . . . A famine prevailed to such a degree, that, compelled by hunger, men ate human flesh, and that of horses, dogs, and cats, and whatever was repulsive to notions of civilization; some persons went so far as to sell themselves into perpetual slavery, provided only they could . . . support a miserable existence; some departed from their native country into exile, breathed forth their exhausted spirits in the midst of the journey.[74]

It was now the turn of Chester to submit to the depredations of William and his army, one presumes before he was deprived of the services of some of his leading officers when they returned to their unhappy wives. With the coming of the Normans to Chester—it was one of the last of the important Saxon towns to capitulate—the city's fortunes revived and a new period of prosperity was set in motion, as its two-mile circuit of city walls indicates. Chester is interesting for things other than Norman now, though there are a few intriguing remains of the period. The church of St John the Baptist retains its sweeping Norman nave arches, noble, almost heroic in their proportions. The same church strikes a more romantic chord with its twelfth-century choir crumbling into ruins. Of the Norman cathedral there remains only one arch at ground level, with several triforium arches above it, handsomely spaced and placed in a wall of irregularly cut blocks; apart from these there are a few patches of Norman wall, incorporated inconspicuously into later work.

By the spring of the year organized resistance to William and his greedy followers was finally broken. The king moved south to be with his queen, reaching Winchester before Easter. He was now in a position to turn his thoughts to other matters. By the late summer he had pulled enough strings and crossed enough palms to get his friend Lanfranc appointed archbishop of Canterbury. Lanfranc confessed to having no feeling for the job; what he really pined for was to return to his place at Bec. But William would hear none of it, and Lanfranc was consecrated on 29 August. Despite his reticence the new archbishop, a man of soft and gentle nature, succeeded admirably. He could be tough, too, and he managed to keep his bishops in line, at best a tricky proposition since they could be, in their way, as rebellious as William's barons.

1071

The Greek presence in Italy was finally eradicated once and for all with the fall of Bari—after two years and eight months of siege. Having seen the Guiscard's forces swell with the arrival of Roger early in the year, the inhabitants, so weakened by starvation, and despondent after watching a catastrophic routing of a Byzantine relief fleet (nine of the ships were sunk), had no choice but to open their gates to the stubborn aggressors on 16 April. More often than not given to pillage and overt cruelty, the Normans were still good rulers. So once the initial violence of the take-over was accomplished, and after the brothers had triumphantly entered the humbled city, life went on pretty much as usual—not the recent usual, but the usual before the siege. Robert and Roger, with Sichelgaita and Judith at their sides, happily ensconced in the port castle, could afford time off to share a victory banquet with their leading supporters. A heavy soup would have been served, followed by a stew of chopped chicken, including entrails and blood, fried with onions in a sauce rich with mint and balsam. There would have been a pie made of ham, sweet with sugar and rich with cheese, and garnished with gherkins, hard-boiled eggs and candied fruits. Add prodigious quantities of strong, southern red wine, and coarse, crusty bread, music, drunken laughter, dancing, a smoke-filled interior, a host of blowsy Bariot young women brought in for the occasion, the usual loud bragging, and probably even a few tests of strength among the men, and—well, it had to have been festive!

The Normans were hearty eaters—a hangover from their northern ancestry. Had they had such amenities available at their victory celebration at Bari they would have enjoyed some of the modern Apulian food, as zesty and hearty as that to which they were accustomed. *Melanzane ripiene* would have, at a single serving, covered several of their dinner courses. Take an eggplant, scoop out the meat and chop it, mix with olives, onions, tomatoes, anchovies, a small amount of breadcrumbs and some capers. Replace the meat and bake until tender. Serve with a meat sauce—à la Bolognese—and *ecco!* food fit for the hungriest warrior and the most fastidious duke, which, even by the ultimate stretch of imagination, we cannot imagine Robert Guiscard to have been. 'The Apulians love to stuff pasta with good things. Take *calzone*, for example; pasta turnovers containing lightly fried onions, olives, *mozzarella* cheese, capers, anchovies, baby mackerel, raisins, and beaten yolk of egg. *Focaccia piena* is a homemade tart consisting of two layers of pastry between which repose black olives, onions, capers, chicory, and anchovies'.[75] This last would have been an especially appropriate dish for the Norman bash considering its proximity to Easter; *Focaccia piena* is a traditional dish for Good Friday. And pity the Normans! They never tasted a southern *pizza Napoletana* or *Siciliana*, slightly heavy on the olive oil and crusty, and covered with a rich variety of almost anything edible. The Hautevilles may have been initiated into this delight through the ancestor of the modern pizza, however, since the 'pizza is one of those almost spontaneous inventions that followed on the discovery of the phenomen of leavening that takes place when certain cereals are cooked in a hot oven (most of all wheat flour), a fact particularly appreciated by Mediterranean peoples from the very earliest times'.[76]

All this about food is appropriate to Bari, which is one of the most animated of Southern Italian cities, most of the activity there centring around pavement cafés, the *Città Vecchia* (the Old City, as contrasted with the modern apartment-lined, tree-bordered boulevarded city), and especially at the quays and fish markets. Animation comes naturally to Bari; it must be a carry-over from that same indomitable good nature and will that enabled its citizens not only to stand against the Norman might for so long but, until the very end, to taunt the aggressors with arrogant humour from their lofty walls. Market-place or fish market, no matter where, there is an excitement, an adventure in sound and gregariousness and, in the case of the fish market, smell. Music, laughter and shrieking automobile horns—much more strident than the sizes of the cars warrant!—hard-bargaining housewives arguing in their shrill dialect with vendors who, without exception, wear expressions of imminent bankruptcy—they are all part of the norm of this prosperous and lively city.

The ambience seems so indigenous to the locale that one gets the impression that the Hautevilles and their followers heard the same sounds, saw the same garishly colourful sights and smelled the same raw odours. On the quays of Bari one feels closer to the eleventh century than in many a Romanesque church or castle; one senses the time link. 'Continuity of effort over many centuries is always impressive, and I have sometimes reflected that two activities which have managed to survive empires are street markets and fish stalls'.[77] To that should be added, before the final 'amen', a plug for the pavement café. The ancients held that no strangers could eat at the same table and remain strangers; once having broken bread together men had little choice but friendship. (The charming Continental tradition of quietly saying goodbye to others in a restaurant is an echo of this old truism.) It is an impossibility to sit in a Bariot eatery without conversing with nearby patrons, probably about nothing important, but always something pleasant. If a child is a part of the company the contact is ensured, and may even lead to an invitation to a home for *un po' di vino*. A child can open more doors and hearts in Italy than in any other place in the world!

With Bari out of the way the brothers Hauteville set their minds to the coming Sicilian campaign. They had learned for themselves the effectiveness of a combined land–sea operation. Now they were ready to go after the coveted island in the same manner. Roger returned to Sicily, while the Guiscard settled down at Otranto to supervise the gathering of the fleet.

To sit under the neatly rowed trees of the Otranto beach, confronted by a barely visible Albania across the smoothest of indigo seas under the dome of clear cobalt blue, idly sipping a glass of red Apulian Aleatico—as slowly as possible, for ecstacy should be stretched to the infinite—is to come as close as one can to absolute tranquillity while still remaining conscious. Perhaps it is better to let history, Normans and all, go its way; only the present should matter. There are few tourists at Otranto, no large hotels, some fishing boats and swimmers and, only now and then, a snarling Vespa to remind one that life goes on. And there is the disarmingly friendly hotel maid who, with inexhaustible patience, taught at least one American family the word for bath-towel and its pronunciation, *asciugamano*—'a-*shioo*-gah-mahn-o'. Incredible!

Otranto had been a principal Byzantine port until it fell to the Normans in 1068. In the period after Robert Guiscard it flourished again as a point of departure for crusaders. The disaster from which Otranto has never really recovered came at the hands of the Turks, who in July 1480 sacked the city and massacred eight hundred of its citizens. The bones and skulls of 560 of these unfortunates can be viewed on request in the cathedral's Chapel of the Martyrs—an oddly unmoving sight and hardly the kind of thing to induce spiritual reverie.

Hands down the most interesting—not to say amusing—sight in Otranto is its cathedral: no great parade of noble arches filing up either side of the nave (though they are handsome); no lofty tower with bells which have pealed away the centuries (though they are full and rich); no wall mosaics of shimmering gold set off by accenting rainbow hues. No! It is the *floor* that is the glory of this eleventh-century cathedral, a consummate tessellated masterpiece extending from the main entrance all the way to the apse. Here, in subdued earthy colours, are the Tree of Life, a medieval bestiary, fables and biblical incidents, a kaleidoscopic succession of kings, heroes, saints and prophets, make-believe and mundane—and most of them in form and attitude right out of the back part of the mind. This floor does not sparkle with the light of Byzantine Ravenna nor of Norman Palermo, for here we walk on quiet blues and watery greens, terracottas, blacks, red-browns and greys. It is the forms themselves that sing, the animals that laugh and the plants that dance.

The cathedral of Otranto was consecrated in 1088, probably built by Robert's son Bohemund, who always loved the little town. The floor, though, was not executed until 1166, conceived and laid by a priest from Southern Italy named Pantaleone. The cleric was an inspired man, not in the sophisticated sense of the Sicilian mosaicists, some of whom were contemporaries and imported by the Normans from Constantinople, but rather in his primitive vision of a world beyond reality, a complete world, but with no basis in tangible fact or object. When one paces the floor at Otranto (which is a little like treading on the Bayeux Tapestry), one wants to whirl and meander, to walk more lightly, maybe to dance. Pantaleone's arabesques and whirlpools, his waves, curlicues and gyrating patterns of broken rhythms weave a continuum of things to see, but combined in a harmony devoid of logic; they constitute a melody, but without tune; there is a rhythm, but no beat.

The Tree of Life, rooted at the entrance, moves toward the sanctuary, weaving, undulating and spiralling to the altar. Camouflaged among the twisting branches and giant leaves are mythical beasts, monsters of outlandish shapes and proportions. A giant stork, stilt-legged and awkward, balances precariously to wave at an unlikely mermaid or chimera; a donkey plays a harp for a dragon, sphinx or centaur, while friendly fish pause to listen and Noah's Ark sails calmly by. An unidentified man talks to a unicorn, while another is hugged by a giant crane-like bird whose lower extremities metamorphose into snakes; a mason constructs a block wall, unconcerned that, within his proximity, Jonah is jettisoned from a dinghy and swallowed by an inadequate-looking fish which 'the Lord had prepared'; and a school of frightened fish scatters every which way. Men ride and walk and posture and climb. They love, work and fight. Here Cain delivers a knock-out blow with a club, so ruthlessly lethal as to leave poor Abel not only *hors de combat*, but in a state of rigor mortis before even hitting the ground (*see page* 119). And Adam and Eve leave the Garden of Eden, Adam with a jaunty, good-natured wave to the avenging angel (*see page* 119). Another rendition of Eve depicts her with breasts so flaccid and pendulous as to make one wonder what attracted Adam in the first place. (The answer to this is easy: he had no reference for comparison.) Solomon is there, as is Abraham, for a change hugging little Isaac instead of preparing to dispatch him in the ritual sacrifice.

And then, surprising from a man born in the Norman-Arab-Byzantine world of Southern Italy, we see, in all his regal splendour, the King Arthur of medieval legend—surprising but not out of place in this merry-go-round world of Pantaleone. This is joyful Christianity, humorous, innocent, and utterly positive in its rejection of despair. Pantaleone's mosaics are an assertion of the Judeo-Christian optimism found on occasion in the Bible:

'But let all those that put their trust in thee rejoice: let them ever shout for joy, because thou defendest them: let them also that love thy name be joyful in thee'.[78]

'Be glad in the Lord, and rejoice, ye righteous: and shout for joy, all ye that are upright in heart'.[79]

1072

Having subdued Bari, and having assembled his fleet at Otranto, Robert headed for Sicily. He had already dispatched Roger to the island, and the two met at Messina. The Greeks had fallen at Bari; Saracen Palermo was to be the next target of a combined land and sea attack. But first Catania was taken by trickery—Roger seeking permission for Norman ships to enter the harbour and then from that vantage point taking over the city from the suprised natives. The brothers then fortified Catania and headed for Palermo. By meticulous teamwork Roger's land forces combined with Robert's navy to bring about—after a long and bloody struggle—the capitulation of the city, the greatest prize of all.

In a glittering triumphal procession Robert Guiscard entered Palermo on 10 January 1072. Famine had broken out in the city. The defending navy was a charred and sunken wreck in the harbour. The Muslim rulers had fled. And an Arab poet was to write:

Weep as you will your tears of blood,
O grave of Arab civilisation.
Once this place was alive with the people of the desert
And the ocean was a playground for their boats . . .
O Sicily you are the glory of the ocean . . .
You were the cradle of this nation's culture,
Whose fire like beauty burnt the world . . .[80]

The Guiscard claimed the island as a duchy for himself. Roger was invested with the title 'great count'. With that double investiture began the new age; it would prove to be the most glowing and the most opulent in all of medieval Europe—and the most envied. Strange that in England, and America too, for that matter, not much is heard of this glory of the Norman world, seeing that the Normans ruled there for over a century, until 1194. Moreover they ruled well, blending their own philosophies, political ideals and aesthetic styles with those of the Greek inhabitants and the former Saracen rulers, creating a new golden age—*the* golden age of Sicily. The island has not succeeded since in so much as coming near to the grandeur, the rampant creativity and paradoxically peaceful toleration among wildly divergent groups that it achieved during the Norman occupation.

Once having quitted the island toward the end of the year, the Guiscard never returned, leaving its administration to his younger brother. As 'great count' Roger was a better diplomat than his older brother, whose main skills were clearly military. The Palermo that Roger took over was a teeming labyrinth of narrow streets divided into quarters, each with its limits and its own character. The quarter near the docks was noisy and dirty, but rich in exotic traffic: cotton from Egypt, brightly dyed linens from the Eastern Mediterranean, and pre-spun, blue-flowered flax plants from the northeast for making domestic linen; brass from Persia, hammered into trays and flasks; wines from Muslim Spain; mosaic tesserae from Constantinople. There was a steady stream of slaves through Palermo from as far away as Russia and Ireland; children and women were especially sought after, but a husky young male never stayed long on the auction block.

Roger's new city was a sensually indulgent sprawl of white, low houses clustered around luxurious palaces, mosques, baths, temporary vendors' stands and every kind of shop. There were fish shops, butcher and jewellery stores, cloth merchants and sandal makers, metal workers, armourers, brothels and eateries of every description. On its streets were Venetians, Arabs, Lombards, Berbers, Greeks, Hebrews, Africans, Pisans and Levantines; to this add the Normans. The noise, the mixture of tongues, foreign costumes and divers racial colours made Palermo perhaps the most cosmopolitan city in the world. And it was, apparently, out of this unlikely confusion of types, traditions and national prides that the Hautevilles set out to mould a unity. The task that had faced King William of England was elementary compared with this. William had walked into a land with at least something of a unifying glue to hold it together; Sicily was nothing but an assemblage of fragments, crystals of differing chemistry, many of them naturally aversive.

It was as though Roger were born to rule, such was the alacrity with which he tackled his job. His reign was a model for the rest of Europe, a model of toleration, fairness, equity and foresight, which other rulers, unfortunately, did not imitate. First of all he guaranteed a degree of continuity by allowing local emirs to remain in their offices, removing only those troublemakers who would be apt to upset the status quo. Arabic continued to be the official language—along with Latin, Greek and French. Islamic laws continued, and the mosques were open to worship. Only those mosques which had been originally Christian and had been taken over by the Saracens were reconsecrated for Christian ritual. And perhaps more important than anything, taxes were alike for Christians and Muslims—high! It would be inaccurate to see Roger's rule as one of unbroken tranquillity. There was trouble, mainly from the Christians themselves, East against West, as old animosities surfaced and resurfaced, not lessened by the great count's insistence that the Greek monks of his realm owed their first allegiance to the Roman pontiff rather than to their more sympathetic Byzantine patriarch. Somehow Roger managed to work his way through the emotion-charged atmosphere, but without the usual Norman brutalities and heartless subjugation of the populace which his countrymen were currently lavishing on England.

To William, since his arrival in England, Malcolm III of Scotland had always been troublesome, probably rightly regarding the English king as a threat to his own sovereignty. Malcolm was married to Margaret (later a saint, no less!), sister of Edgar Atheling ('atheling': a prince of the royal family). He had, in 1070, already devastated Durham and Cleveland. Now, in 1072, to discourage further encroachments by the Scottish king, William carried hostilities back into Malcolm's territory. Malcolm's posturing melted away. He pledged himself as William's vassal, giving his eldest son as hostage. Undoubtedly he was persuaded to this act by reason of the construction of Durham Castle, or perhaps he realized that William was prepared to carry out further invasions of his territories unless he came to heel.

The area around Durham had been sparsely settled by Romans as a means of keeping open the communications to the northern frontier. There are a few meagre remains of prehistoric settlements in the area, but it was Saxon times before any kind of heavy population moved in. During the Norman period it became a most important outlying city indeed, its significance attributable to the frequent raids by the Scottish kings as well as the natural rebelliousness of the nearby Northumbrians.

Of the original castle built by William little remains, though certainly it was a motte-and-bailey construction. The general plan of the keep and its sprawling courtyard follows the pattern of the original, the keep itself (rebuilt in 1840) replacing what was once a timber tower within a shell wall. Because of the importance of Durham in the protection of the realm it was declared a palatinate, with the prince-bishop enjoying full administrative powers. He occupied a prestigious religio-political position, unequalled until well into the nineteenth century. (Even today the bishop of Durham stands to the immediate right of the sovereign during the coronation.) This meant, of course, that he was expected to respond to any emergency of a defensive nature, to furnish an army and even to lead it into battle. Today the castle is lavishly ornamented by coats of arms and other personal signs identifying the long line of powerful bishops who held sway there, and who added to and modified their fortress-palace. Extensive elaborations on the castle were performed by Hugh de Puiset, bishop from 1153 to 1195, who erected magnificent adjoining buildings, of which the Romanesque doorway to his main hall stands as one of the most beautiful of Norman works in the country. It is a masterpiece of non-figurative sculpture, combining three different orders of capitals, modest yet so eloquently Romanesque, a style echoed in the crypt of the chapel which is part of the original Norman building.

The city of Durham is located on a stony peninsula formed by a remarkable meander in the River Wear. As a result it is fortified by a kind of moat, a convenience furnished by Nature, which proved so efficient that the cathedral and its adjacent castle were spoken of as 'half church of God, half castle against the Scots'. William, in selecting this narrow neck of land for his castle, had chosen his site well.

But the year was not entirely given over to military considerations, since one of the triumphs of Norman English ecclesiastical architecture was begun at Lincoln in 1072. (Unfortunately only a fragment of that original lofty structure still stands.) Lincoln was an important centre to the Normans from the moment they touched English soil; in fact, Remigius (or Remi), the first bishop of Lincoln, was also the very first Norman to be given a bishopric after 1066. He had been an almoner of the Benedictine abbey of Fécamp, and as such had supplied William with a ship and some knights for the Conquest. It was possibly a tit-for-tat payment of the debt that secured Remigius his bishopric. In 1068 William had erected an imposing castle at Lincoln, when returning from his first expedition to pacify the north.

We know next to nothing of the earlier Anglo-Saxon minster church of St Mary of Lincoln (only its name still lives in the designation of the cathedral close as 'Minster Yard') on which site Remigius built his cathedral. And of that church only the western front (*see page* 119) and the lower three storeys of the western towers remain. Remigius' church was smaller than the present one, about 310 feet in length, as opposed to the 481 feet of today's cathedral, though it followed pretty closely the style of the Norman churches across the Channel. Yet the façade is unique, a design unparalleled either in England or Normandy. The usual Norman simplicity is shattered by three enormous arches which have been cut into the front, the centre one higher than the two flanking, all of which are deeply recessed and serve as frames for the three main entrances. These are in turn flanked by smaller arches to either side, thereby bringing the stepped effect of the arches to a logical though perhaps less than satisfactory, conclusion. The carved frieze which extends across the entire façade above the doorways was the work of Lincoln's third bishop, Alexander, probably just after a disastrous fire in 1141. Alexander's frieze managed to survive even an earthquake in 1185, which brought down much of Remigius' original church. There is a tapestry effect about the front of Lincoln Cathedral, an overall texture, an exactly repetitive pattern. It is the best part of the church, and all the reminders that it is symbolic of the gate of heaven through which man must pass to fulfil his destiny are meaningless, a superfluous intrusion of a self-consciously conceived symbolism into an uncomplicated statement rendered in lovely honey-tan stone. The western wall of Lincoln Cathedral, so Norman in its strength and in the proportion of its great recesses, so sensitive in its repetitious frieze, is a visual experience. It needs, quite simply, to be looked at. And that is all.

1073

When Robert Guiscard quit Sicily in 1072, he returned to find his mainland realm in disarray, part of it in open rebellion led by his vassal Peter of Trani, and his own nephews Abelard and Herman, sons of his brother Humphrey. Never one for passively waiting, Robert sprang into action and by 2 February 1073, had already taken Trani, whereupon the other insurgent cities quickly returned to the fold.

Trani is a city whose streets are so rich with Norman memories that they seem at a glance more suitable to knights on horseback, archers, pilgrims bound for the Holy Land, or brawling crusaders. A maritime city, it had already in 1063 attained a degree of renown by publishing the first medieval code of maritime laws—the *Ordinamenta maris*. Since the days of the Romans it had served as a thriving east-coast port. Even its cathedral (*see page* 120), so splendidly dominating the quay of the old city, with the three apses staring imperiously eastward toward Yugoslavia, is rooted in the Roman past.

In the dawning centuries of Christianity, a tomb-shrine dedicated to Saint Leucius had been built on the site. As happens to saints and soldiers, memory of him faded somewhat and in the sixth century the people of Trani erected a new Byzantine-style church to the Virgin, but without destroying the lower ancient shrine. The Virgin's church is now the crypt of the present cathedral. Shortly after the time of the Guiscard (who died in 1085), a young pilgrim arrived in Trani from Epirus. He carried a burdensome wooden cross and sang 'Lord have mercy on us!'—*Kyrie Eléison!*—which had an immediate effect. And for good measure he worked miracles. Crowds stampeded to him, to hear, to touch and perhaps to be cured from diseases both physical and spiritual. Despite the acclaim the young man, Nicola Pellegrino (Pilgrim), did not last long in his ascetic pursuits, dying in 1094. Within five years he was canonized by Pope Urban II, whereupon poor Leucius was finally superseded as the patron saint of the city. The local people commenced yet a third church, directly over the other two and dedicated to their San Nicola Pellegrino. It is an attractive 'sandwich of devotion' that can be seen in Trani today—a splendid Norman cathedral astride a Byzantine forerunner built four centuries earlier, and both of them superimposed over a small Roman tomb-shrine.

Understandably the pride and triumph of the cathedral of San Nicola Pellegrino are the central western doors, bronze, and with a centuries-old patina as green as an unripe Norman apple. Four flanking arches on either side, not as high as the centre one, and blind in that they frame no sculpture or decoration but simply echo the show-piece—though two of them do have minor side aisle doors—serve by their very plainness to emphasize the splendour of the nave entrance. This has the added advantage of an intricately carved stone border of fantastic and dynamic little figures—jugglers, animals, satyrs darting in and out of a tangle of foliage. Ascending the flight of heavy Romanesque steps, we approach the doors with respect, eyes raised to catch a first close glimpse. There is an aura of sanctity about them because they are at a level above the meaner streets, the piazza facing the porch, and the blue sea behind. We become *pellegrini* ourselves, in the true sense of the word, before these doors which materialize from the top down as we move upward to their level. For eight hundred years they have hung there

Main portal, Trani Cathedral, Italy

(they were positioned in 1179), facing the sunset whose glow penetrates their surface, a green skin so rich as to appear velvet rather than bronze. That late afternoon wash of light flooding down from the mountains in the west—and made even more limpid by the contact—terminates on the eastern edge of this ancient land, against these doors which now seem to light up from within, changing the green from apple to ocean moss, the shadows to a blue-green as deep as the troughs of the gentle surf which are their natural backdrop. No god of the theatre could have set his stage better; no Apollo, for all the magic rheostats at his command, could have managed with more moving, silence-producing ingenuity, the gentle slackening of light, the blush of pink, and the final sudden plunge into darkness which has been the regular twilight production for centuries.

The name of the creator of the doors we know was Barisanus of Trani, who was actually from Bari. And that is about all we do know, except that he also cast the doors for Ravello Cathedral, as well as the side entrance doors at Monreale, just outside Palermo. The doors are massive (sixteen by ten feet), cast in sections and artfully assembled to hide the joinings. There are saints and angels, warriors in combat on foot and on horseback, each panel separated by borders of abstract floral decoration. Barisanus must have used material which he saw about him every day for his inspiration, a Norman baron for Saint George or a Norman hunting party riding to hounds for Saint Eustace and his companions. Barisanus' doors, so heavily encrusted with foliage and medallions, birds, and fantasies of every kind, even including a pagan centaur shooting an arrow, may not be as elegant as the Byzantine-styled doors of Monte Sant'Angelo, but they are, in their directness, eloquently expressive of the very *bronzeness* of the bronze, more monumental, more masculine, power-fully evocative of the virile toughness of the age and the people who com-missioned them. To see them is to walk into a medieval bestiary or to move through the company of saints.

A few blocks from the cathedral, a little harder to find—but then all one need do is look a bit dazzled or confused; it is never long before a friendly, often knowledgeable Italian will offer directions, sometimes even taking you in tow personally to lead you to the most obscure nooks of interest—is the church of Ognissanti (All Saints). It typifies the ease with which the Italian approaches his monumental heritage. Like the cathedral, Ognissanti is located on a quay, but this one a fishing port—complete with boats, nets, fish stalls, smell and all. It is a sweet church, small, Norman and twelfth-century, and belonged once to the Order of the Knights Templar; it was, in fact, located in the courtyard of their hospital. The hospital is gone now. All of this cannot be of much importance to the fishermen, who have a hard, sometimes perilous living to earn. They have desecrated the exquisitely proportioned apses by driving hooks into that venerable stone, from which they hang their nets to dry. Perhaps they are right. History is good only so far as it can be used.

In the process of putting his house in order, the Guiscard reclaimed the town of Andria, which had been Norman since 1046 and which had, in his absence, been tempted to break free of the Hauteville yoke. Today it is a thriving city, industrial, and at first sight not very interesting, especially if one hits it during the afternoon siesta when, following the city-wide clatter of falling *persiane* (those very Mediterranean slatted shutters), the seventy thousand inhabitants simply dematerialize, an uncharacteristic quiet descends and the streets become as dead as another Pompeii, or Machu-Picchu—or an Arizona ghost town.

Along with a superb ducal palace in Andria there is the severely Norman church of San Francesco, hidden away on a side-street, unnoticed and unsung; it would have remained unseen by us, too, but for an especially gregarious, indescribably dirty, eleven- or twelve-year old urchin who, with the handsomest smile in all of Southern Italy and the most imperial manner imaginable, became a self-appointed guide—and then, with haughty disdain, refused a tip! No tip please, but would we come by and see his mother's needlework? Or taste some home-made wine? Or perhaps we would like a wrist-watch?— Cheap? Already at twelve, *un piccolo trafficante*!

But thanks to Francesco—he claimed that was his name, and who could doubt anyone with eyes like his?—we saw the small church of his patron saint. Have no doubt, we were to see it all, down to the most charming detail, a small bas-relief over the street entrance. There in the brownish stone stands a spindle-legged angel, jug-eared, bald, and wearing the surprised expression reminiscent of a tiny child suddenly confronted by an audience of doting parents during a Christmas pageant. The angel seems to be arising out of a flower, perhaps cardboard or papier-mâché. Six wings are in evidence, as is told in the account of Francis' ectasy during which he was afflicted with the wounds of Christ's passion. 'He . . . saw a seraph coming down from heaven with six luminous wings. And the seraph slowly approached Francis, so that he could discern and clearly see that it bore an image of a crucified man, and its wings were so placed that two were raised over the head, two were extended for flight, and with two it covered its body'.[81]

In every way Francesco's angel fits the traditional description of the miracle of the stigmata, except that his arms are not outspread as though nailed to a cross. Instead, we see two tiny arms and hands emerging from between two sets of wings, as frail looking as the legs, and dangling rather helplessly, as though he does not quite know what to do with them. But the seraph itself is enclosed in a cruciform which carries out the general idea.

Having restored order to his satisfaction, the Guiscard meant to turn his attention to Richard of Capua, by now his chief rival for power, and whose star seemed to be alarmingly in the ascendant. After all, Richard was a Norman; and Robert knew his Normans well. From the

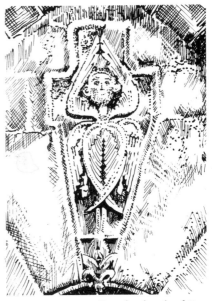

Seraph, church of San Francesco, Andria, Italy

Hauteville point of view the prince of Capua had been getting a little too cozy with Pope Alexander II, a power politician if ever there was one, and even more so with Cardinal Hildebrand lurking just behind the throne. As Robert pondered his next move there occurred one of the few happenings in his life over which he had absolutely no control. He was suddenly struck down by fever. There is no reason to doubt that his wife, Sichelgaita, was genuinely concerned for him; but she was also concerned for her son by him, Roger Borsa, so named for his habit of incessantly re-counting his money—*borsa* meaning purse. Sichelgaita must have been very much apprized of the feeling of the Norman hosts for the Guiscard's first son, Bohemund.

Understandably, she feared as she watched her stepson, in every way the image of his father and only now growing into the massive giant of a man who was going to become one of the most famous of all crusaders and the first Norman prince of Antioch. Yet, concerned as she was for her husband, she was even more torn up for her penny-pinching son. She called Robert's vassals together at Bari and, since she was not the kind of person one lightly refused, persuaded them to swear allegiance to Roger Borsa, thereby effectively side-tracking the ambitious and adept Bohemund. The older son must have been frustrated beyond words by the vassals' compliance (and to a woman!), especially since Roger Borsa was only thirteen years old.

As it turned out, the Guiscard did not die but Pope Alexander II did, to be succeeded by Cardinal Hildebrand who, as Pope Gregory VII, ruled as one of the most outstanding pontiffs of all time, whose innovations and political stands were to set the course for the rest of Church history. But such a man was bound to arouse controversy; and Gregory's position was open to attack by his enemies because he was proclaimed pope by the Roman mob *before* his formal election by the cardinals (which was, however, fully in accordance with Nicholas II's Election Decree).

Suspicion between Normans was always mutual. Just as Robert Guiscard looked with apprehension on Richard of Capua, so *that* prince's hackles rose every time he glanced southward. It was no time at all before a military alliance was in the offing between Richard and the new Pope Gregory VII. In a last effort to head off such a troublesome agreement an attempt was made to arrange a meeting between the Guiscard and Gregory at Benevento. Unfortunately the adversaries were so mutually suspicious that they never managed to pull it off—Robert flatly refusing to enter the papal palace, perhaps fearing assassination, and the pope arrogantly refusing to meet outside the city walls, regarding such a gesture as undignified. Gregory had the eminence of his office to consider; the Guiscard would kowtow to no one. It would be well to get this new pope in the habit of accepting imperial hauteur, since Robert was already envisioning himself sitting on the Byzantine throne, and to this end had betrothed his daughter, Helena, to Constantine, son and heir of Emperor Michael VII. Clearly a power struggle between the Roman pontiff and the duke of Apulia was in the offing.

Chapter Six

The rain of greed and avarice
Has nourished pride and wickedness
And led the whole wide world astray
And none will follow on God's way.

Piere Cardenal, 'Once on a Certain Nameless Town'.
Translated by Bergin; in *An Anthology of Medieval Lyrics*

1075

Pope Gregory must have felt a bit hemmed in. To the north a twenty-four-year-old Henry IV sat on the throne of Germany, king but not yet emperor, and eager to make the trip to Rome for the imperial coronation. Impossible to manage through childhood and adolescence, Henry had finally taken over the reins of government from his regent mother. Having endured the regency for ten years he smarted under any kind of domination from others, especially the Church, and was defensive in the extreme against anyone whom he saw as interfering with his imperial rights. So far as he was concerned, the reformist measures of recent popes were merely blatant attempts to throw off the remaining element of lay participation in the investiture of Church dignitaries. Henry would brook no interference; and so long as he took that stand, he could be certain that he would never hear the *Te Deum* of his coronation service in Rome. Now, making matters even worse, there was a pope on the throne of Saint Peter who, lacking imperial approval, had, in his view, no business being there and was, furthermore, throwing his weight around by condemning all lay investiture to spiritual office—unequivocally on pain of excommunication! Gregory's thinking on the importance of the papal office was contained in the *Dictatus papae*, formulated some time in 1075, of which the following are typical extracts:

> That the Pope is the only one whose feet are to be kissed
> by all princes.
> That he may depose Emperors.
> That he himself may be judged by no one.
> That the Roman Church has never erred, nor ever, by the
> witness of Scripture, shall err to all eternity.[82]

Obviously this new man in Rome needed to be taught a lesson in both modesty and co-operation. To make sure that Pope Gregory understood the meaning of coming against imperial determination, Henry promptly invested two German bishops with Italian sees. He had already appointed an anti-reform archbishop of Milan in 1072, in an effort to instruct the now dead Alexander II and because it was vital to his power in Italy to have the co-operation of the bishops.

Politics in Italy and in the emperor-less Holy Roman Empire were beginning to take on some of the fantastic characteristics of a Wagnerian opera. The Guiscard had been slowly absorbing the territories of his hated brother-in-law, Gisulf of Salerno, a papal ally. Robert's brother Geoffrey and his son had been happily devastating papal lands of the Abruzzi. Amalfi had already flopped over to the duke of Apulia, mainly out of fear of Salerno. The Byzantine emperor Michael VII was crying for help against the Seljuk Turks, a call which Gregory could not afford to ignore, schism or no; this was too good a chance to reunite the Eastern and Western Churches under his supreme pontificate. As Gregory saw it, he first had to neutralize Robert in the south. Then he would be free to move in a veritable crusade against the heathen Turks—himself the saviour of Christendom riding at the head of an army for Christ! Hostilities between the pope and Robert Guiscard reached such an acrimonious peak that a last-ditch effort to avoid bloodshed was attempted—another meeting at Benevento. Gregory planned to make a show of force there, to arrive at the head of an enormous army; but it disintegrated at Viterbo from internal tensions before even setting foot on Norman soil. So the meeting was as futile as the 1073 'conference' had been.

But worse was to follow. Gregory, the supreme Roman pontiff, was attacked by a dissatisfied party of the Roman aristocracy while saying mass on Christmas Eve, and dragged off to a secret prison. Once they found out where he was, he was rescued by the same populace who had precipitated his election as pope; but the humiliation had been genuine and the fright intense. And still greater trouble was coming his way.

1076

Henry IV now moved explicitly into the offensive against Gregory. In response to a letter from Gregory complaining about his investiture of the North Italian bishops and threatening him with the loss of his throne if he did not comply with the papal decrees, he convened a council of German bishops at Worms in January. From it both he and they wrote letters of defiance to the pope, Henry addressing him as 'not now pope, but false monk' (referring to the popular acclamation that had preceded his election), and calling upon him to descend from the papal throne. Meanwhile he was conspiring with the Eastern emperor, and even trying to entice Robert Guiscard to join his camp. In return, at his Lent synod, Gregory deposed Henry in a pronouncement that could serve as a primer for angry popes of the future. 'O blessed Peter, prince of the Apostles . . . I deprive King Henry . . . who has rebelled against thy Church with unheard-of audacity, of the government over the whole kingdom of Germany and Italy, and I release all Christian men from the allegiance which they have sworn or may swear to him, and I forbid anyone to serve him as king'.[83] Then waxing to the drama, Gregory thundered from his throne an excommunication, not only of the king but of Robert Guiscard. And finally, making matters absurdly impossible, the Guiscard, with Richard of Capua's help, was in the act of besieging his own brother-in-law, Gisulf of Salerno, Gregory's last friend south of Rome.

1077

Before invading England William the Conquerer had started building his great Abbaye aux Hommes in Caen (*see page* 120). Now he was in a position to dedicate it. Lanfranc, who had squared the papacy over William's and Matilda's uncanonical marriage, had been made abbot, and his intellectual touch is found everywhere in the abbey, which is dedicated to Saint Étienne (Saint Stephen). Few church façades are more striking than the unadorned west front of St Étienne, today much as it was when consecrated in the presence of the royal couple—that is, if one can ignore the later Gothic spires which add too much height for the comparatively narrow width. The front has been called organic in its logical upward growth, and in that it completely suggests the interior space which it masks. When the mass and solidity of the façade is considered, one understands the strength, simplicity and vigour of Norman Romanesque. It is austere, but magnificently so.

As one would expect, the interior of William's St Étienne is equally glorious and simple. Its spaciousness is such that we feel we have entered a perfectly proportioned container set aside for ceremony, a vast interior that wants to enclose the very heavens. So delicate is the balance between positive structural solids and the negative voids of its recesses and arched shadows. The Norman builders had no interest in the transcendence of space, the stretching out of mass. They would leave that for the Gothic designers. Yet here at St Étienne we see them begin the process of dissolving the Romanesque wall until it becomes a composition of positive and negative space, of light and shade, in terms as solemn and simple as the Gregorian chants which echoed through its vaults. If William's church was built as penance for his 'sin' of marriage, surely he was instantly and totally absolved. How clear, and yet mysterious! How intellectually complete, absolutely logical! What a perfect penance! A supplication to the Divine.

All was not gravy for William this year, however. In a temper because he had not been assigned the proprietorship of Normandy which had been promised him, the king's eldest son, Robert Curthose, 'went to France, and with the assistance of Philip, committed great and frequent ravages in Normandy; he burned the towns, put to death the people, and gave his father no little annoyance and anxiety'.[84]

After a winter of appalling hardships and starvation, Gisulf's city of Salerno capitulated to Robert Guiscard, who had been blockading it since the previous October. Not much is left there from Robert's time, but there is the dominating eighth-century Lombard castle, mistakenly called *il Castello dei Normanni*. Salerno's school of medicine, traditionally thought of as the first of its kind, and the most celebrated of the Western world during the Middle Ages, was later to administer to William the Conqueror's son Robert Curthose, by then duke of Normandy and returning from the First Crusade with an infected arrow wound. The school was already old when the Guiscard took over, and lecturers from every corner of the world enhanced it with their presence.

In precisely the year that William the Conqueror was dedicating his abbey of Saint Étienne at Caen, Robert Guiscard was starting his cathedral of Salerno, which would in 1085 be consecrated by Pope Gregory VII in keeping with the on-again-off-again relationships of the age, friendly with Robert and, in fact, rescued by him from Henry IV and sheltering in Salerno. An inscription is still visible on the cathedral façade stating that it was built by the Guiscard, 'greatest of conquerors', with money out of his own pocket—presumably money which he had, in turn, lifted from other people's pockets.

Two elegantly massive lions guard the main entrance, which does not lead into the church at all, but instead into an enormous courtyard (*see page* 153), itself one of the glories of Romanesque architecture in Southern Italy. All of Europe boasts no finer prelude to entering a cathedral than this spacious court, a quiet respite from the clatter of the crowded, hyper-animated streets of Salerno, a calming preparation for entering Robert's crowning architectural achievement. (One can experience a gentle brush with history by entering the court by means of a side door off the Via Roberto Guiscardo.) The effect of the court is one of refinement, ringed as it is by unmatching but cleverly assembled classical columns purloined by the builders from the ancient city of Paestum, twenty-seven miles to the south. There are twenty-eight of these handsome columns, which support arches of Arab-Sicilian style that spring vertically from stilt-blocks before starting to curve. A lovely arcade above lends a delicate touch to this superb, most sensitively proportioned court with its enlivening fountain, the original of which was hauled off to Naples to grace a public park. In the deep shadows of the colonnade rest a few ancient Roman sarcophagi, which were re-used during the Middle Ages.

The handsome bronze doors of the cathedral proper came from the foundries of Constantinople and were, at one time, inlaid with silver. The interior which lies beyond is not the most interesting of Norman buildings; it has been somewhat changed from that which Robert knew by a devastating earthquake in 1688 and some inept restoration. However, it does not deserve the almost total disparagement shown by the majority of guidebooks.

While the Guiscard was in the act of taking Salerno—and, incidentally, arguing with Gisulf over custodial rights to the city's most treasured possession, a tooth of Saint Matthew—an event was taking place in Northern Italy which has been passed off from one generation to another as the ideal moral lesson proving the evils of temporal ambition. The meeting of King Henry, would-be emperor, and Pope Gregory VII at Canossa (in Emilia, and not to be confused with Canosa di Puglia) turned out, at least superficially, to be about the only personal triumph the pope would experience; it has long been a favourite of romantic painters and illustrators of children's books. Henry had found the going tough in Germany, where his princes were more inclined to obedience to popes than to kings. They had pushed their lord so determinedly that Henry had relented, at least on the surface of it, and came into Italy to seek out the pope for a lifting of the ban of excommunication and deposition. Gregory himself reported his meeting with Henry at Canossa:

> . . . We received certain information that the king was on the way to us. Before he entered Italy he sent us word that he would make satisfaction to God and St. Peter and offered to amend his way of life and to continue

obedient to us, provided only that he should obtain from us absolution and the apostolic blessing . . . Finally, of his own accord and without any show of hostility or defiance, he came with a few followers to the fortress of Canossa where we were staying. There, on three successive days, standing before the castle gate, laying aside all royal insignia, barefooted and in coarse attire, he ceased not with many tears to beseech the apostolic help and comfort until all who were present or who had heard the story were so moved by pity and compassion that they pleaded his cause with prayers and tears.

At last, overcome by his persistent show of penitence and the urgency of all present, we released him from the bonds of anathema and received him into the grace of Holy Mother Church . . .[85]

In actuality the victory was Henry's, and Gregory knew it. He had gained nothing but a momentary moral victory. Cock of the walk again, Henry merely returned to his homeland and carried on as usual, lashing out at his vassals, browbeating the archbishops, and in general displaying the petulance which was so much a part of his character. He had his kingdom back, was once more in 'the grace of Holy Mother Church', and could therefore exercise the prerogatives of top chicken in the feudal pecking order. True, he had not yet been crowned emperor. But that would come.

What Gregory did not anticipate, and had no reason to at the time, was the effect on the German princes of his lifting the ban on Henry. Those who had rebelled against Henry and were in the papal camp now claimed that Gregory had betrayed them. Without consulting him they promptly elected a king of their own, Rudolf of Swabia. Henry's supporters rallied to his cause, and a full-scale civil war broke out. It took Gregory three years to decide whom to support: he eventually opted for Rudolf (again excommunicating Henry and declaring him deposed), too late as it turned out, for Henry already had the upper hand, and in any event Rudolf was killed a few months later.

Following the meeting at Canossa, Pope Gregory returned to Rome to hear, from Gisulf himself, of the fall of Salerno. More unsettling was the news that the Guiscard and Richard of Capua had joined forces yet again and in Richard's interest were hammering away at Naples. It was all bad news for the pope. Then there were those two young men, Robert's nephew and Richard's son, both named Jordan, both making every effort to cut a true Norman *bella figura* by besieging papal lands in the Abruzzi. But the unkindest cut of all to Gregory was the news that in December Robert Guiscard himself, duke of Apulia through the good graces of the papacy, had laid hands on Benevento, considered a papal city since the time of Charlemagne.

1078

Robert and his friends had already, since 1074, been living under a ban of excommunication. Clearly it meant nothing to them. In fact, the assault on Benevento held the excommunication pronouncement up to ridicule, and they remained sublimely indifferent when, on 3 March, 1078, Gregory excommunicated them again.

It must, however, have been a terrible jolt to Robert when within a month Richard of Capua, following a last-minute reconciliation with the pope, died. He was succeeded by his son Jordan, who had no choice but to make peace with Gregory, since he was a papal vassal and could not inherit his throne without the official blessing. Within a few months the pope was a guest at Capua, and with Jordan instigated a revolt against Robert within his own duchy. What a reversal of fortune! Robert was going to miss Richard!

There came on King William of England this year a flood of unpleasant if not downright embittering experiences, most important of which was the start of a sustained revolt in Normandy, headed by his eldest son Robert Curthose, who allied himself with Philip I of France. Robert was not the most loyal of men, and even among Normans he seems heavyhanded. He was short and stocky, devoid of any of his father's cleverness—tricky, perhaps, but not shrewd. It was with no illusions that William achieved a peace of sorts with his untrustworthy son who, as his birthright, was still demanding control over Normandy and Maine. Robert had tried to wrest Rouen from his father's grip and, failing that, had run off and was now openly hobnobbing with Philip of France. This led to the only quarrel recorded to have taken place between the Conqueror and Matilda. Better had they argued about William's weight than about their traitorous, ill-natured offspring. For, no longer cutting the figure of a conqueror, William by this time was becoming—well, distinctly corpulent; it was more than middle-aged spread. The picture of the tiny Matilda standing up to her hulking spouse in defence of her undeserving son, perhaps pacing the floor before him, or shaking her index finger under his nose, is at once heroic and comic. Always an admirer of flair, William must at least have felt a grudging if secret admiration.

1080

Much to his chagrin Pope Gregory had to face the fact that he needed friends. With a hostile King Henry IV to the north, he at last turned south for aid. After tedious but deadly serious negotiations, Robert Guiscard and the pope met face to face at Ceprano, brought together by Desiderius, abbot of Monte Cassino, a devoted Benedictine and a man pulled against his will, into the political maelstrom of the day. Things were patched up, and in the nick of time, for Henry was on the move again. He had held a series of councils of nobles and bishops, the last attended also by Lombard bishops. At each council Gregory was declared deposed, and at the last a successor was nominated. Now Henry was crossing the Alps, headed for Rome to implement the decisions—and, incidentally, aiming to be at last crowned Holy Roman emperor, by the 'rightful' pope, and in St Peter's Basilica.

Pope Gregory VII may have relished the feeling of having made a new friend in Robert, but it was going to be some time before the alliance would bear fruit. It was at this time that Robert, always an admirer of things

Byzantine, seriously turned his conquest-lusting eyes towards Constantinople. He was sure that with proper planning he could take the centre of Eastern culture and last remnant of the Roman Empire. And what an ego-trip, besides! From highwayman to emperor in one lifetime! Constantinople was ripe for the taking, with its power eternally sapped by the proverbial Byzantine intrigues. The Guiscard even had the ideal excuse—family honour. The betrothal of his daughter Helena to Michael VII's son Constantine had never matured into a marriage, and was not going to for the simple reason that Michael had been deposed and packed off to a monastery. Some years after the fact, Anna Comnena venomously maintained that Helena was not as favourably endowed as she had been advertised, and that the young Constantine, 'being still immature, shrank from this alliance at the very outset, as children do from bogeys'.[86] On the breakdown of the marriage plans Helena had been incarcerated in a convent. If they would only keep her there the Guiscard had the ideal cause for a 'just' war. What better reason for sending in the troops than a father—even a sixty-five year old father—protecting the good name of his daughter and the honour of his family?

If Robert Curthose gave him no comfort, William could derive some satisfaction this year from the marriage of his daughter Adela to Stephen I, count of Blois. Adela is more important in the long run than Robert. She was an intelligent woman—the great Anselm was her teacher and friend—and a benevolent patroness of churches and monasteries. But, more important, she was the mother of Stephen, king of England, who was to claim his right to the throne through her, and against the more just claims of his own cousin, the Empress Matilda, daughter of King Henry I.

1081

Alexius Comnenus I, an unfortunate emperor destined to reign for thirty-seven troubled years, siezed the throne of Constantinople to preside over the slowly deteriorating remains of the Eastern Roman empire. One of his first difficulties was holding off the formidable attack of the Hauteville Normans.

By spring of this year Robert was in Brindisi, having commandeered an enormous army and a superbly trained navy. He intended Brindisi to be his jumping-off place against the Eastern empire in his war to avenge his family honour. Anna Comnena's assessment of Robert's motives is probably closer to the truth. 'That man Robert, who from a most inconspicuous beginning had grown most conspicuous, and amassed great power, now desired eagerly to become Roman Emperor [since the Byzantine Empire was the remaining half of the ancient Roman Empire, Anna always spoke of the Byzantines as 'Romans'], and with this object, sought plausible pretexts for ill-will and war against the Romans.'[87] Robert had already sent an advance party under his towering eldest son Bohemund, who was waiting for his father at Butrinto (in modern Albania). By this time Bohemund had grown prodigiously tall; he was massive chested, a possessor of the Hauteville broad shoulders, and had thick blond hair, after the manner of his ancestors.

Now, Bohemund took after his father in all things, in audacity, bodily strength, bravery, and untamable temper; for he was of exactly the same stamp as his father, and a living model of the latter's character. Immediately on arrival [on Byzantine soil], he fell like a thunderbolt, with threats and irresistible dash upon Canina, Hiericho, and Valona, and siezed them, and as he fought his way on, he would ever devastate and set fire to the surrounding districts. He was, in very truth, like the pungent smoke which precedes a fire, and a prelude of attack before the actual attack. These two, father and son, might rightly be termed 'the caterpillar and the locust'; for whatever escaped Robert, that his son Bohemund took to him and devoured.[88]

There is something likeable about this magnificent tough, and one tends to sympathize with him for having been short-changed in his inheritance, a circumstance largely engineered by his stepmother Sichelgaita. But he was Robert's son to the core, loyal and courageous and, one is led to believe, immensely patient.

The harbour at Brindisi, where Robert gathered his forces, was probably used as early as the seventh century BC. Ancient Brundisium was a major Roman centre, the chief port linking Illyria (that history-neglected land on the Adriatic Sea north of Greece) with the Eastern Mediterranean. Mark Antony knew Brindisi, as did Julius Caesar, Pompey and Virgil (who died there in 19 BC). The city was the terminating point for the Via Appia Antica, its overland link with the centre of the empire, Rome. A column (one of two originals) still stands at the head of a flight of steps leading down to the quay, and marks the end of the great highway. Robert (like Alexander the Great ruminating at the tomb of Persian King Cyrus) must have wondered at that column, a pathetically inadequate symbol of might. And there would be others to come who might think on the fragility of power, and wonder at the quirks that push men to achieve it. Robert Curthose, for one, was to choose Brindisi as the point of departure for his crusade, but spent so much time enjoying the flesh-pots of this bustling port that his followers deserted him in droves. Better had he spent his time dwelling on human frailty and sibling ambitions, as it turned out!

Even in those coldly practical days there was always a place for imagination and fantasy in art and architecture, though, as turmoil was an inescapable condition of the times, it more often took the form of one kind of violence or another. Just the year before the Guiscard had arrived in Brindisi to supervise

Portal, Monastery of St Benedict, Brindisi, Italy

the pulling together of his fleet, the monastery of San Benedetto had been founded. Now, while he worked and waited, impatient to set sail for his earthly fulfilment, the monks laboured in quest of their destiny. The monks' massive bell-tower shadows their quiet cloister retreat where they could, in this minute portion of God's own empire, contemplate the meaning of eternity and the futility of temporal power. They built for themselves a handsome church, strong enough, it has been proven, to stand against the depredations of man. And over its south portal they carved a vigorous Norman bas-relief, swirling with action, of men fighting outsized animals, some of them winged.

Though neither building was there at the time of Robert Guiscard, there are two others of interest in medieval Brindisi, and for both we owe a debt to the Knights Templar—'The Poor Knights of Christ and the Temple of Solomon'—one of the great military orders of the Middle Ages. Early in the twelfth century two knights, Hugues de Payns and Godeffroi de Saint Omer, founded the Templars with the pious purpose of protecting pilgrims flocking to the Holy Land after the First Crusade (see 1099). They swore to protect the public highways and to forsake worldly chivalry 'of which human favour and not Jesus Christ was the cause'. The Portico of the Knights Templar, to the left of the cathedral at Brindisi, is a striking relic of that noble organization.

But the delightful small, circular church of St John at the Sepulchre is even more striking. Weather-eroded and colourless on the outside, guarded by two storm-beaten lions, it is, internally, perfection—perfection awash in golden light, endless in its roundness and absolutely stunning in its proportions. The Romanesque portal gives no hint of the austerely simple interior which, to achieve its effect, has no need to rely on mosaic, stained glass or sculptural makeshifts. There are a few faded frescoes, however, and it must be assumed that in its medieval heyday there were others.

In May Robert sailed his fleet out of the protective, antler-shaped harbour of Brindisi and headed eastwards. Despite the efforts of three powerful rulers to stop the enterprise, Robert was determined. Understandably Pope Gregory VII, Emperor Alexius I of Constantinople, and German Emperor Henry IV were all opposed to the venture, the last even offering as compensatory bait his son Conrad as husband for one of the Guiscard's remaining daughters. Some of Robert's own men had tried to dissuade him from undertaking the expedition, arguing that the party responsible for poor Helena's predicament was not Alexius, but rather his predecessor, against whom Alexius had pulled off a successful coup. But Robert, theatrical to the teeth and ambitious to the very ends of his blond hair, demanded vengeance. He

Church of St John at the Sepulchre, Brindisi, Italy

joined forces with Bohemund, and the two of them, their army huge by any standards of medieval measurement, set out to take Durazzo. But there they met unexpected resistance, the defenders benefiting from the timely arrival of a sympathetic Venetian fleet.

1082

William the Conqueror, who could reasonably have expected to be more comfortably situated at this time of his life, must have felt that his world was turning to ashes. Having patched things up with his renegade son, William was now forced to arrest one of his heretofore staunchest supporters, his own half-brother, Bishop Odo of Bayeux. An odious man, he was dangerous at best, and apparently guilty of a treachery that William found especially galling. His perfidy was not recorded, but some historians suggest that he was ambitious for the papal throne and may have been luring knights out of William's service into his own—a not unlikely theory, considering the man. Whatever his disloyalty, he was arrested by the king's men at Carisbrooke Castle on the Isle of Wight, and imprisoned at Rouen, where he was to remain unpardoned until the Conqueror's death. That William was especially bitter is evident; he at first refused to include Odo in the general amnesty that he declared on his deathbed. The infamous half-brother was saved only by impassioned pleas made on his behalf by those standing by.

It was a flowering Adriatic spring before the Guiscard's Normans were able to occupy the city of Durazzo. Robert, Sichelgaita and Bohemund were together during the siege as well as at the moment of triumph. One is tempted to wonder what the dinner-table conversation must have been like among these three—Bohemund knowing that his stepmother had thwarted his claims to Robert's office; she utterly protective of her own son Roger Borsa; and the Guiscard caught in the middle. For the rest of their lives Bohemund and Roger Borsa remained inimical half-brothers.

The struggle for Durazzo is interesting historically as there were Englishmen present, fighting, unfortunately, on the losing side. They were a part of the emperor's Varangian Guard who in the good old days at the turn of the century had been Vikings, stalwart northerners who fought at the emperor's side whenever he took to the field. But changes had come over the guard in recent years. By the time of Durazzo it was composed mostly of disgruntled Anglo-Saxons who had left England after Hastings, enlisting in the service of the emperor, and now seeking revenge on the hated Normans. Their goal was futile, however, and their ending worse; when they sought refuge in a chapel of the Norman's own Saint Michael, it was set afire by those very Normans, cremating the lot of them.

When both Illyria and Kastoria fell into the Guiscard's hands the way to Constantinople was open. Then, in April, Robert received pleas from Italy of such urgency that they could hardly be ignored. Two situations of emergency proportions were in the offing. Encouraged by a fifth-column loyal to Alexius, Robert's whole duchy was up in arms. Equally threatening, the German emperor Henry IV, with his newly nominated antipope in tow, was soon to be hammering on the gates of Rome. Italians, Lombards, even some of Robert's own compatriots, were flocking to Henry's standard, thinking that the future was surely his; for the Guiscard had, so far as they were concerned, deserted Italy for the headier luxuries of the exotic East. Robert could not afford to turn his back on either his own duchy or the papal cause he had sworn to uphold. To break his oath now would be politically suicidal as well as sinful. He returned to Italy to honour his vow, leaving Bohemund to hang on to their conquests. They would resume the march on Constantinople when his and the pope's enemies had been punished—as well, presumably, as his more intimate adherents, for Robert had sworn that he would not bath until the pope was safe! For the moment Gregory waited in Rome, a voluntary prisoner in his palace-fortress, the Castello Sant'Angelo.

1083

A great circular stone drum, the ancient tomb of the Roman emperor Hadrian, has dominated a wide curve of the Tiber since the second century AD. It was during the plague in Rome, in 590, almost exactly one hundred years after his Gargano visit, that Saint Michael visited this tomb, alighting as was his preference, on the high rounded top. Pope Gregory the Great (the first pope to take that name) had issued the order that forty processions were to be held in the city in an effort to please God and persuade Him to lift the plague. The population had been decimated. Suddenly the warrior angel was seen to swoop down, sword in hand, and gently light on the ancient monument. He surveyed the scene, then sheathed his weapon, an eloquent gesture as captured in the bronze commemorative statue atop the tomb by eighteenth-century artist van Verschaffelt. The sheathing of the sword indicated to Pope Gregory that God was satisfied and that the heavenly siege had been lifted. Indeed, the pestilence abated. A chapel was erected on the spot where the angel touched down, and it was from this incident that the name Castello Sant'Angelo was derived. Over the years one pope after another added building after building as a kind of superstructure on Hadrian's tomb until by the late Renaissance the ancient original served merely as a foundation for a luxurious palace, which is connected to the Vatican Palace by a fortified corridor, the *passetto*.

By the beginning of June, Henry IV was in possession of the Vatican. Pope Gregory, in his fortress of the Holy Angel, barricaded behind bolted doors and vowing not to waver in his resolve to tame the German emperor a second time, awaited the coming of Robert Guiscard. Gregory, though a virtual prisoner, knew that he had Henry in a bad place. Rome was faithful to the pope, and so long as that condition prevailed Henry was not going to get his imperial diadem. Henry held only the Leonine City—that part of Rome containing the Vatican, which had been fortified by Pope Leo IV after a ninth-century sacking of the city by the Saracens. Gregory could afford to wait for his Norman allies, and since stubbornness was one of his most noteworthy characteristics he would find the wait not intolerable. He did not know, of course, how long a wait he had in store!

First Robert Guiscard needed to put down revolts in his own realm; pope or no pope, that task came first. He succeeded in quelling the rebellions, but only after summoning brother Roger from Sicily with reinforcements. With things quiet at last the brothers set out for Rome, only to receive disquieting news from Sicily. Jordan, Roger's much-loved bastard son, who had in the past always acted in his father's interest, had now sullied his reputation by allying himself with several disgruntled knights bent on overthrowing Roger's authority. Jordan had already taken that earliest of Norman strongholds on the island, San Marco d'Alunzio. Once again the pope would have to wait. Roger returned to Sicily, made short work of restoring order, and then, though sparing his son, showed that in future he would tolerate no backsliding in allegiance. He had twelve of Jordan's fellow conspirators blinded.

For the rest of his life Jordan remained loyal to his father. Despite his bastardy he was Roger's favourite, and seems to have been the only one of his children (like Robert's Bohemund) to have inherited the Hauteville gusto for living. We know little about him, partly because his life was so short—at this time he had only eight more years to go—and partly because his memory is so completely overshadowed by that of Roger's legitimate son, also called Roger, who lived long and gloriously. We get a picture of a likeable Jordan, though; vital, swaggering, and honourable within the limits of the age.

Without Roger to reinforce him, with an army fed up with moving from one war zone to another—and having accomplished little since sailing so expectantly from Otranto to conquer the Byzantine Empire—the Guiscard seemed to be in no hurry to move north, though he clearly meant to honour his oath of fealty to the pope. The mind boggles at the picture of the unwashed Guiscard lolling about Southern Italy, crossly contemplating the plight of a disagreeable pope, yearning to rejoin Bohemund on his eastern venture, and literally offending those unfortunate enough to be ushered into his presence.

King William of England was also having his fair share of misery. William of Malmesbury recorded that King William wept for many days when his beloved Matilda died this year. That William loved her as much as he could have loved anyone is clear. He is generally conceded always to have been faithful to her, which is more than adequate indication of either her sex appeal or her above-average ability to demand loyalty—maybe both. According to her wish she was buried in her church of the Holy Trinity in Caen. In time Matilda's tomb was desecrated and her coffin destroyed. Her diminutive remains were saved, however, and reinterred under the original stone slab which is still in place before the high altar. Even now the nuns of the abbey pray daily for the repose of the soul of their benefactress-duchess as they are admonished to do by the inscription on the tomb cover.

1084

Henry IV was tired of waiting. By spring he finally came to the realization that Pope Gregory was at least as stubborn as he was himself. Confident of the support of the Roman people, Gregory thundered out new excommunications from behind locked doors; compromises were attempted; synods were held; a papal legate was imprisoned. Some attempts at reconciliation were hilarious: 'a ludicrous suggestion by some of the Roman nobles for a compromise, by which Gregory would not actually perform Henry's coronation but would pass him down the imperial diadem on a stick from the battlements of Sant'Angelo, met with the contempt it deserved'.[89] Henry decided this shilly-shallying must stop and planned to march on the Normans in the south. But the Romans, tired at last of Gregory's intransigence, sent the emperor word that they would no longer resist imperial mastery of their city. They thus sealed their own fate. When the Normans did arrive it would be as conquerors, not liberators.

Henry, escorting his antipope elect, entered Rome in triumph. Gregory was summarily deposed, the anti-Pope Clement III consecrated, and he in turn performed practically the only function of his brief rule, which was, of course, the very reason for his being; he crowned Henry and his wife emperor and empress on Easter morning, 31 March, in St Peter's. By 24 May Robert was camped outside the walls of Rome, at the Porta Capena, near the ancient Circus Maximus. But the new emperor, his wife and army and, needless to say, his antipope, had already fled. To the Romans the future must have appeared bleak indeed. And they were right. They had betrayed their pope. And now the papal protector was at the walls of their city. They sensed—knew—that his vengeance would be awesome.

On May 28 Robert gave the order to attack. Immediately making for the Castello Sant'Angelo, he liberated Pope Gregory, who 'returned him thanks for the toil he had undergone in coming to his aid, absolved him from his sins as a reward for his obedience, and implored for him the eternal benediction of Almighty God'.[90]

For three days the orgy of destruction raged on, a calamity unequalled since the days of the barbarian invasions that had brought the great Western Roman Empire to its knees. The Palatine and the Capitol were levelled. Rome became a roaring inferno. The citizens rose up against their enemies, which only fuelled the Normans' anger. Having sung his mass of triumphant liberation, Gregory watched his rampant deliverers bring down entire quarters of his city. The Romans had been his first supporters. Now he saw them bludgeoned, raped and hurled into the flames. He heard their screams as they were put to the sword; man, woman, child, it made no difference. Many of them were taken and sold into slavery. It was an unleashing of barbarism in the name of Christianity.

Just minutes away from Robert's camp site (prior to his triumphant and destructive entry into Rome) is the Clivus Scauri, 'one of the few corners of Rome where a medieval pilgrim would have little difficulty in recognising his whereabouts'.[91] It is a narrow street, spanned by a series of medieval arches which act as buttresses for the church of SS. Giovanni e Paolo, which is one of the most interesting in Rome, and which was a new church in 410 when Alaric sacked the city. Perhaps the Guiscard would remember this street, as Georgina Masson asserts, if he were suddenly reincarnated today into the city which stands, paradoxically, as the symbol of his greatest power and his most shameful disgrace.

1085

After Robert's sack of Rome, Gregory knew that he would never be able to live there again—a city which some chroniclers claim was left in twelve feet of ashes! He was taken to Salerno, in time to consecrate Robert's new cathedral there—and there he died, on 25 May. His last words, 'I have loved righteousness and hated iniquity, therefore I die in exile', a parody of Psalm 44 (in the Vulgate), were bitter to be sure. Yet he never projected a picture of a man anything but arrogant, one intractably convinced that the Church should and would triumph over all man's pretensions. The Apostolic Church had, he wrote in 1081, 'the power, granted by a unique privilege, of opening and shutting the gates of the celestial kingdom to whom it will'.[92] And he always maintained that priestly office was intrinsically superior to any temporal power. Still, Gregory never saw his prohibitions against Henry IV as final. He was always hopeful that Henry might, presumably by divine inspiration, mend his ways. But that did not happen in Gregory's lifetime. When he was laid to rest in the southeast apse of the new Norman cathedral of Salerno he was totally burned out, and utterly unaware of his achievements. But he had, in fact, firmly set the medieval papacy on its path to the heights of power it was to achieve under the great popes of the next two centuries.

Once again on the prowl against the Byzantine Emperor Alexius, Robert Guiscard settled on the island of Corfu, intending to wait out the coming of spring. His three sons—Bohemund, Roger Borsa and Guy (the latter two were sons of Sichelgaita)—were with him. And it was there on this veritable launching pad against Constantinople that his army was struck by the worst of all disasters: epidemic—probably typhoid fever. Bohemund was struck first, and retired to Bari to recover. Then it was the turn of the Guiscard. While he was aboard ship, sailing to join Roger Borsa and an advance party at Cephalonia, the dread sickness came upon him. The ship put in at a calm little bay still called Phiscardo in his memory. He died there on 17 July, outliving Pope Gregory by less than two months. For all his grasping, violent, many times heartless ways, we know, thanks to Dante Alighieri, that he found his way to heaven. In the fifth sphere of paradise Dante contemplates the souls of the Cross of Mars, the great warriors of God:

> Then William of Orange, and then Rinoard
> drew my eyes after them along that cross.
> And then the good duke Godfrey, and Robert Guiscard.[93]

Roger Borsa arrived, but too late, finding his brother Guy and his mother already overcome by grief. Roger gave in to his grief, too, 'but soon summoning reason to his aid and collecting himself, he sent for all his followers . . . and then made them take the oath of allegiance to himself'.[94] Roger Borsa then proposed to conduct the Guiscard's remains to Italy. 'During the crossing he was caught in such a severe storm, although it was summer, that some of the ships were wrecked, and others dashed on the shore and beaten to pieces. The ship carrying the corpse was also half wrecked and the crew only just managed to save the coffin and convey it safely to

Venusia . . . Robert died in the twenty-fifth year of his reign as duke and at the age of seventy'.[95]

One would have expected the Guiscard to prefer burial in his magnificent new cathedral of Salerno. But he left that to Gregory VII, having himself decided to be laid to rest in the company of his three elder brothers at Santìssima Trinità at Venosa. Thanks to the English chronicler William of Malmesbury we have a record of Robert's original epitaph, in which he was proclaimed the 'terror of the world'—a questionable boast. It was as though Robert would prove to his brothers, at least in death, which of the four was the greatest. But material achievements are transitory at best; and so was the Guiscard's tomb, as it turned out. Along with those of his brothers, it vanished, their contents eventually united in a single container. So here are the four of them, closer in death than ever they were in life, their monument surmounted by a fresco of the Crucifixion and the words, 'The city of Venosa shines with the glory of such sepulchres', so ambiguous as to be meaningless.

Considering Robert Guiscard's beginnings, one must give him credit above that reserved for most men. To the accusation that he was violent to excess his defenders can point out the nature of his times. Not quite a peasant, nor true nobility either, Robert had terrified two emperors, had one of the most important of medieval popes (Leo IX) in thrall, and the papal giant of the age, Gregory VII, under his protective umbrella. And although the name 'Guiscard' was a reference to his military prowess, not to his statesmanship as is often claimed, he managed to weld Southern Italy, never very far from out-right anarchy, into a political entity. He may not have been a statesman of great stature, but the effect of Robert's rough-and-tumble rule is not without certain salutary results, some of them not suspected even by him, such as the rapid development of trade in the later eleventh century, especially in Italy. Analogous to Robert's successes, perhaps encouraged by Norman activities in Sicily, Spain accelerated her battle of liberation from Saracen occupiers. Robert Guiscard would be missed.

1086

As though making one last superhuman lunge for greatness in the final year of his life, King William of England commanded into existence the Domesday Book, born of necessity rather than for reasons of scientific or altruistic curiosity, one of the most far-reaching, patient and comprehensive evaluations of material wealth that history has ever known. According to the *Anglo-Saxon Chronicle*, William

> sent his men over all England into every shire and had them find out how many hundred hides [normally 120 acres of land] there were in the shire, or what land and cattle the king himself had in the country, or what dues he ought to have annually from the shire. Also, he had a record made of how much land his archbishops had, and his bishops and his abbots and his earls . . . So very narrowly did he have it investigated that there was no single hide nor virgate of land, nor indeed (it is a shame to relate it but it

seemed no shame to him to do so) one ox nor one cow nor one pig left out . . . And all these writings were brought to him afterwards.[96]

By William's thinking the Domesday Book was absolutely indispensable. King Cnut of Denmark, reviving Scandinavian claims on England, was reportedly on the march. Robert Curthose was still flirting with King Philip of France (William's power over the combined realms was becoming worrisome to the less powerful French king); and William's half-brother Odo of Bayeux, although languishing in a Rouen prison, might still possibly become the centre of another 'rid-England-of-the tyrant' rebellion. In the face of all these threats William clearly needed surety from a wide range of his subjects. But more than anything he needed money, a lot of it, and fast, in order to pay the large number of mercenaries in his employ.

The vast amount of information that his teams accumulated as they fanned out across the country enabled him to impose maximum taxation on his subjects during the last year of his reign. The survey was so complete that it remained unique, never anything like equalled by the efforts of later monarchs who, presumably, would have liked to accomplish the same thing. But few of them had William's sense of organization or his energy.

While the Domesday Book was being compiled to take care of his fund raising, William in August summoned to a high-level meeting at Salisbury not only his councillors but also 'all the people of any account who were occupying land'. From these he wrung an oath of allegiance, thus binding to himself a selection of important landowners considerably wider than the cadre of tenants-in-chief who had already, in return for their estates, sworn homage and fealty to him. The Salisbury Oath was an important constitutional precedent and as such was an outstanding landmark in William's reign—even though what was perhaps its main cause, the Scandinavian threat, had already ended with the murder (in July) of Cnut by his own dissatisfied followers. When William summoned his retainers to Salisbury it was not to the city we now know by that name, but to its original site two miles north, known today as Old Sarum. Once an Iron Age hill-fort, this place had been frequented by the Romans, the Britons and the Saxons before being more or less abandoned until the arrival of the Normans.

One of the most interesting men in a century dominated by interesting men rose this year to the primacy of the Church. Much against his will Desiderius, abbot of Monte Cassino, was proclaimed Pope Victor III. A member of the ruling family of Benevento, Desiderius had seen his father killed by Normans in 1047, an event that was enough to convince him that the worldly life was not for him. He sought the isolation of the cloister, and by 1086 had been head of Monte Cassino for twenty-eight years. But since he was a Lombard prince, his services were still wanted in 'the world'; he was twice extricated from his monastic cell to serve his native city and later was summoned to the service of Pope Leo IX. Desiderius, to his own frustration, had a natural political talent; he understood that the stay of the Normans in Southern Italy was not going to terminate soon, so he felt compelled to remain on good terms with them.

Cathedral courtyard, Salerno, Italy

*Throne of Elia,
Basilica of San
Nicola, Bari, Italy*

Valletta Harbour, Malta

Durham Cathedral from River Wear, England

Interior Durham Cathedral

Amalfi Cathedral, Italy

1087

In May a band of merchants, scruffy and itchy with lice after long days at sea, disembarked at Bari from a boat they had boarded at Myra, a city on the south coast of Asia Minor. They received from the joyous population an accolade exceeding anything they might have anticipated. There was a festival in the streets: wine, food and dancing. The sound of drum and stringed psaltery penetrated every blind alley and statued niche of the ancient city. Revelry and licence were in the air, itself aflutter with flags, pennants and gaudy streamers. Smoke hung over the city from innumerable ovens, bonfires and braziers along with the heady smells of baking breads, spitted and roasting meats, and deep-fried pastries. Mummers performed their rough, and often racy, stylizations on the porch of the cathedral. Street players set up their portable stages on the trucks of wagons, performing more serious vignettes than the slapstick mimes—improvisational scenes from the life of Saint Nicholas of Myra, known from this year hence as Saint Nicholas of Bari. Nicholas had found a new home-base, thanks to these merchants who had just sailed into Bari harbour; they had brought with them the relics of that much revered fourth-century saint, stolen from the cathedral of Myra.

Saint Nicholas, bishop of Myra, had reputedly died a martyr and had been laid to rest in his cathedral. The Italian merchant-thieves had broken into his tomb with hammers, discovering a marble urn, probably a sarcophagus. On smashing the marble they came upon a sacred liquid, the *manna di San Nicola*, and then escaped with their booty.

The basilica of San Nicola was started as soon as the relics had been received by the jubilantly celebrating people of Bari. The choice of its site was the result of a 'miraculous' occurrence: the oxen pulling the relic-bearing wagon suddenly refused to move further, indicating that the spot for the new church had been found. Because of this 'miracle' the porch pillars of the basilica rest not on the backs of the usual lions, but on oxen which have lost their original bronze horns. 'It would not be a bad idea to restore these horns and so re-establish the identity of the two odd-looking creatures, two porch ornaments which are unique in Italy.'[97]

The outside of the basilica of San Nicolas is plain, broken by a too small rose window—the day of the large wheel of glass on the western façades had not yet arrived. But the interior of the church is a triumph of Norman Apulian architecture—heavy, sombre, yet strangely dignified, housing a much copied ciborium (canopy) of

Basilica of San Nicola, Bari, Italy

exceptionally pleasing, if weighty proportions. The effect of the whole is impressive, with enormous arches bearing considerable loads of masonry, and all of the stout columns exquisitely carved. One feels the weight, but it is not cumbersome, though two clumsily expedient fifteenth-century transverse supporting arches span the nave, unfortunately interrupting the overall architectural majesty.

Behind the high altar is a throne, that of Abbot Elia, the founder of the church and the man who started work on it (*see page* 153). The throne is more a reminder of political history than an assertion of religious pomp and circumstance, the seat being supported by Saracens who are stripped to the waist and grimacing with pain as they hold it aloft, giving every indication that they are having a tough time of it. It was a neat propaganda touch in this Norman church—the 'inferior' subservient people supporting the ascendant 'superior' people on their backs. Between the supporting figures is another, a man adjusting the seat with one hand while bearing a club in the other; he is the master, no doubt a Norman.

The crypt of the basilica houses a silver altar, beneath which rests the saint submerged in the *sacra manna* still believed to be a cure-all for almost every ailment and disability. Male, female and child pilgrims flock to the shrine for their little bottles of the sacred fluid. Today the shrine is especially popular with Sicilians, Russians and Greeks, all of them claiming Nicholas as their patron saint. Before the Revolution, Russian Orthodox pilgrims flocked to Bari, believing that Nicholas had become the heir of Mikoula, the god of the harvest and that he would one day 'replace God, when God becomes too old'. In addition he is the protector of sailors, fishermen, robbers, wolves (the animal kind), pawnbrokers and children, the last association giving rise to the Dutch, German and Swiss idea that he is the giver of presents. Thus, by a curious development, we have the transformation of Santa Claus and of Saint Nicholas into the Father Christmas of Christian English-speaking nations.

Finally losing patience with the constant raids from the French into the Norman Vexin, William gathered his forces, crossed the Channel, and sallied into French territory. His wrath was typically extravagant, and he scoured the country with his usual policy of total destruction. The town of Mantes was given over to pillage. In the midst of the carnage, the looting, the burning buildings and falling timbers, William was either injured or taken ill. Some chroniclers claim that his horse fell and he suffered an internal injury on the pommel of his saddle. Others report that he was overcome with fatigue and heat and then, with the consequent low resistance, became sick. Whatever, the cause, he was incapacitated. He returned to Rouen, but the noise and confusion of that thriving city were too much for him, so he was moved to the priory of Saint-Gervais just to the west. He was obviously dying.

Within the framework of the age in which he was living there is nothing surprising in that William would try to set things right with his God. He confessed and received absolution, professing tormenting guilt over the 'rivers of blood' that he had caused to flow. He directed that lavish distributions of alms should be inaugurated in his name, with special generosity shown to the clergy at Mantes, the same city he was harassing when he was reduced to his present state. Then he commanded that those whom he had imprisoned should be liberated, even reluctantly including his half-brother, Bishop Odo.

Present at William's bedside were two of his three surviving sons: William Rufus and Henry Beauclerc. Robert Curthose was enjoying the sophisticated pleasures at the court of his father's antagonist, King Philip of France. Even the fact that his eldest son consorted with his enemy did not sway William from a promise he had made to bequeath the duchy of Normandy to him. Then, true to the customs of the day when kingdoms—and inhabitants—were considered personal property, he affirmed that William Rufus was to have England. Thus the Conqueror, that paragon of organization and political acumen, bequeathed an unfortunate division of his kingdom from his duchy, a source of consequent dissension among his family.

Having disposed of his duchy and his kingdom, William then addressed Henry Beauclerc. To him he willed a mere five thousand pounds in silver. Along with the money the dying king spoke what might be considered a self-fulfilling prophecy. Henry, he predicted, would enjoy a brilliant career and would surpass both his brothers in fame, wealth and power. Later he received the last rites of the Church. On the morning of 9 September, when the bell of distant Rouen Cathedral rang out, William asked what it meant. He was told it signalled the hour of prime, the call to prayer at sunrise or six o'clock in the morning. He commended his soul to the Virgin Mary, invoking her intercession for him; and immediately died.

In the process of living William had become more than a leader of men: he was a knight among knights, a lord among lords. More cultivated than Robert Guiscard, William was also a better statesman. Though temper-ridden and reckless, he was a consumate general, capable of displaying determination and standing with an iron will against all kinds of opposition. He had created for himself a single domain that spanned the Channel and, what is more, ensured that both parts were well governed. He had supported Lanfranc's reform of the English Church, and then maintained with the Church relations more cordial than were achieved by many of his successors. Being born a bastard, though in no way unique, can hardly be considered a plus. William, however, was a great man—great because he made of his age what his imagination and muscle allowed; but he did not create his age. Achieving a position of power, he became a superstar of his century. There would be others yet to follow, just as the Guiscard would have his successors, in both cases the successors sometimes proving more glamorous and enlightened that their two crusty progenitors.

William may have been dramatically ushered into death by the sound of the great bell of Rouen Cathedral; but his death-chamber, nevertheless, immediately afterwards became the scene of demeaning pandemonium and licentiousness. His magnates,

> mounted their horses and departed in haste to secure their property. But the inferior attendants, observing that their masters had disappeared, laid hands on the arms, the plate, the robes, the linens, and all the royal furniture, and leaving the corpse almost naked on the floor of the house hastened away.

> . . . Behold this mighty prince, who was lately obsequiously obeyed by more than a hundred thousand men in arms, and at whose nod nations trembled, was so stripped by his own attendants, in a house that was not his own; and left on the bare ground . . .[98]

To make matters still worse, William's funeral service in his church of St Étienne at the Abbaye aux Hommes in Caen was gruesomely undignified and singularly reminiscent of his coronation day. The bizarre and macabre series of events began just as the cortège was entering the city. Abbot Gilbert

> . . . with the whole convent of monks, met the hearse in solemn procession, accompanied by a sorrowing multitude of clerks and laymen, offering prayers. But at this moment a sudden calamity filled the minds of all with alarm. For a fire broke out in one of the houses, and, shooting up prodigious volumes of flames, spread through [a] great part of the town of Caen, doing great damage. The crowds . . . hastened with one accord to extinguish the fire, so that the monks were left alone to finish the service they had begun, and they brought the corpse into the abbey church, chanting psalms . . . When the corpse was lowered into the stone coffin, they were obliged to use some violence in forcing it in, because through the negligence of the masons it had been made too short, so that, as the king was very corpulent, the bowels burst, and an intolerable stench affected the by-standers and the rest of the crowd. The smoke of incense and other aromatics ascended in clouds, but failed to purify the tainted atmosphere. The priests therefore hurried the conclusion of the funeral service and retired as soon as possible . . . to their respective abodes.[99]

One wishes this were the end. But no! In 1562, during a Calvinist disturbance, the tomb of the Conqueror was rifled and his remains scattered with the exception of a single thigh-bone. Retrieved and reburied, even this pathetic remainder was not allowed eternal rest. During revolutionary riots in 1793 the tomb with its single content was demolished once again. The simple slab over the tomb tells that this was the spot where William, duke of Normandy and king of England, had been buried. So William fared worse than his Queen Matilda, whose church looks down on his from its higher place across the city of Caen.

Change was in the air throughout the Western world. Three of the greatest men of the Middle Ages had recently died and left incalculable legacies, all of them contradicting tradition and all of them setting both the seeds and the traps for the future: Gregory VII had taken a great step forward in establishing the primacy of the Church, and the separateness of that institution from lay organizations; though it may not have been his intention, Robert Guiscard had set the foundation for a kingdom in Southern Italy and Sicily; and William I of England had established the beginnings of a Norman 'empire' that would eventually extend from Scotland to the borders of Spain. All in all, the last three years had been important ones.

PART TWO

Kings
in
More Than Name

. . . haughty people . . .
Whose will can never know
More than the old and worst customs of all . . .

Petrarch, *Sonnets and Songs* CXXVIII
Translated by Anna Maria Armi

Chapter Seven

There is but one lot for rich and poor: both become the prey of death and corruption.
Trust not then, O sons of men, in princes who deceive. . . .

Ordericus Vitalis, *Ecclesiastical History of England and Normandy.*
Translated by Forester

1087

In the two years since the death of Robert Guiscard his youngest brother Roger, the great count, enjoyed steadily increasing powers in Italy and Sicily. According to the Norman ethic loyalty to a brother (questionable in itself, even in the palmiest days) was certainly not to be confused with loyalty to that brother's son; and much of Roger's newly acquired strength was due to his unashamed and unhesitating picking away, bit by bit, at his nephew Roger Borsa's patrimony.

For Roger Borsa the task he had inherited from his father was wellnigh impossible. Of dreary mediocrity, quite lacking in drive and unduly submissive to the Church, he was in every way totally different from his older half-brother Bohemund, a Hauteville to the soles of his feet and proud of it. Much more the demigod, more talented in every way, and certainly better equipped to rule, Bohemund had every reason to be disgruntled when he saw his birthright pulled out from under him through the machinations of his stepmother Sichelgaita. It was not to be expected that he would remain content with the corner of Apulia which he had forced Roger to cede to him within a few months of the Guiscard's death. He was, indeed, destined to make his own way in the world: but not here. The ultimate theatre of his fame was the Outremer, that revered land of Christ's nativity and passion which with every passing year was increasingly rent by Muslim-Christian conflicts.

While the Hautevilles in Italy and Sicily had their personality quirks and faults, and though they found a concept as basic as loyalty difficult to understand, there is something rather likeable about them and their amiable brawling. The same cannot be said for their countrymen in England, disagreeable, cruel and unprincipled. But then the Normans of the north were confused by the existence of two contradictory sets of ground-rules, the one governing the kingship of England, the other the duchy of Normandy. Unlike Normandy, England had, at this time, no rigid rule of primogeniture. The kingship might be acquired by conquest, but was normally restricted to members of the royal house; it was also strongly reinforced by election and designation by the previous ruler.

William I died on 9 September. William II was crowned on the 26th, the eve of the Feast of Saints Cosmas and Damian, the brother-patrons of doctors and surgeons. Archbishop Lanfranc, William Rufus' teacher and mentor, favoured his pretensions and officiated at the ceremony. Standing on the royal

162

dais in Westminster Abbey, William Rufus was seen by his magnates as short, hefty like his father—in fact given to corpulence—and of florid complexion, which accounted for his nickname 'Rufus'. He was around thirty years old. Blond, with eyes that sparkled impishly in humour and threateningly in anger, he was a man of astonishing strength. He was noted for being an expert rider and a master lance-man. He seems to have had a tendency to stutter. Though he really cared for little besides hunting and fishing, William Rufus settled into his reign with relish, achieving a peak of instant benevolent, if misguided, amiability by restoring various forfeited honours, including the earldom of Kent to his Uncle Odo, bishop of Bayeux, unwisely released from prison by the Conqueror's deathbed decree.

1088

The land was immediately beset with typically Norman troubles. The *Anglo-Saxon Chronicle* records that 'in this year this country was very much disturbed, and filled with great treachery, so that the most powerful Frenchmen [sic] who were in this country intended to betray their lord the king and to have as king his brother, Robert, who was count [sic] of Normandy. At the head of this plot was Bishop Odo . . .'[100] The majority of the English bishops were loyal to the throne, along with the native population, which says something for their belief in orderly succession, an interesting reversal of recent history. William the Conqueror had struggled in the face of native uprisings; now the position was reversed as the English rallied to the defence of their designated ruler. The lords had been presented with the sharp dilemma of a not infrequent feudal situation, that of being vassals to two masters—a king of England and a duke of Normandy. They longed for a single ruler to unite the two sides of the Channel again, that they might rid themselves of the necessity of a double loyalty.

The major threat was from Bishop Odo's earldom of Kent, and from Sussex where Odo's brother, Robert of Mortain, ruled from his well-garrisoned castle at Pevensey. Within six weeks William Rufus had besieged Pevensey and captured both his uncles. Then he turned his attention to Odo's city of Rochester, the nucleus of the revolt which, by an agreement forced upon his uncle, was to be delivered over to him. Even in these straits Odo showed his treacherous nature when, probably by design, he 'fell' into the hands of the city garrison, who then prepared to stand with him against the royal forces.

The castle standing in Rochester at the time of the 1088 siege was the first castle on the site, and had been put there by order of William the Conqueror. This was replaced by a castle built for Rufus by Gundulf, bishop of Rochester, the same Gundulf who had been in charge of building the White Tower in London. 'Gundulf's castle consisted of a walled enclosure surrounded on the landward sides by a ditch or moat of which the impressive remains can still be seen along the east between the castle and cathedral . . . Enough of these walls still stand incorporated in later work to show that Gundulf's castle was in fact the present one—that is, of the same shape and extent'.[101] The castle in question occupied the southwest corner of an ancient Roman city and used parts of the Roman walls as foundations for the new. To the modern student of history, though, the glory of Rochester is the great castle keep, which was not built until the time of Henry I.

Though Gundulf's walled enclosure around the castle may not have even been begun by the time William II laid siege to his Uncle Odo at Rochester, the then existing earthworks must have been a formidable deterrent against the current methods of offensive warfare. The defenders held out until they were driven to surrender by starvation and sickness. They were compelled to seek terms, which William II reluctantly granted, this being one of the few occasions in his hideous reign when he showed compassion. The rebels were divested of their holdings in England, Odo suffering the supreme deprivation of losing for yet a second time his recently re-acquired earldom of Kent. Realizing that his days of duplicity were at an end, at least in England, he fled to France where he hoped to continue with impunity to plot against Rufus. Any meeting with his nephew, the jealous Robert Curthose, must have been difficult to say the least, since one of the reasons why Odo's rebellion collapsed was that Robert failed to provide promised support. As for Rufus, it was his greatest moment: 'In 1088 [he] enjoyed a popularity such as was never again accorded him . . . In return for . . . help the king made handsome promises of good government, good laws, relief of taxation, and free hunting. The promises were, of course, forgotten when the danger was past'.[102] When Archbishop Lanfranc rebuked him for failing to live up to his promises, the king raged at him, 'Who can be expected to keep all his promises?'[103]

1089

With Bohemund and Roger Borsa thundering at one another and succeeding only in catering to the endemic unrest of Italy and Sicily, it would be tempting to think of the great count as comfortably ensconced in his palace in Palermo, content with the realization that he had already left his mark on history. Contentment, however, was not typical of any Hauteville deserving of the name, especially one suffering the worst of all misfortunes: Roger had not yet produced a viable heir. He had one legitimate son, Geoffrey, but that unfortunate man was a leper and living in the seclusion of a remote monastery. There was Jordan, of course, a stalwart son in every way worthy of his father; but he was illegitimate and his claim to Roger's place would be hotly contested. Roger, still reflecting the radiant good looks that his contemporaries found so attractive, his florid countenance weathered by outdoor activity, his hair still golden-red, was now nearing sixty years of age. He was concerned that the best he had to bequeath to his people was an inevitable power struggle. So, with a bravura typically Hauteville, he took his third wife, Adelaide.

A pall of deep mourning was cast over Europe when the great Lanfranc, one of the most effective churchmen and scholastics of the Middle Ages, died on 24 May. Though his image was made lasting mainly through his teaching of law and theology, he had shown himself both a fervent supporter and an outspoken critic of royal methodology, to the Conqueror's frequent delight and Rufus' habitual chagrin. An expert organizer, he had accomplished a master-stroke of diplomacy when he obtained the Conqueror's permission to manage Church affairs through synods manned exclusively by ecclesiastics, which led to the eventual separation of the religious from the secular courts. He was also a reformer, and as such could show a side both intransigent and narrow, unmistakably displayed in his intolerance of England's traditional native saints—'rustic saints' he called them. But under him the religious houses that dotted the English landscape again became the centres, indeed the treasure-houses, of civilization. William the Conqueror had been beholden to his archbishop for foiling a conspiracy against him in 1075, as had William Rufus just this past year. But harder times were coming.

1091

Anselm, successor to Lanfranc as abbot of Bec but not yet archbishop of Canterbury (that office remained vacant for four years) proved himself more than worthy of his predecessor. Like Lanfranc, Anselm was Italian by birth, born in Aosta in 1033. At twenty-seven years of age he had entered Lanfranc's monastery at Bec, becoming prior when Lanfranc moved to Caen, and abbot in 1078. His fame as a teacher spread, and he soon cast even Lanfranc into shadow, though they remained loyal friends throughout the years.

From the royal point of view there were conveniences in leaving the post of archbishop of Canterbury unfilled. A boorish but intelligent man, given to blasphemies and anticlerical jibes, and (worse than anything else as far as his lords were concerned) one who affected the distinctly feminine style of no beard and long hair, William Rufus felt an understandable relief at not having an archbishop underfoot forever chastizing him for his profligacy; and then there were the hardly trifling revenues from that office flowing into the royal coffers. Yet for some reason or another

> Anselm was invited, nay urgently . . . required to come to England . . . When he came to the royal court all the nobility eagerly met him and received him with great honour. The king himself rose from his throne, and met him at the door of his hall with joy; he fell on his neck and led him by the hand to his seat. They sat down, and for a while exchanged cheerful conversation. Then Anselm asked the others to go apart so that he could talk privately with the king . . . He began to rebuke the king for those things which were reported about him: nor did he pass over in silence anything which he knew ought to be said to him. For almost everyone in the whole kingdom daily talked about him, in private and in public, saying such things as by no means befitted the dignity of a king.[104]

Between beratings William Rufus fell sick. Terrified that he would go to hell should he die with Canterbury vacant, he persuaded Anselm to accept that see. Persuaded is hardly the word; the good man was seized by the bishops of England and invested under duress. Both the king and his archbishop were to rue the event!

As though a heckling archbishop of Canterbury were not daunting enough, William Rufus had need to keep in mind his two ambitious brothers. Because Robert Curthose was the more amiable he was also less dangerous, though still deserving of a close watching. But Henry—nicknamed 'Beauclerc' for his business acumen—deserved to be feared. William Rufus could not put out of his mind his father's deathbed prediction that the youngest would outstrip the two elder brothers. This did not prevent the three of them from joining hands on occasion, as they did this year to put down revolts on the Welsh and Scottish borders which had again reached flashpoint, an ever-recurring problem known even to the Romans and which was precisely the reason why Emperor Hadrian had constructed his great wall across the island roughly on the modern border between England and Scotland. The best that William Rufus and his brothers could achieve—either together or separately —was an uneasy peace on the borders, and some new castles which it was hoped would psychologically as well as physically discourage incursions into their territory.

Santa Maria, Mili San Pietro, Sicily

Great Count Roger of Sicily was experiencing his own highs and lows. The low point of the year occurred when his favourite son, the illegitimate Jordan, died in Syracuse of a sudden fever. With one notable exception (his rebellion in 1083) he had been a good son, steadfast in his loyalty, fighting for his father. The grieving Roger laid his son to rest in the lovely little church of Santa Maria in the town of Mili San Pietro. Off the beaten track, Mili San Pietro is only a few miles down the coast from Messina, then inland by a tortuous road through steep Sicilian mountain valleys for a few miles more. When Roger had founded the Basilian monastery there in 1082 it had seemed the perfect location for the monks to practise their Orthodox Eastern faith in rugged isolation. Today it is very much broken down and so degraded that it serves as part of a wildly poverty-stricken farm, knee-deep in mud during the rains and clouded with dust during the summer droughts. Yet the people who run the farm are pleasant and cheerful, and a young man, presumably a son, is perfectly willing to stop his back-breaking work—work not too far removed from the kind of farm labour done in the eleventh century—to point out a broken niche, a cracked staircase or a sagging arch. There are vestiges of frescoes, meagre in the extreme, and a stone recording Jordan's death and burial. Despite the poverty of its surroundings and the proximity of a barn housing cows wallowing in filth, there is a beauty about this simple Norman church obvious to anyone having the patience to seek it out. Hidden from sight, it is nestled in the cradling hills, banked on one side by lemon trees, and lower than the travelled road. It takes a dedicated sightseer's persistence to find Santa Maria at Mili San Pietro. But the reward is great, for in its day it must have been one of the sweetest of the small Norman churches of Sicily.

New lands beckoned to Roger this year, tempting him with added acreage and wealth. Noto, the sole remaining vestige of once formidable Saracen power in Sicily, fell to him. With this last isolated pocket of resistance out of the way, the great count was free to turn his attention elsewhere.

An archipelago of three small islands, Malta lies in the centre of the Mediterranean Sea. Malta, Gozo and Comino, all of them dry and rock-barren but habitable, stand as natural fortresses dividing the eastern Mediterranean from the western, the north from the south. The strategic importance of this tiny group has been recognized from very ancient days, as numerous pre-historic ruins indicate. Saint Paul was shipwrecked on Malta, as is reported in the *Acts of the Apostles* by Saint Luke who was with him.

The inhabitants of Malta are among the most hospitable people of the twentieth century, though they tend to explain away that compliment with a shrug and a reasoning to the effect that, having so often been conquered, they have come to love foreigners and to welcome them to their barren land. (This is not to deny an occasional short-changing of new arrivals at the pier and airport by pleasant-faced, eagerly helpful taxi-drivers, however.) According to Luke, the Maltese were no different in biblical days. It is hard to imagine that Paul, a prisoner on his way to Rome to face charges of subversion—a favourite accusation through the ages to rid ourselves of nuisance personalities—found himself at first sheltered in the palace of Publius, the Roman governor of the island. Luke and Paul remained in Malta an additional three months, or through the winter, in Mdina (pronounced Em-*deen*a), which was the Roman capital. 'And it came to pass, that the father of Publius lay sick of a fever and of a bloody flux: to whom Paul entered in, and prayed, and laid his hands on him, and healed him'.[105] By this demonstration Paul converted Publius, who later became the first bishop of Malta, and eventually of Athens, where he died a martyr and for his pains became a saint. Paul and Luke sailed on to Rome, where Paul later achieved his martyrdom. A cathedral was built in Mdina, possibly on the house of Publius.

There is a great deal of argument about the actual spot of Roger's landing on the island. That he landed near Valletta, or perhaps even in its stark, sun-drenched harbour, is certain (*see page* 154). Having claimed the tiny island, Roger is said to have originated the Maltese flag by halving the Hauteville standard of quartered red and white squares to supply a banner for the conquered forces who now joined his own. The defeated leader's eyes were on the flag of the Hautevilles, gleaming proudly in the sunshine. 'If only we had a banner to march with . . .'

'I will give you a banner,' Count Roger answered promptly. 'Your very own banner.' He beckoned, and the standard-bearer brought the flag to his side. Count Roger reached up, took the standard with its squares of red and white, and tore it down the middle. Then he handed the strip of cloth, now reduced to one red square and one white, to Bin-Said [the leader]. 'Here is your flag, and I charge you, never stain it save with your own blood. Now hoist it up, and march!'[106]

With that he marched on Mdina, his forces swollen by new followers. He was unlike any ruler the Maltese had ever encountered, the very image of what they imagined a Viking to be. But best of all, he was a Christian! One of his first orders was to rebuild the cathedral church of St Publius which he found in ruins, given over to vermin and a tangle of wild foliage. It 'rose from the ruins like a declaration of faith, strong, handsome, unambiguous, eternal'.[107] The cathedral of St Publius dominates modern Mdina like a great baroque bubble augmented by needle spires. Roger's church was more modest in size than the present one, but was destroyed by earthquake in 1693, only the apse surviving. The present cathedral, designed by Lorenzo Gafà, begun in 1697, is one of the more interesting churches on an island not notable for fine architecture. Inside and out it reflects a rich Baroque, but calm rather than flamboyant, tasteful within a style that can easily slip into vulgarity. Roger's apse is still there, and so are the old west doors of black Irish bog-oak, heavy and solid, now serving inside the cathedral as vestry doors. The dome is both bold and dynamic, without a trace of timidity, indeed almost arrogantly asserting its claim as the finest of Maltese Baroque. Just down the street from the cathedral piazza is the interesting Palazzo Falzon—the 'Norman House'— medieval and handsome, but hardly Norman other than in its style. The oldest part of the house dates from the fourteenth century.

Except for the one low spot of the year—Jordan's death—it was a good period for Roger. He was the undisputed master of this whole area of the Mediterranean world, so strong that subservience on his part was no longer called for. He could talk as an equal even to the pope; as more than an equal in fact. Like the Guiscard before him, Roger was seen as the pope's protector, and had been since 1088 when the new Pope Urban II made his bid to take over his throne and city. Anti-Pope Clement III and his protecting German troops were at the time once again in control of Rome, making life so dangerous for the legitimate pontiff that Urban had to be consecrated at Terracina. Urban, former cardinal-bishop of Ostia, was a smooth-talking and scholarly man, adept at diplomacy. Seeking Roger's help, he went personally to Sicily. Roger arranged a temporary peace between his squabbling nephews Bohemund and Roger Borsa, thus making possible a Norman escort to Rome, where the pope was forthwith deposited in November 1088. But by the following year Urban was once again in exile in Southern Italy, not able to return to Rome for another four and a half years. During that time he learned to see Roger, the great count, as a responsible ruler, an able negotiator and a masterful general, who had gained the respect and trust of most of his subjects, regardless of their religion or race, which was a good deal more than Robert Guiscard had been able to claim. Furthermore, he had brought Sicily back into the Christian world. What pope could ignore that?

Yet there were bones of contention between the two: Roger continued to endow Basilian monasteries in a gesture obviously catering to the Greeks in his realm. And he tended to usurp papal authority by making appointments within the Church, precisely the kind of thing against which Pope Gregory VII had railed so adamantly. Urban must have seen that the apex of Norman power was fast approaching. Probably nothing in medieval Europe, or the East either for that matter, would be able to touch the magnificence and brilliance of the Palermo court that was birthing. Sicily's moment was coming; Urban knew it and Roger knew it. And so, probably, did the envious and jealously sniping rulers to the north and east.

1093

A great corner-stone of history was laid in 1093 when a cathedral was started at Durham, the first large building in northwestern Europe to be ceilinged entirely with ribbed vaulting. 'Durham has been said to assail the traditional primacy of France, as Constable and Turner anticipated Impressionism, and it stands not as a national but as a European landmark'.[108] After the Conquest the bishops of England, as well as the abbots and priors, set about to build Norman-styled structures, buildings which they intended should rival the great monuments then under way in Normandy. They were ambitious men, and the motifs they employed were typically Norman, though there is a discernable exchange of ideas in both directions. 'In time it would be possible to speak of an "Anglo-Norman" school of Romanesque architecture, a common style of building extending from the north of England to the southern marches of Normandy . . .'[109] and Durham Cathedral must be recognized as the greatest achievement of that Anglo-Norman school, easily holding its own with the finest churches of the Continent, such as those at Jumièges and Caen.

Though Durham Cathedral is considered the earliest English example of grand-scale ribbed vaulting, curiously enough the style was not further exploited, most other new churches continuing to be covered with the traditional flat wooden roofs. It would take the Gothic French to understand the awesome potential of the ribbed vault, and extend it to its future limits of symbolic architectural expression.

Even before William of Saint-Calais' new cathedral, Durham had already been an important pilgrimage shrine of Saint Cuthbert, a man of decidedly bucolic slant. Five hundred years before the better known Saint Francis was hymning his Brother Sun and preaching to his sisters the birds, Cuthbert had become known as the patron-protector of sea birds. 'Indeed his memory is reverenced by northerners to the present day. He has given his name in popular parlance to the eider duck, "Cuddy's ducks", to a local variety of sea-weed, "St. Cuthbert's Beads", and to many spots on the coastline of Lindisfarne and of Farne. According [to some sources] St. Cuthbert tamed the eider ducks of

Farne; in the breeding season they are tame to this day.'[110] Cuthbert's remains had been brought to Durham from Chester-le-Street in 995, to be housed in two successive wooden churches until a stone one was built during the reign of King Cnut. Now they would be housed in the new cathedral. But Cuthbert is not really at Durham. Today his abbey at Lindisfarne resounds to no more than the cries of gulls, the high-pitched whistle of the North Sea squalls and the rhythmic, marauding waves beating ceaselessly ashore. That sweet saint smiling at a gracefully circling gull, strolls the dunes of Lindisfarne. Gently, a loving patron, he talks to and strokes the tame, trusting eider duck beneath his arm. 'Cuddy's duck' it is; what other saint can claim so much?

Durham became a Benedictine monastic community, sheltering, along with Cuthbert's mortal remains, those of the Venerable Bede who had died at Jarrow in 735. His relics were stolen from that place around 1020 by a monk-sacrist of Durham. With the city lying directly on the invasion route from Scotland even the clerics needed to be tough fighting men. Cast in this mould were the second and third Norman bishops of Durham, William of Saint-Calais and his successor Ranulf Flambard. These political prelates sought many outlets for their ambitions, and both of them found one in building. William of Saint-Calais' career was not unchequered; he was a known con-spirator in Bishop Odo's 1088 plot in favour of Robert Curthose and was subsequently exiled to Normandy. During the three years that he spent there he had ample time to see the splendid churches springing up, which must have encouraged him to bolster his ego and fame by building his own. When he returned to England in 1091 he did not hesitate to destroy Cuthbert's shrine in preparation for his architectural marvel, which he perched proudly, arrogantly—almost defiantly—seventy feet above the River Wear (see page 154).

Bishop William of Saint-Calais laid the foundation stone for Durham Cathedral on 11 August 1093, watched by a host of guests, including King Malcolm III of Scotland, slayer of tyrant Macbeth, he whose tomorrows crept at such a petty pace. Because of its location Durham seems made for storms and violence, and the site a natural for a church-fortification. Remembering that the bishops of Durham were also warriors, and were expected to rise to the call of arms in the frequent emergencies that afflicted the area, it seems the most logical thing in the world that a church and castle would be situated on this romantic promontory formed by an abrupt meander of the Wear. The medieval town grew up first on the steep peninsula (in effect that is what it is) called Dunhol, which became softened to Duresme in Norman times, and thence Durham. Such a famous pilgrimage spot would not long find the narrow confines of the site adequate, and it soon overflowed beyond its original limits. Eventually it jumped the river, which necessitated the building of several bridges, three of which are old, one—Elvet Bridge—being twelfth-century. An agreement was reached that Bishop William would take responsi-bility for the building of the church, while the monks of the community would be charged with the monastic buildings. When William died un-expectedly in 1096 the monks took it upon themselves to make the church the first order of their responsibility. By 1099 the choir and transepts had been completed. This was the year that Ranulf Flambard took over the see of Durham; the building proceeded apace.

A typical power seeker of his age, Ranulf was nicknamed Flambard by the barons of William I in reference to his prodigious talents for mischief-making. He had been born in Normandy, the son of a little-known parish priest. Apparently he was disliked from virtually the moment he set foot in England, where he came at an early age to enter the service of the Conqueror. Having probably played some role in the compilation of Domesday Book, he was granted an important administrative office under William Rufus, and may have exercised the functions later carried out by the king's chief justiciar. According to the chroniclers he was allowed all the leeway even he could want 'to plunder, pull down, and destroy every man's goods for the benefit of the king's exchequer',[111] and for the rampant extortions visited on the general populace during the last years of Rufus' reign when 'money alone held sway with the men in power.'[112]

Ranulf was as tyrannical as his master, and managed to obtain for himself many preferments, culminating in the see of Durham. On the accession of Rufus' brother Henry he was imprisoned in the White Tower, from which, according to legend, he escaped by climbing down ropes smuggled to him in a cask of wine, and found refuge with Robert Curthose in Normandy. But Ranulf soon wormed his way back into good stead with the king of England, and was allowed to resume his position as bishop of Durham. Even then he went on making himself a subject of conversation: his private life was the topic of much colourful gossip. Yet posterity owes Ranulf a nod of gratitude; following on William of Saint-Calais' basic design he completed his great cathedral, the finest Norman expression of the 'Church Triumphant' in all England, and the clearest demonstration of that vigorous style—at the same time calm and agitated, simple yet ornate—which we have come to know as truly Norman.

To walk into Durham Cathedral (*see page* 155) is to enter sculpture, gorgeously massive, typically divided into three clearly defined tiers, and a monument to the concept of restrained yet rich decoration. For decoration is everywhere, not localized to the arches and mouldings, but also featuring inventive herring-bone, chequer-board and stripe patterns carved deep into the surfaces of ponderous round columns. There are spiral flutings and vertical patterns, diamond repeats, zigzags and (as though to emphasize the orna-mentation) an occasional plain, undecorated column. And all of this is lighted by windows larger than we are accustomed to find in churches built at a time when walls were designed to bear imposing weight and were therefore minimally perforated. The impression is one of overwhelming solidity and embellishment that is luxurious but never mawkish. 'Nowhere else can one be overwhelmed so easily by the strength of Norman architecture. Nowhere else is such confidence shown in the proportions or the placing of ornament'.[113]

Saint Cuthbert's body was restored to the place of honour behind the high altar that it had tenanted in the earlier cathedral. The Venerable Bede found his permanent resting place in the twelfth-century Galilee Chapel, slender-columned and almost oriental-looking, which was built at the western end of the church. One explanation of why the Galilee Chapel was built here, so close to the sheer drop to the River Wear that it could have no west door, is mooted in the legend of Saint Cuthbert's abhorrence of women.

For all his love and understanding, his kindness to birds and beasts, Cuthbert was said to have been a notorious misogynist, a worthy forerunner of the twentieth-century male chauvinist. His dislike of the opposite sex allegedly stemmed from the time when, living by choice as a lonely hermit, he was accused by the daughter of a Pictish king of fathering her child. Cuthbert, outraged, called to the heavens to clear his name. The earth opened and swallowed up the princess, the kind of vindication to give any accuser pause, any king second thoughts, and possibly the mild Cuthbert more than superficial shock. Understandably horrified, the king begged Cuthbert to return his daughter, which the saint agreed to do, but only on condition that no woman would be allowed to approach him again, an excessive reaction, it would seem, especially in light of the rather extreme proof of his innocence. It was therefore decreed that no woman would ever be allowed to enter any church that was dedicated in his name; and that included even Mary, the Mother of Jesus! (At Durham there survives an inlay of black Frosterley marble beyond which women were not allowed to pass.) So when Bishop Hugh de Puiset, nephew of the future Empress Matilda, tried to build a *Lady* Chapel at the eastern end of the church, Providence intervened: walls cracked, pillars fell, the floor buckled and arches sagged. Clear such an undertaking was not appropriate.

There are other tales concerning Cuthbert's eternal aversion to women. 'A woman called Sungeoua, wife of a local dignitary named Gamelus, was said to have taken a short cut home through the [Durham] cathedral cemetery when she collapsed, paralysed by a stroke. Gamelus rushed his wife home, but she died that night'.[114] Even Edward III's Queen Philippa is said to have been frightened enough by the wrath of the saint to vacate a room in the priory, which she had occupied in ignorance of his aversion, and to wander about, lightly clad, in the cold night air begging forgiveness. All of which leaves one wondering whether Cuthbert's highly touted patronage of birds and beasts extended only to males.

Over eight centuries of terrible devastations have been visited on Durham Cathedral as a result of political and religious controversies and in the vague name of taste. As usual the hand of Henry VIII wreaked its reforming havoc. In 1650 Oliver Cromwell incarcerated in the cathedral four thousand Scottish prisoners he had taken at the Battle of Dunbar. They were exhausted and starving and can perhaps be more easily forgiven than their captor for the damage they inflicted, their worst desecration being the breaking up of the fine medieval choir-stalls for fuel. In the following centuries various well-meaning and sometimes tasteless

Door Knocker, Durham Cathedral, England

architects visited their particular forms of ugliness on the great building, in sundry ways mutilating England's handsomest Norman church. Despite the depredations it still stands stupendous on its promontory, and today is closer to its original form than at many other times in its history.

There are many things for the visitor to see at Durham: the monastery dormitory, the kitchen and cloister, the monks' garden, chapter-house and deanery, even a small prison. The monks' door leading from the church into the cloister—the Norman ironwork on the cloister-side is especially handsome—is framed by a richly decorated Norman arch. There is a twelfth-century painting of Saint Cuthbert in the Galilee Chapel, appealing in its Romanesque dignity and geometry. And on the north door is the famous grotesque mask knocker, bronze and properly leering, to which a criminal might cling, thus claiming sanctuary until he either agreed to his case being tried, or confessed his crime and 'abjured the realm'. The north side of the cathedral is parked by the expansive palace green, lined by old almshouses, libraries and the bishop's castle. How could any visitor feel cheated?

1094

Schemes, rumours, clerical unhappiness, an explosive situation in Wales and a widespread plot by his nobles goaded William Rufus into a binge of disinheritings, killings and physical mutilations. Thoroughly frightened and no longer capable of organized rebellion on a significant scale, his nobles watched him become more than ever the image of a tyrant. The common people suffered as well. They had practically no way of dealing with the excesses of their cold-blooded, self-indulgent king. Performing their daily back-breaking labours in the fields, going home to dreary, unheated, un-ventilated huts which they often shared with their poultry and smaller live-stock, they suffered profoundly. The monarch seldom stopped anyplace for more than a night or two, at most a week, 'and with him moved all the paraphernalia of government—his treasure, his business documents, his chancellor and clerks with their writing materials, and the multifarious staff of his household. This ambulatory court, living on the country through which it passed, was a cause of serious grievance . . . And such was the terror that its coming inspired that the inhabitants, we are told, would hide themselves in the woods and other places until the danger had passed'.[115] Such was passive resistance during the Middle Ages.

Despite all of this, William Rufus' reign was not totally lacking in achieve-ment. Building was rampant throughout the realm. 'Rufus laid the foundation stone of St Mary's York in 1089, in which year Gloucester abbey was begun. In 1092 the cathedrals of Salisbury, Worcester and Lincoln were consecrated; in 1093, Winchester cathedral was ready and Durham inaugurated; the next year Battle abbey was dedicated and in 1095 a magnificent band of prelates gathered at Bury to translate the incorruptible body of St Edmund into the new abbey . . . Never had such weighty and sumptuous buildings been seen in all parts of England. The grandeur of these churches survives today as the most obvious and widely appreciated achievement of Norman England'.[116]

173

Chapter Eight

Before the dread voyage   none deems it fit
Wiser in spirit   than the world's way
To ponder deeply   ere parting hence
What sins or good deeds   his soul has done
That after his death-day   deemed shall be

The Venerable Bede
In Sutherland, *The Oxford Book of Literary Anecdotes*

1095

Never in history has there been a more unlikely series of events than the incredible mass movements of the crusades—migrations they were—from West to East, and then back again. The violence, the blood, the suffering and costly destruction—all in the name of the Prince of Peace!—that spanned a period just short of two hundred years, appalls and staggers the imagination. From a serious (if misguided) altruism brought on by a profound (if bigoted) religiosity, to an undisguised and hypocritical greed and lust for power, is a difficult intellectual transition to make nine centuries later. Even the eloquent Edward Gibbon has trouble wrestling with the problem: 'the Christians, both of the East and West, were persuaded of their lawfulness and merit; their arguments are clouded by the perpetual abuse of Scripture and rhetoric . . .'[117] Just a quarter of a century before, severe penances had been meted out to those who had taken part in the Battle of Hastings, in spite of the fact that William I had sailed under the papal banner. Warfare may have been the most telling sign of the times; yet the Church had always been uneasy about it.

We can finger the man most responsible for the gradual acceptance of war as desirable, guaranteed to open the portals of paradise to anyone who gave his life in its performance: Gregory VII, who as Cardinal Hildebrand had arranged the presentation of the papal banner to William the Conqueror. But tracking down the origins of the crusading idea is more complicated than simply pin-pointing Gregory. The Old Testament is replete with bloody tales of violence committed in the name of a demanding God. The Muslims had set the example with their *jihad*—holy war. And now that example was being reversed in Spain with the beginning of the Christian reconquest. By the time Pope Urban II raised his inspired battle-cry at Clermont, the crusading spirit, if not rampant, was already becoming commonplace.

Urban II may have been the driving force behind the First Crusade; but there was another who had goaded him into action. Peter the Hermit had landed in Bari in 1089 on his way home from Jerusalem. He carried a letter from the patriarch of that city begging for Western help against the Muslims who were allegedly harassing Christian pilgrims and desecrating their shrines. Peter had promised the patriarch that he would 'rouse the martial nations of Europe in [his] cause'.[118] As luck would have it, Pope Urban II was in

174

Southern Italy, wandering around the neighbourhood of Bari during one of his prolonged exiles from the Eternal City. It was in the crypt of San Nicola of Bari that Peter is said to have exhorted the pope to rise to the defence of the Holy Land. Clearly a fanatic, Peter the Hermit was a Frenchman from Amiens, a former monk, dumpy-looking and swarthy; and, like people who come to resemble their pets, it was said that he had a face that strangely mirrored his donkey's. He rode everywhere on the poor beast, 'poor' in that enthusiasts for Peter's mission had plucked it hairless in their quest for relics. Peter's family was well-to-do; he had even done military service under the counts of Boulogne, and had been married. But he had decided to forsake all that; 'and if it be true that his wife, however noble, was aged and ugly, he might withdraw with the less reluctance from her bed to a convent, and at length to an hermitage'.[119]

In March Urban held a council at Piacenza, where, according to Gibbon, two hundred bishops, four thousand clergy and thirty thousand laity were addressed by ambassadors from the Greek emperor, Alexius Comnenus. The balance of power in the East had been drastically upset, they claimed, by the advance into Syria of the Seljuk Turks (a northern steppe nomad people), whose defeat of the Byzantine Christians at Manzikert in 1071 was so provocative a threat against Constantinople as to cause Alexius to reach to the West, Church schism notwithstanding. In the same year the Turks captured Jerusalem, which for many years previously had been stabilized by a stand-off between Byzantine and Arab forces, and began to harass Christian pilgrims from the West. Military help was what Alexius needed. His delegates pleaded with the Westerners 'to repel the barbarians on the confines of Asia rather than to expect them in the heart of Europe'.[120] At Piacenza they were assured that help would be forthcoming. But first the shrewd Pope Urban II needed time. Prudently he proposed a second synod, and in November called a council to meet at Clermont in south central France.

With Pope Urban's call Clermont became a magnet, pulling entire communities from neighbouring lands. The inns packed guests in more than double their usual number. Though there were no top-ranking lay lords present, there were lesser ones with their families; and military leaders and their troops. The splendid court of the Roman pontiff arrived in state; and the college of cardinals heeded the call. In addition there were thirteen archbishops and over two hundred bishops, some of whom were strained to find properly luxurious accomodation. Colourful tents mushroomed round the city and beyond, the military being more self-sufficient, or at least more adaptable, than the princely. The riff-raff had a field day: the pickpockets, con artists, pimps, prostitutes and touts all profited as they never had in their lives. Adventure was in the air, this time with divine approbation. When else but in Old Testament times had men whose careers were devoted to making war been allowed to exercise their talents in the name of an exacting God, the one true God?

At last Pope Urban II—erect, handsome, his eyes sparkling in fanatic fervour—made his appearance and mounted the scaffold which had been erected so that he could be seen throughout the central market-place. He had hardly begun his harangue before cries of *Deus vult!* ('God wills it') began echoing through the *place*, rising with each of his exhortations until the city itself seemed to rock with the chant that was more explosive than devotional. A master rabble-rouser, Urban laboured 'to spread the flames of war from the Atlantic to the Euphrates',[121] from the start stressing the sacred bond between man and his personal God.

> . . . O sons of God . . . you must hasten to carry aid to your brethren dwelling in the East . . . For the Turks . . . have attacked them . . . and have advanced as far into Roman territory as that part of the Mediterranean which is called the Arm of St. George [the Bosphorus and the Sea of Marmora] . . . Wherefore with earnest prayer . . . God exhorts you as heralds of Christ . . . to hasten to exterminate this vile race from our lands and to aid the Christian inhabitants . . . For all those going thither there will be remission of sins if they come to the end of this fettered life while either marching by land or crossing by sea, or in fighting the pagans. This I grant to all who go, through the power vested in me by God . . . Let those who are accustomed to . . . wage private war against the faithful march upon the infidel . . . Let those who have long been robbers now be soldiers of Christ. Let those who once fought against brothers and relatives now rightfully fight against barbarians. Let those who have been hirelings for a few pieces of silver . . . now attain an eternal reward . . . Let nothing delay those who are going . . . Let them settle their affairs, collect money, and when winter has ended and spring has come, zealously undertake the journey under the guidance of the Lord.[122]

Urban had successfully launched his Holy War. Hearing the encouraging answering bellow *Deus vult! Deus vult!* he knew that 'a new spirit had arisen of religious chivalry and papal dominion; a nerve was touched of exquisite feeling; and the sensation vibrated to the heart of Europe'.[123] But the effect was more than he had bargained for; he was unprepared for the frenzy of the response, as no doubt he was unprepared for the suggestion that he lead the expedition himself. He declined. Adhemar, bishop of Le Puy, was appointed in his stead and as such was the first to accept the crusader's badge, the red cross. The acceptance of Urban's call to arms became almost ecstatic; it was like a sudden, miraculous epidemic of

Pope Urban, Cleremont-Ferrand, France

fanaticism, radiating from his rostrum, until all of Europe was infected by the plague—a kind of divine madness. 'He had in fact launched a movement greater than he knew . . . For, though with all of [the lords] except Bohemund genuine religious fervour was the strongest motive, soon their terrestrial schemes and rivalries would create troubles far beyond the papal legate's control. Still more uncontrollable was the response shown by humbler folk throughout France and Flanders and the Rhineland'.[124]

By the thousands the witnesses present swore to set out to free the sacred places of Christ's ministry on earth. Most of them sought eternal reward, but not a few of them consoled themselves with visions of freedom—the criminal from prosecution, the peasant from his lord, the monk from his chill cell, the knight from his vassal duty. Moreover there was a large reserve of landless knights, younger sons—such as had enjoyed fighting in Southern Italy—for whom prospects at home were bleak, and who welcomed any adventure and the possible chance to improve their fortunes. Men of means divested themselves of land-holdings and money, sometimes disinheriting their own families to defray the expenses of the journey. Princes bought up the property of their vassals for mere pittances, sometimes with no intention of ever allowing God's warriors or their families to buy it back. The pilgrims—and they thought of themselves as pilgrims going to Outremer to worship and only incidentally to fight for the restoration of their shrines (there was no word either in Latin or the vernacular languages for 'crusade' or 'crusader' until the thirteenth century)—knew one thing for sure: they needed ready cash.

Some men, either unable to resist the pleas of their wives, or themselves unable to bear the thought of separation, encouraged their wives to make the pilgrimage with them; indeed, it was not uncommon for entire families to take the pledge to make the sacred journey. Then there were those who were left at home, bearing as heavy a cross as the pilgrims, lamenting the losses of their lovers and husbands, cursing the cross that lured them: 'The cross brings me grief, and praying to God does not help me. Alas! O pilgrim cross, why has thou so destroyed me? Alas, how sad am I! How fiercely am I burning with love!'[125] It would have been almost sacrilegious for a wife to claim that she had taken her marriage vows seriously, and that no man—prelate or otherwise—should put them asunder. Accept her husband's pledge to crusade she must; beyond that she could only hope to be remembered in Outremer.

With the fixing of the departure date for August 15 (the Feast of the Assumption) of the following year, and with all the hoop-la, the indulgences and the promises of eternal reward, with the prospects of gaining wealth on the one hand and the realistic impoverishing on the other, the seeds were being sown for a destruction of the Christian values which had for so many generations been the very backbone of the faith. Furthermore, one needs no proof beyond the First Crusade that the 'lunatic fringe' is not unique to our time. The movement eastward 'began with grotesqueries, comic and horrible. A band of Germans followed a goose they held to be God-inspired. Peter the Hermit . . . preached a private crusade—known as the Peasants' Crusade—and promised his followers that God would guide them to the Holy City. In Germany Walter the Penniless emulated Peter. Motley hordes of enthusiasts . . . marched through Germany and the Balkan lands, killing Jews by the thousands on their way, plundering and destroying'.[126]

The crusade should have been a natural for the restless and adventurous Normans, always on the look-out for new lands to conquer and new wealth to acquire. One would think that it would have appealed to the wanderlust that was such an inherent part of their make-up. With the exception of Bohemund, however, the top southern Normans, always finding sufficient cause, turned deaf ears to the pope's call. Even in the north certain prominent leaders managed to wriggle out of God's service. William Rufus for one had troubles of his own; there was no way, he reasoned, that he could leave his kingdom for an extended period.

Roger of Sicily was a likely prospect; but the pope, seeing him as papal protector, made no more than cursory demands on him. Besides that, Roger was tired of crusading, be the objective heavenly or mundane. The Arab chronicler Ibn al-Athir maintains that Roger's refusal to move was based purely on finances, and that he encouraged others to go on a crusade that he himself would not undertake because he saw it as unprofitable. And, indeed, there seemed no reason why Roger should have looked elsewhere for joy. His earthly happiness reached such crescendo proportions on 22 December when Adelaide presented him with the second son of this marriage that Roger gave him his own name. A first son, Simon, had been born two years before. Should anything happen to him (as it did) there would be another to succeed. His line was ensured. Suddenly luxuriating in the knowledge that a kind of im-mortality was available to the living, and with understandable self-indulgence, Roger called for spectacular celebrations, elaborate services in the cathedral and sumptuous feasts. It was a good welcome for the new Roger who, as it turned out, surpassed his father, reaching exalted heights of grandeur and creating a court of such opulence and brilliance as to be the talk and envy of Europe.

1096

In August of 1096 a disinherited Bohemund, restless, disenchanted, and chafing for more rewarding enterprises, was in the company of the two Rogers—his half-brother and his uncle, the great count—outside the walls of Amalfi, a troublesome city which had not yet become a Norman satellite. It is one of the most spectacularly situated cities in Italy, lodged midway along the drive that bears its name and hangs precariously from vertical cliffs. The traveller negotiating the Amalfi Drive—a small car is in order!—enjoys the fleeting sensations of one moment driving an car, the next piloting an aero-plane, and now and then helming a boat. There is hardly a thrill in Italian travel to compare with bursting through the approach tunnel to Amalfi's beach and tiny harbour, animated by tanned, bikini-clad bathers and a parade of steamers from Naples, Sorrento and Salerno; and this after having driven through some of the most intoxicating scenery that man and Nature, between them, have managed to contrive! There are yet other scenic pleasures in store, especially for the walker: the Valley of the Mills offers picturesque alleys and tiny piazzas, fountains, arcades, mills, a torrent—violent after a rain—and many a southern Italian smile and *buon giorno*.

As an independent republic Amalfi had so far managed to hold out against the Norman might (and did so until 1131). The fame of this utterly charming city nestled in the shadow of the protecting Monte Cerrito had reached its height during the three centuries before the Norman take-over. At one time Amalfi was able to make the questionable boast that it possessed the largest arsenal in the world. Amalfi's maritime code, the *Tavole Amalfitane*, probably in use from the eleventh century, was recognized as the general law of the Mediterranean until the end of the sixteenth century. The *Municipio* (Town Hall) displays what is probably a fifteenth-century copy of this interesting document. At its peak Amalfi claimed a population of seventy thousand (it is only about sixty thousand today) and trading successes to match. With money pouring into its treasury Amalfi was able to construct its most important monument, the cathedral of Sant'Andrea.

From lofty heights Amalfi Cathedral looks down on a spacious, colourful piazza (*see page* 156), enlivened by the Baroque fountain of Sant'Andrea, restaurants, tourist kitsch shops, and various dispensers of alcoholic joy. The piazza, in fact the whole town, seems hemmed in by steep valley walls; these, barely a few feet from the cathedral steps, suddenly open on the sweeping, animated beach and oleander-lined promenade. The *campanile*, standing separate and unsociably aloof, and slightly off the vertical as though vaguely tipsy, is all that is left of the original eleventh-century cathedral. It displays patterns of interlocking Saracenic-looking blind arches and an effective—and terribly Mediterranean—use of yellow and green tiles. The pattern of arches is repeated in the shady Cloister of Paradise adjacent to the cathedral and entered through the atrium.

Puffing up the long flight of stairs leading to the thirteenth-century cathedral is a little like climbing towards some difficult-to-attain gigantic confection, such is the sugar-and-spice effect of the black-and-white striped façade. And to enter the atrium is not unlike being swallowed up by a sweet. The fine bronze doors of the main entrance, like those of the underground church of Monte Sant'Angelo, were cast in Constantinople by one Simeone di Siria, and given to the church by the same rich Amalfi merchant, Mauro di Pantaleone. Beneath the high altar, in a barbarously Baroque interior, reposes the body of the apostle Saint Andrew, minus his head which was detached by Pope Pius II in the fifteenth century for reasons which would make sense only to that age. The corpse, like that of Saint Nicholas of Bari, is said to exude a fluid—'the sweat of Saint Andrew'—believed to possess miraculous powers.

For the travel- or crowd-weary who might find Amalfi a bit of a strain, Ravello offers a lovely respite. Shady, high and wonderfully quiet—no snarling Vespas or soot-belching antique trucks—with a vista that is one of the marvels of the Mediterranean, it is the ideal place for a rejuvenating Campari and soda, an *espresso* or a *cappuccino*: in such tranquil surroundings there is nothing so good as any one of these drinks with a *tramezzino*. The Italians do wonderful things with these half-sandwiches, filling them with such niceties as sliced artichoke hearts, capers and sometimes a dash of herbs.

Students of architecture will find at Ravello a stunning reminder of Trani. The cathedral doors there are of bronze (made by the same Barisanus who did the Trani doors) and are composed of sixty small panels each containing at least one figure. The ensemble, dating from 1179, is attached to heavy wooden bases. Inside the cathedral the medieval enthusiast will find as handsome a Cosmati pulpit as can be found anywhere. The Cosmati family of the Middle

Ages worked in Rome, gathering up the various coloured stones found in the ruins of antiquity, cutting them into small bits and arranging them in geometric and swirling patterns on floors, pulpits, paschal candles and columns. Cosmati work is not really mosaic work, though there are similarities, and the difference can be determined on sight. Cosmati is purely decorative, non-representational, and the patterns are boldly assertive, with the tesserae cut to the shape of the space they occupy. It was natural for this particular kind of craft to spread to Southern Italy, in view of the tradition of Byzantine mosaic work so exploited by the Normans. At any rate the pulpit at Ravello is worth a good long look, as is the phial allegedly containing the blood of San Pantaleone, who died in the persecutions of Diocletian. There are similar relics of the saint at Constantinople and Madrid, and those of Madrid and Ravello are supposed to liquefy on his feast day, 27 July.

So here was Bohemund at Amalfi, at the foot of the towering hills that pedestal Ravello. But he hoped for more out of life than simply fighting his relatives' battles. He was intrigued by the prospects of the crusading movement. But he was too shrewd to offer an instant, later-to-be-regretted response to Urban's call. As the launch date for the First Crusade approached—it finally got under way in November, not far enough off schedule to cause concern—more and more pilgrims were passing through Southern Italy, bound for ports from which to sail to the Holy Land. Bohemund became convinced of the seriousness of the enterprise and optimistic about its chances of success. Without warning one day he dramatically appeared at the siege of Amalfi wearing the crusader's red cross on his shoulder. His example was followed by so many of those engaged in the siege that the great count and Roger Borsa no longer had adequate forces to prolong it and went home.

Events were to prove that Bohemund's quest was more for territorial gain than everlasting salvation; and who can blame him, seeing the short shrift he had received at home? By late summer he had gathered around himself over five hundred knights, including five other grandsons and two great-grandsons of Tancred de Hauteville. There was also an appropriate number of foot soldiers. Bohemund's army was probably the best equipped of all those that went on the First Crusade. His men were accustomed to fighting both Greeks and Saracens—not to mention other Normans—and many of them were adept in both Arabic and Greek. The rabble that had followed Peter the Hermit and Walter the Penniless, and were already either skeletons in Anatolia or prisoners unwillingly answering the muezzin's call, had been a motley and ill-armed crowd. The later bands, led by northern nobles, were better equipped than these superstitious mobs, but they were also accompanied and encumbered by the riff-raff element. Of such, Bohemund probably had the fewest.

In Normandy Robert Curthose was doing his bit for the cause, making one of those colossal errors of judgement for which he was notorious. One wonders who his advisers were! He had committed himself and donned the red cross. To raise money for his part in the giant scheme he mortgaged off his dukedom to William Rufus —a singularly ill-chosen broker—for a paltry ten thousand marks, and so 'proved, in the . . . administration of the duchy of Normandy, how incompetent he was'.[127] Did Robert really believe that he would get Normandy back? William Rufus had probably known all along that sooner or later Robert would make a decisive mistake, thus allowing the reunion of England and Normandy under one ruler.

1097

As though by a magic gesture from Urban, Europe was on the march. From every point on the compass the pilgrims set out, eyes always to the East, their thoughts on the Holy Sepulchre and salvation. Once the lunatic fringe had departed—and foundered—the better organized groups got under way: Raymond of Toulouse marched down the Dalmatian coast to the Via Egnatia, then turned towards Constantinople; starting at Lyons, Robert Curthose passed through Genoa, Florence and Rome, and embarked for Constantinople from Bari; Godfrey of Bouillon started at the most northerly point, Regensburg, moving through the savage kingdoms of Hungary and Bulgaria. He, too, was headed for Constantinople. And with the balmy temperature of spring Bohemund, who had crossed the Straits of Otranto from Brindisi, moved his troops along the ancient Via Egnatia. Emperor Alexius had asked for help; now he had more than sufficient cause for alarm.

'The principal force of the crusaders consisted in their cavalry; and when that force was mustered . . . the knights with their martial attendants on horseback amounted to one hundred thousand fighting men, completely armed with the helmet and coat of mail'.[128] The weight of the army was the cavalry, the flower of European manhood, whose sole occupation was the gentlemanly art of making war. It was thus that the Arabs, perhaps rightly, saw the Westerners: 'Among the Franks—God damn them!—no quality is more highly esteemed in a man than military prowess. The knights have a monopoly of the positions of honour and importance among them, and no one else had any prestige in their eyes'.[129] There was also the noisy rabble that formed the unruly infantry, though a few of the more dependable might be used as scouts, archers and guides. This undisciplined and ill-assorted mob numbered, according to Gibbon, in the neighbourhood of six hundred thousand, 'besides the priests and monks, the women and children'.[130]

In an effort to reassure Alexius about his intentions Bohemund left his followers at the modern Kesan under the watchful eyes of his nephew Tancred, and went on alone with only a few select knights. The other armies had already arrived at Constantinople, to be stunned by a city the like of which they had never seen or imagined. Nothing in the West could touch the scintillating glory of Constantine's city, situated squarely on the confluence of the Bosphorus, the Sea of Marmora and the Golden Horn, the last simply a four-mile long harbour of the Bosphorus. ' "Oh, thrice-happy City, eye of the universe, ornament of the world, star shining afar, beacon of this lower world . . ." So sighed in the twelfth century a Byzantine author forced to absent himself on a diplomatic mission'.[131]

It was generally conceded that Alexius had little dignity except when enthroned. It was therefore in the audience hall of the Blachernae Palace (one of at least three palaces for imperial luxuriating), robed in stiff brocade shot

Instanbul (Constantinople) with Hagia Sophia

through with gold and covered with cascades of pearls and precious stones, that Alexius I Comnenus received his European visitors in their travel-dirtied chain-mail tunics. The edges of the emperor's robes were embroidered with heavy gold patterns, and the whole draped over with a purple cloak fastened at the shoulder by a massive jewelled brooch. He wore silk shoes (that must have impressed the crusaders!), a crown of pearls, and cradled his sceptre.

By nature a suspicious man, Alexius had become increasingly more wary of the Westerners' intentions. He had noticed that many crusaders had their entire families in tow, and had become rightly convinced that they would try to carve for themselves principalities, dukedoms, earldoms and the like from the territories they had vowed to wrest from the infidels. Well and good, so far as Alexius was concerned; these Western barbarians could act as effective buffers between him and the Muslims. But he had no intention of allowing them to acquire territories which had been until recently part of the Byzantine Empire. In what amounted to open bribery, Alexius showered his guests with wealth, revictualled their troops, and agreed to send his own as escorts through Byzantine lands—on one condition: they must all swear fealty to him and agree to return whatever former Byzantine lands they captured.

The leaders of the crusade were housed in sumptuous apartments where they could bathe and enjoy the blandishments of attentive servants and the luxury of exotic Eastern foods. While their betters were enjoying the temptations of state entertainment, the common folk were wandering the crowded, cramped streets, visiting the native quarters, as well as the Latin quarter called the Galata, seeing the churches and prowling around the monuments of the Eastern Roman Empire. Yet by the time they left Constantinople they were happy to be on their way.

That vast, splendid city, with all its wealth, its busy population of merchants and manufacurers, its courtly nobles in their civilian robes and the richly dressed, painted great ladies with their trains of eunuchs and slaves, roused in them contempt mixed with an uncomfortable sense of inferiority. They could not understand the language nor the customs of the country. Even the church services were alien to them. The Byzantines

182

returned their dislike. To the citizens of the capital these rough, unruly brigands, encamped for so long in their suburbs, were an unmitigated nuisance . . . The opening of the Crusade did not augur well for the good relations between the East and the West.[132]

Bohemund was acknowledged, perhaps grudgingly, the *de facto* head of the European forces. Following the example of the others, he had taken his oath of loyalty to Alexius; Raymond of Toulouse, however, had sworn to only some of the conditions. With formalities accomplished and agreements made, the crusaders crossed the Bosphorus into Anatolia. By June 19 they had taken Nicaea, the holy city of the First Ecumenical Council of AD 325, over which Constantine the Great himself had presided. Alexius' troops played an important part in the siege. In accordance with their agreement he then took possession of that city. Already the political balance was shifting positively in his direction. The European armies then moved southwards and slightly to the east, to meet the Seljuk field forces at Dorylaeum (the modern Eskisehir). With the defeat of the Turks there on 1 July, they continued towards Heraclea.

Pity the uneducated rabble of Europe who so trustingly followed their lords, poor people so ill-informed of the distance involved in their trek that while still traipsing across Germany and Northern Italy they had begun asking their leaders whether such-and-such a city were not Jerusalem, or that mountain village Bethlehem. At least Bohemund's men had not to be disabused on that score, accustomed as they were to the nomadic life of the soldier in the seething Italo-Sicilian arena, and so able to take long hauls and forced marches, hunger and want in stride. Besides, many of them were veterans of the previous de Hauteville sallies into Greek territory when Robert Guiscard had had it in mind to be emperor. More than a few times Bohemund's troops sustained assaults by the mounted Turks, who rode lighter horses and relied more heavily on infantry. At last, with the taking of Heraclea, the road to Antioch was open. By the end of October the Europeans were encamped at the foot of the ancient walls, initiating what was to prove a agonizingly long siege indeed.

Bohemund may never have heard of William the Conqueror's half-brother Odo, bishop of Bayeux. With impending siege on his mind he would have been little interested that this year the former earl of Kent, past master of shady politics, among the most militant of churchmen, and at one time the most trusted of William's magnates, died at Palermo, whither he had journeyed on his way to crusade. He was buried in the cathedral.

William Rufus had done well to rid himself of his unprincipled uncle. He had also done well not to have volunteered for the crusade, what with various weighty problems at home, not the least of which were the perennial uprisings of the Welsh, into whose territory Norman conquerors had made inroads but had mostly achieved only a tenuous hold. Ferociously stubborn, the Welsh were determined to resist the Norman yoke, an act they were never able to complete; but neither were they completely overwhelmed, and until the late thirteenth century they were able to give their overlords anxious moments and misery-laden seasons. It was because the Welsh were difficult to manage, that

Pembroke Castle,
Wales

Arnulf de Montgomery arrived in the westernmost area of Wales near Milford Haven, whose Welsh name, Aberdaugleddau, indicates an estuary formed by the union of the Eastern and Western Cleddau rivers. At the end of a creek connected to Milford Haven, Arnulf built the first Pembroke Castle, a typical motte-and-bailey structure, bounded on one side by the creek and on the other by the River Pembroke, a site which may have been occupied as early as Roman days. Scandinavian sea rovers in their early encroachments may have settled on the same land; at least they gave names to the adjacent islands of Skomer and Skokholm.

Soon, through additions and modifications, Arnulf's castle became reputedly almost impregnable; because of its western location, it was one of the most vital Norman fortresses in Wales. Today its evolutionary descendant stands atop a limestone cliff, dominating the old town and facing Monkton Priory—founded by Arnulf in 1098—across the southern tidal inlet. Pembroke Castle was too formidably positioned to become involved in the almost daily violence of the Norman-Welsh conflicts, maintaining its reputation for invincibility until the time of Oliver Cromwell. He was the first to take the fortress, though he needed six weeks to do it, and brought the garrison to submission only by cutting off their water supply.

Because of its proximity to Ireland, in addition to its strategic location within Wales, Pembroke Castle was added to and redesigned almost constantly during the next centuries. The irregular shape of the outer curtain walls came, eventually, to follow the shape of the natural rock foundation, the walls in some places reaching a thickness of fifteen feet, and were protected by five stout towers and a gatehouse.

At the time Pembroke was built militarists were growing dissatisfied with the rectangular keep, so difficult to protect from within and with corners so vulnerable to sapping from without. Crusaders began returning from the Levant, 'where the development of projectile engines such as the trebuchet, which could hurl stones weighing half a hundredweight, made it necessary to develop patterns of wall surface off which the projectiles might skid. A cylindrical tower was one solution. Quite the most impressive and complete example in Britain is the round tower of Pembroke Castle...'[133] This awesome feature of the castle complex was put up in about 1200 by William Marshal, earl of Pembroke. Fifty-three feet in diameter, it still maintains a height—discouraging to besiegers—of close to eighty feet, with a wall twenty feet thick at the base giving access to all four floors by means of a circular staircase within its ponderous thickness. The keep—donjon—was originally topped by battlements and a dome carrying a kind of crow's-nest whence cross-bowmen and archers could protect both the bailey and its guarding curtain wall. In case the bailey were taken, Pembroke's keep was encircled by a projecting wooden gallery—a brattice (its supporting beams' put-holes are still clearly visible)—from which all sorts of injurious articles could be dropped on enemy heads. Made of unsquared and undressed limestone rather crudely coursed, the keep is stunning to behold even in its derelict state.

Adjacent to the dominating keep in the inner bailey is the Norman hall, striking in its ruins, and one of the first important structures to be built on the site after the original motte-and-bailey. A later Earl William Marshal built the hall with an eye to greater comfort and accommodation than had previously been provided. One end of the hall forms the dividing wall between the inner and outer wards, and there is a large fireplace inside, an architectural feature just then making its appearance. The successful fireplace depended first on the invention of the chimney, which was a long time coming—Rochester Castle was one of the earliest to employ this modern device. But the flue as a specific architectural form was not developed until the fifteenth century, early fireplaces venting merely through the wall.

Adding to the invincibility of Pembroke Castle is the unique 'Wogan', a natural cavern below the castle halls, which was used as a storehouse and supply entrance from the River Pembroke—and sometimes, one might think, as an escape hatch. Of the man-made additions to the cave there is a type of herring-bone masonry which is pre-Norman at least, perhaps even Roman.

In a period of rampant construction and the development of progressive styles and methods, the most ambitious secular building was the great hall of Westminster, which was built for William Rufus in 1097-9. Like other Norman kings, William held court during the great Church festivals, wherever he happened to be at the time. He was at Westminster for Whitsun 1099 and was able to use the new hall for the first time. His carping comment about Westminster Hall seems characteristic

Westminster Hall, London

of this grumpy, ill-tempered man: 'Not half big enough—too large for a room, too small for a hall'.[134] Little remains of Rufus' 'small' hall beyond the walls, which have been resurfaced. Yet in some of the wall passages can be seen traces of red and blue paint with decorative black lines, from which we can get some idea of the brilliant and luxurious colours which embellished medieval buildings.

Lovely as William Rufus' Westminster Hall may have been in the past, its real glory today is its magnificent timber roof, erected by Richard II in 1394. Hugh Herland, a master carpenter in the king's service was probably responsible for the creation of this roof, which may well be the finest in Europe. Herland's new 'miracle of Gothic carpentry' allowed the floor space to be cleared of any timber post-supports, thus providing the hall with an uncluttered span of sixty-seven and a half feet. The elimination of ground support had never before been attempted. Hugh Herland managed to support the heavy ridge-piece of his upper triangulated structure by a series of arched timbers, cantilevers, and hammer-beams, 'so called from the horizontal baulks, nearly two by three feet thick and ending in carved angels. An enormous area can be spanned by this device of making arches spring from brackets fixed to the wall. No other supports are needed, although the walls have to be strongly buttressed outside ... The hammer-beam was an English triumph'.[135] Though the roof was extensively damaged by the ravages of the death-watch beetle, and slightly by bombing during World War II, it still stands silently aware of its days when it served as a seat of English law. Among those tried in its vast closeness were Sir Thomas More, Charles I and Queen Caroline, the unhappy and frustrated consort of King George IV.

1098

Bohemund de Hauteville had long-range designs on Antioch. From the moment he had arrived there in October 1097 he had realized the potential of this ancient and holy city and its surrounding plain. Here was a place, he figured, where he could settle down and carve out his own future without the restraining, jealous hand of Roger Borsa to impede him. Others unfortunately had the same idea, the most potentially dangerous being Raymond of Toulouse. This count of Provence was the oldest and richest of the European leaders, notoriously tough while at the same time willing to support and capitalize upon outbursts of religious hysteria. He had only one eye which, as far as his numerous devotees were concerned, enhanced the mystical aura which enveloped him. Accompanying him on crusade were his wife and son, as well as Adhemar, papal legate and bishop of Le Puy.

Only twenty miles from the beaches of the Mediterranean Sea and on the left bank of the River Orontes, Antioch enjoyed a place of honour on a blessedly fertile plain rich in vines and a variety of grain. Fruit trees of divers kinds—olives, figs, citrus and pistachio, along with white-fruited mulberries—grew in abundance. Just as important, this fortunate city was situated on the main route from Christian Constantinople to Arab Outremer, in a position to sift trade from Egypt, Palestine, the Upper Euphrates and all of Asia Minor, trade in such exotic items as glass and carpets, silk, soap and pottery.

Despite repeated attacks against the walls of Antioch no dent was made in that venerable city's defences. It was not that the crusaders did not fight bravely. In the month of February, for example a particularly bloody battle had taken place some little distance from the walls; an eyewitness described its din as resounding to heaven, while showers of spears and arrows darkened the air. The besiegers were finally reduced to such straits of hunger and want that they even went so far as to expel 'women from the army, the married as well as the unmarried, lest perhaps defiled by the sordidness of riotous living they should displease the Lord. These women then sought shelter for themselves in neighbouring towns'.[136] And lavish as the agricultural cultivations around Antioch may have been when the besiegers had arrived the previous October, by June of this year the land had been stripped of its wealth. Desertions became the order of the day; Alexius' liaison officer quietly slipped away home, and on 2 June Stephen of Blois turned his back on the siege and led his troops off to the coast, returning to France by boat.

Seeing his troops hungry, indeed watching his army shrink daily through desertions and deaths, Bohemund finally realized that victory could be gained only from within. He also knew that the Atabeg Kerbogha of Mosul was on the march from the east to relieve the city. Bohemund found his turncoat, an Armenian converted to Islam, named Firuz, who entered Antioch to activate its betrayal. In the darkness of early morning on 3 June he then 'admitted over the wall twenty of our men by means of rope ladders. At once, without delay, the gate was opened. The Franks who were ready, entered the city'.[137]

According to the oath that Bohemund had made to Alexius it was his duty to turn Antioch over as part of the empire. But when Kerbogha laid siege to Antioch on 7 June, the defenders agreed that they would support Bohemund's claims on the city provided that he managed to repel the attacker. Raymond of Toulouse alone dissented, arguing that only he, who had not sworn full fealty to Alexius, could honourably claim the city. A brilliant victory over Kerbogha on 28 June confirmed Bohemund's position. As for the oath to Alexius, where had he been when they had need of him? He had never shown up. Even when one of the crusaders was dispatched to summon him to claim his city he did not respond. Alexius had in fact been *en route* to give promised aid but, on hearing erroneously that the crusaders had been vanquished, had turned back to Constantinople. So Bohemund acquired Antioch by default.

While his stubborn nephew was confronting both Turks and Greeks (and Raymond) in Outremer, Great Count Roger was enjoying his successes at home. In Salerno he and Pope Urban II reached an agreement 'which has led to more speculation and heated controversy than any other incident in the whole history of Sicilian relations with Rome'.[138] It had to do with the rights of investiture, that same knotty problem that had plagued the relationship of Pope Gregory VII and the German Henry IV. In a letter dated 5 July, Pope Urban allowed that Roger and his immediate heirs were granted the rights of approval over all papal legates in Roger's territory. Furthermore, Roger was granted absolute powers to select which bishops he sent to future Church councils. This achievement of Roger's pre-dated a similar papal agreement made a few years later with King Henry I of England.

1099

Weary, blood-soaked and violently devout, the crusaders stormed their way into Jerusalem on 15 July amid scenes of appalling butchery. With Raymond of Toulouse at their head (Bohemund had stayed behind in Antioch to nurse his fledgeling realm) they had managed to construct a great tower and move it along the high walls of the city. The Saracens responded with frantic defence. 'With *fundibula* they hurled small burning brands soaked in oil and grease against the tower and the soldiers in it. Therefore many on both sides met sudden death in the fighting'.[139] Some crusaders were already in the city

> where there was such a massacre that our own men were wading up to their ankles in enemy blood . . . Our men took many prisoners, both men and women, in the temple. They killed whom they chose, and whom they chose they saved . . . [They] rushed round the whole city, seizing gold and silver, horses and mules, and houses full of all sorts of goods, and they all came rejoicing and weeping from excess of gladness to worship at the Sepulchre of our Saviour Jesus, and there they fulfilled their vows to him'.[140]

The spectacle of the dead, the maimed and dying has gone down in history as one of the most dishonourable deeds of man. 'Still more dreadful was it to gaze upon the victors themselves, dripping with blood from head to foot, an ominous sight which brought terror to all who met them'.[141] With a willingness as amazing as it is suspect, the crusaders turned from the slaughter to devotion as 'they began with sighs and tears, with naked feet, and with every sign of humility and devotion, to visit each of the holy places . . . and in particular, the church of the Resurrection and of our Lord's Passion'.[142]

When Raymond of Toulouse declined the nomination as lay ruler of the city on the pious grounds that he could not reign where Christ had suffered, the position was offered to Robert Curthose. He should have accepted. But he was anxious to get back to his dukedom and his brotherly squabbles. Godfrey of Bouillon was finally chosen as the 'advocate of the Holy Sepulchre'. Then, at Christmas time, Bohemund fulfilled his pilgrimage to Jerusalem, and he and Godfrey knelt before the newly appointed patriarch to swear fealty to him as legate of the pope, receiving from him the investiture of Antioch and Jerusalem. Bohemund had reason for pride; he had certainly proved himself worthy of the Guiscard. With the patriarch of Jerusalem as his witness, and before the crusaders of the European West, he owed allegiance to no overlord other than the pope or his legates. Neither Alexius nor Raymond could now question his right to Antioch. On New Year's Day, 1100, he proudly strutted off to take final possession of his city, styling himself, as he would for the rest of his days, 'Prince of Antioch'.

It was probably just as well that the man who had called this holy bloodbath into being never knew of its completion. Pope Urban II died on 29 July, fourteen days after the fall of the sacred city. If it had been his intention to free Jerusalem from violence and religiously fired zealots he would have been bitterly disappointed: centuries of crusaders of all creeds would ravage the most holy of all cities to this very day.

Chapter Nine

If fortune does any wrong to you,
It is her right, indeed, you must not blame her,
Even though she strip you of your shirt:
For you had nothing the day that you were born.

Alain Chartier, 'Most Foolish Fools, Oh Foolish Mortal Men'.
In *An Anthology of Medieval Lyrics.*
Edited by Flores

1100

William Rufus, a keen exponent of the chase, was in the New Forest at the end of July indulging his passion for the hunt. That whole area of western Hampshire had, a few years back, been afforested by order of William I and has ever since been known as the New Forest. Set aside by royal decree for the exclusive use of the court, poaching in it was prohibited by savage laws, infraction of which was punishable by maiming or hanging. The Conqueror's laws were perpetuated by his successors. The New Forest is not all forest in the usual sense but rather, because of the chalky nature of its soil, a combination of bog, heath and scrub woodland. Today it comprises 92,365 acres, 16,000 of which the Crown still reserves the right to enclose and plant.

Normally an early start for hunting would have been made. But on the night of 1 August the king slept fitfully, disturbed by a dream that he was being bled by a surgeon,

> and that the stream, reaching to heaven, clouded the light and intercepted the day . . . Shortly after, just as the day began to dawn, a certain foreign monk told . . . that he had that night dreamed a strange and fearful dream about the king: that he had come into a certain church, with menacing and insolent gesture, as was his custom, looking contemptuously on the standers-by; then violently seizing the crucifix he gnawed the arms, and almost tore away the legs . . . The image endured this for a long time, but at length struck the king with his foot in such a manner that he fell backwards; from his mouth as he lay prostrate, issued so copious a flame that the volume of smoke touched the very stars.[143]

On having the monk's tale related to him Rufus put up a showy front. 'He is a monk', he laughed. 'Like all monks he dreamed this to get something. Give him a hundred shillings so he won't be able to say he dreamed in vain'.

Shaken nevertheless, the king postponed setting off, first reinforcing himself with an overindulgence in wine. It was well after the midday meal when the hunting party finally rode out to the area chosen for the hunt. The royal party decided to dismount, and leaving the dogs with the horses, they pushed their way through the thick growth on foot. Finally Rufus stepped into a clearing, edged on one side by a dank swamp. He paused, hoping to make a quick kill. With him was a young nobleman, Walter Tirel, count of Poix in Ponthieu, already trusted enough personally to accompany the king. The other few members of the king's immediate party, armed as was Rufus with longbows and arrows, concealed themselves among the trees while the beaters drove the game towards the clearing. Two fine stags trotted into the space. According to the chronicler William of Malmesbury, William exercised his royal prerogative and shot first; but, blinded by the low sun glaring into his eyes, he had to be content with watching the beast limp off only slightly wounded. At this point Walter Tirel shot at the second stag, and it has usually been assumed that it was his arrow that hit William Rufus. His companions were stunned to see the king pitch forward to the ground, driving the arrow deeper into his heart. An alleged site of his death, traditionally accepted since the late seventeenth century, is marked by the Rufus Stone, near Stoney Cross.

Tirel may have been innocent, at any rate of a purposive shot; he stuck to his story of innocence right to his deathbed. Nevertheless, he knew that suspicion would rest heavily upon him. Leaping astride his horse, he sped off into the dusk, bound for Poole where he boarded the first boat for Normandy. The rest of the royal hunting party scattered, leaving their dead king where he had fallen. It was two hours before a peasant—in tradition a charcoal burner—found the body, recognized it, and carried it on a cart to Winchester, where it was interred the following morning beaneath the central tower of the cathedral. In the eyes of William's clerical critics the collapse of this tower seven years later implied divine retribution for the burial in the cathedral of so notorious and unrepentant a sinner.

Rufus' brother, Henry Beauclerc, was also hunting in the vicinity. The unseemly eagerness with which he responded to the emergency (assassination?) has raised serious questions concerning his own role in the affair. He rode at once to Winchester and seized the treasury. Without waiting for the burial—he did not even view the body—he was crowned king at Westminster on 5 August, a mere three days later. Few historians absolve him of complicity in his brother's death, from which he had everything to gain.[144] At any rate it was not long before Walter Tirel returned to the island to be much honoured by the new king.

Elected and crowned, Henry set out to woo his subjects, in a grand the-bad-old-days-are-over exercise. The hated Ranulf Flambard was imprisoned in the Tower of London (he escaped a year or so later). Debts owed to his brother Rufus were cancelled. A charter of liberties was issued, and Henry promised to adhere to the laws of Edward the Confessor. At his urgent request the exiled Archbishop Anselm returned at once to England and all seemed well between Church and Crown—but only for a time; another period of exile was in Anselm's future. An attempt to close the chasm between the two nations may be seen in Henry's marriage to Edith, daughter of Malcolm III of Scotland. Although on her marriage she took the continental name Matilda, her former name is the clue to her importance. She was a member of the Saxon royal house, a great-niece of Edward the Confessor.

William the Conqueror and Matilda were not noted for having produced a good-looking family; and Henry cut no better a royal figure than his brothers. He had the family thickset frame, the barrel-chest, the tendency to portliness. A heavy shock of black hair covered a high forehead and shadowed rather soft eyes. He was of medium height. Notwithstanding his benevolent negation of the abuses of Rufus' reign, Henry showed himself to be a cruel man on more than a few occasions. He was avaricious and lustful, admitting to no fewer than nineteen bastard children—eight males and eleven females. Blindings, mutilations and castrations were common punishments dispensed by this king who would tolerate no disloyalty or dishonesty. Because they were not as close to him as was the peerage, the common folk regarded him with affection, for despite his somewhat poisonous personality he was an excellent king and an efficient administrator.

Almost the only one with anything to lose by William's untimely death was Robert Curthose, who this summer was scurrying home as fast as possible to claim his 'rights'. He brought with him his new bride, Sybil of Conversano, a woman of some social consequence since she was the great-niece of Robert Guiscard and Roger of Sicily. She was also wealthy enough to redeem Robert's pawned duchy. Robert had done well at the crusade, enhancing his reputation. Nevertheless as a result of his usual combination of bad luck with inattention to the main chance, (he had relaxed too long in Sicily before concluding his homeward journey), he arrived back only to find his youngest brother already the established and annointed king of England.

1101

Furious at having been cheated out of what he considered his rightful place, Robert tried to bludgeon his way to the throne by invading England in 1101. Although he had considerable support he did not succeed, the best he could do being to reach an agreement with his younger brother; by a settlement made at Alton, near Winchester, Robert disavowed all claims on the English throne, and Henry virtually all his claims to Normandy. Like Rufus, Henry was willing to sit back and wait. Given time, he knew that inevitably Robert would himself destroy whatever chances he had of taking over the kingdom.

It was a sad 22 June in Southern Italy and Sicily when, at seventy years old, tired and unwilling (or unable) to indulge further in the rough-and-tumble life which he had found so exhilarating, Great Count Roger de Hauteville died in the castle he had built at Mileto and which he loved above all others. Odd that he, the youngest of Tancred de Hauteville's giant litter, had become the most successful of the lot. He could feel deserved pride in his achievements, not the least being the fact that he had been sought after as son-in-law by three different kings, even though he ranked lower than all of them and was officially a mere vassal to his nephew, Roger Borsa. He was one of the strongest men of his age, and one of the most interesting. He was buried at Mileto, in the abbey of Santìssima Trinità, which he had also founded. It is gone now, destroyed in an earthquake in 1783, and the shattered sarcophagus which held the great count's body is in the National Museum in Naples.

Unlike Bohemund, his muscular giant of a nephew, Roger had been born to govern, even managing to enlist former enemies into his service. And unlike those crusading Europeans who were so gleefully settling into the Holy Land, and who were at first too arrogant to learn anything from the infidel, he appreciated Muslim military skill. He had created what was virtually a Muslim army, instilling into them a pride in their cultural heritage and religion. Archbishop Anselm, while visiting Italy when in exile from England, had approached Roger's camp during a siege of Capua in 1098. Churchman that he was, he had attempted to proselytize the Arabs among Roger's forces. 'They were impressed by him and his words, but declared that they could not turn Christian if they wished, for the Count was wont to punish severely any of them who abandoned his religion'.[145]

Roger was not a crusader; what he did was for personal gain. Yet his take-over and governance of his island realm was seen as a crusade because he had taken the island from the infidel. But unlike his compatriots in Outremer who were successful only at the start, he perpetuated his success, laying such a firm foundation that the inheritance of his sons Simon and Roger II was more than assured. The basis of Roger's rule was so far-seeing that the second Roger could emulate it, build on it, and eventually raise himself to royal status. And 'here . . . lies the cornerstone of Roger's achievement . . . While the rest of the continent, with a ridiculous combination of cynical self-interest and woolly-headed idealism, exhausted and disgraced itself on a Crusade, he . . . had created a climate of enlightened political and religious thinking in which all races, creeds, languages and cultures were equally encouraged and favoured. Such a phenomenon, unparalleled in the Middle Ages, is rare enough at any time; and the example which Count Roger of Sicily set Europe in the eleventh century might still profitably be followed by most nations . . . today'.[146]

Roger's widow lost no time in assuming the government, acting as regent in the name of their son Simon. But the situation was extremely bleak; Simon was only eight years old, and Adelaide herself without governing experience. Perhaps even more difficult for her was the poor reception she was accorded on the basis of her sex. No Norman was willingly going to knuckle under to a woman, regardless of how much he cherished her husband's memory. She continued to devote most of her time to mothering her two sons, entrusting the government to various Greek, Arab or Norman officials.

1105

The Bocage (literally grove or woodland) is an open country occupying a vaguely defined area of lower Normandy, hilly and dotted with productive meadows and small industrial towns, apple orchards, some dense forests, and farms for raising dairy cattle and Breton ponies. The forests are especially attractive—with a variety of conifers, spruce, oak, beech and larch—but most characteristic of the Bocage are the wide areas of rolling countryside, where fields and orchards are bordered by hedgerows enough to satisfy the most homesick Englishman. War comes easily here, and to the Bessin immediately to the north; it was here in the Bocage that the antagonism between Henry I and Robert Curthose was finally resolved at the small town of Tinchebrai, industrial now and rebuilt since the 1940s. The whole area was devastated during World War II—'the warfare of the hedges'—in some of the fiercest fighting of the entire European campaign.

Henry had come to Normandy to muster what loyal troops he could for the showdown. By this time he had had enough of Robert's meddling, his gadfly tactics, his letter to the barons of England pointing out that he was the eldest of the Conqueror's sons and therefore entitled to the throne. Admittedly Robert had a case, even more so when he reminded them that in a treaty made with William in 1091 each of the brothers was designated the other's heir. Henry could cite only that he had been 'born to the purple', meaning that he was the one son of William I and Matilda who had been born of a royal father and mother, his brothers having been born before the Conquest.

Robert's was a lost cause from the start. But he was abetted by malcontents in the realm. One was Ranulf Flambard who, dispossessed of his Durham see by Henry, had by this time shinnied down the ropes from the White Tower to freedom and Robert's welcoming arms.

It seems so simple to say that Henry gathered 'all the nobility of Normandy',[147] but the facts show that the procedure was far from casual. Henry had to do his persuasive groundwork such as besieging castles, burning

Bayeax Cathedral, France

193

crops and savaging towns. A man as wily as he also bought over many of Robert's neighbours or vassals. Bayeux suffered under Henry's cogent use of arms and torches—Bayeux, the city of his disreputable Uncle Odo and the cathedral of which that bishop had been so proud.

Situated on the River Avre, Bayeux has the questionable distinction of being on a well-worn invasion route. The Viking Rollo built a church there and, it should be remembered, married Popa, the daughter of a Frankish count of Bayeux. Duke Richard I of Normandy built a castle; it was, unfortunately, destroyed in the eighteenth century. King Harold, if he swore an oath of loyalty to William the Conqueror at all, as the latter so tenaciously maintained, perhaps did so here. One of Bayeux's favourite sons was Alain Chartier (*c.* 1385–*c.* 1433), who wrote the poem which graces the start of this chapter. He was also the author of the classic poem of unrequited love, *La Belle Dame sans Merci*, a tale soon translated into English.

Bayeux's Romanesque cathedral had been consecrated on 14 July 1077, with Odo, William and Matilda, Lanfranc and Thomas of Bayeux, archbishop of York, in attendance. It can have occurred to none of them that the cathedral would so soon be almost completely gutted by Odo's own nephew.

What we have left is the result of rebuilding over the centuries, a conglomeration of styles, and even whims, from the handsome Romanesque western towers—part of Odo's original building, and an eloquent testimony of what his church was!—topped by their Gothic spires, to the incompatible lantern and *flèche* of the central tower, the misguided work of the last century by a man perhaps aptly named Crétin. So often in Norman work there is an insistence on humour that verges on the stubborn, as though a good laugh were almost as important to them as a good miracle; a veritable medieval bestiary of monsters, apes and dragons all bring on smiles, one likes to think, even among the saints. But that kind of levity cannot last. With the coming of the Gothic Age art becomes more dour. The Romanesque builders enjoyed their religion, their buildings and their God more than almost any other people with the possible exception of the ancient Greeks. It is as though they said of their churches, these are for the glory of God. But even He must have a sense of humour, a feeling for the absurd, a contempt for pretention. Even He can laugh—He created mankind, didn't He?

When the young Count Simon of Sicily died this year the way was unexpectedly opened for the ascension to his place in the sun of one of the most enlighted and able rulers of the Middle Ages. Roger II, not quite ten years old, was abruptly pushed into his brother's place. It would be hard to imagine a better ruler for Sicily, even remembering that the unfortunate Simon was not given a fair chance. All things considered, Roger II's rule was to prove beneficial to his subjects, and a primer to posterity of toleration among races, cultures and religions. Roger grew up infinitely more sophisticated in his tastes, more worldly in his view, and more consummate a politician than ever his self-trained father had been. He could thank his Italian mother for this. Adelaide raised him in an essentially Mediterranean world, his Norman heritage for all practical purposes forgotten. His teachers were Muslims, Greeks and Italians, and their subject matter enlightening.

Mainland Italy, too was on the upswing, suddenly seeming a brighter place with the return of Bohemund, as blond and blue-eyed as ever, and entertaining some pretty grandiose ideas of his own. Everywhere he went he was acclaimed; he was a hero, all but a living legend. And he was at his affable best, moving up and down Apulia, drumming up a horde of young adventurers willing to risk a trip to fabled Outremer. In spite of the relative success of the First Crusade, that troubled area continued to churn with unrest and open hostilities, erupting first here, then there in disastrous, hate-building warfare between Christian intruders and native Islamic peoples. Who knew what stirring experiences, even romance, awaited the young and strong of heart, those who, for reasons of age or whatever, had been denied the valiant heroics of the First Crusade? Bohemund even attracted the attention of the new Pope Paschal II, and on a visit to the pontiff incited him, not against Islam, but against his fellow-Christians. Alexius, it seems, was again the object of Bohemund's hatred.

As Prince of Antioch Bohemund had not had much time to enjoy his new prestige. Within a few months of his take-over, in the course of an expedition against the Danishmend Turks of the Upper Euphrates River, Bohemund had been captured and held for ransom. For reasons of their own not many people were especially interested in seeing him freed; even his once trusted nephew Tancred was enjoying his place as acting head of Antioch and was noticeably unanxious to relinquish his new status. The only one interested in freeing Bohemund was Alexius—provided that *he* could hold him in thrall. Both the emperor and Raymond of Toulouse, who had carved out a power centre for himself, had designs on Antioch. In 1103, after three years of captivity, Bohemund was finally ransomed, none the worse for wear, but owing no thanks to any of the three aforementioned. He arrived in Antioch understandably bitter, and realized immediately that he would need massive help to hold off not only the ubiquitous Saracens, but Alexius and Raymond as well. After suffering a defeat by the Saracens in 1104 he returned to Italy to drum up reinforcements.

It must have been joy to this Norman son of Italy to be back in his old haunts. There were acquaintances

Molfetta Harbour with Cathedral, Italy

195

to renew, familiar places to revist: Bari, still safely in the Norman fold; Brindisi, from which he and the Guiscard had sailed so confidently on their bid for empire; and his favourite Otranto, hallowed in his memory as the place in which his father's remains had been received back into Italy. There were also Barletta and Bitonto—and Molfetta.

Molfetta is a bustling port, housing a large fishing fleet which puts out to sea as far as the coast of Yugoslavia for its hauls. Octopus and *calamari* (cuttlefish) are among the favourite catches here and, as you would expect, are served up at almost any *trattoria* with an Italian flourish and a seasoning that would cause the most jaded mouth to water. The tiny *calamari* (like tiny squids but for the little interior plastic-like cuttlebone which must be removed) are a nuisance to prepare. But once the bone is removed and the fish carefully cleaned in salt water, it is necessary only to drop the little beasts in hot olive oil flavoured with a dash of garlic and perhaps a bit of parsley—the Italian word *prezzémolo* is such a beautiful word!—and, *ecco*! Superlatives are inadequate. For the person not prone to counting calories, a thin batter may be applied by dipping before frying, and then—well, superlatives are even more inadequate.

Molfetta's cathedral of San Corrado—the *Duomo Vecchio* that is, since a new cathedral was begun in 1795—may have been in the process of going up when Bohemund was roaming the area to gather recruits for Outremer, since it was consecrated in 1150. (Some authorities maintain, however, that it was *started* in 1150.) So he never had the thrill of seeing the twin towers, 'dazzling as if carved in chalk',[148] arising almost too vertically over the white town huddled at their feet. The towers are Romanesque; but one gets the feeling that the whole ensemble is a combination of Saracenic, Byzantine and Southern Italian, all brought together to satisfy eclectic Norman tastes.

Standing at the head of a piazza right on the edge of the sea, the building is roofed by three domes, oddly not exactly repetitious, a discrepancy which serves to impart a rather exciting vitality to the composition. The construction began with the eastern dome, set by means of an elaborately decorated cornice on four pendentives. The later two domes were set on drums, through the utilization of squinches, a not unsatisfactory deviation from tiresomely exact repetition. Furthermore, there is—and it is easily perceptible to the naked eye—a deviation in the constructional axis of the building causing a curve in its alignment. And the four central piers are not in a perfect square, which causes the central dome to be more oval than circular. As a matter of fact, only the eastern dome—the first—is a precise circle, at least so far as the eye can see.

Molfetta Cathedral, Italy

Externally the cathedral offers further delights. Grotesque masks and the most ferocious of lions look down from walls on which are shallow interlacing arches of Saracenic inspiration. Even the cathedral neighbourhood is charming for the tourist bent on exploring shadowed recesses and alleys. There are passages as cool as the sunlit piazza is hot, quiet enough to echo each step, as hidden as a thought, as secret as a memory. But do not think that you are passing unnoticed! Behind those slatted *persiane* are watching eyes, eyes that nothing escapes; not the fondling lovers who think they are alone in their own intimate world; not the tourist basking for a moment in the misguided notion that he has escaped the twentieth century; not even the street boy filching a piece of fruit or a plastic Jesus from the gaudy display stand in front of a tiny shop. For everything is on display in Italy; the ruins, the age, even the poverty and somehow made to look bewitching.

1106

Once back in Europe Bohemund got off to a good start. He was received by King Philip of France, who was so impressed by the reputation that had preceded this strapping defender of Christendom and by his heroic tales, that he offered him the hand of his daughter Constance. He was also introduced to King Henry I of England. Pretty good for a rough-neck southerner just in from the eastern edges of Christendom! It was a triumphal progress through Europe for Bohemund, its best result being that it allowed him unlimited opportunity to denigrate Emperor Alexius. Bohemund saw the Byzantine emperor as supremely perfidious, and solely responsible for the traitorous attacks made on innocent Christians as they passed through his territory. He appeared, in effect, as a pagan. And Bohemund's listeners, impressed by the sincerity of his manner and the directness of his steady blue eyes, were only too willing to adopt that erroneous view. It should have been perfectly clear to them that this genial giant was also a showman who had not given up his father's dream: one day he meant to be emperor! But unfortunately for him and all those who backed him, his star had already passed its zenith and even in Antioch he was soon to be humbled.

Resuming his campaign in Normandy, and as part of his scorched-earth policy, Henry I laid siege to the castle at Tinchebrai. It was here that Duke Robert came upon him. The contestants squared off for battle. Henry had decided to fight mostly—but not entirely—on foot, in the hope that the engagement would prove decisive. Nobles and knights shouted their troops together. Banners fluttered in the sun over both armies. Coats of mail were adjusted, alignment of arrows checked, bowstrings tested. Swords were unsheathed and hefted, felt with gingerly caressing thumbs and forefingers. Axes and halberds cut the air in deft practice swings as men feinted and ducked, parried and dodged in anticipatory practice for the coming brawl. The men thus armed were the most important of the close-encounter foot soldiers. Many of them were mercenaries; the practice of using paid troops to augment or substitute for a feudal army was just then developing.

Robert moved first. Disadvantaged by having a smaller number of troops, he chose to be the aggressor. He came on relentlessly, 'with the greatest boldness; and being skilled in the wars of Palestine, he fiercely drove back the royal troops, carrying himself like a man of wonderful and long-tried valour. Then the cavalry of the Britons . . . dashed from the opposite side upon the duke's soldiers, and forthwith scattered them, whereupon the army was immediately dispersed and vanquished . . . A wonderful event this! . . .'[149]

The fate of England was in the balance; yet the battle to decide that fate lasted barely one hour. By winning, Henry resolved the matter once and for all. There was nothing ignoble about Robert's capture. Sword in hand, he had been surrounded by enemy forces and dragged down. He had fought to the end. He could expect honourable treatment, at most to be held for ransom. He was in for a surprise. 'To imprison a great noble for life was rarely done; to imprison an elder brother almost never'.[150] But this is exactly what Henry did to Robert. The disarmed duke of Normandy was hauled off the field, and marched into twenty-eight years of what is euphemistically called 'honourable captivity', leaving behind a Norman-Italian wife and a fatherless son—William Clito. So it was that Robert Curthose, who 'had refused the kingdom of Jerusalem when it was offered to him, preferring to be the slave of rest and idleness in Normandy, rather than labour for the Lord of kings in his Holy City . . . [was] condemned . . . to eternal idleness in an eternal prison'.[151] The date of the Battle of Tinchebrai was 28 September, by an odd coincidence the fortieth anniversary of the landing at Pevensey of William the Conqueror, father of the two principal contestants.

Just one month before Henry Beauclerc's quick, kingdom-saving victory, another Henry, older and accustomed to as many defeats as victories in life, died at Liège. The Holy Roman Emperor Henry IV—licentious from youth, deposer of popes and supporter of antipopes, a public penitent in the snow at Canossa, the despoiler of Rome, an arrogant braggart when things were going his way, but a leader unwilling to stand against an angry Guiscard—finally gave up. Towards the end of his life Emperor Henry suffered the supreme humiliation. His elder son Conrad had been in constant rebellion against him, and in response to the threat he had had his second son, Henry, crowned in 1098. Conrad died in 1101, but his brother soon emulated his disloyalty, capturing Henry IV and forcing him to abdicate. Henry escaped. It was while he was striving for a come-back by negotiating with France, England and Denmark, and trying to raise an army, that he died, leaving the empire to his son, Henry V.

This new man in Germany, Henry V, was just as hard-nosed as his father; his fortunes were shortly to become intertwined with those of the king-duke of newly reunited England-Normandy. The papal throne was occupied by Paschal II, not an illustrious man and not noted for strength, but a good man, and a reformer; his eagerness for reform (investiture was still an issue of contention, especially with the new German ruler) always far outstripped his capacity to effect it. In Sicily an eleven-year old, at the moment in the hands of tutors of divers backgrounds while his mother acted as regent, was headed for kingship. And one of the ablest of England's kings sat on his throne, confident and cruel, an inveterate womanizer, and trustworthy only so long as it benefited him. For a century that had barely started, the prognosis indicated exciting times ahead.

1107

An enormous, finely cast bronze bell had been ordered for the Benedictine abbey at Bury St Edmunds. The central tower of the huge church was about ready to receive it. And a fine tower it was, too, not unexpected considering that the abbey was one of the wealthiest in all England. Pilgrims flocked to this place in Suffolk to pray at the tomb of King Edmund, whose body had been brought there early in the tenth century, and from whom thereafter the town took its name. King Cnut founded the abbey there in 1020. Edmund had been impaled with innumerable arrows and then beheaded by the Danes in 869 or 870 and his martyrdom was followed immediately by impressive miracles. Edmund's body had been recovered, but according to the legend a forty-day search was needed to locate the decapitated head, then found only after following directions laid down by a talking wolf. And the head was, just as miraculously, joined to the body after being placed by it—the kind of story that appeals to people, religious and secular alike. In a world of harsh realities and unrealized dreams, the simple story of a king martyred for his refusal to renounce his faith, and further, the rightness of his act proved by miraculous manifestations, gave some looked-for meaning to the inequities of life—hope where otherwise there would have been no hope. Even kings could be victims of barbarity. Even kings were beholden to powers beyond the known.

The simplicity of Edmund's story did not prevent his memorial abbey from acquiring grandiose aspirations. And the great bell which was mounted in the abbey tower sometime between 1107 and 1121 was suspended there as a symbol of these pretensions, seen—and heard—by all. On the other hand, the dreams entertained by the abbots of Bury St Edmunds were typical of those enjoyed by a host of other heads of religious houses that dotted Europe. Wealth and power were prime factors of coenobitic success, never mind that there had been many reformers in the past and that others were now on the way. Bernard (later Saint Bernard of Clairvaux) was already seventeen years old, preening himself for his cue to flounce on stage, eyes glowing with the fire of true reform, hair bristling in agitation, and a voice positively stentorian with rage. He was destined, at twenty-two years of age, to join the newly founded abbey of Cîteaux, dedicated to an austere and unqualified adherence to the ancient precepts of the Benedictine rule.

Monastic reform was in the wind again. Two centuries earlier the reformed Benedictines of Cluny had spearheaded a monastic revival that profoundly affected the whole Western Church and eventually rescued the papacy from the slough of impotence and scandal in which it wallowed during the tenth century. But for monastic or other religious orders success always signalled danger; new monasteries became popular, had worldly gifts pressed upon them, and eventually fell back into the slackness they had been founded to banish, becoming veritable clones of a morally debauched society, isolated from it by cloister walls of sanctimoniousness and unadhered-to vows, while at the same time enhancing their power and wealth. The monasteries springing up across England with the new reforms were distinctly Norman, though they maintained a solid English practicality; but their roots were in Italy—at Monte Cassino.

Saint Benedict of Nursia had been born about 480 near Spoleto. Having been sent off to Rome for schooling by his well-meaning, well-to-do parents, he was totally demoralized by the general depravity of that degraded city. He fled to the mountains of the Abruzzi, finally settling down at Subiaco, where he lived for three years in a cave—the *Sacro Speco*, which is still shown to the modern pilgrim. Benedict's sanctity attracted others and in time a group gathered around him. He was prevailed upon to take on the job as acting head of a local community and later built twelve small monasteries to accommodate his followers. But local jealousies and hostilities caught up with him. He left Subiaco with a few chosen companions, finally settling at Monte Cassino, where he destroyed an old temple to Apollo—a neatly symbolic act against the pagan 'Lord of the Silver Bow'.

Benedict's Monte Cassino became a centre of culture during the medieval centuries, a nucleus of learning and a storehouse for the preservation of ancient writing, art and historical memorabilia. It was here that Benedict wrote his famous Rule, a concept of the monastery as a self-governing entity, a self-sustaining oasis of sanity in an insanely hostile world. When Benedict died he left a wise legacy, but not a totally original one it would seem. In compiling his Rule he had drawn upon the earlier wisdom of the Desert Fathers, of Saint John Cassian and Saint Augustine of Hippo. What Benedict left was a Rule both beneficient and authoritarian, a outline for a working community, a pattern for a life both comfortable and austere. A balance of prayer, study and manual labour was the secret of its success. His 'monks were to be no mere ritualistic bookworms—he wanted them to get dirt under their nails'.[152]

Though Benedict's Rule was adopted and followed in innumerable religious houses, these remained totally separate from each other. The first centralized 'order', that is a coalescence of separate religious houses under the rule of priors who were in turn under the authority of an abbot from a mother house, was established following the foundation of the reformed Benedictine monastery of Cluny, in Burgundy. As other new foundations sought to emulate it, and existing houses begged to be 'reformed' by it, a centralized system developed by which all the dependent priories owed obedience to the abbot of Cluny.

On a good day, the monastery at Monte Cassino commands an un-obstructed view from Naples to the environs of Rome across a fertile valley that has been used as a thoroughfare by legions of tourists and soldiers since before recorded history. After Benedict's death in about 547 abbot followed abbot, efficient and inefficient, honourable and otherwise, those dedicated to the Rule and those self-seeking. At last, in the eleventh century, Monte Cassino found one of the best of the lot, (excepting only the saint himself), Abbot Desiderius, who had in 1086 unwillingly answered a call to become Pope Victor III. He had already constructed a gorgeous, mosaic-encrusted basilica on Monte Cassino which had been dedicated in 1071 by Pope

Alexander II. Hildebrand had attended the ceremony, as well as Saint Peter Damian—a brilliant theologian, wearer of an iron girdle and an eater of coarse bread and stale water—and a host of Norman leaders. The church was utterly destroyed by allied bombing in 1943, for which the writer as a key participant carries a lifelong guilt.

But perhaps even more remarkarble is Desiderius' little church of Sant'Angelo in Formis, just three miles east of Capua. In 1073 Desiderius reconstructed an old church on a small hill, the site of a temple of Diana. But there is nothing of this pagan deity at Sant'Angelo in Formis. The church is approached through an atrium, a later addition and really rather unattractive, not at all the kind of thing to prepare one for the jazzy wonders to be found inside. There is, however, one mitigating item: a lovely painting in the tympanum over the main entry, a representation of Saint Michael, the favourite angel of every card-carrying Norman. (Desiderius and the Normans were the best of friends). There overhead is the archangel in all his masculine splendour, lance in hand, the defender of Christendom, looking more Byzantine than Italian in his colourful dalmatic, jewel-encrusted and geometric. And that is exactly right; the stylistic groundwork to prepare us for the inside. A revival of Italian painting was taking place at the time, an upsurge of local activity albeit under the direction of Byzantine artists called from Sicily and sometimes even from Constantinople. The frescoes show a strong reliance on eastern prototypes. They are more decorative than realistic, though a feeling for the realistic was not foreign to these artists, in spite of the stiffness of the figures, the flatness of a treatment more abstract than representational.

Going into the rectangular, three-aisled basilica is a little like walking into a Christmas tree, so alive are the colours. It is all there, from Desiderius presenting a model of the church of Sant'Angelo (the building rendered in a strange, flat perspective) and wearing a square halo, indicating both his stature as a holy man and that he was alive when the painting was done, through the Old Testament and the New, and a gallery of prophets, to the Last Judgement. Desiderius occupies another place of honour, too, in the apse, all the closer to the lively figure of the enthroned Christ. The Son of God is not the friendly, fatherly figure of later days, the head of the human family, the benevolent keeper of His house. Here He is a little dour—not sour, not forbidding; simply

Abbot Desiderius, S. Angelo in Formis, Italy

unsmiling. His hand is raised in blessing, and He is clothed in rhythmic geometry, robes whose purpose, one gets the feeling, is to create a stylized panoply of lines, a cascading cadence of lights and darks in imitation of Romanesque sculpture and, by extension, Byzantine mosaics. His eyes are large, staring, but not hostile; in their depth they mirror a kind of pity. There are the usual adoring angels floating about, some of them in three-quarter view, difficult in a style that seems to want to insist on painting's literal flatness.

Up and down the nave are scenes from the Testaments which, despite their two-dimensional approach, still manage to convey their messages realistically, and seem as pertinent as a modern newspaper. The good Samaritan is there helping the wounded traveller. Christ befriends the adultress, He looking kind, coaxing, as though persuading her to a better life, she distrustful and hesitant. Her accusers huddle together in attitudes suggesting both frustration and shame—one of them in the front even looks a bit conniving, as though planning to keep the incident in mind for future reference. Christ heals the blind, and raises Lazarus from the coffin, while the attendants hold their noses against the odour of decomposition—a touch of realism so accurate as to be almost offensive. For in spite of the stylistic manner of these paintings—the rhythmic lines rather than three-dimensional folds, the flat backgrounds devoid of scenic effects, the two-dimensional quality of the figures them-selves—techniques meant to create a hierarchical, out-of-this-world aura, they can be at the same time stunningly realistic. That was the way with the Middle Ages. Everyone knew the stories. The figures they prayed to, the Christ and the saints they worshipped may have been unapproachable in that they were not of this world, but they had been flesh and blood and they had therefore suffered the same limitations as the rest of us. It was later that these same figures were raised to heights of rarefication so unrealistic that they became all but unapproachable on any level.

On the upper nave wall we see Christ riding into Jerusalem, while His

Condemnation of Christ, S. Angelo in Formis

future tormentors lay their clothes in His path and a boy waves a palm from the heights of a tree. The ass on which the Saviour rides is the most lifelike thing about the painting (limited, however, by the fact that the front quarters look more like the usual rendition of a costume donkey). Christ gathers with His apostles for the Last Supper around a strangely tilt-topped table so that we can have a good view of all the utensils thereon—good story-telling. After the dinner He ties on a makeshift apron and washes His apostles' feet. In the Garden of Gethsemane Judas administers the famous kiss while a dalmatic-attired priest watches. There is a graphic violence about this scene: swords, pikes and gestures of the struggle. And yet the composition—an interesting combination of Byzantine and Western styles—somehow distances us from the action. An unfrightened Christ is derided and finally made to carry His cross to Calvary, where He is crucified. An interesting touch: while Pilate washes his hands of the blood of this just person he seems to look after Christ who is moving away in company with Simon of Cyrene, watching the receding figure longingly, almost wistfully. We read into art what we choose to read; but it does seem clear that the artists saw Pilate sympathetically, perhaps as a politician unable to stand up to his responsibilities and filled with regret at the realization of the injustice he has been party to—or perhaps simply of his own ineptitude. (A more charitable view of Pilate than the Western Church is accustomed to is not unknown in other parts of the world. While Western Christians hold him responsible for the condemnation of Jesus, the Ethiopian Church regards him as blessed.)

The crucifixion scene, the ultimate sacrifice always so important in Christian dogma, is totally iconographic, a departure from the other biblical tales at Sant'Angelo in Formis. Christ is on the cross, yes, attended by the conventional mourning angels above and by John and Mary below. But He is erect, proud, alive, not at all the pathetically abused, slowly dying sacrifical victim of later works. And unlike other representations of Him at Sant'Angelo, this depiction shows just a trace of a smile about His mouth. It is a lovely concept of the greatest moment of the Christ story. The apostles and women of Jerusalem mourn, the soldiers haggle over His robe, all heaven laments, and yet there He hangs, erect, living—and smiling.

Solomon and David, royal in their Eastern-inspired robes, display scrolls telling of their predictions of Christ's coming to earth. Other prophets, simply attired as befits their stations, behave similarly. Noah builds his ark, and Cain commits the first fratricide; and Saint Pantaleone, boneless and unprotesting, is rolled down an abstract hill on a wheel to his martyrdom. (He was finally beheaded, thus, presumably, enabling some anonymous devotee to collect the miraculous blood-milk on display at Ravello.)

On the west wall of the basilica, as was the convention of the day, Gods sits in awesome majesty, judging, dividing the damned from the elect, while angels trumpet the Day of Wrath. 'The most remarkable representations of the Last Judgment occurred in Italy in the regions influenced by Byzantine art . . . But the earliest fresco of the subject is at S. Angelo in Formis . . .'[153] Here, as on hundreds of other Western walls, hell looks to be a more exciting place than heaven; artists can do only so much with prayerful attitudes and choir practice; the dark part of the mind knows no limits when it comes to the surreal.

The Benedictines in Italy had their competitors, among others the Basilian monks, who were more than tolerated—they were encouraged—by the Norman rulers of Sicily and Southern Italy. These followers of Eastern Orthodoxy adhered to the Rule of Saint Basil (fourth-century), whose teachings were familiar to, and admired by, Benedict. A stunning, little-frequented Basilian monastery was founded in the wilds of Calabria by Saint Bartholomew of Simeri.

Bartholomew was born in Calabria in the mid-eleventh century. At an early age he was already disenchanted by the world and became a disciple of a hermit named Cyril. He finally went off on his own—1,900 feet above the Calabrian coast near Rossano, where he built his first monastery in 1101, thanks in part to the backing of Great Count Roger. This monastery church still stands (*see page* 205), restored, silent and alone. The *signora* who produces the key to allow the occasional visitor into the church is a patient southern Italian, knowledgeable about the church, and resentful that more tourists do not find their way up the absolutely treacherous road to this remote spot of Basilian isolation. She argues rightly that the government displayed a staggering propensity for folly by spending large amounts of money to restore the church while leaving the perilously winding road—hairpin turns, unguarded drop-offs and axle-breaking pot-holes—so ill-kept as to discourage tourist traffic. At heart we cannot dispute the lady's logic. But how nice to have such a lovely old Norman-style church to ourselves! The view itself is enough to make the sceptic turn to God, and the *signora* enough to make one vow to write to the government tourist office.

It is a fine three-apsed, small-windowed church. Blind arches buttress the apses while adding a touch of vertical nobility. Inside the nave arches spring vertically from sturdy columns, spanning a floor which becomes almost giddily amusing with its mosaics of unicorns and centaurs and other fantasies not too unlike those of the cathedral floor at Otranto, and nearly as elaborate.

Bartholomew called his monastery Santa Maria Odigitria ('Holy Mary Who Knows the Way'), but it was later changed to Santa Maria di Patir, or simply the Patirion, meaning of the Father, a reference to Bartholomew. He must have been a remarkable man, associating with Pope Paschal II, and journeying to Constantinople to collect icons and books for his monastery and, incidentally, to meet Alexius and his Empress Irene. With the spread of his life-style after his death he is generally considered to have been the organizer of Basilian monasticism in Southern Italy. Bartholomew of Simeri died at Rossano on 19 August 1120.

When the Benedictines envisioned their abbey at Bury St Edmunds they had an Italian tradition of grandeur to fall back on. To the Norman, scale was bound up with grandeur and majesty, as well as tasteful, abstract decoration and balanced proportions. Bury St Edmunds would boast the most extensive nave, the most sweeping arches, the most noble height in East Anglia if not elsewhere. Certainly the number of monks housed in a given community as well as the number of the surrounding population dictated to an extent the size not only of the living quarters, but of the church itself. And Bury St Edmunds was an extremely popular pilgrimage centre.

Bury St Edmunds, England

Patirion, near Rossano, Italy

Harbour at Barfleur, France

*St Bartholomew
the Great, London*

Norman Gate, Bury St Edmunds, England

So Bury became by far the largest abbey church in East Anglia; its façade was more majestic than even nearby Ely Cathedral. In time it was overwhelmingly the most influential abbey in its quarter of England. For now, however, the monks who were hanging their fine new bell in the visible-for-miles central tower had no way of knowing that their glorious abbey was not destined to survive the Reformation, not being needed thereafter as a parish church. Today we see little more than a skeleton—a few columns, an arch or two, a broken crypt, a few inarticulate scraps of frescoes—the whole reduced to a municipal park of sweeping lawns, a fragrant rose garden, a tranquil picnic ground as quietly removed from the bustling city it centres as this particular working abbey was from its medieval lay community. (*See page* 205.) But what a skeleton it is! With the finished ashlar surface of the walls and columns long since dismantled, the rubble core—a kind of petrified marrow—takes on a soft look, curved rather than vertical, an architectural rib-cage. The flesh is gone; only the bones remain, rain-soaked and sun-dried, eroded by the leprosy of the elements augmented by the vandals who are always among us—who are us. Resembling some medieval Stonehenge, the ruins rise almost organically from the soil, the centre of worship of an all but forgotten saint. It is visual poetry, this noble wreck, but the poetry of a forgotten tongue—or no tongue at all—a silent symphony, breathtaking in a motionless, awful drama.

By contrast two virtually intact gateways remain which, through the fine quality of their ashlar surfaces, give us more than just an idea of what the abbey was in its heyday. The more interesting of the two is a magnificent Norman block of a gate, solid as the stone of its making. These masters of proportion here again showed their skill, sensitively balancing the negative window spaces of the upper tower with the more solid and heavily decorated power of the lower portion. The archway's gable points upward to a wall arcading that brings the attention to rest on the middle storey. Imagine the tower without that arcade—or without the three blind discs under each of the upper windows, for that matter—and you have just another ordinary tower, old perhaps, but not especially interesting. As it stands, with its gargoyles grimacing above, its wide entrance arch at ground level, and a superlative arrangement of openings and solids in between, it may well be the handsomest Norman relic in England, the more eloquent for the scanty ruins to which it leads. The other gateway, built after 1327, is more flamboyantly Perpendicular, so it has none of the sober majesty, the foursquare dignity of the Norman, which is known as the Tower of James. The abbot who put up the Norman gate did so in lieu of a pilgrimage to the shrine of Saint James of Compostella in Spain—one way of avoiding a disagreeable trip! Incidentally, it also acts as the belfry for the neighbouring church of Saint James.

The history of humanity's intrepid march toward the Bill of Rights, the Rights of Man and the United Nations is not uninvolved with the story of Bury St Edmunds. The chronicler Roger of Wendover records that in November 1214 the barons of King John Lackland met in the church, ostensibly in honour of the Feast of Saint Edmund, but instead held a secret meeting during which they swore on the high altar to force the detested king to grant them the liberties originally referred to in Henry I's coronation charter, or they would make war on him. This was a run-up to the famous sealing of Magna Carta a year later; hence the town's boasting self-designation 'the cradle of the law'.

1108

King Philip I of France, who died on 29 July, was not likely to be missed in the political field, except perhaps in retrospect by Henry I whose enterprises in Normandy had benefited from his lack of energy. He was succeeded by his son Louis VI—brother-in-law of Bohemund of Antioch—at twenty-seven, already a seasoned military campaigner and cynically hardened. As his nickname, 'the Fat', suggests, he had an inordinate appetite for food and drink; but he was also devoted to physical exercise. His good relations with the Church are attested by his chief minister and biographer, Abbot Suger of Saint Denis: 'And so the famous youth Louis, jolly, gracious, and benevolent, to such an extent that he was considered simple by some, now an adult, illustrious, and zealous defender of the paternal kingdom, looked out for the needs of the churches, and, what had not been done for a long time, strove for the security of the clergy, the workers, and the poor . . .'[154] In spite of this contemporary evaluation and compliments from modern historians, Louis VI 'was as gross as his father . . . a sensualist . . . an avaricious man . . . He let himself be bought . . . [He] trafficked in justice . . . [and] sold his support to the side which bid the higher'.[155] Inherited enemy Henry I of England would find that he had met his match!

The year that saw the accession of Louis VI to the French throne saw the final shattering of Bohemund de Hauteville's dream of empire when he was obliged to go down on his knees to acknowledge the Byzantine Emperor Alexius as overlord of Antioch. The end was inevitable.

Bohemund had been almost too successful in his last attempt to gather sufficient manpower to move against Alexius. By 9 October of the previous year he had already landed his troops, perhaps exaggeratedly estimated at 34,000, on the eastern coast of the Adriatic. His eyes were on Durazzo, still, as in his father's day, the main barrier on the road to Constantinople. With his usual optimism he anticipated no tough resistance from the Greeks defending the city; and once they were out of the way the route east would be clear. But by September of this year—one year after landing—Bohemund was still bogged down outside the walls of Durazzo, the road to his dreams blocked by the Greek army, and the way back home cut off by the Greek navy augmented by sympathetic Venetians. His own troops were diseased; famine had taken its toll. He had no choice but to appeal to the emperor, and accept his claims.

Bohemund was like a mighty tree that had been felled. A towering presence in a forest of mediocrity, he had been singled out, admired and envied. Now here he was, cut down to size by a man punier than himself, stripped of dignity and, as he saw it, his reason for being. To return to Antioch under the conditions laid down would be to disintegrate slowly, to become a virtual nonentity, remembered but no longer admired—and certainly not envied. Instead he chose to return to his roots in the heel of Italy, a sulking, pathetic man. There had been something grand about his and his father's dream. But that was all in the past. For now there was but a short time left, only three years as a matter of fact. Bohemund remained in Southern Italy with his wife and two sons, the second destined to rule over Antioch as Bohemund II. His successors were to govern that eastern outpost until 1287 (ninety-three years beyond the demise of the Norman dynasty in Sicily), when Bohemund VII died without issue. Even then the last Bohemund was ruling over a distinctly tattered principality, since the Mamelukes had taken the city of Antioch twenty-one years earlier.

1110

With all the elaborate fanfare, the trains of personal effects and gifts, the armed guards and courtiers that befitted a future empress, Princess Matilda, the eight-year old daughter of Henry I of England, was sent to Germany as the betrothed of King Henry V, the aspiring (but not crowned until 1111) Holy Roman Emperor. The marriage did not take place for another four years. The intiative for the betrothal probably came from Henry V, but it was still a magnificent coup on the part of the king of England. Now, destined to be empress, Matilda provided one more feather in her father's cap—better, a jewel in his crown. Prestige is important to kings, emperors, popes and presidents —more important to them, if the truth were known, than to their subjects and constituents—and there is no doubt that the Anglo-Norman monarchy was enhanced by the proposed union of the two houses. It was by manoeuvres such as this, along with a marvellously efficient system of collecting taxes, that the English Norman kings, like their countrymen in Sicily, became the most powerful rulers in Western Europe, as well as the wealthiest. Henry V did less well out of the union. Matilda gave him no heir, and although she herself became heir to her father's possessions on the death of her brother in 1120, Emperor Henry V did not live long enough to take advantage of the circumstance. In fact, Henry's reign, like that of his father, was mainly characterized by a series of quarrels with the inflexible Pope Paschal II over the ubiquitous problems of investiture. That cause of strife was finally laid to rest with the Concordat of Worms of 1122 when compromise was reached between Henry V and the new pope, Calixtus II, but only after the customary abductions, the placing of an antipope in the chair of Saint Peter, the crowning and *re*-crowning and excommuncation of the emperor. After the turmoil of generations Europe must have heaved a collective sigh of relief, if not of boredom!

1111

It must have been with a feeling akin to deliverance that both Anna Comnena and her father Emperor Alexius heard of Bohemund's death. His last years had not been easy ones, even at fifty-three chafing as he was for the more active life, and apparently suffering the strains of paranoia. By odd coincidence Bohemund's death had been preceded, just a week or so

Tomb of Bohemund, Canosa, Italy

before, by that of his hated half-brother Roger Borsa. Roger was laid to rest in Salerno Cathedral, where his sarcophagus still stands in the south aisle. He was succeeded by his son, the weak and listless William.

Bohemund was carried to his last resting place at Canosa di Puglia by his worshipping mother. Alberada should have derived some sort of perverse satisfaction out of the realization that her son had survived not only his undeserving, usurping half-brother, but also his conniving step-mother Sichelgaita, who had died in 1090 and been buried at Monte Cassino. The grieving mother built the tomb for her son against the south wall of the cathedral of San Sabinus, tucked away well below street level, somewhat of a curiosity, rather oriental in appearance (ironically appropriate for this frustrated would-be Eastern potentate) and closed by heavy bronze doors. The huge metal sheets, which squeak eerily when opened, are embossed with arabic ornamentations and eulogies. The right leaf is composed of four panels beautifully decorated with patterns and panegyrics, and so expertly assembled as almost to defy the eye to determine the seams. The left-hand leaf was made in one enormous slab, with the name of the caster—Roger of Melfi—clearly indicated on it.

Bohemund had been baptized Marco, but because his father had become enthralled by stories of a giant named Bohemund he was affectionately dubbed with the same name. And so his name remains in death, carved on the flat tombstone—small for such a big man!—in large block letters 'whose coarse magnificence still catches the breath, one word only: BOAMUN-

DUS'.[156] The tomb is not elegant, but it is simple, square, and surmounted by a dome. The inside is plain, with a potted aspidistra or two, and a few scattered, shrivelled orange peels. It is at once tawdry and powerful. The spots of light coming from above and the two small columns do nothing to lessen the starkness of the dank interior. And the word on the tomstone is 'pathetic in its inference that everyone would know who Bohemund was, which was once true, but now his name means nothing save to a few scholars and to the people of Canosa'.[157]

Saint Sabinus was a sixth-century bishop of Canosa, renowned for his charity and certain gifts of prophecy. The cathedral that bears his name is worth a visit for anyone interested in things Norman. There is a high pulpit dated about 1050, and a Norman nave lined with columns from classical ruins and topped by mismatching capitals, a not infrequent, sometimes charming, practice in those days of purloined building materials. There is a superbly interesting episcopal throne supported by two elephants, unusual even for so inventive a people as the Normans. Some claim that the cathedral was built by Bohemund, and this could be so since Canosa was one of his favourite haunts, a jumble of narrow twisting streets through which he liked to carouse. Certainly that would explain why Alberada chose this town instead of his home-base of Otranto to inter her son. But that is a problem we cannot solve. And the inscription on her own tomb (instructing the visitor who is seeking Bohemund to go to Canosa) does nothing to elucidate it.

1112

At seventeen years of age Roger II of Sicily achieved his majority and assumed the running of the government. In the summer he was officially knighted at Palermo. Receiving the accolade of the new knight, he looked every inch the coming ruler of consequence: tall and powerful of body, though not yet fully matured; his voice was loud and full, his gaze steady; his mouth displayed a firm line of tenaciousness; his hair was fair, but darker than that of his forebears—he was after all half Italian. He had left behind him the direct, simple style and manner of the Normans. He was, instead, more in tune with the flattery and ceremonial manners of the Eastern peoples who formed a large percentage of his subjects and court. From his early education he had 'learned the subtle craft of the long-civilised races, and his mind was fashioned to a tolerance which was as much the result of temperament as of policy'.[158] His subjects would find him a strong ruler, but not a fighter in the physical sense, a man who preferred diplomacy to armed struggle, political manipulation both open and surreptitious to ruinously expensive and endlessly repetitive military encounters. It is not that Roger II cowered from the use of military might; he simply preferred trying other ways first. When his magnates saw him walk from the old palace of the emirs in company with his mother after his knighting ceremony, they saw a fledgeling ruler of enormous potential, an audacious and imaginative young statesman, a Christian tolerant beyond most Christians of his day. He would need a period of breaking in. But by and large Sicily was in good hands—the best it would ever know.

Chapter Ten

. . . Thou, O Lord Jesus, shall bring down the highlooks of the proud,
Thou shalt tread under foot both lion and dragon.

Bernard of Clairvaux to Cardinal G .
In *Life and Works of Saint Bernard*. Translated by Eales

1113

King Baldwin I of Jerusalem (crowned on the death of his brother Godfrey in 1100) was short of funds. He was also short of a wife. In spite of the fact that in his youth he had dallied for a time in holy orders, his court had taken on none of the austere characteristics of that life-style. He had already cast aside his second wife, an attractive Armenian princess with a penchant for the muscular embraces of almost any stalwart male who came her way, including, as gossips had it, a band of Muslim pirates into whose clutches she had not reluctantly fallen. Eventually she was too much even for the generally free-thinking Baldwin, and was exiled from his court.

Word drifted down that Adelaide, dowager countess of Sicily, was also casting an eye about for a mate. She was newly freed from her work as guardian of her son Roger; and everyone knew that Sicily, and consequently Adelaide, was enormously wealthy. Baldwin was noticeably down-at-heel at the moment, the costs of maintaining forces in the face of steadily increasing Muslim hostility being what they were. Would it not be to everyone's advantage to effect a union between the two houses? Adelaide was singularly alluring with all that money, not to mention that she had behind her the power of an island people fairly bristling with a nascent passion for expansion. Both advantages outweighed the sobering facts that she was hardly of nubile age, and that Baldwin was still childless. Baldwin tendered his proposal to Roger, a proposal that made sense, especially the provision that Roger would inherit the kingdom of Jerusalem should no issue result from the marriage. Adelaide was granted an impressive dowry in addition to her own wealth, all of it more than sufficient to bail Baldwin out of his onerous financial troubles. So it was that Adelaide left Sicily in August with enough gold to fill the fleet of nine ships with which she travelled. The ship in which she herself sailed was splendidly decorated with gold that shone brightly in the sun. No visiting potentate had ever created so ostentatious an entry into the harbour of Acre. There were a few who judged her advent into the Holy Land as vulgar, but pragmatic fighting men realistically saw that no other nation could afford such wealth, vulgar or not. Baldwin's position was strengthened, which was precisely his intention. His reception of his redemptive bride was properly demonstrated with musicians, an obsequious court waiting to receive her, and lush carpets strewn in the royal path.

Within just five years Adelaide was back in Sicily, scorned by a husband who, with extraordinary facility, had disposed of her wealth and then, on grounds that she could not produce an heir for him, had convinced Pope Paschal II that their marriage should be annulled. Shame destroyed Adelaide. She had been duped; and so had Roger. It was only on demanding his divorce that Baldwin finally admitted that he had, in fact, neglected to divorce his Armenian princess who was now residing in Constantinople, 'where she found the permissiveness of the capital a good deal more to her taste'.[159] Adelaide died within a year. Roger was angry for his mother. But more, his own pride had been hurt. Jerusalem should have been his; now it had slipped beyond his grasp. And what was more, the act had been contrived with papal blessing! The treatment of his mother he would not forgive; the depriving him of the kingdom he had aspired to he could not forget.

By contrast, things were going well for Henry Beauclerc in England. His daughter was about to marry Emperor Henry V of Germany; his son William had already married Matilda of Anjou—a good marriage—and was maturing into his role as future king. The realm was about as peaceful as one could hope a Norman kingdom to be; Henry could afford to be generous. His young nephew, Stephen, had already been accepted as his favourite after William, and was now living in England as ward of the king. Stephen was the third son of William the Conqueror's daughter Adela, who had married Count Stephen of Blois, the defector from the siege of Antioch. (Apparently of stronger character than her husband, Adela had demanded that he clear his name of his infamous defection. He returned to the wars where he died a hero's death in 1102.) Son Stephen made no claims on the family wealth; he had bigger things in mind. It is likely that he was even educated to royal pretensions by his ambitious mother. For her part she entered a convent in 1109.

This year Henry, who had already knighted his young nephew, went so far as to grant him lands which had formerly been part of the estate of the count of Mortain who, misguidedly opting for the cause of Robert Curthose, had been captured at Tinchebrai, imprisoned and divested of his holdings. Stephen could feel comfortable with his new country, as well as in the realization that he was the royal pet. But at this time he entertained no delusions. Prince William was being groomed to wear the crown. One move on Stephen's part to demolish or in any way interfere that plan and his perquisites would vanish on the instant.

1115

This year marks the start of the public life of one of the most prominent of medieval reformers and saints, Bernard of Clairvaux. By this time Bernard had already been a monk at Cîteaux for two years, having joined that secluded life when he was twenty-two, and having taken with him an uncle, all of his brothers and most of his friends, all told some thirty well-to-do men of his neighbourhood near Dijon. Until Bernard and his eager friends and relatives arrived on its doorstep, Cîteaux was in tough straits; it was a joyful day when the abbey's enrolment swelled from seventeen or eighteen to nearly fifty! In an extremely short time a sort of enlistment fad was created, and soon Cîteaux was the mother house of a group of satellite houses all dedicated to the literal practice of Benedict's Rule—work, prayer and contemplation. Then, in 1115, Stephen Harding, the gentle abbot of Cîteaux, who had received his early monastic initiation at Sherborne Abbey in Dorset, dispatched Bernard with instructions to set up a new monastery at Clairvaux—the Valley of Light.

For years to come Saint Bernard was the most zealous and most active—as well as the loudest—of medieval reformers. Under his influence Cistercian houses sprouted up all over Western Europe, until people began to wonder whether the whole world was turning Cistercian. Within his lifetime this man came into conflict with most of the major figures strutting across the political and ecclesiastical stage. Convinced that his work was divinely inspired, he feared no-one. He insisted a monk's place was in the monastery, yet was himself constantly on the move for his principles. He focused the eyes of the world on the Cistercian order, which he saw as the one sure way to heaven.

Paul of Caen, a kinsman (some alleged the son) of the great Archbishop Lanfranc, had reason to be proud of his accomplishment. In 1077 he had taken over the derelict abbey of St Alban in the ancient Roman city of Verulamium, which had long fallen on hard times, largely abandoned and much looted for building materials. For half a century the abbots of the run-down monastery had been stockpiling materials, especially Roman bricks from the old city, with the intention of some day building a new abbey church. On assuming office, Paul of Caen immediately undertook the job, entrusting the work to the master, Robert the Mason, to whom, in appreciation, he made a grant of lands and a house in the city now called St Albans. And well he might have rewarded Robert, for he created one of the finest churches in England, finished around 1089, but not dedicated until 1115.

An interesting man in his own right, Paul of Caen was a zealous reformer, who plunged into the task of enforcing wrenching changes within the house whose governance he had inherited. He reformed the chants, making the brethren sing more innovative ones which were bridging the Channel from the Continent. He demanded that the laws of silence be strictly adhered to, and that the inmates' eating habits be simplified according to the Rule. (It would seem that St Albans had fallen on lax as well as hard times.) But more than anything else he is noted for rebuilding the entire abbey, not just the church— except for the bakehouse and the buttery, which he apparently found satis- factory. He was contemptuous of the former Saxon builders, calling them *rudes et idiotas*, but not above parsimoniously using some of their columns in the triforium of his south transept. Under Robert the Mason's direction and Paul's encouragement and patronage, St Albans Abbey rose proudly and sparklingly new, a worthy tribute to England's first martyr.

The Venerable Bede tells Alban's story in his *Ecclesiastical History of the English Nation*. During (or possibly before) the early fourth-century perse- cutions of Roman Emperor Diocletian, Alban was a pagan resident of Verulamium. Evidently an extremely impressionable man, he sheltered in his house a Christian priest, by whom he was in a few days converted to the new faith. With the arrival of a search party Alban changed clothes with the priest, thus allowing him to escape. In due course Alban was found out, tortured and sentenced to be beheaded. He was led outside the city, across the River Ver—which miraculously dried up to allow him to pass—then up a gentle slope, to 'a place adorned, or rather clothed with all kinds of flowers . . . worthy from its lovely appearance to be the scene of a martyr's suffering'.[160] When Alban prayed for a drink a spring burst forth at his feet. As though all of this were not sufficient to convert even the most antagonistic pagan, as the axe severed Alban's head the executioner's eyes dropped out! With such goings-on we can be sure that a church was built on the site of the execution which, Bede tells us, became a favourite pilgrimage centre where miracles occurred. In 793 Offa, king of Mercia, claimed to have discovered the relics of Alban and immediately established in place of the original memorial church a Benedictine monastery which after the Conquest became one of the most important religious houses in England. By contrast the city of Verulamium was reduced, over the years, to a park.

The church put up by Paul of Caen was patterned after William the Conqueror's St Étienne, but on a larger scale. Enormous portions of Paul's church are still visible both inside and out, and handsome they are with their white plaster walls and painted patterns overlaying Roman brick. Standing in the nave is to experience a 'crash' course in comparative art history, so distinctly Norman is the north side, and the south so clearly Gothic. The four giant arches supporting the central tower are Norman and the most note-worthy feature of the inside, while the same can be said for the tower itself from the outside, which is stridently Norman except for the battlements at the top. Though Paul may have curled a lip at his Saxon forerunners, their monolithic columns in the triforium are attractively used and are not incompatible with the Norman style, though some may find the bridge from Saxon to Gothic a bit difficult. The relics of Saint Alban were housed in a coffin which sat on a pedestal, part of which is still on display behind the high altar.

As a centre of learning St Albans was famous for its scriptorium and extensive library, which catered to and helped produce such noteworthy scholars and chroniclers as Roger of Wendover, and Matthew Paris his continuator, a prolific writer who was also a gifted artist and cartographer. Of the abbey buildings all have disappeared but the huge gatehouse, the size of it commensurate with the church, which is the second largest in England.

*Interior of
St Albans Abbey
Church, England*

Winchester alone exceeds it, and then by only six feet. (Winchester lays claim to having the longest nave—560 feet—of any medieval cathedral in Europe.) St Albans has many interesting houses, some of them centuries old.

1120

Henry I of England had educated his son William carefully, knowing from experience the catch-as-catch-can rigours of succession and the fickleness of his magnates. By any standard Henry was the picture of a successful ruler. He was secure on his throne; the succession was accounted for; the realm was at peace. He was a fortunate man. Had he been more inclined to philosophical and historical reading, he might have been familiar with Herodotus' *History*, a work from ancient Greece not unknown at this time. Thus he would have known of Solon's warning to the boastful Lydian king, Croesus: 'In every matter', Solon lectured the arrogant monarch, 'it behooves us to mark well the ending; for oftentimes God gives men a gleam of happiness, and then plunges them into ruin'.[161] So it was with Henry Beauclerc. His son William was 'destined to the succession . . . But God saw otherwise; for this illusion vanished into air, as an early day hastened him to his fate'.[162]

Henry, his family and court, had been to Normandy. He was determined to return to his island kingdom before the winter storms imprisoned him on the mainland until spring. Just before twilight on 25 November he set sail from Barfleur. William, 'who was now somewhat more than seventeen years of age, and, by his father's indulgence, possessed everything but the name of king, commanded another vessel to be prepared for himself . . .'[163]

William sent his young wife Matilda along with his father. When Henry's ship set sail the prince and his companions, who were still loading on shore, called out that they would soon catch up and indeed overtake it, since their vessel was of new and superior design. Even aware that the young were already well into their cups in anticipation of their return to England, but at the same time accustomed to Norman drinking habits, the king was not alarmed.

It was after dark when the young people launched their ship. (*See page 206.*) 'She flew swifter than the winged arrow, sweeping the rippling surface of the deep: but the carelessness of the intoxicated crew drove her on a rock, which rose above the waves not far from shore'.[164] The culprit may have been a rock called Quilleboeuf, which at ebb tide would have been very close to the surface, if not barely above it. Suddenly sobered, the crew and the young nobles worked together to save the ship. Some of the crew were washed overboard. A smaller boat was finally launched and the prince, as highest ranking person aboard, was taken into it. It was cast free of the wreck and would certainly have made it to shore had not William heard his illegitimate sister, the countess of Perche, calling to him not to leave her aboard the sinking vessel. 'Touched with pity, he ordered the boat to return to the ship, that he might rescue his sister; and thus the unhappy youth met his death through excess of affection: for the skiff, overcharged by the multitudes who leaped into her, sunk, and buried all indiscriminatingly in the deep. One rustic alone escaped; who, floating all night on the mast, related in the morning the dismal catastrophe. No ship was ever productive of so much misery to England . . .'[165] It is said that no one ever saw Henry Beauclerc smile again.

Unexpectedly widowed, William's young wife was returned to the abbey at Fontevrault, from which she had been taken to become his bride. And the chronicler Henry of Huntingdon fairly crowed in celebration of this latest manifestation of divine justice. William and his companions, he wrote, were jaded youths: 'all or most of them were said to have been tainted with the sin of sodomy. Behold the terrible vengeance of God! Sudden death swallowed them up unshriven, though there was no wind and the sea was calm'.[166] Only the previous January Henry had wrung from his barons an oath to uphold William's right of succession. He was left now absolutely disconsolate and unable to absorb himself in the work of the realm, which was carried on for a time by his chief minister, Roger, bishop of Salisbury.

1121

But even in his grief Henry could not long remain inactive. He was soon persuaded out of his lethargy, tempted in part by the prospects of taking a new wife (Matilda had died in 1118). More than anything Henry wanted a son to guarantee the continuation of his bloodline. His new bride, Adela of Louvain, was in every way a good and attentive wife, lovely and understanding; but she bore him no children. The situation seemed hopeless to him. He had Robert Curthose safely in prison (but a prisoner was always a potential risk); more seriously, Robert's son, William Clito, the last surviving descendant of the Conqueror in direct male line was waiting impatiently to press his claims on the crown. Then there was Stephen of Blois, also a grandson of William I, alerted by the death of the prince to new possibilities. And there were in addition, Henry's numerous illegitimate children of both sexes, perfectly willing to stir up a witches' brew of trouble should the succession not be assured within Henry's lifetime. Eventually Henry had to make what seemed to him the best arrangement he could.

In the spring of the year King Henry was on the move again, heading toward Wales and an Easter court at Berkeley Castle. He probably stopped off to visit Cirencester on his way, staying a night or two at the partially finished abbey which he had founded in 1117 and which was destined to become one of the wealthiest Augustinian houses in England during the Middle Ages. Or he may have stayed at the manor house there, near the source of the Thames, in a building whose original charter came from the Conqueror himself. But the prime motive for Henry's royal progress was the need to be seen, sparked not by idle vanity but by reasons of state.

Henry moved westwards in a slow, elaborate and colourful procession of ministers, secretaries, cooks, musicians and entertainers, knights with their horses and squires, a few bastard children, assorted soldiers and just plain court hangers-on. In progress over the rolling water-rich landscape of the realm, Henry could look with pride on the evidence he saw of a working feudal society, and with arrogance on the bent backs of his industrious subjects working the fields with their oxen. The peasants at this time of year would be tending the wheat or rye, oats or barley just then breaking ground, giving special attention to the latter which, in addition to being ground into meal for making bread, was converted into malt for beer. The Middle Ages were awash with beer, partly because so much food was salted for preservation. Beans were being planted, an important item in the diet of the poor. Such was the country through which Henry moved with his court—rolling hills, spectacular with flowering apples and cherries, mulberries, plums, crabapple-like medlars, and half-domesticated bullaces, budding forests and newly tilled fields—until he arrived in Gloucestershire.

The property that Henry was heading for at Berkeley—looking down on the Severn estuary and with a breathtaking view of Wales and its troublesome inhabitants—had once been owned by Earl Godwin, father of William the Conqueror's defeated rival, King Harold, who may have had some kind of small dwelling there. The castle occupying the site in Henry's time was not at all the one we know today, but rather a wooden structure old enough to have been listed in Domesday Book; we even know the name of the owner at that time—Roger, who took the name de Berkeley. For us the finest thing is the keep, started around 1117 and finished about 1153. It is a great solid structure, formidable in every sense of the word, entered by means of a most handsome Norman doorway opening on a staircase, rising, dramatically dark, to a second Norman entrance into the keep itself, infamous in history as the prison and execution site of the unfortunate King Edward II.

The murder of Edward is the most notorious historical event that has taken place at Berkeley, shameful in its rationale, despicable in its method. Edward's unpopular government was usurped by his treacherous wife Isabella, daughter of Philip the Fair of France, and her lover Roger Mortimer of Wigmore. After some months' imprisonment at Kenilworth, Edward was forced to renounce the throne in favour of his son Edward III. He was moved to Berkeley and subjected to deprivations in the hope that he would die of natural causes. Two attempted rescues were foiled; eventually it seemed clear that his continued existence was too dangerous for the new regime, and Mortimer suggested to Edward's gaolers the obvious remedy. It was soon rumoured that his death had been effected by a 'hoot brooche putte thro the secret place posterialle'—a method of leaving the corpse unmarked and also showing disgust at Edward's homosexual tendencies.

Berkeley Castle remains a residence of the descendants of the original twelfth-century owners, a record for this sort of thing, bettered only by the proprietors of Dunster Castle in Somerset who trace their lineage directly to the Domesday Book owners. It has about it, therefore, an aura of being 'lived in', hard to find in most ancient English homes. Perhaps the most splendid thing about Berkeley Castle is its setting. Seen from the extensive gardens in the lower meadow the rose-pink sandstone and iron-grey tufa of the building turns almost purple in the sunset, with the great walls softened by red valerian sprouting from the chinks. It is of Nature wrought, carved out of its site, a great fortress. 'Nature would seem to have taken back to herself the masses of stone reared seven-and-a-half centuries ago. The giant walls and mighty buttresses look as if they had been carved by wind and weather out of some solid rock-mass, rather than wrought by human handiwork'.[167]

1122

Poetry comes easily to Southern France, that warm land of green hills, flowers, rivers, vineyards and a most benevolent sun, a land of love, art and free-thinking intellectuals. Stretching from the placid, shimmering River Loire in the north to the towering, snowy Pyrenees in the south, Aquitaine is an area rarely matched for beauty, providing a landscape and climate especially conducive to the enjoyment of simple pleasures—a picnic by a lazy, quiet stream, a wave to a passing cyclist, a good natured mix-up over foreign currency with a garage attendant. There are the lovely coastal cities of La Rochelle, Royan and Bordeaux, the latter two intimately bound to the north-flowing River Garonne. Angoulême, Poitiers and Bourges, inland and thriving, all have their places in world history. Aquitaine has endured a complicated, sometimes wrenching, history, as intriguing as the names of some of it's leaders: Lupus, Pippin the Short, Waifer, Charles the Bold, Louis the Stammerer, William the Pious and Eblas the Bastard. One of the most interesting of its rulers was William IX, duke of Aquitaine and count of Poitou; and William was the grandfather of the most fascinating of them all—glamorous, feisty, intelligent Eleanor of Aquitaine, wife to two kings and mother of two, the most sought-after heiress of her time.

William IX had felt compelled to take an active part in the First Crusade, but on returning home was not readily amenable to further religious palaver. So when he found his wife Philippa engrossed in a new religious movement of untoward strictness he promptly became enamoured of another lass of less taxing inclinations. His new countess already had a daughter by a former marriage, a bright girl and a pretty one by the name of Anor. William had a son, the future William X; what better way to conserve the family fortune than to wed the two? It was from the union of Anor and young William that Eleanor was born in about 1122. She was named after her mother and called Alia-Anor—another Anor—which history has elided to Eleanor.

In his day William IX was labelled public enemy number one of chastity and female virtue, the founder of an 'abbey of debauchery', a gay dog, a deuce of a fellow, and a man who flaunted his masculine tastlessness to the embarrassment of all. More importantly, he is also considered to have been the first of the troubadours. Not overtly concerned with some dim future beyond this world, he brought into vogue a new vernacular poetry which in his compositions evidences his own libertine tendancies. If Eleanor was trained in any tradition at all, it should best be labelled liberal, growing up as she did listening to her grandfather's racy verses. At times he can be downright licentious in his unabashed pursuit of love, a pilgrim to sensuality devoid of spiritual implications:

> One happy morn in memory bless's
> We laid our foolish war to rest.
> She granted me her greatest treasure,
> Her love, her ring—joy beyond measure!
>   Oh, would to God I live so long
> To have my hands beneath her cloak![168]

The *doubles entendres* come thick and fast and must have been lurid in William's day. Yet we sense only William's delight in women, not his scorn; and though much of his poetry is obviously written for the appreciation of ribald male listeners, some of it gives hints of the coming *amour courtois*, and was clearly intended for mixed audiences. Such was the carefree, almost hedonistic intellectual heritage to which Eleanor of Aquitaine would fall heir.

Young Roger in Sicily was growing into his situation. As his father had picked away at the inheritance of weak Roger Borsa, so now Roger II wrung concession after concession from Borsa's son William, who was beloved of his people but a poor ruler, weak, and at times incompetent to the point of inertia. Eventually Roger claimed all of Calabria and even those halves of Palermo and Messina which had remained ducal property since the time when the Guiscard and his brother had divided their conquests fifty-fifty. Already enjoying a lively trade with the eastern Mediterranean, Sicily could now claim both sides of the Straits of Messina, thus putting an end to pirating in the narrow channel and improving Roger's trade status throughout the vast sea. The fact that Roger was vassal to Duke William of Apulia was a mere technicality; on the basis of sheer landholdings he was infinitely wealthier and more powerful.

Never really much of a soldier, Roger invariably preferred to rely on diplomacy. But with at least some Norman blood coursing through his veins he felt the need now and then to emulate father Roger and uncle Robert Guiscard with a conquest or two. Expansion was what any true Norman needed to prove his worth, and this year an excuse (if one was needed) presented itself. In the summer a Saracen fleet from North Africa, aided by the Almoravid Muslims of Spain, attacked the coast of Calabria, particularly punishing the town of Nicotera on the Gulf of Gióia. This lovely coastal area was despoiled of what wealth it had, much of it being loaded aboard the waiting Muslim ships, the rest being simply destroyed. The woman were raped and a large part of the population dragged off into slavery. Roger leaped to the challenge. He assembled an expedition of three hundred ships, more than a thousand mounted knights and thirty thousand foot soldiers, if we can believe enemy reports. Because he was admittedly not the best of soldiers Roger delegated command of the Sicilian forces to a certain Admiral Christodulus. But it was the admiral's second-in-command, Lieutenant George of Antioch, who was destined to be the star of this unsuccessful venture against the Saracens, and whose name henceforth became most admired and feared in the entire Mediterranean world.

1123

The failure of the first expedition of revenge that Roger II launched against the Saracens of North Africa was unparalleled in the history of the southern Normans. His Sicilian land forces were thoroughly trounced while trying to take the Arab city of Mahdia, and while defending the temporarily conquered fortress of ad-Dimas. So far as his navy was concerned, of the three hundred ships that had sailed so confidently from Sicily only one hundred returned. It was a bitter pill for Count Roger to swallow, sweetened only by the knowledge that through the ill-fated mission he had gained a new champion, a man of dedicated loyalty, and peerless in his political and military abilities: George of Antioch. He was the new darling of Sicily, and was to be the first of a line of admirals who remained loyal to the Norman monarchy until the very day when it fell to the German emperor in the closing decade of the century. Despite being only second-in-command against the Saracens on a mission that was a fiasco, George received the accolades.

George had been born in Antioch, probably sometime around 1090, of Greek parents named Michael and Theodula. Both he and his father found their way into the service of the sultan of Mahdia; in time he was promoted to the position of financial administrator, a job that not only made him skilled in finance and the Arabic language, but also gave him a working knowledge of all the Mediterranean trade routes and an insight into the inherent weaknesses of the Muslim states. When the rule of Mahdia changed hands following the death of the sultan, George turned his eyes elsewhere. And where would an up-and-coming young (he was only around eighteen by now) genius turn in the first years of the twelfth century but to Sicily? Certainly language would be no problem to him; he already spoke Greek and Arabic—he could learn Norman French.

On disembarking at Palermo George discovered a country poised on the brink of a golden age. The year of his landing was 1108, four years before Roger II took the government into his own hands. Later in the same century an Arab traveller from Spain, usually known to us as Ibn Jubayr, was to wax unashamedly rhapsodic, reporting Sicily as 'an island having many towns, cultivated places and hamlets . . . The prosperity of the island surpasses description. It is enough to say that it is a daughter of Spain in the extent of its cultivation, in the luxuriance of its harvests, and in its well-being, having an abundance of varied produce, and fruits of every kind and species'.[169] This assessment was later endorsed by Roger II's close friend and advisor, the scholar Edrisi (Abu Abdullah Muhammad al-Edrisi), who wrote of caravanserai, baths, gardens, 'all the pleasures and all the comforts of life; a flourishing commerce, an industrious population, fertile corn-fields . . .'[170] It was a country rich in vineyards and timber—stone-pines, cedars, cypresses and towering palms—almonds, apples and every kind of citrus, fig and fish. At the piers of Trapani George saw the sloppily rigged fishing boats with brightly coloured sails, not unlike those of the north coast of Africa. Enormous nets festooned the docks, hanging there to be dried and repaired. To this day Trapani is the centre of the island's tuna fishing industry, the fisherman putting out their nets—sometimes three miles long—called *isole* (islands) under the direction of a master fisher known by the Arab-derived name of *il rais*—boss.

The teeming streets of Palermo were strangely familiar to George of Antioch. Dressed as he was in the Arab long robe, multicoloured and full, he fitted unobtrusively into the Palermitan street traffic. Ibn Jubayr reports that the natives affected Arabic dress, especially the women with their rouge and perfumes, their heavy gold jewellery, and elegant gowns. On their feet they wore gilt boots. The peasants, of course, wore simple tunics and clogs but, newcomer that he was, George had no eye for any of that. The market-places he strolled through were very much as they are today—animated and shrill, filled with Moorish sounds and the cries of vendors similar to those he had heard in Al Kahira (Cairo). He saw pyramids of oranges and lemons, racks of figs, olives of all kinds, celery, fennel and artichokes. The inns adjacent to the markets and the stalls presented mouth-watering displays of foods both Eastern and Western, and sometimes a combination of both. By the time he set foot ashore George was no doubt pining for a good grilled lamb or a stew, or perhaps a complicated couscous. The Berbers of North Africa invented this dish, made with meat and vegetables with yoghurt, and sometimes sweetened. The Sicilian couscous is made with fish, and presumably was in George's time, which must have been a bit of a jolt to him.[171] Clams steamed in olive oil seasoned with garlic and parsley would have appealed to George of Antioch, had he been able to resist the smoky perfume of shrimps cooking over open grills. But newly arrived from Arab lands, George craved sweets more than anything else; and the streets of Palermo were gaudy with baroquely designed sweets guaranteed to bring to joyous flower even the most deadened taste-buds. And the pasta! This very ancient food was much in evidence—Edrisi attests that the macaroni was excellent. Even in pasta the Italian and Muslim cultures merged. 'An indubitable survival is represented by that national dish the *maccheroni alle sarde*, so truly mediaeval in its complication and the com-bination of opposites in the sauce, or dressing, which consists of chopped onions fried in butter, with broccoli, salt anchovies, currants and fresh sardines. The macaroni is served in a flat dish gorgeously coloured on top with saffron, sometimes patterned in red with tomatoes, and garnished with fried sardines arranged like the spokes of a wheel',[172] all of which tastes a good deal better than one would think from the sound of it.

Not long after touching ground at Palermo, George of Antioch presented himself at the palace, tall and broad-shouldered, the very picture of a Greek gentleman of standing, with dark hair, steady black eyes and an aquiline nose—and speaking perfect Arabic. He knew he was bound to impress; and his self-confidence was justified, for he was taken into service on sight. In time he came to Roger's appreciative attention, and was eventually appointed second-in-command for the first attack on the Saracens of North Africa, giving that ill-fated mission its only meagre success through his superior knowledge of the Tunisian coast.

A man named Rahere enters our history, briefly, and concerning only a single work—but what a work it is! Strange that neither William of Malmesbury or Henry of Huntingdon even mentions his name. There are two legends about him—that he was jester to the king, and that he was a noted musician—neither of them supported by documentary evidence. Still we have some sketchy facts about his life, pitifully little considering that he was responsible for building the finest Norman church in London.

Around 1120, Rahere, who was probably a cleric, though one with a reputation for partying and general high living while still holding a prebend at St Paul's, had felt called upon to make a pilgrimage to Rome. According to some sources he had been especially moved by the tragically premature death of the English heir apparent in the disaster at Barfleur and decided that it was better late than never for a change in his own life-style. His early fifteenth-century tomb in the church of St Bartholomew the Great in London shows him gowned as a canon, tonsured, average in height, not handsome but of pleasant appearance, thin—almost gaunt—the kind of person who might be given to both levity and austerity. While making the rounds of Rome's pilgrimage spots—the catacombs, the martyrdom sites, Santa Maria in Trastevere—Rahere visited the church of San Bartolommeo on Tiber Island.

Well within the area of the ancient city, Tiber Island has long associations with the healing arts, an important detail in Rahere's story, and is not without miraculous origins. During a plague in the year 291 BC a Roman embassy was sent to the shrine of Asclepius at Epidaurus in southern Greece to procure there a statue of that god of healing. The returning ship bearing the image was just sliding up to its dock at Rome when a large serpent was seen to slither off its deck and swim to the small island, an incident immediately recognized as a divine indication that a temple should be erected there; serpents were sacred to Asclepius for, by annually renewing their skins, they were considered mysteriously related to the art of healing. (Asclepius is usually represented as carrying a staff enwrapped by two serpents—the caduceus, symbol of the modern medical profession.) In further commemoration, a part of the island at about water level was constructed into the shape of a ship's prow, which can still be seen there. But it must be sought out by going to the left of the church of San Bartolommeo and following the steps down to the embankment. No expense was spared in building the Temple of Aesculapius (as he was called in Rome), with expansive protective colonnades where the sick could spend the night, just as they did at Epidaurus, in hopes of a curing visit from the god. In time the island became a centre of temple worship of various kinds, but that of Aesculapius was always the most popular. It was not until the eleventh century that a Christian church was erected on the island, when German Emperor Otto III (he died in 1002 at the ripe old age of twenty-two) built one on the site of Aesculapius' temple. He dedicated it to an old friend of his, Saint Adalbert, bishop of Prague, who was martyred by the Prussians in 997. Otto also deposited in his new church some relics of the apostle Saint Bartholomew.

It was while Rahere was praying over these relics that he was stricken with a devastating attack of malaria. Tossing in his bed, sweating profusely, crying out in alternating attacks of fever and chills, he thought he was dying. In sudden panic he screamed an oath that, should God grant him renewed life, he would return to England and build a hospital to provide succour for the poor. He recovered and set out for home. But that is not the end of his story. While resting along the way he had a vision of Saint Bartholomew who commanded him also to build a church. Rahere was good to his sworn word and to the instructions of the saint. On his arrival in London he set himself to establishing the hospital and church of St Bartholomew the Great, in a suburb known as Smedfield (Anglo-Saxon Smoedfeld: modern Smithfield), the earliest hospital in Britain and the oldest parish church in London.

The church was served by Augustinian canons, of whom Rahere was the prior. Apart from its hospital activities the priory's most important secular function seems to have been the yearly cloth fair held in its churchyard. St Bartholomew's has always been involved in the lives of the common people.

The hall for the butchers' guild was built in Bartholomew Close, and the priory church still serves as the church of the Worshipful Company of Butchers. But the history of St Bartholomew's has not been all roses. The Lady Chapel was used as a fringe factory as recently as 1885, actually spilling over into the apse of the church itself. Prior to that it was used as a printing office where American polymath Benjamin Franklin served an apprenticeship. Worse than either of these two desecrations, the north transept was leased in the seventeenth century to a blacksmith whose hammer and anvil could be heard with annoying clarity in the church. And then—supreme abomination! —towards the end of the last century the cloister was turned into a stable!

Of all London's churches St Bartholomew's is the most Norman. (*See page* 206.) What we see there (except for the fourteenth-century Lady Chapel and the upper storey of the church proper) is mostly Rahere's, but not the entire original building by a long shot. Large portions of its 310-feet length were demolished during and after Henry VIII's dissolution of the religious houses. It is still enormous, however, and of a nobility unknown to more frivolous architectural styles. For in St Bartholomew's there is none of the airiness of Gothic, none of the melodic counterpoint of Baroque and Rococo; it is straightforward, direct as the stone from which it is made, a grand statement of belief, the Great C Major Symphony of Norman architecture. Like that final symphony of Franz Schubert it is dual in nature, coldly sombre and yet comforting. It is as though the designer of St Bartholomew's church had 'learned everything from God', just as Schubert's school conductor felt the young composer had done. The church rises out of the earth—not from, but *out* of—slowly, solidly. Heavy it may be, but not crushingly so; solid but not rigid. Of the soil, it is by heaven inspired, utterly beautiful and susceptible to no change—and deserving infinite contemplation. It is as characteristic of Norman blood as are the chevron patterns and fine proportions, the round-arched triforium openings and their handsomely decorated mouldings. No light ever fell on columns more stoical, no shadows ever hid the undersides of arches more noble, no decorations ever dispensed a joy more subtle. In sur-roundings like these it is a treat to see and hear the Sunday morning service, the processional and recessional of the choir, red–robed and justifiably famous. For the church should be seen in use, with music resounding through its vast spaces. It was an act of faith that built it; it is belief that maintains it.

The exterior of the church resembles that of the White Tower—the black flint walls accented by white ashlar at the corners and around the arches, with emphases of black and white chequered patterns. One enters the churchyard from the west, by means of a gatehouse which marks the western extremity of the original church, and then through the yard to approach the south aisle door. Inigo Jones was christened at 'St Bart's' in 1573, and the church register (Number 4) relates that 'William Hogarth was borne in Bartholomew Closte next door to Mr Downinges the printers, November ye 10th 1697 and was baptized ye 28th November 1697', in the font which is still in the great church. (Hogarth was later a governor of St Bartholomew's Hospital to which he gave two of his own murals—'The Pool of Bethesda' and 'The Good Samaritan'.) The original central tower probably disappeared in the severe earthquake of 1382, after having already been struck by lightning in 1264.

1125

Henry of England was suffering restless nights. From the look of things William Clito, son of the still imprisoned Robert Curthose, might well come to be the next occupant of the throne, exactly the situation most abhorrent to the king. (Had he been able to see into the future Henry would have slept more soundly on this issue at least. William Clito, the man with the strongest claim to the English throne, was to die just three years later, in 1128, of wounds suffered in battle, thus clearing the way, as Henry thought, for his own direct line to be maintained.) Intellectually and physically Henry laboured mightily to rebuild the grand design for his succession; but nothing seemed to work; no suggestion by his advisors was acceptable, no amorous dalliance with his wife Adela seemed potent enough to produce an heir. Then, without warning, good luck descended upon the royal head as though poured from a divinely manipulated cornucopia: Henry learned that his son-in-law, Emperor Henry V, was dead. Matilda, still a young woman, was a widow, attractive, aristocratically tall, fair skinned, and an empress. Henry suddenly saw a way out. Perhaps it would be best to call her back to England. She could provide a grandson-heir—or could she? As of yet there was no evidence that she could.

1126

Apparently enjoying her role as dowager empress, Matilda resisted her father's summons. She was nearly twenty-five years old now and one of the most unlikeable women in English history. True, it could not have been easy seeing herself as no more than a political pawn, but in that role she was no different from most of the other well-bred young women of her day. She may have had reason for the petulance that seemed to come so naturally to her, but she was also headstrong and demanding, totally out of sympathy with any cause that she did not understand or that did not benefit her directly. She would be involved in controversy for the rest of her life. When she finally did her father's bidding, she 'brought back three things from Germany: the richly jeweled crown she had worn, the [alleged] sword of Tristan, and the most imperious temper that ever plunged a nation into conflict'.[173] She was, in short, the model *par excellence* of Chartier's *La Belle Dame sans Merci*.

Matilda eventually joined her father in Normandy, and they reached England at Michaelmas (29 September). Her residence with the king and queen (her stepmother) must have generated a domestic situation about as comfortable as that of Guiscard, Sichelgaita and Bohemund! Immediately Henry showed his hand when, 'by the king's command, all the nobles of England and Normandy swore fealty to her, [including] Stephen . . . son of Adela, the king's sister . . .'[174] By this time Stephen must have had in mind an eventual grab for the throne. He had as good a claim as William Clito could muster, except that William's was a shade firmer in that his relationship to the mighty Conqueror was through the male line. And in the practical sense Stephen's was better than Matilda's; on the basis of her sex alone he could anticipate with relish the difficulties she would have trying to manage the barons. Normans never worried about fighting among themselves, and Stephen was no doubt confident that he could successfully take on his cousins. The words of his oath to uphold Matilda must have caught in his throat though; his actions in years to come were to indicate that they had.

1127

With his eye out for a new—and this time a potent—son-in-law, Henry next pulled off a truly remarkable coup by marrying his daughter to Geoffrey, count of Anjou. It was a political triumph, since it effectively weaned Anjou away from the French orbit where, because of family ties, it had circled happily for generations. But even as irritable tempered as she was, one can hardly blame Matilda for seeing this new development as a disaster, and one to which she would not take willingly. She had, after all, been an empress for eleven years, living in a glittering, wealthy court whose traditions extended back to the days of Charlemagne. She outranked all the queens of Europe. Even now, no longer the wife of an emperor and married to a mere count, she insisted on being addressed as 'Empress', as she did for the rest of her life. And apart from the disparagement involved in so lowly a union, Matilda also suffered the annoyance of suddenly finding herself married to—well, a boy, barely fifteen years old! Never mind that he was already marvellously handsome—even at his age he was being called *le Bel*—cutting (according to legend) a romantically dashing figure as he sported a sprig of *planta genista* (broom) atop his helmet. The nickname Plantagenet may have arisen, however, because he planted a lot of broom to provide coverts for game. Whatever its origin, the name has been applied, in general, by historians to the longest ruling dynasty of England (although Geoffrey's son Henry II and grandsons Richard I and John are usually called Angevins, and rulers during the fifteenth century Lancastrians or Yorkists). The first known use of the name was by Richard, duke of York (father of the kings Edward IV and Richard III) in 1450.

It was in this same year that Henry granted to Archbishop William of Corbeil of Canterbury the castle at Rochester 'in perpetuity'. The charter, which still survives, empowered the archbishop to add to Gundulf's original 'a fortification or tower within the castle and keep and hold it forever'. The chronicler Gervase of Canterbury notes that Archbishop William built a 'noble tower'.

The great keep, or donjon, is always the dominant feature of any Norman castle, being the military strongpoint and place of last refuge as well as the general living-quarters. At Rochester Castle (*see page* 239), a seemingly impenetrable fortress housing luxurious accommodation, these functional ideas are carried to the ultimate, at least within the framework of the Norman Romanesque style. There is something imperious—even challenging—about the blocky 125-feet height of Rochester keep, invulnerable on its knoll and secure in its bailey, defending the old Roman road which still served as the main link between Dover and London. Here, just in the castle's shadow, is the junction of the River Medway with the Thames; heavily trafficked, it needed a bully's protection. Rochester keep is the tallest in England, as though built to

*Interior
Rochester Castle,
England*

express the importance of its defensive role; this staggering statistic is best appreciated by standing at its base and looking upwards. Built chiefly of Kentish ragstone, rougher looking for the smooth-cut ashlar dressings and quoins shipped from Caen, the soaring walls lend a mottled ruggedness to the overall effect, a texture implying that the building is as durable as the stone itself. It seems a great, square-carved natural rock, pierced in strangely ordered rows by openings to allow its inhabitants an occasional view of the brighter, less secure world outside.

At ground level Archbishop William's keep measures seventy feet square, and sits on a splayed plinth which increases its measurements accordingly. The outside walls are twelve feet thick at base, narrowing to ten at the top. There is a basement, and above that three residential floors, the second being the main living area, higher-ceilinged than the others and boasting a gallery achieved by incorporating two storeys into one. Above is a third floor, only slightly less lavish than the one below. The joist holes for the beams to support the wooden floors are clearly visible, and a number of the living and storage rooms are incorporated within the thickness of the exterior walls. All the stages had windows, those on the lower floor smaller for security reasons, those above becoming increasingly large, handsome and ornamental. From top to bottom the keep is divided by a cross-wall which, at the luxurious second storey, is pierced by elaborately decorated arches. The cross-wall has a well shaft running through all three floors. Archbishop William understood the meaning of the word luxury; his keep is one of the earliest that has efficient fireplaces on every floor, round-arched, chevron-decorated and each one large enough to house a small crowd.

The 'perpetuity' of Henry's charter to William of Corbeil lasted short of a century as it turned out. Rochester Castle remained in ecclesiastical control until 1215, when it was held by rebels against King John and he successfully laid siege to it. But it proved a hard nut to crack. Despite five massive stone-throwing machines, John failed to breach the walls, and he at length realized that he must resort to a sapping operation. An area was dug out beneath the southeast tower and parts of the foundation removed, to be replaced by timbers. The king wrote to the justiciar, urgently requesting 'forty of the fattest bacon pigs of the sort least good for eating to bring fire beneath the tower'. They were, if results prove the point, fat indeed, for the burning fat ignited the timbers and brought the tower crashing to earth. This disaster, combined with the ravages of starvation, finally caused surrender.

During the next twenty years considerable expenditure of money was made in an effort to restore the battered fortress. The fallen tower was replaced, this time by a more up-to-date round tower, defensively more efficient because there were no corners to tempt would-be sappers; also, siege missiles tended to glance off the curved surface. In 1264, during the Barons' War between Henry III and a group of his disloyal magnates, such severe damage was inflicted that the castle was allowed to rot uattended for another century. Even Nature seemed in league with the destroyers when a 'great wind' did its share. Not until that prodigious builder, Edward III, decided to restore it, between 1367 and 1370, was the castle put back on a functioning basis. The Peasants' Revolt of 1381 brought further harm to the venerable pile, which was once again repaired by Richard II. From then on its history was more or less downhill, with the castle falling steadily into a derelict condition through neglect. In the eighteenth century plans were afoot to turn it into an army barracks, which proved uneconomical, 'for it was clearly less well adapted to keeping soldiers in than keeping them out'.[175]

In the south Duke William of Apulia died, opening the way for Roger II to claim all of Southern Italy. He had a reasonable claim since William had no heir of his own and, always in dire need of cash, had in return for a subsidy in 1125 declared Roger his sole heir. It was a foregone conclusion that Roger's claim on Apulia would be contested, but opposition or no, William's death left him the most powerful—and the most wealthy—figure in Italy. What Roger had not anticipated, however, was that William had left several 'sole heirs' to his realm, among them Bohemund II of Antioch. Most of these could be casually brushed aside, but the pope, suzerain of all of Southern Italy and desperately anxious to prevent a Norman unification, could not be so easily dismissed. On hearing of his cousin's demise Roger wasted no time. He sailed against Salerno, intent on claiming the duchy as his due. Although at first entry was denied him, by patient negotiation he took the city in a near-bloodless coup ten days after his arrival there, and forthwith called himself duke of Apulia. Amalfi immediately submitted to his authority; but he still needed papal recognition, a thing not readily forthcoming. Honorius II (pope since 1124) had already forbidden him to take the position of duke. Roger marched on Benevento, perhaps hoping to win it over, but found the pope holding court there. So, surprising everyone, he left the 'siege' in charge of local magnates, instructing them to keep the papal troops at bay while he, Roger, made a progress through his domain.

It was a triumphal procession through territory new to Roger, but important in the story of his family, from its beginning at Monte Sant'Angelo high on the Gargano Peninsula, and including the fields of Civitate and Cannae, the cities of Barletta, Trani and Bari, all places where Norman history had been made, where blood had been shed, where treaties had been sworn and oaths broken. All these places he claimed as his own. Sitting tall astride his charger he cut a figure both demanding and benevolent. He knew his strength and, once they had seen him, so did his people. Young, handsome, not so blondly Viking-looking as his predecessors—a plus as far as Southern Italians were concerned—he dispensed the largess of his presence throughout Apulia. His subjects looked on him and smiled, then waved, and finally cheered. Everywhere in Apulia he was fêted and honoured, kowtowed to and given promises of loyalty. Before winter had set in he was safely back in his palace in Palermo. Let the pope and his shakily aligned allies fight sentiment like that! Roger seemed to have the upper hand, though he knew as well as anyone else that when the chips were down he could count neither on the barons, nor on the villagers—fair weather friends all!

But Pope Honorius remained steadily hostile. Because he knew his history of the papacy, and of the role the Normans had played in it, his best bet was to stay as friendly as possible with them. Yet the last thing he needed was a powerful, stubborn, headstrong Norman duke, more powerful than all of his quarrelsome compatriots put together, right on his southern doorstep.

1128

Midsummer occasioned one of the most monumental face-downs of the Middle Ages. The scene: Southern Italy, a spot on the Bradano River southwest of Matera. Southern Italy had witnessed the breakdown of will-power in stronger men that the pope. It had seen other armies turned back, exhausted by heat and defeated by the terrible humidity, if not by the diseases endemic in the area. The papal armies were camped on one side of the river, Roger and his troops—two thousand knights and fifteen hundred archers according to some—on the other. Honorius had planned to crush Roger, but clearly he had underestimated the young man's determination, if not his power. Neither made the first move: the pope perhaps out of fear, knowing he could not count on a scratch army of dissident Normans he had managed to bind insecurely together, Roger out of preference. After a month's stand-off,

Ponte Leproso,
Benevento, Italy

the pope, clearly in trouble with his own cohorts who were already bickering among themselves, saw the hopelessness of his situation and sent word that he was ready to negotiate, aware that it meant his ultimate defeat. Roger's domain was going to be enlarged; and there was simply nothing Honorious could do about it. Better to cater to this ambitious southerner now; someday he might need Norman help, as his predecessors had in the past.

A negotiation site was set up in the papal city of Benevento. After three days of conferences accord was reached. There followed an altercation that almost doomed the agreement. Stubborn as only a man with Hauteville blood in his veins could be and reminiscent of the Guiscard's behaviour towards Gregory VII in 1073, Roger refused to allow his investiture as duke of Apulia to take place on papal territory, fearing the symbolic interpretation that might later be made from it. The antagonists finally agreed to meet outside the city walls on the neutral Leproso Bridge, which probably got its name from a nearby leper refuge.

Twenty thousand torch-bearing spectators made a stirring backdrop when, after dark, the two men walked from opposite sides of the Sabato River, followed by their attendants, the one group robed and glittering with gold and jewels, bearing crosses and censers, the other more simply attired in the gear of fighting men, carrying lances and girded with swords. The brige, spanning the river on handsome, round Roman arches, slopes upwards towards the centre. An engineering marvel in ancient days when, bearing the Via Appia, it formed part of that road's junction with the Via Latina and the Via Traiana, and had seen its share of historical action. But for sheer drama nothing in its past could equal this moment when Roger, at the apex of the bridge, placed his hands in those of the pope, the customary gesture of homage, swore fealty, and was invested by Honorious with the duchies of Apulia, Calabria and Sicily. Roger emerged from the meeting one of the most powerful of European rulers. He was only thirty-two years old.

It is both pleasant and intriguing to visualize the impossible, to imagine the celebration enjoyed that night by Roger and his men. One would hope that he gave more than a nodding salute to his *buona strega*—his good witch who had watched over him and pulled him through these last perilous months. Even from ancient days Benevento has been involved in affairs of witchcraft; and if Roger's witch was anywhere at all she would have been there. Had it been invented by his day Roger would certainly have toasted his witch with a goblet of *Liquore Strega*, that delicious, highly intoxicating speciality of the city of Benevento.

Troia Cathedral, Italy

1129

It is a fact that even while the new Duke Roger was being invested at Benevento his domains were already in revolt. So in the spring of 1129 Roger crossed the Straits of Messina and once again careered through Southern Italy, with an impressive army, while his fleet of sixty ships under the new emir, George of Antioch, bottled up the port of Bari. By the end of summer all the southern cities had succumbed to Roger, except for Troia, beautifully perched on its foothill to the Apennines. Like its namesake of Greek history-myth, Troia put all its bravado behind stout fortress walls (erected against the Normans just over a century before by the unappreciated and long-forgotten Greek, Basil Boioannes). Its citizens did not maintain their defiant posture long after suffering the indignity of being betrayed by their leader, self-seeking Rainulf of Alife, who was married to a half-sister of Roger.

Had Roger chosen to enter Troia at this time—and, having other things on his mind, he almost certainly did not—the citizens would have proudly escorted him to their gorgeous new cathedral, which is predictably Apulian Romanesque, but with a difference: it happily combines northern Pisan influences with that basic style. The cathedral of Pisa, most famous for its leaning bell-tower, had been finished now for eight years. Already influences had spread southwards; an example is the circular and diamond-shaped decoration under the blind arches of the lower storeys at Troia. There are delightful Saracenic motifs at work here, too, especially in the magnificent rose window of the western façade, the real glory of Troia. The most delicately pierced stone-work, unsymmetrically balanced and so satisfyingly complete, creates a pattern of lace-like intricacy worthy of the best Muslim sculptor. The whole upper façade is an astonishing creation, complex, ornate, with bulls and lions and a bestiary of medieval fantasies so logical in form as to seem almost organic—a flowering, a dazzling climax growing out of the sturdy support of the lower section. Rarely have blind arcades been used to such advantage as here, lined up to support the higher magnificence, which is carried on bluntly round Romanesque arches unencumbered by superfluous decoration.

As though the rose window were not enough, the cathedral boasts yet another masterpiece, an enormous western bronze double door (*see page* 239). The giant bronze slabs are by the hand of the Oderisius of Benevento, and were apparently cast in that nearby city in 1119. Oderisius employed the niello technique, that very Byzantine inlaying of silver, lead and copper in a bronze backing as outlines for figures, allowing full expression in these bronze pictures, as well as in the door pulls and assorted reliefs which, in their ornateness, seem a compatible accompaniment to the polychrome upper storey.

All the majesty of Troia Cathedral is not spent on the exterior. It carries to the inside, now restored to its original form from the sinful excesses of Baroque remodellers. As a result there is not much decoration to distract the eye from the basic architectural form. What Troia offers is a subtle majesty, a dignity, enough ornamentation—but not a surfeit, and mainly on nave columns—to balance the plainness, along with the usual Norman mastery and tender expression of space. Even the hordes of shrill little street boys who congregate around every visitor cannot destroy the solemnity of the vast interior.

The boys see you coming. They simply materialize, humorously mal-evolent angels of the back streets and alleys of this attractively medieval town. They would have you believe that they are experienced guides, knowledgeable historians, advisors on places to eat (slim pickings in Troia!)—veritable tourist agents all. It takes enormous courage to stand against these good-natured young *furbi*—con artists in the literal sense. They will chant you through the narrow, sometimes stepped, medieval streets and cobbled piazzas, all the way to the top of the 1,450-feet hill which their city crowns. If cities may be likened to crowns then surely the cathedral represents Troia's topmost jewel, its star—and maybe the shrilly chanting gang of kids its devilishly angelic choir!

1130

On the death of Honorious II Rome was again caught in the turmoils of papal schism. Anacletus II, like Gregory VII a Pierleoni and therefore of partly Jewish origin, was pitted against the more liberal Innocent II, both of them having been chosen by obviously uncanonical elections, and both of them putting forth questionable claims. Innocent rallied most of Europe to his cause, including a fulminating Bernard of Clairvaux, while Anacletus found only one source of support, but a good one: Roger of Sicily. By going against the grain of Europe Roger knew precisely what he was doing. He saw a kingship in his future. An inveterate politician, Roger backed the claims of Anacletus, to the horror and outrage of the rest of Europe's rulers, not to mention the anathematic denunciations of Bernard. Recognizing a friend when he saw one, Anacletus dutifully performed a tit-for-tat favour by issuing a papal bull from Benevento on 27 September, granting to Roger and his heirs the royal crown of Apulia, Calabria and Sicily, an investiture which was immediatly ratified by Roger's barons. Roger had his throne—and on it he would remain. Even the eventual failure of Anacletus to become the generally accepted pope could not take from him what he had been given.

The crowning of Roger II was accomplished with a maximum of fanfare in Palermo Cathedral. His barons were all there that Christmas Day, along

Cappella dell'Incoronata, Palermo

with their retainers, as well as representatives from both the Latin and Greek churches and notables from almost every nation. He was anointed by a cardinal, and crowned by Robert of Capua, the newest member of his camp and his leading vassal. The ceremony was performed amid incredible pomp, the actual crowning taking place in the north chapel known as Santa Maria l'Incoronata.

Heavily crowned with gold and precious stones, robed in rich gold-edged brocade and shimmering with jewels enough to rival the most sumptuous Byzantine mosaic and dazzle the assembled court, with sceptre in hand and looking from head to toe a king, Roger was escorted out of the chapel to the adjacent Loggia dell'Incoronata—a kind of royal exhibiton stand, still there though much fallen on hard times—where he acknowledged the acclamation of his people. For the first time in their long, turbulent and tragic history the Sicilians could salute a king of their own. Staring up at their bejewelled monarch, they sensed their new identity. Were they not now citizens of the third largest kingdom in Europe? And was not their kingdom the wealthiest of them all? The strongest? The Normans might not be the most appealing of breeds, but they had brought Sicily to this happy situation, easier to accept in that Roger seemed so unlike his Norman ancestors. He was the picture of a Mediterranean prince, but tall and robust, with graceful Oriental overtones in his manner and personality—a genuine child of a rich Sicilian heritage.

Roger rode slowly through the streets of Palermo, the most exotic city of Europe, now even more so, festooned as it was with flowers and brilliant hangings. The parade seemed endless to the ecstatic onlookers, with its musicians, its lively prancing steeds resplendent in blindingly polished gold and silver harnesses, and bearing knights in gleaming armour sitting erect in their saddles, proud of their part in the proceedings but not above a suggestive wink or silent whistle at certain members of the cheering throng. At the palace Roger, garbed in the jewelled manner of a Byzantine emperor—that old dream of empire was a long time dying—entertained his magnates and visitors lavishly, with rich foods both Eastern and European, with music and dancing. Roger's contemporary biographer, Alexander of Telese, records that the palace floors were covered with sumptuous carpets, that all the dishes and cups were of pure gold, and all the servants clad in silk. It is no wonder that in time Roger came to be thought of as having been crowned by Christ himself, as depicted in a mosaic in George of Antioch's church of the Martorana (see 1143).

Short-lived though it might prove in the end, the kingdom that Roger had brought into existence on this Christmas Day was to show itself the most enlightened of the Middle Ages, the most civilized amalgamation of races and cultures, and aesthetically the richest, most productive and most enduring in appeal. Henry of England, Lothair of Germany, and Louis VI of France, all relatively secure on their thrones, were backwoods reactionaries compared to Roger, and the son and grandson who were to succeed him. This new dynasty would create in its Mediterranean kingdom a model for the future, a height—more, an apex—to which later ages could but aspire. Yet it is a singular fact that few people of the twentieth century even know that the Normans were in Italy and Sicily, much less that they created one of the high points of Western civilization, certainly the greatest moment of that impoverished island.

Chapter Eleven

The world is perishing, growing old, and is failing.
The world has the laboured breathing of old age.

Saint Augustine

1131

Like so many prelates, popes and kings before him, Anacletus groped desperately through the dark corners of Europe for friends. But search as he might he could turn up only one: King Roger of Sicily. Anacletus had his throne all right, and the city of Rome. And that was about all he had. On the other hand, the rival and legitimate Innocent II had no territory or seat to call his own, but he did have friends to spare—almost everyone, it seemed, but Roger. Lothair II of Germany, not yet crowned emperor, was champing at the bit to get this papal schism over with so that he could properly receive his diadem, while the two candidates for the papacy continued to spar back and forth, both of them tiara-ed and over-costumed, undercutting here, slandering there, and pronouncing anathemas, excommunications and denunciations in all directions. And over-seeing all the confusion, and dogged in his persistence, was the emaciated-looking Bernard, trumpeting more loudly than ever his spare frame would imply. In truth Innocent had no better a case than Anacletus, but Europe united behind him, thanks largely to Bernard. Even standoffish Henry I of England took sides, flopping over to the majority view after meeting Innocent at Chartres, a parley engineered by Bernard who persuaded him to fly in the face of a long friendship with Anacletus, a former papal legate to the English court.

With an emir such as George of Antioch to help him fight his battles King Roger of Sicily was nearly unbeatable. However, while he was returning to his island after a successful punitive mission on the mainland it was Nature that almost did him in. Off the north coast of Sicily Roger's ship was harassed by a violent storm. Winds, rains and lashing waves damaged the boat sufficiently to alarm the royal passenger into swearing that should he be delivered from the wrath of the sea he would build a great church at the place where he touched shore. He made shore safely and, good to his word, immediately set to work on his cathedral of Cefalù, a glory of stone and mosaic and, if the truth is admitted, a political statement of turgid strength. Whether or not the story of the storm is true, the building of the new cathedral was certainly in accordance with Roger's policy of strengthening his alliance with the Church within his kingdom. He also further bound anti-Pope Anacletus II to himself by requesting the creation of the new bishopric.

Cefalù—Cephaloedium, named after the enormous rock which the Greeks saw as head-shaped and at whose feet the city huddles—was a thriving city. Both the Saracens and the Normans saw the defensive potential of the giant rock 'on whose large circular summit is a fortress, than which I have never seen any more formidable. They hold it in readiness for any sea attack that a fleet from the lands of the Muslims—may God render them victorious—might make upon them unawares'.[176]

For maximum impact Cefalù Cathedral should first be seen from afar and from the west. The eye should be allowed a leisurely wander across the curve of sandy beach, the fringe of green trees and semi-tropical growth, before obeying the imperious call of the jumble of walls and tile roofs that is augmented by the hunched backdrop of the towering rock from which the city gets its name. There, in the midst of the sun-yellowed city, rises Roger's cathedral. No Norman church stands more proudly beautiful than this, 'dominating the houses below as effortlessly as its sisters at Lincoln or Durham'.[177] For sure it has been tampered with over the years, but nothing can dull its lustre; it remains a high point of Norman art anywhere. Is it any wonder that Roger wanted it as his final resting place? He made plans to be buried there, causing two porphyry tombs to be placed in his new church. But again his motives seem to have been political: to enhance the new bishopric and to flaunt its glory in the face of the claims of Pope Innocent II and his supporters. And perhaps it was because political aims shift and political weapons alter, that Roger in the end did not lie at Cefalù but at Palermo.

As at Trani, one approaches Cefalù Cathedral from below, humbly, up a flight of stairs that rises from the piazza to the church level. One must look up to it. And this is fitting, for Roger's masterpiece stands as one of the most perfectly conceived churches in the world. Forget the later additions—the portico which was rebuilt by Ambrogio da Como in the fifteenth century, for example. Nothing can mar the dignity, the uncomplicated refinement, the tinge of elegance.

If the outside of Cefalù Cathedral is satisfying, then the inside is fulfilling (*see page* 240). Later accretions have overloaded the arches, oddly slender for Romanesque. But in this cathedral the main glory is not the columns but the mosaics. Their shimmering, anonymous glory makes us understand—as perhaps few other works of art can do—the *idea* of the Supreme Judge ensconced in His paradise which is literally out of this world. 'I am the light of the World' proclaims the book He is holding in His left hand, while

Cefalù, Sicily

His right—lest we despair altogether in the face of such majesty—is raised in a comforting gesture of blessing. He is not quite pure Byzantine; nor is He as Italian as some others. There is something unsympathetic about many Greek Pantocrators, untouchable, menacing. And the Italian Judge is so often cheerful, friendly, perhaps too understanding to be truly effective. This Christ means to rule; but He also wants to save. He means to judge; but He also pardons. He gives the Law; but He allows for interpretation. 'There is nothing soft or syrupy about him; yet the sorrow in his eyes, the openness of his embrace, even the two stray locks of hair blown gently across his forehead, bespeak his mercy and compassion'.[178]

Mary is there in an attitude of prayer, and for once we understand the reasonableness of the artist's showing the mother in that unnatural pose. The first four of the seven archangels are present, too—Michael (but of course!), Raphael, Gabriel and Uriel—their depiction ranking among the most accomplished products of the masters who worked in the cathedral shortly after the middle of the twelfth century. Decked out like Byzantine potentates, they are brilliantly attired and bejewelled, and inclining their heads gracefully in Mary's direction. Then there are divers saints, apostles and fathers of the Church, each one mosaically stiff, shimmering with a miraculous light. It is all quietly grand, dignified and, on prolonged contemplation, hypnotically beyond our material realm. We relate to this. We relate to these formal figures; their stiffness does not stand in the way of communication. Nor should it be confused with inflexibility. They are, quite simply, of another time—and certainly of another place. The Cefalù apse is a vision of heaven, a manifestation of divine order, a place of light.

Below the stunning mosaics are two thrones—one for the bishop and one for King Roger. Even though only the eastern end of the church up to the transepts was finished by the time of his death in 1154, it is fun to contemplate the pride Roger might have felt when, enthroned and the centre of mundanile adulation, he could contemplate with an upward glance the Divinity he had called into being. It is no wonder that he wished to lie, finally, basking in the warmth of that heavenly radiation of light!

As though to affirm another viable culture of Roger's day, there is preserved in the old quarter of Cefalù a Muslim *lavabo* or public laundry, where women still congregate to wash clothes and exchange gossip, and where children meet to exercise their amazing propensity for wasting time and boundless energy.

Saracen Lavabo, Cefalù

1132

The new year is barely under way before rumours have it that German King Lothair is preparing to march on Rome in an effort to end the papal schism and install Innocent II on his throne, in turn to be crowned emperor by him. Since Roger was the only European ruler to have supported Anacletus II, he found himself standing alone among his peers—and even among his mainland barons. Insurrections followed one after another. When Lothair entered Italy in August, Roger's barons increased the pressure on their new king, causing him to dart from one revolt to another as though he were fighting a series of brushfires. Worst blow of all was that Robert of Capua, Roger's vassal-in-chief, the man who had placed the crown on his head just two years before, was one of the leaders of these sporadic revolts.

Around this time—the dates are usually ambiguously given as 1100-36—the tiny church of San Nicolò at Sciacca was completed. The foundation for it had been established by Countess Judith, first wife of Roger I, who had died a young woman. It is a lovely church in a simple, direct way, with three eastern apses and the undecorated look we expect from a Norman building. It nestles against the hillside in a rather run-down area of Sciacca, dwarfed by the three- and four-storey apartment buildings surrounding it, not one of which deserves a second glance, such is the encompassing charm of their tiny neighbour. San Nicolò is very much a part of the noisy, active life that swirls about it. One is tempted to see it as an echo of Judith herself; we picture her as small—she was French, after all—and quiet, but very strong-willed. The recollection of the cruel winter of 1062-63 that she endured with Roger outside the walls of Troina is enough to convince anyone that she was indomitable, though not a Brunhilde like her sister-in-law, Sichelgaita. And that is the spirit of this little church: unassuming, low key, and yet as strong as the rugged blocks of which it is made.

Besides San Nicolò there is not much in Sciacca to attract the hedonistic-ally inclined twentieth-century tourist—some sixteenth-century walls and two ruined castles from roughly the same period. A convent now occupies the site of the former Saracen palace and boasts a painting of Roger I establishing the foundation. Some nearby Roman baths. And that is all.

At the instigation of Bernard of Clairvaux twelve Cistercian monks and an appointed abbot, William, set out for Yorkshire, where they established the first Cistercian house in northern England. (An earlier Cistercian house had been founded at Waverley in Surrey in 1128.) 'They set up their huts near Helmsley . . . by a powerful stream called the Rie in a broad valley stretching on either side. The name of their little settlement and of the place where it lies was derived from the name of the stream and the valley, Rievallis, Rievaulx'.[179] Before many years Rievaulx was in a position to establish daughter abbeys, in places such as Melrose and Dundrennan, both in Scotland.

More Gothic than Norman-Romanesque in appearance (*see page 241*), Rievaulx is magnificently situated on a westward slope that rises from the River Rye. Water, so fundamental to any settlement, was not supplied by the river though, but from a series of springs in the hillside, which flowed to a conduit house whence it was distributed by pipe to the different buildings of the abbey. There was a stone channel which carried the water under the refectory and the reredorter (latrine) to the river—all very practical.

Ailred, Rievaulx's third and most famous abbot, was in charge from 1147 until his death in 1167. Under him there may have been as many as one hundred and forty monks and at least five hundred lay brothers. Keeping the abbey in mind and with *The Life of Ailred of Rievaulx* by Walter Daniel in hand, we can form an accurate picture of the life of the typical Cistercian community. Walter, disciple of Ailred, tells us that he was of English stock, born at Hexham in Northumberland, and brought up at the court of Kind David of Scotland. He was a close companion to the king's son Henry and, one presumes, not unfamiliar with the courtly flesh-pots—even Walter Daniel delicately insinuates that Ailred may not have been a virgin. Walter Daniel described the life of the abbey. The habits of the 'white monks', he said, were made

> . . . from the pure fleece of the sheep. So named and garbed and gathered together like flocks of seagulls, they shine as they walk with the whiteness of snow. They venerate poverty, . . . are welded together by . . . firm bands of charity . . . The remnants of their former meal are dished up again, except that, instead of the two cooked dishes, fresh vegetables, if they are to be had, are served. When they rest on their beds, each of them lies alone and girdled, in habit and tunic in winter and summer. They have no personal property; they do not even walk together . . . Everything they do is at the motion of the prelate's nod and they are turned aside by a like direction. At table, in procession, at communion and in other liturgical observances all of them, small and great, young and old, wise and ignorant are subject to one law . . . Women, hawks and dogs, except those ready barkers used to drive away thieves from houses, do not enter the gates of their monastery. By their exceeding love they stifle among them the bane of impatience, and every growth of anger and the smoky emanations of pride.[180]

The Benedictine abbey of St Mary at York was one of the richest and most influential of the northern monasteries. Round about this time certain of the brethren, led by their prior, Richard, had become distressed that Abbot Geoffrey was too easygoing in his interpretation of the Rule of Saint Benedict, especially in matters of diet and dress. A crisis was reached when the archbishop of York was invited to visit. A riotous scene ensued, after which it was suggested that Richard and his adherents leave the abbey. The archbishop eventually granted Richard a tract of land on the River Skell. Richard was elected abbot, and the great Fountains Abbey was founded.

'Literally without a roof over their heads, cast into a place "fit rather to the lair of wild beasts than the house of human beings", the brethren sought the shelter of a large elm and knocked up a shack with a roof of turf. The archbishop provided bread, the Skell drinking water; apart from a mention of herbs and leaves, we hear of no other sustenance'.[181] Of water the brothers indeed had an abundance, there being half a dozen springs on the abbey property. Thus the place was called Fountains, 'where, at that time, and afterwards, so many drank of waters springing up to eternal life, as from the

Doors, Troia Cathedral, Italy

*Rochester Castle
Keep, England*

239

Interior Cefalù Cathedral, Sicily

*Rievaulx Abbey
Church, England*

Barletta Castle, Italy

241

Cardiff Castle, Wales

Castle Rising, England

Fountains Abbey, England

fountains of the Saviour'.[182] More than once the monks were tempted to give up, but time and time again luck moved their way. Bernard sent over an old hand at building and organizing. Riches and scholars moved in their direction. It was not long before Fountains was sending out daughter houses of its own.

Nowhere more so than at Fountains Abbey will you find a clearer picture of life in a rich and powerful medieval monastery. The church is there, simple enough to please even Bernard, but overshadowed by a tower which, contrary to the rules of an order that insisted on unobtrusive towers, soars 170 feet heavenward and is divided into four storeys. Saint Bernard notwithstanding, it is a handsome piece of architecture, vertically offering a welcome balance to the basic horizontal line of the rest of the abbey. Norman columns flank the nave of the church, but the arches between them are Gothic, early for England. The abbey rejoices in a comfortable marriage of the two styles, the Norman perhaps holding a slight edge with the weight of the side aisle round arches.

It is a ghost abbey, a skeleton structure, but the more eloquent for its ruination. The hum of Cistercian industry, the plaintive chant of the services, the soft, guarded laughter of the monks enjoying their brief periods of social relaxation no longer echo down the cloister corridors or filter through the restraining arches that now seem so singularly devoid of life. The living quarters are still there in stately ruins a downfall that began in 1540 when the church and cloisters were stripped of valuable materials and furniture. The monks' dormitory is unmistakable, as is the refectory with its row of washing places along the wall outside an uncharacteristically ornate doorway. There is the kitchen with its back-to-back fireplaces. What must have been a moderately comfortable visitors' quarter is located just off the end of a solid, but graceful twelfth-century bridge. There are a mill, an infirmary and latrines, the latter efficienctly located over running water. A warming room adds a nice touch, no doubt much needed between All Saints' Day and Good Friday, the only season when heat was allowed, and only in this one part of the community! The 125-feet square cloister reinforces the impression that Fountains was indeed a wealthy abbey, though this centre of communal life was not so large as that of some other contemporary Cistercian abbeys, such as Rievaulx or Byland. The singular, enormous *cellarium* (undercroft) three hundred feet long and with twenty-two bays is where the lay brothers ate, strolled and enjoyed a moment (but only a moment) of recreation. The size of this enclosure, which was beneath their sleeping quarters, is testament to the importance in the Cistercian Order of this particular element.

Situated so picturesquely in a greensward literally carved out of a forest, Fountains Abbey is the perfect objective manifestation of the Cistercian philosophy of work, prayer and reclusion. Isolated in north Yorkshire, the brothers would have no difficulty realizing one of Bernard's most insistent injunctions, *ama nesciri*, love to be unknown. But not all the brethren who found their way to the Cistercian abbeys remained as anonymous as Bernard would have liked. Some versions of old story books tell us of a monk from Fountains, a large man, notorious for his strength and for his skills as an archer. He is said to have fought the boldest outlaw of his day to a draw. The two became devoted companions, and their adventures have been read by millions through the centuries as the tales of Robin Hood and Friar Tuck.

The isolation that Bernard insisted upon could, at times, be awkward, by its very nature creating difficulties in a building programme already fraught with dangers. But it was not in architecture that the great Cistercian contributions were made, but rather in farm planning, agriculture and horse and cattle breeding. These monks were excellent land managers, knowledgeable in problems of irrigation, crop rotation, land clearance, husbandry and the marketing of their products. As they became more adept at management they acquired more lands, often by grant, which, because they were so large and so far removed from the abbey were leased out to tenant farmers. But their greatest wealth came to be in wool; the wildernesses in which their monasteries were established (or which were artificially created by the destruction of surrounding villages) became profitable sheep runs. The Cistercians contributed their entire wool yield for one year for the ransom of Richard I (*see* 1193).

1133

Throughout his reign Henry I maintained the active building programme inaugurated by his father; but Henry's buildings were better than William's in that more of them were made of stone. It was in this year that he established an Augustinian priory at Portchester near Portsmouth, and, probably in this same year also, a castle on the site. He had perhaps decided to refortify Portchester at the time of his struggles with Robert Curthose when troops supporting Robert landed nearby. Raids and invasions were commonplace at Portchester, where a fortress was first built by the Romans in the third century, one of a chain of forts around the southeast coast of Britain, an augmentation and support for the Channel fleet—the *Classis Britannica*. These forts extended in an unbroken line from Brancaster (Norfolk) in the north to Portchester on the south coast. Portchester is the only Roman fortress in Northern Europe whose walls still rise to their full original height—about twenty feet. More than that, of the twenty original semicircular towers that interrupted and guarded the walls, fourteen remain intact. It is no wonder that Henry, utilizing a ruin as only a good Norman could, built his strong keep there. He knew what he was doing. The work was half done for him before he even set foot in the place.

It is believed that a small Saxon community may have existed within the walls of the fort after the fifth-century Roman departure from Britain, and some historians maintain that these squatters built a church there which was destroyed by Viking raiding parties. But there is no physical evidence of this. The existing church that is there now was built in 1133 for the Augustinian canons, whom Henry installed. The Augustinians were a little late on the English scene, and never did enjoy the same political power and wealth as did the Benedictines. But for a while during the twelfth century they were much in vogue, sought after and patronized by monied families, which may have been part of their undoing—too many houses in competition with one another so that eventually very few survived with any degree of affluence. But they left their marks, and one of the finest in Hampshire is at Portchester.

The 'canons regular' were followers of the Rule of Saint Augustine of Hippo (who had formulated it to govern the life of the clergy of his household) and are differentiated from 'monks', who adhered to the teaching of Saint Benedict, and from 'friars' who principally followed Saint Francis and Saint Dominic, though the latter was avowed to the Rule of Augustine. Unlike the Benedictines, the canons regular geared themselves to the life of the pastor, believing that there was more to living than simply cloistering one's self away and praying for things to get better. The very fact that they were priests indicates this, since a priest's work deals with parishes and communities. They were following the example of Augustine of Hippo, who was not the kind to lock himself away in a cloister or raise himself atop a column in the desert. The Augustinian Rule was later made the basis of that of the Dominicans who, like other Friars, were dedicated to preaching, again an outward-looking activity.

The canons did not last long at Portchester. It was decided to strengthen the fortress there, and a house of active canons on the premises struck the authorities as being singularly inappropriate, or at least an embarrassment. They were moved inland to Southwick in 1145 and their church at Portchester was reduced to a simple parish church.

The church at Portchester is a small church, low, in keeping with the unostentatious life-style of the canons regular. The community buildings are gone now, but their joining with the south wall of the church can be clearly traced. Inside there are wall paintings of the sixteenth century, a Norman baptismal font, and some nice examples of twentieth-century stained glass. There is a Roman baby's coffin, a Norman piscina and a sampling of Elizabethan wood carving. But the overall effect remains low-key, quietly Norman, emphasized by the handsome Norman entrance.

Henry I was responsible also for a two-storey keep which rose menacingly in the opposite corner of the old Roman fort. Its walls are twelve feet

Portchester Castle, England

thick and the original entrance, following the Norman custom, was on the first floor, with a cellar at ground level below. The building was topped by a steep, angled roof, marks of which can still be seen. Henry's keep was enclosed within a second inner bailey which was entered by its own gate and draw-bridge, evidences of which are still there. Later builders added two more storeys, and Richard II converted it into a small but comfortable palace; un-fortunately much of his building is now in ruins. There are kitchens and gatehouses, however, which can be identified with little difficulty.

All in all Portchester is a fascinating ruin—one of the best in England—for its historical associations as much as anything else. It was, for example, a principal point of embarkation for Henry V's troops in his 1415 French campaign during which he won the Battle of Agincourt. It was used during the reign of Elizabeth I, and from the late seventeenth century was brought into service to house prisoners of war. During the Napoleonic Wars there were over four thousand men imprisoned within its confines.

With his realm at peace, with his building programme proceeding apace, Henry I felt that his cup of good fortune was full to the brim. Then suddenly, on 5 March, it ran over when daughter Empress Matilda gave birth to a son, the future Henry II, ruler of England and much of western France. Henry was to be followed by two more brothers, Geoffrey and William. 'When an inheritance was at stake it was desirable to have a quiverful of sons, for infant mortality was high and afflictions of adolescence frequently fatal'.[183] Mis-matched as the parents were, no one thought Henry's conception anything but close to the miraculous. Matilda had left Geoffrey (or he had demanded that she leave) several times, but succession-thinking Henry I always drove her back. With such an unpropitious start it was no wonder that Bernard of Clairvaux, on seeing the infant Henry, thrust him away 'with a melancholy air, predicting that he would come to an evil end'.[184]

But Henry and his descendants would have more to think about than the gloomy prophecy of a politics-dabbling monk. There was always that widely circulated story about the wife picked up by one of the early counts of Anjou, Mélusine, who was reputedly a witch. Common gossip had it that she seldom went to mass, and when she did she never stayed through the consecration, but would instead spring suddenly from her place just before that most sacred part of the service. Her husband, suspecting that something was amiss, utilized the help of four hefty men to force her to remain in her place for the duration. As befits any witch worthy of the name, Mélusine was cleverer than her beefy guards; she managed to fly out the window, leaving them red-faced and holding only her cloak, surrounded by an awe-stricken congregation and the unmistakable smell of brimstone in the air. Through the lifetimes of Henry II and his sons, allusions were made to this spectacular performance (certainly worthy of an Academy Award!). And it was not only outsiders and antagonists who made slighting comments. When Henry had become king and his sons were at odds with him and with one another over matters of power, succession, and just plain bloody-mindedness (which was much of the time) they attempted to excuse their family disloyalties as some mysterious streak planted in them by their eerie ancestress. Because of her intrusion into their bloodline, they said, they were doomed to strive against each other, brother against brother, sons against father. It was indeed fortunate that Henry I was unable to see into the future. So far as he was concerned this year all was well. His arranged marriage between Matilda and Geoffrey had paid off. His line was secure and he need have no further worry.

It was a successful year for Lothair of Germany, too. Things worked out as planned. He marched his troops across the Alps, then down the boot of Italy to Rome, where he installed Innocent II on his papal throne in the church of St John Lateran, choosing this church because the obstinate Anacletus still occupied the Vatican. Innocent immediately lived up to his part of the bargain and crowned Lothair emperor. Having accomplished his personal objectives, but not confident enough to take on Innocent's opponent, Roger of Sicily, the new emperor departed for his homeland forthwith, leaving a vaguely surprised and dangerously vulnerable Innocent quaking in his chair. He had reasons for his discomfort as it turned out. Within only a few months, he was forced to flee the city, leaving Anacletus once again in undisputed control. If there was any comfort at all for Innocent it was in the realization that he was not alone in his disillusionment; there was that bevy of Norman barons in Apulia who had hoped that Lothair would help them to throw off the yoke of their allegiance to Roger. As a prelude to the emperor's arrival some of the historically important cities of Apulia were already in open revolt against royal authority—among them Melfi, the first Norman capital, and Venosa, the place of the Hauteville family shrine.

More diplomat than soldier, and comfortable in his palace at Palermo, Roger sat out events. With the threat of imperial interference out of the way, Roger determined to move against his disloyal mainland barons. His superbly trained Saracens, a body of men whom he knew could not be subverted by smooth-talking barons and who entertained no fear of papal anathemas, started their campaign at Venosa, the centre of the Hauteville cult, a symbol not wasted on Roger's vassals. The Saracens fanned out from there to take in Barletta, Matera and finally Montepeloso, which was totally given over to the torch and sword. By 19 October when Roger set sail again for Palermo, Apulia was a smoking shambles, with every important city ravaged and its defences wrecked. The gods were not one hundred per cent with Roger, however. 'Twenty-three vessels laden with countless spoils and thousands of captives accompanied him; a storm rose in the night, and they went down with all their cargo.'[185] Roger may have thought that this was the end of his troubles with his barons, to a man every one of them more Norman than himself; but he was wrong. It would take him one more excursion to the mainland the following year before he finally brought Southern Italy to heel. In the meantime the area needed rebuilding.

When visiting Barletta—so tranquil, such a friendly place!—it is not easy to imagine that city being put to the torch. The cruel massacre that inevitably followed the successful siege, and the general turmoil, suffering and grief do not come easily to mind. While not catering to tourists with first-class appetites, it is a peaceful coastal town that offers adequate accommodation, a few good restaurants, and two nice beaches. There is interesting fare for the active sightseer, not the least being an ugly bronze statue thought to be of an Eastern emperor, stolen from Constantinople in the crusaders' rape of that city in 1204 and consigned to the waves of the Adriatic when its transporting galley sank off the coast. Rescued, it now stands forlornly, pointlessly and unattractively in front of the Gothic church of San Sepolcro on the busiest corner in Barletta, the Corso Vittorio Emanuele and the Corso Garibaldi—a sixteen-feet monument to imperial bad taste.

Barletta dates back to the third century BC, but never attained prominence until the Normans moved in. Like Trani's streets which are so reflective of the Middle Ages and seem to echo with the clashing sounds of departing crusaders, Barletta's labyrinthine alleys impart a feeling that by merely walking through them one is brushing cheek by jowl with stalwart pilgrims to the Holy Land, or sharing air and space with an arriving or departing merchant from the East. There are later eras represented at Barletta, too; the fourteenth-century Angevin period, for example. The Palazzo Bonelli was built in the age of Robert of Anjou, king of Naples, and is just as handsome now as it was then. Baroque palaces and churches add an ornate richness. And if one expects to find a castle in an Italian town it would naturally be in the centre of the medieval quarter: so it is at Barletta.

The massive *castello* (*see page* 241) squatting defensively on the edge of the Adriatic is largely the result of Hohenstaufen determination to protect their holdings, inherited when the direct Hauteville bloodline ran out. Built on a solid Norman foundation of stone, their castle is imposing and seemingly undefeatable, an impression due largely to the four solid, lance-shaped bulwarks at the corners, which were added three centuries after the cruelly ambitious Charles of Anjou had done his share of enlarging and strengthening between 1282 and 1290. There are stout walls, and staircases so sweeping as to satisfy the most swashbuckling twentieth-century romantic. A bridge still spans the moat, and there are dark rooms and dungeons enough to conjure the direst imaginings.

The cathedral of Barletta, Santa Maria Maggiore, stands a stone's throw away and, like that of Trani, has a *campanile* semi-attached by a wide arch to a front corner. The oldest part of the basilica dates from 1140, just a few years after Roger's destructive whirlwind rush through Apulia. Originally it had three apses, but these were modified in the fourteenth century to a polygonal apse with five radiating chapels. There is a mood of sobriety about Barletta Cathedral, a chill in the air, a sombreness in the shadows. If a musical-literary analogy is apt, there is nothing here of Palestrina or Pergolesi; nor of the elegantly simple lines of Bernard de Ventadour, who was by now just three years old and growing up in the French Limousin. No; this is a more richly resonant organum (a sung accompaniment to plainsong) by Perotinus, heavily melodic but not overbearing, unadornedly simple but never boring. Its very plainness has a sumptuous quality.

Legend says that Richard Lionheart contributed to the building of Santa Maria Maggiore, and there is a eulogy in medieval Latin to that crusader-king cut into the centre stone above the left doorway, which he is supposed to have donated. Inside the church, on a north aisle capital, there is a figure of a man in a boat and an unreadable inscription. The enthusiastic verger will insist that it is most certainly a representation of Richard, though it is not known that he ever set foot in Barletta.

Italian vergers—*sagrestani* seems so much healthier a word—have about them a special charm; and the verger at Barletta deserves an award beyond the usual smile, the muttered *grazie* and the few lire tip. This *sagrestano*, true to his breed, is never in evidence, especially when you feel genuine need of his presence. A search is usually called for, in this case via a side street to his lair off the end of the south transept. In all probability he will be found there chatting with his wife and indulging himself with *un espresso* and *un tramezzino* —one of those appetizing half-sandwiches of incredible flair, remember, which Italians concoct from such mouth-watering delectables as artichoke bottoms, mushrooms, thin sliced salami, pimientos, capers, mozzarella cheese, if not an occasional bit of gorgonzola. Introductions are performed, extra *espresso* brewed in a trice—*peccato!* there is no drink for the *bambini*. The slightest interest on the part of the tourist will elicit a stream of enthusiastic lore, much of it pure hearsay, but all of it interesting, about this moody old church. No matter that the building is closed for remodelling—that has been going on for years, apparently one of the longest remodelling jobs in history. The *signore* and his family must see inside. And have we seen the crypt? The old metal lamp? The soaring canopy? There is nothing in our time to touch the effusive hospitality of the southern Italian when he feels he has encountered a kindred spirit. Most tourists recognize with amused forbearance that guides, official and otherwise, dwell on matters which they have been led to believe the tourists want to hear, and say things to reinforce the travellers' preconceived fallacious notions. The Italians are the most sterling performers of this questionable art; but they do it with such verve, with such conviction and, when necessary, with such drama. 'Many see through the deception and yet applaud the adroitness of the performer. It takes a great man to do such things. Anybody can made an omelette with eggs. Only a genius can make one with-out'.[186] The *sagrestano* at Barletta is so in love with his church, so warm in his hospitality and so enthusiastic in his (sometimes) misinformation that he all but defies his listeners to leave the premises without the certainly that the figure in the boat up there is beyond doubt the English King Richard I. And should you entertain the vaguest doubt, you have the verger's word for it!

1134

'Woe to him who is not old enough to die!' wrote the most famous political prisoner of his age, Robert Curthose, in the Welsh language which he taught himself as he whiled away the monotonous hours of his long captivity. Cardiff Castle (*see page* 242) was his final place of detention, and when he died there this year he was around eighty years of age. His younger brother Henry was soon to follow him to the grave.

Robert was entombed in Gloucester Cathedral, where the fine Norman choir forms an expansive canopy for a handsome painted wood effigy representing him. As depicted he appears less good looking than he probably was, certainly younger than his eighty years, and with his legs crossed in the customary position symbolic of his role as a crusader—the one really successful role of his life. But even his part in regaining the sacred soil did not spare him the ultimate curse of contracting worms in his woodwork. On a last visit to Gloucester the writer was informed by a straightfaced, charming volunteer worker at the cathedral that Robert's effigy was not currently on exhibit. 'He became infested with worms and needed refurbishing'.

If ever there was a wasted life, Robert's must be a high contender. Talented, intelligent, a winning personality and courageous, he was defeated not so much by the forces of life or by identifiable antagonists as by his own impetuosity, pettishness, lack of imagination and loyalty. And while he could not blame himself for having a brother as calculating, patient, expedient and vindictive as Henry, he was himself responsible for having provoked Henry. He was no doubt chagrined, perhaps even shocked, by the pointless, boring and futile outcome of his life; but surely he was not surprised. After all, his father had predicted it on his deathbed. But then Robert had not heard him; he had not been there. He had been in France conspiring with the French king against his own dying father.

A wasted life is a tragedy, Robert's no more or less than any other. Even his final poem (it may well be genuine) smacks of tragedy. He could see an oak tree from his window at Cardiff; apparently it became a symbol for himself— noble, yet rooted to a single earthly spot. For twenty-eight years he had been his brother's prisoner. Now his poetry sounds both sombre and angry.

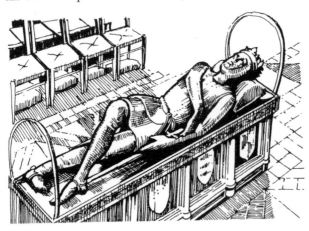

Effigy of Robert Curthose, Gloucester Cathedral, England

Oak that hast grown up on the grounds
Of the woody promontory fronting the contending waves of the
   Severn sea;
Woe! to him that is not old enough to die.

Oak that hast grown up in the storms
Amid dins, battles, and death;
Woe! to him that beholds what is not death.[187]

1135

'King Henry is dead!' mourns a chronicler of the times, 'the glory once, now the grief of the world. The Deities lament the death of their fellow divinity . . . England, who, springing from her cradle, had shown exalted on high beneath the sceptre of his divinity, now sinks in shade. She, with her king, Normandy, with her duke, waxes faint . . .'[188]

Both England and Normandy plunged into anarchy with the unexpected death, brought on by Henry's exercising the kingly right of gluttony: apparently he ate too many lampreys after a hunt in the Forest of Lyons near Gisors in the Norman Vexin. Henry may deserve some of the contemporary eulogies, many of them made more glowing and enthusiastic by the horrors of the period that followed his passing, but he can be faulted for being

> . . . one of the most repulsive among the kings who have reigned in England . . . His chief vices . . . were lust, avarice and cruelty, and while he shared these with many of his contemporaries, his methods of indulging them were his own . . . His cruelty was revolting. Though he cannot with certainty be convicted of fratricide, there is strong evidence that he connived at the murder of one brother, and he kept another in close confinement for nearly thirty years. He allowed two of his granddaughters to be blinded when they were hostages in his hands, and his punishments of malefactors was hideously savage . . . Henry was of course not isolated in his brutality, but he was perhaps exceptional in the false geniality with which it was cloaked.[189]

The Forest of Lyons is amber-lighted and shadowy, a chilly semi-wilderness of glorious beech trees extending for more than forty square miles. There is a fine twelfth to thirteenth-century ruin of a Cistercian abbey in a dense, wooded setting, and the market town of Lyons-la-Forêt, a tranquil village of half-timbered houses and usually empty streets, surrounded by a lush beech growth. Slow, meandering streams feed the rich forest, which was always a favourite hunting ground of Norman dukes and was in the twelfth century a good deal larger and denser than today. But it is still wild and appropriately sombre—easily acceptable as the stage for the last drama in the life of a king who, despite his personality, was kindly regarded by his people.

Henry was tired and cold when he returned from the hunt. The end of November is not the most salubrious of months in northern France, with biting winds, cold fogs and rains, early twilights and bleak skies that chill and depress. Scudding clouds seem only to accentuate the skeletal leaflessness of the trees, grotesquely twisted, some of them, by winds, and standing silhouette-black in the grey atmosphere of damp cold. But the hunt had been invigorating for the sixty-seven-year old king, a healthy escape from the pressing cares of government and a welcome change from the heated father-daughter arguments which were now so much a part of his life, 'sundry disagreements, which had their origin in various causes, between the king and the Count of Anjou [Geoffrey], and which were fomented by the arts of his daughter. These disputes irritated the king, and roused an ill feeling, which some have said resulted in a natural torpor, which was the cause of his death'.[190] So Henry's digestion at this point was probably not all that good. On top of that he had wanted to return to England before the onset of winter storms made the crossing unpleasant if not impossible. But after thirty-five years of ruling it became increasingly difficult for him to act assertively. So he 'continued in Normandy, though he often proposed to return to England, an intention which was never fulfilled'.[191]

Tonight was one time, however, when Henry could act with positive assurance. Braced as he was by the excitement of the hunt, and now as warm and dry as a rough hunting lodge would allow, he was mellowed with a couple of tankards of wine. One wonders, though, how medieval wine could mellow anyone if we can believe contemporary accounts of a liquid that verged on the poisonous: 'The wine is . . . sour or mouldy; thick, greasy, stale, flat, and smacking of pitch' wrote Peter of Blois of courtly tippling just a few years later. 'I have sometimes seen even great lords served with wine so muddy that a man must needs close his eyes and clench his teeth, wry-mouthed and shuddering, and filtering the stuff rather than drinking.'[192]

Henry demanded his favourite food; a platter of lampreys. A primitive, scaleless, eel-shaped fish, the lamprey is at best difficult to digest 'a source of most noxious humours, and a strong exciter of others of a kindred nature'.[193] Henry knew that they always disagreed with him. His physician had warned him against them. The feast, as prophesied, brought on the expected symptoms causing 'a sudden and extreme disturbance, under which his aged frame sunk into a deathly torpor; in the reaction against which, Nature in her struggles produced an acute fever, while endeavouring to throw off the oppressive load. But when all power of resistance failed, this great king died on the first of December . . .'[194]

In view of what followed his people had reason to mourn. In spite of the fact that he had been perpetually in need of larger amounts of money and therefore had been terribly oppressive in demanding fines and taxes, he had been liked. He had surrounded himself with good administrators, men as ruthless as he, and had run an efficient government. The twelfth century was not an easy one for heads of state, and the general lawlessness demanded stringent response. 'It is worth mentioning how severe Henry, king of England, was upon ill-doers. He caused nearly all the moneyers of the whole of England to be emasculated, and the right hands of those workers of iniquity to be cut off, because they had privily corrupted the coin.'[195] His sobriquet 'the Lion of Justice' was well-deserved.

Chapter Twelve

. . . The good seed has fallen into a good, nay, an excellent, soil; I hope in the Lord that it will take root, spring up, multiply, and bring forth fruit with patience.

Bernard of Clairvaux to King Roger, in the *Life and Works of Saint Bernard.*
Translated by Eales. Edited by Mabillon

1135

As careful as Henry I had been regarding the continuation of his line on the throne of England, he had not counted on the determination of his trusted favourite nephew, the likeable Stephen of Blois, to whom he had granted the county of Mortain almost thirty years before. The oath that Stephen had taken in company with the other barons of the realm in 1126 to uphold the claims of Matilda now stood for little. True grandson of William the Conqueror that he was, Stephen sprang into action at the news of Henry's death and sped across the Channel. Finding both Dover and Canterbury closed to him, he moved on to Winchester where he enlisted its bishop, his brother Henry of Blois, in his cause. The treasury was turned over to Stephen, allowing him to make the most pleasant discovery that Henry I had penuriously amassed a wealth far beyond anyone's expectations. Such resources would help swing the barons to Stephen's side, it always being advantageous to rally around the one with the cash. The leading churchmen held a conclave to debate Stephen's claims; and on 22 December, barely three weeks after the death of Henry I, Henry of Blois, Bishop Roger of Salisbury (Henry I's chancellor and chief administrator) and a small group of barons watched while 'William . . . archbishop of Canterbury, who had been the first to swear allegiance to the late king's daughter, consecrated, alas! the new king; wherefore, the Lord visited him with the same judgement which he had inflicted on him who struck Jeremiah, the great priest; he died within a year . . .'[196]

By swearing fealty to Stephen, and thereby repudiating their vows of 1126, the barons present committed a treachery similar to that of which William the Conqueror had accused King Harold Godwinson. In the doubtful event that any of them suffered pangs of guilt, Pope Innocent II eased their consciences by approving Stephen's accession. Stephen issued what had by then become a customary coronation promise to forswear the 'evil customs' of his predecessors. This charter was usefully vague, but it was not long before he began to make specific promises and concessions.

For the superstitious onlookers there were omens aplenty to give rise to uneasy feelings concerning the future of the realm. The benediction (according to some chroniclers the kiss of peace) was inadvertently omitted during the service; and it was noticed that the Communion Host suddenly disappeared. The future did not look propitious.

Stephen's principal weaknesses were lack of determination and aggressiveness. He was a charmer of the first water. Acclaimed by some as the handsomest man in Europe, he was tall, broad-shouldered and deep-chested. He was good-natured; people found it difficult to dislike him—except Matilda, naturally. Brave and honourable on the battlefield, he was gallant in court, and wealthy, with valuable fiefs both in England and Normandy. Through the gracious help of his trusting uncle, Henry I, he had married in 1125 the heiress of Count Eustace of Boulogne, yet another Matilda. (The student of history, perhaps confused by the incessant repetition of names—the countless Rogers, Roberts, Matildas—may be interested to note that after the Conquest the Normans demanded that names be chosen only from a list of about two hundred recognized saints.) Apart from her wealth, the new Matilda was of royalty descended, being the great-great-granddaughter of the English king, Edmund Ironside (died 1016), and the granddaughter of Malcolm III, king of the Scots. Stephen had everything going for him but his own indolence, and his voice, which was so weak that he is known to have delegated at least one rallying speech to a subordinate.

On the other hand Empress Matilda had nothing going for her except her father's designation. So far as the barons were concerned her temperament was reason enough for them to recant their oaths, but it was clear that their main complaint was one of sexual bias. But Matilda had yet another strike against her: the barons now considered her an Angevin. She was, after all, countess of Anjou. And Angevins were traditional enemies of Normans. In any case, quite apart from these disadvantages, Matilda was not in the right place at the right time. Stephen was not only in England but had been crowned king. As it turned out, however, Stephen failed to exploit his inital advantage. And for five years Geoffrey and Matilda on the other side of the Channel did little more than make minor raids into Normandy.

Sicily this year had its share of royal death with that of Queen Elvira. We know very little about this daughter of Alfonso VI of Castile, other than that she was married to Roger for eighteen years, bore him seven children, and that he was broken-hearted by her demise. It would seem that she had been a model of feminine piety. But the chroniclers are largely silent.

Roger's bereavement—'he shut himself up in his room for several days, and refused to see even his dearest friends' [197]—did not prevent him from firmly asserting his control over the kingdom. By the end of the year there was a Hauteville at the head of every important fief in Southern Italy: the king's eldest son, also a Roger, was duke of Apulia; second son Tancred was prince of Bari; and the third, Alfonso, was prince of Capua in place of the traitorous Prince Robert, who was even now in Naples fighting against the king's interests. It is obvious that Roger was girding himself to resist an expected invasion of his realm by Lothair of Germany.

1137

And he had good cause to do so. By 1136 Emperor Lothair had already crossed the Alps. Roger waited out the events in Palermo, living the most luxurious court life in Europe, enjoying his family and gardens. By doing absolutely nothing he was doing the right thing. He knew the history of German invasions of Southern Italy, all of them frustrated by the terrible summer heat, malaria, dysentery and, unless the enemies chose to remain in hostile lands over the cold winters, the frantic need to vanish back to their side of the Alps before snow closed the passes. Roger was counting on Lothair to learn from history. Roger had unlimited time; Lothair had not. Roger also had unlimited amounts of money which, at the proper time, could be distributed among the invading German soldiers.

Like every German emperor before him, Lothair still saw Southern Italy as his by imperial right. By February of this year he had reached Bologna. Persuaded by Pope Innocent II and Saint Bernard (who was convinced that Roger was the heart of the papal schism) many influential Italian cities swung over to support Lothair. With Anacletus still sitting in Rome, it remained extremely doubtful whether Innocent would ever get his throne back unless Anacletus' main support, Roger, could be eliminated. Better for Lothair to bypass Rome altogether, rid the world of Roger, and then watch the antipope's cause collapse for lack of support. So at Bologna Lothair divided his army, taking one half down the Adriatic coast himself. He proposed to meet in Bari the other half commanded by his son-in-law, Henry the Proud of Bavaria, who would move through the central and western side of the peninsula. All very well in the planning stage.

Lothair moved unhampered, aided in fact by some diversional activity by Pisa and Genoa who, like packs of hounds, hoped to get in on the kill. But Henry of Bavaria ran into unforeseen difficulties along the way, which were not helped by the obvious hostility which he and Innocent openly displayed for one another. Monte Cassino, wisely remaining loyal to the Normans—after all the abbey was situated in Norman territory—defied both papal and imperial orders by slamming the gates in the face of the conquering army. The monks did pay a small contribution in gold to encourage Henry's departure for his projected meeting with his father-in-law. Pausing only long enough to assert his mastery of Benevento, Henry joined Lothair in Bari in time for Whitsun. Lothair had arrived on schedule, having on his way thoroughly sacked Monte Sant'Angelo, the shrine of the Norman patron angel. A friend of the pope he may have been, but that did not prevent him from robbing the shrine of all its silver, gold, jewels and fine vestments. Whit Sunday, May 30, saw the reassembled German army in the basilica of San Nicola of Bari, piously hearing High Mass sung by the emperor's pope, Innocent II.

Even when the Pisan and Genoese fleets attacked Roger's mainland capital, Salerno, he did not move. Roger's appointed governor of Salerno—oddly enough an Englishman known as Robert of Selby, 'the first of a long line of his compatriots who, as the century wore on, were to travel south to take service with the Kings of Sicily'[198]—held out against the enemies until Lothair himself arrived in August. Robert then came to terms with the emperor, thus sparing Roger's mainland capital from devastation. Furious at having been done out of their hard-earned looting rights, the Pisans set sail for home, but not before dispatching a ship to Palermo to re-establish ties with Roger. So far so good for Lothair. Not imperial right, but conquest had established Southern Italy as his and his alone.

But winter was approaching. Lothair had no further time for Southern Italy. Besides he was tired and ailing. The best he could do was to try to secure what he had gained, for which reason he appointed Rainulf of Alife (Roger's brother-in-law!) as duke of Apulia, over and against the claims of Roger's son. Then giving up all pretence of putting Innocent on his coveted throne, Lothair set out for home, determined to cross the Alps before the snows made them impassable. He got as far Breitenswang in the Tyrol. He could go no farther. He died there, in a peasant's hut, at seventy-two years of age. By this time Roger had already undone the imperial plans by winning back a large part of his own domain. In time he would get it all.

One of Lothair's last acts in conjunction with Innocent II was to send Bernard of Clairvaux as emissary to King Roger, hoping that the abbot, with his prestige and unrelenting logic, would be able to break the schism by weaning the king away from Anacletus' cause. Bernard sensed that Roger might be willing to relent, knowing that as long as he supported a man whom most people saw as the antipope, the German emperors would continue to stir the always simmering pot of Southern Italian politics. Evading the issue of the legality of the last papal election, Bernard addressed the delegations from both popes which he and Roger had agreed should be present, moving everyone to Innocent's side—except Roger, who re-affirmed his support of Anacletus. If he were going to switch sides he needed assurances that the pope would confirm his hold on the crown and his son's title to the duchy of Apulia which had just been given to the papal-imperial appointee, Rainulf.

Just as the Church was having its troubles with the papal schism, so too was little headway being made in pulling England and Normandy together under a single head. Matilda and Geoffrey continued to harass Stephen's lands, but achieved only minor successes. Finally Stephen felt the need of crossing over for a direct confrontation. In general he was well received, and he did homage for Normandy to King Louis VI of France, which shows that Louis accepted his position. But his trip in the end achieved nothing. The English barons and knights were not all that solidly behind him, so for his engagements against Geoffrey of Anjou he had to rely on mercenaries from Flanders, who did more to hurt his cause than help it. He eventually made a truce with Geoffrey, agreeing to pay him a fixed sum annually. He returned to England at the end of the year, writing his foray off as a waste of time, effort and money.

At thirty-eight years of age William X, duke of Aquitaine and count of Poitou, suddenly and mysteriously died while on pilgrimage to the shrine of Santiago de Compostela. Saint James had a reputation for looking after his pilgrims, which partly accounts for the prevalence of scallop shell emblems which were worn by such a large segment of the European population, badges signifying that they had performed the rigorous pilgrimage, tough but considerably less so than a pilgrimage to the Holy Land. William X was an attractive man, liked by his people, and stubbornly unconventional, being the only prominent figure in Europe except King Roger to support anti-Pope Anacletus II. For him to die while on a mission to the kindly Saint James—one of Christ's Apostles who had, in Spain at least, been transformed into a warrior saint and who was just now getting up steam for a concerted drive to oust the Arabs who had already occupied Spain for nearly five centuries— seems odd. But then even Bernard of Clairvaux would admit that sometimes God's ways were past understanding.

William's death galvanized King Louis VI into action. Louis, despite his present condition—so fat at fifty-six that he could not even tie his shoes, much less mount a horse to defend his kingdom—was a good king. He was quick to seize an opportunity that would enable him to expand French territory, and also to threaten the position of Geoffrey of Anjou. How absolutely convenient that William's heir was a fifteen-year old daughter, Eleanor, now the king's vassal! If Louis the Fat were suddenly to come into ownership of Aquitaine and Poitou his royal demesne would be virtually doubled, with Geoffrey and Matilda caught squirming in a giant French pincer. Nothing would do, decided the ailing king, but that his gangling, pleasant-looking but retiring sixteen-year old heir, Louis, should become the instrument of his plan by taking Eleanor, duchess of Aquitaine, as his bride.

Young Louis' education was pitiful preparation for his future as king of France. Ascetic by nature, he had been educated in the secluded cloister of Notre Dame, from which he had been retrieved by the accidental death of the heir apparent, his older brother Prince Philip, to be further educated for what lay ahead by the famous Abbot Suger, who was himself building a monument just outside Paris—Saint Denis, the first truly Gothic church. Adolescent Louis was a decent sort, sensitive, not especially intelligent and of extremely narrow religious beliefs. If he was uneager and unsuited to wear the crown of France, he was equally ill-equipped to manage the headstrong, coquettish, gorgeous and sensual Eleanor of Aquitaine. From the moment he saw her he became her passionately-in-love plaything. The nuptials were celebrated in Bordeaux's cathedral of St André, today one of the most famous in France, but bearing little resemblance to what it was in the twelfth century. The vows were recited before the high altar: the ascetically thin Louis, shyly admiring his wife; Eleanor, ravishing in her beauty, already staring back at him directly, her full mouth edged by lines of a determination that would in years to come bring such misery on herself and such glory to her country and her blood.

By August the marriage party was in Poitiers, enjoying a rest on the slow, stately progress to Paris. It was here the word reached them that ailing Louis VI was dead, and that honeymooning Louis VII was now king. His retainers insisted that Louis get back to Paris post-haste, and Eleanor with him. It was a long trip and, forced as it was, a hard one. The newly weds were exhausted by the time they approached the gates of Paris. But they and especially the exquisite Eleanor, were welcomed appropriately, which perhaps made the strains of the trip seem worth while.

1138

All the schismatic politicking of the past years, the threatened and actual invasions and counter-marches proved to be exercises of wildest futility when anti-Pope Anacletus II, his health broken by the endless struggle, died on 25

January. Anacletus was a decent man—as was Innocent II—but he had been placed in a position to which he believed himself entitled, and for which he suffered much. Time has not dealt kindly with him, largely as a result of writers who have supported his opponents, mostly Catholic apologists and biographers of Bernard. When he is mentioned at all Anacletus is usually vilified. Needless to say Bernard was delirious on hearing of his death. '... Thanks be to God who hath given [the Church] the victory', he sang, 'has crowned her labours, and glorified her in them. Our sadness has been turned into rejoicing, our mourning into gladness. The winter is passed, the rain is over and gone; the flowers appear on the earth, the time of pruning is here, the useless branch, the rotten member has been cut off. The wicked man who made Israel to sin, he has been swallowed up by death, and given over to the pit of hell ... As Ezekiel says, *Destruction has come to him and he shall be no more for ever*.[199] All of which goes to prove that, apologists and whitewashers notwithstanding, Bernard had in him a streak of viciousness which on occasion he displayed without shame.

For a brief time a certain Victor IV took Anacletus' place, but his heart was not in it. He laid down his tiara before the year was half gone. Roger of Sicily then declared for Innocent II, even though that hardened old winner stubbornly maintained his distance and was shortly to excommunicate him. But the schism was over.

In England neither King Stephen nor Matilda could gain a decisive advantage. The country was tragically at the mercy of the barons—robber barons all—who were themselves being wooed by both sides. As one would expect, the period of the seventeen-year civil war became more than ever one of active unchecked castle building.

The family of de Albini (or d'Aubigny) was an old Norman family from near Coutance on the Cotentin Peninsula. Their record goes back to the time of the battle at Val-ès-Dunes, when the lord of the family fought against William the Conqueror, and as a result lost his castle. (One of his sons, Roger, made a noteworthy grant of property to the abbey of Lessay in 1084; another, Richard, was the abbot of St Albans from 1097 to 1119.) Though they attained their first notoriety by fighting against William, eventually the family came to terms with royalty—two grandsons of William's unfortunate opponent doing extremely well for themselves in England when they wisely opted to support William Rufus and then Henry I against Robert Curthose. One of these two de Albini brothers, William, stood particularly close to Henry I, who granted him the honorary office of butler, as well as a daughter of the strong Bigod family of East Anglia. He also confirmed to William a former grant (made by William Rufus) of certain lands including Rising, about four miles northeast of King's Lynn. An old quatrain, which natives of the area have no difficulty making rhyme, says

Rising was a seaport town
When Lynn was but a marsh;
Now Lynn is a seaport town
And Rising fares the worse.

While it is doubtful that Rising's foundations were ever washed by the sea, it is known that the lords of Rising did enjoy a good share of the valuable custom taxes of Lynn, found useful to this day by the dukes of Cornwall.

William de Albini's son, William II, fared even better than his father. He married the widow of Henry I, Adela of Louvain, this year, now that a decent period of mourning had passed, thereby raising himself to the summit of power among the Anglo-Norman aristocracy. Dowager Queen Adela brought him lands, honours and wealth, and the accompanying prestige, as well as the castle of Arundel in Sussex and the earldom of Lincoln. A profitable marriage!—with all the profit not on William's side. Adela gained one of the most macho men of the time, a man known as William of the Strong Hand because he was supposed to have pulled out the tongue of a lion.

Castle Rising, which William II de Albini started to build this year, is one of those elaborate stone structures which gives the modern visitor a reasonable picture of what castle life in the twelfth century was like. It was set inside a formidable fifty-nine feet high earthworks, which in its turn was protectively reinforced by two additional ringwork enclosures, one to the east and the other to the west, the three of them covering an area of just over twelve acres. The eastern outer bailey defended the main approach to the castle, the road passing through it to the still existing gatehouse. The magnificent keep is of course in the inner bailey. It rises fifty feet, and contained sumptuous apartments for the lord and his lady, along with other accommodation. Beyond that there were, also in the inner bailey, additional quarters that were required 'not only by the great itinerant household of the lord earl but also by the several households of his lady, of his sons when they reached the appropriate age, and of visiting magnates, as well as the more modest establishment of his resident constable . . . hall, chambers, chapel, kitchen, buttery, pantry . . . stables and the like'.[200] We know little of the castle's outer defences, but the spectacular keep is sufficient to satisfy even the most demanding student of the Middle Ages.

Approach the great keep (*see page 242*) through the remains of the gate house—actually at one time strong enough to be considered a barbican, with flanking walls and a portcullis. From the gatehouse one gets a splendid view of the keep, looking down into the bailey from high on the rampart. The keep is oblong, squatter than the tower-shaped keep such as we find at Rochester. Enter through the handsomely ornamented arch, up wide stairs to the fore-building, whose strange, high-pitched roof strikes the one jarring note in the entire complex. The carving over the

Stairs to keep, Castle Rising, England

door illustrates convincingly the idea that castles were coming to be thought of as more than just defensive bulwarks but as homes as well. The slowly increasing role of the woman in the society may have been partly responsible for this change, so clearly demonstrated at Chepstow and Rochester.

The great hall has lost both floor and roof, and thus its appearance challenges the historical imagination. One is forced to remain in a small entrance lobby—not part of the original plan—and look into what was once the forty-seven by twenty-three feet hall, to reconstruct in the mind's eye a floored, tapestried and furnished room of state. It takes more than a little imagination too, since the visitor is staring into the depths of the two-chambered storage cellar below. The task is not unrewarding, though, especially in that the lobby itself is distinguished by a two-light window, richly carved and made even more remarkable by the interlaced pattern of its central shaft.

Demeaning the original beauty of the castle is the fireplace in the great hall, built 'sometime in the philistine Tudor age [when a] splendid entrance . . . was blocked and a fireplace inserted, presumably in the "squatter" period of the keep's history, when the principal apartments had become uninhabitable, and the glory had departed'.[201] What a doorway it must have been!—magnificently proportioned height to width, round arched with alternating chevron patterns and ribs, flanked by receding columns. No one contests that the inhabitants needed warmth. But was it necessary to destroy one of the handsomest interior doorways of Norman England in order to achieve this?

Within the keep there is an inner cross-wall, slightly off centre, running straight through the castle on an east-west axis and vertically from cellar to roof. The great hall occupies the larger, northern side of the division. On the first floor, level with the great hall, are several other rooms, the so-called great chamber with accompanying service rooms, a kitchen (which may be the most interesting room in the castle, with its oven and hearth, its circular chimney shaft and floor-level drain) and a small chapel—a tiny retreat from the clatter of castle life. (Think of the racket a man in armour created by just walking!) A fine fireplace in the great chamber (which was originally connected to the great hall by a wide door) assured at least a modicum of heat during the damp Norfolk winters. There is one habitable room on the second level, directly over the chapel and awkwardly reached by a long corridor built in the castle's outside eastern wall. There is an upper room as well in the fore-building, a thirteenth- and fourteenth-century addition.

William de Albini and his wife led a luxurious life at Castle Rising. Floor or no, one can envisage the great hall, window-lit in the day hours or smokey with torches at night, crowded with the lord and his lady, his retainers and favourite knights, her ladies-in-waiting, assorted children and dogs and bustling servants. Backed by a round-arched recess in the long wall of the great hall, William presided over the vast silver-littered table extending along the east-west axis. The niche was designed, apparently, solely with that idea in mind, to dramatize the position of the powerful lord of Castle Rising.

Musicians grouped in a corner amused the diners by playing and singing popular ballads, some tender for feminine appeal, others unashamedly bawdy and suggestive, and still others, in the growing fashion of the day, full of tragically unrequited love. Songs of the troubadours, originating in Southern France, Catalonia and Northern Italy, and bearing their message of the exaltation of the lady, began spreading after 1130 throughout Europe (the singers were called *trouvères* in Northern France and Flanders, and *minnesingers* in German-speaking regions) and were being imported into England.

> Alas! how much of love I thought I knew
> And how little I know;
> For I cannot stop loving
> Her from whom I may have nothing.
> All my heart, and all herself,
> And all my own self and all I have
> She has taken from me, and leaves me nothing
> But longing and a seeking heart.[202]

Sometimes itinerant companies of mummers or dancers provided interludes, or an impromptu wrestling match would enliven the party, maybe even Lord William himself accepting a challenge and—remember the fate of that poor lion!—winning. The gradual improvement in the status of women had brought about changes in men as well. They were expected to be more refined than their fathers; and, though still basically professional fighters, were abandoning the image of the two-fisted, swashbuckling braggart. Robed in yellow, blue or green, William would have worn a belted gown reaching to the floor, with points at the hem. Friends his own age dressed with the same dignity, but the younger men, wary of too much decorum and restlessly on the prowl, dressed in *mi-parti*—garments in several colours—a style then in vogue. Women were encouraging men to wear their hair long; and certainly more of them were shaving. Chivalry, already well-started in Spain and Southern France, was now spreading through Europe and into England.

The women were dressed similarly, in close-fitting brightly coloured clothes intended to emphasize their bodies, their carriage, their elegance, especially in the dance. Not to be outdone, they aped the colours of the men, some of them sporting sleeves tight to the wrists and then amplified by folds hanging to the ground. The married woman could be identified by a scarf or veil, and she might wear a belt over her dress, for belts were thought to have magical power. In any event the belt helped produce a slim-waisted image. Wolfram von Eschenbach, writing a little later in Germany, insisted

> You know how narrow
> Ants always are in the middle
> But the maiden was slimmer still.[203]

Castle Rising remained in the estate of the de Albinis until the thirteenth century when, in 1243, it passed over to the Montalt family. Queen Isabella, widow of King Edward II, whose murder at Berkeley Castle was probably done with her connivance, lived here off and on for twenty-seven years after the death of her lover, Mortimer. When she died in 1358 Castle Rising went to her grandson the Black Prince, then to his son Richard II.

1139

That Stephen could never be an effective king was becoming more and more evident even to his most loyal supporters. Bold and courageous he was; but he was also an appeaser, giving away his royal prerogatives and setting poor precedents so easily that his unruly barons learned to pay little heed to him as a legitimate ruler. To make matters worse for him, Matilda and her half-brother Robert of Gloucester arrived in England in late September. Robert hastened to his stronghold at Bristol, while Matilda stayed with her step-mother at Arundel Castle whence Stephen, with totally misplaced chivalry, allowed her passage to Bristol, going so far as to provide an escort for her!

Even before Matilda's arrival Stephen had by his unwise actions pre-disposed many to swing over to supporting her. He set the stage for intense family feuds and regional rivalries, by dignifying the military governors of numerous local shires with the title of earl, thereby negatively affecting his own position. What had been in the first year of his reign a monolithic coalition of support was thus broken by local and intense jealousies. Bishops and other Church dignitaries also became involved in dissension.

Roger, bishop of Salisbury and the ostentatious builder of the cathedral on the ancient hilltop city now called Old Sarum, had long held a vital role in the administration. King Henry had first come across Roger at Caen. Impressed by the speed with which the priest could read the service—time was of the essence to English kings—he brought him to England and made him first chancellor and then justiciar, a position of enormous power and prestige. Not highly educated, Roger possessed natural organizational abilities and business talents far exceeding those of most men. It was not long before he rose to a position of trust unmatched in the realm, ruling in effect when Henry was in Normandy. It was Roger who created the exchequer system through which, born manipulator that he was, he managed to amass great personal riches. He built for himself the castle of Devizes, one of the grandest in all England. Like Henry, Stephen placed a noticeable reliance on Roger; how could he do otherwise since Roger had openly espoused his cause. But the favour Roger had enjoyed had allowed him to build up a dynastic power base; his nephew Alexander had been made bishop of Lincoln and another nephew, Nigel, was bishop of Ely. Moreover Roger's son by his mistress, another Roger, called 'le Poer', was Stephen's chancellor.

The three bishops may certainly have aroused Stephen's suspicions. Roger of Salisbury had been stockpiling arms and provisions, and all three had acquired large retinues of knights. At a council held in Oxford in June Stephen used a (possibly arranged) brawl between Bishop Roger's men and those of one of the barons to have the two Rogers and Alexander seized. (Nigel escaped to his uncle's castle at Devizes.) Stephen conveyed the two Rogers to Devizes, and his threat to hang the chancellor and starve the bishop gained for him not only Devizes but also Bishop Roger's castle at Sherborne.

One look at Sherborne Castle would be enough to accelerate any king's suspicions. Certainly it is of striking proportions and defensive potential. The symmetrically polygonal outer defences of curtain wall and deep moat enclose an area of about three and a half acres, the whole complex topping a knoll and surrounded on the north and east by marshes. The gatehouse on the southwest survives from Roger's time, the only one of three to do so. Remains of many of the domestic buildings can still be seen within the bailey. Part of the keep endures in ruins, dramatically set in a sweeping green lawn. The great hall, kitchen, chapel and courtyard can be identified with certainty. But the parliamentary order to dismantle the castle after the Civil War was all too efficiently carried out. One of the more charming aspects of the castle is a semicircular bay, probably of the fifteenth century, with a groined vault supported by a re-used centre column. Tantalizing fragments of stairs, vaultings, chevron patterns and interlacing blind arcades, a decorated capital here and there, a pathetic bit of paving and evidence of latrine pits allow the romantic imagination free reign to reconstruct the combined luxury and insecurity of Roger's life-style.

Roger of Salisbury had obviously spared no expense. No wonder Stephen coveted such wealth. Many English kings have been pressed for money, and Stephen more so than most, what with his realm in a perpetual state of anarchy. Once 'having got hold of the bishop's treasures, he used them to obtain in marriage for his son Eustace the hand of Constance, Lewis the French king's sister',[204] thereby setting up a family alliance with that monarch. Roger did not survive the extortion long. He died in December, living a virtual prisoner in his castle at Salisbury. But the usurpation of Roger's wealth and his ensuing death was of little help to Stephen. By this time the country was divided, with the empress in the west and Stephen in the east. The Church was quarrelling with the State; even Stephen's brother Henry of Winchester was negotiating with Matilda. The stage was truly set for that period of anarchy and misery described in a famous passage of the Peterborough continuation of the *Anglo-Saxon Chronicle*.

> Every powerful man built his castle . . . When the castles were built, they filled them with devils and wicked men . . . I have neither the ability nor the power to tell all the horrors nor all the torments they inflicted upon wretched people in this country; and that lasted the nineteen years while Stephen was king, and it was always going from bad to worse. They levied taxes on the villages every so often, and called it 'protection money'. When the wretched people had no more to give, they robbed and burned the villages, so that you could easily go a whole day's journey and never find anyone occupying a village, nor land tilled. Then corn was dear, and meat and butter and cheese, because there was none in the country . . .

> Wherever cultivation was done, the ground produced no corn, because the land was all ruined by such doings, and they said openly that Christ and his saints were asleep.[205]

Unaccustomed to security in his papal chair, Pope Innocent II could delude himself that intransigence was the best attitude to strike in his dealings with Roger of Sicily. After all he had allowed no compromise with Anacletus, and, by surviving him, had come out on top. Now he hoped to bring down the other half of that accursed team. But Innocent was manipulating himself into a situation from which extrication was going to prove impossible. In the meantime Roger could match his stubborn determination against papal intransigence any day. He was not concerned even when, at a Lateran Council in April, Pope Innocent lashed out with sentences of excommunication against him, his sons and any southern bishop who had been consecrated by Anacletus.

By June Innocent was on the march again, egged on and accompanied by Robert of Capua, Roger's turncoat vassal, who had been confirmed in his principality by Innocent and Lothair in defiance of Roger's claiming it for his son Alfonso. But Roger regarded this new display of determination as little more than show. In negotiation with the pope he remained hard-nosed, refusing to recognize Robert of Capua's claim in return for Innocent's acceptance of his own kingship. Tiring of fruitless negotiations, Roger laid his trap. He marched off—a ploy—knowing that Innocent and Robert, frustrated into action, would once again rattle their swords.

Towns were ravaged, fields fired and the earth scorched between Capua and Monte Cassino as Innocent and Robert moved. Galluccio is a typical out-of-the-way southern Italian village with little to interest the outsider but scenery—spectacular craggy mountains, water-gushing ravines and vineyards. The tourist can visit Galluccio, make a complete circuit, and not encounter a soul. Yet here it was, in this strangely inappropriate town, that Innocent and Robert made their shocked, unscheduled halt. There, high up on the mountain, just to the left but hard to see against the sun, were Sicilian soldiers. They were being watched! Innocent was stunned, and suddenly frightened. They had walked into a trap. He called for immediate retreat; but it was too late. Roger's son, the young Roger, not long out of his teens now, swooped down the mountain side with a thousand knights, making directly for the centre of the papal ranks. The word decimation best describes what followed. Trying to outrun one another, the pope's men were mown down. Some were drowned in the Garigliano River. In the every-man-for-himself débâcle Robert escaped. But Innocent fled ignominiously to the tiny basement chapel of San Nicola in the equally tiny church of the Annunziata. It was in this sordid little hideaway that he was in due course found and taken prisoner.

Just north of Naples, roughly fifty miles via the Autostrada del Sole from Rome, is the town of Mignano. Like Galluccio it has little to offer the tourist. It does boast an attractive castle, however, part of it Norman; and it was to here that Roger conveyed the pope with the respect that his office commanded. But he was also persuasive. And Innocent finally had to face the fact that 'here was the greatest humiliation suffered by the Papacy at the hands of the Normans since Duke Humphrey de Hauteville and his brother Robert Guiscard had annihilated the army of Pope Leo IX at Civitate, eighty-six years before'.[206] Once that realization had sunk in Innocent II owned that he had no choice but to meet the demands of this hated Norman king. One can sense his anger at having to recognize Roger's kingship, and consequently the validity of his enemy Anacletus' bull which had permitted it. The walls of Mignano Castle must have reverberated with Innocent's outrage when Roger insisted that further conditions for freedom were papal confirmation of young son Roger as duke of Apulia, as well as of son Alfonso's claims on the princedom of

Capua. The pope was never one to lack for words, though. He celebrated mass, 'in the course of which he preached a sermon of enormous length on the subject of peace, and left the church a free man'.[207] But he knew, as did Roger, as did every political observer, that the treaty of Mignano was nothing less than unconditional surrender.

It is almost impossible to imagine events of such historic magnitude taking place at two such unlikely places—Mignano is perhaps a slightly more believable venue than Galluccio. The castle at Mignano, much altered since Roger's day, stands on a quiet commercial street in what is basically a non descript town. But Galluccio lays claim to being the most improbable site for events involving persons of such importance as a king and a pope. And the church of the Annunziata, from the

Chapel of S. Nicola, Galluccio, Italy

outside more a barn than a church, is in character with its surroundings. To make matters even worse, the chapel of San Nicola—hiding place of one of the most unyielding of medieval popes—is hardly more than a cellar, entered by an unassuming door in a corner of the building and (at least when visited by the writer) knee deep in stagnant water. Only dim frescoes of unidentifiable saints and heavenly beings scaling off the walls and ceiling give so much as a hint of former beauty, if such there was.

With the pope humbled and Robert of Capua abandoned, Roger was clearly in control of Southern Italy. Resistance melted away. When he returned to Sicily in November the mainland was quiet, his barons subdued. Unlike the insecurely situated ruler of England, Roger was at the height of his power. And that called for a celebration!

1140

April 28—Palm Sunday—may be regarded symbolically as the day when the Norman-Sicilian amalgamation of the dominant Latin, Byzantine and Islamic cultures of Roger's kingdom burst forth into glorious flower, the most dazzling and brilliant showcase of interfaith harmony that the world will perhaps ever know. On that day, in the presence of King Roger, dignitaries of both the Latin and Greek Churches, royal favourites, leading court members and foreign visitors, was dedicated the Cappella Palatina, located, as its name indicates, in the Palace of the Kings at Palermo. It is hard to imagine Roger *not* robed in his magnificent mantle, now fortunately preserved for us in the Kunsthistorische Museum in Vienna. Woven of red silk and half circular in

Roger's robe,
Kunsthistoriches
Museum, Vienna

shape—to be worn around the shoulders—it is embroidered in gold and pearls showing floral designs and two tigers attacking a pair of camels. Oriental in feeling—the animals are emblazoned with arabesque patterns—it is worthy of a rich emir interested in impressing on witnesses the grandeur as well as the cosmopolitan influences of his court. There is a border design along the bottom edge of the mantle, an inscription in Neski characters (a cursive Arabic script) which places and dates the robe—'the *Tiraz*, Palermo, 1133'. The *Tiraz* (royal workshop), which had been active since the days of Arab hegemony, was peopled mostly by women. They were expected to gratify the men of the court when they were not at work at their looms, a diversionary addendum to their jobs and a 'tradition . . . the Normans, eclectic as ever, had appropriated with enthusiasm; and it was not long before *Tiraz* became a useful, if slightly transparent, cover for the royal harem'.[208]

To see the Cappella Palatina, to be absorbed by it, is like becoming light itself. It is a miracle of light, a source, a font of all colours, so rarefied that one is willing to accept it, no questions asked, as a bit of heaven temporarily located on our mundane level. Even the monumentally disastrous restorations of the eighteenth century need not distract us; the romantic viewer will zero in by instinct on the twelfth-century miracles, some of which were added by Roger's son and successor William I. A few of the thirteenth-century additions may jar on us, but nothing can spoil the gut-level experience of this brightest jewel of Norman-Sicilian art.

If Cefalù is heavenly—and it is—then the Cappella Palatina is divine. (*See page 275.*) There is such colour in this chapel, such an orgy of pattern and texture and inventive design that it seems to take on an energy of its own. It is the stuff of miracles, of visceral experiences and visions. Of the earth, it is as ethereal as a wisp of incense, as radiant as a candle flame. Of light and shimmer, it is as solid as bronze, as positive as its builder. If ever pictorial form becomes melodic, then the Palatina's flowers, shrubs, trees and water waves weave visual tunes to rival the delicate polyphonic masterpieces which were sung here at the time of the Norman kings. Organized part-music—the organum—has met its optical match here with harmonies and counterpoints of form and colour. It is an Alleluia, a Credo, a Gloria all at once. No vielle, flute or lute, with all their strength and sinuousness, can rise and diminish, weave and float and soar beyond the structured harmonies, the meticulous rhythms and delicate counterpoints of Roger's chapel. On entering one feels somehow lighter, elated as if by music, subject to a kind of levitation that is not lessened by the ornate dadoes, the balustrades and the noble flights of stairs.

The supreme craftsmen who painstakingly cut and grouted these countless tesserae into pictures and designs straight out of Byzantium, defy us to resist looking upward, past their glorious encrustations to the wooden stalactite ceiling—a touch of pure Islam—created by Arab artisans, said to be the earliest datable work of Arab painting in existence. 'Nothing affords more striking proof of the irrepressible vitality and insidious charm of Arab art than this ceiling, with its representation of Persian and pagan subjects: winged genii that cannot be interpreted as angels, dancing voluptuous houris that cannot possibly be mistaken for martyrs, gazelles, antelopes, elephants, and other Far Eastern animals . . .'[209] One needs almost microscopic vision to see, much less study, the myriad tiny figures, animals, plants and beasts from another world, which cavort and race amid the ornately carved pendants.

Over and above everything, it is the mosaics which finally arrest the attention (see page 275), absorbing us in their reflective splendour. This is church art, to be sure. But it is also palace art. And any king, prelate or emperor would be satisfied to possess just one of the Palatina's sumptuous works, much less the dozens upon dozens that adorn it. Saints and angels, virgins and martyrs, God the Father and God the Judge; they are all there, there in an aureole of glistening light that dazzles but does not blind—a light that negates the dust and accretions of centuries.

As though to match the glories of the Cappella Palatina, the court preacher Theophanes Cerameus, a Greek, addressed the king on that Palm Sunday

in terms more adulatory than Western court chaplains were accustomed to use, and the praises of the new foundation were sung in an imagery somewhat florid and Oriental.

'A joy day is this feast because of the numerous assembly of illustrious men, but its greatest adornment is the presence of the King who sits before us not in the glory of the Crown alone but also in the glory of high deeds, and yet not trusting in these but fast and sure in the faith of God through whom he has become so great . . . Yet thy deeds of valour, O King, thy victories granted from God, thy deeds of fame and trophies are to other ages by other men appraised and shall be for ever: so long as the sea is bounded by the dry land, they will praise thy deeds to the end'.[210]

The individual works—the illustrations from the Bible, the abstract trees (see page 275) and decorative flowers, the patterns, the immense paschal candle-stick, the stately pulpit—all these things can be studied individually, bit by bit. But the whole must be experienced in time, just as music is an experience in time. Awash in the most luxurious colours—reds, blues, emeralds, and above all gold—it must be felt rather than seen; absorbed rather than merely looked at. No single thing stands alone. No mosaic is an isolated island. 'The mosaic glides around the edges and corners, spreading like a glaze over all the surfaces. All the angles and corners are rounded so as not to separate but to link walls standing at an angle . . . The encrusted surfaces receive their sole articulations by their own folding, as it were, and by ornamental caesurae of the mosaic itself'.[211] The end result is mysterious rather than revelatory. Science tells us that all colours in light combine to make white light. Here in this not large house of worship, by means of quite ordinary earthly materials of stone, plaster and wood, the myriad colours of creation seem to coalesce into white light, the pure Light of the World—God.

In July Roger met with his barons on the mainland, at Ariano, where he presented to them his sweeping Ariano Assizes. In these declarations of law Roger upheld the rights of all his people—Greeks, Arabs, Normans, Lombards, Jews—to live according to the customs of their fathers, except in the few instances where they might perhaps be in conflict with the new ordinances. Furthermore, Roger asserted again and again the God-given authority of kings, claiming that any negation of his law, which was a manifestation of the will of God, was treason, and punishable by death. The Ariano Assizes covered many other problems of government and the administration of justice, but these were their two most prominent features. Many of his laws were based on the Justinian Code.

Since he had been brought up in the Byzantine-orientated court of his father, the great count, it is not difficult to understand why Roger the king, more an oriental potentate by nature than a Western leader of hard-to-manage, independent minded vassals, would try to merge the complex European feudal system with the Eastern imperial order. And for the most part he carried it off. In addition, Roger established a standard coinage for the entire kingdom—the ducat—which was to dominate the commercial and banking worlds for the next several centuries. (For purposes of foreign trade it is still coined in Austria, Czechoslovakia and The Netherlands.) As though all of this were not enough, it was during this year that the first Cistercian monastery was founded in Southern Italy, in Calabria, a result of the patching up of the long animosity between Roger and Saint Bernard. Reduced to *sotto voce* by age, Bernard was tired, burned out; he had mellowed. 'Far and wide the renown of your magnificence has spread over the earth', he had written the year before. 'For what lands are there to which the glory of your name has not reached? . . . Endeavour as much as in you lies to refer this same glory to Him from who it comes, if you do not wish to destroy it, or to be destroyed by it'.[212]

This, then, was Sicily's greatest moment. Roger was king: all powerful, inspiring love, fear, hate; accessible yet terribly remote; a near divinity yet human enough to want—to need—revenge; a lover of art, the despoiler of cities; a man of letters, a man of the flesh; a Westerner and at the same time an oriental—practical and pragmatic. It is no wonder that a few years later he would be represented in mosaic in George of Antioch's church, the Martorana, crowned, not by a bishop, cardinal, pope or (as was actually the case) by his vassal-in-chief, Robert of Capua, but by Christ Himself. Of course!

Chapter Thirteen

King Stephen was a worthy peer,
His breeches cost him but a crown;
He held them sixpence all too dear,
With that he call'd the tailor lown.

He was a wight of high renown,
And thou art but of low degree:
'Tis pride that pulls the country down,
Then take thine auld cloak about thee.

Shakespeare, *Othello*, Act II, scene 3

1140

Bristol was enriched this year by the foundation of a new large abbey, despite England's raging civil war and despite further the city having declared for the basically unpersonable Empress Matilda. The new Augustinian foundation, established by the provost of Bristol, Robert Fitzharding, was correspondingly magnificent. The abbey church of Augustine (since 1542 the cathedral church of the Holy and Undivided Trinity) is the only 'hall church' in England, having its aisles the same height as the nave, without triforium or clerestory. Furthermore, the later choir is the earliest English example of Gothic lierne vaulting (from the French, meaning 'tie': a short intermediate 'rib' which does not spring from an impost block but passes from one intersection of principal ribs to another). By its very nature the lierne vault makes for an architectural form basically foreign to Norman. As far as the church itself goes there is little of the Norman left—an occasional wall section, the south transept, including a fine night staircase built into its wall, the lower part of the main gatehouse, the east walk of the cloister, and a few other odds and ends. But they are not the best that Bristol's cathedral can show us. Hardly to be classified as either an odd or an end is the stupendous Norman chapter house, which remains pretty much as it was when just completed.

Entering from the Norman vestibule, with its low vaults and pleasing combination of both pointed and round arches, one moves suddenly into an expanded world of interlocking arches and woven stone (*see page* 276), of contrasting textures and competing patterns, a vibrant microcosm where stone is chiselled into twisting, turning ornamentations unmatched in any other Norman interior in England or France. It is as though the stones of its making were at one time soft, allowing the masons to mould rather than construct, to weave rather than carve, to twist into zigzags, to bend into arches, to advance and recede surfaces for rich effects of light and darkness. And all of this encloses space so perfectly proportioned as to make one smile with pleasure. It is wonderfully rich visually, so full of the marvellous vitality that we cannot help but associate with these vigorous people from across the Channel. By the time the church and its chapter house were consecrated in 1165—King Stephen was already dead eleven years and the throne taken by the Angevin line—the Plantagenets. And though this new blood continued to expand the realm under Henry II, the spirit of architectural forms became less virile, less Norman, until its vitality was ultimately sapped. There were yet great things to come, but nothing to surpass this meeting room of Augustinian fathers.

1141

By the beginning of the year Stephen had created such an atmosphere of distrust, that some of his staunchest supporters were deserting him, some of them motivated more by inordinate self-interest than by any desire to strengthen the realm. One of the most notable of these was Ranulf, earl of Chester. He had a certain attachment to Matilda's cause since he had married the daughter of her half-brother, Robert of Gloucester; but he also had decided it was in his interest to establish his own independent state spanning the island from coast to coast. Heretofore the civil war had comprised mostly minor skirmishes and sieges, but at the first major struggle of the conflict, which followed the seizing of the royal castle of Lincoln shortly before Christmas 1140 by Ranulf, war broke out in earnest. Besieged by Stephen, Ranulf slipped out of the castle and sought help from Robert of Gloucester. The besieging army thus itself became besieged. Before the deciding battle on 2 February 1141, Candlemas Day (the Feast of the Purification), Stephen

was hearing mass . . . during which, as he was offering to God the usual waxen taper . . . it broke as he placed it in the hands of the bishop Alexander. The king took this as a sign that his own power was broken. The pix, also, in which was contained the body of the Lord, fell upon the altar . . . the chain by which it was suspended having broken; and this also was an omen of the king's downfall. Then this valiant king went forth to battle . . . All the king's knights were defeated and fled . . . They who did not flee were taken prisoners . . . King Stephen kept his ground like a lion, standing single-handed in the field, so that no one dared approach him . . . wielding in his hand a battle-axe, with the frequent blows of which he repelled the continued attacks of his assailants . . . Even while thus alone, it was no easy matter to take him prisoner. Thus Stephen, king of England, was captured . . . and was miserably brought into Lincoln . . . God's judgement having thus dealt with the king, he was carried off to the empress . . .[213]

The castle Ranulf had taken over at Lincoln had been built by William the Conqueror in 1068 on an ancient Roman camp, and covered an area of almost fourteen acres, including the walls and ditches. Entry to the bailey was through the eastern gateway, the passage of which still stands, though the façade is fifteenth-century. The Lucy Tower—so called to honour Lucy the Countess, who may have built it and who was married to Ranulf's father (he was her third husband)—was probably the keep Ranulf had appropriated. It tops a mound that rises abruptly from the floor of the bailey and is approached, as it was in Stephen's day, by a long flight of stairs. It is easy to see why the castle was so valuable, with its twenty-feet high walls shaped to fifteen sides on the outside and twelve on the inner. A seven-feet wide arch spans the entry at the top of the steps. It is a simple archway, a great blunt curve with only one string of chevrons decorating its outer edge. Every inch of it looks defensive, a no-frills, frankly muscular, stocky entrance that would take some storming. The whole mound today is overgrown with foliage and vines. these make the keep appear no longer menacing but still solidly discouraging, dissuading.

There is another mound within the bailey, probably the one William had used for his original castle. Over the years it was modified and added to until it is now a forty-feet square tower known as the Observatory Tower (since it was used as such by an astronomically minded nineteenth-century governor of the local gaol at that time housed within the castle precinct).

When the captured king was brought to Gloucester Matilda was over-joyed. He was sent on to be held in Bristol Castle, the strongest fortification Matilda possessed. Now nothing could prevent Matilda from assuming her designated place on the throne of England as her father had dreamed—nothing but her own personality, of course. She rushed to Winchester to claim the crown and, incidentally, what little was left of the royal treasury. Matilda had to work to convince Stephen's brother, Bishop Henry, to take her side, but not very hard since he too had been slighted by the tactless king. A month or so later Henry, by virtue of his rank as papal legate, convened at Winchester a council of most of the bishops and some abbots; they declared for Matilda, despite the fact that they had previously sworn fealty to Stephen.

There is some uncertainty about Matilda's movements while these preliminaries were taking place. From Wilton, near Salisbury, she moved to Oxford and St Albans. Her goal, of course, was London, where the coronation ceremony must be held. But the citizens of London had already sent a delegation to Winchester to argue Stephen's cause. It was only with reluctance that, around midsummer, they admitted Matilda to their city. And it was there that her triumphs suddenly evaporated.

By this time Matilda had already justified the fears of those who had at first shied from her as queen. '. . . Success made her so elevated in mind and haughty in speech, that, through her intolerable pride of sex, she incensed the yet-hesitating minds of the nobility against her. The citizens of London, also, although at first they had favourably received her, yet, disgusted at her pride, again rejected her'.[214] The last straw had come when she demanded of the citizens a huge sum of money. Beyond that she had become so arrogant (she abused even her half-brother Robert of Gloucester) that Bishop Henry, who seems to have acquired the habit of switching sides, was driven to regret having been the leader on her behalf and abandoned her cause.

By August Matilda was back at Winchester where she had gone to tongue-lash Henry. She laid siege to Henry's palace, but soon found herself besieged by Stephen's loyal wife, and fighting for her own survival. Eventually, in September, Matilda was forced to flee to Gloucester; her half-brother Robert, who was fighting a rearguard action, was captured and imprisoned at Rochester. In contrast to the treatment Stephen had received from the empress,

Robert was accorded an unexpected hospitality, being granted free run of the town. In these circumstances Robert himself was apparently in no hurry to be returned to the company of his overbearing sister. But Empress Matilda knew that Robert lent credibility to her campaign, even though it was now all but spent. The rout from Winchester had 'cooked her goose'. She had no choice but to agree to a release of King Stephen in exchange for Earl Robert.

Thereafter the civil war dragged on, the situation substantially the same as it had been before the battle for Lincoln. In places the countryside became depopulated. Famine set in. The fleecing of the people continued. England had never known such evil conditions, even in the early days of the Norman occupation. There seemed no end to the trouble. '... Everyone robbed somebody else if he had the greater power ... They were all utterly accursed and perjured and doomed to perdition'.[215]

1142

Once his struggle with Bernard of Clairvaux was patched up, King Roger established a Benedictine abbey in Sicily, at Palermo. San Giovanni degli Eremiti—St John of the Hermits—is within easy proximity of the palace; its abbots became the royal chaplains and confessors, and its cemetery the burial place of the royal family, except for the kings themselves. In time it became the most richly endowed and wealthiest of all monasteries in Sicily.

For his new Latin foundation Roger took over a former mosque. Surrounded by a thick growth of green trees and parked gardens, its five domes, standing on high drums in the Arabic manner, seem to float on the greenery, arresting even the most callous tourist fatigued, perhaps, by lesser domes. One need not agree with those historians and critics who see them as unattractive and unnoteworthy. Their spacing in relation to one another is superb; each stands alone, yet they form a unit, spanning the small church five times over, an eloquent testimony to Arab tastes and refinement. The adjoining cloister— so quiet and shady—reminds one of the successful union of Christian and Arab motifs, not to mention philosophies and manners. For the cloisters, later by half a century than the church, are Norman. Sitting in this quiet oasis in a noisy modern city, and seeing the cupolas rising from the verdant growth surrounding them, 'one is reminded for the hundredth

S. Giovanni Degli Eremiti, Palermo

time that in Sicily Islam is never far away. And it is, perhaps, in the church and cloister of what was once the leading Christian monastery of the Kingdom that its presence is most keenly felt'.[216]

Henry fitzEmpress, eldest son of Empress Matilda and Geoffrey Plantagenet, made his first Channel crossing to England this year. Before dying, a tired and bitter king, he was to get to know that Channel well. But for the moment this nine-year old, destined to a personal success as notable as his mother's utter failure, was brought to Matilda's stronghold at Bristol and entrusted to the tutor Master Matthew. At Bristol he met the philosopher Adelard of Bath, one of the first to introduce Arabic scientific knowledge to Western Europe, and who dedicated to Henry his treatise on the astrolabe. When he returned to the Continent in 1144 one of his tutors was the grammarian William of Conches. Henry became adept at both Latin and French, and may have had some knowledge of other languages. He encouraged the arts—Wace composed his poetical epic history of the dukes of Normandy, the *Roman de Rou*, at his request.

The question arises: why was Henry brought to England at this time? 'The Angevin cause needed a new figurehead to replace the discredited Matilda. It was a baptism of fire'.[217] Matilda was indeed discredited, after the disastrous rout from Winchester. Now to make matters even worse, King Stephen had her holed up in the castle at Oxford and was besieging her there. It is interesting that her husband Geoffrey refused so much as to lift a finger to help her. He had pretensions of his own, and they were sighted not on England but on Normandy. The indomitable empress, however, had no need of rescue. One snowy night, with a small party she walked boldly through Stephen's lines and on to Abingdon, fleeing thence by horse to Wallingford. It was Matilda's most spectacular moment of personal courage; but thereafter all hope of placing her on the throne was abandoned, even by Earl Robert. The only chance for eventual Angevin succession rested on the young Henry—and that would take some growing up.

1143

While Henry was being drilled by his masters the woman who was to have a greater effect on his life than any other person was doing her share not only to refine the capital city of Paris but to set the entire country on edge. That Eleanor of Aquitaine was a woman of taste was obvious from the moment she arrived in grey and dreary Paris. She set about trying to brighten up the old palace on the Île de la Cité, hanging tapestries which she had commissioned, and bringing in amenities of foreign places—'musk; sandalwood to sweeten the vast and cheerless rooms; light silk veils; rose preserves; ginger to purify the breath'.[218] Her effect on the courtly life was pronounced. 'Most important of all, Eleanor had lost no time in sending for the troubadours. Life would have seemed drab to her without them. She needed their songs, the strains of viol and tambourine, of flute and cithara, and above all the poetic interplay of words, the repartee, light-hearted and sometimes slightly daring, which had always found favour at the courts of her father and grandfather and which she had been anxious to introduce into France'.[219]

On September 24 Pope Innocent II died, to be followed in rapid succession by Celestine II and Lucius II, each of whom ruled less than a year. Further intensifying Innocent's sense of failure, the Romans, in a move that had been coming on for generations, had declared their city a republic by reviving the Roman Senate and denying all temporal power to the popes just weeks before his death, perhaps hastening it. Resentment, anger and confusion reigned. Indeed, Pope Lucius II died while personally leading papal forces against republicans in a Roman street battle.

Possibly as a result of a successful foray on the north coast of Africa, the emir of emirs, George of Antioch, founded a church in Palermo, Santa Maria dell'Ammiraglio. It is now familiarly called the Martorana in memory of one Geoffrey de Marturano, who some years later founded a Benedictine nunnery which eventually became associated with George's church. Inside, the Martorana stands as a classic of its time: outside, as a travesty encrusted with Baroque trapping and further defaced by rebuilt eastern and western ends.

The mutilations of sixteenth- and seventeenth-century 'modernizers', though they destroyed what must have been marvellously luminous apsidal mosaics, did not dim the lustre of the centre part of George's original church, which seems to burn with an inner light, a self-perpetuating fire of creativity. Here under the central dome we find none of the majesty of the Cappella Palatina, nor any of the glorious loftiness of Cefalù. This is intimate art, representing the basic stories of the New Testament—the Annunciation, the Nativity, the Presentation at the Temple, the Death of Mary—human stories all, family happenings, tales that are familiar to everyone because they are largely built on ordinary human experiences. In the manner of the day Joseph is shown truer to life than in some modern glamorized representations; here he is a mere appendage to the nativity scene, not really crucial to it, perhaps even a little forlorn in his realization that he is, after all, superfluous and in the way. Mary, on the other hand, is intimately involved with her Baby, pleased with her chosen part, glowing in her role of life source. Then, on the wall opposite, we have the other end of the life span—death. An outsized Christ is there at the Virgin's death, holding her soul in the form of a small child. Thus in the reversal of symbols so uniquely medieval we have the full life cycle—the mother as producer, holding her creation; the dying mother being held by her Divine Son who is the great Creator.

Two of the most fascinating of all the mosaics to survive the cruel restorations and rebuilding of the Martorana face us as we stand at the foot of the nave looking east. (*See page* 276.) On our right is King Roger himself, being crowned by none other than Christ. The king is every inch pure Byzantine, an Eastern potentate who bends ever so slightly to allow the crown to fit more securely. His beard is pointed, his hair drawn back; his expression is softer than Roger was perhaps wont to affect in the generally stand-offish, untouchable mien he bore. Yet one feels he would be recognized if he were encountered in a palace corridor or at a royal reception. He is dazzlingly outfitted in a long blue

Cappella Palatina,
Palermo

Cappella Palatina,
Palermo

Mosaic, Cappella
Palatina, Palermo

Chapter House, Bristol Cathedral, England

*Christ crowning
King Roger,
Martorana,
Palermo*

dalmatic and a golden pallium—sacerdotal implications. This is not just a ruler of an undisciplined rabble: Roger the king is on speaking terms with divinities. For all this, however, it is not Roger de Hauteville. Contemporary accounts tell us that he was tall and tended towards overweight. We do not know him as the gentle, mild-mannered, self-negating ascetic here shown insignificantly as only two-thirds the size of Christ. If he was not quite a physical giant, he was one psychologically at least, a despot capable of incredible cruelty and unpredictable generosity. A lifelike representation? No. But it is as true a likeness of Roger—a Norman of Byzantine pretensions and interests, a well-educated, philosophical monarch reigning over a viciously corrupt nation of mixed origin—as we are likely to find, psychologically truer than the majority of verbal accounts of his time. And the artist remains anonymous.

On the opposite side of the nave of the Martorana, on our left as we enter, is another interesting portrait, but this one not without its humour. Here we have George of Antioch, looking not unlike some strange shelled creature, grovelling at the foot of Mary to whom he dedicated the church. Unlike George, she is undamaged by time, and is holding a scroll on which is written in Greek a prayer for George both on earth and in the hereafter. She is a miracle of dignity, the vertical lines of her robe as elegantly refined as the flutings of a doric column. But there is nothing stagy about this Virgin, nothing pretentious or other-wordly, except the resplendent gold background. She leans towards George, her hand held in a manner bidding him rise. She is absolutely of the earth yet heavenly, all the more so in the face of the absurdly reconstructed body of the founder of the church rolling about at her feet.

Bell-tower, Martorana, Palermo

During a nineteenth-century restoration of the Martorana a Kufic inscription was discovered on the bottom rim of the dome at the feet of the archangels represented thereon, oddly enough of a Byzantine hymn to honour the Virgin. Why a Greek hymn written in Arabic? Many reasons have been suggested but John Julius Norwich comes up with the most intriguing possibility of all—'that this hymn was the particular favourite of George of Antioch himself, and that he loved it best in the language in which he had heard it first, half a century before, in his Syrian boyhood'.[220] To this day the church of the Martorana remains as it was founded, Greek in ritual and administered by Greek clergy. And so it was when visited by Ibn Jubayr, who was in Palermo in December, 1184, on his return journey to his native Cordoba.

277

One of the most remarkable works of the infidels that we saw was the church known as the Church of the Antiochian . . . The spectacle of [this] one must fail of description, for it is beyond dispute the most wonderful edifice in the world. The inner walls are all embellished with gold. There are slabs of coloured marble, the like of which we had never seen, inlaid throughout with gold mosaic . . . In its upper parts are well-placed windows of gilded glass which steal all looks by the brilliance of their rays, and bewitch the soul. God protect us (from their allurement). We learnt that its founder, after whom it was named, spent hundred-weights of gold on it . . . This church has a belfry supported by columns of coloured marble. It was raised cupola over cupola, each with its separate columns, and is therefore known as the Columned Belfry, and is one of the most wonderful constructions to be seen.[221]

1144

The 'conquest of conquests'—the fall of the city of Edessa to the Muslims —created so great a wave of consternation throughout Christian Europe that it led within a few years to the Second Crusade, one of the most mismanaged and ill-advised mass-movements in history. Violence was nothing new to Edessa, a city of northwestern Mesopotamia—the Urfa of modern Turkey. For centuries it had swung back and forth between Christianity and Islam, the earliest locale of Syriac-speaking Christians. Taken by the Muslims from the Byzantine Emperor Heraclius in 638, it continued to shift with changing dynasties and local Arab chieftains until, in the second half of the tenth century, it made peace with the Christian Byzantine Empire once again. By that time there were reportedly more than three hundred churches in Edessa, and the mosaic-lined cathedral was described as one of the wonders of the age.

After the expansion into Syria of the Seljuk Turks in the eleventh century Edessa changed hands several times between them and the Christians. In 1098, during the First Crusade, Baldwin of Boulogne (later king of Jerusalem) founded the Latin county of Edessa, which for the next half century formed the eastern bulwark of the Christian kingdom of Jerusalem. Then, in the 'conquest of conquests', Edessa was besieged and finally stormed by Imad-ud-Din Zengi, ruler of Mosul in Mesopotamia. The glow of the success of the First Crusade of 1099 had long since faded, and contemporary writers acknowledge that the defeat was the result not only of poor morale among the Frankish troops, but in fact of the noteworth absence of such soldiery. The only permanent standing army that existed in Outremer was composed of the two military orders, the Hospitallers and the Templars. They could hardly have been expected to hold out against the great and ever-growing might of the brilliant Zengi. It was time for a new crusade; but at that moment the only powers capable of mounting such an offensive in the name of Christ were involved with problems of their own.

Geoffrey Plantagenet was acclaimed duke of Normandy in the cathedral at Rouen, an investiture later confirmed by King Louis VII, but only after

Geoffrey, as a concession to the king, had deeded over the mighty castle at Gisors in the long-disputed Vexin. This distinct break between England and Normandy, the first since 1066, made Stephen's position even more difficult. But it was a fact of life he had to face. His capture at Lincoln had severely shaken the loyalty of his vassals. 'The long-term solution . . . was the reuniting of England and Normandy after Stephen's death . . . The answer to the problem, already becoming clear, was to recognize Henry as heir'.[222]

The early dukes of Normandy had resided at Rouen, but after the time of the Conqueror they tended to favour Caen, and later (having acquired other continental territory) Poitiers, Le Mans and Angers. At the time of Geoffrey, Ordericus Vitalis described the city as 'populous and enriched by commerce, its busy port and flowing rivers, and pleasant meadows, making it a cheerful residence. It abounds in fruits and fish, and is affluent in its supplies of all commodities, is surrounded on all sides by woods and hills, is strongly fortified by walls, trenches, and bulwarks, and its public and private buildings, its houses and churches, make a fine appearance'.[223]

The cathedral in which Geoffrey received his investiture for the most part no longer exists, having been burnt down in 1200. It had been built by William the Conqueror's great-uncle, Archbishop Robert, on the site of the ancient Roman forum. A few remnants of the original remain: the north tower of the western façade is mostly of Geoffrey's time (although the upper portion is a later addition), as are the two portals to either side of the main entrance. The southern tower—the Tour de Beurre (it was built out of 'donations' exacted for the privilege of eating butter during Lent; many European cathedrals seem to have similar towers, similarly named, proving only that a prodigious amount of butter was consumed during the medieval Lenten seasons)—is essentially Norman in spirit, squarish with high mullioned windows.

The western façade of Rouen Cathedral is mostly Gothic in style, an intricate filigree of flamboyant stone tracery which seems to wind and twist through and among an array of statues which, though actually in relief, appear to be completely in the round. The upward pull on the eye is irresistible. There is so much to see that even conscious effort to resist must give way to aesthetic demand as the sculptors, Jacques and Rouland le Roux, force our eyes to move over their sixteenth-century fretwork, upwards, always upwards, finally reaching the material point of finiteness at the spires. Although not without certain aesthetic problems and questionable details, the whole is fascinating, a shimmering mass of light and dark that makes one appreciate Claude Monet's infatuation with its impressionist possibilities.

Obviously the proliferation of the automobile has wrought changes. But not that many. The cathedral *place* still holds its dignity. It still maintains its animation and colour. Above all, from the *place* we can still bear witness to the subtly changing façade of the cathedral as the sun follows its diurnal odyssey, indeed even in the artificial light of night. From the *place* the church can be darkly moody and scintillatingly alive—but never threatening, despite its size—when it is shimmeringly awash in a Norman rain, intermittently illuminated by flashes of white lightning. Then it is most in keeping with the violent turmoil of its Norman heritage, most obviously a product of the quarrelsome people who produced it. John Ruskin saw it as a 'proper' Gothic building. (How typical of him to be so debatably judgmental—'proper', indeed!) It is lovely and tawdry, solid and delicate, masculine and effeminate, decadent and—yes, dignified. Overall, despite the fact that most of it is post-Romanesque in style, it is terribly Norman in its contradictions, from its north Tower of Saint Roman—so solid, almost dour—through its swirling Gothic-ness, to the alternatively much criticized and praised nineteenth-century cast-iron and bronze flèche—the Ravens' Glory—no masterpiece admittedly, but a wonderful 492 feet high launching pad for a soar into space.

The cathedral houses many tombs and memorials of Norman and French notables: Rollo, first duke of Normandy who died in 933, and his son William Longsword; Richard Lionheart and his elder brother Henry the Young King; and Empress Matilda. There is a tomb-memorial of Louis de Brézé, grand seneschal of Normandy, erected by his wife Diane de Poitiers and designed by Jean Goujon. Since Diane (mistress of King Henry II) was not the kind to remain sexually inactive for any length of time, acceptance of the inscription prophesying 'the most faithful spouse as she was in the marriage bed so will she be in the tomb' requires a grain of salt.

The rue Saint-Romain along the north side of the cathedral is lined, opposite the church, by half-timbered medieval houses, leaning jauntily, slanting and bulging at their joinings, lucky survivors of the last European war. It is fun to pick out the houses built before 1525 both here and in the district just to the east, in the area between the churches of St Maclou and St Ouen. The older buildings protrude over the street as they rise in their successive storeys, an overhanging of the public space and a consequent darkening of the narrow streets which was forbidden by law after 1525.

Joan of Arc was condemned to death in the archbishop's chapel in the rue Saint-Romain on 29 May 1431, in one of history's sorriest displays of blatant political expediency. Joan's first place of detention in Rouen is also still extant, known as the Tour Jeanne d'Arc, and a sombre, sinister looking place it is. She was finally put to the stake and burned in the market-place—the Vieux-Marché—now, alas, tastelessly filled by an extremely ugly, unfunctional modern church. It was so much nicer when it was an open square!

1146

Pope Eugenius III must have sensed from the start that he was going to have a rough time of it. The first thing to happen to him after his election to the papacy (in 1145) was that the Romans would not allow him to enter St Peter's until he confirmed the new republican government which had been established in the city two years before. Even so, the reconciliation proved impermanent, and Eugenius soon had to leave Rome again.

Thereafter the principal catalyst in Rome's continued revolt against papal shackles was, oddly enough a young priest and Augustinian canon named Arnold of Brescia, whom Eugenius himself had unwisely sent to Rome to do penance there. A man of great personal integrity, Arnold had become an outspoken adversary of the corruption of the clergy and the temporal power of popes. Eugenius, for the time being, settled at Viterbo. As well as his problem with the republicans in Rome, he had need to respond to the devastating news of the fall of Edessa. Unlike Pope Urban II, who had 'sent forth a voice like a heavenly trumpet and undertook to summon sons of the Holy Roman Church from the ends of the earth',[224] to free the Holy Land, Eugenius III was demoralized by total disinterest in his clarion call for a new crusade. A Cistercian, he turned to his former teacher Saint Bernard who could trumpet more shrilly. He was billed as guest speaker at an Easter meeting at Vézelay to which King Louis VII summoned his vassals.

Vézelay then had a population of close on ten thousand, though today it is made up of only a fraction of that number. Its Benedictine abbey put Vézelay on the map, especially after the acquisition of some relics of Saint Mary Magdalene, when enormous numbers of pilgrims were attracted to the hillside town. At the time of Bernard's call to arms the church was a new one (*see page* 293), the original having been destroyed during an insurrection which resulted in the murder of the abbot. (Vézelay was to be the scene of yet another 'taking of the cross' when English King Richard I and French King Philip II jointly vowed to go on the Third Crusade in 1190.) Rich in memories, Vézelay stands quietly on a hillside on the left bank of the River Cure, proudly dignified, like an old dowager aware of her wealth—her magnificent church—and of her former importance. Vézelay has been passed by in time. Tourists, too, bypass the town, speeding past within only a few miles, thus failing to enrich their own lives in the reflected glory of more than one moment of greatness. Most of Vézelay's medieval ramparts are still intact, and they testify to the impressive role the town once played. And its dignity is still manifest. But that is all.

When word spread of Bernard's planned appearance, Vézelay became congested with the curious and expectant from all over France, so many that the new Romanesque church of the Madeleine was not large enough to accommodate them. A wooden platform was hastily erected on a hillside, and remained there until it was destroyed during the Revolution of 1789. It was probably Bernard's greatest triumph. So tired and frail that he 'seemed already to be touched by death',[225] and yearning for the quiet of his cloister, he spoke so forcefully that the crowd demanded crosses on the spot, cloth crosses to be stitched to their tunics as emblems of membership in this new club. Bernard himself doffed his robe and tore it into strips to be sewn into the desired shape. Barons, lesser nobles, knights and peasants, all vowed to free again the Holy Land from the evil clutches of the infidels. Even Louis VII rose and 'with great eagerness of spirit received the cross . . . and volunteered for military service across the seas'.[226] He had in fact made up his mind long before.

So, also, had Eleanor. She was not about to be left behind, one of Bernard's 'widows . . . whose husbands are still living', whom he seemed so eager to brag about. There was no way that Louis could have left this headstrong woman at home. Though the chroniclers of the day do nothing to dispute her sincerity, Eleanor had surely heard the fabulous tales of the fairyland luxuries of Outremer. One suspects that she had reasons other than spiritual for her adamant insistence on going.

With this initial success—greater than Eugenius had dared to hope for— Bernard moved across France and eventually into Germany, where he collared

Speyer Cathedral, Germany

Conrad III of Hohenstaufen, successor to Emperor Lothair II, at Christmas time. The meeting took place in the cathedral of Speyer, a fortress-like Romanesque structure, heavy with round arches and dome. Like the rest of Bernard's listeners the king of the Germans (as yet—and forever—uncrowned emperor) was unable to resist his exhortations.

By this time Pope Eugenius was feeling that Bernard's zeal was misguided, that he was going a little too far. The pope had wanted Conrad III in Italy, not in the Holy Land. He still had not taken his rightful place on his pontifical throne, and he needed help in quelling the antagonistic Roman populace. Besides that, like his predecessors, he harboured ideas of taming the upstart king of Sicily; and only a German emperor could do it. Conrad had this year married off his sister-in-law, Bertha of Sulzbach (who changed her name to the more suitably Greek Irene for the occasion), to the Byzantine Emperor Manuel Comnenus, who had succeeded to the throne in 1143. Roger, although now the acknowledged master of the Mediterranean, could do nothing but view the German–Greek marriage as an alliance which threatened his Sicilian hegemony.

Bernard's crusading call stirred up a host of intermural suspicions in Europe's structure of royal houses. Roger certainly did not want to see the German king in Outremer where he could meet Manuel face to face over a conference table. On the other hand, knowing that it would be dangerous for him to leave his realm, no argument of logic or religion could have persuaded Roger to take the cross himself. He made only a token offer. Nor were Louis and Eleanor of France keen on the idea of Roger in Outremer, since Roger continued to claim Antioch (currently ruled by Eleanor's uncle, the high-living Prince Raymond of Poitiers) on the grounds that the state had been founded by his cousin Bohemund. Then, after Roger's cousin Bohemund II had died in 1131 while fighting the Muslims and Raymond had accepted an invitation to marry his widow Alice, Roger's henchmen had tried to kidnap him as he passed through Southern Italy on his way east. Arriving safely, Raymond married, instead of Alice, her nine-year old daughter Constance, becoming the ruler of Antioch and relegating the ambitious widow to obscurity. Again Roger had been done out of his claims.

Roger was relieved when his unenthusiastic offer to take part in the Second Crusade was turned down by the pope. As it was, the crusade worked in Roger's favour by distracting Conrad from trying to settle his Italian problem, and by forcing Manuel to grapple with a situation familiar to his grandfather Alexius I—the enormous onslaught of pillaging, ill-mannered, undisciplined Europeans flooding across his territory. That the English, involved in their civil war, would not take part in the crusade was a foregone conclusion.

This year Roger's kingdom began to take on empire proportions when George of Antioch captured Tripoli. Roger's forces had been harrasing North Africa for years, but here, finally, was something they could put their hands on and, it was hoped, something they could hang on to. While it proved to be a less permanent holding than Roger wished—in fact almost gossamer in its intangibility, held for little more than ten years—it still marked a high point in his might and a short period of economic and strategic advantage. Now more than ever he had command of the middle Mediterranean, as well as economic control over a large portion of North Africa by virtue of the fact that he dominated the major caravan routes.

1147

War fever swept the face of Europe. Bernard of Clairvaux was at his vocal best: 'Let not your former warlike skill cease, but that spirit of hatred, in which you are accustomed to strike down and kill one another . . . Take the sign of the Cross, and you shall gain pardon for every sin that you confess with contrite hearts'.[227] Barons encouraged their relatives and friends to accompany them to Outremer, in the meantime selling their property to raise money for the adventure. Troubadours wandered the countryside and visited courts, singing both laments and exhortations to battle, with refrains that became the slogans of crusading songs: 'He who goes with Louis will never have fear of Hell; his soul will go to Paradise with our Lord's angels'.[228]

The Germans sent out a more than slightly rag-tag army; the ill will it engendered in its passage was reaped by French who followed. By the time Louis reached Constantinople the Eastern Christians were thoroughly fed up with the destructive hordes passing through their realm. The German-Greek alliance was not helped when Conrad III's nephew, Duke Frederick of Swabia—later known as Barbarossa—still in his mid-twenties, gratuitously burnt down a monastery at Adrianople (modern Edirne) and murdered the innocent monks in revenge for an attack by local brigands. It was too much for Emperor Manuel. Though he welcomed Louis and Eleanor and entertained them at his court, he was plainly anxious for them to be on their way as quickly as possible. No sooner had they left when word came that the German army, already in Asia Minor, had been massacred by Turks and reduced to about a tenth of its original size. Conrad and Frederick had escaped, but it must have occurred to them right then that the crusade was doomed. Even more disturbing to Manuel, who already had troubles enough with Westerners, was the report that King Roger of Sicily had sent his fleet against Byzantine territories.

George of Antioch's assault on the Byzantine Empire cannot be described as anything other than an unprovoked attack. Sailing from Otranto, that favourite jumping-off place for points east, George of Antioch took Corfu without a struggle; the islanders, apparently resentful of Manuel's oppressive taxation, gave in to George and allowed him to establish a garrison there.

Having stablized Corfu, George of Antioch guided his marauding fleet quickly around the Peloponnesus and moved against Athens. He then sent a raiding party ashore to hit Thebes, the centre of the Greek silk manufacturing industry, where he reaped splendid booty. Once piracy gets in the blood the appetite is voracious. It was recorded that he was like some monstrous sea creature, swallowing everything that came before him. He kidnapped a large number of the women silk workers, many of them Jewish, to augment the royal *Tiraz* in Palermo. Thebes he plundered 'to its last penny and loaded his vessels so with captives, with gold and silver, and silken vestments, that his vessels sank as low as the third oar-bank in the water'.[229] Next on George's hit-list was wealthy Corinth, which held out so tenaciously in its fortress-like Acro-Corinth that he was forced to abandon hope of a breakthrough, though his lack of success did not prevent him from flinging a final petulant taunt at the defending commander to the effect that he was 'feebler than a woman and only fit to spin wool'.[230]

When George of Antioch returned to Sicily, he sailed into Palermo harbour a triumphant hero, 'his ships resembling the galleys of rich merchants rather than the pirate-craft that they actually were'.[231] Aside from the profits of looting, George had accomplished two worthwhile political gains: he had taught Manuel Comnenus a lesson lest he have designs of moving against the Sicilian kingdom; and he had taken Corfu into the Norman orbit, thus depriving that over-burdened emperor of his best launch point for an attack.

Twelfth-century history focuses on Outremer, the Mediterranean, Europe and England; it zeros in on capital cities, urban centres and those remote areas that grow up around strongholds or sites of natural resources; the personalities making history are royalty, nobility, Church fathers, an occasional saint, and the peasant only *en masse*. Small wonder that we give little time to another breed of men who did their bit to establish their idea of a way of life far from battlefields and castles and cities, seeking a new order, but finding it so difficult to create one in an age of upheaval and budding nationalities. The monks went about their business of setting things right with their God, working the land—especially the Cistercians—and practising the new science of animal husbandry, praying for a world gone mad, and hoping for a swift salvation.

Among the religious orders formed (or reformed) during the twelfth century was that of Savigny. The original Norman abbey, set up in 1112 on land given by Raoul of Fougères to its first abbot, one Vitalis (who had already spent around seventeen years living as a hermit in the forest of Savigny) was based on the Benedictine Rule. Like Cîteaux, Savigny encouraged agricultural work, held annual chapters for its daughter houses and incorporated lay brothers into the communities. Some thirty houses were established in France and England; had chance taken Saint Bernard to Savigny instead of to Cîteaux, it might have attained the prestige of the Cistercians. As it was, although successful enough, Savigny fell under the shadow of the ubiquitous Saint Bernard and in 1147 its third abbot, Serlo by name, effected a merger (or rather a take-over by the greater order).

One of the English Savignac houses was Buildwas, founded in 1135 by Roger de Clinton, bishop of Coventry. Its site was then in a remote part of the Severn valley, but today it is close to Ironbridge, which takes its name from the world's first bridge made of that material, a delicate span that crosses the Severn in fine late eighteenth-century style.

If the great cathedrals of the world represent the 'Church Triumphant', then Buildwas (*see page* 293)—like more than a few other small abbey churches—shows the more tender side of Christianity, its frank simplicity, its innocence, the personal love felt for a personal God and for His Son. Look to the cathedrals and the cities' basilicas if you seek the magnificent; but come back to the village parish church and the isolated monastery to find the divine essence, the simple belief in the Lord's Prayer and the unpretentious affection for the Ave Maria. This quality shows especially in Buildwas, in its simple round columns, so expertly cut and joined. And when the sun creates contrasting shadows across the floor of what was once the nave of the abbey church of Our Lady and St Chad (a seventh-century English saint), now a velvety carpet of lush green grass—beautiful but, alas, no longer tiled to echo the sandalled footfalls—surely it is then that the spirit of the Ultimate Light possesses every stone and chink, every weed struggling from untended crevices. The outer aisle walls of Buildwas are gone now, and the sun streams through in a way never intended, like a divine light penetrating the darkness, creating horizontal shadow arches, a rhythm of dark and light as persistent as the passage of years and the decay of churches. It bursts forth from the well of the universe in a flood of whiteness—gold and pink at sunset—through an area that was meant to be secretive, hidden, echoing mystery and flat-sounding chants. The church was never sizeable enough to incorporate a triforium gallery, nor rich enough to have its interior dressed up with frivolous decoration. Starkly simple it was, and dark—some would say depressing— cool, with even the eastern end devoid of large windows; all the better to enable the monks to contemplate the mysterious, to approach the unapproachable, to commune with the unknowable. Contrasts are the excitement of life: and if the monk saw his God as the true Light of the World, then what better place to experience the vibration of light than in its shadow? Light never seems so bright and clear as when we emerge from darkness. The phrase 'when I sit in darkness, the Lord shall be a light unto me'[232] might well have had added significance for the devout monk or lay brother breathing the incense-laden air made heavier by candle smoke, kneeling in the shadow of those mighty columns that shoulder so easily the Herculean load of bluntly pointed arches and the bank of clerestory windows above.

Geoffrey Plantagenet's ducal investiture of 1144 had brought temporary peace to strife-torn Normandy. Then this year fourteen-year-old Henry fitzEmpress—perhaps deciding that peace can be boring and craving a bit of action—decided to pull off his own private invasion of Stephen's realm. With a handful of like-minded companions and a small party of mercenaries whom he hired on credit (he must, indeed, have had a way about him!), he sailed for

England and attacked the castle of Cricklade, where he was promptly beaten back. Enthusiasm and boldness may be all very well, but hardly the equivalent of experience and strategy. Henry, frightened, and realizing he was in over his head, appealed to his mother and Uncle Robert of Gloucester for help, neither of whom rose to the occasion. Henry 'then, cheekily, applied to his other uncle, King Stephen, who sent him some money, so that he might pay off his mercenaries and go home'.[233]

With such heady events taking place it is small wonder that historians give practically no attention to the fact that Earl Robert died in October. He had not been chosen of fate. Had he been a legitimate son of Henry I 'he would have been unquestioned king of England on his father's death, and the claims of Matilda and the pretensions of Stephen would have been unknown to history. By all the evidence he was well fitted to rule. He was a man of honour, generosity, and dignity. He was cultured and sagacious'.[234] And perhaps his worst stroke of ill luck was having the bad-tempered Matilda for a half-sister. She, with her principal support snatched away, gave up the struggle and retired to Normandy, to the city of Rouen, where she lived out the rest of her days. From the point of view of Stephen's enemies she was no great loss, having been little more than a figurehead around whom they could gather ever since her brief moment of power in 1141. Any Angevin hope now lay with Henry.

1148

The most grievous of losses—that of a child—bereaved Roger when his thirty-year-old son, Duke Roger of Apulia, died of unknown causes. He had been a stalwart fighter all his life, a good politician, and a mirror of Hauteville pride. Young Roger was the fifth of the king's six children to die before him. Only William, the fourth son, remained to take over the vacated dukedom—and with luck to succeed his father. The Arab poet Abu-ad-Daw wrote a lament for the gallant young man, perhaps a small comfort to the grieving father in the manner of a friendly stroke:

> His tents weep for him, and his palaces; the swords and the lances are for him like women mourners. Hearts are rent with grief no less than garments; the hands of the brave have fallen; valiant souls are filled with dread; their words fail the eloquent.[235]

Roger had some additional consolation, though, when George of Antioch (always coming through at just the right time!) took the north African city of Mahdia, a final revenge for the disastrous debâcle there in 1123. The Sicilian hold on the city was strengthened by George's mild conditions of surrender—he allowed his troops only two hours of pillage. Other north African cities were taken—Susa, Sfax, Gabès—so that by the end of the year Roger's authority on the coast extended from Tripoli to Tunis. It was the apogee of his power, though it was to last only a short time.

Chapter Fourteen

If I were fire, I'd burn the world away;
If I were wind, I'd knock it to the ground;
If I were water, then it would be drowned.
If I were God, I'd make it Satan's prey . . .

Cecco Angiolieri, 'S'io fossi fucco, arderli lo mondo'.
Translated by Donno, *An Anthology of Medieval Lyrics*
Edited by Flores

1148

Hearing of the appalling ill luck that befell the latest host of crusaders, chronicler Roger of Hoveden observed: 'In the year of grace 1148, being the thirteenth year of the reign of king Stephen, the armies of the emperor of Germany and the king of the Franks, which, graced by those most noble chieftains, marched onward with the greatest pomp, were annihilated, because God utterly despised them'.[236] Henry of Huntingdon went further, pinpointing the sins that so angered a righteous God: 'They abandoned themselves to open fornication, and to adulteries hateful to God, and to robbery and every sort of wickedness'.[237]

But ill luck and providence had little to do with it. More mundanely, the blame for this new crusading fiasco can be put down to poor planning, internal bickering, the ravages of Nature, and marauding Turks. Louis VII, at the head of his French army, and Conrad, leading the sad remnant of German troops, struck out across Asia Minor for the southern coast. At Ephesus Conrad became so sick that he was persuaded to return to Constantinople. Upon recovering he would meet Louis in Syria. By the time the French contingent made it to Laodicea they were near exhaustion due to unrelenting heat and constant skirmishes with Turks who were seemingly everywhere—and invisible as well, until they attacked. But they struggled on. Daily the journey became more perilous; precipitous mountains and bottomless gorges, the same treacherous landscape that had so daunted the first crusaders.

And the weather! They were either frying in the sun or freezing at night. Horses died in such numbers from heat and strain that quantities of the pilgrims' much-needed baggage had to be destroyed. The French advance guard was all but wiped out by the ever-present Turks.

By this time Eleanor must have had profound regrets that she had ever decided to make this pilgrimage. Her love of travel had bested her judgement. Now, suffering hardships of travel unlike anything she had ever imagined, she was realizing her dreams of seeing exotic places and (according to inflammatory rumours—hilarious or shocking, depending on the gossip's inclination) indulging her fantasies and satisfying her need to attract attention and create scandal. Twentieth-century playwright James Goldman capitalizes on one of Eleanor's alleged flamboyant escapades designed to create sensation and

add to her notoriety. Years later, when the Second Crusade was all but forgotten, Eleanor engages in a fictional discussion with husband King Henry II:

> HENRY: You always fancied travelling.
> ELEANOR: Yes, I did. I even made poor Louis take me on crusade.
> How's that for blasphemy? I dressed my maids as Amazons and rode bare-
> breasted halfway to Damascus. Louis had a seizure and I damn near died
> of windburn, but the troops were dazzled.[238]

It was a sadly depleted force for Christ that finally gathered with equally
weakened German troops at Attalia on the south coast of Asia Minor. A
decision was then reached to go on to Antioch by sea. As a large enough fleet
could not be mustered the nobles, knights and the kings' households boarded
ship, leaving the rest to follow along on foot. Only half of the latter reached
Antioch late the following spring, their more unfortunate fellows having been
either killed or enslaved *en route*.

Sorely disappointed at the small number of Europeans who were arriving,
Eleanor's uncle, Prince Raymond of Antioch, still managed to put a good face
on it and welcomed them with open arms. He saw at once that capturing
Edessa was out of the question, at least for the moment. Instead he suggested
Aleppo, reasoning that the pressures on his own realm would thus be relieved.
But Louis had vowed to get to Jerusalem and did not want to be side-tracked.
He was anxious to assist the sacred city which was suffering increasingly
severe Saracen raids. But Eleanor took her uncle's side. She did not want to
leave Antioch.

It was like coming home again to arrive at a thriving, bustling city of
churches, bazaars, entertainments and—at last!—decent food. Besides, Prince
Raymond was attractive, tall, well-mannered and gallant. Better than anything
else, he could converse with Eleanor in her native *langue d'oc*, which Louis, for
lack of time or interest, could not seem to master. While the period of
uncertainty lasted Eleanor gave herself up to the blandishments of bazaars and
historic sights, always in the scintillating company of her charming uncle, who
was a worldly fiftyish. She enjoyed long intellectual conversations with him in
private, during which she let it be known that she was not happy in her
marriage, that Louis was 'more monk than man' and that she was contemplating ending their marriage. Raymond, seeing her for the comely, intensely
alive woman she was, encouraged her to have the union dissolved. Tongues
wagged that Eleanor was seeing rather too much of him, that he had
incestuous designs on her. Louis became jealous. That, as well as his learning
that Conrad had already reached Jerusalem, determined him to move on.
Eleanor made protests and excuses against going with him, raising the always
convenient point among royalty that, since she and Louis were related in the
fourth and fifth degrees, they had no business living together anyway. Some
of the chroniclers report that Louis became enraged at her arguments. He is
supposed to have abducted her from her room in the dead of night and
whisked her off to Jerusalem.

Contrary to her expectations, Eleanor liked Jerusalem. The city was in dire
need of friends, so once again the Europeans were welcomed as saviours. They

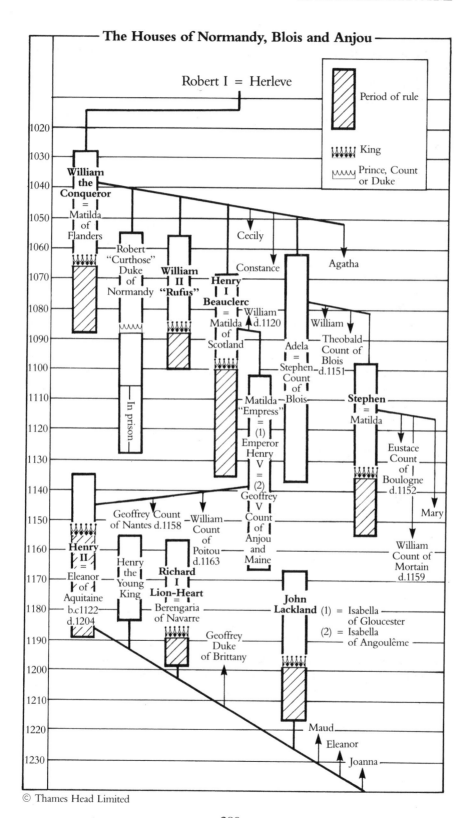

The Houses of Normandy, Blois and Anjou

Robert I = Herleve

Period of rule

King

Prince, Count or Duke

1020
1030
1040
1050
1060
1070
1080
1090
1100
1110
1120
1130
1140
1150
1160
1170
1180
1190
1200
1210
1220
1230

William the Conqueror = Matilda of Flanders

Robert "Curthose" Duke of Normandy

In prison

William II "Rufus"

Cecily

Constance

Agatha

Henry I Beauclerc = Matilda of Scotland

William d.1120

William

Adela = Stephen Count of Blois

Theobald Count of Blois d.1151

Matilda "Empress" = (1) Emperor Henry V = (2) Geoffrey V Count of Anjou and Maine

Stephen = Matilda

Eustace Count of Boulogne d.1152

Mary

Geoffrey Count of Nantes d.1158

William Count of Poitou d.1163

William Count of Mortain d.1159

Henry II = Eleanor of Aquitaine b.c1122 d.1204

Henry the Young King

Richard I Lion-Heart = Berengaria of Navarre

John Lackland (1) = Isabella of Gloucester (2) = Isabella of Angoulême

Geoffrey Duke of Brittany

Maud

Eleanor

Joanna

© Thames Head Limited

289

were escorted to its centre by the Knights Templar, who had gone almost to the gates of Antioch to meet them. First on the agenda, Louis was taken to the Holy Sepulchre: he had refused either to eat or sleep until he had made that visit. '. . . There, in a transport of joy, Louis cast down the burden of his sins . . . and laid his offering upon the holiest altar in the world . . . It was only after [a] circuit of the city that the king and his *mesnie* were lodged at last in the ancient Tower of David, where the patriarch had provided richly for their entertainment'.[239] And there the harmony ceased.

1149

Arguments, bickerings, petty jealousies, indecisions, a futile attack on the city of Damascus, all of these combined with the heat and the impatience of the men at arms to bring the Second Crusade down in shameful disarray and a final humiliating retreat. After lingering a year in Jerusalem, Louis and Eleanor departed for home, sailing from Acre in separate ships. As part of the fall-out of chronic Sicilian-Byzantine hostilities Eleanor's ship was captured by the Greek navy, only to be rescued by the Sicilians; and Eleanor ended up in Palermo. She must have been intrigued by the Byzantine character of the court there, the royal harem, the Saracen army, the Greek churches and the Arab members of the court. It is doubtful whether she had yet heard of the death of her Uncle Raymond who had been killed at just about the time she was leaving Acre. It is even more doubtful that she was looking forward to meeting her husband in Calabria, where he had finally landed. Having been welcomed ashore by a commiserating Roger II, he was now impatiently awaiting his wife. On top of all she had been through, and devastating her plans for divorce, Eleanor was pregnant. The royal couple visited Pope Eugenius III at Tusculum where he had a lot more on his mind beside his exile: and Arnold of Brescia was still stirring the crucible of Roman insurrection.

> Now he openly attacked the cardinals, saying that their assembly, because of their pride and avarice, hypocrisy, and manifold wickedness, was not the Church of God, but a house of business and a den of thieves . . . He said that the pope himself was not . . . an apostolic man and a shepherd of souls, but a man of blood, who upheld his authority by fire and slaughter, a tormenter of churches, an oppressor of innocence, who did nothing . . . but feed on flesh, and fill his own coffers and empty those of others.[240]

But even in his hardships the pope had time for the troubled royal couple. He tried unsuccessfully to gloss over their marital problems, for he saw that Louis 'loved the queen passionately, in an almost childish way. The pope made them sleep in the same bed, which had been decked with priceless hangings of his own; and daily during their brief visit he strove by friendly converse to restore love between them'.[241] Eugenius forbade under pain of anathema any further discussion of problems of consanguinity between Louis and Eleanor. But Eugenius did not understand. The rift was unhealable. Eleanor was a sexually dissatisfied woman.

Once back in Paris Eleanor knew that Louis would have to take the initiative in any annulment proceedings. Eleanor's latest pregnancy (she had earlier presented her husband with a daughter) had come to term. Another girl!—Alice, future countess of Blois. After fifteen years of marriage she still had not given Louis a male heir. Perhaps, annulment was a duty.

While Louis and Eleanor were experiencing the nadir of their marriage, Roger of Sicily was reaching the apex of his career through his diplomatic skill and in spite of intended annihilation from two co-ordinated challengers, Manuel of Constantinople and Conrad of Germany. During the two winters that Conrad had spent with Manuel, his brother-in-law had been agreeable to elaborate plotting to rid the world of the Sicilian upstart: the island was to be returned to the Byzantine fold, as well as Southern Italy, which Conrad conceded to Manuel. For this reason Conrad hurried back to Germany to prepare for the concerted assault on Roger's kingdom. With Venetian help Manuel at last succeeded in taking Corfu, his one success in the Sicilian offensive. Meanwhile troubles in Germany kept Conrad distracted.

Never mind that Roger lost Corfu. The year ended with both emperor and king totally incapable of moving a muscle against him. One suspects that Roger had stirred up opposition forces in both lands to such an extent that Manuel cancelled his Italian invasion plans in order to deal with a Balkan uprising; and Conrad postponed his because of threatening intrigues on the part of Count Welf of Bavaria, a professed rival for the imperial crown.

The royal sun might seem to be setting in France and to have reached its zenith in Sicily; it was, some thought, just rising in England. At Whitsuntide this year young Henry Plantagenet was knighted at Carlisle by his uncle and most eminent kinsman, King David of Scotland. This event sparked a renewal of England's intermittent civil war, with the people at large the main sufferers again, since both sides resorted to a scorched-earth policy. After unsuccessful operations in the north, Henry fled south, where Stephen and his son Eustace did everything in their power to corner him, setting themselves 'to lay waste that fair and delightful district, so full of good things, round Salisbury; they took and plundered everything they came upon, set fire to houses and churches, and, what was a more cruel and brutal sight, fired the crops that had been reaped and stacked all over the fields, consumed and brought to nothing everything edible they found'.[242] The ferocious determination of Stephen's attacks indicates the seriousness with which he viewed Henry's presence and new position as head of the opposition. He correctly saw the young knight as a viable substitute for his own son Eustace as king of England. In the end Henry was advised to return to Normandy.

1150

On landing in Normandy Henry was greeted effusively. It was no accident that Geoffrey Plantagenet chose this time to invest his son with the title of duke of Normandy. Henry was enthusiastically received by the barons.

They saw in this macho seventeen-year-old an end to the incessant warfare that had been ravaging the duchy since his birth. Indeed, the barons on both sides of the Channel, remembering the palmier days of Henry I, had had enough of anarchy. The peasants simply wanted to be let alone, to plough their fields and tend their animals in peace. England in particular was crying out to be rescued.

> Heir to thy grandsire's name and high renown,
> Thy England calls thee, Henry, to her throne;
> Now, fallen from her once imperial state,
> Exhausted, helpless, ruined, desolate,
> She sighs her griefs, and fainting scarcely lives:
> One solitary hope alone survives.
> She turns to thee her dim and feeble eye,
> But scarce can raise the suppliant's plaintive cry;
> 'Save me, oh save me! Henry; or I die:
> Come, saviour, to thy own; by right divine
> Fair England's royal diadem is thine'.[243]

It seems remarkable that through all the disruption that had been and was taking place in England, building work of any sort could be continued. Yet it was in this year that work was completed on one of the most monumental architectural crowns in the kingdom: the church of Tewkesbury Abbey. Now the second largest parish church in England and one of the finest of all Norman churches (that part of it that is still Norman, at any rate), it received its crowning central tower, a massive structure forty-six feet square and one hundred and forty-eight feet high (though the upper stages were not added until 1160).

According to tradition Tewkesbury Abbey occupies a site initially settled by a seventh-century monk named Theoc, who built his isolation cell there on the bank of the River Avon near its confluence with the Severn. In the eighth century Benedictine monks built a monastery, but nothing remains of it today, and little is known of it except that it was so badly slighted by Danish raiders that it was assigned a daughter role to a more prosperous parent organization in Dorset. With the Conquest it passed into Norman hands, and was eventually given by William Rufus to his cousin Robert fitzHamon, who founded the present abbey, though he did not live to complete it. One of Henry I's many illegitimate sons, Robert Fitzroy, carried on the work of the building, which was consecrated in 1123.

The largest Norman tower in existence is the most striking feature of the church. The lower storey forms a solid base for the upper two, which, being later, are more ornate, though still distinctly Norman. The massive block rises imposingly from the central crossing, superb in its arrogance, almost lyrical in its two-stage transition from sheer bulk to a cube of pierced walls and blind arcades. It is bound to appear majestic, since the church is almost precisely the same grandiose size as Westminster Abbey, though there the resemblance ceases; unlike Westminster, Tewkesbury has retained most of its Norman character, at least on the outside. It has much the same feeling as the gatehouse at Bury St Edmunds, so brazenly massive below, and lighter, more

Church of
The Madeleine,
Vézely, France

Buildwas Abbey Church, England

Sculpture over door, Malmesbury Abbey, England

Support for Tomb of King Roger, Palermo

Kilpeck Church, England

Bitonto Cathedral, Italy

Goodrich Castle, England

Cathedral, Caserta Vecchia, Italy

Street in Anagni, Italy

decorative—but never effeminate—above. At the very top the battlements and four corner pinnacles—these last the sole touches of frivolousness or caprice—are the only non-Norman parts of the church, having been added in the sixteenth century.

Unfortunately, the inside of Tewkesbury Abbey is not of the same calibre. No doubt magnificent at one time, with its impressive parade of stout columns holding up ponderous round arches, it has been ruined by a later disrespectful age that replaced what was probably a simple flat wooden roof, in keeping with the supporting architecture, with the most complex lierne vaulting. In no way is it a happy marriage, for it pits two incompatible styles, the results being to dwarf the awesome giant columns, thereby detracting from the vaulting itself. The foremost of Norman characteristics, flawless proportion, has been thrown out of balance, with ribs soaring stridently from the capitals of the columns, inconsiderately blocking out light from the clerestory windows and occupying what was once an expanse of welcome plain wall above the triforium. The historical imagination suffers unless one can keep one's eyes focused lower, to view only what is Norman architecture as handsome as can be found anywhere. The destruction of the upper nave, fine as the additions may be within the framework of their style, is a classic example of what can happen when arrogant rebuilders, lacking any semblance of sensitivity to form, and suffering from a conceited disrespect for the worthy accomplishments of the past, set their minds to improve without knowledge or taste—and end by creating a superstructure totally inconsistent with the building they have used as their starting point.

The windows at Tewkesbury are mostly modern or of the fourteenth century. And there are several apsidal chapels dedicated to personages familiar to our story, such as Saint Margaret of Scotland, Saint Edmund the Martyr and Saint Nicholas. The western front is remarkable in its use of a soaring round arch which, firmly planted on the ground, rises vertically and terminates in a single vast curve at the very roof. The whole space thus defined is glassed, thereby compensating for the partially blocked clerestory windows with an augmenting flood of western light. Of the monks' quarters in the abbey little remains. But one can still see the interesting row of restored fifteenth-century rental shops which were owned by the abbey and which, no doubt, added measurably to the coffers of what was one of the richest foundations in all England.

Tewkesbury Abbey Church, England

1151

In August young Henry fitzEmpress was brought to the court of France by his father to do homage to the king for his duchy of Normandy. Louis received his visitors courteously, thereby recognizing Henry as the legitimate duke, which must have sent a shiver through Stephen of England; he had counted on Louis' support for the claims of his own son Eustace. The meeting was complicated, however, by what was a vulgar and undignified confrontation between Geoffrey Plantagenet and his royal overlord. Playing the aggrieved vassal to the hilt, Geoffrey dragged his own turbulent vassal, Rigaud Berlai, into court in chains, charging Louis with egging him on to ravage the marches of Anjou. Geoffrey refused to proffer homage, or to allow his son to, until he had redress. The affair was finally settled, but not before Geoffrey had been excommunicated by Bernard of Clairvaux, and when offered absolution in exchange for his prisoner, prayed publicly that if what he was doing was a sin God should not forgive him. In a fury of both anger and astonishment, Bernard claimed that he foresaw an early end for any man who could utter such blasphemy.

More important than this temper-ridden confrontation was the meeting of Duke Henry with Queen Eleanor. He was verging on eighteen, she nearly thirty. But she was enchanted the moment she saw him. His education appealed to her. She arranged several private meetings for intellectual conversation, though in the light of her reputation (and the events of the ensuing months) she may have had other ideas in mind. At least more than a few chroniclers and later historians have intimated as much.

Henry was large for his age, broad-shouldered, deep chested—robust. He was not especially handsome, but his ruddy colour and reddish hair made the not unhealthy Louis look positively peaky by comparison. He was an extremely physical young man with an energy born of a nascent sexuality that was bound to intrigue the love-deprived queen. His legs, well formed in their tight hose, and his muscular arms showed him to be a man of action and, though he was soft-spoken and courteous, a lover of athletics and the violence of arms and the hunt. When Henry came into Eleanor's view her future suddenly looked brighter than it had since before the crusade. But the prospect of gain was by no means one-sided. Henry, with his royal ambitions and training, could use a worldly queen. She had travelled the breadth of Christendom had known notables from all the 'civilized' courts, visited exotic places. 'Her knowledge of places and personages, of affairs, of gossip and intrigue, made her a helpmate nonpareil for an ascendant king . . . Eleanor was unquestionably a prize with a dower meet for any king'.[244]

Their stay in Paris accomplished—and more of a success than either of them suspected—Geoffrey and his vigorous son left for Angers. It was a warm September, with blue skies backing scudding clouds. The grain was tall in the fields, made more brilliantly yellow by patches of glowing mustard; grapes were heavy on the vine, and there was still a glory of wild flowers, toned down from springtime exuberance but still in profusion. All was well with the world for father and son. In a moment of levity, as well as wishing to shed the dust of the road, they doffed their clothes and plunged into a refreshing pool along a tributary to the placid Loire, just south of the city of Le Mans. After the horseplay of an enjoyable 'skinnydip' they climbed out refreshed and ready to move on. During the night Geoffrey was taken with chills and high fever. Three days later he was dead. He was buried in St Julien's Cathedral at Le Mans. His duties accomplished, Henry hurried off to Angers to claim his new realms of Maine and Anjou.

In the south neither Pope Eugenius III nor Roger of Sicily was sitting in enviable comfort on his throne. Though Pope Innocent II and just about everyone else in Christendom had recognized him king of Sicily, Roger had yet to win over the new pope. And the matter concerned him since he needed papal sanction to assure the succession of his one remaining son, William. Feeling the advance of years, Roger took matters into his own hands, papal approval or no: he had William consecrated and crowned co-king on Easter Day in Palermo Cathedral. The resident Archbishop Hugh officiated. Henceforth young William would be king along with his father, sharing the responsibilities and learning the ins and outs of the feudal laws of the realm. All of this did nothing to assuage the almost paranoid fears of Pope Eugenius, who would have been well advised to see the Sicilian Normans as Pope Gregory VII had come to see Robert Guiscard seventy-one years earlier: as friends—better, as protectors. But so far as Eugenius was concerned Roger was totally untrustworthy; and this business of admitting a co-ruler into the governing machinery of his realm was proof enough. More than ever the papacy needed the armed might of the German king (the yet uncrowned emperor) to rid itself of this dangerous, at times belligerent, foreigner.

1152

King Stephen suffered his greatest personal loss with the death of his wife on 3 May. Matilda of Boulogne had loved Stephen from the time she had married him in 1125, and had remained loyal to him through the many years of anarchy. She died at Hedingham Castle in Essex, and was buried in the abbey at Faversham which she and her husband had founded. She had reason for exhaustion. Her assault on Winchester by which she had routed Empress Matilda was not the first time she had taken the field in defence of her brave but unwise husband.

As comfort went in the twelfth century, Matilda at least had the benefit of dying in amiable surroundings. Built by Aubrey de Vere, grandson of a man of similar name who had accompanied William the Conqueror on his invasion, Hedingham stands as one of the most striking of the tall Norman keeps. The second Aubrey had been lord great chamberlain of England under Henry I, a title held by his descendants until the eighteenth century. The third Aubrey fought at Antioch with Bohemund de Hauteville where he proved himself worthy of that best of crusaders, and then took the side of Empress Matilda against Stephen, being clever enough to emerge from that struggle with his family, property and rights intact.

Hedingham Castle dominates the town and the surrounding countryside so imperiously that it seems only fitting that the town has adopted its name. From the outside it gives an impression of ponderousness, of brute strength, standing 'to this day as an ideal picture of a Keep—on a mount, high above old trees, with two of its square corner turrets still rising up to nearly 100 feet. It is besides probably the best-preserved of all tower-keeps of England. In proportion, style, and detail that of Rochester is its nearest relation, and the two may well be the work of the same architect or *ingeniator*, as the designer of fortifications was called'.[245]

Like Castle Rising it had a fore-building which, in this case, is gone now, though the steps are still there. The marks of its roof-raggle where it attached to the main structure can be clearly seen. There was no interest on the part of Aubrey de Vere in creating a pleasing façade other than through the simplicity of its basically fine proportions and the quality of its splendid oolite masonry. No decoration other than chevron patterns on the window arches of the top storey, no pleasant little flights of whimsy or design capriciousness entertain the visitor.

Castle Hedingham, England

At Hedingham one gets an idea of what the rooms of an important twelfth-century Norman castle were like. No castle interior is more apt to thrill the tourist who seeks it out and climbs the circular stairs to the great hall, a room two storeys high and traversed on a higher level by a gallery passing through all the window bays, to form a magnificent circuit of the hall as well as to provide some advantageous nooks and crannies for viewing the domestic action below. This great room, with its gallery like a triforium of a medieval church, and its enormous fireplace, conjures a vision of twelfth-century comfort unattainable elsewhere. Hedingham has an advantage over many other castles in that it has wooden flooring, though not the original (which was totally burned out when the keep was gutted by a fire in 1918).

The sweeping arch which spans the great thirty-eight by thirty-one feet hall soars two storeys upwards, acting as a main support for the floor above. And a magnificent curve it is! There is a similar arch below, in its turn supporting the floor of the great hall, but it lacks the vastness of space necessary properly to display its noble dignity. The arch of the great hall has been singled out as the finest of its kind in the world.

For anyone who does not understand the meaning of majesty in architecture a mere glance at the central span of Hedingham's hall will make instantly clear what words have difficulty in defining. Unlike the fine but heavily arched cross-walls that divide the great halls of other castles, such as Rochester, Hedingham's flying arch creates an expansive, uninterrupted floor space, moving in a slow curve from one side of the room to the other, anchored on either end by a wall column and clearly performing its function of supporting the upper floor. If Aubrey de Vere set out to achieve an aristocratic grandeur in architecture, he was eminently successful in his central hall. But he also managed to create a hospitable interior, an open room where bulky piers of cold stone are not in evidence, where spaciousness allows for gracious living. Undeniably the hall, the focal point of castle life, has about it an amiability, an airiness, a richness of light and, with those wide fireplaces (there is also one on the floor below, which must have been a garrison room), offers a warmth unknown to most other castles of the period. The mind boggles at this point, however: there are no chimneys—only small vents through the outer wall which must, at best, have offered only a minimal chance for allowing smoke to escape. The provision of storage space is proof of a growing feminine influence in castle planning, as the walls of Hedingham are honeycombed with closets. Oddly enough, neither kitchen nor chapel is located within the keep, a singular omission for such a distinguished fortress-home. There is a well shaft in the northeast corner with openings on every level. The chapel, kitchen, a hall and other outbuildings which made up the intimate life of every castle were all located around the keep on the two-acre bailey.

Hedingham Castle has played an active part in England's history, especially during the reigns of kings John, Henry III, Henry IV and Henry VII. It is open during the summer months, but only on certain days, so prospective visitors would do well to check in advance. Among interesting features of Hedingham are the exceptionally legible masons' marks on many of the stones. Individual masons of the period can be tracked around England by means of these trade marks, each one unique and exclusive.

On 21 March, the Friday before Palm Sunday, the archbishop of Sens called a conclave of august churchmen to consider the intricate problems of the long anticipated annulment of King Louis VII's marriage with Queen Eleanor. Bernard of Clairvaux, as always thoroughly distrustful of the queen (he recalled only too well her appalling upbringing by her libertine father), had already convinced Pope Eugenius III that the laws of consanguinity made the separation imperative—the usual excuse for these political shenanigans. The synod was held mainly for the purpose of ironing out political problems and feudal laws as they applied to the two principals and to the country as a whole. Bernard's rhetoric aside, the fact of the matter was plainly one of inheritance of the crown: Eleanor had been lax in her duties by not supplying her husband with a male heir. There were the two daughters, Marie and Alice, but they simply would not do. France needed a son to take the helm. Look at the horror abroad in England due to the pretensions of a woman! So far as Eleanor was concerned, she simply wanted to be free. The parting was amicable. The two princesses were declared wards of the king; Eleanor's domains were restored to her, and both the principals were assured that they might marry again should they desire. With these agreements the annulment was announced— news which must have hummed sweetly in the ears of young Henry Plantagenet. It was momentous for both France and England, oddly ignored (though not entirely) by the chroniclers. Eleanor herself would have been hard put to see the agreement as 'a step of inconceivable folly on the part of the French King, and direct cause of the bitter conflict between France and England which was to embroil the two countries for the next 300 years'.[246] Freed at last, Eleanor suddenly found herself the object of much unwanted male attention. As the most experienced and intelligent woman of her day, still young—she was just about thirty—the possessor of wealth beyond most men's imaginings, and a former queen, she was made to realize immediately how very vulnerable she was to every kind of pressure, including outright kidnapping. Planning to stay at Blois for the first night on her journey home to Aquitaine, she was obliged instead to press on to Tours and then to Poitiers, to avoid the plot of Count Thibault of Blois to detain and marry her.

But she was not yet free of her admirers. Henry's younger brother, Geoffrey of Anjou, aged sixteen, ambushed her train as it neared the River Loire, planning to take both her and her possessions by force. After out-manoeuvring this second valiant she found her way to her own lofty castle at Poitiers where she was safe from youthful brigandish vulgarity. But not from Henry. In May, perhaps beckoned by Eleanor, Henry showed up at Poitiers. While she had never laid eyes on Louis until he had arrived at Bordeaux to marry her, Eleanor 'had already had a view of this bridegroom and was prepared for the bold, stocky, deep-chested, high-hearted, rufous young duke who came riding his stallion over the bridge . . . On the 18th of May, scarcely eight weeks after the decree, the erstwhile queen became Duchess of Normandy . . . The Duchess of Aquitaine was thus . . . swept into the orbit and encompassed by the destiny of her former lord's hereditary enemy'.[247]

Now, with the added power Henry had amassed in land, wealth and men, his chances of ultimately capturing the English throne seemed considerably improved. Louis of course was furious. He asked himself the obvious question: what had happened to his right as Eleanor's feudal overlord to arrange her marriage? Henry only recently had made vows of fealty to Louis and had received the kiss of peace. Was this his way of exercising a vassal's duties? Louis summoned Henry and Eleanor to appear at his court to answer for their infringement of feudal law. They ignored the command—Henry was planning to visit England—and Louis therefore invaded Normandy.

We do not know the inheritance provisions Duke Geoffrey Plantagenet had made for his sons. His intentions were explained verbally to his magnates on his deathbed. Whatever they were, son Geoffrey was not satisfied. The flair he had demonstrated in his attempted kidnapping of Eleanor would seem to have been the showy efforts of a young man desperate to make his mark, perhaps to spite an up-and-coming elder brother. Geoffrey now joined the king of France in his attack on Normandy, and was forced just as quickly to concede to his brother's superiority. Henry also quickly countered the royal army, recapturing border towns and establishing a defensive line. Eventually Louis, unwell and disillusioned, arranged a truce and returned to Paris.

At the beginning of 1152 the future of the kingdom of Sicily appeared suddenly threatened; Conrad of Hohenstaufen was at last ready to press his claims on Southern Italy and to rid the world of the Norman kingdom and its creator once and for all. Pope Eugenius needed no persuasion to give moral backing. Manuel Comnenus was pledged to swoop in from the East, and had convinced his Venetian allies that they should join this new 'crusade'. But fate was on Roger's side; and fate alone settled the last crisis of his life.

At fifty-nine years of age, on 15 February, Conrad III died at Bamberg, surrounded by doctors, some of them Salernitans. He was buried in the cathedral of Bamberg by the side of Emperor Henry II, a man who had suffered similar frustrations and humiliations in his dealings with the unmanageable Normans. Even had he lived in less turbulent times it is doubtful whether Conrad would have been a successful ruler. There is a persistent note of melancholy hanging over the memory of his reign; rejection was the keynote of his life. He had been repudiated by both Pope Innocent II and his rival, the anti-Pope Anacletus II. Then, when he was crowned king of Germany, he was not totally accepted even there, never managing to rule without the threat of being unseated. And, worst irritant of all, he had never been allowed the pleasure of receiving the imperial diadem. 'He was the first Emperor-elect in two centuries . . . not to have been crowned in Rome—a failure which somehow seems to symbolise his whole reign . . .'[248]

On his deathbed Conrad passed over his own son because of his youth, appointing his nephew as successor. This was the Frederick Barbarossa—'Red Beard'—who had so appalled Emperor Manuel by killing innocent monks and torching their monastery while on the Second Crusade. So the duke of Swabia became King Frederick I and future Holy Roman emperor. By boat and horseback he came to the city of Aachen, where he was crowned and seated on the throne of Charlemagne, to the applause of all present.

While Roger can hardly be expected to have lamented the death of Conrad III, he must have deeply mourned the passing of George of Antioch, his emir of emirs, who died either this year or the year before. The high admiral had done much for Roger, and is certainly one of the more likeable figures of our story. A swashbuckling leader of the Sicilian navy, he was also an intelligent

Ponte dell'Ammiraglio,
Palermo

man, a linguist, as sensitive to human suffering as a twelfth-century man of authority could afford to be, as well as being a lover and patron of the arts. His Martorana stands, one hopes forever, on the enormous architectural plinth which it shares with San Cataldo; but his lovely bridge over the River Oreto is, perhaps, more truly his memorial. The bridge spans the dry river bed—the river has been diverted—in a march rhythm of seven arches, proudly pointed and rising progressively to the centre. George would be proud to know both that his bridge still stands in his name (it is called the Ponte dell'Ammiraglio) and that, in Italy's great Revolution it formed the stage for the first battle between the royalist Neapolitan forces and Garibaldi's Thousand on 27 May, 1860. It seems somehow appropriate that this should be so.

1153

By the turn of the new year, reinforced by the additional men and wealth of Eleanor's dowry, Duke Henry gathered together thirty-six ships, pointed them towards England, and sallied forth. He was in the nick of time, too, since his adherents had been clinging desperately to the hope that he would arrive before they were forced to surrender to a desperate and determined King Stephen. Henry's followers manning Wallingford Castle in Oxfordshire had been suffering a protracted siege, and had even gone so far as to notify him that they would be forced to capitulate if he did not relieve them soon. Henry totally disconcerted his enemies by an unexpected strategy.

Instead of galloping to the aid of Wallingford Castle as expected, Henry turned the tables on Stephen by attacking Malmesbury in Wiltshire. Before the king could get there, caught off guard as he was, Henry had taken the town and was besieging the castle. Since Malmesbury was the royalist equivalent of Wallingford, Henry knew that Stephen needed to defend it with all his strength, and to do so would be obliged to raise the siege of Wallingford.

It was a bitterly cold winter, with sudden downpours of freezing rain swelling the streams and rivers. Famine was abroad; there seemed no end to the hardships that Nature was inflicting on the unhappy land. By the time Stephen arrived at Malmesbury he was fearful that his own barons were being tempted to desert. His troops were so numbed by cold that they could hardly hold their weapons. There were two sorry armies facing one another across the swollen River Avon, chilled to the bone, cold-infected and wet to the skin. The colourful, loose-flowing surcoats which the knights took to wearing about this time over their hauberks, clung soggily to their armour. This new shift was shaped like a tube, belted, and slit up the sides so that it could be worn in the saddle. The knights barely had the energy to support their shields, brightly painted with devices which were family emblems and now just starting to be passed from generation to generation. On both sides of the Avon everyone was so uncomfortable and lacking in energy, the weather was so bad and so cold, and the deprivations so severe that a temporary truce was called—with Stephen getting the worst of it. Malmesbury Castle was to be demolished, though the story is told by at least one chronicler that the engineer in charge of the demolition handed it over to Henry intact.

A modern market town, Malmesbury started as a tiny hermitage built in the shadow of a rough stockade on the fringes of the Selwood Forest. An Irish scholar named Maildubh, seeking a place for solitary contemplation, had arrived there about 635 but, defeating his own purposes, was forced by circumstance to take in paying students. A town grew up around his settlement, and it was not long before the hermitage became the nucleus for a thriving abbey. Aldhelm, its first abbot, a learned scholar and prolific writer, introduced the Benedictine Rule there.

Located so far west, Malmesbury was not noteworthy in the swim of English politics and violence—until 1153, that is. The West Saxon King Athelstan was one of its major benefactors, and was buried there. One of our more reliable medieval chroniclers, William of Malmesbury, as his name indicates, was a monk of the abbey. And according to legend there had been Oliver the Monk, an early would-be Wright brother, who made himself a pair of wings with which he attempted a flight from the lofty western tower. He plummeted to the ground without so much as an ounce of lift and hobbled about the abbey a cripple for the rest of his life. In the later Middle Ages Malmesbury Abbey sank into a slow and sorry decline, and at the dissolution of the monasteries was bought by a rich clothier named Stumpe, who used the buildings as workshops.

All that is left of the great abbey church of SS Peter and Paul at Malmesbury is the fine Norman nave with flanking aisles, and splendid Romanesque sculptures on the east and west walls just under the porch vaulting arch. On one wall (*see page* 294) there are several apostles, surmounted by a flying angel who is crowded into the space immediately below the arch, seemingly a bit cramped, but not lacking in verve for the smallness of the space allotted to him. In truth, all the figures seem to lack elbow-room, a condition which does nothing to impede their style and dignity, though it does make for slightly leaning attitudes. They are all men with large feet and hands, expressively positioned heads, and robes delineated by swirling, rhythmical lines indicating folds but in no way attempting to imitate them. Marvellous figures they are, much more aware of the angel zooming overhead (and who would not be?) than they are of us as we crowd through the door beneath them. Faithful or merely curious, it makes no difference what our stand; they treat us all with equal—well, not quite disdain—perhaps tacit disinterest. But even that statement must be mitigated; tacit except for the one apostle just left of centre. He inclines his head downwards, holding his hands in a gesture which implies some surprise at seeing us there. He is not annoyed. We have not distracted him from higher thoughts or churchly argumentation. He is simply more friendly than the others. Perhaps he is Saint John, the most loved disciple of Christ, sitting comfortably among the other less gregarious apostles. He does not smile; neither does he frown. He accepts the fact that we are there. We smile up at him. How can we help it? Powerful figures these; stone—almost blatantly stone—the finest Romanesque sculpture in England. Certainly not men at our level; it is only our century that likes to reduce everything to the democratically mundane and ordinary.

The truce between Henry and King Stephen having run out, the two stalked one another around the English countryside, periodically exchanging roles of hunter and prey. Several times mediators tried to bring about a settlement, but the pay-off opportunity did not present itself until Stephen was driven into a dispirited malaise and finally immobilized by the unexpected death of his son Eustace. Though he had another son, William, Eustace was the one whom Stephen had trained and guided to succeed him as king.

While Henry and Stephen were sparring cautiously with one another across the breadth of England, always refusing to come to direct and decisive encounters or negotiations, Eustace had been careering about Cambridgeshire on a rampage of wanton destruction calculated to bring Henry into open battle. But Henry did not accept ready-made situations; he created them. The picture of a frustrated, worried and impious man, Eustace ravaged the very land he hoped one day to inherit, finally lighting on Bury St Edmunds. In a tantrum of murder and mayhem brought about by the abbey's refusal to give him money to pay his troops, he torched the surrounding countryside, destroying the monks' crops. Some said it was divine vengeance that struck him down shortly afterwards by causing him (by one account) to strangle on a dish of eels. It was then that Stephen abruptly tired of the struggle. The negotiators moved in, and on 6 November king and duke were persuaded to meet for a reconciliation at Winchester. Out of this unanticipated meeting emerged one of the strangest, yet workable, treaties of the Middle Ages.

Robert of Torigni, a contemporary chronicler who was at this time prior of Bec and was, next year, to become abbot of Mont-Saint-Michel, reports the unusual agreement that Stephen should remain king for his lifetime or for as long as he wished, in return for a sworn recognition by Stephen and the assembled magnates, of Henry's hereditary right to succeed him. 'What boundless joy, what a day of rejoicing when the king himself led the illustrious prince through the streets of Winchester, with a splendid procession of bishops and nobles, and amidst the acclamations of the thronging people; for the king received him as his son by adoption, and acknowledged him heir to the crown! . . . Thus through God's mercy, after a night of misery, peace dawned on the ruined realm of England'.[249]

At Stephen's Christmas court the Winchester decisions were given greater legal force in a charter he issued from Westminster. As well as repeating the main provisions of the treaty, the charter made careful arrangements to safeguard the landholdings of Stephen's surviving son William.

One can imagine Louis VII's secret thoughts at this turn of events. He would never have been so generous in the annulment settlement had he had any premonition at all of what less than twelve months was to yield. It was bad enough that Henry's and Eleanor's lands had been united, making those two vassals richer territorially than he, their overlord. Now the prospect of adding all England to their holdings, not including the spheres of influence in Scotland, Wales and Ireland—well, it was intolerable! And that Henry should return to his waiting duchess in glory, the acknowledged future king of England, the successor of the great William the Conqueror, and the vindicator of his mother the empress was more humiliation than any monarch should be expected to endure. Henry was able to hold out a promise to his duchess far in excess of anything she herself had dreamed—and her dreams were opulent enough! Acknowledged heir to England, Henry returned to his future queen riding a swelling wave of success. He came to her at Angers, where she had set up a court of culture at the heart of his undisputed holdings.

The residential castle at Angers, vastly modified by King Louis IX (Saint Louis) between 1228 and 1238, is as formidable an example of feudal defensive architecture as one can find. Its seventeen towers, lower now than they once were, rise from 130 to 195 feet. Sitting so comfortably by the River Loire, the black slate castle seems to wish to appear forbidding. It almost glowers. But this posture is only an act. The beautifully curving Loire, the clear skies and verdant growth of Anjou do not allow for that sort of negative put-down. The herd of timid deer grazing so calmly in the now dry moat seem much more indicative of the twentieth century than of a medieval one.

Castle at Angers, France

Within the precinct of Angers Castle a modern gallery has been erected to display one of the finest collections of fourteenth-century tapestries in existence. On order of Louis I, duke of Anjou, Hannequin de Bruges designed a series of 'Apocalypse' tapestries, which were executed by Nicolaus Bataille, the most famous weaver in Paris. Perhaps it was the nature of the times that caused Duke Louis to choose such subject matter—plagues, wars, rains of fire, famine, pollution, the most dreadful visions of horror, relieved by an occasional vaguely optimistic passage.

For those who like to draw contrasts, Angers' former hospital of St John (established in the twelfth century) houses a series of magnificent modern tapestries, the *Chant du Monde* by Jean Lurçat. Over 260 feet in total length, woven in glowing colours and with intense swirling lines, the tapestries depict a world in which war is eliminated, space is conquered, plants bud and bloom and re-seed, and animals cavort. Also, while comets leave trails of flames across the heavens, Man performs the dance of life under a burning sun, a splendid song to Man's ultimate conquest—of himself.

There was nothing provincial-seeming about the Angers of Eleanor's and Henry's day. The cathedral of Saint Maurice is of their century, arched by the first Gothic vaulting in Anjou, dating from just about the time that Eleanor was awaiting the return of her duke. There are none of the usual deadeningly hollow echoes here, the walls still being covered by tapestries first-rate (mostly Aubusson) as they were in the past. The play of light from the twelfth- and thirteenth-century stained glass windows reflects, intensifies and complements the tapestries; its effect is fortunately not lessened by the inferior windows of the next three centuries which, alas, seem to strive to become paintings rather than stained glass. We study the early windows with undisguised admiration, with love, with a feeling of spiritual fulfilment. The Angers Virgin and Child is a masterpiece of the brittle art of glass, unbending in its assertion of its material, of such dignity of concept—though not without a sweet naïveté—that we hesitate to stare at it for too long lest we appear gauche. The woman is a queen and mother, just as Eleanor was shortly to be. She looks us straight in the eye, almost unaware of the Baby who is struggling to raise His tiny hand in blessing. The slightly garish clash of purple, green and cobalt merely accents the Virgin's Byzantine affectation. But this Virgin is no mosaic. No! The Virgin of Angers is glass, a true source of light to her modern vassal who stands in the dim shadows at her feet. She is light itself—penetrating, soothing, calming, and not without humour in her wide-eyed stare. Her creators, it would seem, were inspired to transcend mere earthly bounds, to go beyond normal tastes and needs and desires. And that was the way with these early Gothic windows.

The city of Angers, among the most handsome of modern French cities, has other churches of the twelfth to the fifteenth centuries, and a fine array of Renaissance wooden houses. For those interested in historical connections, a section of its main boulevard is called the rue Plantagenet. Weaving is still practised as a major industry at Angers, along with the production of slate, wine, oil, leather and fruit liqueurs.

No twelfth-century woman was better equipped than Eleanor to capitalize on the knowledge that she had absorbed from her childhood, from the Capetian court and from her travels through the Eastern capitals of the world. She soon attracted to her court a generation of men of letters and art, all eager to gain their name through her patronage. While Henry Plantagenet was in England forcing Stephen to the bargaining table, Eleanor, free at last from the narrow surveillance of the conservative French nobility, sent out the word to creative men. These harbingers of the future streamed into Angers. Eleanor and her artists and thinkers and singers removed the hampering shackles, creating a frame of mind not unrelated to the later ages of Reason and Enlightenment. 'The colourful *langue d'oc* was heard far more frequently than French or Latin, and, according to fourteenth-century biographers of the troubadours, it was at this time that the most gifted and tender of all these poet-singers, Bernart de Ventadour, first visited Eleanor's court'.[250]

Bernard de Ventadour, young, handsome, loving, talented—and poor—was welcomed by the temporarily grass-widowed duchess, herself eager for a little dalliance and receptive to the troubadour's songs of praise. True to the style of the day, Bernard fairly languished in his love for the lady. 'I may go without clothes, naked in my shirt,' he wrote to his duchess, 'true love protects me from the chill wind . . . I have taken thought of myself, from the time when I first begged the most beautiful for her love, from which I expect so much good that in exchange for these riches I would not take all of Pisa'.[251]

The son of a furnace stoker and baker at the castle of Ventadour in the Limousin, Bernard had learned the art of the troubadour from the master of the castle, Viscount Eblas III, a vassal of Eleanor's. He had indeed learned his art well—in more ways than one. He outstripped his tutor as both troubadour and lover of the castle's mistress, going so far, according to the slanderous (or envious?), that he was forced to take to the road. Though we think of Bernard as the most ethereal of poets of love, he had an unmistakably sensual side:

> . . . And I can find no fault in her
> If she but graciously consent
> One night, while shedding all her clothes,
> To set me in some chosen place
> And make a necklace of her arms.

Elsewhere there is a real cry of passion:

> And I will kiss her mouth a thousand times,
> That one month hence the traces can be seen![252]

Admittedly all this must not be taken too literally—exaggeration was the name of the game. The *chansons* may have defied credibility and ignored logic, but they do have a sentimental tug, a joy, a freshness, a sadness almost to despair that is built of intimacy. They have a true-to-life honesty that points the way out of some of the more sombre, tight-lipped tendencies of the Middle Ages. The escape from medieval abstraction may have been tortuous, but it was none the less inevitable. Bernard de Ventadour and his fellow troubadours and artists were anticipating a more sensual world than ever the Church-dominated Middle Ages approved.

With this new burgeoning of wordly pleasures perhaps it was just as well that two entrenched defenders of rigid morality passed away this year: Pope Eugenius III and Bernard of Clairvaux. As for Eugenius, who died at Tivoli, seldom has a pope experienced a more troubled reign and seldom has a more unlikely candidate for a success story filled the chair of Saint Peter. And yet, contrary to all expections he managed to rise above the quicksands of episcopal treachery and contemporary politics, in many ways asserting the primacy of the Church and his own place as its leader. Very few of his eight years as pope were spent in Rome, owing to the volatile Roman populace's response to the many voices of reform, especially that of Arnold of Brescia. Many times Eugenius must have mourned the change of attitude on the part of the flock he had been elected to lead. Eugenius—and Bernard, too—must have stared into the mirror of contemporary disillusionment reflected in the tale of *Aucassin and Nicolete*, a story set in Provence but showing Northern French characteristics. It was not long in penetrating every corner of medieval Europe, every court, sacred or secular, indeed the very Church itself.

In Paradise what have I to win? Therein I seek not to enter, but only to have Nicolete, my sweet Lady that I love so well. For into Paradise go none but such folk as I shall tell thee now: Thither go these same old priests, and halt old men and maimed, who all day and night cower continually before the altars, and in the crypts; and such folk as wear old amices and clouted frocks, and naked folk and shoeless, and covered with sores, perishing of hunger and thirst, and of cold, and of little ease. These be they that go into Paradise, with them have I naught to make. But into Hell would I fain go; for into Hell fare the goodly clerks, and goodly knights that fall in tourneys and great wars, and stout men at arms, and all men noble. With these would I liefly go. And thither pass the sweet ladies and courteous that have two lovers, or three, and their lords also thereto. Thither goes the gold, and the silver, and cloth of vair, the cloth of gris, and harpers, and makers, and the princes of this world. With these I would gladly go, let me but have with me, Nicolete, my sweetest lady.[253]

We may wonder whether Bernard of Clairvaux, on hearing of the pope's death, had any misgivings concerning the undignified display of pique which he had vented on the election of that pontiff. For when word arrived at Clairvaux Bernard was himself on the verge of death. He was sixty-three years of age when he finally succumbed, dropsical but mentally alert, on 20 August.

The student of the twelfth century understandably becomes a little bored and sometimes irritated with the endless eulogizing of this saint. In truth Bernard was first of all a politician, a fact which calls all his spiritual attributes into question. Bernard was fanatical, utterly uncomprehending of any kind of disagreement. He manipulated, hounded and persecuted. He hesitated not at the prospect of spilling blood; witness his call to the Second Crusade, and his encouraging of Lothair to war against Roger of Sicily. Yet there is no doubt of Bernard's sincerity. His concern for Man approaching the *dies irae* of his imagination was genuine, as was his love for his brothers, though the latter was sometimes curiously manifested. It is his ingenuousness that, if he is likeable at all, makes him so. He believed; and he believed strongly.

Almost immediately on Bernard's death a movement was started for his canonization, which took place in 1174. It remains difficult to dislike the man totally—and just as difficult totally to understand the saint. It is certainly hard to accept Dante's assertion of Bernard as

> . . . the living love
> . . . who in this world, through contemplation,
> tasted the peace which ever dwells above.[254]

If there is any satisfaction to be gained by the ways of the world, both Bernard and Eugenius might have had such a pleasure had they lived two years longer. Then, in June 1155, they would have seen Arnold of Brescia finally condemned, hanged and burned, and his ashes thrown into the Tiber.

1154

The great cathedral at Cefalù had been designated by Roger II as his final resting place. A large but simple porphyry sarcophagus had been waiting nine years to receive him. But Roger never found his way to Cefalù after his death on 26 February 1154. For one reason or another (mostly political) he was buried in the cathedral of Palermo, tawdry by comparison to Cefalù, and in a different porphyry sarcophagus. In the south aisle of the cathedral Roger now rests in company with his daughter Constance, her husband Emperor Henry VI, and their son—Emperor Frederick II. But none of their tombs was originally in this part of the cathedral. 'Not until after the remodelling, or rather the ruthless destruction, of the interior of the old cathedral by Ferdinand Fuga in 1781-1801 were the tombs transferred to their present unsuitable location in the two western-most chapels of the right-hand aisle.'[255]

Roger's tomb (*see page* 294) is the handsomest of the group, simple, unadorned, with a pitched top and resting on marble supports carved to resemble youths kneeling under the weight of the great load they bear on their shoulders. And it is arched by a heavy marble canopy glittering with mosaic, dignified by good taste and with only a touch of ostentation. European Roger—he of Byzantine tastes—would have approved once he had accepted the fact that history was not to allow him to rest in the place of his choice.

Roger had expanded his empire beyond the dreams of either his father or his uncle, Robert Guiscard. If they had ever thought in terms of Africa, for example, they never let it be known. They may have thought of kingship— almost certainly Roger I did—but never for themselves. Roger II was the man who achieved it. And we must agree with John Julius Norwich when he maintains that territorial expansion alone is not a valid measure of success; neither is the dignity of office. The great glory of Roger's reign is the government he imposed over diverse peoples, languages and religions, wherein each was allowed to maintain its identity and dignity and still be embraced by laws geared to everyone's interest. While establishing a high, quasi-religious aura around the crown, Roger promulgated his law by creating strong institutions; to build these he imported a galaxy of the ablest men he could find, and from their labours rose the most successfully integrated kingdom of the Middle Ages. Roger then surrounded himself with an almost mystic splendour that lent credence to the popular idea that he was, if not divinely appointed, at least divinely inspired.

There is a quality about Roger that one cannot help but like. Yet he remains remote; we do not even know the cause of his death. From where we stand his father appears more likeable, perhaps because we know more about him. He was more into the struggle—and struggle is more intimate, more exciting, and usually more interesting than attainment. Roger II managed well in a world that was ill-prepared to receive him and that he seemed ill-prepared to govern. At the beginning one would have thought he was doomed, pushed into a society treacherous by any standards, a physical age where muscle was used to settle matters which should have been dealt with through the philosophical reasoning to which it gave persistent lip service. He was the absolute opposite of his warlike forebears. He laboured mightily to bring about a better world, especially a more equitable one; even the Arab writers point out that he honoured and respected them as he did his own people. And, these writers point out further, he was loved in return. That Roger admired the Muslims is clear; but he also used them. The most intellectually distinguished of them was Edrisi—'the Strabo of the Arabs'—who, thanks to Roger, has been granted a place of honour in the annals of Western history. Having been trained at Córdoba, he became a close friend and guide to Roger in his scientific speculations. Roger loved geography and mathematics, and commissioned Edrisi and a team of scholars to compile a treatise on his own kingdom and also the rest of the known world. This, based on existing sources both Arabic and European—including Ptolemy and Orosius—and almost certainly on contemporary travellers' accounts, is generally known as *The Book of Roger*. The text was originally illustrated with maps (now mostly lost or partially damaged) and is pariculary valuable for the information it gives on Roger's Sicily. It was completed in 1154. Edrisi also made a silver globe and planisphere, but neither has survived.

Thanks to Roger and his translators—with a healthy boost from their brethren in Spain—much of Greek learning, which had long been lost to the West was re-introduced into Europe. Edrisi wrote that Roger was 'the best and most celebrated among monarchs . . . He unites high intellect and goodness; to these are joined his resolution, sharp understanding, deep spirit, foresight, his skill in all measures, which betray a masterful intellect . . . His sleep is as the awakening of other men. I cannot enumerate his knowledge of the exact and technical sciences, nor set bounds to his wisdom'.[256] Roger's story is magnificent. It needs no glamorization by writers, artists or musicians—as in composer Karl Szymanowski's hokey opera *King Roger*.

However fine Roger's intellectual achievements, his success was in the end limited; the integrated society he created did not last. 'For a few more years yet Norman Sicily . . . was to increase its influence and prestige from London to Constantinople. Two more Emperors were to be humbled, one more Pope brought to his knees . . . But already the internal fabric of the state was showing signs of decay; . . . the kingdom, though still golden in its splendour, embarks on its last, sad decline.'[257]

Roger's sole surviving son, King William I, labelled by posterity, perhaps a little unfairly, the Bad, received his kingly crown for the second time from the hands of Bishop Hugh of Palermo on Easter Sunday. No doubt he felt confident, for he had inherited his father's chancellor, Maio of Bari, whom he immediately promoted to be emir of emirs, 'one of the most fateful acts of his entire reign'.[258] Unlike his father, William was content to leave the administration of the realm to his ministers; and Maio adopted a policy of excluding the naturally rebellious Norman barons from any positions that might afford them political leverage, thus contributing massively to the inevitable ruin of the realm. But Maio brought about the decline in other ways as well. A southern Italian, he encouraged the growth of the Latin Church at the expense of both the Greek Church and of Islam, thus upsetting a balance of power that had been carefully nurtured and maintained by the two Rogers. An increasing number of Western churchmen were attracted to Sicily, men who were by nature intolerant.

Roger had raised his people to new heights of prosperity and pride; King Stephen of England had reduced his to new depths of deprivation and misery. They were both honourable men, Stephen and Roger, honourable within the context of the twelfth-century meaning of that word. Roger was not a soldier by nature; his talents lay in politics and diplomacy. On the other hand Stephen 'was a man of activity, but imprudent; strenuous in war; of great mind in attempting works of difficulty; mild and compassionate to his enemies and affable to all; kind, as far as promise went; but sure to disappoint in its truth and execution . . .'[259]

It was not without a sigh of relief that England greeted the news of the passing of King Stephen on October 25. Disheartened by the deaths first of his queen and then of his son, he had become daily more lethargic in spirit. Twice before he had lain in a coma verging on death. This time, while he was at Dover Castle, he fell into a similar condition, violently ill of 'a chronic flux of haemorrhoids', and unable to be moved. Thus was brought to an end the unhappy reign of this most physically attractive but tragically ambitious man. The judgement of history has been less than flattering. He was cursed with an innate weakness; always lacking the proper drive to be a successful king, he acquiesced, made concessions, waffled, bought off the opposition and gave away properties. Eventually he came into conflict with the Church itself, which had originally upheld his claims. But he cannot be blamed for the fact that whereas Innocent II had supported his claim, later popes, especially Eugenius III, favoured the Angevins. His ill-treatment of Roger of Salisbury in 1139 had been less damaging to his relations with the Church than to the administrative system so painstakingly built by Henry I. But twelfth-century satirist Walter Map's statement that Stephen was a near idiot inclined towards evil is too strong. His great sin was that he lacked ruthlessness. He was succeeded by a strong king, active, enlightened—and ruthless. History makes a comparison in favour of the latter.

Henry Plantagenet found himself preparing to cross the Channel sooner than he had expected when parting company with Stephen barely twelve months before. But this time he was accompanied by his stunning wife, pregnant with her second son (her first, William, had been born in 1153 but was to survive only until 1156), and sad to leave her beloved Southern France. Yet she was anxious to fulfil her destiny by the side of her loud, robust man who was more active physically and sexually than ascetic Louis ever pretended to be. God was on Henry's side, it seemed, eventually granting him a covey of sons. Henry had further reason for swagger. He was on his way to assuming control of an expanse of territory vastly larger than any anticipated by his great-grandfather William the Conqueror. Furthermore his arrival was anticipated with nation-wide eagerness.

Henry was delayed at Barfleur by poor sailing conditions. But he was determined on a coronation before the end of the year so that a festive Christmas court would be the first one of his reign. He finally set sail in defiance of the elements, not quite making Southampton as intended, but arriving close by, and all his scattered ships making safe landfalls. 'From Mont-Saint-Michel-in-Peril-of-the-Sea, the archangel had stretched forth his mighty arm and brought that precious company up living from the deep.'[260]

He must have cut a wonderful figure, this new king; and his queen was no doubt the object of many a praising glance. Eleanor, always ready with a winning smile and the manners of a cultured and impeccably noble lady, was exactly the right counterpoint to Henry's mien. What he lacked in fineness of feature and finesse of manner he certainly made up for in vitality, an athletic quality that was not lost on his barons, and a natural restlessness that made him appear to stalk rather than walk. His very arrival on the island in the teeth of winter storms which would have deterred a more timid man was taken as a symbol of the new regime, an omen of the energetic pursuit of justice and order that his courtiers came to rely on.

Henry insisted that they head straight for London, visiting only those towns which lay *en route*. The skies were cloudy and heavy with damp and cold, but the people came out of doors to feast their eyes on the richly caparisoned procession and to cheer their glamorous new royal couple. Through Hampshire and on towards London they were accorded the joyous welcome Henry expected.

Approaching London from the south, the royal retinue crossed the Thames from Southwark by means of a wooden bridge on the site of present-day London Bridge. Eleanor realized at once that she would like London—except for the climate. It was an active city, she could see that, a centre of the representational and architectural arts, a point of convergence of the rich literature of Europe. By this time Westminster had become a populous suburb already linked to the city of London, but both of them bearing vivid testimony to the nineteen-year struggle between Stephen and the Angevins. The royal couple found that Westminster Palace 'had been so despoiled by the followers of Stephen that it could not be occupied. The Plantagenets were obliged to take residence in Bermondsey . . . at the busy east end of the city, below the old bridge and nearly opposite the Tower . . .'[261] Even Edward the Confessor's triumphant Westminster Abbey was dingy with neglect and not far from dilapidation. But that was no reason to delay the coronation proceedings.

Henry had his work cut out for him. Institutions had to be restored; the legal system needed revamping and strengthening. The central government, which had fragmented under Stephen, had to be pieced back together. Warfare against the bands of mercenaries and bandits who terrorized the roads of the realm was a first priority. The economy needed revitalization. Just as Edrisi could eulogize the late Roger II, so could Henry of Huntingdon praise the living Henry II even before he landed on England's shore.

> Fresh genial warmth shall burst the icy chain,
> In which, benumbed and bound, the land has lain;
> England with tears of joy shall lift her head,
> And thus shall hail her saviour . . .[262]

Everyone rejoiced, anticipating a brighter future, except Bernard de Ventadour—now moved to Toulouse. His loss seemed irreparable, a loss perpetuated in the *Carmina Burana* manuscript, and popularized through the music of Carl Orff:

> Were the world all mine
> From the sea to the Rhine,
> I'd give it all
> If so be the Queen of England
> Lay in my arms.[263]

PART THREE

Shame on
a
Defeated King

*Who lives in this world and isn't a King
or Emperor, or Pope, or at least a Duke,
These people get no say in anything.*

Guiseppe Gioachino Belli,
'The Sovereigns of the Old World'.
In *Sonnets of Giuseppe Belli*
Translated by Miller Williams

Chapter Fifteen

'. . . Provided they themselves are willing.'

('. . . Si ipsi consentire vellent'.)

1154

Henry II's defiance of tides and weather was not lost on his subjects; from the moment of his landing in England he became legendary, looked upon as a man who had challenged divine providence—and had won. As he moved northward towards London Henry marshalled an ever-growing body of nobles and churchmen, a good army of them Stephen's former adherents, nervous now in their roles as sustainers of the new royal family. 'Curtmantle' they called him, making fun of his short French-styled cape. But Henry could afford to ignore the gibes. Riding the crest of his acclaim, he was in no mood for vindictiveness; nor did he have need of it. So convinced was England of Henry's abilities that for the six weeks between the death of Stephen and Henry's landing no challenge had been made to his authority. Archbishop Theobald of Canterbury deserves the lion's share of credit for keeping the explosive baronial tempers and ambitions under control until the new king arrived. Norman by birth, and a former abbot of Bec, Theobald was an independent thinker, willing on more than a few occasions to stand against royal authority. It was Theobald who had brought Henry and Stephen together at Winchester for the reconciliation that ended the civil war and put Henry on the throne sooner than he had anticipated. In the course of his tenure at Canterbury, Theobald was the patron of three of the most eminent men of his day: Thomas Becket, who this year was just about to enter Henry's service; Vacarius, an Italian jurist who was the first to teach Roman law in England; and the scholar and chronicler John of Salisbury.

The London in which Henry and Eleanor found themselves was a thriving medieval metropolis, guarded on the east by William the Conqueror's White Tower, and on the west by two great castles, Baynard and the Tower of Montfichet.

There runs continuously a great wall and high, with seven double gates, and with towers along the North at intervals. On the South, London was once walled and towered in like fashion, but the Thames, that mighty river, teeming with fish . . . has in course of time washed away those bulwarks, undermined and cast them down. Also upstream to the West the Royal Palace rises high above the river, a building beyond compare, with an outwork and bastions, two miles from the City and joined thereto by a populous suburb.

On the North are pasture lands and a pleasant space of flat meadows, intersected by running waters, which turn revolving mill-wheels with

316

merry din. Hard by there stretches a great forest with wooded glades and lairs of wild beasts, deer red and fallow, wild boars and bulls . . .

There are also round about London in the Suburbs most excellent wells, whose waters are sweet, wholesome and clear . . .

Among these Holywell, Clerkenwell and Saint Clement's Well are most famous . . . In truth a good City when it has a good Lord![264]

London may well have been 'a very noble city', but Eleanor, for one, must have found it close to unendurable. After all, had she not been raised in Aquitaine, 'opulent in every kind of wealth'?[265] With opulent Bordeaux as its capital and Poitiers, a neighbouring city just to the north, with their lordly and comfortable castles infinitely more hospitable than the draughty fortresses she was likely to know in England, Eleanor could have been nothing but displeased with the prospect of life there. Acknowledging the plaudits of her welcoming subjects, she had no way of anticipating just how agonizing and bitter her stay in this island realm would prove to be.

The hastily contrived coronation of Henry and Eleanor was magnificently enacted on the Sunday before Christmas in 1154 in a tawdry if not delapidated Westminster Abbey. Seventeen years of anarchy had left pockmarks on the venerable, solidly Romanesque building, the pride and joy of Edward the Confessor. The truth of the matter was that Westminster had fallen on hard times, with many of its properties ravaged or stolen during the anarchy.

The nobles were all there on this 19 December, for once in apparent agreement that the twenty-one-year-old taking the crown was the best that England could expect after her years of trial. They carried the royal regalia: the *Curtana*—the sword of Edward the Confessor—blunt-pointed, the emblem of the sword of mercy; the orb and sceptre; the crown; the ring of the Confessor; the cross of King Alfred. There were the Church hierarchy, including a smattering of abbots and priors. Jewels and furs abounded, even on the lesser nobility who trod the cloth that marked the path of the procession. There followed the bailiffs and mayors, the sheriffs, knights and wealthy citizens. Henry and his queen walked to the service, enjoying the acclaim of the crowd. Henry was not unattractive. The picture of courage and energy, of fearlessness, of action, he

was a man of reddish, freckled complexion with a large round head, grey eyes which glowed fiercely and grew bloodshot in anger, a fiery countenance and a harsh, cracked voice. His neck was somewhat thrust forward from his shoulders, his chest was broad and square, his arms strong and powerful. His frame was stocky with a pronounced tendency to corpulence, due rather to nature than to indulgence, which he tempered by exercise. For in eating and drinking he was moderate and sparing, and in all things frugal in the degree permissable to a prince. To restrain and moderate by exercise the injustice done him by nature and to mitigate his physical defects by virtue of the mind, he taxed his body with excessive hardship, thus, as it were, fomenting civil war in his own person.[266]

But it was the glamorous Eleanor who attracted the eyes of the masses. Radiantly beautiful she was, with the brown eyes of Southern France, the clear alabaster skin, dark hair, soft and in four plaits in the most up-to-date fashion. She had not changed much since her marriage to Louis VII of France, unless one looked more closely than one was able to in the coronation crush. If anything she was even more beautiful. Wearing a form-fitting tunic of white, overlaid by a gold-bordered pelisse edged with fur and with ermine-lined sleeves, she trailed a long train which was borne by two adolescent pages.

Close by her husband as he sat on the curved, wooden faldstool, Eleanor listened attentively to the sermon. Prayers for the success of the new regime echoed among the slow-curving arches of the vast church, even permeating the quiet cloister itself where the capitals depicting Biblical scenes enlivened brooding shadows and reflective silences. One capital still survives, showing the Judgement of Solomon, precisely at that moment when he orders his soldier to divide the living baby while the heart-broken mother implores him to spare the child and give it to the pretender. 'The use of this subject at Westminster was probably intended not only as an illustration of the well-known Biblical event, but also as an allusion to King Solomon's wisdom which should be an inspiration to all rulers'.[267]

Eleanor could smile with satisfaction when Theobald of Canterbury lowered the crown to Henry's head, reminding him that he assumed the rule of the land only with the consent of the ruled—'si ipsi consentire vellent'. Then Henry mounted the steps of the dais to take the throne of his forefathers, while shouts of *vivat rex!* and *waes hael!* from Normans and Saxons respectively rent the newly established quiet of the realm. The young king and his queen stood in their glory as the *Te Deum* was intoned by the monk attendants calling on God to look after the fledgling regime.

With Eleanor at his side, one son ready to start crawling about the palace halls and another on the way, Henry was, even at the time of his coronation, in an enviable position of strength. Almost all classes were anxious for stability and strong government after the years of civil war and rapine. As it turned out, Henry's main problems during his reign were with the intransigent Thomas Becket who was to succeed Theobald as archbishop of Canterbury in 1162, and later with his own quarrelsome and greedy sons, each of whom was to demand his patrimony before Henry was willing to relinquish it. Henry was destined to spend prodigious energy and a good part of his time in suppressing revolts from both within and without his family. But from the moment he took the crown it was clear to his adherents that Henry's main interests were Continental. So far as he was concerned Normandy and England were annexes of Aquitaine and Anjou, and he needed to spend as much time in his French duchies as in England. He had cause for optimism. Had he not been brought to England as a saviour whose destiny was to lead those ill-used people back to a saner world?

Probably sometime in the 1150s—the date remains obscure—a church was completed at Kilpeck in the western county of Herefordshire that vividly illustrates the eclectic propensity of Norman builders. The southern marches between Wales and England are relatively little known to the tourist, perhaps because they are perilously adjacent to place-names that seem so difficult—so

Welsh—most of them suffering an insufficiency of vowels and 'all those *dreadful* consonants!'—as one Englishwoman put it to the author. There are orchards and fields, sturdy Hereford cattle—white-faced and sad-eyed—undulant landscapes, gardens of hops for English beer. And there are the meandering rivers, Severn and Wye, so rich in salmon. The people are as charming as English people can be, busy with their bee-keeping and growing what they claim to be the best cider apples in England—although this is disputed in Devon and Somerset. Cider-making is an ancient art in Herefordshire, not surprising when one remembers that there are over 350 varieties of apples grown there, fruits which 'have been given strange and picturesque names . . . like 'Slack-my-girdle', 'Sheep's Nose', 'Duckbill', 'Cider Lady's Finger', 'Cat's Heads' or 'Old Foxwhelp'.[268]

Located eight miles southwest of Hereford, Kilpeck was probably the site of the cell of a local Saint Pedic (or Pedoric)—'kil' meaning cell or retreat. A church was established on the site in very early times, and a village of about six acres grew up around the hallowed spot, located to either side of the present church drive. The Saxons revamped the tiny shrine, parts of which are still incorporated within the existing building; and a small fragment in the northeast angle of the nave is pre-Conquest. William the Conqueror gave Kilpeck to a kinsman, William fitzNorman, who built the motte-and-bailey castle nearby to the west, now a sorry ruin but still recognizable.

It was William fitzNorman's grandson Hugh—by this time styled de Kilpeck—who built the parish church of SS Mary and David (originally associated with a Benedictine monastery) with a nave only 31 1/4 feet long, which he constructed of rubble walls with ashlar dressings. The sculpture throughout is representative of an eclectic school that developed in the West Country, especially in Herefordshire, and which 'owed its origin to a recorded journey of Oliver de Merlemond . . . to Santiago de Compostela in about 1135. He must have had in his retinue a sculptor who, on his return to England, made use of the sketches he had made on the journey, for in . . .

Kilpeck . . . motifs derived from churches on the pilgrimage route are used side by side with Anglo-Norman and Viking decorative elements'.[269] Celtic interlacements, Byzantine-looking figures, semi-oriental patterns and Viking bravura could also be mentioned. But the church, very little altered since the twelfth century, must be considered Norman. It is a priceless bit of heritage, and ranks high among Norman churches surviving in England.

The inside chancel arch is stunning, comprised of heavily semi-circular arches of chevrons, lozenges and pellets supported by columns fashioned into six 'apostle' figures,

Kilpeck Church, England

three on each shaft. Marvellously naïve, North Italian in origin, they are large-headed and stony stiff, each standing unconcernedly on the halo of the one below. It is hard not to respond to these charming little figures, so rooted in our material world, but in presence and fixity so indicative of another more ordered and stable existence.

The west end of the building is extremely handsome, with a magnificently carved window high up on the wall and grotesque crocodile heads which could have been lifted directly off the prows of Viking longships so similar are they to figure-heads. But the south doorway (*see page* 295) is the gem of the building—the gem of a gem so to speak. Here are wraith-like forms dredged out of the designer's unconscious, a mythical Garden of Eden, an outlandish menagerie, a botanical garden of the soul. On the right of the door, in a plethora of abstract vines and growing arabesques, the serpent of the Temptation rises towards the tympanum. On the left, head down, it crashes to earth, the symbol of the fall of evil, surrounded by menacing shapes such as the two Norman warriors one above the other who help form the engaged column. Nowhere in Europe can we find such a peculiar mixture of ideas, such a combination of motifs, such virility of forms, interesting especially in that none of them can be traced directly back to Normandy. There is both a joy and a melancholy, a verve and a brooding quality about the architecture and sculpture of Kilpeck. And the horizontal course of decorative and often comic masonry, resting on a brow of carved corbels illustrates this paradox.

When King Roger II of Sicily died this year, he thought he was leaving his domain in good hands. And to a degree he was. For one thing, his surviving son, who became King William I, was a good fighter when the occasion arose, a worthy attribute in those days of unrelenting violence when a man had to be prepared to fight for his life at a moment's notice. He was a handsome man in a primitive way, with a great black beard and fierce eyes. He was said to have been strong beyond the imagination of most men. 'He could separate two linked horseshoes with his bare hands; once, we are told, when a fully-laden pack horse stumbled and fell when crossing a bridge, he picked it up unaided and set it on its feet again'.[270] He was given to corpulence though, which tended to maximize his majestic presence. He was a haughty man, and his greed in the acquisition of wealth was complemented by a streak of stinginess. Munificent in rewarding loyalty, he was quick to punish betrayal, relying mostly on torture or banishment. However for all his marks of personal strength William was vastly inferior to his father in character, energy and imagination. He seemed content to allow others to run the government while he lolled about in Byzantine splendour in a number of pleasure palaces that ringed the Conca d'Oro, the plain in which his capital city was built. But then William, who had had three elder brothers, had never been reared to wear the crown. Only their premature deaths had thrust him onto the throne, unprepared, seemingly unwilling, lazy, and a lover of voluptuous pastimes. He had been married young, to Margaret, princess of the house of Navarre, but he paid her little attention, despite the fact that she bore him four sons. 'His life was more like a sultan's than a king's, and his character embodied that same combination of sensuality and fatalism that has stamped so many Eastern rulers. He never took a decision if he could avoid it, never tackled a problem if there was the faintest chance that, given long enough, it might solve itself.[271] And King William I had problems: with his barons, those in the South seeming by instinct to be more rebellious; with the Eastern Empire, riddled with Byzantine intrigue, its ruler entertaining hopes of regaining lost Italian and Sicilian territories; with the Holy Roman Empire, its German ruler cherishing thoughts of regaining ownership of Southern Italy, which he considered rightfully his; with the Church, now headed by Pope Adrian (or Hadrian) IV, the only Englishman ever to occupy the papal chair.

1155

Nicholas Breakspear, born about 1115 at Abbots Langley in Hertfordshire, had been elected pope without the attempted elevation of a rival (a refreshing change) on 4 December 1154. He was strongly influenced by religion, his place of birth being a dependency of Saint Albans Abbey. He was elegant in manner, pleasant, good looking and wise, clearly headed for success, perhaps greatness. As a student he went to Paris, city of commerce and intellect, and raucous with the irrepressible levity of hordes of students, all hearty drinkers and promiscuous lovers. For a man like Nicholas Breakspear, bent on the religious life, it may have been hard to take—but not too hard.

After studying in Paris Nicholas joined the Canons Regular of Saint Rufus near Arles, where he later became prior. He served as a cardinal under Pope Eugenius III. Taking over the papacy in December 1154, after the very short reign of Anastasius IV, he immediately lashed out at the citizens of Rome for having accepted the control of a republican—as opposed to a papal—government and for having harboured the dissident Arnold of Brescia, a rabble-rouser of the first water, albeit a learned one. Moreover, Arnold's followers had attacked and wounded a cardinal. With that Adrian lowered the boom: on Palm Sunday 1155 he proclaimed Rome under interdict.

Except for the baptism of infants and absolution for the dying, the interdict meant that no religious services were allowed in the city—no masses, marriages, or even funerals. This had never before happened in Rome, which was at the moment expecting its annual influx of pilgrims during the Easter season. It was bad for business. But there were sincere moral trepidations as well in the heart of every Roman. Religion was too important a facet of life to ignore this judgement by Christ's vicar. By the middle of Holy Week the citizens marched on the capitol. Arnold was driven from the city and the pope lifted the interdict. There was not a citizen of Rome who did not see this new pope—and a foreigner at that—as a man of enormous courage, political acumen and stubborn tenacity.

Adrian had his chance to prove just how right they were when he struck out at William I of Sicily, no doubt seeing him as did the later chronicler of the period, Hugo Falcandus, who designated him 'the Bad'. It had been a year now since William had taken the crown of his father, and he had not yet requested the pope, his suzerain, to confirm his title. Stung by this implied rebuke, Adrian in turn refused to recognize William as a legitimate ruler.

By nature indolent, William could be goaded into action. Pope Adrian's refusal to recognize him as legitimate king of Sicily was one such prick that caused the slow-moving giant to react: he marched on the Papal States, to be frustrated and finally forced into retiring, not by the pope, who on the surface seemed formidable enough, but by an even more dangerous adversary, the thirty-two-year-old German, Frederick Barbarossa, who had been in Italy since October 1154 endeavouring to establish his claims on Northern Italy and, more importantly, to force the pope to crown him emperor.

Frederick was a man with a will to match the pope's. Political realities made these two stubborn men natural antagonists; but logic indicated to both of them that they ought, somehow, to reach an accommodation. Unwilling to compromise in any way on anything, Frederick would give way to no one—pope, Sicilian king, or Byzantine emperor. He was determined to achieve the imperial crown (unlike his Uncle Conrad who never did) and to subjugate Italy to his will. All of this boded no good for the future of the peninsula, for the wish of the Byzantine emperor, Manuel I Comnenus, to regain control of Southern Italy, or for the royal claims of William I. Probably still more galling to William was the fact that Frederick was an extremely attractive man, immensely broad-shouldered, with narrow waist, thick reddish-brown hair and, as his sobriquet indicates, a fine red beard. Easygoing and quick to laugh, he was capable of a dedication that William would never know. And underneath it all there lurked a man of inordinate cruelty.

Of all the figures strutting the political stage in the middle of the twelfth century, William I was the least enviable: a king, a pope and an emperor were each, if not out to get him, at least entertaining thoughts of depriving him of a large part of his inheritance. United they would have been invincible. As it was, unable to act together, they might make life miserable for him, even pull him down a peg or two. But, though Sicily's great day might have passed with King Roger, there were still some marvels to create, some enlightenment to dispense. William and his son of the same name, but of diametrically opposite nickname—the Good—were there to see to that.

In the world of medieval power politics Frederick proved a good choice for German king and future emperor. He was not at all the compromising, frustrated kind of king that Conrad had been. He opened negotiations with Emperor Manuel Comnenus, and even tried to wangle an Eastern bride for himself—after dismissing his wife on the usual trumped-up grounds of consanguinity—an acceptable means of gaining power and establishing alliances, certainly preferable to sending armies against one another. But as far as practicality was concerned, in the end such an alliance would have been impossible to maintain for the simple reason that both king and emperor wanted desperately to get their hands on Southern Italy and Sicily.

In October 1154 Frederick had launched the first of six historic excursions he was to make into Italy, no small feat in those days before Alpine tunnels and highways. The object of this march was to assert his hereditary, always locally disputed, claims over Northern Italy, to tame Milan's over-mighty commune, and to have his own head adonized by the imperial crown, which could come only from the pope's hand. A chronicler reported on Milan's increasing power:

Now this city is considered . . . more famous than others not only because of its size and its abundance of brave men, but also from the fact that it has extended its authority over two neighbouring cities situated within the same valley, Como and Lodi. Furthermore . . . Milan, elated by prosperity, became puffed up to such audacious exaltation that not only did it not shrink from molesting its neighbours, but recently even dared incur the anger of the prince, standing in no awe of his majesty.[272]

For months Frederick rampaged through Northern Italy, strutting and flexing, the very paragon of Teutonic determination and arrogance. One edifying lesson after another was offered up to the always free-thinking, but never determinedly cohesive Italians. But he was not strong enough to take on Milan—at least not on this trip. Instead he made an example of Tortona, an ally of Milan, by razing the city to the ground. Then he turned south.

There was something so ferocious about this red-bearded king—straight from hell he must have seemed—that the Romans, hearing of his victories in the north, were stampeded into instant panic. They, who just recently, encouraged by Arnold of Brescia, had set up a republican government modelled after that of ancient Rome, suddenly saw themselves on the verge of being swept back into papal-imperial control. New Pope Adrian, a stubborn man, and totally defensive of Church interests, was not all that secure himself. He knew only too well the hair-raising stories of imperial treatment of former pontiffs: after all there were still some alive who remembered the year 1111, when Pope Paschal II had been physically seized and held prisoner for two months until he agreed to imperial terms and granted Henry V his crown. And everyone knew of those classic earlier imperial-papal face-offs between Gregory VII and Henry IV, first one side then the other gaining the advantage until, getting the worse of it, Gregory finally had to appeal to the Normans of Sicily, at last coming to the conclusion that he was better off using them as friends and protectors than standing alone. Now here was Frederick, the new quick-tempered young German king, marching on Rome, head ready—though not bent—to receive the imperial crown. Investing a would-be emperor was always a tit-for-tat exercise. If Frederick wanted his crown badly enough then surely he would be willing to make concessions in turn, or at least to perform some of the dirty work that every pontiff needed done.

Adrian was aware that Frederick must hate Arnold of Brescia as much as he did himself, as much as any properly Christian ruler should. After all, Arnold was a persistent challenge to the status quo, a master of insurrection and, in papal eyes at least (and one would hope in imperial eyes as well), steeped in heresy and evil doctrine. Adrian's legates prevailed upon Barbarossa to capture Arnold and turn him over to papal authorities. Arnold

was brought by King Frederick . . . to the Roman judge who had been appointed, and was put in chains. And the ruler ordered his case to be judged, and the learned teacher was condemned for his teaching.

But when he saw that his punishment was prepared, and that his neck was to be bound in the halter by hurrying fate, and when he was asked if he would renounce his false doctrine, and confess his sins after the manner of the wise, fearless and self-confident, wonderful to relate, he replied that his own doctrine seemed to him sound, nor would he hesitate to undergo death for his teachings, in which there was nothing absurd or dangerous. And he requested a short delay for time to pray, for he said that he wished to confess his sins to Christ . . . And after a short time, prepared to suffer with constancy, he surrendered his body to death. Those who looked on at his punishment shed tears; even the executioners were moved by pity for a little time, while he hung from the noose which held him. And it is said that the king, moved too late by compassion mourned, over this.[273]

Arnold's body was then burned, and the ashes thrown into the Tiber so that no relics would survive that might encourage the development of a cult around his memory.

Frederick was now in a better position to negotiate for his imperial crown. A meeting was set up between the spiritual and temporal rulers, at Campo Grasso near Sutri. Adrian arrived at Barbarossa's camp in his papal finery, accompanied by a properly impressive retinue of bishops, cardinals and attendants. He was greeted by a company of German barons, all spit and polish for the occasion, friendly, almost acquiescent, demonstrating not at all the kind of arrogance Adrian had been led to expect. Finally his cavalcade rode into the presence of the king.

Protocol dictated that Frederick walk forward to the mounted pope, lead the horse by the bridle to the negotiating area, and then hold the stirrup for the pontiff's dismounting. Frederick, aware of tradition but unwilling to act as Adrian's groom, simply held his ground. The pope, confused and irritated, dismounted unassisted and took his throne on the dais. Then Frederick advanced and knelt to kiss the papal slipper, an act more demeaning, one might think, than holding the papal stirrup. When he rose to receive the kiss of peace from Adrian, it was withheld, and Frederick was told that he would never receive it until he had shed his pride (though one wonders who displayed the greater pride here) and performed the required act of submission to his titular overlord. Bull-headed Adrian 'knew that what appeared on the surface to be a minor point of protocol concealed in reality something infinitely more important—a public act of defiance that struck at the very root of the relationship between Empire and Papacy'.[274] Frederick finally acquiesced, and, two days later, was re-enacted the whole ritual, the king this time holding the pope's stirrup; and, with the kiss of peace finally bestowed, the summit meeting for shaping strategy began. After confirming existing agreements and concluding new ones, the two moved on towards Rome, each at least convinced that he had done the best he could under difficult circumstances. But the Romans were not quite ready to receive a new emperor.

Before Adrian and Frederick arrived at the city they were met by a delegation of Roman citizens sent out by the senate, armed with brave words making it explicitly clear on what conditions both pontiff and would-be emperor would be received into their city. Republican-minded as they were—a testament to the influence of Arnold of Brescia—they pointed out that it was only with the agreement of the Romans that Frederick's forerunners had become emperors and that he himself could receive the crown. With that thought in mind, he would do well to swear to the city's future liberty. Frederick had had enough of menial bullying before the spokesman had anything like finished. Holding up his hand for silence, he pointed out that the power and dignity claimed by the senate was that of ancient rather than of present Rome, and that time and again imperial visits to Rome had been made in response to senatorial pleas for help. He declared himself 'the lawful possessor' of the city and defied the senators to overturn his might. Following Frederick's speech the delegation withdrew in confusion and hangdog embarrassment. Adrian advised immediate action. The next day, 18 June, Frederick bent his head to receive the crown of empire and the papal blessing in St Peter's Basilica while the Roman senate was still gathering to decide on the best way of preventing that event from taking place. Infuriated when the news spread that Adrian and Frederick had outsmarted them, the citizens rose in revolt, pouring across the Tiber, swarming through Trastevere, the Leonine City—that part of Rome occupied by St Peter's Basilica—the Vatican and the Castello Sant'Angelo. The attack on the Leonine City constituted and affront to his authority, and anxious lest the citizens go after the pope, Frederick ordered his soldiers to prepare for battle. The combat lasted from ten in the morning to nightfall, with the Romans finally overwhelmed. With that Frederick took his army away from the city, more to avoid the humid malaria- and dysentery-producing climate than his angry subjects. After attacking and defeating the city of Spoleto, and meeting with unctiously servile emissaries from Byzantine Emperor Manuel Comnenus, who vainly hoped for some sort of joint action against William of Sicily, Frederick headed home for Germany. He was back in Bavaria in September well ahead of the winter snows that render Alpine foot travel so treacherous.

Frederick's retirement from the Italian theatre stimulated Manuel Comnenus to step up his campaign against William of Sicily. And he did so with vengeful troops led by Michael Palaeologus, a prince of the royal blood, who had tried to entice Frederick and any other interested party into war against William. His forces were joined by those of Robert of Loritello, a typically dissatisfied Norman aristocrat and first cousin to King William. Certain that he was destined for a higher position than he now enjoyed, Robert perpetually smarted under the pre-eminence of William's grand admiral, Maio of Bari. With the title of emir of emirs and second only to the king, Maio of Bari was the palace professional who generated the most offence to the feudal aristocracy. The barons called him an upstart son of an oil merchant, a would-be usurper of the throne, a seducer of young girls and even of the king's wife; whereas he seems to have been a cultured and sensible politican, a patron of poetry and the arts, someone who believed in Roger's ideas of strong kingship and saw that aristocratic pretensions were already helping to ruin Sicily. Michael Palaeologus' army and fleet of ten ships, in combination with the usual disgruntled Norman barons, made up a force enough to attack the city of Bari where a sizeable number of die-hard Greek loyalists waited, hopeful of a power shift that would restore them to their past glory. The gates were opened to the attackers who in a short time also had the citadel under control.

By this time Frederick must have been having second thoughts about returning to fight for what he believed to be his patrimony rather than see it fall into the hands of the rival emperor. Fortunately for Sicily, Frederick had opted to return to Germany. Had he moved against William at this time in conjunction with Byzantine forces he would have solved his problem with William once and for all. Frederick must have been even more sorely tempted to turn south following the arrival of the erroneous news that King William had died. The Apulian coastal towns were demoralized by the same rumour. William was in truth seriously ill; but he had many years of successful rule yet ahead of him. In the meantime he had some faithful supporters. Count Richard of Andria was one of them, fighting like a man possessed to keep the town of Giovinazzo within the royal hegemony. Eventually it fell, just one of many Greek conquests that made it seem that all Apulia would return to the greedy clutches of Manuel Comnenus. (Richard was to die a scant few weeks later.)

Like so many of the coastal and inland cities and towns of Apulia, surrounded by extensive landscapes of olive trees, Giovinazzo, with its old and new *quartieri* and small port, gives, as does Venice, the feeling that the twentieth century has passed it by. The harbour, with its brightly painted boats —red, blue, yellow, green—asserts itself on eyes that are tired of earth colours, soft olive greens and grey stone. Giovinazzo cannot claim a piece of history the way the nearby towns of Trani and Barletta can; the best it can hope for is to ride in the wake of stormy Bari, only ten miles to the south. Even its cathedral (consecrated in 1283) seems provincial in its robustness, and the rugged, weather-beaten Romanesque sculpture on its outer walls. As for cathedrals, no city of the Terra di Bari can boast of one more magnificently robust than Ruvo di Puglia, around which the battles for Apulia swirled as they did around all the settlements along the eastern coast of Italy.

Located well in the centre of an area that holds more of interest to historians and lovers of architecture than most areas twice its size, Ruvo stands close to the top of the list of indispensable Italo-Norman Romanesque cathedrals. Just a skip inland from a most romantic coastline, surrounded by towns whose ancient buildings are of bleached white local limestone, and competing for tourist attention with the charming fishing ports that line the Adriatic north and south of Bari, Ruvo stands barely a chance of attracting the modern traveller's attention. But Ruvo is a must for the tourist who looks to find the 'real' Southern Italy, who wants to be surprised by the almost Moroccan orientalness of obscure Southern Italian streets; for the visitor who seeks mood rather than glamour, and the kind of dramatic contrasts resulting when southern sun pits itself against deep shadows that can be as cool as ocean froth, then again as hot as the centre of a piazza. True, the one simple hotel is hardly enticing; and when that bible of travellers, the Michelin green guide for Italy, avoids mention of the town even on its map, the short westward drive inland from coastal route SS16 does seem an exercise in futility, especially with Bari a mere twenty miles south, and Bitonto a piddling twelve to the north. Too bad for the lazy traveller!

In the dim prehistory of the Italian peninsula Ruvo was already an important centre of the Peucettii, a people responsible for a handsome pre-Greek ceramic industry making cups and wineskin-shaped *askoi* (pitchers), gorgeously painted with elaborate geometric ornamentation. With the Greek establishment of Magna Grecia, these natives adopted the more 'civilized' new styles, assimilating them with apparent ease and modifying them to their own tastes until Ruvoware became the most celebrated in the region. (The century-old Museo Jatta has a collection of over seventeen hundred of these local and imported Greek ceramics. An appointment is necessary to see the collection.) Ruvo enjoyed *municipium* status under the Romans, when it was known as Rubi, and was a station on the Via Traiana, a well-travelled feeder road to the port city of Brundisium (Brindisi.) According to tradition Ruvo was destroyed in AD 463 by the Goths, to remain pretty much in the doldrums until the coming of the Normans. It is known today for its fine eating grapes and almonds.

Ruvo Cathedral, Italy

In a city not famous for much else, Ruvo's cathedral of Santa Maria is the deserving attention-getter. Walking through narrow, twisting streets, cooled by shadows cast by buildings to either side, and usually followed by a swarm of wise-cracking, good-natured *birichini*—the impish little urchins who run Neapolitan *scugnizzi* a close second for raffish charm—one comes suddenly on the cathedral, worn-looking, low, seeming smaller than it actually is because it is situated some feet below the street at what was the level of twelfth-century Ruvo. It is best to see it early in the afternoon, when the population (at least the adult population) is sleeping off the effects of copious noon meals behind heat-frustrating shutters. For the sightseer who fears neither heat nor *birichini* there is no experience quite like that of communing with a relatively unknown cathedral, church or castle, an experience which must be achieved largely on one's own since there is little written about them. 'They remain in delightful obscurity, the timeless activities of small harbours going on all round them and weekly markets being held in their shadows. They are the most beautiful surviving memory of the Norman conquest of Southern Italy'.[275] (It must also be pointed out that during siesta they are closed!)

Magnificent round arches frame the heavy doors which open on to Ruvo Cathedral's interior, recently restored to remove frivolous Baroque excesses so often found in southern churches, additions which did nothing to help the simple, direct Norman designs and a great deal to hurt them—despite Oscar Wilde's aphorism 'nothing succeeds like excess'. The three superb exterior arches, heavily Norman in shape but carved with un-Norman intricacies, are set in shallow round-arched niches which form strong Romanesque preludes to the corresponding nave and two aisles.

With a fairly typical Italo-Norman exterior, at least in feeling, the cathedral displays two lions, one to either side of the central door; but these lions are perched on small platforms held aloft by crouching slave figures. The lions support columns, which in their turn support menacing griffins with human skulls between their paws, flanking the arch which springs from their perches. A fine rose window tops the façade, balanced majestically on the apex of a double-arched window. Any tendency to façadal monotony is negated by a series of small arches riding on corbels of sculptured masks, the whole serving as a blind arcade just under, and acting as visual support for, the long line of the nave roof. The motif is repeated inside. The campanile is isolated from the church and is unusual for this part of the Norman world in that there is no architectural link between the two structures, such as the connecting arches we find at Trani and Barletta.

A visit to the interior may not be an exciting brush with history; but it is certainly a sobering experience in the *time* of history. Dark, rather dreary, but marvellously proportioned as is to be expected of a Norman building, it smacks of a solidity to balance the precarious existence of the times. Here was a place of refuge as unchanging as God's justice, as positive as salvation, as free from evil as the very portals of heaven. It was a safe haven of reaction and comfort in an age when the investigative sciences of the new-forming universities were unsettling old beliefs and shaking dogmas. And those crusaders lucky enough to return from Outremer could not help but have been influenced by the Arabic thought they had encountered in that exotic land, philosophies such as that of Avicenna, whose medical writings by this time had entered Europe and were being translated—rather badly—into Latin. Even closer to home was Spain, where Muslims were far ahead of Christians in scientific and mathematical studies, and through contact with them the Christian West learnt of vital inventions such as Chinese paper and the so-called Arabic (in fact Indian) numerals that included the concept of a zero.

It was in Moorish Spain that ancient manuscripts were being copied and from there introduced into European libraries. Expansion of knowledge by its very happening spawns disturbing challenges to the existing order of things. The intellectual world was in healthy turmoil, and this affected all reigning princes, not least those Normans. Turmoil can be good for art; serenity of spirit does not of itself breed fine art. 'I never yet met with a Christian', wrote John Ruskin, 'whose heart was thoroughly set upon the world to come, and, so far as human judgement could pronounce, perfect and right before God, who cared about art at all'.[276] For the common folk these cathedrals, and Ruvo among them, were securely anchored in tradition while serving as foretastes of that 'place of refreshment, light and peace'[277] for which they yearned, a welcome contrast to the winter of this world.

As Ruvo was caught up in the swirl of Norman-Greek hostilities around Bari, so was the city of Bitonto, roughly twelve miles away, and close enough to Ruvo for the respective citizens to hear each others' church bells. The only way to see Bitonto is on foot, for there are wonderful stepped streets and low-hanging arches, all in all a fine medieval *quartiere*. One may chance on bits of Roman Butuntum (previously a Greek colony) but they are all but non-existent, since it was virtually destroyed by Byzantine Greeks in 975. It was the

Normans who rebuilt the city in the eleventh century. There is a Benedictine Abbey of San Leo (ninth-century, remodelled many times, and finally restored in the twentieth century), some thirteenth-century churches and much manifestation of former wealth in some grand *palazzi* of later centuries. And of course there is always Bitonto's superlative olive oil! With Bari so near, Bitonto has never developed tourist amenities, so it is best to bed down elsewhere. But the tourist who avoids Bitonto misses what is considered by many to be the finest of Apulian Romanesque architecture, its cathedral. It was begun by Normans in 1175, and took only twenty-five years to complete, for its day an incredible splurge of creative effort.

Church building during the Middle Ages was not just a matter of religion; civic pride was at least as great a motiviation. Medieval interests turned to rivalry among cities, prompting them to try to outdo one another in the splendour of their buildings, especially their churches, thereby justifying their vanity with religious motivation. This rivalry, which often exploded into actual warfare, is as demonstrable in Italy as anywhere else. But the southern Normans went even further than most, adding a new dimension to their one-upmanship: they aimed to rival the Eastern Empire, whose capital city of Constantinople, with its billowing domes and sparkling mosaics reflecting in the shimmering waters of the Golden Horn, would have seemed unmatchable to anyone less intrepid. The Normans in Apulia could not hope to challenge the magnificence of Hagia Sophia or the Blachernae Palace (their kings could and did, but only with the help of imported Byzantine craftsmen), but they did create a glory of their own.

Bitonto Cathedral is a superlative Norman effort, reflecting more than any other the Italo-Norman style, as opposed to the Arab and Byzantine, which were equally well represented in William's kingdom, reflecting the cosmopolitan nature of his realm. It was in Sicily that the styles were most expertly amalgamated—in buildings such as Cefalù Cathedral, the Cappella Palatina, and the cathedral at Monreale (yet to come). More often than not the buildings of the mainland reflect less catholic tastes, are less intricately involved with uniting the four elements of the realm. Bitonto Catheral could be nothing but Italo-Norman (Apulian) and that is its great strength.

Southern Italian churches are fun to 'discover' because they have a way of either suddenly appearing before the seeker, or of offering tantalizing brief previews of themselves at the far ends of narrow and twisting streets. They maintain themselves as centres for town activities, focal points of markets, festivals and religious holidays that may be as old as their history. The people who live in the shadow of Bitonto Cathedral and countless other historic buildings in the smaller towns of Italy have a place in history and know it.

Standing in the cathedral piazza one feels a bit cramped, hemmed in. But that is only the initial experience, created by the fact that the main façade of the building is so large it seems to dwarf the open space. It is not long before one's attention is distracted by abundant niceties: the open gallery high on the south wall (*see page* 295), for instance, its columns gleaming in the sun and on which rest wonderfully intricate capitals, no two the same. They are masterpices of the sculptor's art and are in every way enhanced by the perfectly proportioned arches they bear, as well as by the deep blind-arched buttresses below, and the

Bitonto Cathedral, Italy

shallow tiny arches of the moulding under the roof line above. As usual, light and shadow, along with an exquisite understanding of proportion are the real strengths of the Norman designer-planners. Bitonto Cathedral creates an experience of *chiaroscuro*; and its size-relationships are breathtaking, from the sweeping, deeply recessed arches at ground level, to the aforementioned gallery of columns and arches strongly outlined against deep shadow, and the delicately pitched little blind arcade under the roof which lends a wondrously refined touch to a generally blank upper wall.

Even the colour of Bitonto Cathedral works in its favour, making it look every inch its age, weathered, dark, stained by centuries of grime that you would not want to see removed for fear of somehow altering its character or emasculating this brawny model of Norman self-assertion and aggrandizement. For the Norman was proud; he was loudly assertive of his own dignity and worth. And Bitonto is positive, its harmony and balance so evident as to go unnoticed simply because there are no weaknesses. The rich rose window is surmounted by a carved hood supported by lions standing on stone columns. Lions are everywhere in Norman art, those symbols of the watchfulness of the Church over her flock, since the lion, according to medieval belief, slept with its eyes open. The lion was also a symbol of dignity, courage, majesty, strength. So we find lions here, as well as in countless other medieval churches, Norman and otherwise, guarding doors, one on either side.

Adjacent to Bitonto Cathedral is an utterly charming little loggia—double-arched above, single-arched below—from which the devoted romantic will find it almost impossible to tear himself away. Tucked between the building to the left and the corner of the cathedral itself, the loggia is guaranteed to bring a smile to the most dour tourist's tired mouth. But it is only a prelude to the joys offered within the cathedral.

Bitonto is as Norman-Italian as an imaginary escargot pizza; but it does admit to exotic foreign influences. In a setting of Islamic swirls, overall patterns and a pigeon-like bird half the size of a man, stand blank-eyed but dignified and unsmiling Romanesque figures, claimed by some to be the family of Emperor Frederick II (1194-1250), but almost certainly intended to represent the Three Magi before Herod. The whole *ambione* is a masterpiece, dated 1229, from the hand of Nicholas, a priest and master sculptor.

Then there are the nave capitals with their monkeys, birds and beasts scampering through carved foliage, delightful in their celebration of the natural world as something more enduring than cities and wars and temporal power. If these capitals are lovely in their Romanesque beauty and decorative charm, then the thirty carved capitals in the crypt are thought-provoking even in their whimsy and fantasy. Eagles and composite animals peer at us from their perches on foliage arabesques of virtuoso design. As always there are the lions, but this time accompanied by little men wearing jaunty tasselled hats. It is a menagerie uncaged, a horticulturist's dream in which the various bird, animal, human and plant forms rejoice in the presence and proximity of the others.

One of the most important figures to emerge from the unrelenting tales of horrors in the Byzantine-inspired revolt in Southern Italy was Prince Robert of Capua. This last prince of that ancient city was one of the leaders of insurrection, a role true to his character of the last thirty years. Robert was at best prone to duplicity, always a traitor, and at worst a man without so much as a shred of redemptive honour. It was he who twenty-five years earlier, with brazen two-facedness, had placed the crown on the head of William's father, Roger II. That act had been an admission by both parties that Robert was Roger's principal vassal. But Robert had almost immediately rebelled against Roger who had deprived him of his principality; in his drive to regain it Robert had decided on intrigue with the king's enemies rather than on reconciliation, and this year was re-invested with his princedom by Pope Adrian IV. In defiance of William's title, this English pope had marched into Southern Italy at the head of his troops with the encouragement of Michael Palaeologus in a rare, but not unique, showing of co-operation between the pope and the Eastern emperor. Things looked black indeed for William, by nature slow to react, but this time genuinely sick in his Palermitan palace. Even some of the barons of Sicily itself were in rebellion, primarily against the rule of Maio of Bari and Archbishop Hugh of Palermo, who between them had assumed complete control of the government during William's sickness. By the end of the year his enemies had control of most of Southern Italy—except for Calabria, but that was probably only a matter of time.

Chapter Sixteen

I would have you know that to attend upon the King is something sacred,
for the King himself is holy; he is the anointed of the Lord.

Peter of Blois; in Plumb and Weldon,
Royal Heritage: the Treasures of the British Crown

1155

Compared with the current chaos in Italy and Sicily, government in England was running smoothly, considering the country's recent history. Henry II's problems were as nothing compared to William's; but he had them none the less. Troublefree as Henry's coronation may have been, the war of succession between King Stephen and Matilda had caused a decided break in normal administrative procedures. Enormous adjustments had to be made, including the reclamation of land deeded over to many barons during the years of Stephen's anarchy, certainly a bitter pill for them to swallow.

At about the time of Henry's coronation one of the finest castles of the realm was erected: Goodrich Castle in Herefordshire (*see page* 296). Made of local red sandstone, looming dramatically against the lush, opaque green of its milieu and the intense blue of the arching sky, the central keep remains one of the best of the Norman great towers, even encircled as it is by elaborate late thirteenth-century additions. Guarded on one side by a steep descent to the River Wye over which it broods with typical Norman dourness, and on the other by a wide rock-cut moat, Goodrich seems invincible. Nothing mars this note of unconquerable obstinacy, even the perfectly proportioned if randomly placed Romanesque windows. The mid-century keep was not the first building on the site, being preceded by a wooden castle perhaps built by one Godric Mappeston (mentioned in the Domesday Book) to guard a popular ford across the river below. The keep we see today was probably ordered by Henry II to replace the earlier out-of-date structure. Goodrich Castle is an elaborate complex, with towers, halls, a kitchen, a gatehouse, barbican, causeway, and a stone bridge dating from the fourteenth century. (At one time there was a drawbridge, the pivotal sockets of which can still be seen.)

Henry had need of efficient castles forbidding enough to discourage the infectious contagion of rebellion, the toxic germ of which could bring down the most robust government. His rule extended through Western Europe from the Pyrenees to the Scottish border. His frontier with Brittany was at this time fluctuating, but he was destined to take in that duchy too. Four different languages were spoken in his realm: English, Welsh, Provençal and Northern French. Then there was always the ever-present Latin of educated men. And the new interest in scholarly pursuits did not make things easier for the leaders. More and more, men were beginning to think in terms other than mere survival. Rulers needed to be aware of these changes. To implement his regime Henry surrounded himself with a body of men, mostly on the youthful side,

Goodrich Castle,
England

energetic and devoted to rebuilding a working government. The most interesting of these appointees was a man fourteen years older than the king, whose friendship was to prove the richest and most tragic Henry would ever enjoy: Thomas Becket.

Thomas was London-born of respectable middle-class parents. His father, Gilbert was from the Rouen area and had become a prosperous merchant; his mother was a Norman too, from Caen. He had two sisters, one of whom became abbess of Barking, but to neither did he seem very attached. Thomas was destined for sainthood, though one would never have guessed it from his early carousing with Henry or from his life-style after becoming chancellor.

By nature Thomas was richly endowed, being tall and fair-complexioned, vigorous, dark-haired and having a prominent nose. He was athletic, a quality that held him in good stead in his relationship with Henry. He is said to have had extremely keen eyesight and hearing, a remarkably retentive memory, and to have been a master rhetorician. At the age of ten he had been sent to Merton Priory in Surrey to be educated by the Augustinian canons there. He never wanted for anything, including contacts with the well-to-do, men a good deal above his middle-class station. After some schooling in London, Thomas had been sent to Paris to round off his education. His complacency was struck two staggering blows when within a very short span of time his mother died and he became impoverished after his father lost his property in a series of disastrous fires. After working as clerk to a relative who was justiciar of London, Thomas eventually landed a similar job in the household of Archbishop Theobald of Canterbury, a curious place for him to be since he was admittedly no scholar, and the archbishop's household was at a high pitch of intellectual activity.

So even as a young man Thomas was made familiar with Church-State affairs; and he was a close witness of Archbishop Theobald's defiance of King Stephen, first in attending the Reims council despite the king's prohibition, and secondly in refusing, on papal orders, to crown Stephen's son Eustace. He acquired a number of benefices and in 1154, after being ordained deacon, was appointed archdeacon of Canterbury, a mainly administrative and highly lucrative office. His appointment, at Theobald's behest, to be the king's chancellor, was a startling rise in the world, an unimagined stroke of luck and a vastly more important promotion than he could possibly have expected. The scope of his job was awesome, certainly daunting to a man of lesser abilities. The chancellor was the king's right-hand man, his personal assistant, his secretary. He was the royal chaplain, keeper of the great seal, prime mover for the king in secular as well as ecclesiastical business, activating the treasury and administering vacant sees. With this new appointment Thomas found himself a most important member of the court. On top of that he became the king's closest friend and confidant, even though, in the loftiness of his new position, he soon learned to surpass his royal friend in luxury; but then Henry always was—and remained—niggardly in his life-style.

With historical hindsight it seems inevitable that Henry and Thomas would clash over policy once Becket had been made archbishop of Canterbury. For the time, however, Becket was bent on being a good chancellor. He may have liked the high life, lavish feasts and luxurious clothes; but he worked consistently hard in the king's interest.

Yet Thomas Becket could not handle all of his lord's problems. Younger brother Geoffrey of Anjou was yapping at Henry's heels, smarting, perhaps, from the 'Mum always liked you more' syndrome or, more likely, simply flexing his combative Plantagenet muscles. But even he was not enough to prevent Henry from thinking of bigger things, events he would set in motion once he had put his younger brother in his place. Already he had dispatched John of Salisbury, secretary to Archbishop Theobald, to Rome. English to the core, Pope Adrian IV listened to John as he pleaded the case of his king to invade Ireland with the intention of incorporating it into his domain. Kings, presidents, chairmen of parties, ayatollahs, dictators—what have you—invade for one purpose: to enlarge their realms. Henry knew this; John knew it; and so did the pope. Adrian turned a receptive ear to the royal legate, with whom he always enjoyed a cordial relationship. John argued that his monarch wanted to spread the doctrine of Christ, that he wanted to raise the Irish to a higher degree of Christian civilization, a bare-faced lie since the Irish were not a whole lot worse off than their English cousins—and all three men knew that, too. Following his audience with John of Salisbury, and in a masterpiece of hypocritical rhetoric, Adrian issued a bull—his famous *Laudabiliter*—in which he proclaimed:

Adrian the bishop, servant of the servants of God, to his most dearly beloved son in Christ, the illustrious king of the English, greeting and apostolic benediction. Laudably and profitably does your magnificence contemplate extending your glorious name on earth and laying up a reward of eternal happiness in heaven, inasmuch as you endeavour like a catholic prince to enlarge the boundaries of the Church, to expound the truth of the Christian faith to ignorant and barbarous peoples . . .

You have, indeed, indicated to us . . . that you desire to enter into the island of Ireland for the purpose of subjecting its people to the laws and of rooting out from it the weeds of vice . . . and to preserve the rights of the churches of that land whole and unimpaired. We, therefore . . . agree that

> . . . you may enter that island and perform there the things that have regard to the honour of God and the salvation of that land. And may the people . . . receive you with honour, and reverence you as their lord . . .[278]

It was not until sixteen years later that Henry actually invaded Ireland. By that time he had reasons very different and more pressing than those he entertained in 1155; but although there was then a different pope—Alexander III—he also welcomed Henry's adventure with enthusiasm.

John of Salisbury's mission to Rome was a mere diplomatic feeler on Henry's part. At the moment his interests lay closer to home. His brother Geoffrey was busy stirring up a hornet's nest in Henry's Continental holdings. Geoffrey was noising it about that he, not Henry, was the rightful count of Anjou as their father had intended Henry to renounce the title once he had secured the English throne. Improbable as the story was, there were enough malcontents to encourage Geoffrey's defiance of his brother. King Louis refused to take sides, preferring, by his neutrality, to promote the quarrel—a shrewd tactic on the part of a man not normally famous for his political acumen, and a positive boon to Henry since the combined strength of Louis' and Geoffrey's forces would have made a formidable opposition. As it was now, there could be only one sure loser: Geoffrey Plantagenet.

1156

By the new year Henry felt reasonably secure in England; but his hold on his Continental duchies and counties was a bit shaky. To rectify this he met King Louis at the Norman-French border on 5 February and there, as was proper, did homage for Anjou and Aquitaine, and again for Normandy. By thus acknowledging his place as Louis' vassal Henry effectively isolated his brother, and by summer was besieging Geoffrey's castles at Chinon, Mirebeau and Loudon, all of them key strongholds which he finally wrested from him. He graciously granted Geoffrey a considerable annuity (some authorities maintain that he even allowed him to keep Loudon), but not enough to encourage further mischief. By the end of the year Henry had established his brother as count of Nantes, a position that he enjoyed for less than two years as it turned out; he died in 1158 at the age of twenty-four.

The revolt begun a year ago in Southern Italy was a short-lived affair. Finally raising himself from his sick-bed, and with Maio at his side, William marched first against the Sicilian rebels who were holed up in Butera in southern Sicily. The city promptly surrendered, the insurrection achieving nothing. William was now free, in the spring of this year, to turn his attention to the mainland. By the end of April he and his army had crossed the straits from Messina to Calabria and were headed for Brindisi, while his navy was rounding the sole of the Italian boot, bound for the same city. When news of William's coming hit town, the Greeks and rebellious native barons watched as their army miraculously melted away. In command of the mutinous troops since the recent death of Michael Palaeologus, one John Ducas now found himself facing forces numerically superior, fresher and better equipped than those few he had left. The battle for Brindisi lasted one day, with the Sicilian forces by land and sea acting in perfect unison. Wanting to make his displeasure clear, William ruthlessly punished the hapless rebels. From Brindisi he pushed on to Bari, which had eagerly embraced the Byzantine cause. Except for the cathedral, the church of San Nicola and a few small religious buildings, Bari was destroyed.

For Pope Adrian William's recovery was a disaster beyond comprehension. Unable to return to a Rome relentlessly hostile since the coronation of Frederick Barbarossa, he had spent much of the winter in Benevento. Now here was William, with no consideration for territorial sovereignty, headed straight for Benevento and his holy personage. Immediately the pope sent out his emissaries, and talks were inaugurated. An accord was reached on 18 June: the Treaty of Benevento (drafted by young Matthew of Ajello—we will hear more of him—and still on file in its original form in the Vatican Archives) ceded to William everything he wanted. He received papal recognition of his kingship over Sicily and Italy south of the principality of Capua, and now, for the first time, extending into the northern Abruzzi and the Marches. For the most part he retained his traditional privileges as far as Church affairs in Sicily were concerned, including his control over ecclesiastical elections. But William, having at last achieved papal recognition together with the accompanying benefits, had also earned the undying hatred of Emperor Frederick Barbarossa, who rightly saw the Treaty of Benevento as a denial of his own claims to Southern Italy and Sicily.

For the moment everything had been taken care of to kingly satisfaction, including the capture of Robert of Capua, betrayed by one of his own vassals, Count Richard of Aquila, who hoped to ingratiate himself in William's eyes—a manoeuvre which Robert, of all people, should have been able to understand!—and succeeded. Robert was sent to Palermo where, by William's order, he was blinded. There were others blinded and imprisoned, including two of William's own nephews; still others, according to contemporary reports, were thrown into pits of vipers. Wives and daughters of the malefactors were forced into harems and houses of prostitution.

For a man who found it next to impossible to bestir himself from the blandishments of his assorted palaces and pleasure pavilions, William had done rather well; so well, in fact, that his success made Barbarossa ever more edgy. Adrian had done well, too. Now he had an ally, and the strongest one around, to support him against any future threats the emperor might have been entertaining. And Maio of Bari had fared pretty well, emerging from the wars stronger than ever. Having been invested with his territories, William took leave of the pope to return to his island capital and its creature comforts; but not without stopping briefly at Naples for the ritual dedication there of two prominent buildings.

Few cities of Europe inspire such difference of opinion as does this teeming metropolis, whose existence goes back to the murky days of Greek myth-history. The siren Parthenope, perishing in suicidal despair from her inability to beguile Ulysses with her song, was reputedly washed ashore at Naples, an ironical reversal of the adage 'see Naples and die'. In Strabo's day (early first century AD) her 'tomb' was a tourist spot, with torchlight races and gymnastic events held there in her honour. True romantics love Naples with a passion felt only for certain cities and endangered species; non-romantics despise it with a disdain reserved only for romantics and modern art. Brash and gaudy, Naples presides raucously over its bay, guarded majestically to the south by Capri and dominated the east by Mount Vesuvius.

Arriving in Italy via Naples harbour is an experience that has to be endured to be believed, unduplicatable in the Western world. And, even if you could manage to tune out the clamour now and then in the interest of sanity, it is one of the most improbable and overwhelming experiences of modern travel. In a matter of seconds one is plunged from the gentle, highly civilized etiquette of boat travel into the world of hard-sell, pestering pedlars, pimps, prostitutes and pickpockets. There is nothing in the world so persistent as a Neapolitan hawker—and no one who smiles so convincingly as he slips a wallet out of the hip pocket of an unsuspecting, utterly beguiled tourist. And the *scugnizzi*—those cheerful little ragamuffins who live by their wits, sing like miniature Carusos and somehow avoid being killed by the most frightening traffic in Europe, not to mention the careening trams to which they attach themselves like funloving little slugs—even the *scugnizzi* are in a class of their own: prepubescent pickpockets to a boy.

Eating a pizza in one of the numerous *pizzerie* of the old quarter or while walking through the bustling traffic—pizza folded in half like a taco and called *un libretto*—is an experience unto itself. And food is all-important in Naples. If one craves to eat *alla Napoletana* one can hardly do better than *mozzarella in carrozza*—'mozzarella in a carriage'—a thick slice of the cheese between two slices of bread, the whole coated with egg and crumbs and fried in olive oil. And where else but in the Naples-Sorrento-Capri triangle can one find a lovely wine—white, mild and clear—called *Lacrima Christi*—'Tear of Christ'?

Anyone who has been to Naples, who has learned to love the lively *spiritosita* and fun-filled dissembling of the population will vouch that the Neapolitans are indeed the most lovable con artists in the world. Youth is ever present—alive, pleasure-bent and carefree, dressed in the mode of the region—flesh-clinging skirts, tight pants and button-popping shirts; but so are care and hard work, gnarled hands and faces creviced from worry and toothless from bad diet. It is impossible to be lonely; there are just too many people, all of them gregarious. Accommodation is never a problem, from pensions to the finest of luxury hotels. But it would be a shame to acquire a room there without a view of the bay and its never-ending parade of vessels from every country entering and leaving at surprisingly frequent intervals. The Santa Lucia area with its noisy Via Parthenope (one gets used to noise in Naples after a while, the way one grows accustomed to dirt) is the ideal rooming area with its choice of several hotels overlooking the Borgo Marinaro—and the Castel dell'Ovo.

Made of rich, mellow, honey-coloured limestone and situated on a tiny, long-inhabited island connected to the south shore of Naples, thus forming the marina, the Castel dell'Ovo was founded by William I on his visit, and rebuilt by the Angevins in 1274. Within the Castel dell'Ovo, only recently opened to the public, one comes on a warren of corridors, one-time barrack-rooms of several centuries of soldiers, quiet cells of Basilian monks who resided there theoretically to maintain the faith of the soldiery, depressing dungeons now being modernized to accommodate art galleries and a theatre. There are the remains of a seventh-century church, and, perhaps most intriguing of all, a remnant of the fabulous villa of the Roman General Lucullus, from whose ostentatious life-style has derived the term 'Lucullan feast' for an especially rich banquet. The last Western Roman emperor, fourteen-year old Romulus Augustulus, who was deposed by the Germanic leader Odoacer in AD 476, is alleged to have been retired to the Lucullan villa, and may have died there at an unknown date.

Frederick II of Hohenstaufen (grandson of Barbarossa) enlarged the Castel dell'Ovo and stored his enormous treasury therein. Later on Charles I of Anjou lived there, as did Alfonso of Aragon. There was an enchanting medieval legend that the poet Virgil, believed to have been a wizard, had constructed the castle upon an egg balanced on the floor of the sea, hence its title. One does not need such romantic invention to enjoy it; all it takes is a summer evening at any one of several restaurants that line the quay of the marina, teeth on edge from squeaking violins and discordant guitars of itinerant musicians who accompany shrill Neapolitan tenors in tediously repeated *O Sole Mio*s and *Santa Lucia*s. There can be no greater pleasure: the food is reasonably priced and more than all right; the boats glide silently to and from their berths; the *scugnizzi* plead for you to cast coins into the water from your table so they can dive to retrieve them; the waiters cluck over you the way only Italian waiters do; the fishermen and flower vendors ply their trades among the tables. It is all so alive, so animated—so Neapolitan—worth a long pause, notwithstanding the off-key tenors, and the price of a bottle of *Lacrima Christi*. It is sad to think that William I, enjoying his triumphs over barons and pope alike, missed the delights of this experience, and right in the very shadow of the castle whose foundation he laid, too! Worse, it would have been impossible for him to savour one of the most succulently appealing of all Italian dishes, *Melanzane alla Parmigiana*—egg-plant (aubergines) with Parmesan cheese—since tomatoes were not introduced into Italy from Peru until the sixteenth century.

Castello Nuovo, Naples

Aside from the gastronomic delights of the area of the Castel dell'Ovo, there are many things of interest to see within easy walking distance. Five minutes away is the huge, reverberating Piazza Municipio with its gardens and walks, useful to travellers for the many money changers and tourist agencies and, adjacent to it, the grimly towering battlements of Castel Nuovo, built by Charles I of Anjou in 1282, its moat now used simply as another car-park. It is alleged that its architect, Pierre d'Agincourt, modelled it after the great castle at Angers, which is a little hard to swallow, though it has somewhat the same forbidding spirit. Still, the 'triumphal arch' gateway of Alfonso of Aragon is worth a good long look; it was designed by Francesco Laurana in 1467 and is rich with heraldic sculptures. The enormous bronze door, by a fifteenth-century Parisian monk, still has a cannon-ball embedded in it from the Italian campaign (1494-5) of Charles VIII of France. A stroll in the opposite direction from the Castel dell'Ovo takes one to the Villa Comunale with its Stazione Zoologica display of submarine life from the Bay of Naples.

The true centre of Neapolitan life, the Piazza Plebiscito, backs the Santa Lucia area. It is a noble semicircular piazza banked on one side by the royal palace, which displays on its front, among the figures of kings of the eight dynasties that have ruled Naples, that of Roger II; on the other side the piazza is flanked by the neo-classic church of San Francesco di Paola, built on the pattern of the Pantheon in Rome—but resembling it very little. The San Carlo Opera House is nearby, commissioned by Charles IV when he was only twenty-one, richly decorated in the neo-classic style and boasting allegedly perfect acoustics. Right across the street from the San Carlo is the Galleria Umberto I, iron- and glass-enclosed; the high decibel discussions among groups of arguing business men add to the din that is second only to that of the Piazza Municipio. But what a place to sit over a Campari and soda with a twist of lemon and watch the flood of Neapolitan life flow past!

For the more exotic minded there is, in the cathedral of San Gennaro, a sacred flagon-shaped *ampolla* of the blood of the saint which miraculously liquifies, and sometimes appears to boil, twice yearly. Folklore tells us that great evil will befall the city should the saint not perform his biannual miracle. On these occasions he is vilified and his church threatened by the populace until he causes the liquification to occur; and Naples goes happily on with its noisy business, secure in the knowledge that all will be well until the next time. In tradition Gennaro (Januarius) was a bishop of Benevento who was beheaded at Pozzuoli, near Naples, during the persecution of Christians by the Emperor Diocletian—but not before he had stayed an eruption of Mount Vesuvius. His powers could have been put to good use in 1944 when the author witnessed the last catastrophic eruption of this 'throat of hell', which changed the familiar profile of the mountain and sealed off its opening, obliterating, perhaps forever, the classic 'pine tree' of smoke still in evidence in every cheap watercolour and wood-inlay picture of the Bay of Naples.

There is probably not a Neapolitan worthy of the name who would deny any of the above (and a good deal more) about their San Gennà, as he is affectionately known, even after his very existence was questioned by the revised listing of saints made following the Second Vatican Council. 'Local personage' was the best it could do for this popular and colourful patron of

Naples. 'The Neapolitans reacted, as always, with surface indifference. On the great main door of the cathedral, however, an anonymous hand expressed the city's real feelings. "San Gennà", it wrote, "futtetenne", which can only be inadequately translated as "San Gennà, don't you give a fuck"'.[279]

There are other 'musts' in Naples. There is the cloister of the convent of Poor Clares (Franciscan nuns) with its eighteenth-century Majolica tiles covering the arbour beams, benches and columns, depicting rustic scenes—people fishing or picnicking, carnivals in full swing—trees and landscapes, one of the strangest non-growing gardens in Christendom. And during the Christmas season there are the famous Neapolitan *presepi*—Christmas cribs—some with hundreds of figures from peasants to royalty, all of them dressed in the clothes of the eighteenth and nineteenth centuries and framed by streets and houses typical of Naples at that time. There is the site of the former residence of the Norman princes—the Castel Capuano—ordered into existence by William I and rebuilt by a Spanish viceroy in 1540, serving now as the Courts of Law and devoid of Norman characteristics.

But for sheer joy, nothing can touch the streets themselves, especially those of the old quarter of Spaccanapoli. And then there is music, not, alas, the hurdy-gurdy which seems so typically Neapolitan, but now the recorded variety, mostly rock and always blaring. Once in a while, however, if one is lucky, one will happen on a hurdy-gurdy, but not as in the old days when 'one was never, literally never, out of hearing of a hand-organ; and these organs, which in general had a peculiarly dulcet note, played the brightest of melodies; trivial, vulgar if you will, but none the less melodious, and dear to Naples'.[280] As though to make up for the absence of the hurdy-gurdy, the *pazzariello* (literally a foolish man) is still in evidence, especially in the Spaccanapoli, where children gather to hear this one-man band, to stare at his costumes of another age, and to laugh at his imitations of *bel canto* singers.

It is hard to imagine William I visiting Naples without stopping off at Caserta Vecchia, just a brief ride to the north. The town sits high—1,310 feet—and presides over a breathtaking view of the great valley below, with its screaming Alfa Romeos and lumbering *carretti* pouring along the Autostrada del Sole between Naples and Rome. Founded in the ninth century by Lombards of Capua, it was a thriving community into the middle of the eighteenth when that inveterate builder, Charles of Bourbon (later King Charles III of Spain) started his sprawling palace at a new Caserta down on the plain, causing the general abandonment of the high Caserta, from then on known as Vecchia—Old. A Norman castle is there, dreadfully ruined both by time and by man. But the fine Norman cathedral of San Michele (*see page* 296) is not ruined.

Started by Bishop Rainulf in 1120, the cathedral would for all practical purposes have been finished just three years before William's visit. Accustomed as he was to the luxurious life of Palermo, even William could not have helped but be impressed by the basilica church 'with its massive architectural scheme that gives it the look of an armoured warrior'.[281] Standing in its lonely square it is the apotheosis of the Romanesque basilica, patterned after the cathedral at Sessa Arunca a short hop north. The soaring cupola rising from the central part of the building, eight-sided and enlivened by two rows of interlacing

Norman arches, was not yet built at the time of William's visit. Decorated by patterned light and dark stone occasionally representing animals such as the lion—the Hauteville emblem—it is, as far as the representations go, a visual throwback to the first Hauteville shrine at Melfi. And there are mosaics of Byzantine inspiration, endless patterns and knots, moulded into circular shapes and centred under the interlacing arches. The front entrance, which was not completed when William was there (it is dated 1160), is considered among the finest of Norman Romanesque achievements in Southern Italy.

Except for the front façade which opens on to a small piazza, the church is hemmed in by buildings which severely reduce the intense light normally available on the southern Italian heights. As a consequence the interior of the church is dim, lighted for the most part by the narrow horseshoe windows along the nave. But what otherwise might have been just another dank interior has become, instead, glorious in its evocation of mystery; for the eye is drawn—along with the spirit—ever forward between rows of monolithic columns towards the sanctuary steps awash in a sea of light. The source of the glory is the great cupola, for among the blind arches of the arcade that encircles the drum of the cupola are eight small windows; and their effect is a dramatic miracle of light at precisely the cathedral's central crossing. The mundane explanation for this focusing of light is that the cupola stands higher than the surrounding buildings that want to hem it in; but whatever the reason, the resulting effect is impressive.

To the right of the sanctuary steps is an inlaid ambo (pulpit-lectern) decorated with the richest poly-chrome mosaics to be found in Southern Italy. Absolutely Muslim in its brilliance and inspiration, it echoes the floor which looks for all the world as if it were an inlaid stone rug derived from the patterns of Eastern fabrics. There is a panoply of exotic animals, a zoo begotten of an ecstatic mind, similar to what we have seen at Otranto and in the church of Santa Maria del Patir near Rossano.

But the best part of Caserta Vecchia is simply walking the nearly deserted streets. One does not expect to meet anyone here, since only about two hundred people inhabit the town, no doubt enjoying the blessed quiet which seems so unnatural to Southern Italy. There are shadowed arches; an arch, in fact, pierces the bell-tower of the cathedral, allowing a narrow street to pass through. There are walls hiding gardens; gates and loggias

Cathedral Campanile, Caserta Vecchia, Italy

open to the air—wonderful on a summer evening!—and looking as though they were lifted out of a painting by Giotto. If you arrive by car, which is much the better way as public transport to the town is not easy to come by, the chances are that yours will be the only one you will see in the area. And if you are hungry there is an *osteria*, vine-and arbour-covered, which serves good food, wine and beer, and presents one of the most stunning views in Southern Italy.

In July William sailed from Salerno. One trusts that he looked hard at the handsome cathedral there, built by his great-uncle, Robert Guiscard, in a day more fraught with struggle than even his own. Once back in Palermo, William relaxed into the torpor that seemed so natural to him, sinking into the arms of luxury, comfortably arrogant in his recent triumphs. He had reason to be. And he had engraved on the royal seal with which the Treaty of Benevento was made official the same proud claim that his grandfather, Great Count Roger, had had engraved on his sword after the Battle of Cerami in 1063: *Dextera domini fecit virtutem; Dextera domini exaltavit me* ('The right hand of the Lord gave me courage; The right hand of the Lord raised me up'.)

1157

On 8 September a son, Richard, was born to Henry II and Eleanor of Aquitaine, the fourth child in five years of marriage. (One can imagine Louis VII—now married to Constance of Castile, who, like Eleanor when married to him, seemed capable of producing only girls—and his steamy thoughts when he heard that his former wife had given Henry a third son!) More than any of Henry's progeny, Richard was to be spoken of as descended from the devil, an allusion to his ancestress, the witch Melusine. His life would not prove especially long, only forty-two years, but it would be adventurous—downright violent is more to the point—sometimes scandalous, and always interesting. Dubbed Lionheart, Richard should have had enormous appeal to his father; and, if the truth were known, he probably did. But there was no way in which these two stubborn, ego-ridden, fearless men could manage to get along. Respect one another they might; but work together—never!

It is remarkable that Henry had the time to sire Richard, or any of his brood for that matter: he was seemingly never at home. Ruling over holdings larger than those claimed by Louis VII of France, Henry was constantly on the move. Though the machinery of government ran smoothly in the hands of competent officials, he was not one willingly to trust others—except for Becket, and his trust there proved almost naïve. Henry felt called upon to visit all quarters of his realm, usually following well publicized itineraries; but he was not above turning up unexpectedly in remote outposts. He would sometimes be absent from England for several years running. More than almost any other prince of his day, Henry had to travel vaster distances and at greater speeds to keep an eye on the workings of his territories.

Prince Richard was probably born in Beaumont Palace at Oxford. The first historical reference to Oxford is in the *Anglo-Saxon Chronicle* under the year 911. It is believed that the town grew up around a shrine (built in the eight century) dedicated to Saint Frideswide, whose legend was written down in the twelfth century by William of Malmesbury. He recorded that Frideswide, apparently of ravishing beauty, was pursued for years by a hot-blooded young Mercian noble named Algar. His suit became such a burden to her, especially when he tried to abduct her, that she called down a miracle from saints Catherine and Cecilia, who caused him to be struck blind—a rather stiff penalty for amorousness. To her credit, Saint Frid (as she is familiarly known among her twentieth-century admirers) restored Algar's sight. Understandably chastened, he left her alone from then on.

Little enough is left of Norman Oxford; even less of anything pre-Norman. The tower of St Michael's Church on the east side of Cornmarket Street is the sole surviving Oxford building pre-dating the Conquest. A bell-tower, it is small, sturdy and heavy, reflecting its probable use as a defensive bastion, an assumption further indicated by its placement in conjunction with the north gate of the old city. Originally it may even have been tied directly to the city wall.

The only remaining parts of Oxford's castle are the earth mound, St George's Tower, and the crypt of the garrison church which stood immediately to its east. The motte is not impressive as these things go, shorn of its tower keep and overgrown with weeds, but it must have been more formidable than it now seems since it was from such easily defended castles that the Normans ruled the land. St George's Tower stands on a line with what was the bailey, is four storeys high, with a spiral staircase ascending to a corner turret, and has walls whose thickness recedes in six stages, those at the bottom being the thickest—nine feet.

The castle is largely forgotten by the twentieth century, unfortunately obscured by a drab modern prison built on the site, and even before that serving as a house for a college of canons which was important to the development of Oxford University in the late twelfth century. The university was perhaps unwittingly started by Henry II himself when, during his dispute with Thomas Becket, he recalled English students from the University of Paris in 1167. Although not the only centre of academic study in twelfth-century England, Oxford had many famous and learned men, and from this time began to assume the status of a *studium generale*.

The Beaumont Palace where Richard was born had been built beyond the north gate by Henry I in about 1130, becoming his favourite residence. The only remembrance of it today is the name of Beaumont Street on which is located the famous Ashmolean Museum. But for a city so popular with the Norman monarchs it is surprising that there is so little Norman architecture in evidence. Most of their buildings were razed to the ground to make way for colleges, or so drastically reconstructed as to be virtually worthless as Norman relics. The church of St Peter-in-the-East still has its fine Norman crypt, but the best Norman architecture is in the cathedral—the smallest in England—which also serves as chapel for Christ Church. It has undergone many changes since it was rebuilt in the second half of the twelfth century, and although parts of it maintain a handsome Romanesque assertiveness, it is a lesson in four hundred years of architectural design from Romanesque through Gothic to the intricate fan vaulting of the late fifteenth century. In the sixteenth century great changes were wrought by Cardinal Wolsey, and then by Henry VIII, though on a diminished scale of splendour, after the politically minded cardinal fell into disgrace. The central spire is claimed to be England's earliest modelled on French examples; and of course underlying the spire is a cruciform floor plan.

Frederick Barbarossa was at a high point in his career, with the king of Denmark and the duke of Poland as his vassals, Bohemia and Hungary firmly in his sphere of influence, and Burgundy recently acquired through his marriage with its heiress. It was time to convene a diet. Besides those subject to him, including many Italians, there were also present at Besançon ambassadors from Spain, England and France. In the midst of an assembly so gratifying, one can imagine Frederick's consternation when legates arrived from Pope Adrian IV and read aloud a complaint from the pontiff protesting against the alleged mistreatment of a Danish archbishop while travelling through Frederick's domains. But what caused Frederick really to lock horns with the papal legates and goaded the gathered princes to near riot was an apparent mistranslation of the papal message, 'that the fullness of dignity and honour had been bestowed upon the emperor by the Roman pontiff, that the emperor had received from his hand the imperial crown . . .'[282] giving the impression that the recent imperial coronation had made Frederick a papal vassal. In the ensuing argument one of the papal legates gave further offence by inquiring 'From whom then does he have the empire, if not from our lord the pope?' So far as Frederick was concerned the papal messengers had spoken 'as though inspired by the Mammon of unrighteousness, by lofty pride, by arrogant disdain, by execrable haughtiness . . .'[283] But this was only the beginning of Frederick's thundering condemnation. '. . . Since, through election by the princes, the kingdom and the empire are ours from God alone . . . whosoever says that we received the imperial crown as a benefice (pro beneficio) from the lord pope contradicts the divine ordinance . . . and is guilty of a lie'.[284] The papal legates were sent scurrying back to Rome, lucky to get away with their lives, their mission unaccomplished, and papal-imperial relations at a new low. On top of it all Frederick chose the autumn of the following year to invade Italy a second time.

1158

Frederick's invasion of Italy was not so simple as he had anticipated. Despite his earlier harassment of the Lombard cities and his interest in protecting the smaller ones against the encroachments of giants such as Milan, and even though some cities hailed him as protector and deliverer, he still had no easy time of it. In some countries self-governing towns were to be a feature of the Middle Ages; and those of Northern Italy were among the earliest to establish their power. It was a new type of government, with burghers replacing, or trying to replace, the feudal, ecclesiastical or dynastic groups of the immediate past. Towns were coming to be governed by elective magistrates, and by assemblies that could pass and enforce laws. Naturally Frederick was anxious to establish in Northern Italy the imperial authority that had long been claimed, but seldom consistently maintained, by the Holy Roman emperors.

Milan was by far the most powerful Lombard city, and the most defiant of imperial control. With the help of its rivals, Frederick laid siege to the city and finally starved it into submission, partial obedience and a half-hearted peace. It was not until November that he convened a diet at Roncaglia, to work out his plans for adequate imperial control of Lombardy—and by implication eventually of all Italy, including the Norman domain. First Frederick disclaimed any idea of ruling as a tyrant. Yet he had rights, he insisted, ancient rights that must be respected. These were carefully defined by the assembled lawyers: he forbade private wars and the formation of leagues among cities; he insisted on his rights to appoint city magistrates and on his ultimate jurisdiction in appeals and criminal cases; the control of mints, markets, highways and taxes was within his rights; in each city he appointed an official, the *podesta*, to rule in his name. Immediately public support for Frederick wavered, even among the cities that had originally supported him. Many of them had been glad to see Milan humbled, but few were happy to accept the authority of imperial officials. A rumbling discontent developed, that was destined next year to explode in further defections.

What with the birth of his son Richard just the year before, and now the death of his brother Geoffrey Plantagenet on 26 July, Henry II was too preoccupied to concern himself with Frederick Barbarossa's second excursion into Italy. As for Geoffrey's city of Nantes, Conan, duke of Brittany, laid claim to it, an act which could only strengthen Henry's opinion that Brittany must be swept into his sphere of influence. There were other territories causing him worry, especially the Norman Vexin now in the possession of King Louis VII of France. In the summer of this year both parties agreed that negotiations should be opened for the resolution of the problem.

As was to be expected, Henry had a specific plan in mind, and Thomas Becket was the ideal man to execute it. Besides being the king's confidant, rough-house companion and chancellor, he was also an aide, sometimes accoutred in full armour—as though he were a knight rather than a clerk in minor orders—accompanying his king in 1156 when he reduced his brother Geoffrey to submission, and against the Welsh in 1157. More important, Thomas was known for his sagacity, for his tact, his graciousness and expertise in diplomatic affairs. In his official capacity as chancellor he was sent on an embassy to France, his purpose to negotiate the betrothal of the English king's eldest surviving boy, Henry, not yet four years old, with the French king's infant daughter, Margaret. The underlying purpose of the mission was to persuade Louis that the Norman Vexin should be Margaret's dowry, to be delivered when, in the future, the marriage would take place.

According to some reports Becket tended, privately, to live rather more frugally than he did in public, though his table, more often than not frequented by honourable and royal company, was notorious for its opulence and service. But we know from one of Thomas' biographers, William fitzStephen, that the retinue accompanying him to Paris was extravagant beyond most imaginations. Two hundred and fifty footmen led the procession into every village *en route*, singing at the tops of their lungs their own English ballads. There followed the chancellor's hounds and greyhounds, an object lesson to the

French on the English manner of the chase. Drawn by five horses each, eight wagons of Becket's household goods rattled over the cobble-stones, two of them carrying barrels of the finest English beer. Each of the wagons was guarded by a chained mastiff, and—a showy touch of caprice—each horse was jockeyed by a monkey. Twenty-eight pack horses followed, bearing Thomas' own chapel furniture and religious paraphernalia, gold and silver plate, carpets and various hangings for his chamber, and twenty-four suits of clothes. (It was reported that he wore his outfits only once and then gave them away.) There were boxes of money to be dispensed to the poor, along with countless gifts and books to soften the hostility of those who mattered.

Some short distance behind marched two hundred squires, carrying their knights' shields and leading the horses of their glimmering-armoured masters, all mounted and arrogantly erect. Falconers marched two by two with their birds perched on their wrists, followed by sons of barons, by cooks, stewards and menial servants. And then—the climax of all this ostentation—came Thomas Becket himself, chancellor to Henry II of England, in company with a few of his friends. Astride a handsome charger, impeccably outfitted in brightly coloured hose and tunic open at the neck against the summer heat, 'sitting tall in the saddle', his long, clean-shaven face and high forehead giving the mark of natural dignity, with eyes glistening, he radiated the impression of a man born to the court. Everyone knew he was the king of England's closest friend; seeing him now they believed it.

By the time Henry crossed the Channel to meet Louis on the Norman-French border everything had been arranged. Young Prince Henry and Princess Margaret were declared betrothed, with the Norman Vexin as the infant bride's dowry. Of course the marriage could not take place for years, the ages of the two principals being what they were, and until such time Louis would retain control. Henry further ensured the certainty of his eventually recovering the Vexin by having it stipulated that should young Henry die before the marriage, Margaret would then marry another of his sons. For the present Margaret would remain in the custody of Henry and Eleanor. The two kings then put their heads together and resolved the problems of Nantes and Brittany to their satisfaction and to the discomfiture of Conan who, though he was forced to cede Nantes to Henry, was at least recognized formally as duke of Brittany. Then, in September, while his queen awaited the birth of yet another son, Henry moved on to Paris to collect his daughter-in-law-to-be.

In contrast with Becket's splendid embassy, he conducted himself modestly, travelling with only a small retinue, and declining the lavish hospitality which was offered him. He was nevertheless received with extravagant honour by King Louis and the barons of France, and, according to Robert de Torigny, the Parisians danced with joy 'both at the good relations of the two kings and at the visit of so notable a guest'. In November King Louis was taken by Henry on a tour of Normandy as far as Mont Saint-Michel on the confines of Brittany. When they stayed overnight at the abbey of Bec, King Louis was heard to remark that there was no one he esteemed so highly as the king of England. 'Wonders never cease,' commented the chronicler.[285]

Chapter Seventeen

'I know there are those . . . [who] say: 'Liberty is a priceless possession.' It is a fine thing to fight for liberty. I admit it. Yet this should be done at the beginning; if one has been subdued and long obedient and and then shakes off the yoke, he seems rather to yearn for an evil death than for liberty.'

Otto of Freising, *The Deeds of Frederic Barbarossa.*
Translation by Mierow and Emery

1159

The strain of five years as pope had taken its toll on Adrian IV. He died at Anagni on 1 September. Perhaps the end came in the nick of time since a complete rupture in his relationship with Frederick Barbarossa seemed inevitable—indeed the wheel had been set in motion just the month before. Even before his meeting with William I at Benevento in 1156 and the humiliation implicit in his admission that he needed the armed support of the abhorred Normans to maintain his papal throne, his health as well as his morale had begun to fail. Now, backed by an enormous army and posturing arrogantly in Northern Italy, Frederick was demanding taxes and other traditional rights of regalia not only from the Lombards, but from parts of the papal territories as well. Falling back on the ultimate and questionable papal device of excommunication, Adrian had threatened the proud emperor in August. Yet he sensed the end was near when 'he confided to his compatriot John of Salisbury, who knew him well, that the burden of the Papacy had now become greater than he could bear, and that he often wished that he had never left England. He died, as many Popes had died before him, an embittered exile; and when death came to him, he welcomed it as a friend'.[286]

But Adrian had already set in motion a vital force of opposition to the emperor, with the collusion of William I of Sicily through his political architect and emir of emirs, Maio of Bari. Maio had been labouring over a year to better Sicily's position within the papal curia and Italy generally. With the willing help of Siena-born Cardinal Roland Bandinelli, chancellor to the pope and a man who had already played leading roles at Benevento in 1156 and at Besançon in 1157. Roland was an enthusiastic supporter of Adrian IV and, since he had helped create the Treaty of Benevento, with its consequent recognition of William as king of Sicily, he could be counted on to support Sicilian causes, especially if they stood against German pretensions. A former teacher, writer on canon law and theology, a cardinal and finally papal chancellor, he was, in Sicilian eyes, an ideal candidate to succeed Adrian IV.

Just before Adrian's death Roland had reached an agreement with the Sicilians, as well as with refugees from Frederick's depredations and harsh vengeances in the north, and with representatives from Milan and several other cities of Lombardy. The anti-imperial conspirators had met at Anagni in August, swearing to a pact that would in time become the nucleus of the

347

powerful Lombard League. Adrian was already sick, and later in the month had his first attack of the angina that was to carry him off.

The birthplace of four popes, Anagni is a picturesque medieval hill town. One cannot afford to drive past Anagni, just off the Autostrada del Sole from Rome to Naples, unless one wants to miss a most delightful picnic spot in the cathedral piazza, a setting absolutely smacking of the Middle Ages and redolent with echoes of history. And, fortunately for the tourist, it is usually deserted.

The cathedral of Anagni, situated so spectacularly on its Piazza Innocente III, which looks out over a sweeping valley eastward in the direction of Fiuggi (a spa noted for its tasteful and restorative waters), had been in existence more than ·half a century by Adrian's time. The

Cathedral Campanile, Anangi, Italy

bell-tower is separated from the body of the church in the manner of the Italian Romanesque, free-standing and not without a kind of forceful masculine elegance. The Romanesque campanile is one of the most beautiful examples of monumental architecture. Within the framework of the style there may be more elaborate towers such as those of the northern cathedrals of Pisa, Florence and Lucca; but none is more majestic. Rising tier on tier, with arched openings becoming more and more airy the higher they go, the tower takes on a lightness, a gravitational contradiction that carries our spirits upward into the dazzling blue of the sky, into purer air. Everyone should have a favourite campanile; without apology the writer claims this one for his own! At noon every day the cathedral custodian, who lives in a house attached to the south wall of the church, enters the campanile to ring the deep-throated bells, announcing to the vast surrounding valleys as well as to the industrious little city itself, that the sun has reached its zenith. All is well. Nothing can mar the comforting tranquillity.

On entering the massive cathedral one moves back through time almost beyond time. Ponderous and heavy it is, a fitting setting for papal thunder and the issuing of excommunications. Both the episcopal throne and the paschal candleholder are signed by Pietro Vassalletto, a marble worker and mosaicist of the twelfth and thirteenth centuries, and famous for his cloister at San Paolo Fuore le Mura in Rome, as well as for certain parts of Santa Saba, Saint John Lateran and other buildings. The crypt is of a later date (consecrated 1255) than the church, and so was never known by Adrian IV. But he would have been proud to see therein, among the meticulously detailed frescoes which at times seem more Byzantine than Italian, his countryman Thomas Becket, identified by the tell-tale physical characteristic of the absence of the upper part of his head—an allusion to the manner of his 'martyrdom'.

The thirteenth-century quarter (*see page* 296) surrounding the cathedral is evocative of the age and is in keeping with the church itself. Arches span narrow streets, the kind of streets one would expect for a chance meeting of Rigoletto and Sparafucile. There are thirteenth-century walls, flights of steps, some sweeping and grand, others narrow and cramped, twisting and secretive; there are dense shadows and intense moments of light. There is something about the medieval quarter of Anagni that is more than yesterday, or today, or tomorrow. More than mere conjuring, it is magic. One feels history here, although other places by the hundreds—especially in Italy—have been more important in the historical scheme. And the medieval arches and the occasional bits of sculpture decoration that the casual tourist encounters are augmented by occasional glimpses caught, between palaces and at the ends of flights of time-worn steps, of the Sacco Valley and the Lepini Mountains.

The election of the new pope on the day after Adrian's burial in the crypt of Saint Peter's was among the more hilariously undignified moments in Church history. Recognizing that any candidate but his own nominee would be sure to lean towards William of Sicily, the emperor now determined to put on the throne his own candidate, Cardinal Octavian, a not exactly efficient dignitary, but one with more than ordinary determination if one believes the following account which, by and large, seems factual. The two-thirds pro-Sicilian majority of the College of Cardinals had already decided to elect the distinctly anti-German Roland Bandinelli. In a letter to the bishop and clergy of Bologna, Roland—Pope Alexander III by the time of writing—gave his version of the electoral proceedings:

> . . . when we had busied ourselves with the election for three days, finally everyone present except three, namely, Octavian, John of St. Martin, and Guido of Crema, agreed . . . upon our person, insufficient for this burden and by no means suited for the eminence of so great an office. With the assent of the clergy and the people, they elected us pontiff of Rome. But two, the aforesaid John and Guido, nominating the third, Octavian, stubbornly supported his election. Hereupon Octavian himself was swept into such audacity and madness that—like a maniac—he violently tore from our neck with his own hands the mantle, with which—according to the custom of the Church—Odo, the first of the deacons, had invested us (though struggling and resisting, because we saw our unworthiness), and bore if off amid a tumultuous uproar. But some of the senators had seen this monstrous act, and one of them, divinely inspired, snatched the mantle from the madman's hand. But he straightway turned his flaming eyes in a frenzy toward a certain chaplain of his, who had come instructed and prepared for this, crying out and signaling that he should quickly produce the mantle that he had craftily brought with him. He did so without delay, and that same Octavian . . . taking off his cap and inclining his head . . . assumed the mantle . . . And we believe that it was through divine judgment that the part of the mantle which should have covered him in front covered his back, as many looked on and laughed. And when he himself frantically strove to remedy this, because he could not find the head-piece of the mantle—being beside himself—he slung the fringes

around his neck, so that at all events the mantle might seem to be attached to him somehow . . . When this had been done, the doors of the church, . . . were opened, and armed men, whom he had manifestly hired for money, rushed in with drawn swords, . . . and that deadly pest . . . was surrounded by a throng of armed men. But the brethren, unexpectedly beholding a deed so monstrous—one unheard of since the world began— . . . betook themselves, together with us, to the protection of the church. And there [in fortified Saint Peter's Tower in a corner of the Vatican] . . . he had us kept under armed guard with all diligence, day and night, for nine successive days lest we should go forth in freedom.[287]

Octavian was enthroned and, as self-styled Pope Victor IV, was led off to the Lateran. Imperial instigation of this ludicrous scene was immediately recognized and Octavian's support began to melt away. By 16 September he was hooted and reviled out of the city and Roland was escorted triumphantly back into Rome from Trastevere where he had been taken by Octavian's henchmen for safe keeping. He was promptly honoured as Pope Alexander III. Paradoxically Alexander's hand was strengthened by Frederick Barbarossa's recognition of the preposterous Victor IV the following year, thus forcing the legitimate pope even further into the arms of William I of Sicily. Frederick obviously at first hoped to control the papacy through Victor, but an attempt at Pavia in 1160 to bring the whole Church behind the antipope failed dismally, and the schism put Frederick squarely in opposition to all the other rulers of Europe, who recognized Alexander. Alexander responded to Frederick's support of anti-Pope Victor by the typical twelfth-century pontifical knee-jerk—excommunication. Of course Victor responded in kind. But despite the support of most European rulers, Alexander was unable to remain in Rome where Victor's family wielded great power. He was consecrated pope in a small town to the south of Rome, and thereafter remained away from the city, first in Southern Italy, and from late 1161 in France.

Alexander, Frederick and Victor were not the only ones having their troubles. After years of the dry rot of neglect, King William's North African empire had begun to collapse. Now only the city of Mahdia was left to the absentee king, but even its days were numbered. It was brimming to the walls with a glut of Christians who had flocked there from throughout William's African empire in the wake of a revolt led by Sheikh Omar, who had taken over the governorship of the city of Sfax from his father, Abu al-Hassan al-Furriani. Too advanced in years for the job, Abu al-Hassan had, several years before, pledged himself a voluntary hostage to the court of William in favour of his son. As early as 1156, when William's kingdom was being threatened by Greek, papal and German forces, Omar, on the advice of his father, called for an uprising in Sfax, during which every Christian there was massacred, and for which 'Abu al-Hassan, praising Allah with his last breath, was led to the gallows on the banks of the Oreto and hanged'.[288] With that the decay began. Other cities followed suit. By the time Tripoli rose in revolt (1158) against the Norman hegemony, William and his emir of emirs, Maio of Bari, must have known that their presence in Africa was doomed. Finally Mahdia was encircled, the siege beginning on 20 July. By January of 1160 William and Maio decided to abandon the North African cause. Their defending garrison at Mahdia was given safe conduct home to Sicily; by their departure Islam regained the last of Africa's Christian cities.

Understandably Maio was blamed for Sicilian inertia in defence of the African part of the empire. Already unpopular because of his too-readily displayed contempt for William's barons—and Normans in general—he sank still further in the esteem of the court at Palermo. We may wonder why he and William allowed North Africa to slip through their fingers so readily. Quite simply, it was too far away to bother with; it would take too much energy, manpower and money to quell the revolts there, and then hold on to the land. Besides that, they had bigger things on their minds, something infinitely more challenging than merely hanging on to a far-off coastline of a hostile continent inhabited by infidels. It was much more important, advised Maio, to expand the Sicilian sphere of influence in Europe, especially now that they had an anti-imperialist pope—and a legitimate one at that—in their camp.

If Maio was aware of the popular distrust and court hatred (and how could he not be?) he gave no indication. While William, as always more indolent than inspired, was lolling in his harems, enjoying his odalisques and his exquisitely oriental pastimes, Maio, as though to celebrate his enviable position of power, was at work on his church of San Cataldo in Palermo, named after a little-known sixth-century bishop of Taranto.

Starkly simple inside (*see page* 393), San Cataldo displays, without complicated decoration but for its Eastern-inspired capitals, the essential structure of Norman-Islamic architecture. Even if the church was once decorated by shimmering wall and cupola mosaics (it was probably left unfinished on the sudden, violent death of its founder), it does not suffer from their absence. Standing in striking contrast to the vivid colouring of the Cosmati-style floor, its austere plainness is perhaps disappointing to those who need decorative distractions. Yet simplicity is its advantage. Now, undistracted by the glories of vibrant tesserae, we can see the form—those magnificently arranged solids in an exactingly proportioned void. Often overshadowed in the tourists' view by its site-mate, the Martorana, San Cataldo is none the less an example unsurpassed of the Norman love and feeling for solidity and proportion. Width to height it is perfection; curve to straight line it is absolute balance; its solid heaviness is wondrously mitigated by a soaring into three undecorated, spherical domes. It is of the same type as the three-domed Apulian churches of the period. It is also Islamic in feeling, with its pierced stone windows and its stone arabesques edging the top of its outer walls.

San Cataldo is a small church, echoing the spirit of Sicily's twelfth-century Normans, a spirit then on the wane, a spirit dispirited, a eunuch of its former being. With the exception of a little gem just outside Castelvetrano—the Santissima Trinità di Delia—the Arabic influence in Sicilian building is ceasing to be apparent. As the days of the Norman kingdom became numbered the island leant inexorably towards the West. The visionary marvel of the great count and Roger II—that successfully eclectic blending of East and West—had just about run its course. But then, after all, when perfection has been achieved, and since perfection cannot move beyond perfection, what more is there?

With the impact on Europe of the loss of William's African holdings, and the petty, but deadly, bickering unleashed by the death of Adrian IV, it is no surprise that the passing away of yet another Englishman should go unnoticed. Nevertheless there is something gravely noble about the life of King Stephen's younger son, William of Blois, and sad about his death. He was only twenty-five years of age, and without issue. He had made no attempt to claim the English throne and was indeed on very good terms with Henry II, fighting at his side and knighted by him in 1158. He died in the king's service during the campaign Henry had mounted to make good a rather specious claim that Toulouse was part of the Aquitainian inheritance. William had been very well provided for in the terms of the treaty made between King Stephen and Henry: he was count of Boulogne and count of Mortain, and held all the lands both in England and on the Continent that his father had held before becoming king. By his marriage in 1148 with the Warenne heiress Isabel he acquired her family's large holdings, notably in East Anglia and Sussex.

The Warennes' Castle Acre in Norfolk was magnificent. But the castle at Lewes in Sussex was more the family abode, probably because it was closer to the source of action and, together with Pevensey, Hastings, Bramber, Arundel and Chichester, formed a line of defence along the Sussex seaboard. Lewes Castle is unusual in that it possesses two artificial mounds. (Lincoln had a second mound, although its existence is not so obvious as at Lewes.) William de Warenne threw up his first motte to overlook the valley of the River Ouse. It is currently known as Brack Mount. Later he built a second mound southwest of the original and nearer the town, enclosing the area between the two to form a large court for domestic buildings. On this new mound

Lewes Castle, England

an elliptical shell keep was raised, and it is this keep that furnishes what spectacle there is to see at Lewes today. A good part of the old facing of the keep is still in place, along with the corbels that held up the sloping penthouse roof that protected its defenders. Fireplace flues can be traced upwards along the walls. The southern tower of the keep is the more noteworthy of the two that were built during the thirteenth century, complete with arrow-loops and some of the old stairs. From the top of the tower one enjoys a fine view of the town and the surrounding countryside at a height of two hundred feet above sea level. Nothing of the domestic buildings of the castle remains but some vaulted cellars. The castle is protected by a fourteenth-century barbican, massive and pointed-arched, and then by an inner Norman gatehouse.

There is a kind of loneliness about Lewes Castle, even though the visitor is aware that he is right in the heart of a quietly thriving town. And there never seem to be many people about—though an Elizabethan house, called the

Barbican House, built against the outer protective gate, is now a museum of archaeology displaying prehistoric, Roman, Saxon and medieval artifacts. In this castle refuge from the industrious town, one can hardly suppress the historic excitement, an experience enjoyed by a group of six non-English-speaking Italian girls who requested the writer to take their picture. They were from diverse cities in Italy, two of them from Bari. Of course they knew of the Norman presence in Southern Italy. But not one of them knew that the Normans had come to England as well. It is not surprising, actually, when one realizes that very few of the English realize that the Normans were in Italy and Sicily. Neither do most people know that Lewes claims to have the lowest death rate of any place in England—whatever that means.

Anne of Cleves lived at Lewes after the annulment of her marriage to Henry VIII, and her half-timbered house is still there, now serving as a folk museum. Another one-time inhabitant of Lewes was Tom Paine, the controversialist and author, whose *Common Sense* was a match that helped ignite the American War of Independence; indeed, his words 'These are the times that try men's souls' became a revolutionary battle-cry. His *Rights of Man*, probably better known in England both then and now, was written in enthusiastic support of the French Revolution.

1160

When King Louis VII's Queen Constance died during the summer, he married again within a fortnight. The indecent haste of the new marriage indicated to Henry II that the French king was determined to produce an heir; and if such should come to pass then Louis would somehow renege on handing over Princess Margaret's dowry of the Norman Vexin. But Henry had his own trump card to play. He had not as yet officially recognized Alexander III as pope. By threatening to withhold recognition he obtained papal sanction for the marriage of the royal children, which took place on 2 November, propelling a totally surprised Louis into a royal purple rage. By a treaty of May 1160 that ended the hostilities between the two kings in Toulouse and Normandy, the Vexin was not to be handed over until 1164, unless the marriage took place earlier 'with the consent of the church'—and this Louis had not expected would be given. But from Henry's point of view the coup was masterful. With the marriage ceremony completed, the Norman Vexin—with the castles at Gisors, Neufles and Neufmarché—was handed over to him by the Knights Templar, the acting custodians. Louis was especially furious at the loss of Gisors, the traditional meeting place of French kings and Norman dukes when they wanted to berate one another. Henry II's course of territorial aggrandizement could hardly have defused the alarm of either Louis or Frederick Barbarossa, both with legitimate fears of his growing strength.

Henry had been on the Continent since 1158 and was to remain there until January 1163. But his building programme proceeded apace throughout all his domains from Scotland to Aquitaine, was pursued by him for the rest of his life, and was continued thereafter by his sons Richard and John. When Henry took the reins in 1154 he could count 225 baronial castles and 49 of his own, a ratio of about five to one. Sixty years later, well into John's time, there were only 179 baronial fortresses as opposed to 93 for the king, now rather less than two to one. Among the first castles to which Henry turned his attention was Norham, in reality a possession of the bishop of Durham, whom Henry encouraged to improve its motte-and-bailey with a stone keep. It still stands,

> The battled towers, the donjon keep,
> The loophole grates where captives weep,
> The flanking walls that round it sweep . . .[289]

though much in ruins, as a silent guard at a ford across the River Tweed—a frontier outpost against the kings of Scotland. Norham, and Carlisle Castle on the Solway, had been built by Henry's predecessors to guard important river crossings on the only two routes practical for armies moving between Scotland and England. While there was no clear boundary between the two countries there was a tacit frontier of sorts beyond which the Norman kings, while coveting the northern lands, were not eager to go. Outpost strongholds needed to remain strong.

The block-like keeps—and Norham is no exception—are invariably the spectacular parts of castle remains. They were for the most part austere, more fortresses than homes, and normally supplemented by various domestic buildings clustered within the confines of the bailey. There are only a few remains of these domestic buildings—those at Oakham in Rutland and at Christchurch in Hampshire being among the more notable—but most are too fragmentary to be very interesting, or have vanished altogether. While not among the most spectacular of castle ruins, in its day Norham must have been at least daunting when its

> . . . warriors on the turrets high,
> Moving athwart the evening sky,
> Seemed forms of giant height;
> Their armour, as it caught the rays,
> Flashed back again the western blaze,
> In lines of dazzling light.[290]

Farther south, in Yorkshire, Henry had in 1151 confiscated the chief stronghold of the most powerful local baron, William le Gros, count of Aumale, building there a tower keep of his own. Scarborough Castle remained in royal possession until the reign of James I. The keep that Henry built and that one sees there today conforms to the style of castle-building that was emerging in the second half of the twelfth century: it is noticeably higher in proportion to its bulk. This is the period of greatest progress from the old earth and timber motte-and-bailey to the rectangular stone keep, which turned out to be the most typical of Norman castle styles.

Scarborough had been inhabited intermittently since prehistoric times, indicated by *in situ* findings left by invaders from the Low Countries or the Rhineland area. Because of its natural defensive position on a prominent headland the Romans built a look-out and signal station here, the ruins of which are still discernible. Called after a Viking adventurer Thorgils 'Skarthi'—the hare-lipped—who had built a fort there around 965, it was harried by Harold Hardrada's forces in 1066. It was under King Stephen, though, that the great harbour was finally protected by a sizeable stone castle, begun by William le Gros around 1135. High on its promontory, the castle remained impregnable until Cromwell's time, though it had a low moment in 1557 when Sir Thomas Stafford, leading a company, outraged by the marriage of Queen Mary to Philip of Spain, occupied the fortress before being led off a week later to the Tower of London and executed.

What remains of Scarborough is largely the work of Henry II, including the curtain walls, and is as impressive and dramatic as any medieval remains in England. On occasion large sections of curtain wall, ravaged by time and storms, have plunged into the North Sea, including the tower where George Fox, founder of the Quaker movement, was imprisoned in 1665-6. Only the east wall of Henry's keep remains intact, but the original form of the whole is clear—four storeys high with the entrance on the second. Having the entrance on the level above the ground floor was sheer practicality, forcing would-be invaders to fight their way upward to gain admission. There was no access to the ground floor from without, also a practical measure since the rooms were used for storage, only now and then as a convenient prison. Every floor was equipped with wardrobe and armour storage areas. The upper floors were of wood. There were few windows.

There can be no doubt that the Norman royal pleasure palaces at Palermo were modelled on Eastern designs. At one time, in fact, they were mistaken for buildings that dated from the time of the Saracen emirs; it was only in the latter part of the last century that they were correctly designated Norman buildings. It is not beyond the imagination to picture the reactions of Robert Guiscard and his brother, Great Count Roger, had they been able to foresee the debilitating depths to which their line would sink within two generations. In contrast to Henry of England, who was building his fortresses for expansion and defence, William of Sicily, in a blatant display of how thoroughly he had adjusted to Byzantine luxury, was planning or building just outside Palermo four palaces set in the park of Gennoard like 'a necklace on a beautiful woman'. He only planned and built them: the enjoyment was left to his son, the future William II. But lovely they were, sumptuously ornate, far enough removed from the

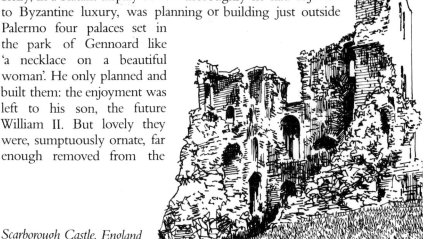

Scarborough Castle, England

smells and noise of the city to act as further inducements to indolence. Alive with running waters that fell with a cooling splash into fish-filled pools, all of them were jewel-set in gardens luxuriant and informal as a natural cornucopia, ever filled with Italianate reds, golds, greens and whites in combinations that seemed to defy the prism.

Of four palaces only La Zisa (from the Arabic *Aziz*—magnificent —an apt description of them all) and La Cuba retain any semblance of former grandeur. As for Menani, it is gone; La Favara—or *Castello di Mare Dolce*, the Palace of the Sweet Sea—is

La Favara, Palermo

derelict, turned into a warren of apartments in the midst of an impoverished area of modern Palermo, and alive with children, their hard-working parents and their pets. Originally and distinctively located in the centre of a lake, it consisted of low buildings surrounding an arcade. It was first built by King Roger, was added to and modified luxuriously by William I, and enjoyed by William II. One can hardly blame the kings for not wanting to leave such a heady oasis as Favara, complete with colourful landing stage and gaily painted barges in which, according to at least one chronicler, William II dallied with his women. Abdur Rahman, from Trapani, tells us:

> Oh, how fair is the lake . . . and the palace in its midst . . . The clear water of the two well-springs is like liquid pearls, and the basin like a lake. The branches of the trees seem to stretch out to look at the fish in the water and smile at them. The big fish swim in these limpid waves, and the birds in the garden sing melodiously . . . The ripe oranges on the island seem fire burning on branches of emerald . . . The yellow lemon seems a lover passing his night in tears for the absence of the fair one . . .[291]

William I's idyllic pleasures were abruptly shattered when his emir of emirs, Maio of Bari, was assassinated on 10 November, Saint Martin's Eve, struck down in the Via Coperta in Palermo by his own son-in-law-to-be, who led a small band of disgruntled nobles. Maio's favouritism towards the Greeks and Arabs in the government, along with his general intransigence, had driven the group to revolt. News of the treachery spread as only such news can to the ever increasing cacophony of rejoicing in the streets. And with the celebration rose the power and popularity of the treacherous leader of the conspiracy, Matthew Bonnellus, a man of no title, but handsome and rich, a member of one of the oldest Norman families in the south, an extensive property owner, and of undeniable appeal to the masses. As he fled to nearby Cáccamo thoughts must have been crossing his mind to rid the island of its king as well. Instead he underwent the hypocritical formalities of a reconciliation.

1161

But being reconciled to the king should in no way be construed as becoming a friend—or even a supporter. Matthew Bonnellus was a Norman. Since Maio's assassination Bonnellus had become the fair-haired boy of Sicily, the liberator of the people from seven years of Maio's iron-handed administration. So it was easy for Matthew to find comrades in treachery, even from within William's family, men who would be only too happy to hurl the king aside and take his place on the throne. There was the king's half-brother Simon, bastard son of Roger II, chafing under the current rule, unable to assuage his resentment that the king had used his illegitimacy as an excuse for usurping his principality of Taranto (given to him by their father). Another was Count Tancred of Lecce, bastard son of William's brother Roger (who had died in 1148), who had been lanquishing in prison since 1156 for his part in the aborted Apulian rebellion. Both of these men, being Hautevilles, were invaluable to Matthew Bonnellus.

The plot was well laid. On 9 March, while William was holding his morning conferences with one of his ministers, the signal was given. With the prisons opened according to plan, and the inmates armed, the conspirators were admitted into the palace, to be met and led on their mission by Simon and Tancred who knew the palatial layout. So far so good.

William was lucky beyond words to remain alive, not to mention saving his throne. He was rescued, but only after a thorough looting of the palace and a heinous massacre. Everything was ransacked and carried off; gold and jewels, money, pots, furniture, countless heirlooms of the Hautevilles, textiles, and royal and ecclesiastic vestments. Most irreplaceable of all was the great planisphere which had been designed for King Roger by his close friend Edrisi, certainly the most brilliant of the scholars attached to the Palermitan court during the ascendancy of the Hautevilles.

The object, which disappeared forever during the riots of this year, was of silver, 'weighing 450 Roman pounds, on which were traced in their equal distances, as far as was known, the gulfs, seas, and other physical and topographical features of the globe . . .'[292] A gorgeous sphere it no doubt was; but by modern standards it was wildly inaccurate, though certainly indicative of men's knowledge at that time.

What was the exact shape of this silver instrument? Edrisi says, 'the world is a ball floating in the clouds of Heaven like the yolk of an egg,' but the only inhabited part of the earth is the upper or, as it seemed, the northern half. That the world was round was surmised by the best minds, Arab and Latin, even if the vulgar opinion held that it was flat. However, as the southern half of the earth was to his mind burned with the sun and unpeopled, Edrisi must have constructed the silver instrument as the upper half of the globe, and not a complete ball, as some have thought.[293]

The looting mobs burned the court records, murdered the palace eunuchs, and made off with the harem. The situation was eventually saved by the people themselves, those who either tired of the excesses or did not take a part in them

Castle at Cáccamo, Sicily

to begin with, and by such loyalists as Archbishop Romauld of Salerno and other churchmen. But the nine-year-old heir to the throne, Roger, was killed by an arrow in the eye during the struggle to rescue the palace staff. The insurgents fled again to Cáccamo. Now thoroughly shaken, but free, William was out for revenge. Few of those who fell into his hands escaped death or mutilation. Matthew Bonnellus, captured after having been lulled into a false sense of security, was blinded and hamstrung, and sent where he should have been sent when he killed Maio—to prison. He died there not long after.

The ancient walled city of Cáccamo is known to have been a going city during the Carthaginian presence in Sicily; it was occupied from the time of Greek hegemony through to Roman and later Saracen rule. A lack of archaeological findings makes it difficult to estimate just how complete a city it was. One would have thought that by taking over the castle at Cáccamo Matthew Bonnellus would not only have found a safe refuge for himself and his followers, but would have deprived the king of a key strongpoint.

If ever there is a castle that looks prohibitively defensive it is Cáccamo— and this despite its fairy-tale contours. Precariously perched atop a massive outcropping of rock, it scowls over the lower city and surrounding valleys. Reflecting the warm light of sunset, it is magical; the heat-drenched light of a midday Mediterranean sun shows it nakedly martial; haze and fog cause it to float, disembodied as though part of a dream; moonlight makes it translucent, ghostly, mysterious. One comes on the castle suddenly, from a distance, catching a breathtaking first sight from the modern road that wends tortuously up from its coastal origin at Termini Imersi.

Exploring the castle's rooms, halls, dungeons, chapels and terraces is another thing, however. The author, having made trip after trip to Cáccamo in all seasons, has never been able to get past the padlocked gate at the foot of the final steep approach to the round-arched entrance. The scenario follows a rigid pattern: local people direct the visitor to an apartment door; ring the bell; when a voice answers, ask for the modern castellan; he is always 'out of town'; disappointment and frustration; then the nagging questions concerning a bureaucracy that will spend so much money restoring and maintaining a monument that is clearly inaccessible.

The last major uprising of William I's reign had come very close to disintegrating the kingdom. It took more than a year for him to restore order in the realm, during which time he destroyed the town of Piazza which had been occupied by the rebels. He then founded in its place Piazza Armerina, its name derived from an army camp established by Great Count Roger on the Armerino Plain. The great count's entry into the original city of Piazza, bearing an image of the Madonna given to him by Pope Nicholas II and still preserved in the cathedral, is celebrated every 15 August.

Tourists flock to Piazza Armerina today mainly to visit the ruins of the fourth-century Roman villa at nearby Casale. What most tourists miss on their visit to Piazza Armerina is the fine little priory church of Sant'Andrea, built in 1096 by a cousin of Roger II, Simon count of Butera. Named after the first of Christ's apostles, Sant'Andrea commands a view of a shallow valley on the north side of town. Its setting is bucolic and, happily for the writer, replete with a parade of sheep and two umbrella-carrying shepherds strolling across the property on a drab, rainy day. There is a lovely strength about the quietly situated church, a solidity that, if the building had been larger, could have been severe. As it stands it seems so gentle, if foursquare, as befits the apostle concerned enough for the masses to bring to Jesus the boy with the loaves and fishes, and who was determined enough in his faith to die on an X-shaped cross, a saltire. Some frescoes from Sant'Andrea are housed in the National Gallery in Palermo.

Having purged the insurgents and brought the rebellion under control, William returned to his lazy, non-governing ways. It was at this time that he built La Zisa, wanting to enjoy the privileges of royalty in opulent splendour. But most of that magnificence is gone now. Alas, La Zisa is being restored, to stand as a show-place of Norman art in Sicily, it never occurring to the faceless powers who dispense funds for such activities that reconstituted 'show-pieces' are entirely modern, at best an estimate, at worst dishonest. The exterior of La Zisa is austere, handsome in a military way, for it was also quasi-defensive architecture in the event of the not infrequent uprisings of the period. Part of the interior has survived, including some mosaics that call to mind the nature scenes of the 'Sala di Ruggero' in the main palace. La Zisa was built over or near a spring, for there are ample provisions for fountains and water similar to the Muslim-built Alhambra in Granada. It is a haven of coolness on a sun-tormented island, a respite from every care, a place of kingly glory. On its entrance arch is a raised inscription:

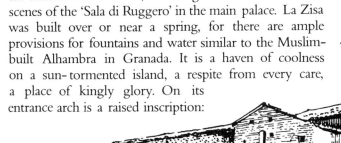

Priory of
S. Andrea, Piazza
Armerina, Sicily

La Zisa,
Palermo

Here, as oft as thou shalt wish, shalt thou see the loveliest possession of this Kingdom, the most splendid of the world and of the seas.
The mountains, their peaks flushed with the colour of narcissus . . .
Thou shalt see the great King of his century in his beautiful dwelling-place, a house of joy and splendour which suits him well.
This is the earthly paradise that opens to the view; this King is the *Musta'iz [the Glorious One]*; this palace the *Aziz*.[294]

It was at this time, too, that William started—though he may not have finished—the stunning mosaic-shimmering room in the main Royal Palace called, misleadingly, the Sala di Ruggero, the Hall of Roger. Here again we find the intrinsic Norman love of the good things of life; secular and decorative, the mosaics evoke the pleasures of life—the sheer delight in nature and the hunt. We see archers, lions and spotted leopards, oriental-looking trees and exotic flowers. The Sala di Ruggero is a fantasy existence, a quest for the impossible, a love of invention, an escape from intrigues, assasinations, conspiracies and the hates of the court. The Great Count Roger might not have recognized the forms of the decorative mosaics in the room named after him, but he surely would have understood the humour, the gold-backed radiant colours of the fanciful flora and bestiary. It is a hymn to the luxurious, carefree life; it is the final secular sunset glory in a kingdom that is being overtaken by a night of decadence, ineptitude and total lack of dedication. It must have seemed even finer before one of its window alcoves was blocked up to locate a fireplace.

For all intents and purposes William the Bad no longer ruled his land; he had abdicated that questionable pleasure to others, especially to Matthew of Ajello—protégé of Maio and the recorder of the 1156 Treaty of Benevento—to Caïd Peter and to the ambitious Englishman Richard Palmer, bishop-elect of Syracuse. Irreversible damage had been done to the kingdom by the last insurrection; and William's pursuit of the 'good life' once he had given orders to his ministers 'to tell him nothing that might disturb his peace of mind'[295] did nothing to remedy the situation.

Chapter Eighteen

HENRY: . . . by the royal customs of our realm
The Church should hold her baronies to me,
Like other lords amenable to law.
I'll have them written down and made the law.

Tennyson, *Becket, Prologue*

1162

Before he died in 1161 Archbishop Theobald of Canterbury had reason to be disillusioned both with Thomas Becket, his former protégé, and the king. Death was a long time coming to the archbishop, staved off by his desire to see either or both of them. But they were on the Continent, in Normandy, and a stormy Channel had deafened them to Theobald's plaintive requests. It was he who had introduced these two friends. It was he who had advanced his student to unexpected secular heights, and who had championed the claims to kingship of Henry fitzEmpress. It was Theobald who had paved the way for Henry and Stephen to ratify the treaty by which Henry's succession had been arranged. It was the archbishop again who had guaranteed the civil peace those six weeks England had been without a crowned king. And it was he who had enthroned Henry as the first Plantagenet king of England. He had written to the king: 'My flesh is consumed and my soul is on the point of departing from my body; but it still lingers in hope and desire of your coming. It refuses to hear the call of nature, nor will it suffer mine eyes to close, until they have had the satisfaction of beholding your face'.[296]

Theobald had already experienced disappointment in Becket. Having pressed for his appointment as chancellor, he had come to view him as little more than an affluent, dandified royal shadow. In his final agony, Theobald had received only excuses from Becket. Although obviously trumped up, the alibis had borne the added weight of the king's personal assurances that his chancellor simply could not make the trip. No doubt Becket had had neither the desire nor the will to extricate himself from Henry's court. And no doubt he had not looked forward to the lecture he would almost certainly have received at the archbishop's deathbed. So on 18 April 1161 Theobald had died in the arms of John of Salisbury, without having seen either of those who surely, if nothing else, owed him the respect due the dying.

How the realization came to Becket that his appointment to the vacant see of Canterbury must shatter his friendship with the king cannot be known for sure. But instinctively he recoiled from the actuality of it. He was with the king at Falaise, birthplace of William the Conqueror, when Henry finally made his plans clear. 'Behold, my lord', the chancellor reportedly responded sarcastically, indicating his rich and modish apparel, 'what a religious and holy person you are minded to install in that exalted seat . . . It might come to pass, too, my lord, should my affairs take this shift, that I might turn out right unlike, and of a different mind, to him who now standeth here before you . . . I therefore pray, in all humbleness, that you go somewhere else'.[297] Thomas knew that if he became archbishop he could no longer be Henry's friend and agent. But Henry's mind was made up. He had his reasons.

The new year found Henry resolved to see his eight-year old son, Prince Henry, crowned co-king as a safeguard to ensure his succession. As the archbishop of Canterbury alone was empowered to perform the coronation ritual, Henry needed a trusted crony, someone who would bow to his wishes and still be strong enough to enforce them should something happen to him. With Thomas enthroned in Canterbury the king could feel assured that his wishes would be realized with minimum resistance.

Henry's mother, Empress Matilda, as well as others, had warned him against making the appointment. His own reticence notwithstanding, Thomas had no choice but to acquiesce in the royal decision. On the Wednesday after Whit Sunday he was elected to his new post, and was ordained priest immediately. Then, the following Sunday, 3 June, he was consecrated and enthroned as archbishop of Canterbury. With that accomplished he adjourned to Trinity Chapel, burial place of Lanfranc and Theobald, at the east end of the cathedral to say his first mass. 'This chapel was his favourite resort when he was in Canterbury. Here he said mass both before his exile and after his return. Here he would come to assist privately at the office of the monks in choir, and he would frequently retire to the same chapel for prayer'.[298]

The rush of events conspired to set in motion a profound change in Thomas' personality. Formerly a convivial, affluent man of the world, he suddenly embraced the role of defender of the Church, becoming more and more dogmatic in his opposition to royal demands, all of which he saw as impinging on ecclesiastic rights. He became austere, and adopted the life-style of a monk. 'Clad in sackcloth of the coarsest kind, reaching to his thighs and covered with vermin, he mortified his flesh by spare diet . . . He often exposed his naked back to the lash of discipline'.[299]

By and large Henry's relationship with the Church, and with Archbishop Theobald in particular, had been good. It would seem, for the most part, that he saw ecclesiastical and royal jurisdictions as complementary, with neither infringing on the traditional rights of the other. Each side was prepared to compromise, with mutual problems settled by arrangements between the king and Church leaders. We can understand Henry's frustration when he was suddenly faced with an archbishop utterly unbending in his defence of 'Church rights', a man who would not countenance any bargaining, any give-and-take between the two institutions. Becket, once he had accepted his new post, took on the job of defender of the Church with the same zeal with which he had defended Henry's interests when chancellor. This was not at all what Henry had had in mind. He had counted on a champion at Canterbury, not an adversary. He remembered only too well the rollicking good times he and Thomas had shared, the drinking bouts, yes, even the battlefield adventures in the king's interests. Now he was faced not only with a cleric but with a man of frightening austerity, a now estranged friend, an archbishop who regarded the Church as his primary concern, the monks, clerics and nuns—even the common people—as his charges, and the king as his son in God.

1163

Becket's first public act as archbishop was to resign the position of chancellor, which seems to have come to Henry as a shock, though one wonders why. By the end of the year 1163 Thomas on several occasions seems to have gone out of his way to thwart the king's wishes, and Henry's hostility towards him became undisguised. Whoever might bear the initial blame, the world was now called upon to watch

> . . . the kicks and blows of angry men,
> Both losing sight of the cause.
> The high names
> Of God and State are now displaced
> By hurt pride, self-distrust, foiled ambition,
> And the rest of our common luggage.[300]

1164

As though his troubles with Becket were not daunting enough, Henry was seriously concerned about the general lawlessness rampant in his realm. One aspect of this crime wave that became inextricably intertwined with the Becket problem was the number of criminals who were clerks in (probably minor) holy orders. It was Henry's demand that the Church turn over its criminous clerks for secular trial, and Thomas' ultimate outright refusal brought the two into face-to-face confrontation, destroying forever any chance that might have existed of their friendship being restored. In January, at Clarendon, Henry, who had the previous month extracted from Thomas a promise to obey the 'customs' of the land, unwisely went on to define them, presenting to a large council of ecclesiastics and lay lords his 'Constitutions of Clarendon', claiming to set out the customs that had been observed in his grandfather's time. It was upon the third clause that the quarrel between Henry and Thomas centred. Its gist was that a cleric accused of a criminal offence should, if he could prove that he was in holy orders, be tried in an ecclesiastical court. However, an official from the secular courts was to watch the proceedings, and a self-confessed or convicted cleric would thereafter no longer be able to claim the Church's protection. It was to be assumed that he would then be liable to secular trial as an ordinary layman.

The meeting at Clarendon was, to say the least, raucous. The house there had once been a hunting-lodge to satisfy the sportive callings of earlier kings; overlooking the valley where Salisbury now lies, it was magnificently located for such activity. By the end of his reign Henry II had built a great hall eighty-three by fifty-one feet internally. Later additions included a chapel, kitchens, a huge wine-cellar and a variety of chambers. But at the time of the meeting that Henry summoned, Clarendon was a good deal less pretentious.

Following an unprecedented session of bullying and browbeating, Henry requiring the bishops to set their seals to the Constitutions and the entire episcopate at first refusing, Becket suddenly bowed to the royal demands, advising the other bishops to do likewise. Although none actually set his seal to the document, they followed Thomas in promising obedience. But almost immediately Becket recanted, infuriating the king as well as the prelates with what could be regarded as nothing less than betrayal. Now desperately enraged against his former friend, Henry summoned a council at Northampton Castle in October, at which various cases were brought up and charges made against Thomas in what seems a deliberate attempt to break him. From the start of the last day of the council events moved symbolically against Thomas, largely as a result of his own behaviour. Upon a rising he had said the Mass of Saint Stephen, the first Christian martyr. Thomas could not have been unaware of the significance of the introit for that day when he intoned the words, 'Princes sat and spoke against me; and the wicked persecuted me: help me, O Lord my God, for Thy servant was employed in Thy justification'.[301] Even more significant was the gospel with its reference to 'all the just blood that has been shed upon the earth . . .'[302]

Wearing priestly vestments under his cloak and secretly carrying a sacred Host, Becket arrived at the castle (no part of which is standing today). His bishops were already gathered at the entrance, among them Gilbert Foliot, bishop of London. Upon dismounting Thomas took the archiepiscopal cross from the bearer who had preceded him. A clerk approached Gilbert.

'My Lord of London, can you stand by while the archbishop carries his own cross?' 'My dear fellow', replied Foliot, 'the man always was a fool and he'll be one till he dies'.

Robert of Hereford, his old master, tried to take the cross from him in vain; Foliot, approaching on the other side, told the archbishop sharply that he was a fool, and he also endeavoured to wrest the cross from him. Roger of Worcester rebuked Foliot: 'Would you prevent your Lord from carrying his cross?', only to be told sharply that he would live to be sorry for those words. The bishops then fell aside and Thomas entered alone, bearing his cross, and passed through the hall himself; the others followed, and Foliot again remonstrated: 'Let one of your clerks carry it'. Thomas refused. 'Then let me have it; I am your dean; do you not realize that you are threatening the king? If you take your cross and the king draws his sword how can we ever make peace between you?' 'The cross is the sign of peace', answered Thomas. 'I carry it to protect myself and the English Church'.[303]

All but deserted by his bishops, Thomas, still holding his cross, waited, expecting the worst.

In an upper room, near enough for the angry cries of 'Traitor!' to be heard by those below, were gathered the barons . . . The archbishop was condemned and sentenced . . . probably to that perpetual imprisonment which he most dreaded. While the king and a few others remained, the main body of the council came down the stairs to pronounce sentence. The archbishop did not rise to meet them, but remained seated, still holding the cross . . .

Finally, after the duty [of acting as spokesman] had been passed around, the Earl of Leicester, a man of good report with all the biographers, took up the unwelcome tale. He began with a long recital of the archbishop's debt of gratitude to the king, and passed on to a minute account of the events at Clarendon. It was clear that he feared to come to the point . . . Hilary of Chichester, to expedite matters, said that the treason was clear, and bade the archbishop hear the judgment. Thomas rose, exclaiming that it was none of their business to judge their archbishop, and strode through the hall towards the door . . . In the press, the archbishop stumbled over a cord of faggots by the central hearth and there was . . . shouting and jeering . . .

There was no pursuit. According to one biographer, Roger of York and Foliot immediately advised the king to take no violent step in the crowded and excited town, but to send for the archbishop at some future date and imprison him . . . In any case Henry made proclamation that the archbishop was not to be molested . . .[304]

Nevertheless Thomas was reduced to lurking in cellars and outbuildings, moving surreptitiously from place to place disguised as a lay brother. Even in France, where he took refuge, he at first survived partly on handouts from a few sympathetic commoners. Words of a sad threnody spread, to be picked up and sung by peasants and monks thoughout the realm. Thomas was another Joseph, sold into another Egypt by the power lust of 'a son of Herod'.

In Rama [a city of the tribe of Benjamin] a cry goes
    up from the weeping Rachel of England.
For a son of Herod shames her:
Behold, her first-born and the Joseph of Canterbury
    is in exile, as if sold into Egypt, and dwells in France.[305]

Thomas finally caught up with Pope Alexander III (himself still in exile from Rome) at Sens. There Henry's representatives to the papal court had a hard time arguing against the archbishop who convinced the pope that he was the upholder of the Church's authority in England. Although Thomas earned some mild support from Alexander III (not as much as he would have liked), he was also warned to be circumspect and unprovocative. He retreated to the Cisterian abbey of Pontigny, where he remained for two years.

1165

The hopes and prayers of King Louis VII of France were finally answered: his third wife, Adela of Champagne, presented him with a son

    . . . Philip-Augustus, Dieu-Donné,
    Given by God on an August night; hinting,
    What's more, at empire, a name full of promise.[306]

The youngster was destined to become a bigger nuisance to Henry than ever his father had been, and an almost fatal scourge to Henry's successors, Richard and John. There was also at this time an addition in the English royal house: Eleanor of Aquitaine gave birth to Princess Joanna, who in time united the two Norman houses of Plantagenet and Hauteville by marrying King William II of Sicily.

As though sensing trouble coming—he can be forgiven for not seeing clearly that the worst of his troubles were to come from within his own family—Henry II and his engineers continued a frantic programme of building and modifying castles especially urgent in this decade because of the need to prove to his barons the futility of remodelling their own castles as a threat to royal power. One part of the country where Henry especially wanted to provide himself with a strong base was East Anglia, an area where baronial power had become excessively strong during Stephen's reign. Henry established a new royal castle at Orford in Suffolk, the only one that he built from scratch. Henry intended Orford (*see page* 393) as a warning to his baronage; his concern is emphasized by the fact that the keep took only two years to build.

The time had come when few people would trust their safety to these defensively outmoded white elephants. A solution had to be found to the familiar problem of sapping. Primarily, however, it was the rapid and deadly improvements in offensive arms which spurred the ingenuity of the military architects, particularly those who had taken part in one or more of the crusades to the Eastern Mediterranean. There they had come face to face with some of the new machinery such as the trebuchet, which was capable of catapulting stones up to half a hundredweight at a time. With the introduction of such destructive mechanisms, defensive thinking had to change; wall surfaces off which projectiles might ricochet had to be developed. The cylindrical tower was one obvious solution. But the far-seeing Henry went the cylindrical tower one better at Orford, maintaining the circular interior, but creating a polygonal outer shape with walls ten feet thick. Utilizing a unique design, Henry set three turrets equidistant around his main ninety-foot high tower from which the defenders could keep watch over all the main faces of the building. If one of Orford's major functions was to cow the king's rebellious nobles, it succeeded better than might be expected and served Henry well in his coming war with his barons, being so heavily fortified that it was not even attacked. But it was not so popular a variant as to become widely used elsewhere. And ten years later Henry built his keep at Dover along traditional, massively rectangular, straightforward Norman lines.

The annual rolls of the medieval exchequer provide documentary evidence of the building of Orford castle, the first for which such detail is available. It is said to have been Henry's favourite. And well it might have been, with its spacious halls on the ground and first floors, its numerous smaller rooms, a beautiful chapel, two kitchens with sinks, drains and flues, storage areas, and a cistern in the western turret. While its design was wholly modern for its day, Orford Castle did follow a pattern of older castles in that its forebuilding housed an entrance staircase on its southwestern face, which led into the hall on the first floor above the basement. The upper hall must have been stunning both in its appearance and proportions. The plan size is the same as that of the one below, but the upper was roofed by a steeply raked conical vault, supported on corbels that can still be seen in the wall around the room about eight feet off the floor. The highest point of this roof extended above the roof platform and was used to collect rain-water, whence it was carried by a still-to-be-seen conduit. Both halls house large fireplaces, indicating that while Henry was thinking principally of defence, he also had comfort in mind. He further safeguarded Orford by surrounding it with an extensive curtain wall (the last remaining section of which collapsed in 1841), broken at intervals by projecting rectangular towers which enabled the walls themselves to be properly surveyed from within. A good part of Orford keep is still intact, indicating its comparatively uneventful military history. It was once taken briefly by the French in 1217; and it changed hands several times during the drawn-out baronial wars in Henry III's time. By 1336 it was obsolete and divested by Edward III. Now again Crown property, Orford stands stranded on its motte, its outer buildings—even its curtain wall—gone, glorying in its isolation, silently bellowing its counter threats to the thundering North Sea on one side, and to his barons' descendants on the other. Few castles maintain such splendid aloneness; no other is so magnificently expressive of the personality of its builder.

1166

On May 7, at forty-six years of age, King William I of Sicily died at Palermo, slothful to the end, enjoying royal perquisites and giving no indication that the affairs of the world—or his conscience—concerned him. He had been stricken a few weeks earlier by dysentery and fever. Archbishop Romauld of Salerno, one of the attending physicians, maintained that he refused to accept the proper medication.

William was not so bad as his sobriquet implies. Yet it is difficult to imagine the depth of genuine grief exhibited by the citizens of Palermo. The entire city went into mourning for three days in tribute to their late sovereign. The women wept openly. The republican (or at least anti-William I) chronicler, Hugo Falcandus, graphically related their mourning: 'All the ladies, the noble matrons and especially the Saracen women—to whom the King's death had caused unimaginable grief—paraded day and night in sackcloth about the streets, their hair all undone, while before them went a great multitude of handmaidens, singing sad threnodies to the sound of tambourines till the whole city rang with their lamentations'.[307] The effusiveness of their sorrow tempts one to suspect paid mourners.

In the final analysis, however, one cannot help feeling a little sorry for William. With three brothers initially between him and the crown, he had received no training for that kind of exalted position. He could build glittering structures—especially for his own use—and could fight when he had to. But he was basically a man unprepared for what life dealt him. He tried to hide his weaknesses behind a Herculean build and a fierce visage replete with an enormous beard. But that was subterfuge, and most of his barons and administrators knew it. William must have been as unhappy with his own personality quirks as were his subjects. He must have found it just as difficult as they to understand his own savage cruelty which dulled the edge of his charitable benevolence. Even for the best prepared, Roger II would have been a tough act to follow. Perhaps it is a wonder that William the Bad did as well as he did. He was buried in the Palatine Chapel, arched by glittering mosaics and marbles, the finest of the Hauteville creations in Palermo. Twenty years later his body was transferred to its present porphyry tomb in the cathedral of Monreale, that last insistence of Hauteville glory raised by his son and successor just before the final Sicilian-Norman darkness fell.

Since at the time of his father's death William II the Good was not yet quite thirteen years old, his mother Queen Margaret was established as regent, assisted by former governmental advisers William Palmer, Caïd Peter and Matthew of Ajello. There was no public opposition to this arrangement, and when William II appeared after his coronation the entire populace was won over by his good looks, and his innocence offset by seriousness.

While a regency under a woman was not the most desirable form of government over a long period of time, Margaret was known to be strong-willed and determined to maintain the royal position until William came of age. However she soon became suspicious of her triumvirate of advisers, and allowed herself to be surrounded by relatives and countrymen—more than allowed, she even invited some of them. Caïd Peter was the first to abandon the foundering ship of state, taking off for Tunis, his place of origin, changing his name back to its former Ahmed and resuming his previous profession as commander of the Moroccan fleet. Only one of the newcomers, Stephen du Perche, cousin to the queen, had any promise at all. He was a good man—barely a man as he was yet in his early twenties—who 'became to the people an angel sent by God to bring back the Age of Gold'.[308] Young, good-looking, able, and idealistically interested in securing the young king's place and bettering the realm, Stephen was appointed chancellor in November by a perhaps more than politically motivated Margaret.

The governmental scene in Sicily became chaotic, what with jostling and infighting among the civil servants and administrators, and especially among the endlessly bickering bishops and archbishops, all of them seeking temporal power. Apart from Stephen du Perche the newcomers were for the most part self-serving, disreputable and completely unconcerned with the beleaguered kingdom. Before long the Sicilians and the old-timers of the court realized that the kingdom was being administered by foreigners, most of them bad. And among the worst of the unwanted adventurers was Margaret's own brother—or half-brother, since he may have been a son of the queen of Navarre, but not of the king—Henry of Montescaglioso, so called after the county which Margaret gave him 'with the deliberate object of keeping him as far as possible from the capital'.[309]

To add to the confusion and Margaret's fears, Frederick Barbarossa was on the march again. By the end of the year he was leading an enormous army into Italy, obstinate in his determination to place his new man, anti-Pope Paschal III (anti-Pope Victor IV had died in 1164), in the Vatican, and then to move southward to take advantage of the Sicilian chaos.

If Queen Margaret had uneasy feelings that those events which one day would be called history were getting the better of her, she could well have taken a lesson from Henry II of England. Never one to ride along with the tide, Henry was resolved to mould history to his design. He was by now inured to the kind of chaotic condition that was developing in his realms. His nominal vassal, King William of Scotland, was in seditious correspondence with King Louis VII of France, who, in turn was stirring the political stew in Wales and at the same time offering treasonous advice to the Bretons. This last nuisance prompted Henry to mount an attack on Brittany, level the castle at Fougères, depose Duke Conan and betroth that unwise man's heiress, Constance, to his own seven-year old son Geoffrey—probably as good a way as any to strengthen his hold over that troublesome area. Having accomplished all this, Henry accepted the homage which the Breton barons wisely offered him, which was, after all, what he had come there for; certainly not just to study the extensive and fascinating prehistoric remains dotting this western appendage to continental Europe.

Abbey Church, Pontigny, France

Then there was the growing resistance to Henry's authority in Poitou, and an incipient rebellion in Aquitaine. The barons of Queen Eleanor's sunny homeland, egged on by the counts of Angoulême and of La Marche, were increasingly alarmed at his usurpation of their rights, augmented by the number of 'foreigners' whom he was sending into their land. They threatened to break free of the duchy and to turn to Louis VII. Henry had no choice but to march on Aquitaine. None of this bettered his relations with Louis who, moreover, continued to give protection to Henry's erstwhile friend Becket.

For a while Thomas had enjoyed the hospitality of the quiet Cistercian abbey of Pontigny, of which today only the church remains, looking, 'as you draw near, almost as if it were some huge barn ... so plain is it and un-adorned ... The note of severity was, in the time of Becket, toned only by the strange, appealing pathos of the narrow aisles, where the pointed arches rise sharply from the high, undecorated columns, a long vista of religious light that is not dim. The S. Thomas chapel has gone, the altar at which the exile ministered is forgotten; only the solemn peace of the great village church—such now it is—treasures the memory of his name'.[310]

There is a quiet calm about Pontigny, a clarity of sky, a depth of green, and a brightness of the yellow mustard fields so much a part of eastern France. On the other hand, at certain seasons Nature unleashes an atmospheric violence that electrifies the countryside, illuminates the shadows and enlivens the very stones of the church—more in keeping with the volatile, tempestuous nature of its most famous resident. No other visitors are likely to be present to interrupt romantic meditations, to intrude on thoughts of a self-exiled Becket biding his time, perhaps contemplating an equally self-induced martyrdom, and surely happy for one of the few periods in his ecclesiastical career. Approached down a tree-lined avenue and through an uncommonly beautiful narthex, the abbey church, more Gothic now than Romanesque, stands as simple and uncomplicated as Becket's philosophy of Church governance. The graveyard and open fields that lie adjacent to the south and east serve to emphasize the tranquillity, the feeling of isolation from the community it serves. The later abbey buildings, occupied now by a school, lend one the wherewithal to visualize the place when it gave refuge to the intransigent would-be saint.

From his seclusion Becket had sought support, writing to any ruler or official who might be in a position to bring some weight to bear on his unyielding king; he belaboured the pope with requests to lay an interdict on Henry's dominions. He wrote to Queen Margaret of Sicily, too, looking for support as well as a possible place of refuge should he need it. Several of her ministers, including Stephen du Perche, were well disposed towards Thomas. 'Even the king's [Henry's] mother, Matilda, "though she was of the race of the tyrants"—the phrase of a worthy monk who went to see her on Becket's part—said not a little in his favour'.[311] The archbishop of Sens, William of Blois (King Louis' brother-in-law and not to be confused with William of Blois, King Stephen's son and the title-holder of Lewes Castle), could well have been prompted, even unconsciously, by a double bias when he fired off a provocative letter to Pope Alexander on Thomas' behalf:

> The whole world is waiting to see what you will do for the exiled archbishop . . . The king of England is doing his best not merely to cripple the church of Canterbury, but to destroy her, and with her all ecclesiastical liberty, so that the authority of the apostolic see will be excluded from his borders and he alone become all-powerful in his dominions. Unless his audacity is checked it may be feared that other kings and lords will do likewise, for men think lawful whatever goes unpunished . . .[312]

The invective heated up at around this time, and after Henry had threatened to confiscate Cistercian property in England if Becket remained at Pontigny, Thomas moved to the abbey of Sainte Colombe in Sens. From there Becket wrote directly to King Henry. He received no reply. He wrote again, with a similar lack of response. His third letter was at once appealing, high-handed and audaciously threatening:

With desire I have desired to see your face and to speak with you; greatly for my own sake but more for yours. For my sake, that when you saw my face you might recall to memory the services which, when I was under your obedience, I rendered faithfully and zealously to the best of my conscience . . . For your sake for three causes: because you are my lord, because you are my king, and because you are my spiritual son. In that you are my lord I owe and offer to you my counsel and service, such as a bishop owes to his lord according to the honour of God and the holy Church. And in that you are my king I am bound to you in reverence and regard. In that you are my son I am bound by reason of my office to chasten and correct you . . .

It is certain that kings receive their power from the Church . . . so, if I may speak with your pardon, you have not the power to give rules to bishops . . . to draw clerks before secular tribunals . . . and many other things of this sort which are written among your customs which you call ancient . . . Forebear, then, my lord, if you value your soul, to deprive that Church of her rights. Remember also the promise which you made . . . when you were consecrated and anointed king by my predecessor, of preserving to the Church her liberty. Restore therefore to the Church of Canterbury, from which you received your promotion and consecration, the rank which it held in the time of your predecessors and mine . . . And further, if so please you, permit us to return free and in peace . . . to our see . . . And we are ready faithfully and devotedly . . . to serve you as our dearest lord and king . . . saving the honour of God and of the Roman Church, and saving our order. Otherwise, know for certain that you shall feel the divine severity and vengeance.[313]

Henry was much more concerned about his political advances on the Continent and the effects those gains would have on his barons than he was about the domestic troubles of the Church. His mind was full of plans for the future and, as always, for his 'eaglets'. Anjou, Maine, Normandy and England—those lands which he himself had inherited from his father and mother—he set aside for his first-born, young Henry. His next son, Richard, was to inherit the territories he had acquired through his marriage to Eleanor—Poitou and Aquitaine. Brittany he had already designated for the third in line, Geoffrey. Apparently neither Henry nor anyone else considered the proposition or desirability of his 'empire' surviving as a political unity. From his point of view everything was in order, better order, in fact, than anyone could have anticipated exactly one hundred years before, when his great-grandfather pulled off his daring Conquest.

1167

However, this year it must have crossed Henry's mind that he would have to revamp his plans, for Eleanor gave birth to the last of her brood: John (nicknamed 'Lackland' because Henry did *not* adjust his plans all that much).

In the give-and-take of Nature, the birth of a member of a new generation often counterbalances the death of a member of the old: Empress Matilda, grandmother to young John and his brothers and sisters, died at Rouen on 10 September, having lived sixty-five feisty years, ambitious to the end for the success of her son and as full of advice as ever. In its own way her epitaph was a sad conclusion to a lifetime of frustration: 'Here lies Henry's daughter, wife and mother—by birth great, by marriage greater, but greatest by motherhood'.

Frederick Barbarossa was also mapping out his future. His march on Rome was precise and productive. And once he had taken Rome, he thought, he would be set to move against the troubled Sicilian kingdom; this time his forces were augmented by a substantial number of ships manned by robust Pisans who wanted to be in on the final kill. The Romans responded in their fashion by turning against Pope Alexander, though they themselves had invited him to return to his rightful place two years before. He escaped from the city, barely avoiding capture by Frederick's troops.

St Peter's Basilica proved to be the site of the Romans' last stand against the overwhelming onslaught of Barbarossa's forces. It was the worst desecration of that seat of Christianity in its history. The inside was stained with blood even to the high altar, while the dead littered the marble floor—all of this the work of the soldiers of a man who stood as the secular head of Western Christendom. Now Frederick appeared to wield absolute control. Defying the judgement of Europe, he saw his personal pope enthroned in St Peter's. He had his overwhelming forces and a battery of Pisan ships at his disposal. Was there anything that could stop him from achieving his dream of annexing Sicily to his Holy Roman Empire, a dream he had been nourishing since that day in Aachen in 1152 when he had been crowned king of the Germans?

How could Frederick have predicted that within a few short weeks his tragically decimated, dispirited and defeated army would be lurching northward behind their disconsolate emperor? It was a rout born either from an ignorance of history or an arrogant conviction of his own invincibility. Following precedents rooted in the past, without warning and at the moment when victory seemed imminent, pestilence, that enemy unseen, the age-old scourge of armies both victorious and otherwise, struck with such brutality that Frederick, who only days before had seen himself as the strong man of Europe, could do nothing but despair. His closest comrades were left behind dead, along with a large part of his army. His Italian enemies formed a league against him even before he was out of their land. He barely made his way back home disguised deflatingly as a servant.

The Lombard League, the affiliation seeded eight years earlier with those agreements reached at Anagni just prior to the death of Pope Adrian IV, was the source of Frederick's present discomfort and was to be the bane of his future. Fifteen north Italian cities (including the until-now disinterested Venice) rallied to the cause. Seeing providential justice in Barbarossa's retreat, and therefore a justification of Alexander III, they made the again-exiled pope their patron and chief—a position more honorary than practical.

Frederick's misfortune was Alexander's boon. By leaving Rome for Benvento in advance of Frederick's arrival, Alexander had escaped the pestilence. He had made up his mind that, having been stung three times by Roman fickleness, he would be content to rule the Church from without the ancient walls of his rightful capital. Though not the type to gloat, he could derive satisfaction, knowing that righteous men throughout Europe saw his deliverance and Frederick's humiliation as divine intervention in a stupidly wasteful, vainglorious struggle, the cause of which must be laid at the foot of the imperial throne. And on top of everything else, Sicily—still awkwardly placed because of the regency—also was delivered from the wrath of a vindictive emperor. Alexander, long friendly with the Sicilian royal house, had good reason to feel a sense of security for the first time since his consecration.

1168

Contrary to expectations, Queen Margaret of Sicily had no such reason to feel secure. A storm of resentment was building against her for having replaced the young king's inherited advisers with a group of her fellow Navarrese and other outsiders. The eye of the storm centred around the young chancellor, the queen's cousin, Stephen du Perche, who by this time had also been consecrated archbishop of Palermo, thereby augmenting his already considerable influence over the court. The peoples' outright hatred of these haughty foreigners was further inflamed by the machinations of Matthew of Ajello and Margaret's own despicable brother, Henry of Montescaglioso. It was not long before a full-scale conspiracy to murder Stephen was hatched. News of the plot leaked out—the feckless Henry of Montescaglioso, loose-tongued as ever, revealed the plans to a judge who dutifully laid them before the archbishop-chancellor. Stephen neatly shifted gear from hunted to hunter. The court had already, for safety, been moved from its regular base at Palermo to the royal palace at Messina—'white like a dove, which overlooks the shore', observed Ibn Jubayr eighteen years later—a city dominated by Christians who, Stephen hoped, would be more favourably disposed to a brother in Christ, even though an alien, than the muslims of Palermo.

Messina was a fine city, second only to Palermo on the island, though apparently not Ibn Jubayr's cup of tea.

This city is the mart of the merchant infidels, the focus of ships from the world over, and thronging always with companies of travellers by reason of the lowness of prices. But it is cheerless because of the unbelief, no Muslim being settled there. Teeming with worshippers of the Cross, it chokes its inhabitants, and constricts them almost to strangling. It is full of smells and filth; and churlish too, for the stranger will find there no courtesy. Its markets are animated and teeming, and it has ample commodities to ensure a luxurious life . . .

Messina leans against the mountains, the lower slopes of which adjoin the intrenchments of the town . . . Its harbour is the most remarkable of maritime ports, since large ships can come into it from the seas until they almost touch it . . .[314]

The thwarted assassination plot was revealed to the entire court which had been hurriedly assembled in the palace. An army had been mustered on the chancellor's behalf and the majority of the conspirators were taken without bloodshed. Stephen du Perche dealt with them remarkably leniently. Despite the urgings of his adherents, most were allowed to remain free—attainted, embarrassed, and presumably shaken (whether from remorse or from the shock of Stephen's generosity is a moot question), but free nevertheless. One conspirator, however, was unworthy of mercy, whether or not he was truly the king's uncle. The nasty, deservedly hapless Henry of Montescaglioso was summarily imprisoned in the castle of Reggio di Calabria, across the straits from Messina, in sight of the pine- beech- and chestnut-clad Aspromonte, the 6,420 feet stage whereon, in 1862, Garibaldi was wounded and captured during his great struggle for Italian independence.

The one large monument of Reggio di Calabria to escape destruction during the devastating earthquake of 1908 is the stalwart castle, built by the Aragonese, though certainly on Norman foundations, worth visiting today mainly for its superb view of the straits, Sicily, and smoking Mount Etna. Reggio is not the most interesting city in lower Italy, but it has one magnificent advantage over most of the others: a splendid museum. For valid reasons this museum is the pride of the city, exhibiting a rich collection of valuable artefacts from ancient Locri, Croton, Sybaris, Hippontium and Caulonia, not to mention collections from the Palaeolithic age. But far and away the most precious items are two statues which, fished out of the sea off the coast of Calabria in 1972, have 'made the Reggio Calabria museum richer in heroic Greek bronzes than any other in the world, proud owner of not one, but two, large Greek statues thought to be mid-5th century B.C.'.[315] The story of their finding is one of the great romantic stories of modern archaeology, mainly because it was entirely coincidental and unexpected, the chance find of a Roman chemist on holiday near Riace on the east Calabrian coast.

Simply incarcerating Henry of Montescaglioso did not end the dissatisfaction against the Sicilian regency. In less than two years the likeable and earnest Stephen du Perche, who had tried to stabilize a Sicily quaking with palace rivalries, was finally driven from power, forced to resign both his chancellorship and archbishopric. With the consent of those who replaced him, Stephen, together with those few followers still left, embarked for the Holy Land, which had been his professed destination at the time of his arrival in Sicily in 1166. Margaret was bound to miss him. As he had done his best for Sicily, so he had done his best by her, not only in the corridors of power but, according to the scandalmongers, in her bedroom as well. Her unflagging efforts to effect his return to Palermo is indicative of the considerable regard she felt for him; but shortly after arriving in Outremer Stephen du Perche died.

Walter of the Mill, one of the conspirators against Stephen, was consecrated in his stead as archbishop of Palermo. This event broke Margaret's spirit, and she gave up all pretence of maintaining any authority in her son's government. When young William came of age in 1171, she retired gracefully, and probably bitterly, into anonymity. Her hand was felt in only one more instance, when she endowed the church of Santa Maria di Maniace, the great Byzantine abbey, much of which still remains.

Walter of the Mill was an Englishman who had been brought to Sicily as tutor of the royal children. Like several other men of England who came to this southern island, Walter was governed by nothing but ambition. Following his stint as royal tutor, he had been deacon of Cefalù, dean of Agrigento and then canon of the Palatine Chapel. He moved in influential circles, and in time became a man of influence himself. He had a way of swaying opinion to his side, of manipulating men and events, of building the kind of power that would, in the end, do more than its share to bring the Norman kingdom of Sicily crashing into ruins, no longer a reality, but only a gossamer moment in history, an idealistic Hauteville dream that brought a short-lived smile to the sunburnt face of a gorgeous island whose 'prosperity ... surpasses description'.[316] Walter of the Mill helped to turn the dream into a nightmare. By uniting behind him the ambitious barons and clergy, he in time managed to create a body of reactionary magnates who cared only for their own aggrandisement and nothing for the state.

This year was wasted largely in fruitless skirmishes between Henry II and Louis VII. There were several declared truces—in fact the year started out on a truce which had been established in August of the previous year and which lasted until Easter—enabling Henry to harass would-be rebels in Brittany and Aquitaine. Then there were his excursions into neighbouring lands, as often as not held by vassals of Louis. These sallies may have been little more than lordly indulgences to Henry, but they were devastatingly painful for the common man—the man who wanted nothing more than to get on with his life.

Poitou, always on the verge of spontaneous combustion, was one of Henry's most quarrelsome counties. Early in the year he escorted his queen through her own demesne, intending to leave her there, a sop to these self-willed people by granting them the venerated presence of their own beloved duchess. In view of the rebelliousness inherent in the provinces under the Plantagenet's iron rule, augmented perhaps by Henry's growing estrangement from his wife, Eleanor was left in the custody of one of Henry's most trusted vassals, Patrick, earl of Salisbury. One day, while Eleanor and Patrick were journeying northwards to Poitiers, their party was ambushed by troops of the Lusignan family. Eleanor, worth a queen's ransom, escaped, but Earl Patrick was villainously stabbed in the back.

Salisbury's death opened a door for a new hero in the service of the Plantagenets, Patrick's nephew, the recently knighted Guillaume le Maréchal—William Marshal. In the same skirmish that killed his uncle, William fought 'like a wild boar against dogs'[317] for his queen, but was finally wounded and taken prisoner. Eleanor heard of his plight and ransomed him, rewarding him with rich gifts, a marvellous stroke of luck for any young, comparatively unknown knight. William was to become perhaps the greatest soldier of his day, occasionally at odds with the royal family, but always loyal. He can also be credited with saving the English throne — not without difficulty—for Henry III, grandson of Henry and Eleanor.

Recovering from her latest brush with kidnappers, Eleanor settled down in the luxurious Maubergon Tower, a palace addition built by her grandfather for his intimidatingly named mistress, Dangerosa.

Next to Eleanor, Poitiers' most famous citizen is probably Saint Radegund (518-587). Daughter of a Thuringian king, she fell into the hands of the Frankish ruler Clotaire I who, even among his own, was notorious for his cruelty and sensuality. Sometime after his (perhaps polygamous) marriage to Radegund he murdered her brother; this proved the last straw for his queen, who deserted him for a holy life in Poitiers. She founded an abbey named Sainte-Croix after about 569, when the Eastern Emperor Justin II sent the nuns an alleged relic of the True Cross. For its reception Radegund's friend, Venantius Fortunatus wrote the hymn *Vexilla regis* (translated by J.M. Neale as the English hymn 'The Royal Banners Forward Go'). The eleventh-to twelfth-century church of Sainte Radegonde preserves her tomb.

Church of St. Radegund, Poitiers, France

Eleanor must have felt that she was back where she belonged, at the very core of her heritage of comfort, elegance and urbanity. At Poitiers, with its sweeping vistas of the promontory overlooking the junction of the rivers Boivre and Clain, she could forget the rigorous, comparatively primitive life-style of Normandy, Anjou and England. She was home at last: away from that other world so overrun by men; away from feudal kings and their incessant violence; away even from her husband whose philanderings were infamous and whose scandalous affair with one Rosamund Clifford was the chief gossip of the courts of Europe. By the time Eleanor had ensconced herself south of the Loire she had 'made up her mind to cut off with the bright sword of the river her portion of the world from Henry's, set up her second son [Richard] as heir to her patrimony, and leave the king to make whatever division he could among his other heirs of what was left of his empire . . . Her vengeance for the Clifford affair was aimed not at the flaxen beauty of the king's folly, but at Henry himself, his mounting ambition, his . . . dreams of empire'.[318]

The idea of an errant husband was not new to any high-born woman of the age. And Eleanor knew as well as anyone the tales of her husband's insatiable lusts. She had turned her eyes from countless episodes. What set her off was his flaunting his new love, his bringing this Rosamund Clifford into the very palaces where Eleanor, noble-born, the most brilliant queen of her day, should have held sway. And we must face this fact—as Eleanor must have done—that at about fifty years of age and having borne ten children (two to Louis and eight to Henry), Eleanor could no longer be as fascinating to Henry's randy eye; he had found himself a beauty, the daughter of Walter de Clifford, a Norman knight with a castle on the Welsh border.

Most peerless was her beautye founde,
    Her favour, and her face;
A sweeter creature in this worlde
    Could never prince embrace.[319]

All well and good. But Rosamund has not always been thought of in such pristine terms. Some contemporaries played on her name by calling her 'Rose of the World' (*Rosa-Mundi*), while Gerald of Wales royally puts her down by calling her 'Rose of Unchastity' (*Rosa-Immundi*).[320]

Marie of Champagne, Eleanor's first daughter by Louis VII, joined her mother at Poitiers. She was a romantic and enthusiastic follower of the Arthurian cult, whose centuries-old Celtic stories were now passing into European circulation. The Arthurian legend was at the root of many new genres of the romantic movement that came into being, especially at Eleanor's court at Poitiers. 'The mood of the age is expressed in the romance which tells of chivalry, just as it is blazoned upon the wonderful tympana and frescoes and capitals in Romanesque cathedrals. And . . . every attempt to trace the origin of this fusion between the elements of chivalry, courtly love and Celtic myth leads one back to the court of Eleanor.'[321] The next five years were to be the happiest in Eleanor's life, for it was in the great hall of the palace—now a part of the Palais de Justice—that Eleanor and Marie presided over their 'courts of love'. Throughout the palace at Poitiers one sees the stamp of Eleanor's presence. Just as in Paris, she left her mark by countless little refinements that made those draughty royal homes more habitable. But the great hall, appropriate for the most lavish medieval bash, with its arcaded walls just as they were in Eleanor's day, conveys everything that needs be said about her graceful taste.

The church of Notre-Dame-la-Grande (*see page* 394) is the most interesting of several in the city. Here is a feeling for overall decoration, a love of texture and pattern, an exquisitely intricate moulding of stone not too far removed from the art of the smithies. Its great glory, the elaborate Romanesque façade, is a triptych, displaying its still saints and aloof apostles, ennobled by indestructible round arches. There is a reliquary feeling about the façade, an ornateness that, when the sun is low in the sky, causes light and shadow to advance and yield, each sculptural highlight sparkling like a facet on a cut jewel. Nowhere else in France is the relationship between Romanesque sculpture and architecture more clearly stated. The effect is never cheerless like the chants sung within; rather, in spite of the sombre figures depicted, it sings the lighter music of an age that was being developed just a short hop away in the great hall of the palace. And the garish interior (*see page* 394), with its myriad painted patterns in colours that challenge the rainbow, carries the song to a crescendo that the troubadour never knew.

When one considers the exotic charm of Notre-Dame-la-Grande, it is hard to imagine Eleanor having had a hand in the cathedral of Saint-Pierre-de-Poitiers, begun in 1162. She must personally have overseen at least part of the work, even though its construction spanned another two and a half centuries. Not an especially inspired design, it nevertheless presents an interesting trick of construction to make it look longer than it actually is—a materialistic fakery that in this instance does not speak well for the tastes of the royal patrons who commissioned the building. By narrowing the nave and aisles and lowering the arches towards the choir, the architect has created an interior that seems to go almost to infinity; it is like looking through the wrong end of binoculars.

At home in Eleanor's palace the principal entertainment was the joyful art of the troubadour. How could it be otherwise? After all, had not her grandfather been the first of this happily languishing clique? The troubadour's objective was to sing of his devotion to a high-born lady, though her identity was never disclosed. The troubadour had to pass through four stages—aspirant, suppliant, acknowledged suitor, and finally lover, whereupon he took an oath of fidelity to his impossible love, which the lady sealed with a kiss, but in theory with nothing more.

Eleanor's 'court of love' (often minimized by modern historians, but still pleasant to contemplate) was essentially a game in which a troubadour would sing a stanza of the problems of his love, to be answered by a stanza of advice from another. After a period of this romantic frivolity, when no decision could be reached, the matter was arbitrated by Eleanor, Marie, or some other lady of the court. One would think that the sufferings of the day—the plagues, crusades, constant wars—would have sufficed for even the most masochistic. But concerns for romantic suffering became an occupational obsession.

> Love my heart doth wound so sweet
>   With its gentle savor;
> Hundred deaths do I repeat,—
>   And wake to joy the braver!
> Yes, my grief is fair to see;
>   I hold my grief adored;
> So good is my grief to me,
>   Good too the reward![322]

Eleanor's court attracted the great poetic names of the day—her old admirer Bernard de Ventadour, along with Bertran de Born, Rigaut de Barbezieux, Pierre Vidal, Gaucelm Faidit, as well as some of the women troubadours. The court of Poitiers was a natural counteraction to the destructive world of men now wreaking such havoc over the face of Europe and beyond. Eroticism was the mood of the day, however, implied if not overt. And the countess of Dia (born about 1140) was unashamed in her preference for her lover as measured against her husband, as these lines from one of her four surviving poems indicates:

> . . . If only I could lie beside you for an hour
> and embrace you lovingly—
> know this, that I'd give almost anything
> to have you in my husband's place . . .[323]

Amid all of this poetry, music and amorous dalliance some very valid questions of love methodology were discussed. On one occasion a petitioner to the court of love wanted to know if true love could survive marriage. Marie of Champagne decreed that true love could probably not survive within the institution of marriage. Because of the stir created by this decree, Eleanor was consulted, and responded 'that she would find it admirable *if* a wife were able to reconcile marriage and true love. She did not, of course, say that, having experienced two very different but equally disillusioning marriages, she could hardly be expected to have an exalted view of the institution'.[324] Nor did she suggest that husbands might make a similar reconciliation.

To the twentieth-century mind these exercises—sung in the northern *langue d'oïl*, the language of the earliest lyrical poetry, as well as in the native southern *langue d'oc*—may seem to have been a mere *divertissement* for the idle rich or for a community of bored women whiling away the time during which their husbands were abroad across the countryside laying waste the properties of their neighbours. But such a view would imply a total misunderstanding of these gatherings. First of all, men were very much in evidence; in fact, Eleanor's favourite son Richard spent a good deal of time with his mother at Poitiers, especially after he was invested with the title to Aquitaine in 1172. Furthermore, it was not merely a group of bored women, but rather the intelligent women of the period actively keeping alive the traditions of the past while making cultural progress of their own. The 'courts of love' were forerunners of the literary salons of later periods.

Marie of Champagne was particularly interested in encouraging writers, men such as André le Chapelain and Chrétien de Troyes, whose finest achievements were his Arthurian romances set to verse. And the Poitiers court had its role to play in the progressive development of music. Medieval man chanted psalms and canticles as part of his religious rituals. These melodies, lingering in the minds of the faithful, were later turned into love songs. Another little known progress attributable to Eleanor's court of love: it is said that an important change in the rules of chess grew out of the courts—the queen became the most powerful piece on the board, supplanting the king in that position, even though the capture of the male continued to be the object of the game, which says something for women's lib, twelfth-century style!

1169

Two years of turbulence between Henry and his vassals, two years of on-again-off-again warfare by Henry II against his overlord Louis VII, sup-posedly came to an end with a conference at Montmirail. Here also the intransigent Thomas Becket faced Henry for the first time since Northampton. Humbling himself at the feet of his king in the presence of the French and English courts, he was raised by Henry, who was obviously moved. Thomas then delivered a long prepared speech, throwing himself on the king's mercy but ending with the ominous and unexpected rider, 'Saving the honour of my God', which clearly meant that it was not the priest's duty to submit to the will of laymen. Henry flew into a rage and the assembly broke up in despair, with Henry more determined than ever to bring Thomas to his knees. As for Thomas, riding through Chartres on his way back to Sens, he had no way of knowing that before very long he would be represented among the Gothic sculpture on the south porch of the cathedral—among the martyrs.

The meeting at Montmirail did allow certain political agreements to be reached, gossamer as they might have been. Henry explained his plans for dividing his kingdom among his sons, a scheme attractive to Louis as it would break up the enormous 'empire' he so feared and envied. He was especially pleased to hear Henry reiterate that Richard was to govern Aquitaine as a vassal of the French crown. And it was proposed that Richard be betrothed to Louis' daughter Alice, whose sister Margaret was already married to young Henry.

Poor Princess Alice! Henry may have been sincere in his plans to parcel out his kingdom to his sons, but no man can accuse him of honesty, sincerity, or even compassion in his handling of the case of Alice. She was to remain for twenty-five years in Angevin custody, unmarried, a tragic pawn in the male-dominated struggles of Western Europe. Wagging tongues at the time, historical gossips—indeed, Richard himself when he grew to marriageable age—put forth the claim (totally believable to those who knew Henry's reputation) that Alice had been seduced by Henry. Why was she kept in English custody all those years? For the simple reason that by holding her a virtual prisoner, Henry prevented the French crown from marrying her off to anyone else, which could possibly have led to an anti-Angevin alliance. Reciprocally, when the king of France wanted to stir up trouble he always had a convenient grievance at hand. When she was finally released and in 1195 married to Count William of Ponthieu Alice was about thirty-three years old, an age when most princesses were already brides of some twenty years.

1170

Showing his determination to divide his lands among his sons, and imitating a practice of the Capetian kings of France as well as of the Hautevilles of Sicily, Henry had young Henry crowned king—really co-king—of England. It was also a colossal display of contempt, this coronation of the young king, aimed at laying low the equally colossal conceit of Thomas Becket. By time-proven formula the coronation of English kings was performed, and still is, by the archbishop of Canterbury. In this instance the ceremony was performed by the archbishop of York, through a prior agreement between Henry II and Pope Alexander III, which Thomas regarded as unparalleled papal double-dealing. (It is true, however, that the pope did send a letter to Archbishop Roger of York, forbidding him to crown young Henry. The letter did not arrive in time to prevent the ceremony.)

By his break with English tradition Henry realized that he would be presenting Becket with a final insult that could only enrage the archbishop. When the king and Thomas met again in July at Fréteval, neither referred to the Constitutions of Clarendon and Becket accepted Henry's invitation to return to England, probably bent on disciplining the bishops who had taken part in the coronation ceremony. Later Thomas is said to have remarked to an associate, 'I am returning to England to die'. He knew what he was doing. It was as if he saw his death as justifying his reason for being. At the same time, Henry never intended the murder of Thomas; but, inadvertently or not, he certainly set the stage for it.

While the struggle between these titans was moving towards its tragic climax in England, calmer political realities were being mulled over in Sicily. A bride needed to be found for the minor King William II. Byzantine Emperor Manuel Comnenus had several years before offered his daughter, a tacit proposal that the whole empire would become her dowry since he had no sons. That extremely tempting proposition, enough to cause any Hauteville king to salivate, was still being considered when Henry II, in 1168, had proffered his three-year-old daughter Joanna as a nuptial sacrifice. Since Henry was hands down the most powerful king in Western Europe, it was finally decided to accept his offer, and papal approval was obtained. Everything seemed in order. Then came December 29, and the chamber-of-horrors sequence of events at Canterbury. Queen Margaret and her advisers decided that little Princess Joanna was not nearly so desirable as they had once thought. Negotiations were broken off and the search for a new queen began again.

Following his meeting with his archbishop in July, there followed several months during which Henry's attention was diverted from Becket and England—for one thing, he was ill, and he also had trouble with Louis VII over the Auvergne, and a threat of war in Berry. One after another, reports came to Henry that Thomas was parading himself about his see like a victor; but the reports were not always the precise truth. The cross Thomas was bearing was often one of humiliation. He tried to see the young king, of whom he was especially fond, having been his tutor for years, only to receive a note admonishing him to stay away. The young Henry had received instructions from his father not to see the archbishop. On the other hand Becket's behaviour was, as usual, often unwise and antagonistic.

It was during a gripe session concerning the unwise Becket that Henry is supposed to have uttered the anguished words, ' "Will no one rid me of this turbulent priest?"—which have been attributed to him on no good authority'.[325] He was angry. He did speak some unwise words in his rage; that much he admitted. His unguarded words, overheard by four of his knights—Reginald fitzUrse, Hugh of Moreville, William de Tracy and Richard le Breton—sparked them into action to 'avenge' their lord. Getting wind of their departure and suspecting the object of their mission, Henry dispatched a party to head them off, but the Channel ports were searched in vain.

Perhaps Thomas had decided the world was too small for both himself and the king. Whatever his conclusions, we again detect in Thomas a kind of yearning for death, as though he saw it as the only option in his struggle with the temporal power, his only way to victory. Historians and playwrights up to the present have noted this.

This man is obstinate, blind, intent
On self-destruction . . .
Lost in the wonder of his own greatness,
The enemy of society, enemy of himself.[326]

And yet, what a singularly magnificent scene his murder—only later called his 'martyrdom'—was! Becket was elaborately vested in his finest ecclesiastical regalia for the occasion. 'I must look my best today. Make haste'. And later: 'There. I'm ready, all adorned for Your festivities, Lord'.[327]

At no time concerned for his own safety, pursued by his resolute assassins, he proceeded with utmost dignity into the cathedral north transept. Tall, elegant, he moved gracefully through the dim shadows and flickering light, arches towering over him, lost in a darkness that no candlelight could penetrate. The air was chill that evening, but heavy with the sweet-dry odour of dying flowers, of spent incense and long-extinguished tapers. He moved unhurriedly, though the metallic sound of armed feet on stone could be heard from the shadows.

Finally catching up with their quarry, but not recognizing him in the dark, the knights demanded to know the whereabouts of the 'traitor to the king and the kingdom'.[328] The moment the attackers approached, Thomas was abandoned by his clergy and monks—except for one Edward Grim, a clerk of Cambridge. Becket separated himself from the shadows and walked down the steps towards his assailants. Seeing him clearly now, perhaps appalled by the terrible deed they were about to perform, the knights must have suffered a pang of awe. The archbishop's face had already assumed the beatific look of the willing martyr.

' "Here am I; no traitor but a priest and an archbishop", and he took his stand by the east wall of the north transept, by a pillar of the arcading'.[329] Becket's last words were, 'I accept death for the name of Jesus and His Church', but they were uttered only after he had been struck to the floor by William de Tracy's sword. Then Richard le Breton struck the head of the dying archbishop so powerfully that he severed the top of his skull and shattered his sword on the pavement. A defrocked priest, Hugh Mauclerc, who had for some reason or other joined the four murderers, stomped on Becket's neck, and with his sword scattered the brains and blood across the already desecrated floor.

' "Let's go, knights," he said then. "This fellow will not rise again" '.[330] But he was wrong.

Later, when quiet was restored and the cathedral cleared of the townspeople who had been attracted by the din and had watched the horrendous spectacle, Becket's monks returned to attend and dress the body, which was then taken to the high altar. When it was discovered that Thomas was wearing a verminous hair shirt and monk's habit beneath his gorgeous vestments he was (if nothing else, the age was an emotional one!) immediately venerated as a saint. Even those who had stood against him and thought, as Edward Grim reported, that he deserved his fate, now accepted his murder as martyrdom.

On the very night of his murder, Benedict, abbot of Peterborough, one of those who later wrote an account of Becket's 'martyrdom', saw Thomas in a vision. Gleaming in immaculate white garments, Thomas rose from his bier and approached the altar as though to say mass. Benedict asked him, 'Are you not dead, lord?' 'I was dead,' came the reply, 'but I have risen'. So started the stream of visions and miracles. Then began the pilgrimages:

> . . . from every shires ende
> Of Engelond to Caunterbury they wende,
> The hooly blisful martir for to seke,
> That hem hath holpen, whan that they were seke.'[331]

The flagstones where Thomas allegedly fell are marked out even to this day, a large rectangle of earthy browns, tans and reds, colours that blend analogously with spilled blood. The body was buried hastily in the crypt by his monks when they were warned by the murderers that it would be thrown to the dogs if they did not immediately and secretly dispose of it. It was not until 1220 that Archbishop Stephen Langton, in the presence of King Henry III, transferred the remains to their new shrine in Trinity Chapel which, so rich in gold and jewels, astonished even the most seasoned pilgrims. But Thomas' rest was not to be permanent. In 1538, eighteen years after visiting the shrine as a devoted pilgrim, Henry VIII ordered the dismantling of the entire structure. Apart from coveting the rich pickings, Henry regarded Thomas with particular spleen, as a prelate who had resisted royal authority.

As for the assassins, Roger of Hovedon claims that they were universally shunned. It is likely, however, that by lying low for a period of time (which gave rise to the legend that they fled to the Holy Land to expiate their sin) they managed to survive until the furore died down. Eventually they wormed their way back into Henry's good graces. There is no evidence that they either profited handsomely or suffered greatly for their crime. But their actions have never been explained satisfactorily to posterity.

With all his contradictions Becket may have represented the Norman *par excellence;* he had inherited from both his parents the tough pragmatism of Normandy, and his father may even have had the blood of the Norsemen in his veins. Thomas was a born leader, courageous and stubborn, dedicated enough to please any William the Conqueror or Robert Guiscard. The very fact that he could swing with such apparent ease from secular dedication as chancellor to defender of the Church as an archbishop indicates his unswerving single-mindedness to duty. As unyielding as his secular master, and fearless when it came to personal safety, he gathered men around him from whom he demanded loyalty. His harshness was legendary, but so was his gentleness.

Enigma or no, incomprehensible as he may be to savants and students alike, the ultimate irony is that the common man, the superstitious rabble, had no problem with Thomas whatsoever. They took to Thomas dead as they had when he was alive. They knew him for what he was: a man of humble origin like themselves, standing against what they saw as naked power, greed and arrogance. They cheered him on from the sidelines, making no bones of their open adoration whether he moved as chancellor or archbishop. In the end they had no desire but to label him a martyr: and the pope had no choice but to canonize him within three years, a remarkably short span of time for such a step to be taken. The people loved him. His biographers admired, sometimes respected him. Through the centuries people have poured into churches on his assigned feast day—December 29—to sing of his great victory.

> Let the heavenly host rejoice at the martyr's glory . . .
> Canterbury has cherished this feast-day devotedly:
> Even as a strife-torn leader thunders out tyrannical commands.
> But Thomas's forthright steps follow in the footprints of Christ,
>   and cannot be deflected . . .[332]

Chapter Nineteen

There under the bare walls of our labour
Death and life were knotted in one strength
Invisible as root and sky.

Fry, *The Boy with a Cart*

1171

The monks of Canterbury were, of course, overjoyed when they realized they had a miracle-working martyr on their hands; for the rest, a tide of revulsion swept Europe, threatening for a while to dash Henry himself into oblivion. Letters were written to Pope Alexander III from all over the Continent, demanding that he smite the 'murderer' down; 'The sword had been thrust into the very pupil of Christ's eye', wrote Louis VII. That Henry was remorseful over the turn of events is undeniable. He donned sackcloth and poured ashes over his head, mourning loudly, and finally went into a three-day seclusion. In the face of Europe's hostility he insisted that Thomas had brought his death upon himself. Henry confessed that he had been guilty of some unguarded words against Thomas, but nothing to authorize the terrible action of his knights. They were the true murderers, he contended; and for their crime they were excommunicated. At first Alexander III was incapable of action. Following a week of mourning he finally made his pronouncements. An interdict on Henry's Continental possessions (which had been declared before the murder) was upheld. Henry was forbidden to enter a church.

There were no doubt many who, contrary to the prevailing view, rejoiced in the archbishop's demise. 'It was, of course, impossible for anyone to admit to a sense of relief at Becket's departure from the world, but it did in fact mean the removal of an obstacle to a sensible compromise over the ancient customs of the realm of England in matters ecclesiastical'.[333] By the time Alexander had finished stalling in the name of propriety and had sent legates 'to see whether the king were truly humbled', Henry was in Ireland, finally exercising his right of invasion based on the bull *Laudabiliter* of 1155, but more than that making himself scarce from the current vilifications. Only a dreamer would believe that Henry wanted anything more than to enlarge his kingdom, or that Adrian had looked to anything more spiritual than a collection of Peter's pence (that yearly tax of one penny per household to go to the Roman Church) and the bringing into line of a somewhat errant Irish Church.

There was, additionally, a more politically legitimate reason for Henry to hie himself off to Ireland. Just the year before, one of his Norman barons, Richard de Clare ('Strongbow'), earl of Pembroke and Strigoil, had gone to the help of one Dermot, king of Leinster, in return for the offer of marriage with Dermot's daughter and ultimate succession to his kingdom. On Dermot's death in May of this year, Richard felt that his eyes-to-the-future action had paid off handsomely. But he had not reckoned with Henry's determination to control baronial pretensions, nor his opportunist need to get away during the Becket aftermath. Henry made himself unavailable to the papal legates and at the same time cut Richard de Clare down to size by himself mounting an Irish expedition in October. He received the submission not only of the various Norman adventurers but of a number of Irish rulers and laid the foundation for the English control of Ireland that was later more effectively established by his son John. (Henry's Irish settlement formed the basis for a strip of eastern coastal land that later came to be called 'the Pale', the one part of Ireland where England retained a more or less unbroken control, giving reasonable meaning to the cliché 'beyond the pale'.) Meanwhile the Church's interests were met by the holding of an Irish synod, whose decrees brought Irish ecclesiastical practices more into line with those prevalent throughout Western Europe. Henry left Ireland in April 1172.

While Henry struggled with the Irish question, a king was being crowned in Sicily. Handsome despite his adolescence, tall and blond like his Viking forebears, the mild-mannered King William II rode through the teeming streets of his raucously celebrating capital on a coronation day that terminated the regency of his inept and embittered mother—to the intense relief of his subjects. 'The character of this last of the legitimate Hautevilles is an enigma—a recluse seldom appearing in public, never seen at the head of armies, devoted to Palermo, surrounded in his summer palaces by eunuchs, concubines, and negro guards, familiar with Arabic speech and learning . . . yet gives the impression of a great personality'.[334] He spoke all the four (five if we include Hebrew) languages of his realm—Greek, Arabic, French and Latin. He continued Roger II's enlightened policy of welcoming scholars and writers from all over the Latin world, especially from Italy and Provence, to mingle with their Islamic colleagues. Troubadours, *trouvères* and Arab *raouis*, flocking to William II's court, did their share to spread the fame of the poetry that radiated therefrom. Then, too, he trusted the Muslims attached to the palace and utilized their services exactly as had been envisioned by the Guiscard, Roger I and Roger II. He seemed to have had everything going for him, including his looks. Even that arch-critic of us all, Dante Alighieri, was beguiled by him, placing William in the Sixth Sphere of Paradise in the company of King David, Emperor Trajan, and Hezekiah.

Despite the hoo-ha attending William's coronation, the fact of the matter was that Sicily was fast being shadowed by the setting sun; night was upon the kingdom. And William, later in his reign, by a single disastrous decision, 'a most amazing piece of policy',[335] brought permanent darkness down on the Norman kingdom in the South. William the Good? Perhaps. But a good ruler? Hardly! Yet before committing his incredible gaffe he had some history still to make, and one sterling monument to his own taste and to the eclectic genius of the Normans to build. And he still needed to find a wife.

With the breakdown in marital negotiations between Sicily and England resulting from the murder of Becket, Manuel Comnenus, still eager to unite the two great Mediterranean powers, offered his daughter Maria to William for the second time. By now she had a half-brother, Alexius, so, with the imperial succession assured, Manuel could not be accused by opposition forces of giving the empire away. For William the offer was not quite so attractive as it had been before the birth of Alexius. Yet it had advantages. With William's acceptance of the proferred bride—one wants to say 'bartered' here—plans were made for her to be royally received in Apulia the following spring.

1172

It was at Taranto that William waited on the designated day in April. Testifying to the importance of the occasion in his eyes at least was the suite that accompanied him—Walter of the Mill, Matthew of Ajello and the young Prince Henry of Capua, William's brother. It was to be yet another couple of weeks before William reached the painful realization that he had been jilted. For Maria never did arrive. Nor was any explanation offered.

Today a centre of oyster-breeding—though this noblest of occupations to gourmets the world over has been seriously threatened in recent years by industrial pollution of the Mediterranean—Taranto is the strategically placed Tarentum of Roman history. The *Tarantini* are among some of the most aloofly gracious people in a land famous for its graciousness. And they have reason to be both gracious and aloof due to a single glorious moment in their history; tradition tell us that it was at Taranto that the alternatingly receptive and spurning, magnanimous and arrogant, common house cat first set foot on the European continent, perhaps from Egypt or Crete.

The history of Taranto goes back much further than the cat's arrival, however, since it was the ancient Greek Taras, another one of many city-states set up in Magna Graecia seven hundred years before Christ. As an ancient Greek city it stands apart from the others in that it was founded by Spartan bastards, born during a nineteen-year period when their fathers were off warring. Ridiculed as bastards at home, they determined to establish a state where they could walk tall, be independent of the more rigid home society and 'do their own thing'. This they did with a vengeance, developing what became the wealthiest Greek city on the Italian peninsula, along with a powerful and legendary cavalry. But their craft production was noteworthy, too, and the Museo Nazionale shows what is reputed to be the largest Greek terracotta collection in the world, all of which has been found in the cemeteries of Taras, most of it comparatively recently.

Tanagra figures are possibly the most charming of ancient terracottas, reflecting an affinity for our own ways of living in that they appear to illustrate what we ourselves seem to be doing much of the time—arranging flowers, gazing into mirrors, dancing, drinking, or just gossiping. Tanagra, in Boeotia, is the most fruitful site for finding these endearingly small sculptures (most of them are a foot or less in height); hence their name. But large quantities are also found in other locations, including Taranto. They are mostly female figures, which is a relief from the endless parade of Greek athletes, and are usually moulded rather than modelled, with heads done separately and attached before firing. The baked statuettes were then painted. Obviously they were made for mass sale, but the third and fourth centuries BC (the period when they were most common) seems to have been one of good popular taste. The terracottas

Castle in
Taranto, Italy

of Taranto are a little different from others in that they are primarily of funerary design and purpose, but none the less charming for all that. H.V. Morton winningly suggests that should we miraculously have met in the twentieth century a typical Tanagra woman—a fantasy which has always appealed to the more romantic museum goers among us—'they, at least, would have been entirely comprehensible; indeed some of them, as they draw their draperies about them, look as if they were standing on the steps of a theatre at night, waiting for a taxi'.[336]

The castle at Taranto is of fourteenth-century Angevin origin, occupying a key point on an island formed from what had been until then a spit of the mainland and the site of the ancient city. Now it is a tangle of streets, none of them more than a few minutes' walk from water, and all of them inhabited by the Greek-looking fishermen of the area. Their quays face the Mare Piccolo, a lagoon on the land side of the island. The dialect heard in the street is rich, having a strangely Greek sound to an English-hearing ear. Apartments are emblazoned by colourful balcony hangings reminiscent of a more exotic Eastern land. Here are the great oyster and mussel beds with their ranks of ropes strung on poles and from which festoons of the molluscs hang, destined to be packed in large sauce-filled barrels.

With a history of illegitimacy from the start, then of betrayal and counter-betrayal (first to the Carthaginian Hannibal and then to the Romans), it is not too surprising that Taranto attracted the proselytizing zeal of Saint Cataldo who, stopping off on his way back to his native Ireland from the Holy Land in the seventh century, decided his job was to clean things up. He remained at Taranto and became its bishop and patron saint. Cataldo rests in the cathedral under the altar in the Baroque chapel bearing his name.

Having recently been stripped of tons of grossly ornate Baroque trappings, the cathedral of San Cataldo has been restored to its Norman Romanesque form, looking very much as it did when it was built in 1071. Basically it is somewhat clumsy in style, with its windowless drum topped by a conical roof over the transept crossing, although the heavy drum is made slightly more interesting by slender columns which offer needed relief by breaking the mass into sections.

Some of the more interesting sites of Taranto and its environs, apart from the promenade (the Lungomare Vittorio Emanuele) with its palms and oleanders, its views both natural and social, for it seems to be in a perpetual state of *festa*, are worth visiting. Castellaneta, perched on the very edge of a sheer ravine, commands a spectacular view of the Gulf of Taranto and the Calabrian mountains. It touts itself as the birthplace of Rudolph Valentino by the most hideous of hideous monuments to the great lover of the early screen—a life-size ceramic creation in livid colours showing the actor in his role of Bedouin sheikh. No Norman desecration of their adopted land could have been worse than this by proud natives in memory of a fellow *compaesano*.

It was at Taranto then that William II waited in vain for his bride. We have no clue as to why Emperor Manuel of Constantinople so snubbed him, except, perhaps, that he was now receiving more attractive offers for her to marry Frederick Barberossa's son. But it was a slight that would never be forgotten or forgiven. To make matters even worse, by the time a sour William had returned to Sicily, his younger brother Henry, who had gone on ahead, had died of fever.

If William, on his return trip, did not go out of his way to visit the newly completed small abbey church of SS Pietro e Paolo, just north of Taormina, then he missed a sight noble enough to swell any Norman's chest with pride—one of the gems of Sicily's vast jewel-box of medieval buildings. Most guidebooks list this church as being just outside (or 'a few kilometres from') the hilltop town of Forza d'Agrò, a description at best misleading since it is far below the town—though admittedly in sight of it—and across a bridgeless Torrente d'Agrò. Numerous citizens of Forza d'Agrò had either never heard of the church or could not comprehend the author's American Italian. At last a Vespa-riding young lad understood perfectly; if we would just follow, he would show us the way.

Careening through narrow streets in a manner difficult to duplicate in a Fiat 124—indeed, an extra layer of paint or dust on either car or houses would have rendered passage impossible—he led us to an unpaved road, and thence to a view-site perched precipitously on the heights. '*Ecco la chiesa'!* He pointed to the depths, to a church barely visible among the lemon groves, flanked to the north and south by very unremarkable looking buildings—farm buildings?—on the opposite side of the Torrente d'Agrò, raging now with spring run-off. It appeared daunting to get to, and probably not worth the effort. That church could not possibly be our objective. The guidebooks say it is at Forza d'Agrò. '*Ma, signore, è vero! La chiesa è al di là del torrente.*' The boy could not be correct. Obviously we were not communicating. So, with the wisdom of ages of tourists, he was put out of mind. It was two months later, in the culmination of one last effort to locate the abbey church, that, having donned boots to ford *il torrente* because it was too treacherously bedded with enormous boulders for a fully loaded Fiat to navigate, and when we were standing at the church itself, that we saw, high above us on the mountain, the recognizable profile of Forza d'Agrò and the point from which our Vespa jockey had pointed out this very church.

The country is lovely along this part of Sicily's east coast, 'a Turnerian world of deep sun-filled spaces, and distant river-side romance of capes and bays, with a few prominent buildings that look like towers, played round by light and shadow . . . White villages gleam on the tops of the little cone-shaped hills nestling in the embrace of the mountain valleys . . . By no means a desolate scene; yet with a certain desolate grandeur about it nevertheless . . .'[337] If the church of SS Peter and Paul does not look exactly desolate, there is a feeling of aloneness about it, not quite abandoned, but a left-out atmosphere that in the end adds to its charm, its tragedy.

It is recorded in a still-preserved deed that SS Peter and Paul was a Basilian monastery richly endowed by Roger II in 1117. An inscription in Greek over the main portal says that the church was rebuilt (restored) at the expense of Abbot Teosterictos between 1170 and 1172 by Gerard the Frank.

Church of SS. Peter and Paul, Agró, Italy

This *protomagister*—master mason—performed a neat accommodation of his own French heritage and the requirements of the Eastern monks he served.

As one would expect, though, the building certainly looks more Byzantine than Latin, with its patterning of stone and brick, its periodic use of banks of herring-bone designs, and its two blind arcades, one above the other, of stunning interlocking arches on the north and south exterior walls. At the apsidal end these two arcades become one, earth-based and soaring in graceful vertical lines to the crown of widely spaced merlons, reminders that in its day such remote abbeys were sometimes called upon to defend themselves. The whole effect is one of a blending of warm natural colours—brown, rose, yellow, terracotta—with occasional white accents which, blending with the vibrant yellows of the lemon groves, stand in stately contrast against the surrounding greens and hazy blues of the mountains. The interior feels Eastern, the only noticeably Western details being some Corinthian-inspired capitals. While the main circular dome is held aloft by a squinch arrangement, the smaller octagonal cupola is supported by rough honeycomb bracketing that undulates out from the sides like molten stone lava. The two towers which once stood at the western end, and between them set limits for the entrance porch, are no longer there, laid low in another age.

Henry of England was never one to be intimidated by the unreal, the things he could not come to grips with either intellectually or physically. He was a maker of history, a doer, not to be cowed by happenings beyond his control or events instigated by others. A story illustrating this side of his character is told about him when, returning from Ireland he landed near St David's in Wales. He visited the shrine of David, patron saint of Wales, which is located in a valley 'called the Vale of Roses; which ought rather to be named

*Church of SS.
Peter and Paul,
Agró, Italy*

the vale of marble, since it abounds with one, and by no means the other. The River Alun, a muddy and unproductive rivulet, bounding the churchyard on the northern side, flows under a marble stone, called Lechlavar, which has been polished by continual treading of passengers . . .'[338] As Henry and his retinue neared the church a woman approached and asked a favour of him. When he refused she called upon the rock Lechlavar to take vengeance on him.

While Henry's brave, superstitious knights turned pale with dread, Henry merely levelled his gaze at her. He knew as well as the warriors surrounding him that Merlin, the magician usually associated with the Arthurian legends, had allegedly predicted that a king of England returning from the conquest of Ireland would die on that rock. He then strode to Lechlavar, his eyes always on the ill-speaking old harridan, mounted the stone and crossed the stream. Henry was cool, amused, a little contemptuous. He sauntered back. 'Who will have any faith in that liar, Merlin, now? he asked his paralysed knights.

St David's lies about a mile and a half inland on the most westerly promontory of South Wales. It is speculated that the area figured largely in the migratory trading routes of prehistoric peoples, since dolmens, menhirs and stone circles abound. Certainly it was well known to Celtic saints in the early centuries of Christianity, Saint David himself being one of these. He lived in the sixth century, and is traditionally reputed to have been the son of a South Wales chieftain. Having established a monastery, he proceeded to govern it with a rule of rigid austerity; manual labour, absolute silence, strict fasts, and abstinence from any drink but water, which latter rule won him the nickname 'Waterman'—hardly the most congenial of saints.

During the Middle Ages the area around St David's became an important tourist haven on the long pilgrimage route to Santiago de Compostella in Spain. Eventually small chapels were built at various landing places; the ruins of St Justinian (locally called St Stinian) are the best preserved of those still standing. At last a cathedral of SS David and Andrew was built, around which grew up a small city. Soon St David's became the richest of Welsh dioceses, an object of pilgrimage on its own, so important that two pilgrimages there were considered the equal of one to Rome.

Local sandstone with a purplish cast was used for the cathedral, the earliest part being built between 1176 and 1198 under Bishop Peter de Leia. It may not be the loveliest of churches, but there is something persuasively winning about it with its strong central tower rising 116 feet. And the inside is imposing, with wide bays, a solid triforium and soaring clerestory windows. The choir stalls of the fifteenth century are especially handsome. The cathedral was badly used during the Reformation and during the Civil War. More the wonder that the Irish oak roof of about 1500 is still in place! Near the church and just to the north stand the ruins of a lovely chapel and tower built by John of Gaunt and Bishop Houghton in 1377, forming part of a college of St Mary.

At the time of Henry's visit to St David's the bishop's palace was far more modest than it was to become in later centuries. A great hall was built with an extremely attractive entrance porch. A chapel, kitchen, solar (sitting room), and a special bishop's chapel were clustered on three sides around an enormous courtyard. The fourth side is delineated by a long wall. The palace complex occupies half of the entire cathedral close, separated from the cathedral by the dividing River Alun. The roofs are all missing, but they are known to have been of lead, the palace not becoming totally derelict until the end of the seventeenth century, though the decay began during the Reformation when Bishop William Barlow, who wanted (but failed) to move the see to Carmarthen, de-roofed the great hall.

Even before leaving Ireland Henry had been aware that papal legates were waiting for him in Normandy, that he was not going to be allowed to wriggle free of his responsibility for Becket's death. He knew, though, that he held the trump card; his successful reform of the Irish Church had proved to the pope as few lessons could that a strong monarchy was a necessary prop to the Church.

After preliminary discussions a formal reconciliation took place at Avranches. Henry publicly swore that he had neither wished for nor overtly ordered Becket's

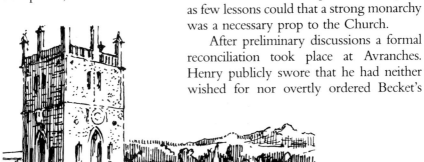

St David's, Wales

Bishop's Palace,
St David's, Wales

death, but admitted that his anger could have inspired the knights' action; he would accept whatever penance the cardinals ordered.

The picture of Henry II, king of England, duke of Normandy and Aquitaine, count of Anjou, ruler of an 'empire' extending from Scotland to the Pyrenees, a man unmatched in political power and one of the wealthiest of European monarchs, kneeling in humility before spiritual authority to be flogged publicly is a scene unmatched in history—even by Henry IV's shivering repentance before Pope Gregory VII in 1077 at Canossa. And yet it is a scene reported by at least one modern historian. The simple chalice carved in primitive imbalance on the stone of Henry's kneeling (*see page* 394) does not do justice to the majestic drama of the event. And the slight remains of the cathedral, an occasional step, a section of the foundation, a few fragments of casually scattered columns—all that is left since an earthquake destroyed the fabric of the building in 1794—along with the explanatory sign that this was the penitential stone, only add to the depressing picture. 'No one records the effect of the scene upon the young king who witnessed the . . . flagellation of his father for a confessed share in the crime against his dead master Becket'.[339] From the north porch of the cathedral Henry could not see across the Channel shoals to the southwest the towering, triangular might of Mont-Saint-Michel. But it was there as it had been for centuries, and may be forever, rising out of the soft sands of the estuary, dominantly proud, the principal monument of Normandy, a symbol of Norman energy built by his maternal ancestors.

The papal legates to Avranches further imposed a private penance and Henry undertook the expense of maintaining 200 knights in the Holy Land for one year. He was also to take the cross for three years, but this condition was later commuted to a promise to found three monasteries. Beyond that certain Church-State issues were settled and Henry promised to abandon any new anti-Church customs that he had introduced, though this pledge was of little value to the Church since, as he later maintained, these had been few.

Even after his reconciliation with the Church, Henry's problems were multiplying, the discontent of Henry the young king being the immediate, though not the only, cause of tensions within the royal family that were approaching flashpoint. Though crowned, the young king had received no lands from his father that would maintain him and his wife. By contrast Richard got his Aquitaine when he was invested as duke in June, much to

S. Cataldo, Palermo

Orford Castle,
England

*Notre Dame la
Grande Poitiers,
France*

Notre Dame la Grande, Poitiers

*Stone of Henry's Penance,
Avranches France*

Cathedral Apse, Monreale, Sicily

*Cloister Capital,
Monreale*

Cloister, Monreale

*North Transept,
Winchester
Cathedral,
England*

Eleanor's relief. And since Duke Conan IV of Brittany had died in 1171, Geoffrey, betrothed to Conan's only daughter, saw his inheritance awaiting him. Thus, of the three eldest sons, only the young king was without territorial possessions, and this in spite of the fact that he was his father's professed favourite. But none of the sons was granted any real power. At this stage of the game Henry could expect no loyalty from the young king—nor from Richard or Geoffrey for that matter. Even his wife found loyalty too dear a price to pay for domestic peace, having been shunted aside once her child-bearing years were over. Young Henry demanded that his father turn over at least one of the lands whose barons had proffered homage at his coronation. But the king, seeing his son as an inconstant, idle spendthrift, albeit charming, had no intention of complying. When young Henry insisted that his father-in-law, Louis of France, wished it to be so, as did the barons of England and Normandy, Henry was alerted to the probability that the king of France was turning his sons against him and that a plot was being hatched within his own family.

1173

Henry needed all the support he could muster, especially when, while making the rounds of his hereditary holdings in an effort to shore up his strength on the Continent, he learned that the young king, a mandatory member of his entourage, had eluded his guards to find his way to the French court at Paris—closely followed by Richard and Geoffrey. They were, all three of them, teenagers, but not one of them the obedient son that Henry desired. This was open revolt. Of those among Henry's sons old enough to play an active part only the bastard Geoffrey Plantagenet, born probably before his marriage remained loyal.

King Louis VII's Easter court became the clearing-house for anti-Henry animosities: old grievances were dredged up; fugitives from the English royal idiosyncracies suddenly materialized in droves. While enjoying the Easter festivities the trio of English princes, encouraged by a trouble-making Louis, swore never to make peace with their father except with the consent of the king and barons of France. Soon war had broken out between Henry on the one side, and on the other his three eldest sons in coalition with a number of Continental lords and English barons. Momentary peace was established for a conference at Gisors, but the offers which Henry tendered, generous when compared to what they would finally reap, were rejected hands down by the three brothers, and the war continued.

Queen Eleanor abetted her sons' rebellion. Henry moved into her domains from the north, scorching the earth from Tours to Poitiers, to the point that eventually Eleanor had to flee the desolate map of her husband's making. As to where she was captured, riding astride and disguised as a man, the chronicles remain frustratingly silent. We know she had been on her way to join her sons in France. Instead she spent the next sixteen years of her life a veritable prisoner of her own husband.

In February of this same year Henry had been further annoyed to hear that Thomas Becket had been 'dignify'd and distinguished . . . from the infamous

Title of a *Traytor*, to the spiritual one of a *Saint*.[340] Pope Alexander III performed the canonization ritual, 'for which the murder would have cried aloud even had signs and miracles been lacking'[341], part of a spate of creative endeavour that took place in the name of Saint Thomas.

1174

William II of Sicily had reached an age when he felt called upon to make his presence felt in the Mediterranean. In line with this urge he responded to a suggestion from the Latin king of Jerusalem, Amalric, that they join forces in a coup against Egypt where the (albeit Muslim) Fatimid population, wanting to throw off the yoke of Muslim Syrian rule, were crying out for help. William rose to the occasion in July by sending a massive fleet, commanded by his cousin Tancred of Lecce to attack Alexandria. The assault was doomed, however, when the unexpected death of Amalric deprived the Sicilians of expected ground support. Three hundred Norman knights were taken prisoner by the king of Syria's vizier, Saladin—by race a Kurd from Armenia who, born in 1138, stepped on the historical stage precisely at the right time to achieve, a few years hence, the final denouement of the Christian presence in Outremer—giving William nothing more than a convenient excuse for harrassing the Egyptian coast intermittently for the next few years. But nothing came of these sporadic raids. William the Good's first attempt at warfare had not proven eminently satisfactory.

All this time William was keeping an eye out for a wife, since his succession and therefore the balance of power had to be assured. Pope Alexander III also had a shrewd eye out. He, too, realized the value—no, the necessity—of finding a suitable wife for William of Sicily. The Roman Church still writhed in the state of schism. Having for years listened to Frederick Barbarossa's claims on Italy and Sicily, Alexander realized better than most the dangers to the Papacy of an empty Sicilian throne. Besides that, here was the emperor on the move again this year, bearing down on Rome with yet another of his antipopes, Calixtus III, in tow. Could anyone doubt that, if successful in this adventure, he would move against William II? Frederick's objectives were all too plain, especially in view of his impudent offer to William of one of his own daughters just the year before. Knowing that a marriage to Frederick's daughter could pave the way to all of Southern Italy and Sicily being given over to German control, William had politely declined the offer.

So far as Frederick's invasion was concerned, he met unexpectedly stiff resistance in the group effort of the Lombard League, holding together to defend their civil liberties in general, and their homes in particular. But Alexander still had cause for anxiety. He revived the idea of a union of the two great Norman houses—a marriage between William II and Princess Joanna of England, the seventh child and third daughter of Henry and Eleanor, a plan that had been dropped at the time of Becket's murder. Both kings responded favourably to the pope's suggestion, and negotiations went ahead.

In the long run more important than any of the year's happenings already mentioned is a legendary event concerning William II. While he was resting one day in the royal deer preserve near Palermo, the Virgin is said to have appeared to him, revealing the location of a vast treasure that had been stashed away in a secret place and which she admonished him to use only for religious purposes. The result of this 'discovery' was the building of one of the most monumentally glorious and sumptuously conceived religious centres in all of Christendom—no, in the world. But, while ostensibly obeying the Virgin's order, William achieved a political as well as a religious purpose.

As archbishop of Palermo, Walter of the Mill had been, especially recently, a good deal less than trustworthy. William was much aware that this imported Englishman, by nature politically conservative and not above seeking his own power base, had taken over the management of a party of unabashed reaction. The power Walter of the Mill wielded was second only to that of the king, and, if the truth were known, was rapidly bearing down on the monarch's lead. The archbishop was clearly not satisfied with limited authority. Young as he was, William was shrewd enough to realize that maintaining any status quo is a foregone lost cause—history is the story of change, not the telling of society at a standstill. Now he saw his chance, under divine auspices as it were, to clip the power of this ambitious archbishop. The creation of another archbishopric nearby would serve the purpose handsomely—as well as asserting the pomp and magnificence of the royal position and person.

For his new foundation William chose the site of a former Greek chapel, Hagia Kyriaka, high in the hills about nine miles southeast of Palermo, close enough to cause Walter of the Mill the desired discomfiture. This Monreale (Royal Mount) was a splendid choice, overlooking as it does the sweeping 'Golden Conche Shell' of the Palermitan basin. The site of this, the last great Hauteville monument in Sicily, was isolated and at the same time within view of the great power centre of the Mediterranean world, reminding the Benedictine monks, whom William imported from La Cava near Salerno, that, cloistered as they were, they were still very much a part of the political world.

The abbey was more than generously endowed by William with large possessions of land, several castles with attendant holdings, dues and taxes, two churches with their agricultural acreage and villages, a mill, a fishery on the island of Fimi and fishing rights (with as many as five boats specified) in the harbour of Palermo. Since medieval folk were such intrepid travellers, one is not surprised to learn of a multitude of deeds guaranteeing hospitality in far flung places for the monks, barley for their horses and freedoms from tolls.

Preparation is needed for entering Monreale Cathedral, and is sumptuously provided. Critics have faulted the exterior (*see page* 395) (specifically the original parts, not those evidences of later ages which admittedly can be pretty grim) as 'unpleasant' and as 'vacuous doodling'. Yet is is anything but that. The rich surface embroidery of interlacing arches serves as visual enticement into a world of pattern and texture, an embellishment of the senses. It is difficult to agree with intellectual put downs of the cathedral's rich surface patterns of red lava on limestone, perhaps 'a little over-ripe and profuse, but very Eastern and effective in the Sicilian sunlight'.[342] The viewer who wants to see the patterning in proper context with the entire abbey buildings must move into the cloister where a monumental view is available along with the gloriously ornate Eastern-inspired cloister itself in peripheral vision.

With the mighty church stark against the cyclorama of the brilliant cobalt Sicilian sky, the view from the cloister represents the world of man's imaginings, the grandeur, the charm and delight, the sheer joy and pleasure in his own creativity. Few places in the world show men—Eastern, Western, Saracenic, Christian, it does not matter—so ready to unite, so willing to pool resources, so loving in their union that it produces an Elysium of joyous togetherness. It is a most fascinating picture book of the inside of the human mind, of man's pleasures and faiths. It is a stage for man's perceptions, a statement of his needs, loves and beliefs. Nowhere in this magnificent quadrangle does one detect a discordant note. Things that should not go together do so successfully; normally contradictory ideas here reinforce one another. And always the energetic spirit of adventure is manifest, for in their own ways these craftsmen were as questing as the rulers and knights.

The capitals (*see page* 395) of the 216 pairs of columns tell the stories: the vintage is trampled while Noah lies drunk under a tree; masons ply their trade, a swineherd tends a pig and a traveller trudges wearily, his bundle hanging from a staff on his shoulder like that of a modern hobo; a banqueting lady accepts a cup of wine from a kneeling page and an acrobat stands on his head. There are elderly prophets identified by name and surrounded by little naked angels—the *putti* of ancient Rome gone Christian. Knights are present in number, fighting, jousting, hunting, while wild beasts counter-attack or scurry for cover amid the acanthus leaves; William offers his church in model form on one capital, while on its companion a baby Jesus reaches eagerly forward from his mother's lap to accept and to touch—a child playing with a doll's house. On another pair the angel Gabriel makes his momentous announcement, while the Virgin acknowledges the reasonableness of it without so much as a blink of an eye; even pagan Mithras is there, enjoying it all with typical heathen abandon. There are birds and fruits and dancing animals; flowers, trees and cornucopias; roaring bulls and dancing dogs; biblical stories, including the complete Nativity cycle; there are mystic symbols and ornamental mysteries—'all the symbolic monsters of the Bestiaries, and a good many other animals besides, elegant winged griffins, uncanny dragons, a serpent drinking out of the same cup as a lamb, real bulls or lions or birds—and a mermaid with a forked tail entwined with some kind of apocalyptic beasts'.[343]

Several artisans' hands are detectable in the cloister—and several traditions too, Provençal seeming to play a more than cursory part among identifiable influences. (*See page* 396.) One sculptor seems more of a virtuoso than his fellows, another a better story-teller, a third a more prolific decorator, and yet a fourth displays a finer sense of grace. And not all the capitals were done during the same period, though surely the cloister was in use (it need not have been completed) by the monks in 1182 when Pope Lucius III issued his bull declaring the abbey church a cathedral, and praising William for creating a building 'the like of which . . . has not been constructed by any king even from ancient times, and such a one as must compel all men to admiration'. But all the capitals work together in the best Rogerian tradition, a mingling of traditions and human experiences which we tend to think of as disparate, all supplementing and upholding one another in the sort of culture mix that we of the twentieth century often strive to achieve.

The columns which support the capitals are wondrously variegated: plain, fluted, twisted, inlaid, carved, embellished with arabesques of staggering complexity. There are zigzags and chequerboards, chevrons and carved spirals. Brilliant mosaic inlays bring light to the cloistral shadows, add lustre to the sun. Such colours were not meant to exist, and yet they do.

There are two sets of great bronze doors that allow entrance into Monreale Cathedral, both of them reflecting the two innate instincts of medieval man: the spirit of creative expression, and the marvellously simple, almost childlike, curiosity, the sense of marvel. Underlying both these characterisitics is the striving for utterance of things that men hold sacred: love, death, creation.

The north porch bronze doors are the work of Barisanus of Trani, whose doors there and at Ravello we have already admired. As one would expect from his heritage, his work at Monreale has more than a mere touch of Byzantium. The flowing lines of his bronze reliefs certainly echo the Romanesque, but the overall hieratic feeling underlying his scenes from the lives of Christ and of the saints and even his fantasies is unmistakable. Barisanus sought stimulus in Early Christian art as well, content not to experiment, but simply to lay out for us his feelings for his dignified saints, his secular subjects, his Madonna, Crucifixion and his Christ in Glory. Always one is aware of his superb sense of decoration, his delight in ornamentation; and even though some of the plaques of his doors were cast from the same moulds as those on his doors at Trani and Ravello, their order is rearranged.

Bonannus of Pisa, who executed the western doors, was a more progressive artist. He did the Monreale doors in 1186, just six years after his famous Porta di San Ranieri in the south transept of Pisa Cathedral, and thirteen years after he designed one of the most popular tourist attractions in the world, the leaning bell tower of the same church. Here at Monreale Bonannus dramatizes on a highly emotional level and in deeper relief than at Pisa, while at the same time bowing to Byzantine predecessors. Unlike Barisanus, Bonannus is the forward thinker, the avant-garde activist of their day. His work lacks the sweetness and elegance of that of Barisanus, but there is an earthy realism about it which is part of the Northern mainstream of art that flowered in Dante, Giotto and the humanists of the Italian Renaissance. Even the superfluous eighteenth-century portico flanked by the Norman towers cannot detract from the excitement of adventurous naturalism displayed by Bonannus' biblical scenes. For the first time in over eight hundred years of Western art we see art in which people are shown beginning to move like people; they are reacting to one another on the stage of a new realism. The splendid Titians and Tintorettos of the High Renaissance are still far away, and of course still further the photographic techniques of the 'New Realism' of the twentieth century. But a new life can be detected, a desire to break free of the mould. And, strangely, none of this naturalism is out of sync with the shimmering interior!

The essential Italian characteristics are all inside the cathedral—mosaics, marble inlays, Cosmati patterns, the two thrones—ecclesiastical and secular— the shimmer, the sparkle and the opulent colours riding a sea of gold to become 'a major part of the composition. This particular style, which seeks to create an atmosphere of enchantment, is obviously strongly influenced by the

East and suits the temperament of two widely opposed regions of Italy'[344]—Sicily and Venice. And yet the style at Monreale has a character all its own. The high point of Sicilian expression, the Palatine Chapel, reflects a civilization that had reached maturity after two generations of determined struggle, often masochistically self-centred while yet contradictorily enlightened. Monreale reflects a child born to the purple, educated in a world of eunuchs and harems, spoiled, pampered, wealthy, but none the less determined to leave its mark. Monreale can reach superb heights, but never quite the peaks of Cefalù, the autumnal harmonies of the Palatine, or the summery brilliance of George of Antioch's Martorana.

It is an interesting fact that at Monreale Thomas Becket is prominently represented just to the right of centre at the apsidal end, identified with certainty by the words *Scs. Thomas Cantur.* However, it is not surprising to find here what is believed to be the earliest representation of *Saint* Thomas, considering that William II's wife was Henry II's daughter Joanna. Monreale may have helped to propagate the cult of Saint Thomas in Italy; there is a chapel dedicated to him in Anagni, and a fresco showing his martyrdom in the church of SS Giovanni e Paolo at Spoleto.

Despite its partial refurbishing after a fire in 1811, Monreale is still impressive almost beyond words, and this also in spite of the flood of light into the cathedral that was not part of the original design. (We can read in a 1540 record of repairs that the windows were originally of cast lead pierced in patterns.) We are still able to appreciate the hushed majesty, the quiet harmonies of the soft grey-greens and blues that echo the hazy colours of the vast Conca d'Oro, the grandeur of the granite columns, the raised choir, the endless parade of mosaic-encrusted arches. We feel the sombreness of a God who, having completed His sixth day of creation, looks sad—no, sagging, hands limp in His lap, tired. And which of us has not been caught un-mannerly?—as in the case of the surprised Adam who, when God presents him with Eve, rudely though understandably remains seated. We relate to the lack of comprehension in the faces of Adam and Eve who, on being driven from the Garden of Eden, look at us with quizzical expressions, as though asking us what *we* think of this brand of divine justice. It is all familiar: the men sawing wood to make the Ark, and then planing the edges of the boards, producing very realistic curls of wood indeed; the bird pecking at a floating corpse during the deluge; one of the sons of Noah having a clumsy time forcing the animals to leave the Ark while, at the other end, his more persuasive father coaxes the beasts—all of them undersized—simply to leap ashore; the nasty head wound on Abel while Cain swings again his lethal club; the masons building the Tower of Babel, carrying a hod or using scaffolds lashed together realistically with leather thongs; Christ standing neck deep in the River Jordan, giving Himself to John's baptismal ritual, looking perplexed—maybe just cold; the smugly expectant faces of the beneficiaries of Christ's miracle of the loaves and fishes; Jesus riding into Jerusalem, unmistakably sceptical of the praises of the palm-waving populace. And what of the Roman soldier who, sheathing his sword after having struck the head from Saint Paul's shoulders, surveys the scene with regret, and an expression of second thought sorrow?

The individual mosaics are of heroic dimensions, too: Christ shot through with gold, performing his miracles and submitting to Mary Magdalen's ministrations; the archangels militantly arrayed in the apse; David in kingly splendour; Isaiah and Habakkuk; Saint Paul enthroned, for once depicted without a sword; William II being crowned by Christ Himself, a kingly link to the divine that we have seen before with his grandfather Roger II in the Martorana. We find William again here as we have seen him in the cloister, presenting his church to the Virgin, with an almost childish insistence that he and no other is the donor. Rebecca is there with her camels, and so are Isaac and Abraham there, and Jacob with his ladder.

But above everything else inside Monreale Cathedral, beyond the colours against shimmering gold backgrounds, beyond the drama of God creating Adam with a piercing ray of light from His creative eye—in its own way as impressive as Michelangelo's famous hands—beyond the majesty of the architecture and the theatrical raising of the apsidal end, it is the Pantocrator (Christ Enthroned) Who finally arrests our attention. 'I am the Light of the World' His book proclaims in both Greek and Latin. Centrally located on the eastern apse, high on the wall immediately above His mother, holding her Child and surrounded by angel attendants, prophets and evangelists, He seems beyond our reach, yet is nevertheless there. He looks down on us from another plane, from a world outside our petty galaxy, from a time beyond our fragile age. No longer is He the Christ of the Passion and Nativity, the angered purifier of the temple. Here He is in His glory, in His own realm, doing what He does best: ruling. 'Thus Christ appears twice upon this wall, once as the Omnipotent Wisdom, the Word by whom all things were made, and once as God deigning to assume a shape of flesh and dwell with men'.[345]

This Christ, though, is no longer the unbending Pantocrator of Cefalù who, though arguably the most beautiful in the world, makes no effort to be one of us. The Pantocrator of Monreale wants to love, to embrace, to save. They are both splendid; but the former commands the greater respect. It is difficult to make even the least criticism at Monreale; but the feeling remains that somehow one is earthbound in William's great cathedral, never really far from the street just beyond Bonannus' doors. Yet, if the Palatine is 'a jewel from the crown of heaven',[346] then Monreale is the whole crown. If Cefalù is the major theme in a visual Ode to Joy and the Martorana a principal chord, then Monreale is the entire symphony. But sometimes the whole is less impressive than the individual parts.

*Pantocrator,
Monreale, Sicily*

403

Chapter Twenty

Solomon says that there are three things difficult to be found,
and a fourth hardly to be discovered: the way of an eagle in the air:
the way of a ship in the sea: the way of a serpent on the ground:
and the way of a man in his youth. I can add a fifth: the way of a King in England.

Peter of Blois. Quoted by Duggan in *The Devil's Brood*

1174

Bathed in warm southern sunshine, La Rochelle is one of the loveliest, most peaceful ports in France, clinging even today to its ancient trade in the import and export of wine. The Old Port is guarded by two imposing towers, neither of which was there at the time of the early Plantagenets: Nicholas on the south (1384) and the Chain Tower (also fourteenth-century) on the north, so called because it anchored the great protective chain which stretched across the harbour entrance. At one time there was a pointed arch between the two towers, spanning the basin entrance. What is left in La Rochelle of historical interest is of later periods than that which concerns us here. Today it is a resort for yachtsmen, its docks crowded, its pavement cafés jammed, but with none of the usual hubbub that one expects in places of such popularity. La Rochelle is also noteworthy as the site where Prince Richard's animosity for his father erupted into open warfare. With his mother Henry's prisoner, young Richard was outraged into taking his first independent political action. Nearly seventeen, Richard the adolescent was fast growing into Richard the man—the Lionheart of history and legend—

> tall of stature, graceful in figure: his hair between red and auburn; his limbs were straight and flexible; his arms rather long, and not to be matched for wielding the sword or for striking with it; and his long legs suited the rest of his frame; while his appearance was commanding, and his manners and habits suitable . . . He was far superior to all others both in moral goodness, and in strength, and memorable for prowess in battles, and his mighty deeds outshone the most brilliant description . . . of them'.[347]

Closer to his mother than to his father, Richard felt the insult done her obliged him to take command of a new rebellion against Henry. First off he descended on La Rochelle whose citizens, loyal to their ageing lord, slammed the gates in his face. His pride wounded by this show of defiance, Richard, in a fury of royal pique, chose as his headquarters the rival city of Saintes, immediately converting the cathedral of St Pierre into an arsenal. But Henry had not lived a life on the go in vain. He was quick to react.

Comfortable in the belief that his father was celebrating Whit Sunday in Poitiers, Richard was suddenly shaken from his complacency by the realization that he was, instead, battering down the gates of Saintes. Richard barely

La Rochelle, France

escaped the assault, but sixty of his knights and four hundred archers were captured by his father. Having sustained such a loss, Richard was diminished as a threat; but he struggled vainly on although his feckless, vacillating elder brother was tottering towards submission.

King Henry was still in every way more daring and decisive than any of his sons. In July, while the young king paced the shores of Flanders waiting for favourable winds to carry him across the Channel to invade England, his forty-one-year-old father showed no hesitation. At Barfleur, 'with more than his customary pandemonium, Henry embarked his mercenaries and his captives [Eleanor and her company] in some forty ships. Then spreading his hands to the stormy sky and uttering one of those challenges that served him for prayer, he called upon heaven to let the sea overwhelm his boats with all their freight unless God meant to vindicate his wrongs'.[348] Heaven obviously favoured him, as it turned out. Eleanor was incarcerated at Winchester, whose town hall even today exhibits certain remnants of the old castle. On occasion she must have attended services in the cathedral there which by her time was already eighty years old.

Winchester had become one of many focal points for the cathedral-building Norman bishops who followed William the Conqueror to England. The remains of the original 1093 building—longer than the present one by about forty feet—which are still visible are unmistakably Norman, especially in the north transept (*see page* 396), which has remained substantially unchanged through the centuries. Built in the typical three-tiered style—main arcade, triforium gallery, and clerestory—it stands classically Norman, beautifully balanced, ruggedly refined, graceful and satisfying. The triforium arches directly above the main supporting arches are formed of two smaller openings, creating a buoyant effect as it were, a sensitive prelude to the higher clerestory windows. While the rest of the church has been modified by later Gothic alterations, the transepts still convince one unequivocally that, while the Gothic may soar with greater lightness and elegance, the Norman Romanesque was born of the earth which it hugs with pride; made of the things of the earth it seems not to want to leave it.

Following her confinement at Winchester, Eleanor was moved succes-
sively to the castle at what is now Old Sarum, or to any of several others in
Hampshire, Berkshire, Buckinghamshire or Nottinghamshire. Despite news of
current affairs occasionally reaching her, she was now effectively shut out of
the limelight. With her imprisonment it may seem that a civilizing light had
temporarily been extinguished.

> Return, poor prisoner!
> Return to thy people, if thou canst.
> And if thou canst not, weep and say,
> 'Alas, how long is my exile!'
> Weep, weep again, and say,
> 'My tears are my bread, both day and night!'[349]

So grieved Bertran de Born, a troubadour-knight normally given to
warlike *sirventes*, in his lament for his imprisoned queen.

Having put his wife away, Henry set out for Canterbury to visit the shrine
of Saint Thomas. He put off his soldier's mantle and shoes, and, donning
simple pilgrim's wool, he made his way barefoot over the cobbled streets of
Canterbury, going directly to the crypt where he spent the night without food
or drink, on his knees, weeping. Then, after hearing early mass, he offered his
bare back for the monks of Canterbury each to lay on three stripes. He thus,
as it were, enlisted Becket's support for himself in the continuing struggle.

While Henry was at Canterbury the king of Scotland, William the Lion,
was on the rampage. Troops in the pay of the count of Flanders, in collusion
with the Scots and English rebels Hugh Bigod and Bishop Hugh du Puiset of
Durham, were harrying the North Country and East Anglia, while their
fellow conspirator, young King Henry, was still indecisively pacing the shores
of Flanders. But within hours of arriving in London Henry II received word
that William the Lion had been taken prisoner near Alnwick.

The joint attack on Henry's kingdom had crumbled, and the bells of
London's churches rang with the news. 'Now God be thanked!' Henry cried
out, 'and Saint Thomas the Martyr, and all the saints of God!'. And indeed,
there were many who believed that William's defeat occurred at precisely the
moment when Henry was being scourged by the monks at Canterbury, so
that 'the reward of his pious action might not seem to have followed the action
itself but rather to have accompanied it, and no one should be suffered to
remain in doubt concerning this point'.[350]

William the Lion is thought to have been imprisoned briefly at Richmond
Castle which looms imposingly over the River Swale in Yorkshire. Built in the
second half of the eleventh century, it nurtured town and large parish church
which grew up in its shadow. Because it was away from the main communication lines of the kingdom, Richmond was largely bypassed by the endemic
turmoil of the twelfth century—even the later violence of the Wars of the
Roses and the Civil War left it untouched. Yet it was designed for defence, as
a fourteenth-century document preserved in the British Museum indicates.
Only Colchester and the White Tower in London display as much masonry
dating from the first decades after the Conquest, and its two-storey Scolland's

Hall is perhaps the oldest of its type in the realm, excluding that of Chepstow. Much of the intriguingly triangular-shaped curtain wall, hugging the knoll on which the castle stands, dates from this early period, including the tower on the east wall where William the Lion is thought to have been detained.

Richmond Castle's keep dates from the second half of the twelfth century. It was started by Conan, duke of Brittany and earl of Richmond, whose daughter was married to Henry's son Geoffrey, and it was finished by Henry after Conan's death in 1171. This new keep was superimposed on an earlier gatehouse, and the large arch that pierces the building at ground level within the bailey was part of that structure. As usual in Norman keeps the main entrance was at the level above the ground floor, in this case opening from the walk on the

Richmond Castle, England

curtain wall. The keep is three storeys high, with the inside wooden floors supported by a stout column, dramatic to look at today, but vexatious in its occupation of the very centre of the main room on each level. There are dramatic staircases within the walls connecting the floors, and leading to the battlements which command a view of the castle compound and the surrounding countryside. Also at Richmond are the ruins of Easby Abbey, a Premonstratensian foundation of 1152, sufficiently complete for its plan to be easily traced. The town boasts a partially Norman church of St Mary, and a small Georgian theatre. There are narrow walk ways known as 'wynds', and one of the largest market squares in Britain.

With the collapse of the insurrection Henry drove his forces into East Anglia where Earl Hugh Bigod had over five hundred knights and a horde of Flemings (sent over in the name of young Henry) crammed into his two castles, Framlingham and Bungay. The fight seems to have gone out of Hugh after the capture of William the Lion, and he sued for peace on 25 July. The other barons joined Henry at Northampton, and King William was led there with his feet tied together under his horse's belly.

Finally satisfied with his victory, Henry set sail from Portsmouth, King William in tow, arriving at Rouen barely in time to deliver it from a combined attack by King Louis and young Henry. An unlikely incident is appended to Henry's rescue: his Welsh troops, on reconnoitring, discovered a supply train *en route* to relieve Louis' forces. Attacking, 'they capture or killed the drivers, unhitched the horses, broke up the wagons, and, if the author of the *Gesta Henrici* is to be believed, poured out all the wine'[351] without drinking it. By 8 September a truce was agreed upon between the two sides.

For a seventeenth birthday present insurgency-minded Richard woke up to the jolting realization that he now stood alone, deserted by both his elder brother and the king of France. Angry, but afraid to lock horns with his father, he was left with little choice. On 23 September, at Montlouis, in the guise of repentance, Richard threw himself at Henry's feet, weeping and begging forgiveness. The king, groping for a sign of filial devotion from any of his sons, personally raised him up and gave him the kiss of peace. King Louis also sued for peace, and by the end of the month the rebellion was over.

Henry was more determined than ever to maintain complete control over his dominions. He stripped his sons of all claims to rule any territory of the realm independently of him, bitter medicine and an object lesson in filial loyalty, but one which, alas, would not be learned. For all their humiliating submission at this time, Henry was never destined to know peace with his 'eaglets' on whom he looked now with disdain, even distrust 'after the manner of a stepfather; and although his sons were so renowned and illustrious he pursued his successors with a hatred which perhaps they deserved, but which none the less impaired his own happiness . . . Whether by some breach of the marriage tie or as a punishment for some crime of the parent, it befell that there was never true affection felt by the father towards his sons, nor by the sons towards their father, nor harmony among the brothers themselves'.[352]

Henry showed more forgiveness to his rebellious barons and vassals than to the members of his own family. Even Hugh Bigod, now approaching the age of eighty, was let off with the levelling of his Framlingham Castle, when he probably expected death, or at least exile. (The handsome thirteen-towered structure that we see at Framlingham today was started by Hugh's son, Roger, and largely dates between 1190 and 1210.) Other barons' castles were destroyed, too, for besides being instruments of insurrection, they stood as emblems of military and territorial aggrandizement, symbols the king could well afford to do without. The heaviest burden of defeat quite naturally fell on William the Lion of Scotland. He acknowledged that he was vassal of King Henry. On top of that, William was forced to relinquish his castles at Berwick, Roxburgh, Jedburgh, Edinburgh and Stirling, by which act he lost effective control of his own country.

By the time of William's humiliation, Jedburgh was already a battered city, standing in the direct line of age-old border skirmishing. Ceded to the English Crown, the castle was dismantled in 1409 by the townspeople themselves who, realizing its very existence encouraged English raiders, saw it as a menace rather than a blessing. But the stately ruins of Jedburgh Abbey still stand, roofless and weather-worn, on the left bank of Jed Water; it is easily the handsomest of the four border abbeys, which include Kelso, Melrose and Dryburgh. By the time of the Treaty of Falaise Jedburgh Abbey was already twenty-two years old.

Originally founded by King David I, Jedburgh Abbey was manned by Augustinian canons brought from Saint-Quentin in Beauvais, France. It was elevated to the status of abbey around the middle of the twelfth century, at which time the church we still see was built, a sterling example of both Norman and Transitional styles. The older part, the choir, is the finer glory. Strong Romanesque arches span distances between stout Norman columns

Jedburgh Abbey Church, Scotland

which rise to support the corresponding arches at triforium level, splendidly imposing. Then, as though having second thoughts about the solidity of the weighty ground-level architecture, the builders created contrast by making their clerestory windows lightly Gothic, a happy blending of the two styles and a welcome relief. Few medieval churches present such a stately array of architectural majesty as the nave cluster-piers viewed from either end of the great aisle; the sunlight streams among them from the side, to repeat the arch patterns on the lush green grass that is the modern stand-in for the original stone floor. 'If a little ghostly, a little ethereal with too great an abundance of daylight intruding'[353], the long view down the nave does nevertheless convey a sense of inherent nobility, magic, and the strength that was obviously necessary even to survive in so contentious a location. Alterations have occurred over the years, and demolitions, but Jedburgh Abbey gives us as clear a picture as any other medieval religious building of the determination and sense of purpose of those stubborn churchmen who came here to practise their rituals and meditate on their faith. There is poetry here and dignity.

In the truce engineered by Henry II following the rebellion of 1173-4 no mention is made of Eleanor. Only the poets sing of her plight:

> You have been snatched from your own lands and carried away to an alien country . . . And now you grieve, you weep, you are consumed with sorrow . . . You cry out and no one heeds you, for the King of the North holds you in captivity . . .[354]

While Eleanor did not actually want for the necessities of life, Henry was not many cuts above penuriousness in his allotment of funds for her support. Occasionally she was released from confinement, but only on the insistence of her sons for family affairs, or for political expediency. For the moment, while she languished during a cheerless Christmas season, Henry held court at Argentan. With his four sons around him, they projected a picture of family harmony—the very essence of the spirit of the season. But it was only an image. They were simply biding their time. In the meanwhile they feasted together on venison and copious supplies of wine and ale, though it is hard to imagine why when one reads that 'the ale which men drink in that place [Henry's court] is horrid to the taste and abominable to the sight'.[355]

1175

While Henry was forcing his sons into line, and travelling to York where his treaty with William the Lion was ratified this year, more peaceful and creative efforts were being pursued near Oxford in the tiny little community of Iffley. It must have been about this time that the church of St Mary the Virgin was nearing completion, built by the Norman Robert de Saint-Rémy. The original Norman church consisted of a chancel, a tower and a nave, the whole not very large and displaying interior Romanesque arches decorated with chevron patterns, a western rose-window surmounted by three Norman windows, and a lovely western portal, along with two lesser ones opening to the north and south. The south portal (*see page*

Parish Church, Iffley, England

413) is especially fine, and its doorway better preserved because it was covered by a porch (dating from the fifteenth or sixteenth century) until 1807. Graphic Romanesque sculpture conveys the idea of good on the right and evil on the left, the latter in the form of wild beasts and monsters including, it is said, a representation of Henry II, presumably there on account of his part in Becket's death. Some of the carving is unfinished, because, it is thought, the workmen bolted after receiving better employment offers from Oxford's St Frideswide's priory, now Christ Church Cathedral. The broad-shouldered central tower, lining up with the outside walls of the church on the north and south sides, is a stunning manifestation of the Norman spirit—bulky, forceful and solid.

1176

Early this year William II of Sicily dispatched a specially chosen party to England to request the hand of the ten-year-old Princess Joanna. The union could be expected to strengthen the mediocre relations between the two kingdoms. The Sicilian ambassadors were thrilled by the child's beauty and sent one of their party back to Palermo to inform the nervously waiting bridegroom-to-be that all was well, that he would be delighted.

Henry ordered the preparation of seven ships to carry Joanna to her new home. He was determined that she should travel in a style befitting the future queen of Sicily—or, more correctly, befitting the daughter of the most powerful ruler in Europe. He ordered her trousseau, including a robe 'that cost the stupendous sum of £114 5s. 5d., by far the most costly garment mentioned in the Pipe Rolls'.[356] In the fashion of the day, the gown swept the floor and had full sleeves from elbows to wrists. It would have been fastened at the throat and shoulders with brooches, and would have had a belt. Perhaps made of silk (robes were also made of either wool or linen), it was richly embroidered with needlework. Presumably it was also encrusted with jewels.

Henry showered the Sicilians with gifts, including precious metals and horses. In August he gave Joanna into their care. Joanna's uncle, Hamelin Plantagenet (Henry's illegitimate half-brother), along with two archbishops and one bishop, accompanied her to Southampton. Her eldest brother, the young king, escorted her through France to Poitiers, where Richard took over until he deposited her at the port of Saint-Gilles-du-Gard, entrusting her into the care of Richard Palmer and the archbishop of Capua. Because of rough seas the princess' sailing party had to hug the coast of Italy. At Christmas they disembarked at Naples to allow the princess to recover from seasickness.

By every standard of the day Henry's cup was full to the brim, and would have been running over but for one mitigating circumstance: it was probably during this year that he lost the only woman whom he truly loved for herself alone. It had been for his Fair Rosamund that Henry had created at Woodstock one of the most romantic retreats in history of which, alas, nothing remains— 'even its site [being] partly destroyed when Blenheim Park [the grounds of the palace where Winston Churchill was born] was laid out in the eighteenth century'.[357] Woodstock had been a royal palace from the time of Ethelred the Unready. Henry made alterations there, some of them exotic, perhaps even inspired by the Palermitan palaces of William II, which were well known to twelfth-century England. Nothing, in his mind, could be too extravagant for

> My Rosamonde, my only Rose,
> That pleasest best mine eye,
> The fairest flower in all the worlde
> To feed my fantasye . . .[358]

He enclosed the palace with a stone wall, and even provided a small menagerie which included a porcupine. Eleanor must have heard lurid stories of Henry's dalliance, but, locked away as she was, she was clearly no threat to the romance. Yet contemporary writers and later poets unblushingly implicate her in a fictitiously scandalous role; and with each reading she becomes more and more the villainess, the woman scorned, who grows increasingly wicked as Rosamund's virtue approaches the angelic. Such is the *Ballad of the Fair Rosamund*, transcribed, perhaps, by Thomas Delon in the fifteenth century after having been sung by minstrels over the years, added to and embellished until we wind up with a wicked-queen-and-innocent-young-lover fairy tale. Woodstock itself, according to contemporary and later romantic poets, was built as a protective bower love-nest, organized like a fairy-tale fortress to defend the favoured courtesan against the queen.

> The king therefore, for her defense
> Against the furious queene,
> At Woodstocke builded such a bower,
> The like was never seene.

Most curiously that bower was built,
Of stone and timber strong;
An hundered and fifty doors
Did to this bower belong:

And they so cunninglye contriv'd,
With turnings round about,
That none but with a clue of thread
Could enter in or out.[359]

Rosamund apparently died of natural causes—and at nearby Godstow Nunnery, not at Woodstock—after taking the veil and living an exemplary life during her last days. That fact was not going to deny the troubadours poetic licence to tell of Eleanor's penetration of the surrounding maze—a good trick, considering that she was under lock and key, probably at Salisbury—and demanding that her hapless and terrified rival drink of a poisoned cup.

Even in death Rosamund did not find the peace she doubtlessly craved after her liaison with the lusty, hyper-active Henry. She was entombed by the nuns of Godstow in the choir of their chapel, draped by an expensive pall and surrounded by lighted candles. But in 1191 or 1192 the stern bishop of Lincoln, Saint Hugh, making his pastoral rounds, was shocked to find Rosamund enshrined there. Although the nuns explained that their meagre prosperity had stemmed from royal alms, Hugh had her body moved to the cemetery 'because she was a harlot'. Even the rather nasty epitaph which was said then to have adorned her grave at Godstow was not rightly hers, having been purloined from a sixth-century Lombard queen of the same name:

Here lieth in tombe the rose of the world, nought a clene rose;
It smelleth nought swete, but stinketh, that was wont to
    smelle ful swete.[360]

1177

At last the eighteen-year-old schism in the Church was brought to an end, with Alexander III victorious. Just the year before, on 29 May, Frederick Barbarossa was laid low—quite literally, as it turned out—by the most disastrous defeat of his entire career. At Legnano, seventeen miles northwest of Milan, his army was routed by the combined forces of the Lombard League, an army superior in numbers and determined to make an end of imperial bullying. But such was Barbarossa's determination and over-confidence that, relying on his cavalry, he galloped to the attack with his inferior numbers, thus losing a battle which some military historians claim foreshadowed the demise of the era of cavalry supremacy. In the end it was the Milanese infantry that stopped him, aided by late-arriving cavalry from Brescia and a regrouped contingent of Milanesi knights. The emperor himself was wounded so badly that at first he was thought to be dead. Seven hundred years later the Milanesi celebrated the victory by erecting a monument on the field of the battle, and

Parish Church,
S. Door, Iffley,
England

Apsidal Sculpture,
St Paul les Dax,
France

La Cuba, Palermo

Rocamadour,
France

Temple Church, London

then again in 1900 with another in their Piazza Federico Barbarossa. Perhaps more interesting, in the mid-nineteenth century Giuseppe Verdi fired his compatriots with a passion of patriotic fervour by invoking memories of Frederick's defeat with his thirteenth opera, *La Battaglia di Legnano*.

Frederick finally woke up to the idea that Europe was not going to follow his lead, that he was the one who was out of step. He acknowledged his new awareness by sending feelers to Alexander III with a view to reconciliation. The price he would have to pay, his ambassadors were informed, was cheap when one thinks of the years of turmoil and upheaval that led to the accord: Frederick would recognize Alexander as the rightful pope, restore confiscated Church properties and conclude peace treaties with Sicily, Byzantium and the Lombard League. For his part, the pope would respond by confirming Frederick's wife as empress; he would recognize their son Henry as king of the Romans (thereby automatically putting him in line to succeed Frederick as emperor) and confirm the position of various prelates who had been appointed by one or another of Frederick's antipopes. It was arranged that the two parties should meet in Venice in July.

On 24 July Frederick, having repudiated his anti-Pope Paschal—and in consequence having had his eighteen-year long excommunication rescinded—was admitted into the city. The cathedral of St Mark was the stage for the imperial-papal *rapprochement* and the formal conclusion of the Treaty of Venice. About nine o'clock in the morning the doge's barge arrived at the quay, bringing the emperor and four cardinals into the papal presence. Frederick mounted the ceremonial platform. Discarding his red robe, he prostrated himself before Alexander, kissing first his feet and then his knees. The pope embraced him and bade him sit at his right hand. 'Son of the Church, be welcome', he said, and then led him into the church while the bells pealed forth and the Te Deum was intoned.

It was a magnificent climax to Alexander III's career. Now, after eighteen years of schism and ten years of exile, he had triumphed. Alexander's victory led to better things for, if nothing else, it now gave him time to ponder on the effect of the schism and its causes. As a result, in 1179, at the Third Lateran Council, new papal election procedures were instituted: henceforth all cardinals would have an equal vote, with a two-thirds majority necessary for election, a rule which has been followed in essence to the present day.

Perhaps to alleviate a nagging guilt for the murder of Thomas Becket, Henry II had been toying for some time with the idea of making a pilgrimage to Santiago de Compostella—though it was not in the cards for him. In anticipation he instructed Richard, as duke of Aquitaine, to keep open the main routes south from Bordeaux to the Pyrenees. Ever since the 1174 agreements reached at Montlouis, Richard and his wayward siblings seemed content to carry out paternal orders—at least so far. It was no doubt in response to Henry's wishes that Richard, in January, took Dax and then Bayonne, browbeating the local populations into oaths of safe conduct for all pilgrims.

Lying on the left bank of the River Adour about twenty-seven miles northeast of Bayonne, Dax was an ancient Gallo-Roman fortified encampment, the defences of which are still visible as a promenade. The church of

Notre Dame, at one time a cathedral, still preserves a lovely thirteenth-century doorway. Across the river the mostly fifteenth-century church of Saint-Paul-lès-Dax, with its sensitively wrought Romanesque reliefs dating from the eleventh century, is the architectural-sculptural gem of the area. The exterior of the apsidal end (*see page* 413), which faces on a public garden and is usually bathed in a light of uncommon limpidity, is banded above a series of blind arches by bas-reliefs telling stories of a singular mixture of subjects. There are fantastic animals, Samson and the Lion, the Women at the Tomb of Christ, the Kiss of Judas, the Last Supper, the Crucifixion, a dragon, and Veronica with the Towel. In terms as direct as only Romanesque art can be, the stories come through to us today with clarity and a sensitivity to the human agony of life. How utterly eloquent is every line etched in the unyielding stone; how calming each plane; how exciting each calculated curve—exciting in that the eleventh-century artist makes us feel the anguish of the execution of Jesus, the inner suffering of the betrayed, the sorrow and shock of the women in terms so persuasive that we have no choice but to respond. There may be nobility in Christ on the cross, but there is debasement, too—he appears as an unheroic hero, a god cut down, a divinity made only too human.

On the night of 2 February the Princess Joanna finally arrived at Palermo. She was met at the gates of the city by an eager William II who, apparently, was instantly smitten. And he was not the only one! Joanna, having been educated mostly at Fontevrault Abbey, spoke French fluently, a distinct advantage for living in the Palermitan palaces. She was as lovely as her twenty-three-year-old husband was handsome; his subjects took her to their hearts as they would have a fairy-tale princess. Joanna's story provides one of the few instances in the Middle Ages when a young lady used as political bait had even a remote chance of genuine happiness. The outlook for her future was bright indeed. Entering Palermo 'together with Gilles, bishop of Evreux, and the other envoys of our lord, the king, the whole city welcomed them, and lamps, so many and so large, were lighted up, that the city almost seemed to be on fire, and the rays of the stars could in no way bear comparison with the brilliancy of such a light: for it was by night that they entered the city of Palermo'.[361] The royal couple were married eleven days later, on Saint Valentine's eve, and Joanna was crowned queen of Sicily immediately afterwards. The ceremony took place in the Palatine Chapel with her countryman, Archbishop Walter of the Mill, officiating.

While a pope and an emperor were patching up a tattered relationship in Venice; while the king of England fretted over the unfilial behaviour of his sons and mourned a lost love; while an eleven-year-old princess adopted a new island home; while these events transpired, a small band of Cistercian monks finally found a new home which was destined to play no role whatsoever in history, its only value today being the drama of its incredible ruins.

The monks had had a peripatetic transitory history. At one point they had settled within earshot of Rievaulx Abbey, an unfortunate location since the brothers of each abbey could hear the others' bells at all hours. The Rievaulx Cistercians were already well established, so it was up to the newcomers—the

Byland Abbey Church, England

Byland monks, as they came to be called—to leave. After a period in the west, they finally found their permanent base at Byland Abbey in North Yorkshire. Despite its historical unimportance, the abbey prospered well, in time growing larger than either of the more famous nearby abbeys, Rievaulx or Fountains.

Most of the layout of Byland Abbey can be appreciated today, though its remains are extremely meagre and not rewarding to the student who seeks opulence in his ruins. But the western wall of the abbey church should be enough to delight the most drama-haunted amateur archaeologist, and the fragments of tiled floors sufficient for the most interested ceramist. As though standing by some mysterious and magnificent force, the single wall of Byland stretches upwards, almost as open as it is solid, its rising movement accentuated by the three vertical shafts of light of used-to-be windows pointing their elongated arches at the huge crescent of emptiness, all that is left of an enormous rose window. In the most breathtaking balance of positive and negative space, the front of what was the longest Cistercian church in England looks almost artificial, like a typical nineteenth-century romantic painting, or even like the false front of a stage set. Surely a good breeze will finally destroy this monument to Cistercian determination! The ruin may not conjure up monkish hymns, or the hushed scuffling of sandalled feet. Even at sunset it appears far too spectacular to allow thoughts of the service of Vespers. Nor does it remind us of the religious will, the devotion, the love, that made such a structure possible. The best we can come up with at Byland Abbey is awe, simple and unadulterated by any other emotion: awe at the nobility of Man in building it. It is that basic.

1178

This year Henry returned to a work that had been interrupted during the rebellions of 1173-4—a massive rebuilding of his fortress at Newcastle upon Tyne. Founded by Robert Curthose in 1080 on his return from a Scottish campaign, Newcastle was regarded as a key to northern defence, judging from the amounts of money which the Pipe Rolls show to have been lavished on it.

The town of Newcastle upon Tyne had been a Roman camp, an adjunct of Hadrian's Wall. When Robert Curthose set to work there, he threw up a motte-and-bailey, which was altered over the succeeding years. Now, almost a century after its foundation, and utilizing the services of a master builder named Maurice, Henry erected a new keep sixty-two feet by fifty-six, which still survives at its original height of eighty feet. Resting on a spreading plinth and reinforced by soaring buttresses and corner turrets (the one on the

Castle keep, Newcastle-upon-Tyne, England

northwest corner, multi-angular instead of square like the other three, is thought to have served as a small catapult platform), the keep has four floors including the basement with its chapel. As usual with Norman castles, the entrance, approached by an outside staircase and a fore-building, is on the first storey and leads directly into the main hall containing a fireplace, an upper gallery, and windows that illuminate the interior with an abundance of light one would not expect in a twelfth-century castle. The king's chamber on the same floor has its own fireplace. All in all it seems like a pretty warm house. Within the castle, stairs connect the floors all the way up to the garrison quarters on the top, giving out onto the roof. The walls are fourteen feet thick, which allowed for various service rooms and an interior latrine.

The castle is now surrounded by the ever-encroaching city so that it is hemmed in on all sides. Indeed, it is even somewhat difficult to find, surrounded as it is by high buildings, railway tracks and an array of bridges, all of which frustrate the romantic historian. But in its day the keep lorded over a vast castle complex while at the same time remaining self-contained and traffic-efficient. All that were needed successfully to resist a siege were provisions; and these had not to be fit for a king. An example: 'At the small Northumberland castle of Wark the defenders were provided with oatmeal and malt, and on this diet of beer and porridge a garrison of fifty men in 1174 succcessfully defied the King of Scotland and his army'.[362]

At this same time Henry was paying lavishly for his modernization of Dover Castle. His updated Dover keep, engineered by Master Maurice and resembling his Newcastle design, was spacious enough to house a huge body of defenders; it had four floors, and rooms built into the outer walls, which varied in thickness at their base between seventeen and twenty-one feet. The keep included a sophisticated plumbing system, a well 240 feet deep, and, appropriately enough, a chapel dedicated to Saint Thomas of Canterbury. All in all, by the time Henry finished with it, Dover was considered to be one of the most formidable strongholds of the twelfth century.

1179

Just as Henry II had had the young king crowned in an attempt to assure the succession, so Louis VII of France planned to crown his son Philip (dubbed Augustus some say for the month of his birth, others say in imitation of the ancient Romans) on his fourteenth birthday, 21 August. But a few weeks before the coronation Philip fell ill, so seriously that there was talk of his dying. The festivities were cancelled. Advised in a dream to seek the intervention of Saint Thomas Becket, Louis headed for Canterbury where he was, with the usual royal hypocrisy, 'graciously received by his "most dear brother" King Henry'.[363] By 1 November Philip had recovered sufficiently to endure the coronation, which was celebrated at Rheims with all attendant fanfare. Only his father was not present; he had suffered a stroke on his way home from Canterbury and, though he held tenaciously to life for another year, his *raison d'être* ceased from that moment. But France was in good hands. Philip was determined to expand the power of the French monarchy. Dogmatic, precise and without humour, he was also notably devious, and was to prove adept at sowing discord among the Plantagenets.

1180

Louis died at the abbey of Notre Dame in Paris, the very place from which he had originally been so cruelly wrenched to fulfil his unanticipated role as king. This strangely inward-looking man, somewhat of an enigma to historians, was laid to rest in the Cistercian abbey of Barbieux where Queen Adela erected for him a noble tomb, reserving a place beside it for herself. A gentle man by nature, much more suited to the cloister than to the palace, Louis had been totally unprepared for the role thrust upon him by the unexpected death of his elder, better coached brother. Like all the politicians of his time (or any other time for that matter) Louis was capable of the most two-faced intrigues, especially when it came to meddling in Plantagenet family affairs. He could wink his religious eye when he needed to in order to see the political situation pragmatically, but his eyes, heart and mind were usually open to religious conviction. He was a strict judge, often more so with himself.

It is not possible to know whether Eleanor heard of the death of her former husband—and if she did, what she thought and felt. But time was to make her rue the advent of young King Philip II, now only fifteen, and who at first relied for support on Henry and his family—the very people he was committed to destroying, and who must have been aware of his commitment. For the moment Philip was too young to seem a danger to anyone. But the Plantagenets, especially Richard and John, were destined to know him well, and detest him thoroughly as he worked ceaselessly to take over their vast continental lands. And he was largely successful.

As though asserting his traditional right to pleasure, William II of Sicily this year dedicated the fourth and last of the luxurious Palermitan royal residences—La Cuba (*see page* 413). It is hard to imagine a more humiliating comedown for a once glorious building than that which has befallen La Cuba; it now stands incongruously surrounded by a modern army base instead of its former lake, with not a flower in sight, not a drop of water, and not a note of music sounding (unless one wants to consider reveille, taps and other martial instrumental pronouncements as music—or even a marching band which on occasion feels the need to strut past, elaborately costumed with the flair that only Italians among modern peoples seem to muster). Sad the palace may be, but La Cuba shows not a sign of dejection. As imperious as a prima donna, defrocked of floral garb, a magnificent centre-piece to a drab piazza given over to parking and parading, it still stands gently proud. Rotting of an internal cancer it may be, but it needs no external cosmetic work to assert its innate beauty, unless one wants to erase the painted goalposts on the wall. The interior is not generally viewable, there is so little of it. But no matter; perhaps we are more fortunate for seeing only the face and figure, barely wrinkled and only slightly bulging, still reflecting the glory of its role as architectural courtesan to a slowly crumbling empire. La Cuba, along with its three sisters—Menani, Favara and Zisa—was a final assertion of grandeur, a last-act *coloratura* aria bearing little resemblance to 'a very goodly pavilion' where Gianni di Procida was discovered with his lady, mistress of the king, in Boccaccio's tale. Discovered in a bedroom of La Cuba and condemned by the king to be burned at the stake, they are finally pardoned for having 'done this sin, if that can be called sin which young people do for love'.[364]

In its day La Cuba was opulent, shimmering splendidly amidst the surrounding lake. It was also a catalyst, encouraging the kind of life that bred an inability to meet crisis, a love of inaction for its own sake—decay. Yet everything about it leads us 'to suppose that the magniloquent terms of the inscription round the top of the building, bidding the wayfarer "pause and admire the illustrious . . . dwelling of the most illustrious king of the Earth, William the Second," . . . are not a mere poetic exaggeration . . .'[365]

1181

Pope Alexander III who, on account of the continued hostility of the Senate, had again left Rome, died in Civita Castellana. Though he had ruled for nearly twenty-two years under debilitating hardships and humiliations, his reign was a distinguished one, one of the most noteworthy in the entire history of the papacy. Even in advanced age he was fearless in opposing royalty if he thought it was warranted, his attitude towards Henry II after Becket's death being a case in point. Throughout his tenure he was determined to hold off secular encroachments on the Church, and even finally humbled Barbarossa himself. He accepted triumph with magnanimity, never lowering himself to trumpeting his victories in vainglorious puffery. Yet when his body was brought back to Rome for burial the procession was marked by violence and very literal mud-slinging. Even in death his Roman enemies were bestially antagonistic.

Alexander was succeeded by Ubaldo Allucingoli, who took the name Lucius III, but because of his age—he was already in his eighties—he was destined for a short reign of scarcely more than four years.

Hamelin Plantagenet, half-brother of Henry II, is generally considered more or less responsible for Conisbrough Castle as we now know it; he held it from 1163 to 1202. It must have been around about this year that Hamelin was rebuilding the castle in stone, replacing the wooden fortress that had been erected by William de Warenne who, it will be recalled, was also responsible for the castle at Lewes and the abbey at Castle Acre. The name Conisbrough may be derived from the Anglo-Saxon Cyningesburh—king's burh (king's fortification)—which would indicate that there was a royal fortress and subsequent settlement here even before William de Warenne received the land from William the Conqueror.

Approached over a drawbridge and through a ruined gateway, Conisbrough sits atop a scarped natural hill, and was enclosed by a curtain wall thirty-five feet high, from which on the south side projected half-round towers; they were not needed on the north wall because of the lie of the land. The wall is splayed at base for strength and to allow rocks and other missiles dropped by the defenders to bounce out towards the hapless attackers.

Conisbrough Castle, England

Hamelin Plantagenet's 'rude yet stately building'[366] carries the evolution of castle design one step beyond Orford which was circular inside and polygonal outside. Conisbrough's keep is round both inside and out, allowing neither easy edges for an assailant's pick nor flat areas for trebuchets or battering-rams. Its wall is fifteen feet thick and splayed at base and has—perhaps as a denial of total commitment to the new cylindrical form—six wedge-shaped tower-buttresses protruding from it like cogs on a wheel. At first glance they seem to serve no purpose other than that of buttresses; but they are hollow at the top, and terminate in turrets communicating with the interior of the keep itself. A small chapel nestles within one of them. Inside the keep proper there are the usual halls and living cubicles, fireplaces, and in the centre of the first floor a singular hole that leads to the basement, providing the only access to that lower level. A curving staircase rises through the cylindrical outer wall, gently curved because of the circumference of the building, and elegant when compared with other castle staircases. By most standards Conisbrough is simple; but it has about it an inherent majesty, a dramatic impact as it rises so deliberately from its horizontal bailey. Dark and dreadful, yes; but stately too. It smacks of events larger than life, beyond reality, events of hazy other worlds.

1182

In the years following the 1174 agreements reached at Montlouis Henry was in the enviable position of having total control over his family, a thoroughly cowed baronage, and a newly established, albeit temporary, friendship with France. Now was his chance to allow his expansive vision free rein. Restlessly moving back and forth across his domain, he scrutinized every governmental detail, studied each new development, destroyed and created, changed tax laws, and initiated more equitable justice for all his subjects. In a day when few men travelled—and then mostly lords and members of the court—and when the arteries of communication were barely more than rough tracks or the unrepaired remains of Roman roads, his movements were constant, often unexpected, and always exasperating for his followers. Enemies were made, of course; but Henry, in every way having the whiphand, and confident as only true power affords, could take care of them.

This was a make-or-break year for Duke Richard, his fortunes now very much on the upswing. At this time his vassals in Aquitaine, habitually occupied in local antagonistic feuds against each other, for once became finally united by their common enmity for him. Loyal to his fiery son, the ageing king moved south, and the two of them together captured Perigueux, the defensive walls of which they immediately razed. It was here that Richard gained his infamous but exaggerated reputation for personal cruelty, oppressiveness and unrelenting violence. He was accused by chronicler Roger of Hoveden of satiating his lusts on the wives and daughters of his subjects, and then handing them over to his soldiers. But Roger's accusations scarcely ring true, standing as they do in stark contrast to the usual (and probably equally exaggerated) picture of Richard as a confirmed and active homosexual.

Trouble was brewing for England's royal family, mainly from a source long anticipated: from one of its own members—the jealous, ennui-ridden, pleasure-seeking, charming young King Henry. All of Henry II's sons, his daughter Matilda and her husband Duke Henry of Saxony, were gathered at the old Norman stronghold of Caen for a Christmas court which, with an attendance of more than a thousand knights, was declared the most splendid ever convened in Normandy. It was a glamorous occasion, and one meant to demonstrate family solidarity (apart from the absence of the queen) to the world, and especially to Philip Augustus. Present among the powerful barons and petty nobles, the bishops, knights, justiciars, princes and troubadours, was middle-aged, war-loving Bertran de Born, viscount of Hautefort in Perigord, now entering the scene as an intimate of the royal family.

Bertran arrived in Caen in the company of Richard, who had no misconceptions of the troubadour-knight's intentions. He knew that Bertran preferred the young king's company to his own, and that the troubadour still bore a grudge just beneath the surface of his winning smile because of his, Richard's, attack on Hautefort Castle in years past, an unsuccessful effort to restore ownership of that contested property to Bertran's rival, his brother Constantin. Because he had abandoned the struggle in a sudden about-face, Bertran had dubbed Richard with the caustic nickname Richard Yea-and-Nay. Richard further knew that Bertran thought of war as a most desirable state:

> Peace does not comfort me,
> I am in accord with war,
> Nor do I hold or believe
> Any other religion.[367]

For this reason Bertran longed to provoke hostilities among Henry's sons. He let the cat out of the bag regarding a castle Richard was building at Clairvaux in preparation for anticipated trouble from his elder brother in his mischievous song:

Between Poitiers and l'Ile-Bouchard and Mirebeau and Loudon and Chinon, someone has dared to build a fair castle at Clairvaux, in the midst of the plain. I should not wish the Young King to know about it or see it, for he would not find it to his liking; but I fear, so white is the stone, that he cannot fail to see it from Mathefelon.[368]

1183

Bertran's melodic stirrings succeeded only too well, though they were probably not so directly the cause of the troubles that beset Henry II as some chroniclers, and even Dante Alighieri himself, would have us believe. Henry's sons must be held responsible for their actions, including the third, Geoffrey of Brittany, dubbed by Roger of Hoveden 'that son of perdition'.[369] By January of this year the family fabric was so hopelessly torn—not that it was ever in a good state of repair—that even Henry himself, often blind to his sons' infidelities, had to face the fact that fratricidal (and even patricidal) war was in the offing. Each of the brothers was so unrelentingly jealous of the others, and jointly so resentful of their father's unwillingness to hand over authority to his quarrelsome brood, that they could not bring themselves to fight for the common good. And all of this in the face of the oath of loyalty that the three of them had sworn to the old king's cause! It was reason enough for Bertran to crow:

. . . It pleaseth me when the scouts set in flight the folk with their goods;
And it pleaseth me when I see coming together after
    them an host of armed men.
And it pleaseth me to the heart when I see strong castles beseiged,
And barriers broken and riven, and I see the host on the
    shore all about shut in with ditches,
And closed in with lisses of strong piles.[370]

The young king had gone south ostensibly as his father's deputy to bring peace between Richard and his disgruntled barons. With his typical father's blindness to his son's perfidy, Henry did not realize—or refused to admit—that the young king would immediately enter into an alliance with Richard's enemies. Henry followed south soon after the young king. As he approached the city of Limoges he was actually assaulted by a shower of arrows from his eldest son's barricades, one of them even piercing his mantle. Feeble explanations were made; it seems inconceivable that Henry believed them, but he did—or so he said. Ultimately he and Richard joined forces against the young king and Geoffrey, which in itself was enough to ensure victory. The revolt was not sufficiently deep-rooted to succeed, and it finally faded away altogether with the unexpected death of the young king.

Chapter Twenty-one

What avail me all my kingdoms? Weary am I now and old;
Those fair sons I have begotten long to see me dead and cold . . .

Thackeray, *King Canute*

1183

Though probably less diabolical than some historians make him, Bertran de Born did insinuate himself into Plantagenet family intrigues sufficiently to earn himself consignment to Dante's *Inferno*. Through marriage both he and his brother Constantin claimed the castle of Hautefort, Constantin with the stronger claim since he had married the daughter of the owner; Bertran had married only the sister. Eventually Bertran became sole lord after driving out his younger brother. There is precious little of Bertran's fortress left at Hautefort. The tourist must look closely to find even traces, the most obvious being a fragment of a Romanesque column with alternating diamond and circle patterns embedded in a seventeenth-century wall of the present château.

Bertran may have been with the young Henry in at least part of the latter's rampage through Southern France, the country of Nature's richest palette. This was the land that the spoiled young king, temperamentally unfit for the role life had thrust upon him, was terrorizing, apparently to the glee of his troubadour follower. True to form it was not long before Henry ran out of money. He headed for the nearest major shrine—Rocamadour—that could profitably be plundered, despite the fact that just two years before its monks had been obliged to pawn their precious tapestries to money-lenders, having sunk so deeply into debt in their effort to care for the excessive number of pilgrims. Henry II himself had visited the shrine in 1170.

Popular but improbable legend says that Saint Amadour was the first French hermit. Tradition tells us that he was especially devoted to the Virgin Mary, and the church of Notre Dame houses a wooden figure of the Madonna reputedly by the saint's own hand. For his retreat Amadour chose an awesome place (*see page* 414), a deep ravine carved by the River Alzou, walled on either side by steep cliffs. On the one side buildings have been stacked almost vertically one above the other, reached only by long, tiring flights of steps. Even the sanctuaries are stacked, with the subterranean church of Saint Amadour (1166) extending beneath the church of Saint Sauveur. The most moving sanctuary is the little chapel of Saint Michael, always so dear to the hearts of the Normans, which is half natural grotto and half man-made. There is a sweet Romanesque fresco of God the Father and His angels in the tiny apse. Young Henry may have come here to spite his father and to steal the wealth of the revered shrine—it was his crowning act of sacrilege and disrespect, for it is said he stole even the precious sword of the Frankish hero Roland—but one stands in awe of such dedication to spite that could move a whole army through a ravine landscape of almost surrealistic quality.

When the young Henry fell sick a few days later, popular judgement inevitably deemed that it was God's punishment for his systematic looting of the sacred shrine of Rocamadour, although Henry II may have had other ideas. He understood that looting was simply a natural remedy for the chronic need of money to continue the fight. As for the campaign itself, it probably did not even suggest to Henry any absence of love on the part of his son. When told, in a popular modern play that 'None of [your sons] has any love for you', Henry responds: 'Because we fight? Tell me they all three want the crown, and I'll tell you it's a feeble prince that doesn't. They may snap at me or plot and that makes them the kind of sons I want. I've snapped and plotted all my life: there is no other way to be a king, alive and fifty all at once'.[371]

By the time young Henry reached Martel he sensed that his sickness was more than a routine summer fever, that he was going to die. There filled his mind then all the guilts, forebodings, regrets and fears of his life, and a desire to wipe the slate clean. Since he had vowed once to go on crusade, he charged a friend to take his crusader's cloak to Jerusalem and place it on the Holy Sepulchre—certainly the easy way out. He sent word to his father that he was dying and pleaded with him to come to his bed so that he could personally ask his forgiveness. Henry, suspecting a trick, refused, and young Henry sent another messenger begging the king to have mercy on his followers and on his mother, the queen. He requested that he be buried in Rouen. Then, lying on a bed of ashes and with stones at his head and feet, a sign of true repentance, he died on June 11. Some said that this was his finest hour, that nothing he had ever done in life became him as much as dying. At any rate Bertran de Born wrote one of his most profoundly felt works in lament.

By nature Henry II was not a demonstrative man; but he had felt for the young king a degree of love beyond any he was able to give to others. He was inconsolable, despite the fact that the young man was utterly treacherous and unworthy of his father's devotion. For a time Henry tended to brood, without interest in affairs of state. His temper, normally short-fused, was now all but instantaneous. If there was any comfort at all for Henry it rested in the fact that the revolt against his authority in Aquitaine was over, and that the long-term hopes of the French to compensate for their loss of Aquitaine and Poitou (by Eleanor's marriage to Henry) with the marriage of Princess Margaret to the heir of the English throne had come crashing down in ruins.

A desolated king and a grief-stricken father, Henry followed the cortège of his eldest son to Rouen. With the funeral over, he received son Geoffrey at Angers, where peace was made between them. Only Bertran de Born remained to be dealt with. Hardly was the young king buried before Henry, accompanied by Richard, marched his troops south to take Bertran's Hautefort Castle. The defenders were put at a disadvantage when Henry resorted to using a *malvoisin*—'bad neighbour'—in his attack, a wooden tower which rose higher than the castle walls. Bertran surrendered and was summoned before the king who, grief-stricken and obviously failing, then forgave him.

Later in life Bertran became a Cistercian monk at the abbey of Dalon, near Hautefort. His name is mentioned now and then in the cartulary and then, in 1215, we find the entry: 'Eight candles were placed in the sepulchre of Bernardo de Born: the wax cost three soldi'.[372]

Henry might be able to forgive; but not Dante! On his guided tour through hell he comes on Bertran who because 'he separated father from son . . . carries his head separated from his body, holding it with one hand by the hair, and swinging it as if it were a lantern to light his dark and endless way. The image of Bertrand raising his head at arm's length in order that it might speak more clearly . . . is one of the most memorable in the *Inferno*.[373]

> . . . I am Bertrand de Born, and it was I
> who set the young king on to mutiny,
>
> son against father, father against son
> as Achitophel set Absalom and David;
> and since I parted those who should be one
>
> in duty and in love, I bear my brain
> divided from its source within this trunk . . .[374]

1184

Monreale Cathedral was the last great Hauteville triumph in Sicily, political or otherwise. But the marvels of that great edifice did nothing to mitigate the sudden turn towards disaster that was now in store for this time-abused island. And it came from a most unexpected source: from the fair, culturally atuned, much beloved King William II himself. But Frederick Barbarossa played a part too. Temporarily weakened after the Treaty of Venice, Frederick soon recouped his losses. This year, with unbounding confidence, he sent ambassadors to Palermo to propose a marriage between his nineteen-year-old son Henry (his designated successor, already crowned king of Germany) and Princess Constance of Sicily, eleven years his senior. Constance was the posthumous daughter of King Roger II and therefore aunt, though a year younger, to William II. She is alleged to have been a beautiful woman, with the blonde hair of her northern ancestors, and a nun, wrested from her convent retreat to fulfil her role as political pawn. Dante accepts this hearsay when she is pointed out to him in Paradise as one who was forced in life to give up her nun's vows to serve the political interests of her family.

Since William had no children by his English Queen Joanna, Constance stood as heiress-presumptive of the kingdom of Sicily. And though Joanna was still only eighteen years old, Barbarossa must surely have been aware that, in the event of William having no heir and Constance succeeding him, if she had become his daughter-in-law he would have accomplished by marriage what emperors of both East and West had been dreaming of accomplishing for generations—the incorporation of the whole of Southern Italy and Sicily into the imperial realm. No one knows what really possessed William to respond as he did to Frederick's proposal; it was not as though he were not free to find another, less dangerous, husband for Constance. But in the summer he announced his accord with the imperial desire, horrifying a majority of his advisors and subjects, and as it turned out sealing the fate of his kingdom.

Perhaps he was planning to attack Byzantium and needed an alliance that would safeguard his kingdom from a flank attack. Walter of the Mill was one counsellor who gave his stamp of approval, though why is anybody's guess.

Duke Richard of Aquitaine was already at odds with his father again. And once again it was on account of territory. Since Richard was, after all, now the future king of England, Henry wanted him to turn Aquitaine over to his youngest brother John, who was still lacking any extensive land he could call his own. Richard knew his father well, anticipating that he could not tolerate any threat to his authority, least of all from a young man champing at the bit to assume what he considered his rightful place on the throne. It was clear to Richard that Henry now had in mind for him the role of the landless vagrancy that had been forced on his elder brother.

On Richard's flat refusal to hand over Aquitaine, John declared his right to take it by force, encouraged by that ever-ready instigator of trouble, Geoffrey. The two declared war against their elder brother—with Henry's acknowledged approval. A temporary lull in hostilties was established when Henry summoned all three sons to England for an uneasy reconciliation at Westminster and at Windsor. It looked as if Henry had perhaps changed his plans. Richard was allowed to return to Aquitaine, arrangements were made for John to go to Ireland, of which he had been nominal 'lord' since 1177, and Geoffrey was sent as 'custodian' of Normandy. This last decision constituted a clear warning to Richard to watch his step.

1185

It was this year that Heraclius, Latin patriarch of Jerusalem, came to England to appeal for help against the Muslims in Outremer. Things were looking very dark there. King Baldwin IV was dying of leprosy, his nephew and heir-apparent was only a child, and rival factions were jockeying to control the inevitable regency. A decisive iron fist was needed now to stand against the new Muslim star and saviour, Saladin, whose destiny it was to live at a time when new enthusiasm for unity was sweeping the Muslim world. The Latin principalities in Outremer had managed to survive because they had hitherto faced only divided Muslim powers. But all that was changing.

The patriarch offered Henry the keys of Jerusalem, the Tower of David and the Holy Sepulchre, and, most tempting of all, the throne of Jerusalem. But the timing of Heraclius' visit was bad. By the time Henry called a meeting of his vassals at Clerkenwell to discuss the patriarch's offer, his sons Richard and Geoffrey were already at war with one another yet again. No wonder the barons advised Henry not to leave the realm lest in his absence it dissolve into chaos. Henry heeded their advice, refusing to abdicate his throne for a distant and more insecure substitute. On the other hand, he promised to send men and money, an offer which the plain-spoken Heraclius rejected as useless, saying that what he sought was a prince.

While in London Heraclius was called upon to consecrate two churches, both of them built by orders of knights who, in their own disparate ways, were active in Outremer. The Knights Hospitallers of Saint John of Jerusalem had chosen Clerkenwell, a district on the north side of the city of London, as the site of their priory—'the well of the clerks', so called 'for thither once a year the parish clerks of London . . . used to gather and perform a series of those dull entertainments, so much beloved of our forefathers, the miracle and mystery plays'.[375] Grand Prior Garnier de Nablus no doubt welcomed Heraclius to his thirteen-acre priory at Clerkenwell, knowing that the patriarch was going to dedicate a church for the rival Knights Templar (if he had not done so already), a circular church like the Hospitallers', built in imitation of the Church of the Holy Sepulchre in Jerusalem. It was important for the Knights of Saint John to hold their heads up in the face of such competition, because to 'the folk of London, the great round churches of the Hospitallers and Templars provided an opportunity to worship at the gates of Jerusalem without leaving London. But they were also reminders, symbols of the earthly Jerusalem; to put the matter bluntly, they advertised the pilgrimage and the crusade'. [376]

From the circular nave of Garnier's church a short choir extended east-wards, underlaid by the crypt. The upper level buildings were destroyed by Wat Tyler's Peasants' Revolt in 1381, during which animosities became so heated that the prior was beheaded in St John's Square. The church was replaced by a rectangular building under the auspices of Prior Thomas Docwra who, raising his priory from the rubble of the revolt, became its most ambitious and active beautifier. Following the dissolution of the monasteries utilitarian-minded Henry VIII used the buildings as storehouses. He intended the property to go to his daughter Mary Tudor, but before she could get her hands on it the stone of its making was purloined for the con-struction of a Thames-side house for the duke of Somerset, uncle of her brother Edward VI, on the site where now stands the sprawling Somerset House. It is said that much of St John's Priory was metamorphosed into the Somerset House by designer Sir William Chambers, also renowned for his part in the layout of the Kew Gardens and for the design of the landmark pagoda there.

The main entrance of Sir Thomas Docwra's priory was the southern gateway, made of red brick with Kentish ragstone and today still exhi-biting his coat of arms. The gatehouse has served many functions through the centuries, housing the offices of Queen Elizabeth I's Master of Revels and serving, in the eighteenth century, as

St John's Gate, London

Crypt, St John's Priory, London

office and shop for bookseller Edward Cave (Sylvanus Urban) and his *Gentleman's Quarterly*'. It was therefore well known to the *Gentleman's* most celebrated contributor, Samuel Johnson. James Boswell tells of Johnson's coming to Clerkenwell for the first time: 'He [Johnson] told me, that when he first saw St. Johns's Gate . . . he "beheld it with reverence" '.[377] It was at St John's Gate that David Garrick is said to have given his first performance, an improvised *Mock Doctor*, an English translation from Molière by Henry Fielding. Then, too, it was allegedly frequented by William Hogarth when it catered to baser tastes as the Old Jerusalem Tavern. Henry II's son, King John, lived here for a month in 1212, and in 1265 Prince Edward and his wife Eleanor of Castile were entertained on the premises. In 1485 Richard III created a scene in the great hall when he denied allegations that he intended to marry his niece.

The finest part of what is left of the Priory of the Order of St John, though, is the crypt. Huddled under low arches below ground level, its ancient stones seem to glow with an inner light; secretive and at the same time inviting, it remains proudly unscathed after the trials of the centuries, including the London blitz during World War II. Its three western bays are pure Norman, complete with identifying masons' marks; the two eastern are of the Transitional style. There is an almoner chapel on the south side; two chapels on the north are used, alas, as a vestry. Descending into the silent crypt one steps into an age of more determinedly stringent faith and worship. Because the slit windows are below ground-level, not much light finds its way into the sombre interior. But it is no matter. It seems an ideal place for quiet meditation beyond the traffic-congested Clerkenwell Road which, having been driven right through the property in 1878, now separates the crypt from the gatehouse. Insulated by the centuries from the hectic modern rush, St John's crypt has turned in on itself and its memories of heroes and grateful pilgrims.

And well it should reflect the glory of the order. As the Christian position in the Holy Land weakened in the thirteenth century, the knights were forced from Krak des Chevaliers to Acre, to Cyprus, to Rhodes, and finally to Malta where they established full territorial sovereignty. It was at rock-bound Malta that they experienced what was perhaps their finest hour by emerging victorious from the Great Siege in 1565, destroying once and for all Turkish Sultan Suleiman the Great's bid for power in the western Mediterranean.

Since losing Malta to Napoleon in 1798, members of the order have devoted themselves to humanitarian works, their most noteworthy being the establishment of the St John Ophthalmic Hospital in Jerusalem, set up in 1882 to combat the eye diseases endemic to the Middle East, and the St John's Ambulance Corps, thereby perpetuating their tradition when

> . . . from the gate of Clerkenwell
> St. John's good knights would ride,
> To fight against the infidel
> And bend the paynim's pride . . .[378]

Patriarch Heraclius also consecrated the New Temple Church in London. Introduced into England by Henry I, the Knights Templar had settled in Holborn near the north end of Chancery Lane. Such was their rapid growth, appeal and strength that it was not long before they needed a larger head-quarters and chose a site closer to the Thames. By the year of Heraclius' visit the order was rich, strong, arrogant and devout, the very embodiment of a romantic union of monk and soldier, and just then conveniently putting the finishing touches on its fine new church, called to this day the Temple. Their wealth was already legendary. Henry II, a man not given to ready admiration of others, was 'impressed by the skill of the Templars in handling money and keeping it safe. He made the London Temple one of his principal treasure-houses: and it passes the wit of man to decide where in the Templar movement treasure on earth ended and treasure in heaven began'.[379]

On entering directly into the Temple through a Norman Romanesque archway, one is struck by the obvious lightening of heavy Romanesque architecture that was taking place in the middle of the twelfth century as a process of transition to the Gothic style. The clerestory and aisle windows are round-arched, earthbound; the arches of the main arcade are heaven-reaching, pointed, and supported by Purbeck marble columns slender enough to presage the coming Gothic. These great columns are new, the originals (Perhaps been the earliest examples of Purbeck marble used on a grand scale) having been split by the heat generated when the flaming roof crashed to the floor during the London blitz on the night of 10 May 1941. The arcading of the triforium is composed of interlaced, semi-circular arches which, in their turn, form pointed arches, a happy combination of Romanesque and Gothic. Around the aisle walls, in a sort of chapter-house setting of stone benches, is an arcade of blind pointed arches supported by free-standing columns. Between the columns, each with its own individually designed capital, are a series of Gothic heads, marvellously grotesque, some ugly and misshapen, others aggressively hostile and threatening, 'traditionally . . . said to represent souls in heaven and souls in hell; they all seem to be at least in purgatory'.[380]

When first built, the round church had a small chancel attached to it, replaced in the thirteenth century by a spacious new choir in the Gothic style which was consecrated in the presence of Henry III in 1240. The choir is a 'hall church', that is, with three aisles, all rising to the same height, though it is not so spectacular an example as Bristol Cathedral. In the northwest corner of the choir two slit windows look into it from the 'penitential cell' wherein 'were confined Knights who disobeyed the Master or broke the Rule of the Temple; Walter le Bacheler, Grand Preceptor of Ireland, is said to have starved to death in this grim chamber less than five feet long'.[381]

The most interesting part of the Temple is the round church (*see page* 414) with its four effigies, resembling grave markers, on the floor. William Marshal, earl of Pembroke, who was 'governor' of the kingdom early in the minority of Henry III, is represented by one, and two of his sons, William and Gilbert, by others. Some of the figures have crossed legs which, according to many historians, indicates that they took part in at least one crusade to Outremer. The effigy of William Marshal may very well date from the thirteenth century; he is known to have been buried before the high altar with pomp befitting his status when he died in 1219.

Having bid Heraclius *bon voyage*, Henry II returned to matters closer to home. He gathered an army in Normandy, brought Eleanor to his side in a supposed display of unanimity, and then sent word to Richard that he would invade Aquitaine unless he, Richard, ceded his holdings back to his mother from whom he had received them. Aware that he was his mother's favourite, Richard found this ultimatum not disagreeable. Henry's trump card deprived Richard of his land and brought him back to his father's court; but it was also a triumph for Richard in that it rehabilitated his mother to all her rights, at least in name. And that could mean only that his rights as future duke were reassured. His security was increased by an agreement Henry made with King Philip II at Gisors the following spring. The Vexin, which Henry had acquired as dowry of the young Henry's wife Margaret, was allocated as dowry of Princess Alice, who was now betrothed to Richard, an agreement politically significant in that it confirmed Richard as heir apparent. As for Alice, that poor lady had years ahead of her yet as a veritable political prisoner. Geoffrey, too, had no illusions about the significance of the agreement. In a mood he traipsed off to Philip's court in Paris where he could conspire to his heart's content with an avowed enemy of his family and perhaps recoup his inheritance.

When Ibn Jubayr visited Trapani on the extreme western coast of Sicily in 1185, preparatory for sailing home to Spain on the last leg of his epic grand tour through the Mediterranean, he tells of being prevented from leaving:

Having agreed on the price of our passage in the ship going . . . to Spain, we turned our minds to provisions for the journey. But . . . there arrived an order from the King of Sicily stopping all ships from sailing from the shores of his island. It seems that he is preparing a fleet, and no ships may sail until the fleet has left . . .

The people of Trapani are making conjectures as to the destination of the fleet this tyrant is preparing . . . Some men say its destination is Alexandria . . . while yet others say Africa . . .

There are others who see the levy as intended solely for Constantinople the Great, because of the momentous news which has come concerning it; news which inspires the soul with bodings of strange events . . .[382]

Ibn Jubayr was correct on his last speculation. In one of those ill-advised political moves that William II seemed so persistently bent on making, he mounted a military campaign against the Byzantine Empire, no doubt dreaming the dreams of Robert Guiscard, Bohemund and Great Count Roger—the conquest of that sad last vestige of the ancient Roman Empire. It was a propitious moment for attack; life in the Constantinople of Andronicus Comnenus, who had usurped power in 1180, was certainly not ennobling. Atrocities were the order of the day, and once again the people were crying for relief. And there was now a new pretender to the throne, a nephew of the late Manuel Comnenus, who had appeared in Sicily and was acting as an instigator of invasion. William's fleet, commanded once again by his cousin Tancred of Lecce, comprised two hundred to three hundred vessels which carried an army calculated at eighty thousand men, including five thousand kinghts and a detachment of mounted archers. At first successful, the Normans took Durazzo and Thessaloniki, amid scenes of carnage and pillage—not to mention church desecration—unmatched even in Norman history. The Byzantine Empire, however, was saved by revolution, touched off by Andronicus' cousin, Isaac Angelus, a descendant in the female line from Alexius I. With the revolution a success, a new spirit of resistance against the Norman intruders was born, ending in a humiliating withdrawal of the tattered Sicilian army, and the evaporation of dreams of a Siculo-Byzantine empire.

For all of his distractions in the East, William of Sicily put his best foot forward as far as the projected marriage of his Aunt Constance to young Henry of Hohenstaufen was concerned. Acting as her personal escort, he accompanied her to Salerno, thence to Rieti, where she was turned over to the imperial emissaries. Then, followed by a train of hundreds of pack animals bearing her dowry, appropriately lavish as befitted a future empress and probably the wealthiest heiress of the Western world, she was conducted to Milan, the designated place of the wedding. There, in the dark and cool—no, frigid—church of Sant'Ambrogio, hastily refurbished after being used as a granary, Constance of Sicily was married to Henry of Hohenstaufen. The unthinkable, the fatal mistake, had been made! Should anything happen to William II before he could produce an heir of his own then the dreaded legal claim could be made on the Sicilian throne by the German imperial house.

1186

For the moment the greatest loser was Pope Urban III. (Pope Lucius had died barely two months before.) As former archbishop of Milan, always the leading Lombard city barking at the heels of the emperor, Urban was unrelenting in his enmity for the Germans. For any pope the greatest nightmare imaginable was an alliance between the two great powers that lay north and south of the papal states. Furthermore, since the future imperial couple were married by the patriarch of Aquiléia, and since Urban had not yet surrendered his see, he regarded the marriage as a pointed affront to his authority. Then, adding insult to injury, the same patriarch of Aquiléia immediately crowned the newly-weds with the iron crown of Lombardy, strengthening the hereditary principle in the imperial succession, and usurping another traditional prerogative of the archbishop of Milan. Clearly papal-imperial relations, improved so startlingly by the Treaty of Venice ten years before, were set in reverse. The patriarch of Aquiléia was excommunicated. Frederick Barbarossa returned to Germany, leaving Italy in the hands of his son Henry, an unprincipled man committed to violence and to having his own way. It would seem that, to save the situation from a total reversion to unrelenting animosities, it would take divine intervention; which may have been precisely what happened the following year.

Truces and meetings between the kings of France and England aside, war was never far beyond the horizon, especially between two such headstrong rulers, and despite the difference of years between them. And peace was not served by the sudden death of Geoffrey while he was still plotting at Philip's court, carried off by a fever or as a result of a tournament accident. Notwithstanding that Philip, 'in a frenzied display of grief was scarcely restrained from leaping into the tomb of his bosom friend, who was buried with circumstance in Notre Dame',[383] he, as overlord, claimed the guardianship of Geoffrey's two daughters, threatening to invade Normandy if Henry did not give them up. It was a good political bludgeon, and both men knew it. They cautiously agreed to a truce until early the following year, thus giving each of them time to plan—and to prepare for all-out war.

1187

Saladin was on the march. Encouraged by weak leadership of the Christian forces occupying the Holy Land under Guy of Lusignan—a man utterly without capacity for kingship—Saladin struck. (Baldwin IV, the 'leper king', had died as expected in 1185, and his child heir the following year.) On 4 July the Muslims shattered the Christian armies in the Battle of Hattin. By 2 October they were in Jerusalem. The news of the fall of the most sacred of Christian cities caused the aged Pope Urban III to die of shock—and just when he was about to excommunicate the German emperor, too! But new Pope Gregory VIII had no time for power games between Aachen and Rome. What with Tiberias, Acre, Nablus, Jaffa, Sidon and Beirut falling to the Saracens in that order, a new crusade was obviously called for. It was of no importance to the West that Saladin, without a hint of vindictiveness, proved himself a magnanimous conqueror, in stark contrast to the barbarous slaughter that had taken place in Jerusalem when the Christians took it in 1099 as part of the First Crusade. Saladin's conquest of Jerusalem ultimately of course led to the Third Crusade; but it had to be held in abeyance for a time, at least until Henry II put his house in order and Philip of France was more comfortable on his throne. With only Tyre remaining in Christian hands, Gregory VIII was insistent that the monarchs of Europe rally to the defence of the Holy Land. Apparently the strain of it all was too much for him; he died within eight weeks of becoming pope, and was immediately succeeded by Clement III, who carried on the exhortations.

Richard had taken the Cross in November; his father and King Philip Augustus followed his example in January 1188. Barbarossa also acknowledged his duty. But for the time being only William II, after establishing peace with Byzantine Emperor Isaac Angelus, acted. Pious though he was known to be, it would be unrealistic to think that religious fervour alone sparked him to dispatch his admiral, Margaritus—the last great admiral of Norman Sicily—to the Holy Land, where he remained until 1189 as virtually the only representative of Christian opposition. For two years he was a supreme irritant, a buzzing gadfly who came closer than anyone to causing Saladin to lose his cool. With only sixty ships in his command, he served as an inaccurate reminder that the Europeans were still determined to preserve their Christian interests. But in the end Margaritus' dedicated show was mostly bluster, finally cut short by events entirely outside his theatre of activity.

With the tenuous peace established between Henry and his eldest surviving son, and once Aquitaine had been turned back to Eleanor's nominal possession, Richard began to frequent the court of Paris, much against his father's will. 'And the king of France held him in such high esteem, that every day they ate at the same table and from the same dish, and at night had not separate chambers. In consequence of this strong attachment which seemed to have risen between them, the king of England was struck with great astonishment, and wondered what it could mean . . .'[384] One would think so!

As though mirroring the growing tragedy of Henry's life, it was a sorry day in England when, visible over a good part of Sussex, the sky above Chichester glowed with a flickering, bloody red arc, animated by torrents of sparks and burning embers that soared heavenwards like a reverse waterfall of light and heat. It was as though the flames of hell had burst free of their subterranean furnaces and were attacking heaven itself in one last effort to pull the promised kingdom into the infernal abyss. The cause of the flush that scorched the vault of the firmament, a devil-created rival to the aurora borealis, was the burning cathedral of Chichester, its wooden roof a gigantic torch that finally crashed in a rush of angry flames and hissing sparks into the nave below. Since the cathedral had been consecrated only three years before, the destruction of the church was disastrously deflating, not to mention a cause for questioning God's justice. But never mind: the stout-hearted natives set to work, replacing the wooden roof with a graceful stone vaulting to arch the nave that stands today, adding Purbeck marble columns at the triforium level to bear the extra weight. More than ever now they could take pride in their creation of a bit of the heavenly abode on earth.

The earliest extant charter concerning Chichester is one of King Stephen, granting certain rights as they existed in the time of William the Conqueror, though we know there was a Romano-British town on the site, the plan of which is still preserved in the layout of streets. The city from the start was one of commercial importance, as numerous royal charters testify, famous for its corn and fish markets. It did not become a cathedral town until 1075 when the see was moved there from Selsey. A twelfth-century Hospital of St Mary is still in existence and is used as an almshouse, its buildings of the later Transitional style. Other old buildings still stand, including St Olave's Church in which Roman building materials were recycled, and perhaps the finest market cross in England, erected by Bishop Story in 1501 at the junction of the four main streets of the town. A fine length of Roman wall—about a mile and a half—follows the general line of the ancient fortifications.

But it is the cathedral which takes precedence over all else. Its history

> can start almost anywhere in South-West Sussex. Chichester from the Selsey peninsula is like Chartres from the Beauce: no other English cathedral, not even Lincoln, exerts such a continuous presence on the flat surrounding countryside, and it is the continuity which is the important thing; the spire becomes as invariable and natural as the sky and sun. What Chichester has in addition, on any kind of clear day—and there are a lot of clear days in Sussex—is the gently rising backcloth of the South Downs two or three miles away, so that God, man, and nature always seem to be in equilibrium . . . Spire and countryside form an equation or a symbol experienced by millions of people every year, which cannot be given a value purely in terms of landscape or architecture.[385]

And this is true; at least from the outside the spire *is* the most memorable feature of the cathedral, though it is now entirely Victorian. (The former spire collapsed in 1861.) 'What we see now is one of the most successful reconstructions of the period and one that fully preserves the intentions of . . . the original architect'.[386] The church is also noteworthy for its detached bell-tower—a feature unusual in England—in the Perpendicular style.

The keynote of the inside is simplicity; and spaciousness, especially in the wide aisles, really double aisles which were formed by incorporating side chapels into the aisles themselves. In rebuilding the eastern end—the retro-choir—after the disastrous fire of 1187, designer Walter of Coventry utilized the coming Early English Gothic, in a tactful and pleasing marriage of the older Norman style to the new modernity. A charming Lady Chapel terminates the building at that end, typically English in its square bluntness and heavy strength.

But then the whole interior is a happy blending of periods and styles from medieval to modern, with the Norman nave surmounted by its Norman triforium taking pride of place. The extended vista of the nave from west to east (the inside of the church is 393 feet long) presents a startling series of space-creating Norman arches, the eternally durable majesty of huge piers, and the balanced interplay of mass and void. Four different styles are wedded in

Christ arriving at Bethany, Chichester Cathedral, England

435

the church—Norman, Early English Gothic, Decorated and Perpendicular—the very four which were, more than any others, to influence church buildings in England for the next eight hundred years.

At one time the interior was aglow with colour, but now, perhaps to our advantage, it is back to natural stone. Sculpture abounds, including the stalwart Arundel screen separating the nave from the choir, the capitals of columns, the wooden choir-stalls, and, most interesting of all, two Romanesque bas-reliefs which are probably twelfth century, but could be eleventh. Two subjects are depicted: the Arrival of Christ at Bethany, and the Raising of Lazarus. At one time they, too, were brightly coloured, and the figures sported jewels for eyes. The panels are crowded with buildings and trappings of the stories, along with the hordes of followers who seem to accompany Christ in most medieval representations: they are clad in the rhythmically swirling Romanesque lines of drapery and there is not a smiling face among them.

Saint Richard of Chichester, who was bishop in the mid-thirteenth century, was one of the most avid beautifiers of the cathedral. A brilliant academician at Oxford University, and a friend of perhaps the most priggish saint on record, Saint Edmund of Abingdon—how else does one describe a man who, on agreeing to an assignation with a young lady, met her with his university teachers in tow and with their help 'beat the "offending Eve" out of her'?[387]—Saint Richard was consecrated despite the opposition of Henry III. Richard's shrine stands at Chichester behind the high altar. He would be shocked—one hopes pleasantly—by the changes time has wrought in his venerable building, especially through the introduction of twentieth-century arts. Painting is represented by Graham Sutherland (Christ Appearing to Mary Magdalene) and Hans Feibusch (The Baptism of Christ). A tapestry of the Holy Trinity behind the high altar is by John Piper, while cast aluminium furnishings in the chapel of St Mary Magdalene are by Geoffrey Clarke and Robert Potter. Most of the glass in the church is of this century, the most stunning being Marc Chagall's window on the theme of Psalm 150—'Praise ye the Lord . . . Let every thing that hath breath praise the Lord'.

1189

We know practically nothing of the death of William II of Sicily other than the date: 18 November 1189. If we are to believe a picture in the manuscript of Peter of Eboli's poem on Sicilian affairs, he died peacefully in his bed, with doctors and servants around him. Since he was only thirty-six years old we can assume that William's death was unexpected, its most tragic aspect being that he died without an heir—exactly the situation most feared by the opponents of the marriage between his Aunt Constance and Henry of Hohenstaufen. For the Normans in Sicily the show was clearly over; the curtain was descending on their stage of operations with a finality that was unequivocal. William the Good was the last legitimate Hauteville to sit upon the royal throne of the kingdom of Sicily.

Objectively, and despite the fact that he left a kingdom at peace with itself and its neighbours, we must conclude that William had not been a good king, certainly less good than his name suggests. There was more than a bit of the hedonist in him, and a good deal of the voluptuary as he sat enthroned among his orange groves, a descendant of the hoary Vikings but possessing none of their adventurous spirit, costumed in the manner of a Byzantine potentate, a Latin Christian ruling a people part Latin, part Greek, part Muslim, and enjoying the typical Eastern perquisites of a harem and eunuch attendants. If we can believe the rhetoric of the day, he was mourned profoundly, as his father had been. But he must stand accused of awesome misjudgements, among which the marriage of Constance stands as one of the most stunning political blunders of any age or place. One must assume that he knew what he was doing—even before Constance had left 'William exacted from his vassals an oath that they would recognize her as heiress of Sicily, should he himself die without children'.[388] If on their extra-terrestrial planes Robert Guiscard, Great Count Roger and Roger II were apprised of William's decision, it must have indeed dimmed the celestial light. The fusion of diverse peoples and cultures which they had worked so hard to achieve had been weakened, mismanaged, and finally dealt a *coup de grâce*.

No thinking person of the twelfth century could have reason to suppose that the succession would be an easy one, especially with the only legitimate heir to the throne now allied with the German imperial dynasty. The picture of a German planted on the throne of the Hautevilles was calculated to bring a shudder of revulsion to the populace of the southern Norman kingdom. Even that paragon of tolerance Roger II had found the Germans offensive because of their allegedly uncouth ways; and Sicilian children were said to have fled in terror from the sound of their guttural language. Instantly on William's demise opposition parties rose against the designated and legitimate heiress; their growth was to result in the crowning of a new king, Tancred of Lecce, bastard cousin of the recently departed king, the following year. But this gesture to show a semblance of unity was merely that—a gesture, window-trimming. It was not important who was crowned king, or who supported whom: the Norman kingdom of Sicily was doomed.

That Henry of England preferred son John to son Richard is obvious. But it is equally obvious that, believing as he did in inherited rights of succession, which he had spent a good part of his life asserting and defending, he planned to allow Richard his ultimate rights. We must in the end assume that Henry simply could not bring himself to give up his own control. He had fought hard for it; it meant too much to him. But Richard was just as determined to have his inheritance as Henry was determined not to relinquish it. Egged on by Philip of France, who always recognized a good family quarrel to exploit when he saw one, Richard was, by summer, in open warfare with his father, who finally holed up in Le Mans, the city of his birth and where his own father lay in final rest. Pressed by Richard, Henry was forced to abandon his refuge. In doing so, he fired the land behind him—a scorched-earth policy to frustrate Richard's pursuit—but was dismayed to see the flames reversed by the wind until the whole town was ablaze. Unable even then to accept the responsibility for the disastrous result of his stubbornness, he is said to have raised his fist to heaven to swear vengeance on his God.

In all of Henry's family the one who remained loyal to the end was the illegitimate Geoffrey Plantagenet. 'You are my true son', Henry had several times said to him, 'the others are bastards'. Geoffrey was with his father at Le Mans, holding the position of chancellor. Now, in his last days, Henry derived a great satisfaction and comfort from this one loyal son.

With Richard hard on his heels, Henry fled northwards with Geoffrey and William Marshal. But when he had almost reached Alençon, and was thus not far from the comparative safety of Normandy, he suddenly changed his mind and decided to ride due south again, to Chinon, which had become the administrative centre of his continental administration. He dispatched Geoffrey to Alençon to alert his troops there of his change of plan. Against the advice of every man privy to his decision, Henry divested himself of most of his escort to make his way more unobtrusively through the rebel-infested area. All his advisers deplored this new move. But 'the explanation for this extraordinary decision is not hard to divine: Henry had no stomach for a fight, he was weary unto death, and was going home to die'.[389]

Originally a Celtic settlement, then a Roman *castrum*, Chinon (*see page* 447) nestles under a ruined medieval castle perched on a lofty, rocky height. Of Henry's castle only the foundations remain, one of three separate strongholds that comprise the whole. But the largely restored fortress offers a magnificent vista of the River Vienne and the town below, and is redolent with a feeling of medieval history. Joan of Arc first met Charles VII here, while down below in the village, in about 1495, Rabelais was born.

With Philip and Richard overrunning Southern France at their own discretion, Henry was finally forced to consent to a meeting, which was convened on 4 July a few miles southwest of Tours. Arriving from Chinon astride his great mount, Henry was obviously in such a state of physical debility that Philip benevolently offered him a cloak to sit upon. Proud even in his direst moment, Henry disdained the offer, preferring to remain in the saddle, claiming haughtily that he had no desire for conversation, that he merely wanted to be informed what terms they offered; he would agree. Propped up in the saddle by one of his retainers, he then with a stoical face heard a dismaying list of demands; he was to do homage to the king of France for all his continental possessions; he was, henceforth, to be totally in the service of Philip. He was to release Alice and give her into the custody of Richard who, it was agreed, would marry her on his return from the anticipated crusade. Richard was to be acknowledged immediate heir to his father's holdings and to receive fealty from all his father's subjects. Henry was to pay an indemnity of twenty thousand marks. Three castles were to be forfeited. As these flagrantly shaming, even cruel, conditions were read aloud, thunder was heard to rumble through the sultry summer air.

Even after this ultimate humiliation custom would be served, demanding that Henry give his son the kiss of peace. As he leaned forth to accomplish this act he was heard to growl in Richard's ear, 'God grant that I may not die until I have had my revenge on you!' By now he was too feeble even to ride.

Watching as his father was borne off in the direction of Chinon, Richard must have been troubled by contradictory thoughts. He knew that he had won the fight that his elder brother, the young king, had been unable to win. But in truth his father had been broken less by political forces than by the world: his life had at last become too much for him.

At Chinon, attended by neither of his living legitimate sons, Henry waited in his castle for death. He asked for a list of retainers who had betrayed him by going over to Richard. Nearly demented by shame and disappointment and feeling totally abandoned, it was too much for Henry to hear the name of his favourite son John heading the list of traitors. 'Now let all things go as they will', he cried. 'I care no longer for myself or for anything else in the world'.[390] He sank into a delirium, interrupted by moments of lucidity during which he took leave of his faithful retainers. Then, at his request, he was carried into the castle chapel, where he confessed and received his last Communion. Geoffrey Plantagenet did what he could to comfort his father, but even he had to stumble from the room, unable further to bear the anguished and delirious ravings. Henry sent a ring as a memento to one of his sons-in-law, King Alfonso VIII of Castile, and gave his bastard son Geoffrey another ring set with a precious sapphire. Several times in his last agony he cried out, 'Shame, shame on a defeated king!' These were his last words, the thought tormenting him like a demon of death. He died on 6 July. To some his death seemed ignominious, 'but it was the ignominy of an ailing lion savaged by jackals'.[391]

Even before Henry was dead some of his more unprincipled knights had begun to plunder him of all they could, knowing that, in his present straits, there would be little enough to parcel out among them. 'Since the saddest state of the unfortunate man is that he once knew happiness, this also completed the tale of his adversity, that amidst his many treasures, both in England and across the sea, greater by far than was wont, he died a pauper'.[392] They fled then, leaving only a handful of loyal friends.

Servants swooped down on Henry's body, stripping it of anything of even the slightest value. The greatest king of his day was left lying naked on the floor, a coincidence strangely reminiscent of the death of his great-grandfather, William the Conqueror. Finding him there, one of his knights, William Trihan, covered him with his own cloak, pathetically concealing his nakedness barely to his knees. It was recalled then that he had been mocked as a young king coming to England by the nickname 'Curtmantle'. 'A band of tattered gold embroidery as a travesty of a crown'[393] and a sceptre were hastily contrived and placed on the corpse. 'It was difficult to find anyone to wind it in a shroud, to fix the horses in the hearse or to follow the funeral procession with fitting obsequies'.[394] The meagre cortège of his saddened retainers wended its way down to the village from the castle heights, along the bank of the Vienne, and through the gently rolling, wooded Angevin hills to Fontevrault, favourite endowment of his wife Eleanor. There Henry was interred in the basilica as he had requested. He was fifty-six years old.

Richard came to Fontevrault, possibly to be sure that his father was actually dead. As he entered the basilica at Fontevrault, night was falling, and the candles surrounding the bier cast a flickering, perhaps mercifully flattering, soft light on the dead man's face. The nuns of this royally endowed abbey had gathered in the spacious stone church for the Office of the Dead, their chant echoing through the lofty vaults. Richard, now a king wanting only a crown, descended the wide stone stairs at the basilica's western end, and then strode the full length of the nave, his steps a metallic resonance on the stone floor. But the nuns, giving no sign of awareness of his presence, were not to be interrupted. Richard gazed down at his father without so much as a trace of outward emotion. He knelt briefly—'scarcely longer than the space of a Paternoster'.[395] It was claimed that 'blood flowed in streams from the nostrils of the body at the approach of his son'.[396] Everyone knew that when a murderer approached the body of his victim the corpse, by supernatural manifestation, indicated the accursed presence by such a sign. Duke Richard—uncrowned King Richard I—knew it too. But business was at hand, and he stalked out of the abbey to get on with the governing. Henry was buried in the choir at Fontevrault (see page 447).

Henry had lived too long—at least from the point of view of his wife and surviving sons. What we see from the distance of time is a man given to excessive passions, a jealous guardian of his own power, loyal and therefore expecting loyalty, somewhat a ruffian, an extreme extrovert, fonder of his position than of his family. He was a hard man to deal with, a tough opponent; but once having reached agreement he would not normally go back on it. He was stubborn, and certain of the rightness of his own judgement, thus finding it difficult to admit, even to himself, that his family could oppose him; and to Thomas Becket, his former friend, he could exclaim in a moment of utter frustration: 'If you would just do what I want you to do!' Yet he can lay claim to a certain greatness.

> Both as a man and as a ruler, the figure of Henry II has come down to us distorted by the loves and hates of an age of the most violent and bitter controversy. Brilliant though scarcely heroic to his friends, to his enemies he was a veritable demon of tyranny and crime, whose lurid end pointed many a moral respecting the sins of princes and the vengeance of the Most High. Eminently a strong man, he was not regarded as in any sense superhuman, but rather as an intensely human figure, tempted in all points like as other men and yielding where they yielded.[397]

Henry cannot be dismissed without some assessment of his place in history as a ruler. His 'achievements remain . . . Henry pursued his great, wise and successful administration, harassed but not, in the end, seriously disturbed or deflected by his conflicts with the Church or with foes within and without . . . His work did not dissolve when he died, a broken man'.[398] He was 'one of the last of the medieval cosmopolitans' but 'it says much for his realism that he did not envisage the survival of his "empire" intact as a political unit, but tried to refashion it as a dynastic federation'.[399] And for the student of English (and therefore ultimately of British) legal and constitutional history his reign is one of outstanding importance.

So it is with the death of Henry II, with the accession of Richard Lionheart and the sudden liberation of Queen Eleanor that the English part of our story ends—in so far as the island kingdom is concerned, at any rate. It becomes less relevant as a part of a Norman chronicle except as it affects happenings in Norman Sicily. So Richard still has a role to fulfil, though a diminished one. As for Sicily: that unhappy kingdom has but five years to go.

Chapter Twenty-two

The Eagle of the Broken Covenant . . .
will rejoice in her third nesting.

Geoffrey of Monmouth, the 'Prophesies of Merlin'.
The History of the Kings of Britain. Translated by Thorpe

1190

Newly crowned Tancred of Sicily was not destined for a happy reign. Although he was a brave and capable man, there was no way he could have succeeded, no way he could have held back the fall of night on his Sicilian kingdom. There is a propitious time for most rulers. There was no such time for Tancred. One of his problems was that he was insufferably ugly, depicted in both words and pictures as a monkey. 'He was, in the most literal sense of the words, an ugly little bastard, whose enemies never tired of poking fun at his dwarfish figure. He looked, so it was said, like a monkey with a crown on its head'.[400] In his youth he had displayed a traitor's tendencies towards his uncle William I. Since then, however, as commander of William II's fleet, he had more than proved his loyalty to the throne. He was energetic and, when once he set his sights, determined. Also on the credit side for him was the fact that Matthew of Ajello, an old man now and still as actively against the Hohenstaufen union as ever, was on his side. Old Pope Clement III, too, could be counted on to support him, anything being better than having the Papal States totally surrounded by the German Empire. On the other hand, Walter of the Mill supported Constance, and it was only grudgingly that he crowned Tancred; Tancred rewarded Matthew of Ajello for assuring his ascendance by appointing him chancellor of the kingdom.

Opposition to Tancred came at once, mainly from the Muslim sector, revolt that took the better part of a year to subdue. Then the barons of Apulia and Campagna reverted to time-honoured Norman procedures and rose up against their new king, joining forces with the supporters of Henry and Constance. One would think that, with insurrection rampant within the realm, Tancred would have looked without for allies; and one of his surest bets would have been the new king of England, Richard, brother to the widowed Queen Joanna. But no! Tancred seemded as incapable of playing his cards properly as William II had been.

Already Richard was hearing alarming stories of Tancred's refusal to acknowledge Joanna's rightful revenue from Monte Sant'Angelo, which had been agreed to as part of her marriage settlement. Furthermore, Richard was well aware that William II had promised Henry II a legacy of no insignificance—gold plate, a number of ships, a table of gold twelve feet long—which his successor was now refusing to yield up. Well, Richard of England would take care of pretender Tancred of Sicily—even now he was limbering up for his crusade, starting out on a route that would shortly take him to Sicily.

Tympanum at Vézelay, France

Richard had been talking about a new crusade since 1187. He had been encouraged by popes Urban III, Gregory VIII and Clement III, not to mention the exhortations of Patriarch Heraclius of Jerusalem. The late William II of Sicily had three years before sent his man Margaritus to the Holy Land (he was now back home), and Emperor Frederick Barbarossa, not to be upstaged by anyone, had himself left in May 1189, leading 'the largest single force ever yet to leave on a Crusade, . . . well armed and well disciplined'.[401] So Richard had set forth early in the year, tearing his subjects from their loved ones to join him in the heroic adventure. The crusade was already running behind schedule for several reasons, not the least being the death of Isabella of Hainault, Philip of France's queen. Richard toured his domains on the Continent, perhaps at this time becoming secretly betrothed to Berengaria of Navarre, thereby establishing a political link with her father, King Sancho VI. Since Richard was already betrothed to Philip's sister Alice, this posed certain problems. The last Philip had heard was that Richard had expressed his willingness to marry the ill-fated Alice. It was to be some time before the admission could be made that the French princess had been jilted.

Richard and Philip met at Vézelay on 2 July, hymned by a crescendo of crusading pilgrims' voices as they approached the shrine of Ste-Madeleine, the great four-square basilica rising on its height, and with its typanum Christ spreading His enormous hands in a gesture at once benevolent and threatening. It could not have been lost on Richard that some forty-odd years before, his mother, then the young queen of France, had come to this same place with her ascetic first husband for the purpose of launching a similar onslaught against the hated Saracens. With any luck his crusade would prove more successful. That their crusade was a completely mutual venture was agreed between the two monarchs; and all plunder was to be equally divided. With their meetings accomplished the armies got under way, parting at Lyons but agreeing to meet at Messina, whence they would sail for Outremer.

Richard could not at once bring himself to make the long voyage to Sicily. Given to seasickness, he procrastinated until he no longer had a choice; he journeyed by land down the length of Italy and then made the shortest crossing possible. But, tactician *par excellence* that he was, he had already issued a series of disciplinary regulations for his fleet, which may be more revealing of his personality than many an observed account by chroniclers.

> Whoever shall slay a man on ship-board, he shall be bound to the dead man and thrown into the sea. If he shall slay him on land, he shall be bound to the dead man and buried in the earth . . . A robber who shall be convicted of theft, shall have his head cropped . . . and boiling pitch shall be poured thereon, and then the feathers of a cushion shall be shaken out upon him, so that he may be known, and at first land that the ships shall touch, he shall be set ashore. Witness myself, at Chinon.[402]

As an adjunct to the tragic disarray that marked the opening of this last decade of the century, Walter of the Mill died early in the year, departing life unlamented by the new king and probably by most Sicilians. Walter had done much for his adopted country, but he must share with William II the blame for the predicament in which the kingdom currently found itself. It had been he more than anyone who had prevailed upon William to agree to the marriage of Constance with Barbarossa's son. Even his most prominent monument, Palermo Cathedral, stands boringly pretentious and in bad taste—though not all of this is his responsibility since the building has been so badly reworked in succeeding years. Only the tombs within, of which his is one, are of any real aesthetic and historical interest.

A worthier monument that Walter of the Mill left for posterity, and one that has captured the modern imagination for reasons which he never would have suspected is the church of Santo Spirito, located, appropriately enough, considering its history, in an enormous modern cemetery. Santo Spirito is a handsome Norman-style building, incorporating some elements of Italian Romanesque—for example, alternating dark and light stone stripes around the windows, and a strong emphasis on horizontal lines on the façade. It is heavy, solid, clinging to the ground to which it seems rooted.

The inside, too, is intrinsically handsome, but at the same time gives the impression of a brutal toughness, of endurance, of a block-solid ponderousness beyond mere strength. And its bluntly pointed arches do nothing to lessen the

Santo Spirito,
Palermo

atmosphere; only the dim light from the side aisle windows grudgingly allows us to observe just a few details at a time, as though the drama of seeing all at once would be overwhelming. The church is not sullen or portentous; that would be a negation of its very reason for being. But it is not difficult to believe that in 1177 Walter of the Mill laid his foundation-stone 'on a day made sinister by an eclipse of the sun'.[403] It was after Vespers at this church on Easter Monday 1282 that the Sicilians revolted against their Angevin rulers. A terrible massacre ensued known as the 'Sicilian Vespers'. After two thousand French citizens were put to the sword, the revolt spread throughout the expanse of the island, paving the way for a take-over by the Aragonese—a mere trade of one form of foreign supression for another, a greater tragedy than one would understand on hearing Verdi's opera *I Vesperi Siciliani*.

Several months after Walter of the Mill's passing another unexpected death occurred, this one in far-away Asia Minor. On 10 June, still *en route* to the Holy Land, Frederick Barbarossa was drowned as he prepared to cross the river Calycadnus. How the accident occurred is uncertain; but the disaster was a bitter disappointment to the Christians who were barely holding out against the Muslims in Outremer. For King Tancred of Sicily, it held little interest. The potentially worst blow of all for Sicily was that the combined French and English crusading armies, responding to an old invitation from William II, were rapidly approaching and were expecting hospitality. Already sitting on a shaky throne, Tancred was now about to come eye to eye with an offended and formidable Richard of England whose sister was being deprived of her dower and confined. And he himself was being cheated out of his legacy from King William—the gold and the galleys he had intended to use on crusade.

It was not until 22 September that Richard crossed the Straits of Messina, entering the harbour in a galley at the head of his enormous fleet and accompanied by a glorious pageant of pennants and trumpeters. Philip II had already arrived and, watching Richard's theatrically staged landing, was more than a little irked by the ostentatious show which contrasted so noticeably with his own quiet, even austere, entrance just the week before.

> So great was the splendour of the approaching armament, such the clashing and brilliancy of their arms, so noble the sound of the trumpets and clarions, that the city quaked and was greatly astounded, and there came to meet the king a multitude of all ages, people without number, wondering and proclaiming with what exceeding glory and magnificence the king had arrived, surpassing the king of France, who with his forces had arrived seven days before. And forasmuch as the king of France had been already received into the palace of Tancred, king of Sicily, within the walls, the king of England pitched his camp without the city. The same day the king of France, knowing of the arrival of his comrade and brother, flies to his reception, nor could their gestures sufficiently express in embraces and kisses how much each of them rejoiced in the other.[404]

Immediately on landing Richard demanded the justice he thought he and his sister were due. Tancred, in no position to argue with the king of England now camped on his soil and backed by the most powerful army in Europe, acquiesced at once. Joanna arrived in Messina on 28 September to rush into the waiting arms of her brother. She had gifts with her—money from Tancred, not stingy allotments but still in Richard's eyes hardly more than tokens. Plainly trouble was brewing; but when it came it was from an unexpected source.

As is often the case where occupying armies are involved, an intense hostility had grown up between the Sicilians and the crusaders. It was probably true that the defenders of Christendom were being bilked at every turn by the natives. On the other hand, women were very much on the minds of the so-called pilgrims, a reality deeply resented by husbands and brothers, not to mention strict fathers. Antagonisms reached such a pitch that a crusader thought twice before going alone into the streets where he had to face native—mainly Greek—hostility. A Norman minstrel by the name of Ambroise, a gifted recorder of the genre picture of the crusade—the soldier's point of view, his courage and suffering—gives us this clear account of the situation faced by the foreigners.

> For the townsfolk, rabble, and the scum
> Of the city—bastard Greeks were some,
> And some of them Saracen-born—
> Did heap upon our pilgrims scorn.
> Fingers to eyes, they did mock at us,
> Calling us dogs malodorous.
> They did us foulness every day:
> Sometimes our pilgrims they did slay,
> And their corpses in the privies threw.
> And this was proven to be true.[405]

Until now Richard had stationed his troops outside the city. But things had clearly come to a head, resulting in the taking and plundering of the city of Messina. In the face of this 'conquest' Tancred was forced to come to terms with the mighty Richard; agreements were reached, monies were paid in lieu of the legacy and Joanna's dower, neither of which for strategic reasons Tancred could afford to turn over to the English. The usual promises of military assistance were made, but in this case perhaps not quite such hollow promises as one might expect. Richard swore that while he was in Sicily he would provide Tancred aid against *any* invader. It was further agreed that one of Tancred's daughters should be married to Richard's nephew, the three-year-old Arthur of Brittany. Then with impetuous *naïveté*, Richard promised that Arthur would be designated his heir should he die without issue. No great imagination is needed to guess what brother John, sulking and plotting in England, thought about *that* when he got wind of it.

Richard knew that Tancred was in severe straits and in desperate need of friends, especially since word had been received that Henry of Hohenstaufen was on his way south to Rome to claim for himself and his wife, Constance, the imperial crowns. After Rome, Sicily? Who could doubt it? Had not Constance the clearest legitimate claim on the Sicilian throne? For the time, however, Tancred could feel confident that he had gained a friend—and such a friend!—to help him stand against German claims.

As the autumn wore on it was decided that the two armies, French and English, would winter in Sicily, the seas being too treacherous to risk sailing two such armadas with their vast numbers of men and animals and their holds full of equipment. On the surface things seemed amicable between the French and English kings, though anyone on the inside surely knew that picture to be false. For Richard's capture of Messina and the subsequent taming of Tancred had generated in Philip a hatred that finally ruined the whole crusade. Philip had taken justifiable exception to Richard hoisting his English banners over the city of Messina, seeing the act as an assertion of a claim by conquest. Had not the kings agreed just last July at Vézelay that they were mutually involved in the whole project and that they would consequently share *all* plunder? Ambroise the minstrel correctly noted this quarrel as the start of an enmity which not only defeated the crusade, but led, in years to come, to Philip's takeover of Normandy. Ambroise wrote of the quarrel

> Which in the French King did create
> Envy that time will ne'er abate.
> And herewith was the warring born
> Whereby was Normandy sore torn.[406]

Richard uttered smooth words in the face of Philip's anger, and piques were soothed. Hindsight allows us to know what the future held for the monarchs and their armies; it would have been better had the whole venture been scrapped in Sicily, thus saving lives and money beyond reckoning.

1191

Wintering in Sicily was not the respite that might be imagined. True, it furnished the crusaders valuable time to build siege-machines, repair ships and simply sport their time away. But these were not the reasons for which the warriors had left their homes and families. To guarantee the loyalty of his men to the cause of the crusade Richard made lavish gifts of the gold that he had wrested from Tancred. (Apparently Philip had a similar problem and solved it the same way.) But tempers were short all around. And enforced idleness was not compatible with Richard's make-up. If ever there was a propitious time for him to leave Sicily it was during the first months of the new year. Word was received that the dauntless queen mother, Eleanor, now in her seventies, had crossed the Alps and was hard on her way to Messina with Berengaria, betrothed of Richard, in tow. Their marriage was to take place sooner than immediately if Eleanor had anything to say about it.

The secret was out; and the news was more than enough to send Philip into paroxysms of rage. That his sister Alice, betrothed to one or another Plantagenet for years, was to be heartlessly cast aside for an upstart Navarrese could be interpreted only as an intolerable insult. 'Let the king of England know', Philip had threatened Richard one day, 'if he puts my sister aside and marries another woman I shall be his enemy as long as he lives!' Growing increasingly irritated with the argument, Richard finally resorted to the ugly,

Chinon, France

*Tomb of Henry II,
Fontevrault, France*

*Tomb of Eleanor
of Aquitaine,
Fontevrault, France*

Abbey Kitchen,
Fontevrault

Château Gaillard, France

and apparently unfounded, rumour that Alice had been his father's mistress— some even claimed she had had a child by Henry that had died in infancy. He asserted that he wanted no part of his father's cast-off mistresses. It was tasteless and insulting rhetoric, and both Richard and Philip knew it.

Philip immediately got to work, feeding Tancred's natural suspicions of Richard to the point that when Eleanor and Berengaria arrived at Messina they were not allowed to disembark, but were instead shunted on to mainland Brindisi. In a five-day meeting at Tancred's castle at Catania Richard demanded reasons for this treatment of his wife-to-be and his mother.

Of Norman Catania there is only a part of the cathedral of Sant'Agata, chaste maid who was martyred in that city in AD 251 and whose imminent death allegedly caused a violent earthquake. The cathedral maintains its three Norman apses (1091) and a few scattered remnants of Norman work peeking from behind later Baroque incrustations. The rest of the city is predominantly Baroque, some of it very beautiful. There are lovely gardens, notably those dedicated to the memory of Vincenzo Bellini who was born there in 1801, and who is buried in the cathedral. Just twenty-one years before Richard's conference with Tancred, Catania had been almost totally destroyed by earthquake; and it was to be devastated again six years hence by Henry VI of Hohenstaufen, coming to Sicily and asserting his imperial rights.

In his five-day meeting with Tancred, Richard, finally divining what fears in his host he had to dispel, brought all his diplomatic skill into play. It followed that the two kings reaffirmed their friendship, and an alleged state of mutual admiration was sealed with another exchange of gifts, Richard receiving from Tancred fifteen galleys and four large transport ships. The two having ostensibly patched up their quarrel, Philip Augustus, realizing that further struggle on behalf of sister Alice was mere tilting with windmills, had no choice but to put on the best face possible and to reach an accommodation with Richard. The two patched up their dispute; Richard was released from his vows. For Philip it could only have been humiliating. 'In a gesture which perfectly expressed his feelings he chose to set sail from Messina on 30 March, just a few hours before Berengaria arrived'.[407]

Determined and persuasive as Eleanor was she could not alter the fact that Lent was in progress when she arrived with her future daughter-in-law; the marriage would have to wait until the termination of that austere season. It was arranged that Berengaria should be placed in the care of the widowed Joanna, and that both women would sail aboard a private vessel in Richard's fleet bound for the Holy Land. Eleanor then returned northwards. Her brief stay in Rome coincided with the imperial coronation of Henry VI and Constance, an event which she could not bring herself to witness. The ceremony took place on Easter Monday, 15 April, officiated over by Pope Celestine III who had been pope for all of one day. (Celestine was an old man and had the remark-ably funny name of Hyacinthus Bobo.)

Tancred must have been sorry to see Richard leave Sicily, although the inconvenience of having this quarrelsome king and his brawling rabble at his very doorstep had been annoying, at times hair-raising. But Tancred realized that Henry VI was well aware that Richard was always spoiling for a fight and would take on the German emperor as unconcernedly as anyone else. No one, including Henry, would lay a finger on Tancred's realm while Richard was still present. But Tancred suspected that Henry would assert his wife's claim to the Palermitan throne on the instant of Richard's departure, on 10 April.

Richard was in buoyant spirits at the prospect of getting on with the crusade. Nevertheless his party had an absolutely ghastly crossing. 'One of his ships was lost in a storm, and another three, including the ship carrying Joanna and Berengaria, were swept on to Cyprus ... Richard's own ship had narrowly escaped destruction in the Gulf of Attalia. Sea-sickness had not improved Richard's temper'[408] by the time he arrived at Limassol. He no doubt surprised many a gossip-monger, and perhaps even himself, by marrying Berengaria on the island of Cyprus on 12 May. The celebration accomplished, and feeling high at the prospects of combating Saladin's Muslims, Richard sailed on to Acre.

For two years now the eyes of both East and West had been focused on Acre. Even with Saladin's most outstanding military architect in charge of its defences, it became clear that, with the Christian armies finally assembled, Acre could not hold out for long, rely as its defenders would on their dreaded Greek fire, a mixture with a naptha base hurled by catapult in pottery vessels. But Greek fire or no, Richard and his crusaders were eager to get on with the fight. He would not have been in such smashing good spirits had he known of the events unfolding on the Italian mainland.

Henry VI moved threateningly towards Southern Italy, precisely as Tancred had anticipated. Norman defection was an endemic factor in Southern Italy, and with the help of disgruntled Norman nobles Henry made swift work of absorbing Tancred's mainland domain. Teano, Monte Cassino, Salerno, Aversa—all fell to Henry, some of them not even clenching a fist in their own defence, such was the perfidy of the Southern barons.

Naples was another story. Here the German army was stopped by this teeming city of forty thousand inhabitants and their commander Richard of Acerra, along with a defending fleet under Margaritus. Then—again—Nature took a hand. Like so many ambitious predecessors, Henry was forced to bow to the combined might of malaria and dysentery—and the consequent defections. Barely in the nick of time, he ordered his decimated forces to set out for home. But he was determined to succeed.

A sick and bitter Henry raised the siege of Naples on August 24 and turned northwards, but not without leaving Constance in Salerno as a pointed reminder that he would, like generals, seasons and bad pennies, return. The Salernitans, hearing of his retreat and fearing reprisals from Tancred for their eager surrender to the emperor, turned on Constance. No doubt she would have been murdered had she not been rescued by Tancred's nephew, Elias of Gesualdo, and sent under protective custody to Palermo. Hostages were valuable in the twelfth century, as they seem to be in the twentieth. But an imperial hostage! In the circumstances Tancred had no right to hope for more.

The Muslims of Acre held out against a prolonged and concerted Christian attack, but finally, with the consent of Saladin, they surrendered. This first victory was one of the few clear-cut wins that the Europeans scored in the entire crusade. As in all the crusades, petty bickering, national jealousies and acute cases of royal one-upmanship doomed the fight for the Holy Sepulchre. Richard, however, was notorious for ferocity. Cutting a magnificent figure, he was likened to a giant reaper mowing Turks down with his sword as one would with a scythe. How long could Philip of France endure seeing Richard strutting through the hero's role, the self-appointed number-one commander of the Third Crusade, macho to his hair ends, popular with his men, and admired for his valour on both sides of the battle-line? Not for long apparently. On 3 August Philip defected.

But Jerusalem was waiting. With properly tumultuous fanfare and bravura Richard led his enormous army across the wasteland surrounding Acre towards a conquest that was never to be realized. Dogging Richard's trail for several days, Saladin prepared for an all-out attack on the enemy host at Ursuf. On 7 September—the eve of Richard's thirty-fourth birthday—the two giant armies, Christian and Muslim, met in a bloody battle. At first it looked as though Saladin's troops would carry the day. There was terrible carnage on both sides until the Hospitallers, goaded beyond endurance by their losses, broke rank and, contrary to Richard's orders, rushed the enemy. Though his orders had been disobeyed, Richard gave them unhesitating support, eventually sweeping all before him. It was the end of Saladin's legendary invincibility.

By contrast Richard was at the pinnacle of his career. Had he not just defeated Europe's most daunting foe? Was there anything to stop him from taking Jerusalem, 'whose capture had been [Saladin's] most glorious triumph'?[409] Jubilant in the flush of victory, he led his 'pilgrims' on, three days later drawing them up before the ruins of Jaffa, the port nearest Jerusalem. Then, on October 30, after a long rest, including several weeks of fruitless bargaining between Richard and Saladin, Richard headed his troops towards Jerusalem. Slogging through mud, in the teeth of rain and violent hailstorms, he brought them to Beit Nuba, within twelve miles of the Holy City. Everyone was ecstatic. The soldiers would soon prostrate themselves at the Holy Sepulchre, walk the Via Dolorosa, climb sacred Calvary. Their lives would be redeemed, paradise assured. But such was not to be.

1192

When Emperor Henry VI retreated sick and discouraged to his own lands both Tancred of Sicily and the pope felt a surge of genuine relief, although aware that the respite was only temporary. Pope Celestine III was in a tough situation, and knew it. Officially and unmistakably he had demonstrated his antipathy to the Hohenstaufen cause by excommunicating to a man the complement of personnel at Monte Cassino Abbey for having been sympathetic to Henry's invasion of the South. At the same time he did not want too strong a Sicily. Perhaps a bargain could be reached.

Pope Celestine III and Tancred met at Gravina di Puglia in June. In exchange for papal approval of his usurpation, Tancred relinquished all claim to administer ecclesiastical affairs in his kingdom, for the first time in its history placing the Latin Church there under total papal control. Backed into a corner as he was, Tancred could do little to keep Celestine from winning one of the papacy's few victories over the Normans.

Worse for Tancred than the agreements reached at Gravina was the follow-up, whereby he was cheated out of his imperial hostage. At Celestine's suggestion Constance was sent to Rome, to remain in papal custody until such a time as Henry and Tancred could perhaps come to some sort of mutual accommodation. On the way to Rome she was, in effect, kidnapped by some of Henry's knights and whisked off to Germany. 'Tancred had been robbed of his trump card. He was not to be dealt another'.[410]

For all his bad luck—to rule the island kingdom at a time of inevitable decline—and his lack of personal appeal, Tancred was a fighter, and a tenacious one at that. He was only too aware that his end as monarch was in sight. But in no way did this prevent him from maintaining the contest for his Norman kingdom. The entire realm was in disarray: highwaymen were abroad; the barons were in revolt, which was probably the only condition in the kingdom that reflected the status quo; and the one person in the world able to help him was having troubles of his own in Outremer.

By this time it was clear even to Richard himself that the crusade was running out of steam. His own followers were having second thoughts about the feasibility of taking and holding Jerusalem. Even should the Holy City fall to them—what then? Who would maintain it as a Christian city, a bulwark against the constantly attacking Saracens? The crusading pilgrims, once having entered the city and worshipped at the Holy Sepulchre, would forthwith take off for home. Besides these misgivings, Richard was worried by rumours that his brother John and King Philip II were plotting against him.

By September the Outremer armies were completely worn out, their leaders, both Saladin and Richard, weakened by sickness and general fatigue. Agreement to a three-year truce was finally reached. The coast of the Holy Land from Tyre to Jaffa was to remain in Christian hands, Jerusalem in those of the Muslims. Christians were free to vist the Sacred City, an opportunity of which many of the crusaders, but not Richard, availed themselves.

Richard set sail for home on 9 October. Trans-shipping at Corfu and, taking only a few knights, friends and Templars, he sailed up the Dalmatian Coast, planning to go overland in disguise, through German territories, reasoning that he would be little expected in that area. Unfortunately his galley was driven ashore somewhere between Aquileia and Venice. Thus he was forced to proceed overland a little sooner than had been anticipated. Word got out in no time that Richard was loose in the countryside, and before long the world shook with apprehension at the news that Richard I of England had been captured in the small village of Eedburg, just outside Vienna. By February 1193 he was a prisoner of Emperor Henry VI.

Now more than ever Tancred of Sicily could do with a friend; but where to find one? Groping for any succour to come his way, that beleagured king concluded a marriage-of-convenience contract with Byzantine Emperor Isaac Angelus. It was agreed that Isaac's daughter Irene should marry Tancred's son Roger, duke of Apulia. Tancred hoped that the world would interpret this link as some sort of military support. No such luck!

1193

Despite the fact that he sometimes acted like one, Tancred was no fool. The political game he was playing with Emperor Isaac Angelus was sound, considered well within the ground rules of the day. Tancred could afford to feel a trifle more secure when his Roger married Isaac's Irene in Brindisi in the spring of the year. But his new-found security, if such it was, was short-lived. Roger was dead before the end of the year, his young Byzantine wife a widow—and destined for greater things. Through all of this depressing year Tancred fought dissatisfaction and disintegration, at best a losing battle, at worst a tragedy. But the strain began to show, until finally he fell ill.

As a further blow to Sicily's chances, old Matthew of Ajello died this year. By and large it had been advantageous for the kingdom to have had Matthew in its service. Certainly he was ambitious, and suspicious along with the rest of them. But he had worked hard, usually with the best interests of the monarchy in mind. There is something quixotic in Matthew's personality which makes him in the end only that much more interesting. Even when he sided with insurgents, as he did in the days of William II's regency when he stood against Stephen du Perche, he seemed more patriotic than anything else. From the start he had been against the alliance of the Sicilian and German royal houses, but had lost the argument in face of Walter of the Mill's erroneous judgement. Perhaps if he had been a younger man maturing at this dismal moment in Sicilian history the kingdom would have been spared.

It was at this time, early in the year, that the event immortalized in the legend of Blondel of Nesle, an old Aquitainian troubadour friend of Richard, is supposed to have taken the palace. According to the story, Blondel, who had once shared the writing of a ballad with Richard, disguised himself as a minstrel and meandered through Germany hunting for his king, singing their ballad under the windows of all the high-rising castles he came upon.

> Your beauty, lady fair,
> None views without delight;
> But still as bold as air
> No passion can excite;
> Yet this I patient see
> While all are shunn'd like me.[411]

Blondel's persistence paid off when, according to tradition, outside Durnstein Castle (destroyed in the seventeenth century) on the River Danube he heard the answering voice of his friend singing the other half of the song.

> No nymph my heart can wound,
> If favor she divide,
> And smiles on all around
> Unwilling to decide:
> I'd rather hatred bear
> Than love with others share.[412]

So, the legend insists, Richard's secret prison was discovered. There is no basis for the legend other than the persistence of it, but 'you may believe it, if you like; it would be easy to believe worse things. Richard was himself a Minstrel and a Poet. If he had not been a Prince too, he might have been a better man perhaps, and might have gone out of the world with less bloodshed and waste of life to answer for'.[413]

Eventually ranson for Richard was agreed upon, the terms hammered out between the English envoys and the Germans during an Easter court in the city of Speyer. Henry VI dictated that among other indemnities would be 100,000 marks of silver (later to be increased to 150,000). Further—and one wonders at the effect in Palermo—Richard was to provide fifty galleys and one hundred knights for the emperor's contemplated attack on Sicily. A rider was added that Richard himself, with one hundred additional knights, was committed to accompany Henry on his southern venture. Although this last condition was never enforced, Sicily's fate was indeed sealed. Until the ransom should be paid, the captive king was moved for safe keeping to the mountain castle of Trifels overlooking the Bavarian Palatinate town of Anweiler.

1194

Few castles are as forbidding as Berg Trifels. It is a typical Hohenstaufen fortress, with a ring of guard towers located on encircling hills, defence walls, an impressive gate, and constructed of precisely cut ashlar. The building was constructed on a natural outcropping of rock, which acts as a partial foundation. Evil it is in aspect, unsmiling, unfriendly and claustrophobic despite its soaring sweep to the heavens. It is said that Berg Trifels is the one historic building in Germany whose reconstruction continued throughout World War II: Hitler had it in mind to imprison both Franklin Roosevelt and Winston Churchill there when Germany proved victorious, the ultimate irony. Richard's mettle must have been sorely tested by its dour oppressiveness. There was barely a glimmer of daylight through the narrow slit windows, meagre openings of freshness admitting only hints of the Bavarian spring. No one can know Richard's thoughts while he was cooped up in that sombre jail, but reports state that his spirits never waivered, and that he passed his time wrestling with—and at night drinking them under the table—two attributes which must have won cloddish admiration.

True descendant of William IX of Poitou, the first troubadour, Richard made use of his unaccustomed leisure to polish up his talents as a poet, which he had discovered

Berg Triffels, Germany

454

as a young man from Bertran de Born. He addressed a song to his half-sister, Marie of Champagne, in which he reproached those barons who had defected to John, as well as those fair-weather friends who were being niggardly in their donations towards his ransom. Whether or not Richard was a great king is certainly open to argument, but he 'composed better poetry than any other king who is known to tourists, and, when he spoke to his sister in this cry of the heart altogether singular among monarchs, he made law and style, above discussion'.[414]

> In no way can a prisoner reveal
> His true thoughts unless he tells his grief;
> But sorrow in a song may find relief.
> I'm strong in friends , but their support is weak;
> Their shame if I, unransomed, cannot leave
> Prison two winters long . . .[415]

Within a few weeks of the death of his elder son Roger, King Tancred of Sicily died in Palermo, on 20 February. A tragic figure he, incomparably ugly and tending, at times, to vindictiveness—witness his shabby treatment of Joanna Plantagenet when she was newly widowed. Yet Tancred had no cause for shame so far as his resolute defence of the kingdom was concerned, no cause to echo Henry II's plaintive cry, 'Shame on a defeated king!' Tancred was one of the few who saw the threat from beyond his island's shores, and was totally unable to convince his fellow Normans that unity was the price they had to pay to save their vested interests. A small enough price, one would think; and yet how often in history men have been unwilling to pay it.

If Tancred was a tragic figure then so was his queen, Sibylla of Acerra, perhaps more so in that she survived to see the end of Norman rule. She fought as best she could to save the throne for her son William III, the only male heir remaining, though unfortunately still a child. The idea of another woman regent on the throne of Sicily was too much for a good segment of the population. And Sibylla was not equipped to fight back. Unprepared for the job thrust upon her at Sicily's worst hour, and utterly inept at politics, she could do no more than trust—or distrust—her advisors, ultimately going down to a pathetically rapid defeat.

Emperor Henry was on the move again. By October he had occupied all of Southern Italy that was important to him, some of it rather brutally. 'Advancing . . . with an army, the emperor, in the name of his wife, obtained, without difficulty, the opulent regions of Apulia, Calabria, and Sicily. It is said that he granted pardon to those who had opposed him under Tancred; but he smote with cruel castigation the citizens of Salerno, and ruined that city, once so famous'.[416] As Robert Guiscard had before him, and for the same reason—betrayal—Henry took the city by storm. Pillage followed. 'The walls were reduced to rubble; by then there was little left for them to enclose'.[417] Such was his revenge for Salerno's having allowed Constance to be sent to Sicily in 1191. Henry then crossed the straits to Sicily. Seeing the futility of her task, Sibylla had already sent young William III and his three sisters to the fortress of Caltabellotta, high in the foothills along Sicily's south coast, where

Caltabellotta, Sicily

she later joined them. On November 20 Henry rode triumphantly into Palermo, a Palermo rampant with an all-pervading defeatism. At Caltabellotta Queen Sibylla and her frightened children awaited the imperial pleasure.

There is only a single pathetic tower remaining of the great fortress that once protectively stood sentinel over this town that seems stacked, rather than laid out, as it clings precariously to its hillside. A dark, almost glowering day, cold and windy, can seem depressingly bleak up there; it is a fitting place for the Hauteville era to end. The town turns up but a meagre cache of Norman things, principally the Chiesa Madre, built by the first Roger just over a hundred years before the extinction of the Hauteville regine. One would hope for something more splendid, more glowing and shimmering, something better reflecting the glory of the Hauteville rule. But we have only that one simple tower, rising forlornly to the grey sky. At least it is still there, vertical, proud, even a bit authoritarian. And that, surely, is in the spirit of the Guiscard and the two Rogers. After all, we have Cefalù, the Cappella Palatina and Monreale to reflect the royal glory; and the Martorana, San Cataldo and the little Santissima Trinità de Delia near Castelvetrano (a splendid little gem of a church nestled in a quiet, shady olive grove) to reflect the ambitions of their followers. In that light the lonely tower at Caltabellotta seems apt, sadly appropriate, a proper requiem. The feeling of pathos is augmented by one of the steep, narrow stair-streets leading to the tower known as the Vicolo di Sibylla.

Emulating Charlemagne, Henry VI chose Christmas as the day of his coronation as king of Sicily. The ceremony took place in Palermo Cathedral, that drastically remodelled monument erected by Walter of the Mill, the man responsible more than any other, barring King William II, for throwing the kingdom to the Germans. Now it was an accomplished fact. The Hautevilles, through William and his innocent, probably unwilling, aunt had made a present of their kingdom to their oldest enemies, signed, sealed and delivered. 'That noble kingdom, which by male succession had stood so long immovable, failed by a female inheritor, and fell, and thus passed away into a province of the German emperor, in the one thousand one hundred and ninety-fourth year from the delivery of the Virgin'.[418]

'A prince of irresistible skill and energy, with a determination which did not shrink from any scruples of humanity or equity',[419] Henry immediately instituted a reign of terror, proving himself a most brutal tyrant, and no doubt making every Sicilian look more fondly on the comparative halcyon days of the Hautevilles. And the day after the coronation, the Feast of Saint Stephen, Empress Constance, on her way to Sicily and very pregnant, was forced to stop off at the small Italian Marches town of Jesi, near Ancona, where she was delivered of her only child. Constance was forty years old now, and lest there be some doubt as to her ability to produce an heir to the imperial throne, a tent was erected in the town square—still today called Piazza Federico II—and the women of the community were invited in to watch the birth process. Proudly Constance showed her son off to the townspeople. And what a son he was! Frederick II, grandson of both Frederick Barbarossa and King Roger II; Frederick II, *Stupor Mundi*, the Wonder of the World; Frederick II, 'the first of Renaissance princes two hundred years before his time'.[420]

After arranging Richard's final release and travelling with him from Germany to England, Queen Eleanor took herself off to her favourite abbey, Fontevrault, where she could, in the quiet of the cloister, contemplate the coming world of God and perhaps dwell with no little fondness on the world of the past. Husband Henry, rugged and recalcitrant in life, now quiet and perhaps more lovable in death, was already there. Eleanor lived at Fontevrault for the rest of her days, and upon her death in 1204 was buried there at her husband's side in a demonstration of unity which they had found impossible in life. By that time Richard and Joanna, who had both died in 1099, were also buried there. (Joanna's tomb has since disappeared, obliterated in the destructive excesses of the French Revolution. The present fourth tomb is that of Isabella of Angoulême, second wife of King John.)

Immediately after her marriage to Henry Plantagenet, Eleanor had dictated a charter for Fontevrault, a charter which bears witness to her personal feelings and warm regard for this particular bulwark against the world. The abbess of Fontevrault at the time was Henry II's aunt, Matilda of Anjou, widowed daughter-in-law of Henry I whose chance to become queen consort of England had been dashed by the 1120 Barfleur disaster. Matilda was the second abbess of Fontevrault, the first being one Petronilla of Chemillé, a brilliant and comely young widow who had attracted many high-born, equally intelligent ladies to her remote feminine outpost. And feminine outpost it was, just the sort of thing to appeal to Eleanor.

Eleanor's patronage, even without the remainder of the Plantagenet tombs, is only too evident at Fontevrault, especially noteworthy in the austerely simple Saint Lazarus Cloister and the Saint Lazarus Chapel, both of them built to attend the needs of the colony of lepers nursed there. The cloister was rebuilt in the seventeenth century, its pleasant proportions retained, and with them the tranquillity and charm. Strong Romanesque arches hem in the central garden, supported on squarish, blocky columns—strong, severe, the kind of thing one would expect from Eleanor. The darkness of the arcade stands in stark and relieving contrast to the brilliantly sunned open garden, exposed as it is to the intense southern light of the Loire.

The great abbey church must look today very much as it looked in Eleanor's time; above all else majestic. It is roofed by large cupolas whose repetition of curved lines, both of themselves and of their supporting pendentives, stands in balanced contrast to the stout columns that bear the enormous weight. This architectural heaviness is emphasized—yet mitigated— by wonderfully complex capitals depicting fantastic animals and biblical stories, all interwoven with leaf-work and geometric traceries. The single nave leads to a climactic apse, flooded in light and ringed by a triforium arcade that is at once masculinely supportive and elegantly feminine.

The Plantagenet tombs, bearing polychrome effigies carved out of single blocks of limestone, are in the south transept. All are, of course, recumbent, but Eleanor (*see page* 447) is much more alive-looking than the others; she is, even in death, reading from a book. The other figures are frankly dead. But death without civilized refinements was not a part of Eleanor's comprehension of life. With what grace does this most elegant lady of her age hold her open book! With what calm aloofness this crowned and wimpled queen affirms her life, more than any of her three companions in death maintaining her affirmation of the existence she found so exhilarating. She was a magnificent lady, Eleanor; and her effigy eloquently mirrors her magnificence.

The most interesting structure in the vast Fontevrault complex is Evrault's Tower(*see page* 448), so-called because a legendary brigand of that name is supposed to have shone a beacon from its height, thus luring lost travellers out of the forest, to be looted at his leisure. Actually Evrault's Tower is the monastery kitchen, the only extant Romanesque kitchen in France. It is eighty-nine feet high and thirty-seven feet in diameter, large for a medieval kitchen. Crowned by a pyramidal roof of overlapping stones arranged to resemble fish scales, the kitchen is octagonal with eight apsidioles (three have disappeared), each topped by a chimney. With six hearths and twenty flues to assure that smoke would be efficiently evacuated, this kitchen supplied meals for the four separate convents that once made up the total complex, as well as for the numerous needy people who daily mobbed the gates of the abbey. The structure is curious, octagonal at base, changing to a square at a second level, and then metamorphosing back to the octagonal to form the pyramidal apex.

1195

The political scene in Sicily comes more and more to resemble a Gothic tale. A few days after the Christmas coronation of Henry VI, a conspiracy, so it was claimed, was uncovered to assassinate him. The entire former royal family and a host of others of the leading families were 'implicated'. All of them were shipped off to Germany as political prisoners. Historians from that day to this have argued the plausibility of the charges, with good points being made for both sides. Regardless of their validity, poor ex-Queen Sibylla, who could have been only happy at relinquishing her throne, was to spend the next five years in not comfortless detention with her three daughters in the convent of Hohenburg in Alsace. Her daughter-in-law Irene fared better, within three years marrying Henry's brother, Philip of Swabia, soon to become king of Germany.

The most pathetic story, or suppositon, concerns young William III, who had realized his kingly destiny for all of ten short months. Some say he was blinded and castrated. We do not know. We are fairly certain, however, that by the turn of the century he was dead. He may have become a monk. In any event he was still little more than a child.

Epilogue

Vanity of vanities, saith the Preacher, vanity of vanities: all is vanity. What profit hath a man of all his labour which he taketh under the sun? One generation passeth away, and another generation cometh: but the earth abideth for ever.

Ecclesiastes, I:2-4

If there is a final place to visit in Norman Italy-Sicily we shall have to search for it, for we have pretty well used them up. And yet we find one, a spot appropriate enough for the final resting place of that last despondent Siculo-Norman queen, Sibylla, located in a wild gorge in the hills above Salerno, itself once a heavily contested centre of Norman activity. If the proud, tragically isolated single tower of Caltabellotta strikes one as appropriate for the last refuge of Tancred de Hauteville's family (odd that the last ruler of the line should have the same name as the founder), then La Cava is equally appropriate as the burial place of his queen.

Established a good century before King Roger's time by Alferius Pappacarbone, a prominent Saleritan who in 1011 sought out this rough vale as a refuge for the hermit's life he wanted to embrace, the place would seem ideal to encourage visions and to mitigate medieval guilts. It is claimed that Alferius lived to be a hundred and twenty, so the austere life must have agreed with him; at any rate, he and three of his followers became saints with many others of his disciples declared blessed. Alferius' abbey grew in importance until it administered the Cava congregation of five hundred abbeys—including, thanks to William II, Monreale. There is a Gothic chapter house at La Cava, along with some fourteenth-century frescoes in the chapel of San Germano. And in the main church the visitor can see a stunning twelfth-century pulpit and a paschal candlestick, both decorated with mosaics. Tino di Camaino's fourteenth-century altar is represented only fragmentally, but there is a nice bust of Saint Matthew by him. Among its treasures the abbey preserves several medieval manuscripts as well as two antique reliquaries: one a lovely eleventh-century ivory casket, the other a cross containing a bit of the wood of Christ's death, presented to the abbey by the first of the crusade-stumping popes, Urban II, when he visited the old basilica in 1092.

The existing complex of the Badia della Santìssima Trinità della Cava is an eighteenth-century reconstruction, but the eleventh-to thirteenth-century cloister survives. There are few places like this cloister, with its double-columned colonnade, its vertically elongated arches and its adjacent eleventh-century crypt 'far below . . . where a faint glimmer of daylight makes the glare of the wax torches ghostly'.[421] The tiny old cloister of the early foundation looks more like a stage setting than a real cloister, what with its two-level floor, its fountain and its high-springing arches. 'The place has not the majesty of Monte Cassino, the mother abbey of the Benedictines; it is wild, rude, and romantic, an abode of warlike ghosts and the war-torn wrecks of dead men'.[422] But it is profoundly quiet, the kind of place one feels was deserved

Badia di Cava, Italy

by the troubled Queen Sibylla. Quite literally it provides a respite from the scorching sun of Southern Italy, a cooling reprieve, a tranquillity that is hard to come by in the densely populated cities—a tranquillity which was certainly unknown to this unfortunate queen.

There is no such tranquil place in England that we can single out as a symbol of the decline of the Plantagenet fortunes—only castles, fortresses and dungeons. Richard Lionheart was forty-two years old when he died after reigning a mere nine and a half years, felled at Chalus, near Limoges, by a chance arrow. Within a few years his successor, John, will have lost to Philip all his continental possessions with the exception of Aquitaine; and the determination of his successors to hang on to that fragment was one of the contributing factors of the Hundred Years' War. Towards the end of his life Richard's attention had been diverted and his time swallowed up by his supervision of the building of one of the greatest of all monuments of late medieval defensive architecture—his Château Gaillard, his 'Saucy Castle', the mocking challenge of the original French all but lost in translation.

460

Above the small town of Les Andelys, Château Gaillard occupies a crucial point on the River Seine between Paris and Rouen (*see page* 448). Beautiful for a fortress, it soars upward from its island-like foundation, at once a threat and a challenge to the French king. Picnicking on the hillside overlooking the citadel—French bread and cheese, a pâté and a local wine do not allow warlike thoughts—it is difficult to remember that the Château Gaillard was Richard's masterpiece, the keystone of his architectonic system to defend the Norman Vexin against his enemy. Legend tells us that this most sophisticated stronghold was built in only one year, when the truth is that it took three, still incredible enough to need no exaggeration considering the amount of stone that had to be transported, the enormous quantities of supplies needed for the army of workers—the masons and lime-workers, stonecutters, smiths, carpenters, water carriers, and unskilled labourers beyond imagination. It is said that Richard, viewing with undisguised delight his newly finished bastion perched so dramatically on its heights looking down on several majestically undulating curves of the Seine, made an all-inclusive gesture and exclaimed, 'She is so beautiful, my yearling daughter!' perhaps giving rise to the one-year-construction legend. Hearing of King Philip's blustering, but transparently dismayed, boast, 'If its walls were made of solid irón I would take them', Richard, not known for modesty, retorted that were they made of butter he would hold them.

Despite the depredations of men and elements, Château Gaillard is one of the most romantically appealing fortresses to survive the Middle Ages. A good part remains, but much of the outer defensive ring has vanished, laid low by that most cunning and determined personal power hunter and vandal, Cardinal Richelieu. There are stables and storerooms, a well and a great hall with an enormous fireplace. One can still see remains of the encircling walls, in places twelve feet thick.

To the southeast the castle is guarded by a hill, which may have had questionable merit as a natural defence, but which offers a vantage point for picnicking and photographing the structure against the backdrop of the sweeping curves of the Seine as it wends its way towards Rouen. That the rock of Andelys had strategic merit was acknowledged by both kings, the fact witnessed in an earlier truce that had expressly forbidden its fortification. But such an agreement would never stand in Richard's way. With typical highhandedness, he simply took the rock by force from its rightful owner, Archbishop Walter of Rouen, who was running a thriving river-toll racket there. In protest when Richard began his castle, the archbishop laid an

Château Gaillard, France

461

interduct on the duchy; but under Richard's command no one paid any attention and work proceeded apace, to the cleric's dismay.

For all its obvious strength, it was a matter of only a few years before the castle fell (in 1204, to be exact) to Philip Augustus, though it took five months of siege to reduce it, unbelieveable hardships for the locals pressed into service, and the combined assault of an exceptionally large battery of throwing machines, a high siege-tower, and an audacious French soldier who sneaked into the castle precinct via a latrine conduit. 'It has been said that the capture of Château Gaillard shocked all Europe, but it is more likely that the shock was the news soon afterwards that Normandy had fallen to the French. But the castle was certainly a prestige symbol: Richard built it as a direct challenge to Philip Augustus on the basis of "Here I am: come and get me" '. [423]

As Richard had intended, the news of the completion of Château Gaillard drew Philip Augustus to the Vexin. Confronting his rival at Gisors late in the year, the Lionheart routed the French monarch, and had the pleasure of watching him flee across the River Epte, only to get doused when the bridge collapsed under him and his knights. A sputtering Philip, to Richard's delight, had to be pulled out by his retainers. Richard could not help but be aware that in 911, nearby on the same small river, Charles the Simple, Philip's forerunner, had granted Richard's northern ancestors their first rights to the land that was later called Normandy, a gesture that in time taxed the patience of many a French monarch. Like Philip, Charles took a header, but his was a pratfall, suffered when he was overturned by a Viking menial who was kissing the royal foot. Richard could not resist crowing in a report to the bishop of Durham: 'Thus have we defeated the King of France at Gisors; but it is not we who have done the same, but rather God and our right (*Dieu et mon droit*), by our means . . .'[424] It is from the original of this letter that the English crown adopted *Dieu et mon droit* as its motto.

England and Sicily—Sicily and England! Two island kingdoms, but how differently they fared. Even at the height of Frederick II of Hohenstaufen's power, and it was formidable (he succeeded to the throne of Henry VI), Sicily was to know neither peace nor prosperity. Nothing would go right for the island or for those people who ruled or wanted to rule it. Even Frederick himself, three times excommunicated, so atrocious were his relations with the popes—this *Stupor Mundi*—even Frederick has all but lost his identity in the general imagination, becoming almost hopelessly confused with his robust, red-bearded grandfather, Frederick Barbarossa—and even with another Frederick II, the great eighteenth-century king of Prussia and friend and host of Voltaire.

So Sicily was fought over through the centuries, never knowing either prolonged peace or short prosperity. Is it any wonder that Garibaldi was welcomed by Palermitans with open arms in the second half of the last century? But his war for the unification of Italy and its islands was not the end of Sicily's troubles, right up to the allied invasion on 10 July 1943. It is an unrelenting tale of violence and poverty, of burning sun and volcanic eruptions, of invaders' greed and native sloth. 'Italy has troubles, and these may become graver in time. The country is unstable and large sections of the population are still blocked off from the light of modern times, but the country gives nevertheless an impression of extraordinary warmth and happiness as well as animation. This is a smiling country, the pleasantest of all European nations to visit or live in, no matter who runs it, how or why'.[425]

England, apparently, was made of sterner stuff than Italy and its island appendage. The line of Plantagenet kings survived until the late fifteenth century (there were twelve more of them yet to come, including John Lackland—England's only King John): beyond the deposed Edward II, whose death must rate as one of history's cruellest moments; beyond even the crisis-ridden reign of Richard II, a man very different from the first king of that name; beyond the popularly over-maligned Richard III, whose father, curiously enough, was the first officially to use the name Plantagenet when he put forward the Yorkist claim to the throne. The legitimate male line of Plantagenet was finally brought to an end with the judicial murder in 1499 of the twenty-four-year-old Edward, earl of Warwick.

Yet the monarchical line continued from family to family, through wars, the acquisition of colonies, the emergence of empire—and its collapse—to the present Windsors. There is a staunch and admirable persistence in this tenacity of the British to hang on to their royalty, even if the royalty sometimes does not deserve it. Even the destructive Civil War and Cromwell's Protectorate could do little more than interrupt the line. Trying to dam the flow of English monarchs, it would seem, is akin to trying to dam the Thames, that slow-moving, inexorable force that turns back on itself twice daily with the tides, yet wends its way majestically through the English countryside the way the parade of kings and queens wends its way through the fields of history. The river has seen it all—the altruism, the violence and the greed, the glory and the shame, the heroes and the skeletons.

Sweet Thames, run softly till I end my song,
Sweet Thames, run softly, for I speak not loud or long.
But at my back in a cold blast I hear
The rattle of the bones, and chuckle spread from ear to ear.[426]

Footnotes

For a complete description of the books listed below see Bibliography

1 Davis, **The Normans and Their Myth** p.27
2 Jones, **A History of the Vikings** p.212
3 ibid., p.1
4 Haskins, **The Normans in European History** p.27
5 ibid. p.28
6 Malaterra, trans. in Gunn, **Normandy** p.65
7 Henry of Huntingdon, **The Chronicles**, trans. Forester p.216
8 Barzini, **The Italians** p.14
9 Allen, **Stone Shelters** p.19
10 Osborne, **The Greatest Norman Conquest** p.31
11 Norwich, **The Normans in the South** p.22
12 Adams, **Mont-Saint-Michel and Chartres** p.44
13 Sumption, **Pilgrimage** p.118
14 ibid. p.123
15 Furneaux, **Invasion 1066** p.48
16 Walder, **Nelson** p. 333
17 ibid. p.512
18 Norwich, **The Normans in the South** p.68
19 Anna Comnena, **The Alexiade**, trans. Dawes p.27
20 Norwich, **The Normans in the South** p.69
21 ibid. p.82
22 **Numbers** 22:23
23 Gibbon, **The Decline and Fall**, Chapter LVI
24 Norwich, **The Normans in the South** p.93
25 **Vita Aedwardi**, trans. and ed. Barlow p.30
26 Norwich, **The Normans in the South** p.95
27 Gibbon, **The Decline and Fall**, Chapter LVI
28 Anna Comnena, **The Alexiade** trans. Dawes p.109
29 Norwich, **The Normans in the South** p.114
30 Pindar, 'Olympian Ode IV' in **The Odes of Pindar**, trans. Conway p.24
31 ibid., 'Pythian Ode I' p.82-3
32 La Fay, 'Sicily, Where All the Songs Are Sad', **National Geographic Magazine** 149, no.3 (March 1976) p.407
33 Goëthe, **Italian Journey**, trans. Auden and Mayer p.128
34 ibid. p.240
35 Abu Zakariya, 'The Spear', trans. Kemp, in **Anthology of Medieval Lyrics**, ed Flores p.292
36 Homer, **Odyssey**, Book XII
37 Morton, **A Traveller in Southern Italy** p.377
38 William of Poitiers, in Douglas and Greenaway **English Historical Documents**, vol.2 p.231
39 Gibbs-Smith, **The Bayeux Tapestry** p.10

40 William of Poitiers, in Douglas and Greenaway, **English Historical Documents**, vol.2 p.231
41 ibid. p.231-2
42 Gibbon, **The Decline and Fall**, Chapter XXXI
43 Gervase of Canterbury, in Coulton **Life in the Middle Ages**, vol.2 p.1
44 **The Anglo-Saxon Chronicle**, ed. Whitelock and Douglas trans. Tucker p.139-40
45 Churchill, **History of the English-Speaking Peoples**, vol.4 p.115-16
46 William of Poitiers, in Douglas and Greenaway, **English Historical Documents**, vol.2 p.233-4
47 ibid. p.649-50
48 ibid. p.233
49 **Corpus Poeticum Boreale**, vol.1, trans. Vigfusson and Powell p.192-93
50 Ordericus Vitalis, **Ecclesiastical History**, vol.1, trans. Forester p.482
51 ibid. p.482-3
52 ibid. p.483
53 ibid. p.484
54 William of Poitiers, in Douglas and Greenaway, **English Historical Documents**, vol.2, p.242-3
55 ibid. p.243
56 Elvins, **Invicta** p.5-6
57 Ordericus Vitalis, **Ecclesiastical History** vol. 1, trans. Forester p.490-1
58 Shakespeare, **Richard III**, IV, 3, lines 2-3
59 Ordericus Vitalis, **Ecclesiastical History** vol.2, trans. Forester p.3
60 Douglas and Greenaway **English Historial Documents**, vol.2 p.432
61 Douglas, **William the Conqueror** p.212 footnote Number 1
62 Ordericus Vitalis, **Ecclesiastical History.** vol.2, trans. Forester p 14-15
63 ibid. p.15
64 ibid. p.16
65 For a contemporary account see **Somerset County Gazette**, April 14, 1978
66 Douglas, **William the Conquerer** p.217
67 Ordericus Vitalis, **Ecclesiastical History** vol.2, trans. Forester p.17
68 Shakespeare, **Henry IV** Part I, III, 1. line 31
69 Nuttgens, **York** p.43
70 Shakespeare, **Henry VI Part III**, I, 4. lines 179-80

71 Ordericus Vitalis, **Ecclesiastical History** vol.2, trans. Forester p.20
72 ibid. p.20
73 ibid. p.21
74 Roger of Hoveden, **Annals**, vol.1, trans. Riley p.143
75 Chamberlain, **Italian Bouquet** p. 379
76 Martini, **Pasta and Pizza** p.188
77 Morton, **A Traveller in Southern Italy** p.111
78 **Psalms** 5:11
79 ibid. 32:11
80 Iqbal, 'Bang-i Dara' in Beny, **Roloff Beny in Italy** p.101
81 Jörgensen, 'St Francis of Assisi', in **Brother Francis**, ed. Cunningham p.186
82 'Dictatus papae', in Tierney, **The Crises of Church and State** p.49-50
83 ibid p.60-61
84 Florence of Worcester, 'Chronicles', in **The Church Historians of England**, vol.2, trans. and ed. Stevenson p. 303
85 Tierney, **The Crisis of Church and State** p.63
86 Anna Comnena, **The Alexiade**, trans. Dawes p.33
87 ibid. p.31
88 ibid. p.37-38
89 Norwich, **The Normans in the South** p.238
90 Ordericus Vitalis, **Ecclesiastical History** vol.2, trans. Forester p.363
91 Masson, **A Companion Guide to Rome** p.346
92 Tierney. **The Crisis of Church and State** p.67
93 Dante, **Paradiso**, Canto XVIII, ll. 46-48, trans. Ciardi
94 Comnena, **The Alexiade**, trans. Dawes p.147-8
95 ibid. p.148
96 **Anglo-Saxon Chronicle**, eds. Whitelock and Douglas, trans. Tucker p.161
97 Morton, **A Traveller in Southern Italy** p.98
98 Ordericus Vitalis, **Ecclesiastical History**, vol.2, trans. Forester p.418-19
99 ibid. p.419-22
100 **Anglo-Saxon Chronicle**, eds. Whitelock and Douglas, trans. Tucker p.85
101 Brown, **Rochester Castle** p.166
102 Poole, **From Domesday Book to Magna Carta 1087-1216** p.102
103 ibid.
104 Eadmer, **Life of Saint Anselm**, trans. Southern p.63-4
105 **Acts of the Apostles** 28:8

106 Monsarrat, **The Kappillon of Malta** p.219
107 ibid. p.220
108 Baker, **The Normans** p.250-1
109 Le Patourel **The Norman Empire**
110 Coulson, **The Saints** p.138
111 Roger of Wendover, **Flowers of History**, vol.I, trans. Giles p.448
112 Roger of Hoveden, **The Annals** vol.I, trans. Riley p.190
113 Baker, **The Normans** p.250
114 **Folklore, Myths and Legends in Britain**, Reader's Digest Association p.345
115 Poole, **From Domesday Book to Magna Carta 1087-1216** p.7
116 Matthew, **The Norman Conquest** p.275-6
117 Gibbon, **The Decline and Fall** Chapter LVIII
118 ibid.
119 ibid.
120 ibid.
121 ibid.
122 Fulcher of Chartres, **A History of the Expedition to Jerusalem,** trans. Ryan p.65-7
123 Gibbon, **The Decline and Fall** Chapter LVIII
124 Runciman, **A History of the Crusades,** vol.1, p.113
125 De Sanctis, **History of Italian Literature,** trans. Redfern vol.1, p.9
126 Bishop, **The Middle Ages** p.92-93
127 William of Newburgh, **The History,** trans. Stevenson p.404
128 Gibbon, **The Decline and Fall** Chapter LVIII
129 Gabrieli, **Arab Historians of the Crusades** p.73
130 Gibbon, **The Decline and Fall** Chapter LVIII
131 Mango, **Byzantium** p.74
132 Runciman, **The First Crusade** p.229
133 Helm, **Exploring Saxon and Norman England** p.161-2
134 ibid. p.159
135 Baker, **Medieval London** p.83
136 Fulcher of Chartres, **A History of the Expedition to Jerusalem,** trans. Ryan p.95
137 ibid p.99
138 Norwich, **The Normans in the South** p.273
139 Fulcher of Chartres, **A History of the Expedition to Jerusalem,** trans. Ryan p.120
140 **Gesta Francorum,** Book IV, trans. Hill p.91-92
141 William of Tyre, in Babcock and Krey, **Records of Civilization,** vol 1. p.371
142 Roger of Wendover, **Flowers of History** vol.1, trans. Giles p.434
143 William of Malmesbury, **History of the Kings of England,** trans. Sharpe p.284
144 See Douglas, **The Norman Fate,** p.p.15 and 18; Grinnel-

Milne, **The Killing of William Rufus,** p.159; Barlow, **William Rufus,** p.420 ff. Brooke, **Saxon and Norman Kings,** p.160-8, presents an interesting discussion, and the suggestion that Rufus was the subject of ritual slaughter by devil-worshippers.
145 Curtis, **Roger of Sicily** p.95
146 Norwich, **The Normans in the South** p.278-9
147 Robert de Monte, **The Chronicles,** trans. Stevenson p.682
148 Morton, **A Traveller in Southern Italy** p.130
149 Robert de Monte, **The Chronicles,** trans. Stevenson p.683
150 Brooke, **The Saxon and Norman Kings** p.172
151 Robert de Monte, **The Chronicles,** trans. Stevenson p.683
152 Burke, **Connections** p.90
153 Réau in **Encyclopedia of World Art,** vol. 4 p.826
154 Suger, 'Life of Louis VI, The Fat', in Ross and McLaughlin, **The Portable Medieval Reader** p.267
155 Fawtier, **Capetian Kings** p.19
156 Norwich, **The Normans in the South** p.286
157 Morton, **A Traveller in Southern Italy** p.141
158 Curtis, **Roger of Sicily** p.102
159 Norwich, **The Normans in the South** p.286
160 Bede, **Ecclesiastical History,** eds. Colgrave and Mynors p.33
161 Herodotus, **History of Herodotus,** trans. Rawlinson, Book I, p.12
162 William of Malmesbury, **The History of the Kings of England,** trans. Stevenson p.363-4
163 ibid p.364
164 ibid
165 ibid p.365
166 Henry of Huntingdon **The Chronicles,** trans. and ed. Forester p.249
167 Sackville-West, **Berkeley Castle** p.29
168 Marks, **Pilgrims, Heretics and Lovers** p.78
169 Ibn Jubayr, **The Travels,** trans. Broadhurst p.339
170 Waern, **Medieval Sicily** p.49
171 For an excellent recipe for Couscous *a la Siciliana,* see Ada Boni, **Italian Regional Cooking,** Bonanza Books, New York.
172 Waern, **Medieval Sicily** p.300
173 Costain, **The Conquering Family** p.14
174 Roger of Wendover, **Flowers of History** vol. 1, trans. Giles p.476
175 Gascoigne, **Castles of Britain** p.108
176 Ibn Jubayr, **The Travels,** trans. Broadhurst p.344
177 Norwich, **The Kingdom in the Sun** p.13

178 ibid. p.14
179 Brooke, **The Monastic World,** p.157
180 ibid. p.157-8
181 Phillips, **Fountains Abbey** p.6
182 William of Newburgh, **The History,** trans. Stevenson p.418
183 Warren, **Henry II** p.11
184 Kelly, **Eleanor of Aquitaine and the Four Kings** p.98
185 Curtis, **Roger of Sicily,** p.168
186 Barzini, **The Italians** p.91
187 Borg, 'Robert Curthose', in **British History Illustrated, V,** no. 1 (April-May 1978) p.46
188 Roger of Hoveden, **The Annals,** vol. 1. trans. Riley. p.225
189 Douglas, **The Norman Fate** p.17-18
190 Henry of Huntingdon, **The Chronicles,** trans. and ed. Forester p.259
191 ibid.
192 Coulton, **Life in the Middle Ages,** Vol. 3, p.2
193 Roger of Hoveden, **The Annals,** vol.1, trans. Riley p.224
194 Henry of Huntingdon, **The Chronicles,** trans. and ed. Forester p.260
195 Robert de Monte, **The Chronicles,** trans. Stevenson p.699
196 Henry of Huntingdon, **The Chronicles,** trans and ed. Forester p.262
197 Curtis, **Roger of Sicily** p.173
198 Norwich, **The Kingdom in the Sun** p.52
199 Bernard of Clairvaux, **Life and Works of Saint Bernard,** vol.2, ed. Mabillon; trans. Eales, p.471
200 Brown, **Castle Rising** p.15
201 ibid. p.44
202 Bernard de Ventadour, 'Can vei la lauzeta mover', **Das Alter Werk,** Telefunken Records 6:35412-1
203 Kybalová, Herbanová and Lamarová **The Pictorial Encyclopaedia of Fashion,** trans. Rosoux p.117
204 Henry of Huntingdon, **The Chronicles,** trans. and ed. Forester p.271
205 **The Anglo-Saxon Chronicle,** eds. Whitelock, Douglas, trans. Tucker p.199-200
206 Norwich, **The Kingdom in the Sun** p.68
207 ibid.
208 ibid. p.132
209 Waern, **Medieval Sicily** p.165
210 Curtis, **Roger of Sicily** p.320
211 Demus, **The Mosaics of Norman Sicily** p.37
212 Bernard of Clairvaux, **Life and Works of Saint Bernard,** vol.2, ed. Mabillon; trans. Eales. p.617
213 Robert de Monte, **The Chronicles,** trans. Stevenson p.714-15

214 William of Newburgh, **The History,** trans. Stevenson p.413

215 **The Anglo-Saxon Chronicle,** eds. Whitelock and Douglas, trans. Tucker p.199

216 Norwich, **The Kingdom in the Sun** p.90

217 Warren, **Henry II** p.29

218 Pernoud, **Eleanor of Aquitaine,** trans. Wiles, p.41

219 ibid.

220 Norwich, **The Kindom in the Sun** p.96

221 Ibn Jubayr, **The Travels,** trans. Broadhurst p.349

222 Warren, Henry II p.32

223 Ordericus Vitalis, **Ecclesiastical History,** vol.2, trans. Forester p.131

224 Otto of Freising, **Deeds of Frederick Barbarossa,** trans. Mierow and Emery p.71

225 Norwich, **The Kingdom in the Sun** p.122

226 Otto of Freising, **Deeds of Frederick Barbarossa,** trans. Mierow and Emery p.73-4

227 Bernard of Clairvaux, **Life and Works of Saint Bernard** vol.2, ed. Mabillon, trans. Eales p.909

228 **Music of the Crusades,** trans. Clare, Argo Records ZRG 673

229 Curtis, **Roger of Sicily** p.230

230 ibid.

231 ibid.

232 **Micah** 7:8

233 Warren, **Henry II** p.34

234 ibid. p.17

235 Curtis, **Roger of Sicily** p.311

236 Roger of Hoveden, **The Annals,** vol. 1, trans. Riley p.250

237 Henry of Huntingdon, **The Chronicles,** ed. and trans. Forester p.286

238 Goldman, **The Lion in Winter,** Act I, sc.4

239 Kelly, **Eleanor of Aquitaine and the Four Kings** p.84

240 Ross and McLaughlin, eds. **The Portable Medieval Reader,** p.340

241 John of Salisbury, **Memoirs,** trans. Chibnal p.61-2

242 **Gesta Stephani,** ed. and trans. Potter p.221

243 Henry of Huntingdon, **The Chronicles,** ed. and trans. Forester p.289-90

244 Kelly, **Eleanor of Aquitaine and the Four Kings** p.100

245 Pevsner, **The Buildings of Britain,** vol. 11 (Essex) p.98

246 Harvey, **The Plantagenets** p.49

247 Kelly, **Eleanor of Aquitaine and the Four Kings** p.105

248 Norwich, **The Kingdom in the Sun** p.150-1

249 Henry of Huntingdon, **The Chronicles,** ed. and trans. Forester p.294

250 Marks, **Pilgrims, Heretics and Lovers** p.156

251 Valency, **In Praise of Love** p.135

252 Marks, **Pilgrims, Heretics and Lovers** p.156

253 **Aucassin and Nicolette,** trans. Lang p.32

254 Dante, **Paradiso,** Canto XXX1, trans. Ciardi 11. 109-111

255 Déer, **The Dynastic Porphyry Tombs,** trans. Gillhoff p.89

256 Curtis, **Roger of Sicily** p.318

257 Norwich, **The Kingdom in the Sun** p.163

258 ibid. p.170

259 William of Malmesbury, **The History of the Kings of England,** trans. Sharpe p.389

260 Kelly, **Eleanor of Aquitaine and the Four Kings** p.118

261 ibid p.119

262 Henry of Huntingdon, **The Chronicles,** ed. and trans. Forester, p.297

263 Waddell, **The Wandering Scholars** p.216

264 William fitzStephen, 'A Description of London', in F.M.Stenton, **Historical Association Leaflets,** nos. 93, 94. p.27

265 Ralph de Diceto, **Historical Works,** vol. 1, ed. Stubbs p.293

266 Giraldus Cambrensis (Gerald of Wales), 'The Conquest of Ireland', in Douglas and Greenaway, **English Historical Documents,** vol.2 p.415

267 Zarnecki, 'The Art and Architecture', in Walter Annenberg *et al,* **Westminster Abbey** p.148

268 Walker, 'The Hereford Cider Festival', **In Britain,** Vol.28, no.5, May 1973, p.40

269 Zarnecki, 'Romanesque Architecture', in **Encyclopedia of World Art,** vol. 12 p.416

270 Norwich, **The Kingdom in the Sun** p.168

271 ibid. p.169

272 Otto of Freising, **The Deeds of Frederick Barbarossa,** trans. Merrow and Emery p.129

273 Ross and McLaughlin, eds. **The Portable Medieval Reader** p.343

274 Norwich, **The Kingdom in the Sun** p.179

275 Morton, **A Traveller in Southern Italy** p.118

276 Ruskin, **The Stones of Venice,** vol. 1, book 2, p.106

277 Memento of the Dead, Canon of the Mass

278 Douglas and Greenaway, **English Hstorical Documents,** vol.2 p.829

279 Murray, **Italy: The Fatal Gift** p.189

280 Gissing, **By the Ionian Sea** p.7

281 Decker, **Romanesque Art in Italy** p.61

282 Otto of Freising, **The Deeds of Frederick Barbarossa,** trans. Mierow and Emery p.183

283 ibid. p.184

284 ibid. p.185-86

285 Warren, **Henry II** p.77

286 Norwich, **The Kingdom in the Sun** p.209

287 Otto of Freising, **The Deeds of Frederick Barbarossa,** trans. Mierow and Emery p.289

288 Norwich, **The Kingdom in the Sun** p.211

289 Scott, **Marmion,** Canto 1, lines 4-6

290 ibid. Canto 1, lines 8-13

291 Waern, **Medieval Sicily** p.115

292 Curtis, **Roger of Sicily** p.313

293 ibid. p.314

294 Norwich, **The Kingdom in the Sun** p.241

295 ibid. p.239

296 Pain, **The King and Becket** p.57

297 Hutton, **Thomas Becket** p.52

298 Morris, **The Life and Martyrdom of Saint Thomas Becket** p.69

299 Hutton, **Thomas Becket** p.60

300 Fry, **Curtmantle,** Act II p.48

301 Introit of the Mass, December 26

302 Gospel for December 26

303 Knowles, **The Episcopal Colleagues of Thomas Becket** p.77-8

304 ibid. p.85-8

305 Anon. 'In Rama sonat genitus', trans. Blachly, **Music In Honor of St. Thomas of Canterbury.** Nonesuch Records H-71292,

306 Fry, **Curtmantle,** Act II p.52

307 Norwich, **The Kingdom in The Sun** p.243

308 Curtis, **Roger of Sicily** p.430

309 Norwich, **The Kingdom in The Sun** p.258-9

310 Hutton, **Thomas Becket** p.126-7

311 ibid. p.138

312 Warren, **Henry II** p.104 footnote

313 Hutton, **S. Thomas of Canterbury** p.120-3

314 Ibn Jubayr, **The Travels** p.338-40

315 Pearce, 'Heroic Bronzes of the Fifth Century B.C. Regain Old Splendor', **The Smithsonian,** vol.12, no.8, November 1981 p.126

316 Ibn Jubayr, **The Travels** p.339

317 'L'histoire de Guillaume le Maréchal', ed. Meyer, in Kelly, **Eleanor of Aquitaine and the Four Kings** p.195

318 Kelly, **Eleanor of Aquitaine and the Four Kings** p.194

319 'The Fair Rosamond', in Edwards, **A Book of Old English Ballads** p.59-60

320 Giraldus Cambrensis (Gerald of Wales) 'De principis instructione', in Kelly, **Eleanor of Aquitaine and the Four Kings** p.191

321 Pernoud, **Eleanor of Aquitaine,** trans. Wiles p.115

322 'Bernard de Ventadour', in Grenabier, **English Literature and its Background,** vol.1 p.1039
323 Bogin, **The Woman Troubadours** p.89
324 Marks, **Pilgrims, Heretics and Lovers** p.181
325 Warren, **Henry II** p.112
326 Eliot, **Murder in the Cathedral,** Part I p.41
327 Anouilh, **Becket, or the Honor of God,** trans. Hill, Act 2, p.124
328 Knowles, **Thomas Becket** p.146
329 ibid. p.147
330 Winston, **Thomas Becket** p.366
331 Chaucer, **Canterbury Tales** Prologue, lines 15-17
332 'Sequence, Solemn Canticun', trans. Blachly: **Music in Honor of St. Thomas of Canterbury.** Nonesuch Records H-71292.
333 Warren, **Henry II** p.113
334 Curtis, **Roger of Sicily** p.431
335 ibid. p.434
336 Morton, **A Traveller in Southern Italy** p.195
337 Waern, **Medieval Sicily** p.190
338 Giraldus Cambrensis (Gerald of Wales), **Itinerary Through Wales,** ed. Rhys p.99
339 Kelly, **Eleanor of Aquitaine and the Four Kings** p.225
340 Bancroft, **Henry the Second,** Act I, scene 1 p.5
341 Knowles, **Thomas Becket** p.153
342 Waern, **Medieval Sicily** p.209
343 ibid. p.227
344 Rossi, **Mosaics,** trans. Ross p.75
345 Symonds, **Sketches in Italy** p.252-3
346 Norwich, **The Kingdom in the Sun** p.77
347 Geoffrey de Vinsauf, **Itinerary of Richard King of the English to the Holy Land,** trans. anonymous p.155-6
348 Kelly, **Eleanor of Aquitaine and the Four Kings** p.233
349 Bertran de Born, in Costain, **The Conquering Family** p.151
350 William of Newburgh, in Douglas and Greenaway, **English Historical Documents,** vol.2 p.380
351 Appleby, **Henry II, the Vanquished King** p.229
352 Giraldus Cambrensis (Gerald of Wales), in Douglas and Greenaway, **English Historical Documents** vol.2. p.417-18
353 Scott-Moncrieff, **Scottish Border Abbeys** p.30
354 Richard le Poitevin, 'Lament for Eleanor', in Kelly, **Eleanor of Aquitaine and the Four Kings** p.238-9
355 Peter of Blois' 14th letter to Henry II's chaplains, **Life in**

the Middle Ages, vol.3 ed. Coulton p.2
356 Appleby, **Henry II, the Vanquished King** p.249
357 Brown, Colvin and Taylor, **The History of the King's Works,** vol.2 p.1010
358 'The Fair Rosamond', in Edwards, **A Book of Old English Ballads** p.61
359 ibid. p.60-1
360 Barber, **Henry Plantagenet** p.66
361 Roger of Hoveden, **The Annals,** vol.1, trans. Riley p.413
362 Helm, **Exploring Saxon and Norman England** p.158
363 Warren, **Henry II** p.147
364 Boccaccio, **Decameron** (tale 6 of the 5th day), trans. Paynes
365 Waern, **Medieval Sicily** p.123
366 Scott, **Ivanhoe** Chap.XLI
367 Bertran de Born, in Kelly, **Eleanor of Aquitaine and the Four Kings** p.260
368 Warren, **Henry II** p.590
369 Roger of Hoveden (previously ascribed to Benedict of Peterborough), **Gesta Regis Henrici Secundi,** vol.1, (rolls series 49), ed. Stubbs p.297
370 Bertran de Born, in Pound, **Confusius to Cummings: An Anthology of Poetry** p.80-1
371 Goldman, **The Lion in Winter,** Act I, p.7
372 Chaytor, **The Troubadours** p.63
373 Dante, **Inferno,** trans. Ciardi: Introduction to Canto XXVIII p.235
374 ibid. Canto XXVIII, lines 127-43 p.239
375 **East London Church Chronicle,** vol. 6, no.3, 1895
376 Brooke, **The Monastic World 1100-1300,** p.165
377 Boswell, **The Life of Samuel Johnson,** p.61
378 D.M.S., **Punch, or, The London Carivari,** April 1932
379 Brooke, **The Monastic World, 1000-1300** p.165
380 Lewer, **The Temple Church** p.7
381 ibid. p.8
382 Ibn Jubayr, **The Travels,** trans. Broadhurst p.353-4
383 Kelly, **Eleanor of Aquitaine and the Four Kings** p.286
384 Roger of Hoveden, **The Annals,** vol.2, trans. Riley p.64
385 Pevsner and Nairn, **The Buildings of Britain,** vol.28 (Sussex) p.128
386 Anderson and Hicks, **Cathedrals in Britain and Ireland** p.49
387 Coulson, **The Saints** p.152
388 Curtis, **Roger of Sicily** p.434
389 Warren, **Henry II** p.625
390 Giraldus Cambrensis (Gerald of Wales), 'Concerning the Instruction of a Prince', in Douglas and Greenaway,

English Historical Documents vol.2 p.413
391 Warren, **Henry II** p.626
392 ibid. 390 p.415
393 Appleby, **Henry II, The Vanguard King** p.344
394 Giraldus Cambrensis (Gerald of Wales), 'Concerning the Instruction of a Prince', in Douglas and Greenaway, **English Historical Documents,** vol.2 p.414
395 ibid. p.415
396 Roger of Hoveden, **The Annals,** vol.2, trans. Riley p.111
397 Haskins, **The Normans in European History** p.92
398 Richardson and Sayles, **The Governance of Medieval England** p.268
399 Warren, **Henry II** p.627
400 Gillingham, **Richard the Lionheart** p.150
401 Runciman, **A History of the Crusades,** vol. 3, p.11
402 Roger of Hoveden, **The Annals of Roger of Hoveden,** vol.2, trans. Riley p.140-1
403 Runciman, **The Sicilian Vespers** p.214
404 Richard of Devizes *et al,* **Chronicles of the Crusades,** sec. 20, p.13
405 Gillingham, **Richard the Lionheart** p.151
406 ibid. p.153
407 ibid. p.160
408 Runciman, **A History of the Crusades** vol.3, p.43-4
409 ibid. p.57
410 Norwich, **The Kingdom in the Sun** p.380
411 Broughton, **The Legend of King Richard I Coeur de Lion** p.70
412 ibid. p.71
413 Dickens, **A Child's History of England** p.82
414 Adams, **Mont-Saint-Michel and Chartres** p.221
415 Richard I, in Flores, **An Anthology of Medieval Lyrics,** trans. Terry p.114
416 William of Newburgh, **The History** trans. Stevenson p.630
417 Norwich, **The Kingdom in the Sun** p.384
418 William of Newburgh, **The History,** trans. Stevenson p.630
419 Curtis, **Roger of Sicily** p.438
420 Norwich, **The Kingdom in the Sun** p.389
421 Crawford, **The Rulers of the South** p.256
422 ibid. p.257
423 Fry, **The David and Charles Book of Castles** p.80
424 Bingham, **The Crowned Lions: The Early Plantagenet Kings** p.132
425 Gunther, **Inside Europe Today** p.159
426 Eliot, 'The Waste Land', in **Collected poems and plays, 1909-1950** p.42 also **The Waste Land and Other Poems,** p.34

Bibliography

Adams, Henry. **Mont-Saint-Michel and Chartres.** Boston and New York: Houghton Mifflin Company, n.d. London: Constable, 1950

Allen, Edward. **Stone Shelters.** Cambridge, Mass. and London, England: MIT Press, 1969

Anderson, William and Clive Hicks. **Cathedrals in Britain and Ireland.** New York: Charles Scribner's Sons, 1978. London: Macdonald and Jane's, 1978

The Anglo-Saxon Chronicle. Translated and edited by Joseph Stevenson. The Church Historians of England, vol. 2, part 1. London: Seeleys, 1853

The Anglo Saxon Chronicle. Edited by Dorothy Whitelock, with David C. Douglas. Translated by Susie I. Tucker. London: Eyre and Spottiswoode, 1961. New Brunswick: Rutgers University Press, 1961

Anna Comnena. **The Alexiade.** Translated by Elizabeth A. S. Dawes. London: Kegan Paul, Trench, Trubner and Company Ltd, 1928

Annenberg, Walter, et al. **Westminster Abbey.** Radnor, Pa: Annenberg School Press, 1972

Anouilh, Jean. **Becket, or the Honor of God.** Translated by Lucienne Hill. New York: Coward-McCann, Inc., 1960. London: Methuen London Ltd, 1961

An Anthology of Medieval Lyrics. Edited by Angel Flores. New York: the Modern Library, 1962

Appleby, John T. **England Without Richard 1189-1199.** London: G. Bell and Sons, Ltd. 1965
    Henry II. The Vanquished King. London: G. Bell and Sons, Ltd. 1962
    The Troubled Reign of King Stephen. London: G. Bell and Sons, Ltd. 1969

Arata, Giulio V. **L'Architettura Arabo-Normanna e il**

Rinascimento in Sicilia. Milan: Bestetti and Tumminelli, 1925

Ashdown, Charles Henry. **European Arms and Armour.** New York: Brussel and Brussel, 1967

Ashley, Maurice. **The Life and Times of William I.** Kings and Queens of England, general editor Antonia Fraser. London: Weidenfeld and Nicolson, Ltd. 1973

Aucassin and Nicolette. Translated by Andrew Lang. Portland, Maine: Thomas B. Mosher, 1896. London: David Nutt, 1887

Baker, Derek, editor. **The Early Middle Ages 871-1216.** Portraits and Documents Series. London: Hutchinson Educational, 1966

Baker, Timothy. **Medieval London.** London: Cassell and Company Ltd, 1970
    The Normans. New York: Macmillan Company, 1966. London: Cassell and Co. Ltd, 1966

Bancroft, John. **Henry the Second, King of England.** Edited by Will Montfort. London: Printed for Jacob Tonson, 1693

Barber, Richard W. **Henry Plantagenet.** London: Barrie and Rockliffe with Pall Mall Press, 1964. New York: Roy Publishers, 1964

Barlow, Frank. **Edward the Confessor.** Berkeley and Los Angeles: University of California Press, 1970. London: Eyre and Spottiswoode, 1970
    'Edward the Confessor and the Norman Conquest.' In **1066 Commemorative Lectures.** London: The Historical Association, 1966
    The Feudal Kingdom of England. London: Longmans, Green and Company Ltd, 1961

Barraclough, Geoffrey. **The Crucible of Europe.** Berkeley and Los Angeles: University of California Press, 1976. London: Thames and Hudson, 1976

Barzini, Luigi. **The Italians.** New York: Atheneum, 1965. London: Hamish Hamilton, 1964. Toronto; London: Bantam, 1976

Basile, Francesco. **L'Architettura della Sicilia Normanna.** Catania, Caltanissetta, Rome: Vito Cavalotta Editore, 1975

Batterberry, Michael. **Art of the Middle Ages.** Discovering Art Series. New York, San Francisco, Toronto: McGraw Hill Book Company, 1974

Beautiful Castles of Britain. London: Marshall Cavendish Books Ltd, 1978

Beckwith, John. **Early Medieval Art** The World of Art Series. New York and Toronto: Oxford University Press, 1964

Bede, The Venerable. **Bede's Ecclesiastical History of the English People.** Edited by Bertram Colgrave and R. A. B. Mynors. London: Oxford University Press, 1969

Belli, Giuseppe Gioachino. **Sonnets of Giuseppe Belli.** Translated by Miller Williams. Baton Rouge and London: Louisiana State University Press, 1981

Benedict of Peterborough. (Now established as work of Roger of Hoveden) **Reigns of Henry II and Richard I.** Edited by William Stubbs. 2 vols. Rerum Britannicarum Medii Scriptores. Roll Series 49. London: Longman, Green, Reader and Dyer, 1867
    Salerna of Ifield. Translated by Kenneth M. Ffinch. Reprinted from the Transactions of the Dartmouth Antiquarian Society, 1935

Beny, Roloff and company. **Roloff Beny in Italy.** New York, Evanston, San Francisco, London: Harper and Row, Publishing, 1974

Berington, Joseph. **The History of the Reign of Henry the Second and of Richard and John, his sons.** London: Printed by M. Swinney: for G. G. and J. Robinson, Paternoster Row: and R. Faulder, New Bond Street, 1790

Bernard of Clairvaux. **Life and Works of Saint Bernard.** 4 vols. Edited by John Mabillon. Translated and edited with additional notes by Samuel J. Eales. London: Burns and Oates Ltd, N.D. London: John Hodges, 1889
The Works of Bernard of Clairvaux, 3 vols. Translated by Lilian Walsh and Irene Edmonds. Cistercian Fathers Series. Kalamazoo, Mich.: Cistercian Publications, 1976. London: Mowbrays 1976

Bingham, Caroline. **The Crowned Lions: The Early Plantagenet Kings.** Newton Abbey: David and Charles, 1978

Binyon, Laurence. **The Young King: A Play in 11 Scenes.** London: Macmillan and Company, Ltd, 1935

Bishop, Morris Gilbert. **The Middle Ages.** New York: American Heritage Press, 1970. Also London: Cassell, 1969
Petrarch and his World. Port Washington, N.Y.: Kennikat Press, 1963

Boccaccio, Giovanni. **The Decameron of Giovanni Boccaccio.** Translated by John Payne. New York: Blue Ribbon Books, 1931

Bogin, Meg. **The Woman Troubadours.** New York and London: Paddington Press, Ltd, 1976

Borg, Alan. 'Robert Curthose.'**British History Illustrated Special Issue: England Under the Normans 1066-1154.** Vol. 5, No. 1 (April/May 1978): 43-46.

Boswell, James. **The Life of Samuel Johnson, L. L. D.** New York: The Modern Library, n.d. London: Oxford University Press, 1970

Bradford, Ernie. **The Shield and the Sword: The Knights of Malta.** London: Fontana/Collins, 1972

Briffault, Robert S. **The Troubadours.** Bloomington: Indiana University Press, 1965

Brooke, Christopher N. **From Alfred to Henry III.** New York: W. W. Norton and Company, Inc,

1961. Edinburgh: Thomas Nelson and Sons, 1961. London: Sphere books, 1969
The Monastic World 1000-1300. London: Paul Elek Ltd, 1974
The Saxon and Norman Kings. Glasgow: Fontana, Collins, 1967

Broughton, Bradford B. **The Legends of King Richard I Coeur de Lion.** The Hague, Paris: Mouton and Company, 1966

Brown, Reginald Allen. **Castle Rising.** London: Her Majesty's Stationery Office, 1978
English Medieval Castles. London: B. T. Batsford Ltd, 1954, 1962
(with Howard Montagu Colvin and Alfred John Taylor) **The History of the King's Works.** London: Her Majesty's Stationery Office, 1963
The Normans and the Norman Conquest. New York: Thomas Y. Crowell Company, Inc, 1968. London: Constable 1969
Orford Castle. London: Her Majesty's Stationery Office, 1964
Rochester Castle. London: Her Majesty's Stationery Office, 1969

Brundage, James A. **Richard Lion Heart.** New York: Charles Scribner's Sons, 1974

Bryant, Arthur. **The Medieval Foundation of England.** New York: Doubleday and Company, 1967. London: Collins, 1966

Burke, James. **Connections.** Boston, Toronto: Little, Brown and Company, 1978. London: Macmillan, 1978

Busch, Harald, and Bernd Loshe, editors. **Gothic Europe.** Inroduction by Kurt Gerstenberg. Commentaries on illustrations by Helmut Domke. New York: Macmillan Company, 1959. London: B. T. Batsford, 1959

Bussby, Frederick. **The History of Winchester Cathedral.** Southampton: Paul Cave Publications, n.d.

Butler, D. **Saint Cuthbert of Melrose, Lindisfarne, Farne, and Durham Apostle of Northumbria.** The Iona Series. Edinburgh: T. N. Foulis, 1913

Cantor, Norman F. **Medieval History: The Life and Death of a Civilization.** New York: Macmillan Publishing Company, 1969. London: Collier-Macmillan, 1969

Carville, Geraldine. **Norman Splendour.** Belfast: Blackstaff Press, 1979

Chamberlain, Samuel. **Italian Bouquet.** New York: Gourmet Distributing Company, 1958

Chaucer, Geoffrey. **The Canterbury Tales.**

Chaytor, Henry John. **The Troubadours.** Cambridge University Press, 1912

Christiansen, Eric. 'Two-dimensional Templars.'**The Spectator,** 16 January 1982

Chronicles of Stephen, Henry II and Richard I. Edited by Richard Howlett. Series: Berum Britannicarum Medii Scriptores. London: Longman and Co, 1884

Churchill, Winston S. **The Birth of Britain.** History of the English-Speaking Peoples, vol. 1. New York: Bantam Books, 1956. London: Cassell, 1956-58

The Church Historians of England. 8 vols. Translated by Joseph Stevenson. London: Seeleys, 1856

Clark, Sidney A. **Today in Cathedral France.** New York: Robert M. McBride and Company, 1948

Colvin, Howard Montagu, general editor. **The History of the King's Works,** vols. 1 and 2. 6 vols. Edited by R. Allen Brown, Howard Montagu Colvin, and Alfred John Taylor. London: Her Majesty's Stationery Office, 1963

Combe, William. **The History of the Abbey Church of St. Peter's Westminster, Its Antiques and Monuments.** 2 vols. London: Printed for R. Ackerman, by L. Harrison and J. C. Leigh, 1812

Conti, Flavio. **Centers of Belief.** The Grand Tour Series. Translated by Patrick Creagh. Boston: Harcourt Brace Jovanovich, Inc. 1977. London: Cassell, 1979
Homes of Kings. The Grand Tour Series. Translated by Patrick Creagh

Boston: Harcourt Brace Jovanovich, 1977. London: Cassell, 1979

Contini, Gianfranco. **Letteratura Italiana delle Origini.** Italy: Sansoni, 1976

Corpus Poeticum Boreale. 2 vols. Translated by Gudranr Vigfusson, and Frederick York Powell. London: Oxford University Press, 1883

Costain, Thomas B. **The Conquering Family.** New York: Popular Library by arrangment with Doubleday and Company, Inc, 1962
　The Conquerors. The Pageant of England. Garden City, New York: Doubleday and Company, Inc, 1949.

Cottrell, Leonard. **This England.** Prepared by Merle Severy. Washington: National Geographic Society, 1966.

Coulson, John, editor. **The Saints: A Concise Biographical Dictionary.** New York: Hawthorn Books, Inc, 1958. London; Amsterdam: Burns and Oates, 1953

Coulton, George Gordon. **The Fate of Medieval Art in the Renaissance and Reformation.** Art and the Reformation, part 2. New York: Harper Torchbooks, 1958. Cambridge: At the University Press, 1953
　From St. Francis to Dante. London: David Nutt, 1906
　Life in the Middle Ages. 2 vols. Cambridge: At the University Press, 1967
　Medieval Panorama. New York: Meridian Books, 1957. Cambridge: University Press 1938. London: Collins 1961
　Medieval Studies. 2 vols. London: Simpkins, Marshall, Hamilton, Kent and Company, Ltd, 1905-1931. Also Boston: Beacon 1959

Cowdrey, H. E. J. **The Age of Abbot Desiderius: Montecassino, The Papacy and the Normans in the Eleventh and Early Twelfth Centuries.** Oxford, Clarendon Press, 1983

Crawford, Francis Marion. **The Rulers of the South.** 2 vols. New York: The Macmillan Company, 1900. London: Macmillan and Co. 1900

Cronne, H. A. **The Reign of Stephen 1135-54: Anarchy in England.** London: Weidenfeld and Nicolson, 1970

Cunningham, Lawrence, editor. **Brother Francis: An Anthology of Writings by and about St. Francis of Assisi.** New York: Harper and Row Publishers, 1972

Curtis, Edmund. **Roger of Sicily, and the Normans in Lower Italy, 1016-1154.** Heroes of the Nations Series, editor H.W.C. Davis. New York and London: G.P. Putnam's Sons; 1912

Cuthbert, Father. **The Friars and How They Came to England.** London: Sands and Company, 1903

Dahmus, Joseph. **Seven Medieval Kings.** New York: Doubleday and Company Inc. 1967
　Seven Medieval Queens. New York: Doubleday and Company Inc. 1972

Dalven, Rae. **Anna Comnena.** New York: Twayne Publishers, Inc, 1972

Dante. **The Inferno.** Translated by John Ciardi. New York: Mentor Books, 1954
　The Paradiso. Translated by John Ciardi. New York: Mentor Books, 1961
　Complete **Divine Comedy.** New York; London: Norton, 1970

Davis, Henry William Carless. **Medieval Europe.** London: Oxford University Press, 1961

Davis, Ralph Henry Carless. **King Stephen.** Berkeley and Los Angeles: University of California Press, 1967. London: Longmans, 1967
　The Normans and Their Myth. London: Thames and Hudson, 1976

de Castries, Duc. **The Lives of the Kings and Queens of France.** Translated by Anne Dobell. New York: Alfred A. Knopf, 1979

Decker, Hans. **Romanesque Art in Italy.** New York: Harry Abrams, Inc. 1959

Déer, József. **The Dynastic Porphyry Tombs of the Norman Period in Sicily.** Translated by Gerd Aage Gillhoff. Cambridge, Mass: Harvard University Press, 1959

Delderfield, Eric R., with D.V. Cook. **Kings and Queens of England and Great Britain.** London: David and Charles 1966

Demus, Otto. **Byzantine Art and the West.** New York: New York University Press, 1970. London: Weidenfeld and Nicolson, 1970
　The Mosaics of Norman Sicily. London: Routledge and Kegan Paul Ltd. 1949. New York: Philosophical Library, 1950

De Sanctis, Francesco. **History of Italian Literature.** 2 vols. Translated by Joan Redfern. New York: Barnes and Noble, Inc. 1968

Dickens, Charles. **A Child's History of England.** London: Chapman and Hall, Ltd. 1906

Dickinson, Clarence. **Troubadour Songs.** Historical introduction, biographical notes and English texts by Helen A. Dickinson. New York: H. W. Gray Company, 1920

D.M.S. **Punch, or the London Carivari,** April 1932

Douglas, David C. **The Norman Achievement.** Berkeley and Los Angeles: University of California Press, 1969. London: Eyre and Spottiswoode, 1969
　The Norman Fate 1100-1154. Berkeley and Los Angeles: University of California Press, 1976. London: Eyre Methuen, 1976
　Time and the Hour. London: Eyre Methuen, 1977
　William the Conqueror. Berkeley and Los Angeles: University of California Press, 1964. London: Eyre Methuen 1977

Douglas, David C. and George W. Greenaway, **English Historical Documents 1042-1189,** vol 2. 12 vols. New York: Oxford University Press, 1953. 2nd ed., London: Eyre Methuen; and New York: Oxford University Press, 1981

Downs, Norton, editor **Basic Documents in Medieval History.** Princeton, New Jersey: D. Van Nostrand Company Inc. 1959
　Medieval Pageant. Princeton, New Jersey: D. Van Nostrand Company, Inc. 1964

Drew, Katherine Fischer, editor. **Barbarian Invasions.** Huntington, New York: Robert E. Krieger Publishing Company, 1977

Duggan, Alfred. **The Devil's Brood.** New York: Coward-McCann, Inc. 1957. London: Arrow Books, 1957, 1960. London: Corgi Books, 1975
    My Life for My Sheep. New York: Coward-McCann, Inc. 1955

Durrell, Lawrence, **Sicilian Carousel.** London; Faber and Faber, 1977

Eadmer. **The Life of Saint Anselm.** Edited and translated by Richard W. Southern. London: Oxford University Press 1962. London, Edinburgh, Paris, Melbourne, Toronto and New York: Thomas Nelson and Sons, Ltd. 1962

East London Church Chronicle. Vol. 6, no. 3, 1895

Eccleston, Thomas. **The Chronicle of Thomas Eccleston 'De Adventu Fratrum Minorum in Angliam'.** Translated by Father Cuthbert. London: Sands and Company, 1909

Edwards, George Wharton. **A Book of Old English Ballads.** Introduction by Hamilton W. Mabie. New York: Macmillan Company, 1910

Eliot, Thomas Stearns **Collected Poems and Plays 1909-1950.** New York: Harcourt, Brace and World, Inc, 1952, 1960
    Murder in the Cathedral. New York and London: Harcourt, Brace, Jovanovich, 1963. London: Faber and Faber, 1935
    The Waste Land and Other Poems. London: Faber and Faber, 1940

Elsy, Mary. **Brittany and Normandy.** London: B. T. Batsford, Ltd, 1974

Elvins, S. W. G. **'Invicta': The Story of a Royal Castle.** Dover: Buckland Press, n.d.

Encyclopaedia Britannica. Edited by Walter Yust. Chicago, London, Toronto: 1948

Encyclopaedia of World Art. New York, Toronto, London: McGraw Hill, 1959

Evans, Joan. **Art in Medieval France.** Oxford: At the Clarendon Press, 1948
    Life in Medieval France. London: Phaidon Press, 1957

Eyton, R. W. **Court, Household and Itinerary of King Henry II.** London: Taylor and Company, 1878

Fawtier, Robert. **The Capetian Kings of France.** New York: St. Martin's Press, 1960 London: Macmillan, 1960

Fenwick, Kenneth, editor. **The Third Crusade.** London: Folio Society, 1958

Ferguson, George. **Signs and Symbols in Christian Art.** New York: Oxford University Press, 1954

Fernandez, Dominique. **The Mother Sea: Travels in South Italy, Sardinia and Sicily.** Translated by Michael Callum. New York: Hill and Wang, 1965. London: Secker and Warburg, 1967

Finberg, Herbert Patrick Reginald. **The Formation of England 550-1042.** London: Hart-Davis, MacGibbon, 1974

Finn, R. Welldon. **An Introduction to Domesday Book.** New York: Barnes and Noble, Inc. 1963. London: Longmans, 1963

Fisher, D. J. V. **The Anglo-Saxon Age.** London: Longman Group Ltd, 1973

FitzStephen, William. 'William FitzStephen's Description of London'. Translated by H. E. Butler. **Historical Association Leaflets** 93, 94. Edited by Frank M. Stenton. London: G. Bell and Sons, Ltd. 1934

Fletcher, Banister. **A History of Architecture on the Comparative Method.** New York: Charles Scribner's Sons, 1948. London: University of London, 1962 (17th Ed.)

Fletcher, Harry Luft Verne. **Herefordshire.** The County Book Series, general editor Brian Vesey-Fitzgerald. London: Robert Hale, Ltd. 1948

Florence of Worcester. **The Chronicles of Florence of Worcester.** Translated and edited by Joseph Stevenson. The Church Historians of England, vol. 2, pt. 1. London: Seeleys, 1853
    The Chronicles of Florence of Worcester. Translated by Thomas Forester. London: Henry G. Bohn, 1854

Folklore, Myths and Legends of Britain. London: Reader's Digest Association Ltd, 1973. (2nd ed. 1977)

Forde-Johnston, James. **Great Medieval Castles of Britain.** London: The Bodley Head, 1979

Fraser, Antonia, editor. **The Lives of the Kings and Queens of England.** New York: Alfred A. Knopf, 1975. London: Weidenfeld and Nicolson, 1975

Freeman, Edward A. **History of the Norman Conquest.** Chicago: University of Chicago Press, 1974. Oxford: At the Clarendon Press, 1877-79
    The Reign of William Rufus. 2 vols. Oxford: At the Clarendon Press, 1882

Fry, Christopher. **The Boy With a Cart: Cuthman, Saint of Sussex.** New York, London: Oxford University Press, 1950
    Curtmantle. New York, London: Oxford University Press, 1961

Fry, Plantagenet Somerset. **British Medieval Castles.** New York: A. S. Barnes and Company, 1974 Newton Abbot: David and Charles, 1974
    The David and Charles Book of Castles. Newton Abbot: David and Charles, 1980

Fulcher of Chartres. **A History of the Expedition to Jerusalem, 1095-1127.** Translated by Frances Rita Ryan. Knoxville: University of Tennessee Press, 1969

Furneaux, Rupert. **Invasion 1066.** Englewood Cliffs, New Jersey: Prentice-Hall, Inc, 1966

Gabrieli, Francesco, translator. **Arab Historians of the Crusades.** London: Routledge and Kegan Paul, 1969

Gascoigne, Christina. **Castles of Britain.** New York: G. P. Putnam's Sons, 1975. London: Thames and Hudson, 1975

Gaunt, William. **Oxford.** New York: Hastings House, 1966

Geoffrey of Vinsauf. **Itinerary of Richard King of the English to the Holy Land.** London: Henry G. Bohn, 1848

Geoffrey of Monmouth. **The Historia Regum Britanniae of Geoffrey of Monmouth.** Translated by Robert Ellis Jones. London, New York, Toronto: Longman, Green and Company, 1929
The History of the Kings of Great Britain. Translated and introduced by Lewis Thorpe. Harmondsworth, England, New York: Penguin Books, 1982

Gesta Francorum et aliorum Hierosolimitanorum (The Deeds of the Franks and other Pilgrims to Jerusalem). Translated by Rosalind Hill. London: Thomas Nelson and Sons Ltd, 1962

Gesta Stephani. Translated and edited by Kenneth Reginald Potter. London: Oxford University Press, 1976

Gibbon, Edward. **Decline and Fall of the Roman Empire.** 3 vols. New York: Modern Library Edition (Random House, Inc) n.d. Harmondsworth: Penguin, 1981

Gibbs-Smith, Charles H. **The Bayeux Tapestry.** London: Phaidon Press Ltd, 1973

Gies, Joseph and Francis. **Life in a Medieval City.** Medieval Life Series.
London: Barker, 1969

Gillingham, John. **Richard the Lionheart.** New York: Time Books, 1978. London: Weidenfeld and Nicolson, 1978

Gimpel, Jean. **The Medieval Machine.** Harmondsworth, England and New York: Penguin Books, 1977

Giraldus Cambrensis (Gerald of Wales). **Itinerary Through Wales,** and the **Description of Wales.** Edited by Ernest Rhys. London: J. M. Dent and Sons, Ltd (Everyman's Library) 1908

Gissing, George Robert. **By the Ionian Sea.** London: Chapman and Hall, 1905

Goethe, Johann Wolfgang von. **Italian Journey 1786–1788.** Translated by W. H. Auden and Elizabeth Mayer. New York: Schocken Books, 1968. Harmondsworth: Penguin 1970

Goldin, Frederick. **Lyrics of the Troubadours and Trouveres.** Garden City, New York: Anchor Books, 1973

Goldman, James **The Lion in Winter.** New York: Random House, 1966. London: Samuel French Ltd., 1970

Graham, Rose 'An Essay on English Monasteries' **Historical Association Leaflet 32.** London: The Historical Association, April 1913

Graham-Campbell, James **The Viking World.** New Haven and New York: Ticknor and Fields, 1980

Grebanier, Bernard D., editor, et al. **English Literature and Its Background.** Rev. ed. New York: Holt, 1949. New York: Dryden Press, 1952

Green, J. R. **Henry the Second.** London: Macmillan and Company Ltd, 1908

Grinnel-Milne, Duncan **The Killing of William Rufus: An Investigation in the New Forest.** New York: Augustus M. Kelly Publishers, 1968. Newton Abbot: David and Charles, 1963

Gunn, Peter **A Concise History of Italy.** New York: The Viking Press, 1972. London: Thames and Hudson, 1971
Normandy: Landscape with Figures. London: Victor Gollancz, Ltd, 1975

Gunther, John **Inside Europe Today.** New York: Harper and Brothers, 1961. London: Hamish Hamilton, 1961

Hall, Donald John **English Mediaeval Pilgrimage.** London: Routledge and Kegan Paul, 1965

Hare, Augustus John Cuthbert **Cities of Southern Italy and Sicily.** New York: George Routledge and Sons, n.d.

Harman, Alec **Mediaeval and Early Renaissance Music.** Fair Lawn, New Jersey: Essential Books, 1958

Harvey, John **The Plantagenets.** Rev.ed. Great Britain: Fontana/Collins, 1977

Haskins, Charles Homer. 'England and Sicily in the 12th Century.' **English Historical Revue,** vol.XXVI, nos. 103 and 104 (July/October 1911)
The Normans in European History New York: Frederick Ungar Publishing Company, 1970. London; New York: Constable and Co. 1916
The Renaissance of the 12th Century New York: Meridian Books, 1957

Heer, Frederick. **The Medieval World.** Translated by Janet Sondheimer. New York and Scarborough, Ontario: Mentor Books, 1961. London: Weidenfeld and Nicolson, 1962

Helm, Peter J. **Exploring Saxon and Norman England.** London: Robert Hale, 1976

Henderson, Philip. **Richard Coeur de Lion.** New York: W. W. Norton and Company, 1959. London: Robert Hale Ltd, 1958

Henry of Huntingdon. **The Chronicles of Henry of Huntingdon.** Translated and edited by Thomas Forester. (Includes **The Acts of King Stephen.**) New York: AMS Press, 1968. London: Henry G. Bohn, 1853

Herodotus. **The History of Herodotus.** Translated by George Rawlinson. New York: Tudor Publishing Company, 1947

Hibbert, Christopher. **Tower of London: A History of England from the Norman Conquest.** Newsweek Book Division's Wonders of Man. New York: Newsweek, 1977

Hinton, David. **Oxford Building from Medieval to Modern.** Oxford: Ashmolean Museum, 1977

Holbach, Maude M. **In the Footsteps of Richard Coeur de Lion.** London: Stanley Paul and Company, n.d. (Preface date 1912)

Hollister, Charles Warren. **Medieval Europe: A Short History.** New York, London, Sidney: John Wiley and Sons, Inc, 1964

Homer. **The Odyssey of Homer.** Translated by Samuel Butler. Edited by Louise Ruth Loomis. New York: Published for the Classics Club by Walter J. Black, 1944. London: Jonathan Cape, 1922

Hooker, Katherine (Putnam). **Through the Heel of Italy.** New York: Rae D. Henkle Company, 1927

Hutton, William Holden. **S. Thomas of Canterbury.** London: David Nutt, 1889
　　Thomas Becket. Cambridge: At the University Press, 1926

Ibn Jubayr (Abu 'l-husayn Muhammad ibn Ahmad ibn Jubayr). **The Travels of Ibn Jubayr.** Translated by Ronald J. C. Broadhurst. London: Jonathan Cape, 1952

Ireland, William Henry. **Henry the Second, An Historical Drama (Supposed to be written by the Author of Vortigern).** Eighteenth century Shakespeare Series, general editor Arthur Freeman. No. 21 of 26. New York: August M. Kelley Publishers, 1971

Italian State Tourist Department. **Italy's Book of Days.** No publishing information given.

Jamison, Evelyn Mary, with C. M. Ady, and K. D. Vernon. **Italy, Medieval and Modern.** Oxford: At the Clarendon Press, 1917

John, Eric, editor. **The Popes.** London: Burns and Oates, 1964

John de Joinville. **Memoirs of Louis IX. King of France.** Translated by Colonel Johnes. London: Henry G. Bohn, 1848

John of Salisbury. **The Letters of John of Salisbury.** Oxford Medieval Texts, general editor D. E. Greenway. Oxford: At the Clarendon Press, 1979
　　Memoirs of the Papal Court. Translated by Marjorie McCallum Chibnall. Medieval Text Series, general editors V. H. Galbraith and R. A. B. Mynors. London, Edinburgh, Paris, Melbourne, Toronto: Thomas Nelson and Sons, 1956

Johnson, Paul. **The National Trust Book of British Castles.** London: Book Club Associates, 1978
　　The National Trust Book of English Castles. London: The National Trust/Weidenfeld and Nicolson, 1978

Jones, Gwyn. **A History of the Vikings.** New York, Toronto, London: Oxford University Press, 1968

Jones, Thomas M. **The Becket Controversy.** New York and London: John Wiley and Sons, Inc, 1970

Jones, William. **Crowns and Coronations: A History of Regalia.** Detroit: Singing Tree Press, 1968 London: Chatto and Windus, 1883

Kantorowicz, Ernst. **Frederick the Second 1194-1250.** Translated by E. O. Lorimer. New York: Frederick Ungar Publishing Company, 1967 London: Constable and Co. 1931

Kelly, Amy. **Eleanor of Aquitaine and the Four Kings.** Cambridge, Mass; London: Harvard University Press, 1977. London: Cassell and Co. Ltd, 1952. New York: Vintage Books, 1950

Kidson, Peter. **The Medieval World.** New York, Toronto: McGraw-Hill Book Company, 1967. London: Paul Hamlyn, 1967

Kightly, Charles. **Strongholds of the Realm.** London: Thames and Hudson Ltd, 1979

Kilpeck Church, Herefordshire. No publishing information given.

Kininmonth, Christopher. **The Travelers' Guide to Malta and Gozo.** Indianapolis and New York: Bobbs-Merrill Company Inc, 1967. London: Alfred Lammer, 1967

Kitzinger, Ernst. **The Mosaics of Monreale.** Palermo: S. F. Flaccovio, 1960

Knight, Charles. **History of St. John's Gate.** (St John's Gate Archives, Box HA)
　　Old England: A Pictorial Museum of Regal, Ecclesiastical, Baronial, Municipal and Popular

Antiques. 2 vols. London: Charles Knight and Company, 1845

Knowles, David. **The Episcopal Colleagues of Archbishop Becket.** Cambridge: Cambridge University Press, 1970
　　Thomas Becket. Stanford: Stanford University Press, 1971

Koch, Hannesjoachim Wilhelm. **Medieval Warfare.** London: Bison Books, and New York: Prentice-Hall, 1978

Kubly, Herbert. **Easter in Sicily.** New York: Simon and Schuster, 1956. London: Victor Gollancz, 1956

Kybalová. Ludmila with Olga Herbenová, and Milena Lamarová. **The Pictorial Encyclopedia of Fashion.** Translated by Claudia Rosoux. London, New York, Sidney, Toronto: Paul Hamlyn, 1968. New York: Crown Publishers, Inc, 1968

La Fay, Howard. 'Sicily, Where All the Songs are Sad.' **National Geographic Magazine** vol. 149, no. 3 (March 1976)

Lamb, Harold **The Crusades: Iron Men and Saints.** New York: Doubleday, Doran and Company, 1930

Lander, Jack Robert. **Ancient and Medieval England: Beginning to 1509.** New York: Harcourt Brace Jovanovich, Inc, 1973

Landström, Björn. **Sailing Ships.** Garden City, New York: Doubleday, 1969. London: Allen and Unwin, 1969

Lang, Paul Henry, and Otto Bettman. **A Pictorial History of Music.** New York: W. W. Norton and Company, Inc, 1960

Leclerq, Jean. **Bernard of Clairvaux and the Cistercian Spirit.** Translated by Claire Lavoie. Kalamazoo, Mich: Cistercian Publications, 1976

Lejard, André. **The Bayeaux Tapestry.** Paris: Vendome, 1947

Le Patourel, John. 'Norman Barons.' **1066 Commemorative Lectures.** London: The Historical Association, l966
　　Norman Barons. Edited by W. P. Coakley. Bexhill-on-Sea and London: The

Hastings and Bexhill Branch of the Historical Association, 1966 **Normandy and England 1066–1144 (The Stenton Lecture 1970)** University of Reading, 1971 **The Norman Empire.** London: Oxford University Press, 1976

Lewer, David. **The Temple Church.** English Churches series. London: Pitkin Pictorials Ltd, n.d.

Liebling, A. J. **Normandy Revisited.** New York: Simon and Schuster, 1958. London: Victor Gollancz, 1959

Lindsay, Jack. **The Normans and Their World.** New York: St. Martin's Press, 1974

Little, Bryan. **Abbeys and Priories in England and Wales.** London: B. T. Batsford, Ltd, 1979

Lloyd, Alan. **The Making of the King: 1066.** New York: Holt, Rinehart and Winston, 1966

Lofts, Norah. **Queens of England.** Garden City, New York: Doubleday and Company, 1977. London: Hodder and Stoughton, 1977

Longchamp, Nigel (Wireker). **A Mirror for Fools, or, The Book of Burnel the Ass.** Translated by H. Mosley. Oxford: B. H. Blackwell, 1961

Loyn, Henry. 'The Ages of Britain IV. The Normans.' **The Observer,** 2 August 1981 **Harold, Son of Godwin.** Cardiff: Hastings and Bexhill Branch of the Historical Association, 1966 **The Norman Conquest.** London: Hutchinson University Library, 1965

Mack Smith, Denis. **A History of Sicily, vol.1 of Medieval Sicily 800–1713.** 2 vols. London: Chatto and Windus, 1968

Machiavelli, Niccolò. **The Prince.** Translated by W. K. Marriot. Everyman's Library. London: J. M. Dent and Sons Ltd., 1958. New York: E. P. Dutton and Co., 1958

Mango, Cyril. Byzantium The Empire of New Rome. New York: Charles Scribner's Sons, 1980. London: Weidenfeld and Nicolson, 1980

Marks, Claude. **Pilgrims, Heretics and Lovers** New York: Macmillan Publishing Company, 1975

Marlowe, Christopher. **Edward the Second.** Harvard Classics, edited by Charles W. Eliot. New York: P. F. Collier and Son, Corporation, 1938

Martini, Anna. **Pasta and Pizza.** Edited by Massimo Alberini. New York: St. Martin's Press, 1977. London: Angus and Robertson, 1978

Massingham, Harold John. **The Southern Marches.** The Regional Book Series, general editor Brian Vesey-Fitzgerald. London: Robert Hale Ltd, 1952

Masson, Georgina. **The Companion Guide to Rome.** New York: Harper and Row, 1965. London: Collins, 1980

Matthew, Donald James Alexander. **The Norman Conquest.** London: B. T. Batsford, Ltd, 1966

Mauclair, Camille. **Normandy.** London and Boston: The Medici Society, 1928

Meadows, Denis. **A Saint and a Half.** New York: The Devin-Adair Company, 1963

Monsarrat, Nicholas. **The Kappillan of Malta.** London and Sidney: Pan Books, 1973, 1975

Morisani, Ottavia. **Gli Affreschi di S. Angelo in Formis.** Naples: Di Mauro Editors, 1962

Morris, John, S. J. **The Life and Martyrdom of Saint Thomas Becket.** London: Burns and Oates, 1885

Morton, Henry Canova Vollam. A Traveller in Italy. New York: Dodd, Mead and Company, 1964. London: Methuen and Co. 1964 **Traveller in Rome.** New York: Dodd, Mead and Company, 1957. London: Methuen and Co., 1957 **A Traveller in Southern Italy.** New York: Dodd, Mead and Company, 1969. London: Methuen and Company, 1969

Murphy, Thomas Patrick, editor. **The Holy War.** Columbus, Ohio: Ohio State University Press, 1976

Murray, Jane. **The Kings and Queens of England.** New York: Charles Scribner's Sons, 1974

Murray, William. **Italy: The Fatal Gift.** New York: Dodd, Mead and Company, 1982

Music In Honor of St. Thomas of Canterbury. Texts translated by Blachly. **Nonesuch Records,** H-71292, 1974

Music of the Crusades. Argo Records ZR6 67

Norgate, Kate. **Richard the Lion Heart.** London: Macmillan and Company Ltd, 1924

Norman, Alexander Vessy Bethune. **Arms and Armor.** New York: G. P. Putnam's Sons, 1964. London: Weidenfeld and Nicolson, 1964 with Pottinger, Don. **Warrior to Soldier 449–1660. London: Weidenfeld and Nicolson Ltd, 1966**

The Normans in Sicily and Southern Italy: Lincei Lectures. London: Oxford University Press, 1977

Norwich, John Julius, general editor. **Great Architecture of the World.** New York: Random House Inc, in association with American Heritage Publishing Company, Inc, 1975. London: Mitchell Beazley, 1975 **The Kingdom in the Sun.** New York and Evanston: Harper and Row Publishers, 1970. London: Faber and Faber, 1976 **The Other Conquest.** New York and Evanston: Harper and Row Publishers 1967. London **(The Normans in the South)**: Solitaire, 1981 **Venice: The Rise to Empire.** London: Allen Lane, 1977

Nuttgens, Patrick. **York, the Continuing City.** London: Faber and Faber, Ltd, 1976

Oman, Charles W. C. **Castles.** New York: Beekman House, 1978

On the Conquest of Ireland by Henry II. (An Anglo-Norman Poem.) Edited by F. Michel. London: W. Pickering, 1837

Ordericus Vitalis. **The Ecclesiastical History of England and Normandy.**

Translated by Thomas Forester. New York: AMS Press (Bohn's Antiquarian Library), 1968

Ormond, Richard **The Face of Monarchy.** Oxford: Phaidon, 1977. New York: E. P. Dutton, 1977

Osborne, James van Wyck. **The Greatest Norman Conquest.** New York: E. P. Dutton and Company, Inc, 1937

Otto of Freising. **Deeds of Frederick Barbarossa.** Translated by Charles Christopher Mierow with Richard Emery. New York: Columbia University Press, 1953

Pain, Nesta. **The King and Becket.** London: Eyre and Spottiswoode, 1964

Payne, Robert. **The Fathers of the Western Church.** New York: The Viking Press, 1964

Pereira, Anthony, **Discovering Sicily.** London: B. T. Batsford, Ltd, 1972
    Naples, Pompeii and Southern Italy. London: B. T. Batsford, Ltd, 1977

Perks, John Clifford. **Chepstow Castle.** London: Her Majesty's Stationery Office, 1967

Pernoud, Regine. **Eleanor of Aquitaine.** Translated by Peter Wiles. New York: Coward-McCann, Inc, 1967. London: Collins, 1967

Peter the Venerable. **The Letters of Peter the Venerable.** 2 vols. Edited by Giles Constable. Cambridge, Mass: Harvard University Press, 1967

Petrarch. **Sonnets and Songs.** Translated by Anna Maria Armi. New York: Grosset and Dunlap, 1968

Pevsner, Nikolaus. **The Buildings of Britain,** 46 vols. Harmondsworth: Penguin Books, 1951-74.
    An Outline of European Architecture. 6th ed. Baltimore and Harmondsworth: Penguin Books, 1960

Phillips, Alan Eric. **Fountains Abbey.** London: Her Majesty's Stationery Office, 1967

Pindar. **The Odes of Pindar.** Translated by Geoffrey S. Conway London: J. M. Dent and Sons, Ltd, 1972

Pitt, Derek, and Michael Shaw. **Portrait of Normandy.** London: Robert Hale, 1974

Platt, Colin. **The Atlas of Medieval Man.** New York: St. Martin's Press, 1979. London: Macmillan, 1979
    The English Medieval Town. New York: David McKay Company, Inc, 1976. London: Secker and Warburg, 1976
    Medieval England (A social History and Archaeology from the Conquest to 1600 A.D.) New York: Charles Scribner's Sons, 1978. London: Routledge and Kegan Paul, 1978

Plumb, John Harold, and Huw Wheldon. **Royal Heritage: The Treasures of the British Crown.** New York and London: Harcourt Brace Jovanovich, 1977

Poole, Austin Lane. **From Domesday Book to Magna Carta 1087-1216.** 2nd ed. London: Oxford University Press, 1955
    Editor. **Medieval England.** 2 vols. London: Oxford at the Clarendon Press, 1958

Pound, Ezra. **Confucius to Cummings: An Anthology of Poetry.** New York: New Directions, 1964

Prescott, Orville. **Lords of Italy.** New York, Evanston, San Francisco, London: Harper and Row, 1972

Previté-Orton, C. W. **The Shorter Cambridge Medieval History.** 2 vols. Cambridge: At the University Press, 1952

Price, Mary R., and Margaret Howell. **From Barbarism to Chivalry.** London: Oxford University Press, 1972

Prior, Peter. 'Herefordshire, A Country Idyll.' **In Britain,** May 1973

Quennell, Marjorie and C. H. B. **Everyday Life in Anglo-Saxon, Viking and Norman Times.** New York and London: G. P. Putnam's Sons, 1927

Ralph of Coggeshall. **Chronicon Anglicanum.** Edited by Joseph Stevenson. London: Roll Series 66, 1875

Ralph de Diceto. **The Historical Works of Ralph de Diceto.** Edited by William Stubbs. 2 volumes. London: Longman and Co., 1876

Renn, Derek Frank. **Norman Castles in Britain.** London: John Baker—Humanities Press, 1968

Rice, David Talbot. **Constantinople From Byzantium to Istanbul.** New York: Stein and Day, 1965. London: Elek Books, 1965

Richard of Devizes. **The Chronicles of Richard of Devizes, concerning the Deeds of King Richard the First, King of England.** Translated by Dr. Giles. London: Henry G. Bohn, 1848. G. Bell and Sons, 1914
    The Chronicles of Richard of Devizes of the Time of King Richard the First. Edited by John T. Appleby. London: Thomas and Sons Ltd, 1963

Richardson, H. G. (with G. O. Sayles). **The Governance of Medieval England.** Edinburgh: Edinburgh University Press, 1963

Ringler, Dick. 'To Go A'Viking' **Oceans Magazine** vol. 13, no. 2 (March-April 1980)

Ritchie, Neil. 'Bohemund, Prince of Antioch.' **History Today** vol.XXVIII, no. 5 (May 1978)

Robert de Monte. **The Chronicles of Robert de Monte.** Translated by Joseph Stevenson. The Church Historians of England Series, vol. 14, pt. 2. London: Seeleys, 1856

Roger of Hoveden. **The Annals of Roger of Hoveden.** 2 vols. Translated by Henry T. Riley. London: H. G. Bohn, 1853
    See also Benedict of Peterborough.

Roger of Wendover. **Flowers of History.** 2 vols. Translated by John Allen Giles. London: Henry G. Bohn, 1968. New York: AMS Press, 1968

Ross, James Bruce, and Mary Martin McLaughlin. **The Portable Medieval Reader.** New York: The Viking Press, 1949

Rossi, Ferdinando. **Mosaics.** Translated by David Ross. New York, Washington, London: Praeger Publishers, 1970

Rousham, Sally. **Canterbury: The Story of a Cathedral.** London: Ebenezer Bayles and Son Ltd, 1975

Rowbotham, John Frederick. **The Troubadours and Courts of Love.** New York and London: Swan Sonnenschein and Company, 1895

Runciman, Steven. **The First Crusade.** Cambridge: At the University Press, 1951
   A History of the Crusades. 3 vols. Cambridge: At the University Press, 1966
   The Sicilian Vespers. Cambridge: At the University Press, 1958

Ruskin, John. **The Stones of Venice.** 3 books in 2 vols. New York: Hurst and Company, n.d. London: Smith Elder and Co., 1873

Sackville-West, V. **Berkeley Castle** Derby: English Life Publications, Ltd, 1978

Salerna of Ifield. A Legend of St. Thomas á Becket. Translated by Kenneth M. Ffinch. (No publishing information) 1935

Schuerl, Wolfgang F. **Medieval Castles and Cities.** Translated by Francisca Garvie. New Jersey: Chartwell Books Inc, 1978. London: Cassell, 1978

Schwarz, Heinrich M. **Sicily.** New York: Studio Publications Inc. in association with Thomas Y. Crowell Company, 1956

Scott, A. F. **Every One a Witness: The Plantagenet Age.** New York: Thomas Y. Crowell Company, 1976

Scott, Martin. **Medieval Europe.** London: Longmans, Green and Company Ltd, 1964

Scott, Sir Walter. **Ivanhoe.**
   Marmion.

Scott-Moncrieff, George. **Scottish Border Abbeys.** Edinburgh: Her Majesty's Stationery Office, 1964

Setton, Kenneth M. '900 Years Ago: The Norman Conquest.' **National Geographic Magazine** vol. 130, no. 2 (August 1966)

Seward, Desmond. **Eleanor of Aquitaine.** New York: Times Books, 1979. Newton Abbot: David and Charles, 1978

Seymour, John **The Companion Guide to East Anglia.** London: Collins Press, 1970

Shakespeare, William. **Henry IV, Part I.**
   Henry V.
   Henry VI, Part III.
   Richard III.

Shearer, Cresswell. **The Renaissance of Architecture in Southern Italy.** Cambridge: W. Heffer and Sons Ltd, 1935

Sherrill, Charles Hitchcock. **Mosaics in Italy, Palestine, Syria, Turkey and Greece.** London: John Lane, the Bodeley Head Ltd, 1933

A Short History and Guide to Pembroke Castle. Tenby, Pembrokeshire: The Five Arches Press, 1977

Shortt, H. de S. **Old Sarum.** London: Her Majesty's Stationery Office, 1965

Simons, Gerald. **Barbarian Europe.** New York: Time-Life Books, 1968

Simpson, William Douglas. **Castles in England and Wales.** London: B. T. Batsford Ltd, 1969

Simson, Otto von. **The Gothic Cathedral.** New York: Pantheon Books (Bollingen Series XLVIII), 1956. London: Routledge and Kegan Paul, 1956

Sitwell, Sacheverell, with Tony Armstrong-Jones. **Malta.** London: B. T. Batsford Ltd, 1958

Slocombe, George Edward. **William the Conqueror.** New York: G. P. Putnam's Sons, 1961. London: Hutchinson, 1959

Somerset County Gazette. April 14, 1978

Southern, Richard William, editor. **Essays in Medieval History.** London, Melbourne, Toronto: Macmillan, and New York: St. Martin's Press, 1968
   Western Society and the Church in the Middle Ages. Harmondsworth: Penguin Books, 1970,

Speaight, Robert. **St. Thomas of Canterbury.** New York: G. P. Putnam's Sons, 1938

Stenton, Frank M. 'Norman London.' **The Historical Association Leaflet** 38. London: The Historical Association, July 1915
   Editor. **The Bayeux Tapestry.** London: Phaidon Press, 1957

Stranks, C. J. **Durham Cathedral.** London: Pitkin Pictorials Ltd, 1968

Strassburg, Gottfried von. **Tristan, with the 'Tristran' of Thomas.** Translated by Arthur Thomas Hatto. Baltimore: Penguin Books, 1960

Stubbs, William. **The Early Plantagenets.** New York: Charles Scribner's Sons, 1924. London: Longmans, Green and Co., 1886
   Historical Introduction to the Rolls Series. Edited by Arthur Hassall. London: Longmans, Green and Company, 1902

Sturluson, Snorri. **Heimskringla: Sagas of the Norse Kings.** Translated by Samuel Laing. New York: E. P. Dutton and Company Inc, 1961. London: J. M. Dent and Sons, 1961

Sumption, Jonathan **Pilgrimage: an Image of Mediaeval Religion.** Totowa, New Jersey: Rowman and Littlefield, 1975

Sutherland, James. **The Oxford Book of Literary Anecdotes.** Oxford: University Press, 1975. New York: Pocket Books, 1976

Sykes, N. **The Pictorial History of Winchester Cathedral.** (No city or date of publication given): Pitkin 'Pride of Britain' Books

Symonds, John Addington. **Sketches in Italy.** Leipzig: Bernard Tauchnitz, 1883

Tennyson, Alfred Lord. **Becket.** New York: Dodd, Mead and Company, 1894. London: Macmillan and Co., 1884

1066 Commemorative Lectures London: The Historical Association, 1966

Tenth-Century Liturgical Chant in Proportional Rhythm: Masses for Christmas Day and Easter Sunday. Nonesuch

Records H-71348. Schola Antiqua, R. John Blackley, director

Tetlow, Edwin **The Enigma of Hastings.** New York: St. Martin's Press 1974. London: Peter Owen, 1974

This England. Editorial guidance of Melville Bell Grosvenor and Franc Shor and staff. Washington: National Geographic Society, 1966

Thompson, A. Hamilton **Military Architecture in Medieval England.** Totowa, New Jersey: Rowman and Littlefield, 1975

Thorpe, Lewis **The Bayeux Tapestry and the Norman Invasion.** London: Folio Society, 1973

Tierney, Brian. **The Crisis of Church nd State 1050-1300.** New Jersey: Prentice-Hall, Inc, 1964

Tomkeieff, Olive G. **Life in Norman England.** London: B. T. Batsford Ltd, 1966

Treasures in Britain. 3rd ed. New York: W. W. Norton and Company Inc, 1976

Trevelyan, George Macaulay. **A Shortened History of England.** New York: Penguin Books, 1978

Valency, Maurice. **In Praise of Love.** New York: Macmillan Company, 1958

Vantaggi, Rosella. **Sicily and Her Art Treasures.** (No city or date of publication given.): Plurigraf, Narni and Terni

Vita Aedwardi (The Life of King Edward). Translated and edited by Frank Barlow. London: Thomas Nelson and Sons, 1962

Waddell, Helen. **The Wandering Scholars.** New York: Doubleday and Company (Doubleday Anchor Book), 1955. Harmondsworth: Penguin, 1954

Waern, Cecilia. **Medieval Sicily.** New York: E. P. Dutton and Company, 1911. London: Duckworth and Co., 1910

Walder, David. **Nelson.** New York: The Dial Press/James Wade, 1978. London: Hamilton, 1978

Walker, Bob Danvers. 'The Hereford Cider Festival.' **In Britain,** vol. 28, no. 5 (May 1973)

Walker, David. **The Norman Conquerors.** A New History of Wales Series. Swansea: Christopher Davies, 1977

Warren, Philip. **The Medieval Castle.** New York: Taplinger Publishing Company, 1971

Warren, Wilfred Lewis. **Henry II.** Berkeley and Los Angeles: University of California Press, 1977. London: Eyre Methuen, 1977

Watkins, Paul. **See Sicily.** London: Format Books, 1974

Webb, Clement C. J. **John of Salisbury.** New York: Russell and Russell, 1971. London: Methuen and Co., 1932

Wells, Herbert George. **Tono-Bungay.** New York: The Modern Library, Random House, 1908. London: Pan Books, 1964

Whittingham, A.B. **Bury St. Edmunds Abbey.** London: Her Majesty's Stationery Office, 1971

Wilkinson, Frederick. **Arms and Armor.** New York: Grosset and Dunlap, l971. London:

A. and C. Black, 1963 **The Castles of England.** London: Letts Guides, 1973

William of Malmesbury. **The History of the Kings of England and of His own Times.** Translated by Joseph Sharpe; revised by Joseph Stevenson. The Church Historians of England Series. London: Seeleys, 1864

William of Newburgh. **The History of William of Newburgh.** Translated by Joseph Stevenson. The Church Historians of England Series. London: Seeleys, 1856

William of Tyre. **A History of Deeds Done Beyond the Sea.** 2 vols. Translated by Emily Atwater Babcock and August Charles Krey. No. XXXV of the Records of Civilization Sources and Studies. New York: Columbia University Press, 1943

Wilson, Derek. **The Tower.** New York: Charles Scribner's Sons, 1979

Winston, Richard. **Thomas Becket.** New York: Alfred A. Knopf, 1967

Winyard, T. **The Priory Church of St. Bartholomew the Great.** Cupar, Fife: J. and G. Innes, Printers, Ltd, 1977

Wood, Margaret. **Norman Domestic Architecture.** London: The Royal Archaeological Institute, 1974

Yewdale, Ralph Bailey. **Bohemund I, Prince of Antioch.** Princeton, New Jersey: Princeton University Press, 1924

Zarnecki, George. **Art of the Medieval World.** New York: Harry N. Abrams, Inc, 1975

Index

A Select Listing of Important People and Places